R. Glenn Hubbard
Columbia University

Anthony Patrick O'Brien
Lehigh University

Apostolos Serletis
University of Calgary

Jason Childs
University of Regina

economics

second canadian edition

 **Pearson**

EDITORIAL DIRECTOR: Claudine O'Donnell
ACQUISITIONS EDITOR: Megan Farrell
MARKETING MANAGER: Claire Varley
PROGRAM MANAGER: Richard Di Santo
PROJECT MANAGER: Pippa Kennard
DEVELOPMENTAL EDITOR: Patti Sayle
MEDIA EDITOR: Nicole Mellow
MEDIA DEVELOPER: Olga Avdyeyeva
PRODUCTION SERVICES: Cenveo® Publisher Services

PERMISSIONS PROJECT MANAGER: Joanne Tang
TEXT AND PHOTO PERMISSION RESEARCH: Integra Publishing Services
INTERIOR DESIGNER: Anthony Leung
COVER DESIGNER: Anthony Leung
COVER IMAGE: © Minerva Studio - Fotolia.com; © gstockstudio - Fotolia.com
VICE-PRESIDENT, CROSS MEDIA AND PUBLISHING SERVICES: Gary Bennett

Pearson Canada Inc., 26 Prince Andrew Place, Don Mills, Ontario M3C 2T8.

978-0-13-443126-0

2   17

Library and Archives Canada Cataloguing in Publication

Hubbard, R. Glenn, author
    Macroeconomics / R. Glenn Hubbard, Columbia University,
Anthony Patrick O'Brien, Lehigh University, Apostolos Serletis,
University of Calgary, Jason Childs, University of Regina. — Second
Canadian edition.

Includes index.
ISBN 978-0-13-443126-0 (paperback)

    1. Macroeconomics—Textbooks. I. O'Brien, Anthony Patrick,
author II. Serletis, Apostolos, 1954-, author III. Childs, Jason, 1974-,
author IV. Title.

HB172.5.H86 2016   339   C2016-906954-0

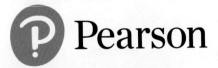

For Adia, Alia, Melina, and Aviana.
—*Apostolos Serletis*

For Marla, Nora, Audrey, Ed, and Leslie.
—*Jason Childs*

Glenn Hubbard, policymaker, professor, and researcher.
R. Glenn Hubbard is the dean and Russell L. Carson Professor of Finance and Economics in the Graduate School of Business at Columbia University and professor of economics in Columbia's Faculty of Arts and Sciences. He is also a research associate of the National Bureau of Economic Research and a director of Automatic Data Processing, Black Rock Closed-End Funds, KKR Financial Corporation, and MetLife. He received his Ph.D. in economics from Harvard University in 1983. From 2001 to 2003, he served as chairman of the White House Council of Economic Advisers and chairman of the OECD Economy Policy Committee, and from 1991 to 1993, he was deputy assistant secretary of the US Treasury Department. He currently serves as co-chair of the nonpartisan Committee on Capital Markets Regulation. Hubbard's fields of specialization are public economics, financial markets and institutions, corporate finance, macroeconomics, industrial organization, and public policy. He is the author of more than 100 articles in leading journals, including *American Economic Review; Brookings Papers on Economic Activity; Journal of Finance; Journal of Financial Economics; Journal of Money, Credit, and Banking; Journal of Political Economy; Journal of Public Economics; Quarterly Journal of Economics; RAND Journal of Economics;* and *Review of Economics and Statistics*. His research has been supported by grants from the National Science Foundation, the National Bureau of Economic Research, and numerous private foundations.

Tony O'Brien, award-winning professor and researcher.
Anthony Patrick O'Brien is a professor of economics at Lehigh University. He received his Ph.D. from the University of California, Berkeley, in 1987. He has taught principles of economics for more than 15 years, in both large sections and small honours classes. He received the Lehigh University Award for Distinguished Teaching. He was formerly the director of the Diamond Center for Economic Education and was named a Dana Foundation Faculty Fellow and Lehigh Class of 1961 Professor of Economics. He has been a visiting professor at the University of California, Santa Barbara, and the Graduate School of Industrial Administration at Carnegie Mellon University. O'Brien's research has dealt with such issues as the evolution of the US automobile industry, sources of US economic competitiveness, the development of US trade policy, the causes of the Great Depression, and the causes of black–white income differences. His research has been published in leading journals, including *American Economic Review; Quarterly Journal of Economics; Journal of Money, Credit, and Banking; Industrial Relations; Journal of Economic History;* and *Explorations in Economic History*. His research has been supported by grants from government agencies and private foundations. In addition to teaching and writing, O'Brien also serves on the editorial board of the *Journal of Socio-Economics*.

Apostolos Serletis is a Professor of Economics at the University of Calgary. Since receiving his Ph.D. from McMaster University in 1984, he has held visiting appointments at the University of Texas at Austin, the Athens University of Economics and Business, and the Research Department of the Federal Reserve Bank of St. Louis.

Professor Serletis' teaching and research interests focus on monetary and financial economics, macroeconometrics, and nonlinear and complex dynamics. He is the author of 12 books, including *The Economics of Money, Banking, and Financial Markets: Sixth Canadian Edition,* with Frederic S. Mishkin (Pearson, 2016); *Macroeconomics: A Modern Approach: First Canadian Edition,* with Robert J. Barro (Nelson, 2010); *The Demand for Money: Theoretical and Empirical Approaches* (Springer, 2007); *Financial Markets and Institutions: Canadian Edition,* with Frederic S. Mishkin and Stanley G. Eakins (Addison-Wesley, 2004); and *The Theory of Monetary Aggregation,* co-edited with William A. Barnett (Elsevier, 2000).

In addition, he has published more than 200 articles in such journals as the *Journal of Economic Literature; Journal of Monetary Economics; Journal of Money, Credit, and Banking; Journal of Econometrics; Journal of Applied Econometrics; Journal of Business and Economic Statistics; Macroeconomic Dynamics; Journal of Banking and Finance; Journal of Economic Dynamics and Control; Economic Inquiry; Canadian Journal of Economics; Econometric Reviews;* and *Studies in Nonlinear Dynamics and Econometrics.*

Professor Serletis is currently an Associate Editor of three academic journals, *Macroeconomic Dynamics, Open Economies Review,* and *Energy Economics,* and a member of the Editorial Board at the *Journal of Economic Asymmetries* and the *Journal of Economic Studies.* He has also served as Guest Editor of the *Journal of Econometrics, Econometric Reviews,* and *Macroeconomic Dynamics.*

Jason Childs is an Associate Professor of Economics at the University of Regina. He received his Ph.D. from McMaster University in 2003. He has taught introductory economics (both microeconomics and macroeconomics) his entire career. He began his teaching career with the McCain Postdoctoral Fellowship at Mount Allison University. After this fellowship, he spent six years at the University of New Brunswick, where he received one teaching award and was nominated for two others. Since joining the University of Regina, he has continued to teach introductory-level economics courses. While in Saskatchewan, he has also consulted with the Ministry of Education, the Ministry of Parks, Culture and Sport, as well as a number of private corporations. Professor Childs' research has dealt with a wide variety of issues ranging from the voluntary provision of public services, uncovered interest rate parity, rent controls, the demand for alcoholic beverages, to lying. His work has been published in leading journals, including the *Journal of Public Economics, Review of International Economics, Computational Economics,* and *Economics Letters.*

Dr. Childs also serves his community as a volunteer firefighter.

BRIEF CONTENTS

CONTENTS

*These end-of-chapter resource materials repeat in all chapters.

PART 2 Macroeconomic Foundations and Long-Run Growth

PREFACE

There have been dramatic advances in macroeconomics over the past 40 years, and the field is changing rapidly. Today, macroeconomics assumes that economic agents (i.e., people) have rational expectations and are forward-looking, relies on market-clearing conditions for households and firms, and relies on financial shocks and mechanisms that amplify and propagate those shocks over time. Yet, in the aftermath of the global financial crisis, a number of economists, the media, and policymakers have argued that modern macroeconomics can't capture the complexity of the world that is to be explained.

We believe that with the increasing complexity and interdependence of real economies, macroeconomics must be relevant and applicable. Our approach in this book is to provide students and instructors with an economics text that delivers complete economics coverage in a "widget-free" way by using with real-world business and policy examples. We are gratified by the enthusiastic response from students and instructors who have used the first edition of this book and who have made it one of the best-selling economics textbooks on the market.

Much has happened in Canada and world economies since we prepared the previous edition. We have incorporated many of these developments in the new real-world examples in this edition and also in the digital resources.

Digital Features Located in MyEconLab

MyEconLab is a unique online course management, testing, and tutorial resource. Students and instructors will find the following new online resources to accompany the second Canadian edition:

- **Videos:** The Making the Connection features in the book provide real-world reinforcement of key concepts. Select features are now accompanied by a short video of the author explaining the key point of that Making the Connection. Each video is approximately two or three minutes long and includes visuals, such as new photos, tables, or graphs, that are not in the main book. Related assessment is included with each video, so students can test their understanding. The goal of these videos is to summarize key content and bring the applications to life. Our experience is that many students benefit from this type of online learning and assessment.

- **Animations:** Graphs are the backbone of introductory economics, but many students struggle to understand and work with them. Select figures in the text have a supporting animated version online. The goal of this digital resource is to help students understand shifts in curves, movements along curves, and changes in equilibrium values. Having an animated version of a graph helps students who have difficulty interpreting the static version in the printed text.

- **Interactive Solved Problems:** Many students have difficulty applying economic concepts to solving problems. The goal of these interactive animations is to help students overcome this hurdle by giving them a model of how to solve an economic problem by breaking it down step by step. These interactive tutorials help students learn to think like economists and apply basic problem-solving skills to homework, quizzes, and exams. The goal is for students to build skills they can use to analyze real-world economic issues they hear and read about in the news. Select Solved Problems in the printed text are accompanied by a similar problem online, so students can have more practice and build their problem-solving skills.

- **Graphs and Exercises Updated with Real-Time Data from FRED:** Select graphs are continuously updated online with the latest available data from FRED (Federal Reserve Economic Data), which is a comprehensive, up-to-date data set maintained by the Federal Reserve Bank of St. Louis. Students can display a pop-up graph that shows new data plotted in the graph. Available in Assignment Manager are real-time data exercises that use the latest data from FRED. The goal of these digital features is to help students develop skills in interpreting data and understand how new data affects graphs.

Highlights of This Edition

The severe global financial crisis that began in 2007 when the housing bubble burst in the United States and the "Great Recession" and European debt crisis that followed still affect the world economy today. In many countries, unemployment has risen to levels not seen in decades. The crisis in the financial system was the worst since the Great Depression of the 1930s. Policy debates intensified as governments around the world introduced the largest packages of spending increases and tax cuts in history. Central banks, including the Bank of Canada, sailed into uncharted waters as they developed new policy tools to deal with the unprecedented financial turmoil while long-running policy debates continued. Huge long-run budget deficits, environmental problems, income inequality, and changes to the tax system all received attention from economists, policymakers, and the public.

The second Canadian edition helps students understand recent economic events and the policy responses to them. It places applications at the forefront of the discussion. We believe that students find the study of economics more interesting and easier to master when they see economic analysis applied to real-world issues that concern them.

The Foundation: Contextual Learning and Modern Organization

We believe a course is a success if students can apply what they have learned to both their personal lives and their careers, and if they have developed the analytical skills to understand what they read in the media. That's why we explain economic concepts by using many real-world business examples and application openers, graphs, Making the Connection features, *An Inside Look* features, and end-of-chapter problems. This approach helps both business majors and liberal arts majors become educated consumers, voters, and citizens. In addition to our widget-free approach, we have a modern organization and place interesting policy topics early in the book to pique student interest.

Students come to study macroeconomics with a strong interest in understanding events and developments in the economy. We try to capture that interest and develop students' economic intuition and understanding in this text. We present macroeconomics in a way that is modern and based in the real world of business and economic policy. And we believe we achieve this presentation without making the analysis more difficult. We avoid the recent trend of using simplified versions of intermediate models, which are often more detailed and more complex than what students need to understand the basic macroeconomic issues. Instead, we use a more realistic version of the familiar aggregate demand and aggregate supply model to analyze short-run fluctuations and monetary and fiscal policy. We also avoid the "duelling schools of thought" approach often used to teach macroeconomics at the principles level. We emphasize the many areas of macroeconomics where most economists agree. And we present throughout real business and policy situations to develop students' intuition. Here are a few highlights of our approach to macroeconomics.

- **A broad discussion of macro statistics.** Many students pay at least some attention to the financial news and know that the release of statistics by government agencies can cause movements in stock and bond prices. A background in macroeconomic statistics helps clarify some of the policy issues encountered in later chapters. In Chapter 4, "GDP: Measuring Total Production and Income," and Chapter 5, "Unemployment and

Inflation," we provide students with an understanding of the uses and potential shortcomings of the key macroeconomic statistics, without getting bogged down in the minutiae of how the statistics are constructed.

- **Early coverage of long-run topics.** We place key macroeconomic issues in their long-run context in Chapter 6, "Economic Growth, the Financial System, and Business Cycles," and Chapter 7, "Long-Run Economic Growth: Sources and Policies." Chapter 6 puts the business cycle in the context of underlying long-run growth and discusses what actually happens during the phases of the business cycle. We believe that this material is important if students are to have the understanding of business cycles they will need to interpret economic events; this material is often discussed only briefly or omitted entirely in other books. We know that many instructors prefer to have a short-run orientation to their macro courses, with a strong emphasis on policy. Accordingly, we have structured Chapter 6 so that its discussion of long-run growth would be sufficient for instructors who want to move quickly to short-run analysis. Chapter 7 uses a simple neoclassical growth model to explain important economic growth issues. We apply the model to topics such as the decline of the Soviet economy, the long-run prospects for growth in China, and the failure of many developing countries to sustain high growth rates. And we challenge students with the discussion "Why Isn't the Whole World Rich?"

- **A dynamic model of aggregate demand and aggregate supply.** We take a fresh approach to the standard aggregate demand and aggregate supply (*AD–AS*) model. We realize there is no good, simple alternative to using the *AD–AS* model when explaining movements in the price level and in real GDP. But we know that more instructors are dissatisfied with the *AD–AS* model than with any other aspect of the macro principles course. The key problem, of course, is that *AD–AS* is a static model that attempts to account for dynamic changes in real GDP and the price level. Our approach retains the basics of the *AD–AS* model but makes it more accurate and useful by making it more dynamic. We emphasize two points: (1) Changes in the position of the short-run (upward-sloping) aggregate supply curve depend mainly on the state of expectations of the inflation and (2) the existence of growth in the economy means that the long-run (vertical) aggregate supply curve shifts to the right every year. This "dynamic" *AD–AS* model provides students with a more accurate understanding of the causes and consequences of fluctuations in real GDP and the price level. We introduce this model in Chapter 9, "Aggregate Demand and Aggregate Supply Analysis," and use it to discuss monetary policy in Chapter 11, "Monetary Policy," and fiscal policy in Chapter 12, "Fiscal Policy." Instructors may safely omit the sections on the dynamic *AD–AS* model without any loss in continuity to the discussion of macroeconomic theory and policy.

- **Extensive coverage of monetary policy.** Because of the central role monetary policy plays in the economy and in students' curiosity about business and financial news, we devote two chapters—Chapters 11, "Monetary Policy," and 13, "Inflation, Unemployment, and Bank of Canada Policy"—to the topic. We emphasize the issues involved in the Bank of Canada's choice of monetary policy targets, and we include coverage of the Taylor rule. We also cover the Bank of Canada's new policies aimed at dealing with the bubble in the Canadian housing market and its effects on financial markets.

- **Coverage of both the demand-side and supply-side effects of fiscal policy.** Our discussion of fiscal policy in Chapter 12, "Fiscal Policy," carefully distinguishes between automatic stabilizers and discretionary fiscal policy. We also provide significant coverage of the supply-side effects of fiscal policy.

- **A self-contained but thorough discussion of the Keynesian income-expenditure approach.** The Keynesian income-expenditure approach (the "45°-line diagram," or "Keynesian cross") is useful for introducing students to the short-run relationship between spending and production. Many instructors, however, prefer to omit this material. Therefore, we use the 45°-line diagram only in Chapter 8, "Aggregate Expenditure and Output in the Short Run." The discussion of monetary and fiscal policy in later chapters uses only the *AD–AS* model, which makes it possible to omit Chapter 8.

- **Extensive international coverage.** We include two chapters devoted to international topics: Chapter 14, "Macroeconomics in an Open Economy," and Chapter 15, "The International Financial System." Having a good understanding of the international trading and financial systems is essential to understanding the macroeconomy and to satisfying students' curiosity about the economic world around them. In addition to the material in our two international chapters, we weave international comparisons into the narratives of several other chapters, including our discussion of labour market policies in Chapter 13, "Inflation, Unemployment, and Bank of Canada Policy," and central banking in Chapter 10, "Money, Banks, and the Bank of Canada."

- **Flexible chapter organization.** Because we realize that there are a variety of approaches to teaching principles of macroeconomics, we have structured our chapters for maximum flexibility. For example, our discussion of long-run economic growth in Chapter 6, "Economic Growth, the Financial System, and Business Cycles," makes it possible for instructors to omit the more thorough discussion of these issues in Chapter 7, "Long-Run Economic Growth: Sources and Policies." Our discussion of the Keynesian 45°-line diagram is confined to Chapter 8, "Aggregate Expenditure and Output in the Short Run," so that instructors who do not use this approach can proceed directly to aggregate demand and aggregate supply analysis in Chapter 9, "Aggregate Demand and Aggregate Supply Analysis." While we devote two chapters to monetary policy, the first of these—Chapter 11, "Monetary Policy"—is a self-contained discussion, so instructors may safely omit the material in Chapter 13, "Inflation, Unemployment, and Bank of Canada Policy," if they choose to. Finally, instructors may choose to omit both of the international chapters (Chapter 14, "Macroeconomics in an Open Economy," and Chapter 15, "The International Financial System"), cover just Chapter 14; or cover Chapter 14 and Chapter 15.

New to this Edition

We have covered a number of new topics in this edition, some of which include:

Chapter 1

- NEW Solved Problem 1.1
- NEW Making the Connection box on central planning
- NEW Making the Connection box on the efficiency equity trade-off

Chapter 2

- Update to discussion of the circular flow model
- NEW Making the Connection box on making a smartphone
- NEW Making the Connection box on the role of government

Chapter 3

- NEW Making the Connection box on lobster as an inferior good
- Reworked subsection on population and demographics
- NEW Making the Connection box on transparent solar panels

Chapter 4

- NEW chapter opener
- Added more explanation to the circular flow model
- Rewrote and updated portions of nominal and real GDP
- Updated GDP deflator example
- Rewrote much of the section on national income accounting to reflect changed reporting standards of StatsCan
- Updated section on division of income and included a comparator from 10 years ago

Chapter 5

- Updated chapter opener
- Replaced Economics in Your Life
- New explanation of Structural unemployment
- Re-wrote Making the Connection box on categorizing unemployment
- New Making the Connection box: Comparing Prices from 100 Years Ago to Now

Chapter 6

- Chapter opener example updated to reflect Bombardier's recent troubles
- Updated Making the Connection box with one on India's growth

Chapter 7

- NEW chapter opener
- NEW Making the Connection box: Why Hasn't Mexico Grown as Fast as China?

Chapter 8

- Updated chapter opener
- Added autonomous consumption

Chapter 9

- NEW Making the Connection box on Canada's mini recession in 2015
- Updated Making the Connection box on predicting shifts
- Updated Making the Connection box on government intervention and recession

Chapter 10

- NEW chapter opener
- NEW Making the Connection box: Apple Didn't Want my Cash
- NEW Making the Connection box: Are Bitcoins Money?
- NEW Making the Connection box: Would You Borrow from an Online Peer-to-Peer Lender?

Chapter 11

- NEW chapter opener

Chapter 12

- NEW chapter opener
- Updated Making the Connection box on recession and health
- Updated Making the Connection box on Greece

Chapter 13

- Improved the chapter opener

Chapter 14

- NEW chapter opener
- Updated Making the Connection box: Exchange Rate Listings
- NEW Making the Connection box: Is a Strong Currency Good for a Country?
- NEW Solved Problem 14.2: Subaru Benefits from a Weak Yen

Chapter 15

- NEW chapter opener
- Changed the Economics in Your Life box

- Deleted the Making the Connection box: The Canadian Province of ... Arizona?
- Updated the Making the Connection box: The Big Mac Theory of Exchange Rates
- Updated Solved Problem 15.1
- NEW Making the Connection box: Greece and Germany: Diverse Economies, Common Currency
- NEW Making the Connection box: The Chinese Yuan: The World's Most Controversial Currency

Special Features: A Real-World, Hands-on Approach to Learning Macroeconomics

Chapter-Opening Cases and An Inside Look News Articles

Each chapter-opening case provides a real-world context for learning, sparks students' interest in economics, and helps to unify the chapter. Each chapter-opening case describes a real situation that students can relate to. Here are a few examples of the topics we explore in the chapter openers in this new edition:

- Red Bull and the market for energy drinks (Chapter 3)
- Economic growth and the business cycle at Bombardier (Chapter 6)
- Will Economic Reforms in Mexico Boost Growth? (Chapter 7)
- Canadian National Railway and the Business Cycle (Chapter 9)
- Can Greece Function without Banks? (Chapter 10)
- Why Would a Bank Pay a Negative Interest Rate? (Chapter 11)
- Bayer Uses a Weak Euro to Increase Sales (Chapter 15)

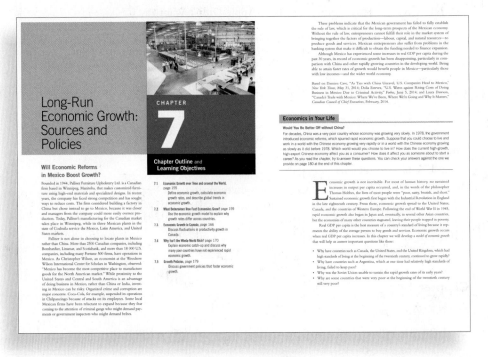

An Inside Look is a two-page feature that shows students how to apply the concepts from the part to the analysis of a news article. The articles selected deal with policy issues and are titled An Inside Look. Articles are from sources such as the *Economist, National Post, and Toronto Star.* An Inside Look presents an excerpt from an article, an analysis of the article, and critical thinking questions.

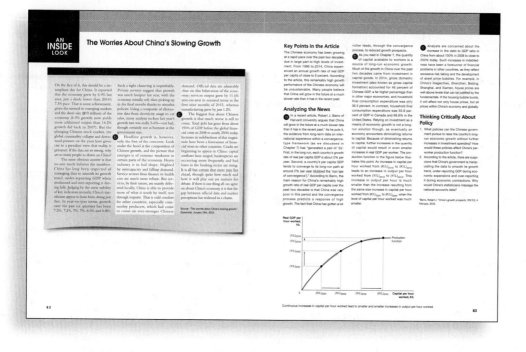

Here are a few examples of the articles featured in An Inside Look:

- As Canadians buy record number of pickups and SUVs, new fuel-economy rules may prove hard to meet (Part 1)
- The Worries about China's Slowing Growth (Part 2)
- CIBC downgrades its 2016 Canadian economic outlook for the second time in a month (Part 3)
- U.S. short sellers betting on Canadian housing crash: 'An accident waiting to happen' (Part 4)
- Four ways the Fed's rate hike will affect our lives up north (Part 5)

Economics in Your Life

After the chapter-opening real-world business case, we have added a personal dimension to the chapter opener, with a feature titled Economics in Your Life, which asks students to consider how economics affects their own lives. The feature piques the interest of students and emphasizes the connection between the material they are learning and their own experiences.

Economics in Your Life

Should You Change Your Career Plans if You Graduate during a Recession?

Suppose you are in the second year of your degree, majoring in economics and geology. You plan to find a job in the energy industry after graduation. The energy industry, particularly the oil and gas sector, has seen much less growth since 2014 and unemployment in the entire economy is still quite high. After meeting with some older students, you learn that many of them already have jobs in the finance industry. Should you switch your major to economics and finance? As you read this chapter, see if you can answer this question. You can check your answer against the one we provide on page 124 at the end of this chapter.

At the end of the chapter, we use the chapter concepts to answer the questions asked at the beginning of the chapter.

Economics in Your Life

Should You Change Your Career Plans If You Graduate during a Recession?

At the beginning of the chapter, we asked if layoffs in the energy industry should cause you to change your major and give up your plans to work for an energy company and switch your major to economics and finance instead. We have learned in this chapter that unemployment rates are higher and layoffs more common in a recession than in an economic expansion. Because you're only in the second year of your degree, you have a few years before you graduate, and by then the recession is likely to have ended and the unemployment rate will have fallen. You should probably investigate whether the layoffs in the energy sector represent a permanent contraction in the size of the industry or a short-term decline due to the recession. If the reduction in the size of the energy sector appear to be mostly related to the current recession, then you probably don't need to change your career path. If you believe the industry will be permanently smaller, then a change might be in your best interest.

Here are a few examples of the topics featured in Economics in Your Life:

- What's the best country for you to work in? (Chapter 4)
- Should you change your career plans if you graduate during a recession? (Chapter 5)
- When consumer confidence falls, is your job at risk? (Chapter 8)
- Should you buy a house during a recession? (Chapter 11)
- Exchange rate risk can affect your savings (Chapter 15)

Solved Problems

Many students have great difficulty handling applied economics problems. We help students overcome this hurdle by including two or three worked-out problems tied to select chapter-opening learning objectives. Our goals are to keep students focused on the main ideas of each chapter and to give students a model of how to solve an economic problem by breaking it down step by step. Additional exercises in the end-of-chapter Problems and Applications section are tied to every Solved Problem. Additional Solved Problems appear in the Instructor's Manual and the print Study Guide. In addition, the Test Item Files include problems tied to the Solved Problems in the main book.

Don't Let This Happen to You

We know from many years of teaching which concepts students find most difficult. Each chapter contains a box feature called Don't Let This Happen to You that alerts students to the most common pitfalls in that chapter's material. We follow up with a related question in the end-of-chapter Problems and Applications section.

Don't Let This Happen to You

Remember What Economists Mean by *Investment*

Notice that the definition of *investment* in this chapter is narrower than in everyday use. For example, people often say they are investing in the stock market or in rare coins. As we have seen, economists reserve the word *investment* for purchases of machinery, factories, and houses. Economists don't include purchases of stocks or rare coins or deposits in savings accounts in the definition of investment because these activities don't result in the production of new goods. For example, a share of Microsoft stock represents part

ownership of that company. When you buy a share of Microsoft stock, nothing new is produced; there is just a transfer of that small piece of ownership of Microsoft. Similarly, buying a rare coin or putting $1000 into a savings account does not result in an increase in production. GDP is not affected by any of these activities, so they are not included in the economic definition of investment.

MyEconLab

Your Turn: Test your understanding by doing related problem 1.6 on page 103 at the end of this chapter.

Making the Connection

Each chapter includes two or more Making the Connection features that provide real-world reinforcement of key concepts and help students learn how to interpret what they read on the web and in newspapers. Making the Connection features use relevant, stimulating, and provocative news stories focused on businesses and policy issues. Each Making the Connection has at least one supporting end-of-chapter problem to allow students to test their understanding of the topic discussed. Here are a few examples of new Making the Connection features:

- Get Fit or Get Fined (Chapter 1)
- The Transformation of Lobster from Inferior to Normal Good (Chapter 3)
- Prices Will Rise (Chapter 5)
- Canada's Mini Recession (Chapter 9)
- Apple Didn't Want My Cash! (Chapter 10)
- Greece and Germany: Diverse Economies, Common Currency (Chapter 15)

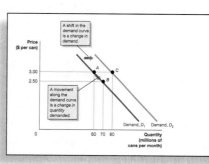

Making the Connection

The Transformation of Lobster from Inferior to Normal Good

When economists describe a product as being inferior they aren't saying it is poor quality, they're just saying that consumers buy less of it when their incomes rise. The same product can be an inferior good to some and a normal good to others. It all depends on the attitudes of people in a given time and place and these attitudes can change.

A lobster dinner in Toronto or Calgary can easily cost $50 or more. In many fancy restaurants, a lobster dinner is the most expensive item on the menu. The high price and honoured place on the menu would suggest that lobster is a normal good—when incomes rise, demand for lobster will rise.

This isn't always the case. In many parts of the Maritimes where lobster is caught, it is considered something you eat only if you can't afford anything better—an inferior good. Historically, in these regions, lobster was fed to prisoners and apprentices as a cheap source of protein, rather than as a fancy meal for the wealthy. Maritimers generally won't brag about having a lobster sandwich for lunch.

Whether a good is normal or inferior depends on social attitudes, tastes, and preferences. The only way to know for sure if a good is normal or inferior is to observe how consumers' behaviour changes as their incomes change.

Your Turn: Test your understanding by doing related problem 1.4 on page 73 at the end of this chapter.

Despite it's high cost in many restaurants, lobster can still be an inferior good.

MyEconLab

Graphs and Summary Tables

Graphs are an indispensable part of a principles of economics course but are a major stumbling block for many students. Every chapter except Chapter 1 includes end-of-chapter problems that require students to draw, read, and interpret graphs. Interactive graphing exercises appear on the book's supporting website. We use four devices to help students read and interpret graphs:

Figure 3.3

A Change in Demand versus a Change in Quantity Demanded

If the price of energy drinks falls from $3.00 to $2.50, the result will be a movement along the demand curve from point *A* to point *B*—an increase in quantity demanded from 60 million cans to 70 million cans. If consumers' incomes increase, or if another factor changes that makes consumers want more energy drinks at every price, the demand curve will shift to the right—an increase in demand from D_1 to D_2 causes the quantity of energy drinks demanded at a price of $3.00 to increase from 60 million cans at point *A* to 80 million cans at point *C*.

1. Detailed captions
2. Notes in the graphs
3. Colour-coded curves
4. Summary tables with graphs (see pages 57, 61, and 234 for examples)

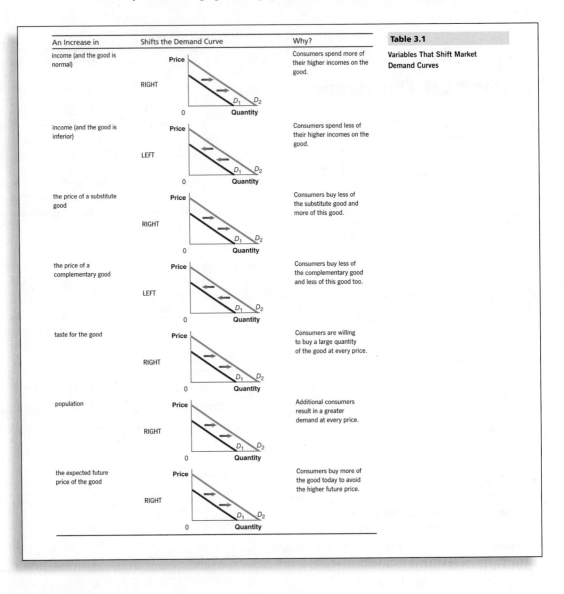

An Increase in	Shifts the Demand Curve	Why?	Table 3.1
income (and the good is normal)	RIGHT	Consumers spend more of their higher incomes on the good.	Variables That Shift Market Demand Curves
income (and the good is inferior)	LEFT	Consumers spend less of their higher incomes on the good.	
the price of a substitute good	RIGHT	Consumers buy less of the substitute good and more of this good.	
the price of a complementary good	LEFT	Consumers buy less of the complementary good and less of this good too.	
taste for the good	RIGHT	Consumers are willing to buy a large quantity of the good at every price.	
population	RIGHT	Additional consumers result in a greater demand at every price.	
the expected future price of the good	RIGHT	Consumers buy more of the good today to avoid the higher future price.	

Review Questions and Problems and Applications

Every exercise in a chapter's Review Questions and Problems and Applications sections are available in MyEconLab. Using MyEconLab, students can complete these and many other exercises online, get tutorial help, and receive instant feedback and assistance on exercises they answer incorrectly. Also, student learning is enhanced by having the summary material and problems grouped together by learning objective, which will allow students to focus on the parts of the chapter they found most challenging. Each major section of the chapter, paired with a learning objective, has at least two review questions and three problems.

We include one or more end-of-chapter problems that test students' understanding of the content presented in the Solved Problem, Making the Connection, and Don't Let This Happen to You features in the chapter. Instructors can cover a feature in class and assign the corresponding problem for homework. The Test Item Files also include test questions that pertain to these special features.

Integrated Supplements

The authors and Pearson Canada have worked together to integrate the text, print, and media resources to make teaching and learning easier.

MyEconLab

MyLab and Mastering, our leading online learning products, deliver customizable content and highly personalized study paths, responsive learning tools, and real-time evaluation and diagnostics. MyLab and Mastering products give educators the ability to move each student toward the moment that matters most—the moment of true understanding and learning.

MyEconLab for Hubbard, *Macroeconomics,* Second Canadian Edition, can be used as a powerful out-of-the-box resource for students who need extra help, or instructors can take full advantage of its advanced customization options.

MyEconLab® Provides the Power of Practice

Optimize your study time with MyEconLab, the online assessment and tutorial system. When you take a sample test online, MyEconLab gives you targeted feedback and a personalized Study Plan to identify the topics you need to review.

Study Plan

The Study Plan shows you the sections you should study next, gives easy access to practice problems, and provides you with an automatically generated quiz to prove mastery of the course material.

Unlimited Practice

As you work each exercise, instant feedback helps you understand and apply the concepts. Many Study Plan exercises contain algorithmically generated values to ensure that you get as much practice as you need.

Learning Resources

Study Plan problems link to learning resources that further reinforce concepts you need to master.

- **Help Me Solve This** learning aids help you break down a problem much the same way as an instructor would do during office hours. Help Me Solve This is available for select problems.
- A **graphing tool** enables you to build and manipulate graphs to better understand how concepts, numbers, and graphs connect.

Pearson eText The Pearson eText gives students access to their textbook anytime, anywhere. In addition to note taking, highlighting, and bookmarking, the Pearson eText offers interactive and sharing features. Instructors can share their comments or highlights, and students can add their own, creating a tight community of learners within the class.

Other Resources for the Instructor

Instructor's Manual

The Instructor's Manual includes chapter-by-chapter summaries grouped by learning objectives, teaching outlines incorporating key terms and definitions, teaching tips, topics for class discussion, new Solved Problems, new Making the Connection features, new Economics in Your Life scenarios, and solutions to all review questions and problems in the book. The Instructor's Manual is available for download from the Instructor's Resource Centre (www .pearsoned.ca/highered). The authors, Jason Childs and Apostolos Serletis, prepared the solutions to the end-of-chapter review questions and problems.

Test Item File

The Test Item File includes 4000 class-tested multiple-choice, true/false, short-answer, and graphing questions. There are questions to support each key feature in the book. The Test Item File is available in print and for download from the Instructor's Resource Centre (www .pearsoncanada.ca/highered). Test questions are annotated with the following information:

- **Difficulty:** 1 for straight recall, 2 for some analysis, 3 for complex analysis
- **Type:** multiple-choice, true/false, short-answer, essay
- **Topic:** the term or concept the question supports
- **Learning outcome**
- **AACSB** (see description that follows)
- **Page number**
- **Special feature in the main book:** chapter-opening case example, *Economics in Your Life*, *Solved Problem*, Making the Connection, *Don't Let This Happen to You*, and *An Inside Look*

The Association to Advance Collegiate Schools of Business (AACSB)

The Test Item File author has connected select questions to the general knowledge and skill guidelines found in the AACSB Assurance of Learning Standards.

TestGen

The computerized TestGen package allows instructors to customize, save, and generate classroom tests. The test program permits instructors to edit, add, or delete questions from the Test Item Files; analyze test results; and organize a database of tests and student results. This software allows for extensive flexibility and ease of use. It provides many options for organizing and displaying tests, along with search and sort features. The software and the Test Item Files can be downloaded from the Instructor's Resource Center (www.pearsoncanada.ca/ highered).

PowerPoint Lecture Presentation

Two sets of PowerPoint slides are available:

1. A comprehensive set of editable, animated PowerPoint slides can be used by instructors for class presentations or by students for lecture preview or review. These animated slides include all the graphs, tables, and equations in the textbook.

2. A second set of PowerPoint slides without animations is available for those who prefer a more streamlined presentation for class use.

Learning Solution Managers

Pearson's Learning Solutions Managers work with faculty and campus course designers to ensure that Pearson technology products, assessment tools, and online course materials are tailored to meet your specific needs. This highly qualified team is dedicated to helping students take full advantage of a wide range of educational resources by assisting in the integration of a variety of instructional materials and media formats. Your local Pearson Canada sales representative can provide you with more details about this service program.

ACKNOWLEDGMENTS

The guidance and recommendations of the following instructors helped us develop our plans for the second Canadian edition and the supplements package. While we could not incorporate every suggestion from every reviewer, we do thank each and every one of you and acknowledge that your feedback was indispensable in developing this text. We greatly appreciate your assistance in making this the best text it could be; you have helped teach a whole new generation of students about the exciting world of economics.

Bijan Ahmadi, Camosun College
Joseph DeJuan, University of Waterloo
Jason Dean, Sheridan/Wilfrid Laurier University
Alex Gainer, University of Alberta
David Gray, University of Ottawa
Suzanne Iskander, Humber College
Nargess Kayhani, Mount Saint Vincent University
Junjie Liu, Simon Fraser University
Douglas McClintock, University of Calgary
Amy Peng, Ryerson University
Julien Picault, University of British Columbia—Okanagan
Charlene Richter, British Columbia School of Business
Elizabeth Troutt, University of Manitoba
Mike Tucker, Fanshawe College

A WORD OF THANKS

We greatly appreciate the efforts of the Pearson team. Acquisitions Editor Megan Farrell energy and direction made this second Canadian edition possible. Developmental Editor Patti Sayle and Project Manager Pippa Kennard worked tirelessly to ensure that this text was as good as it could be. We are grateful for the energy and creativity of Marketing Manager Claire Varley. Nicole Mellow ably managed the extensive MyLab and supplement package that accompanies the book. We thank Charlotte Morrison-Reed and Susan Bindernagel for their careful copyediting and proofreading.

Economics: Foundations and Models

CHAPTER

1

You versus Caffeine

As you study economics, you will start to see the complexity and interconnectedness of the world around you. Something as simple as your morning cup of coffee is actually the result of hundreds of individual choices made by people you have never met.

If you are like 65 percent of Canadians, you had a cup of coffee this morning—you might even be drinking one now. In Colombia, over 3500 kilometres away, someone decided to plant coffee, somebody else picked it, and another group of people brought it to a port. A different group of people loaded it onto a ship, and other people sailed the ship to North America. The coffee beans were then unloaded, transported to a roaster, roasted and ground, and packaged, all by more different people. Finally, the coffee arrived at your local coffee shop, where yet another group of people brewed the coffee for you. This amazing sequence of events happens without any one person or group of people planning it. Yet you get the benefit of all this work by all these different people for less than $5. It's amazing to consider all that's involved in something so simple.

This interconnectedness of people's choices can have major implications for you. Changes in weather patterns, like 2015's El Niño, can dramatically reduce the amount of coffee growers can produce. This change in the weather, so far from Canada, changes what all Canadians have to pay for their morning cup.

Chapter Outline and Learning Objectives

1.1 Three Key Economic Ideas, page 2
Explain these three key economic ideas:
    People are rational.
    People respond to incentives.
    Optimal decisions are made at the margin.

1.2 The Economic Problems All Societies Must Solve, page 5
Discuss how a society answers these three key economic questions:
    What goods and services will be produced?
    How will the goods and services be produced?
    Who will receive the goods and services produced?

1.3 Economic Models, page 9
Understand what economic models are and aren't, and why they are a good idea.

1.4 Microeconomics and Macroeconomics, page 12
Distinguish between microeconomics and macroeconomics.

1.5 The Language of Economics, page 12
Define important economic terms. (It's not *all* Greek.)

Appendix A: Using Graphs and Formulas, page 18
Review the use of graphs and formulas.

Economics in Your Life

How Much Will You Pay for a Cup of Coffee?

The price of coffee is likely to go up in the next year or two. There was a time not long ago when a cup of coffee cost less than a dollar. Suppose you are waiting in line to buy the cup of coffee you count on to keep you awake during class. Is the price likely to be higher than it was last week? We all complain when the price of something we buy regularly goes up, but what determines that price? Consider what might change if the price of coffee doubled over the next six months. As you read this chapter, see if you can answer this question. You can check your answer against the one we provide on page 14, at the end of this chapter.

I n this book, we use economics to answer a wide variety of questions. Just a few examples:

- How are the prices of things you buy every day determined?
- How do government spending and taxation affect the economy?
- Why do governments control the prices of some goods?
- Why are some countries wealthier than others?

Economists don't always agree on the answers to these questions and a lot of others. In fact, there are a number of lively debates on a lot of different issues. In addition, new problems and issues are constantly arising. So, economists are always at work developing new methods to analyze economic questions.

Scarcity A situation in which unlimited wants exceed the limited resources available to fulfill those wants.

All the issues we discuss in this text illustrate a basic fact of life: People have to make choices. We all have to make choices because of **scarcity**. Scarcity means that we don't have enough resources to do everything we want to. Our needs and wants are infinite, but our planet and time are finite. You likely had to choose between spending money on tuition or taking a trip to Europe. Even the richest people in the world have to deal with scarcity of time. Bill Gates, one of the wealthiest people in the world, has to choose between working with his charitable foundation or spending time with his children. Every hour he spends on charity work is an hour he can't spend with his family. **Economics** is the study of the choices consumers, business managers, and government officials (in short, *people*) make in their efforts to make the best use of scarce resources in achieving their goals.

Economics The study of the choices people make to attain their goals, given their scarce resources.

We begin this chapter by discussing three important economic ideas that will come up throughout this book. *People are rational; people respond to incentives;* and *optimal decisions are made at the margin.* We then introduce you to the three basic economic decisions that all societies have had to find answers to since society began: *What* goods and services will be produced? *How* will the goods and services be produced? and *Who* will receive the goods and services produced? Next, we introduce you to the idea of economic models and their role in analyzing economic issues. **Economic models** are simplifications of reality used to analyze real-world economic issues. We will explain why economists use models and how they construct them. Finally, we will discuss the difference between microeconomics and macroeconomics and introduce you to some of the other important terms that are part of economists' language.

Economic model A simplified version of reality used to analyze real-world economic situations.

1.1 **LEARNING** OBJECTIVE

Explain these three key economic ideas: People are rational; people respond to incentives; and optimal decisions are made at the margin.

Three Key Economic Ideas

As you go through your day-to-day life, you interact with many people directly and thousands more indirectly. Whether you are looking for a part-time job, downloading the latest app, or getting a quick cup of coffee, you are interacting with other people through markets. A **market** is a group of buyers and sellers and the institutions (rules) or arrangements by which they come together to trade. Most of economics involves analyzing what happens in markets. Throughout this book, as we study how people make choices and interact in markets, we will return to three important ideas:

1. People are rational.
2. People respond to incentives.
3. Optimal decisions are made at the margin.

Market A group of buyers and sellers of a good or service and the institutions or arrangements by which they come together to trade.

People Are Rational

Economists generally assume that people are rational. This does not mean that economists think that people are computers with no emotions. It means that people make decisions and take the actions that they *believe* will make them happy. Economists tend to think people consider the costs and benefits of something and only do the things with more benefit than cost. When you buy a cup of coffee, an economist assumes that you thought the benefit was worth at least as much as the time, effort, and money you had to spend getting it. You might be wrong, it could be the worst cup of coffee you have ever had, but when you paid $2, you believed it was worth it. Put simply, economists don't think people deliberately do things to make themselves worse off.

People Respond to Incentives

Many factors go into determining the benefit of something. You might see benefits in terms of religious fulfillment, jealousy, compassion, or even greed. Economists emphasize that consumers and firms consistently respond to *economic* incentives. This fact may seem obvious, but it is often overlooked. For a great example of this, take a look at your local bank and then think of banks shown in American movies. Banks in American movies often have bullet-resistant shields and security guards to deter bank robbers. Bullet-resistant plastic shields and armed security guards are unheard of at Canadian bank branches. Why? The shields are expensive, costing up to $20 000. The average loss during a robbery is around just $1200. The economic incentives for banks are clear: It is less costly to put up with robberies and tell staff not to resist robbers than to take additional security measures. Some people are surprised by the lack of security in Canadian banks, but economists aren't.

In each chapter, the *Making the Connection* feature discusses a news story or another application related to the chapter material. Read the following *Making the Connection* for a discussion of whether people respond to incentives even when deciding whether to skip a workout.

| **Making the Connection** | **Get Fit or Get Fined** |

Obesity is a growing problem for Canadians—almost 60% of us are obese or overweight. Being obese increases the risk of a wide variety of health problems including diabetes and heart failure. One reason for obesity in adults is a lack of physical activity—a lot of people find it hard to make themselves go to the gym.

Fortunately, there's an app for that. Pact™ uses incentives to encourage people to go the gym and eat healthier foods. The app charges you $5 or $10 (depending on the amount you sign up for) every time you skip a scheduled workout. If you make your workout target, the app gives you a share of money paid by people skipping their workouts. The idea is to increase the marginal benefit of going to the gym while increasing the marginal cost of skipping a workout. The marginal benefit rises because not only do you get all the benefits of a workout, you'll get paid. When the marginal benefit of something increases, people will do more of it. The marginal cost of skipping a workout increases too. Skipping a workout might make you gain weight, but with the app it makes your wallet lose weight—the cost of skipping a workout now costs you at least $5. When the marginal cost of something rises, people will do less of it.

While no formal studies of the effect of the app have been conducted yet, a lot of users will tell you it works. The app's designers understand that people respond to incentives.

Your Turn: Test your understanding by doing related problems 1.3 and 1.4 on page 16 at the end of this chapter.   MyEconLab

Optimal Decisions Are Made at the Margin

Economics is sometimes referred to as the *marginal science* because of how economists tend to think about decisions. Some decisions are "all or nothing." When you finish your undergraduate degree, you can choose to either get a job or go to graduate school. However, most decisions are not the all-or-nothing type and involve doing a little more or a little less. For example, when you have a job, your choices are not whether to spend everything you earn or to save it all, but how much to save.

Economists use the term *marginal* to mean "extra" or "additional." Should you spend your next hour watching Netflix or studying? The *marginal benefit (MB)* of watching another hour is the enjoyment you receive. The *marginal cost (MC)* is the lower grade you receive because you studied less. You aren't the only one who has to make decisions at the margin. Netflix has to decide how many seasons of a popular show to make available to its subscribers. Should the company make another season available? The marginal benefit of this would be the extra revenue it gets from new users and existing subscribers who would have left the service if that season weren't available, and the marginal cost would be the extra wages, royalties, and equipment costs (server space) needed to make the season available. If your goal is to make the *net benefit* (benefit minus cost) as big as possible, then you have a really simple decision rule—*do more of any activity with a marginal benefit greater than the marginal cost*. As long as MB > MC, do more. If you've gotten as much net benefit as possible, you'll find that MB is pretty close to MC. In fact, MB = MC is an easy way of deciding when to do no more of something. When it comes to a firm's profit (revenue − cost), if producing the next unit increases revenue (MB) more than costs (marginal cost), making that unit will increase your profits. If producing the next unit increases costs more than revenue, making that unit will actually reduce profits. If producing the next unit increases revenue by the same amount as it increases costs, stop! You've now maximized profits and net benefits.

People often apply this rule without really thinking about it. Usually you will know whether the extra enjoyment of another hour spent watching a program is worth the additional cost of spending one hour less studying for your economics midterm without a mathematical formula. However, business people often have to make careful calculations using analysis tools like spreadsheets to determine whether the extra revenue of increased production is greater than or less than the additional costs. Economists refer to this sort of analysis as **marginal analysis**.

In each chapter of this book, you will see the special feature *Solved Problem*. This feature will enhance your understanding of the material by leading you through the steps of solving an applied economic problem. After reading the problem, you can test your understanding by working out the related problems at the end of the chapter and in the study guide. You can also find more *Solved Problems* and tutorials at MyEconLab.

Marginal analysis Analysis that involves comparing marginal benefits and marginal costs.

Solved Problem **1.1**

Binge Watching and Decisions at the Margin

Suppose you've decided to take a break from studying economics to watch an episode of your favourite show on Netflix. The episode ends on a cliff-hanger and you now have approximately 12 seconds to decide if you should watch the next episode to find out what happens or get back to studying. Your friend sitting beside you argues that you should watch one more episode because you'll receive a decent mark (say 70%) if you watch and don't study anymore that night. Do you agree with your friend's reasoning? What, if any, additional information do you need to have to decide if you should watch the extra episode? When would watching the extra episode be a good idea? When would it be a bad idea?

Solving the Problem

Step 1: **Review the chapter material.** This problem is about making decisions, so you may want to review the section "Optimal Decisions Are Made at the Margin," which is on page 4. Remember to "think marginal" whenever you see the words additional or extra.

Step 2: **Explain whether you agree or disagree with your friend.** We have seen that any activity should be continued up to the point where marginal benefit is equal to marginal cost. In this case, that means watching episodes until the point where the extra enjoyment you get out of knowing what happens next is equal to the damage not studying does to your performance in your economics class. Your friend has not done a marginal analysis, so you shouldn't agree with her, *yet*. Her statement about your mark based on the amount you have studied so far doesn't help you decide to watch the next episode. She could be right that watching the episode that is starting really soon is a good idea, but she has not provided you with any proof—you need more information to know for sure.

Step 3: **Explain what additional information you need.** You need more information to make the optimal decision. You need to know the additional enjoyment you will get from watching the episode. You also need to know how much your mark will rise if you get back to studying. In short, you need to know the marginal cost (the change in your mark) and the marginal benefit (extra satisfaction).

Step 4: **Compare marginal cost and marginal benefit.** Once you know the marginal cost and the marginal benefit of watching the next episode, compare the two. If the marginal cost is greater than the marginal benefit, then watching the next episode is a bad idea. If the marginal cost is less than the marginal benefit, then watching one more episode is a good idea.

Your Turn: For more practice, do related problem 1.5 on page 16 at the end of this chapter.

MyEconLab

The Economic Problems All Societies Must Solve

Living in a world of scarcity means that we face **trade-offs**: Doing more of one thing means that we have to do less of something else. The best way to measure the cost of something is the value of what we give up to get it. The value of what we give up to engage in an activity is called the **opportunity cost**. To be accurate, the opportunity cost of something (such as a good or service) is the value of the next best alternative. What is the opportunity cost of spending an extra hour studying? It depends on what you would have chosen to do if you weren't studying. If you would have spent the hour watching TV, then that is the opportunity cost, never mind that you could have spent the same time studying. The easiest way to demonstrate what opportunity cost is all about is with an example. Let's say that a federal government employee, who is currently earning $80 000 a year, is thinking about leaving his or her job to start a consulting company. The opportunity cost of starting the consulting company is the $80 000 salary that is no longer received from the government, even if the person doesn't pay him- or herself a salary in the new business.

Since all societies face trade-offs, they must make choices when answering the following three fundamental economic questions:

1. *What* goods and services will be produced?
2. *How* will the goods and services be produced?
3. *Who* will receive the goods and services produced?

Throughout this book, we'll return to these questions. For now, we briefly introduce each one.

1.2 LEARNING OBJECTIVE

Discuss how a society answers these three key economic questions: What goods and services will be produced? How will the goods and services be produced? Who will receive the goods and services produced?

Trade-off The idea that because of scarcity, producing more of one good or service means producing less of another good or service.

Opportunity cost The highest-valued alternative that must be given up to engage in an activity.

What Goods and Services Will Be Produced?

How will a society decide whether to make more economics textbooks or more video games? More daycare spaces or more sports arenas? Of course, "society" doesn't make decisions, individual people do. The answer to the question of what to produce is determined by the choices that consumers, firms, and governments make. Due to the structure of the Canadian economy, every day you help decide what goods and services firms in Canada and around the world provide. When you choose to spend your money at the movies instead of at the bookstore, you encourage firms to make more movies and fewer books. Similarly, Bombardier must decide whether it will devote resources to producing new planes or trains. The federal government must also make decisions about what to produce. Will it devote resources to the military or increase payments to parents with children? In each case, consumers, firms, and governments deal with scarcity by trading off one good or service for another. Each choice made comes with an opportunity cost, measured by the value of the best alternative given up.

How Will the Goods and Services Be Produced?

After figuring out what to make, societies must figure out how to make it. In the Canadian context, we generally think of firms or governments making this decision. Producers of goods and services face a trade-off between using more workers and using more machines. For example, movie studios have to choose whether to produce animated films using highly skilled animators to draw each frame by hand or to use fewer animators and powerful computers and software instead. Firms also have to decide whether to produce in Canada using few workers and many machines or produce in developing countries using many workers and fewer machines.

Who Will Receive the Goods and Services Produced?

In Canada, who receives what is produced depends largely on how income is distributed. Individuals with the highest incomes have the ability to buy the most goods and services. Governments levy taxes and use part of the money to provide income to some people. Governments also use the money collected in taxes to supply goods and services that are not being provided in other ways. The debate over how much taxation and government spending is appropriate will continue as long as societies must address the three fundamental questions.

Centrally Planned Economies versus Market Economies

Societies answer the three questions—what, how, and for whom?—in different ways. We'll talk briefly about the two extremes, but remember that all countries use a combination of both.

Centrally planned economy An economy in which the government decides how economic resources will be allocated.

One extreme is the **centrally planned economy**, in which an individual or group of people (generally the government) directly answers all three questions. From 1917 to 1991, the most important centrally planned economy was the Soviet Union's. In the Soviet Union, government agencies decided what to produce, what production techniques to use, and who would get the goods once they were made. People managing factories and stores reported to the government. These managers had to follow the instructions of government even when what they were producing wasn't what consumers (people) wanted. Centrally planned economies like the Soviet Union's have not been successful in producing low-cost (plentiful), high-quality goods and services. As a result, the material standard of living of the average person in a centrally planned economy tends to be low. All centrally planned economies have also been dictatorships. Dissatisfaction with low living standards and political repression finally led to the collapse of the Soviet Union in 1991. Today only a few small countries, such as Cuba and North Korea, still have largely centrally planned economies. Recently, Cuba has begun to move away from central planning.

Making the Connection | Central Planning Leads to Some Odd Products

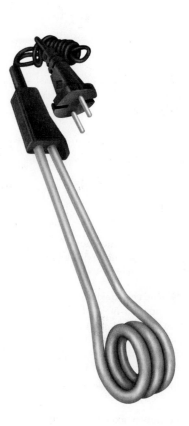

Central planning in the Soviet Union ended up putting some very strange products in the hands of consumers. The really odd ones came about as central planners tried to make substitutes for products consumers saw in the West and wanted to have for themselves. One example is the Zaporozhet, a Soviet-era car made from pressed cardboard, which could come with an optional hatch in the floor for ice fishing.

But a little something we now take for granted presented a special challenge to Soviet-era central planners. An electric kettle or coffee maker is such a common product now that you can buy one for the money made in less than two hours of work at minimum wage. But they were a lot more exciting and expensive when they were first introduced. Having seen or heard about such products, Soviet consumers wanted to be able to get them at home too. The metals, and later plastics, that electric kettles were made of weren't cheap and plentiful in the Soviet Union, so central planners came up with an alternative.

The boiling wand (in the picture) is just a heating element pretty much the same as what would have been used in an electric kettle with a handle. The idea was to submerge the end of the wand in the liquid you wanted to heat up and plug it in—the coil would heat up and so would your water for tea.

Of course, an open heating element presented a huge risk of fires, and Soviet-era quality control in manufacturing meant they were also subject to electrical shorts and other dangers. People still tell stories about Soviet travellers causing power failures by plugging in their boiling wands.

Central planning's bad products aren't limited to history. North Korea's central planning approach has led to the worst airline in the world—it describes its own food simply as "edible" and passenger boarding is accompanied by military marching music.

Sources: Based on *Popular Mechanics*, http://www.popularmechanics.com/cars/g499/8-strange-examples-of-soviet-design; and *Australian Times*, http://www.australiantimes.co.uk/best-and-worst-airlines-in-the-world.

At the other end of the spectrum is the **market economy**. Market economies rely on privately owned firms to produce goods and services and to decide how to produce them. A *market* is all potential buyers and sellers of a good or service as well as the rules that determine how buyers and sellers interact. Markets, rather than governments, determine who receives the goods and services produced. In this type of economy, firms must produce goods and services that people want to buy or they go out of business. In that sense, it is ultimately consumers who decide what will be produced and how. In a market economy, all trades must be agreed to by all the people involved.

In a market economy, people's income is mostly determined by what they have to sell. For example, if you're a civil engineer and firms are willing to pay you $85 000 a year, that's what you will have to spend on goods and services. If you own a house that you rent out to your friends or own shares in a company, your income will be even higher. Market economies have two distinguishing features: (1) markets directly reward people's hard work, and (2) decision making is shared by everyone in the market. Overall, in a market economy the answers to the three basic questions are provided by everyone.

Market economies do have drawbacks. Luck, both good and bad, plays a role in determining a person's income, and sometimes markets don't work the way we would like them to. In particular, markets are not good at providing important goods and services such as roads, national defence, or health care.

Market economy An economy in which the decisions of households and firms interacting in markets allocate economic resources.

The Modern Mixed Economy

We've seen that there are flaws in how both centrally planned economies and market economies answer the three basic questions. As a result, all modern economies are "**mixed economies**" that use elements of both centrally planned and market economies.

Mixed economy An economy in which most economic decisions result from the interaction of buyers and sellers in markets, but in which the government plays a significant role in the allocation of resources.

In Canada, most of the things you buy in stores—electronics, coffee, food, etc.—are produced by privately owned firms in response to the demands of consumers: The availability of these goods results from a market system answering the three basic questions. At the same time, other goods and services are provided by the government, such as roads, national defence, health care, etc. Even the United States and China, often cited as extremes of market economy and central planning respectively, are mixed economies that rely on a combination of both the market and central planning to provide people with a variety of goods and services.

Most debates about central planning and markets focus on the proportion each plays in answering the three questions. Very few people actually still advocate for a total market economy or a completely centrally planned economy. Keep this in mind when listening to the debates of leaders of political parties.

Efficiency and Equity

Productive efficiency A situation in which a good or service is produced at the lowest possible cost.

Allocative efficiency A state of the economy in which production is in accordance with consumer preferences; in particular, every good or service is produced up to the point where the last unit provides a marginal benefit to society equal to the marginal cost of producing it.

Voluntary exchange A situation that occurs in markets when both the buyer and seller of a product are made better off by the transaction.

Market economies tend to be more efficient than centrally planned economies. Before we can understand why this is, we must explore two types of efficiency: *productive efficiency* and *allocative efficiency*. **Productive efficiency** occurs when a good or service is produced at the lowest possible cost. **Allocative efficiency** occurs when a country's resources are used to produce the mix of goods and services that consumers want. Markets tend to be efficient because they rely on **voluntary exchange**. When an exchange is voluntary, both the buyer and the seller are made better off by the transaction, or they wouldn't have agreed to it. The voluntary nature of exchange promotes competition that encourages producers to find cheaper methods of producing the goods and services they want to sell, as consumers always wish to pay less. This leads to productive efficiency, as firms that can't match others' low costs go out of business. Competition also promotes allocative efficiency. A firm that uses scarce resources to produce goods and services that consumers don't want to buy goes out of business.

Markets and competition promote efficiency, but they don't guarantee it. Inefficiency can arise from a variety of sources. It often takes time to achieve an efficient outcome. When Blu-ray players were first introduced, firms didn't instantly achieve productive efficiency, as they had to experiment to find the lowest-cost method of producing them. Some production processes cause environmental damage. In this case, government intervention can actually increase efficiency; without government action, firms will ignore the cost of damaging the environment, leading to the production of more goods than is in society's best interest.

Equity The fair distribution of economic benefits.

An economically efficient outcome is not necessarily a desirable one. Many people prefer economic outcomes that they consider fair or equitable, even if those outcomes are less efficient. **Equity** is harder to define than *efficiency*, but it usually involves a fair distribution of economic benefits. For some people, equity involves a more equal distribution of economic benefits than would result from an emphasis on efficiency alone. For example, some people support raising taxes on people with higher incomes to provide funds for programs that aid the poor. Although governments may increase equity by reducing the incomes of high-income people and increasing the incomes of the poor, efficiency may be reduced. People have less incentive to open new businesses, to supply labour, and to save if the government takes a significant amount of the income they earn from working or saving. The result is that fewer goods and services are produced, and less saving takes place. As this example illustrates, *there is often a trade-off between efficiency and equity.* Government policymakers often confront this trade-off.

Making the Connection | The Equity–Efficiency Trade-off in the Classroom

Imagine your professor decided that it was really unfair that students in her class all received different grades. After all, understanding economics comes more easily to some students than to others. In order to account for this, she tells you that your grade will be equal to the class average no matter how well, or poorly, you do on the midterm and final exam. If every student knows this, there's likely to be a problem. In this extreme case, the marginal benefit of studying becomes much lower, while the marginal cost stays the same—meaning few students will study and the class average will be much lower than it would be if everyone's mark were based solely on their own performance. The result is a much less efficient use of time and an entire class with low grades.

Economic Models

1.3 **LEARNING** OBJECTIVE

Understand what economic models are and aren't, and why they are a good idea.

Economists rely on economic theories, or models (we use the words *model* and *theory* interchangeably in this text), to analyze real-world issues from coffee prices to immigration. As mentioned earlier, economic models are simplifications of reality. Economists are not the only ones using models: An engineer may use a computer model of a bridge to test its resistance to earthquakes; a biologist may make a physical model of a nucleic acid to better understand its properties. The main point of a model is to allow people to focus on the interactions between two or more things. Thus a model makes ideas sufficiently explicit and concrete so that individuals, firms, or the government can use them to inform decisions. For example, we will see in Chapter 3 that the model of demand and supply is a simplified version of how the prices of products are determined by interactions among buyers and sellers in markets.

Economists use models to answer questions. For example, consider the question from the chapter opener: "How much will you be paying for a cup of coffee?" While this seems like a fairly simple question, it is actually quite complicated. To answer complex questions like this one, economists use several models to look at different aspects of the issue. For example, they may use a model of how wages are determined to analyze the flexibility different firms have in their cost structures. They may use another model to consider how often people will change their purchasing patterns. Yet another model might be used to explore how growers will react to a change in the price of raw coffee. Sometimes economists can use existing models to analyze an issue, but in other cases, they must develop a new model. To develop a new model, economists generally follow these steps:

1. Decide on the assumptions to use in developing the model.
2. Formulate a testable hypothesis.
3. Use economic data to test the hypothesis.
4. Revise the model if it fails to explain the economic data well.
5. Retain the revised model to help answer similar economic questions in the future.

The Role of Assumptions in Economic Models

Any model, in any discipline, is based on assumptions because models have to be simple to be useful. We cannot analyze an economic issue unless we reduce its complexity at least a little. For example, economic models make *behavioural assumptions* about the motives of consumers and firms. Economists assume that consumers will buy the goods and services that will maximize their well-being or their satisfaction. Similarly, economists assume that firms act to maximize their profits. These assumptions are simplifications because we know they don't describe the motives of every firm or every consumer exactly. Many firms are now considering corporate social responsibility in making their production choices. How can we know if the assumptions in a model are too simple or too limiting? We discover this when we form hypotheses based on these assumptions and test the hypotheses using real-world information.

Forming and Testing Hypotheses in Economic Models

An **economic variable** is something measurable, such as the wages paid to Tim Hortons employees. A *hypothesis* in an economic model is a statement about an economic variable that may be either correct or incorrect. Most hypotheses take the form of predictions.

Economic variable Something measurable that can have different values, such as the price of coffee.

An example of a hypothesis in an economic model is the statement that extreme weather in Colombia will increase the price of coffee in Canada. An economic hypothesis is usually about a *causal relationship*; in this case, the hypothesis states that weather patterns associated with El Niño *cause* higher prices for coffee in Canada.

All hypotheses need to be tested before they are accepted. To test a hypothesis, we analyze statistics on the relevant economic variables. In our coffee example, we would gather data on coffee prices and other variables that we think might have an impact on the people buying or selling coffee. Testing a hypothesis can be tricky. For example, showing that coffee prices rose following an El Niño year is not enough to demonstrate that El Niño weather *caused* the price increase. Just because two things are *correlated*—that is, they happen together—does not mean that one caused the other. In this example, perhaps the price increase was caused by an increase in the wages paid to coffee shop employees. Many different economic variables change over any given period of time, which makes testing hypotheses a challenge.

Note that hypotheses must be statements that could, in fact, turn out to be incorrect. Statements such as "high coffee prices are bad" or "high wages for baristas are good" are value judgments rather than hypotheses because there is no way to disprove them.

Economists accept and use an economic model if it leads to hypotheses that are confirmed by statistical analysis. In many cases, the acceptance is tentative pending the gathering and analysis of new data. In fact, economists often refer to a hypothesis having been "not rejected," rather than "accepted." But what if statistical analysis rejects a hypothesis? For example, what if a model generates the hypothesis that weather associated with El Niño leads to higher coffee prices in Canada, but analysis of the data rejects the hypothesis? In this case, the model must be reconsidered. It may be that an assumption used in the model was too simplistic or limiting. Perhaps the model used to determine the effect of weather on Canadian coffee prices didn't take into account Canadian weather patterns—people drink more hot beverages when it's cold outside. If we also have a much warmer winter in Canada, we might not see an impact on coffee prices.

The process of developing models, testing hypotheses, and revising models occurs not just in economics but in disciplines like physics, chemistry, and biology. This process is often referred to as the *scientific method*. Economics is called a *social science* because it applies the scientific method to the study of interactions among people.

Normative and Positive Analysis

Throughout this book, as we build economic models and use them to answer questions, we need to keep the distinction between *positive analysis* and *normative analysis* in mind. **Positive analysis** concerns facts or logic. Positive statements are concerned with what is and can potentially be disproven. **Normative analysis** is about value judgments, or what *ought* to be. Economics is about positive analysis, which measures the costs and benefits of different courses of action.

Positive analysis Analysis concerned with what is.

Normative analysis Analysis concerned with what ought to be.

We can use a provincial government's minimum wage laws to compare positive and normative analysis. At the end of 2015, Ontario had the highest minimum wage of any province in Canada (though the Northwest Territories had a minimum wage of $12.50). At that time in Ontario, it was illegal to pay a worker less than $11.25 an hour. Without the minimum wage law, some firms and some workers would voluntarily agree to a lower wage. Because of the minimum wage law, some workers have a hard time finding work, and some firms end up paying more for workers. A positive analysis of the minimum wage law uses an economic model to estimate how many workers lose their jobs (or are unable to find one) when the minimum wage increases, the impact of an increase on firms' costs and profits, and the gains to those workers who find jobs at a higher rate of pay. After economists complete this positive analysis, the decision as to whether an increase in the minimum wage was a good idea or a bad idea is a normative one and depends on how people view the trade-offs involved. Supporters of minimum wage laws feel that the losses to employers and to newly unemployed workers are more than offset by the gains to workers who see their pay increase. Opponents of minimum wage laws think the losses are greater than the gains. The assessment depends, in part, on a person's values and political views. The positive analysis an economist provides would play a role in the decision but can't by itself decide the issue one way or another.

In each chapter, you will see a *Don't Let This Happen to You* box like the one below. This box alerts you to common pitfalls in thinking about economic ideas. After reading this box, test your understanding by working out the related problem 3.5 at the end of the chapter.

Don't Let This Happen to You

Don't Confuse Positive Analysis with Normative Analysis

"Economic analysis has shown that an increase in the minimum wage is a bad idea because it causes unemployment." Is this statement accurate? In 2016, legislation in Alberta prevented anyone from paying a worker less than $12.20 an hour. This wage is higher than some employers are willing to pay some workers. If the minimum wage were lower, some people who couldn't find a job would be able to find work at a lower wage. Therefore, positive economic analysis indicates that an increase in the minimum wage causes unemployment (although there is a lot of disagreement on how much). *But,* those people who find jobs benefit from the increased minimum wage because they get paid more.

In other words, increasing the minimum wage creates both losers (those who end up unemployed because of the minimum wage legislation and the firms that have to pay workers more) and winners (people who get paid more than they would have before the minimum wage increase).

Should we value the gains to the winners more than the losses to the losers? The answer to this question involves normative analysis. Positive economic analysis can only show you what the consequences of a policy are, not whether a policy is "good" or "bad." The statement at the beginning of this box is incorrect.

MyEconLab
Your Turn: Test your understanding by doing related problem 3.5 on page 17 at the end of this chapter.

Economics as a Social Science

Since economics studies the actions of people, it is a social science. Economics is similar to other social science disciplines like psychology, political science, and sociology. As a social science, economics is all about human behaviour—particularly decision making—in every context, not just the context of business. Economists study issues such as how families decide how many children to have, why some people have a hard time losing weight, and why people often ignore important information when making decisions. Economics also has much to contribute to questions of government policy. As we'll see throughout this book, economists have played an important role in formulating government policies in areas such as the environment, health care, and poverty.

Making the Connection | ## Should the Government of British Columbia Increase Its Minimum Wage?

The current minimum wage in B.C. is $10.85 per hour, despite the fact that Vancouver is one of the most expensive places to live in Canada. Should B.C. increase the minimum wage? Like most questions about economic policy, the answer is, it depends. There are costs and benefits to increasing the minimum wage.

An increase in the minimum wage tends to reduce the number of entry-level jobs. When firms have to pay workers more, they hire fewer people. Entry-level jobs, which tend to be filled by young people, can be the first step in developing a successful career. Youth unemployment is a growing problem in a number of countries, such as Spain and France, that have restrictive labour laws. Moreover, a person's early employment history has a huge impact on lifelong earnings.

Should B.C. raise its minimum wage?

Higher labour costs are also difficult for some firms to deal with. Having to pay more for labour means that firms that are able to substitute machinery for workers will have an advantage over those that can't. Increasing the minimum wage tends to give larger firms an advantage over smaller ones, because they can afford the complex machinery to replace people. (Do you think a small retail store could afford the self-scan checkout you see at major retailers?)

Increasing the minimum wage also offers important benefits. Those who can find or keep their jobs get bigger paycheques. An increase in income can go a long way toward improving the lives of people who depend on minimum wage work for their livelihoods. People with lower incomes may spend more of what they earn than those with higher incomes, so increasing the minimum wage may create more economic opportunities for other people as well.

Whether B.C. should increase its minimum wage rate is a normative question. The answer to that question will be based on how the people of B.C. feel the costs and benefits compare.

MyEconLab   **Your Turn:** Test your understanding by doing related problem 3.3 on page 17 at the end of this chapter.

1.4 **LEARNING** OBJECTIVE

Distinguish between microeconomics and macroeconomics.

Microeconomics The study of how households and firms make choices, how they interact in markets, and how the government attempts to influence their choices.

Macroeconomics The study of the economy as a whole, including topics such as inflation, unemployment, and economic growth.

Microeconomics and Macroeconomics

Economic models can be used to analyze decision making in many areas. We group some of these areas together as *microeconomics* and others as *macroeconomics.* **Microeconomics** is the study of how individual economic agents make choices, how these choices come together to determine what happens in a single market, and the impact of government interventions on market outcomes. When you're talking about microeconomics, you're generally talking about *one* person, *one* firm, or *one* market. Microeconomic issues include explaining how consumers react to changes in prices and how firms decide what prices they should charge. Microeconomics is also used to analyze other issues, such as how individual women decide whether to have children, who is most likely to take illegal drugs, and how to reduce pollution in the most efficient way.

Macroeconomics is the study of the economy as a whole. When you're talking about macroeconomics, you're generally talking about a country, province, or region. Macroeconomics focuses on topics such as inflation, unemployment, and economic growth. Some of the big questions in macroeconomics are why economies experience a cycle of booms and busts, why some economies grow much faster than others, and why prices rise faster in some places than in others. Macroeconomics also involves a lot of different policy issues, such as whether and how the government can intervene to prevent recessions.

The division between microeconomics and macroeconomics is not always clear-cut. Many situations have *both* a microeconomic and a macroeconomic aspect. For example, the level of total investment by firms in new machinery and equipment helps determine how quickly an economy grows, which is a macroeconomic issue, but understanding the decisions made by each firm about what to invest in and when to do it is a microeconomic issue.

1.5 **LEARNING** OBJECTIVE

Define important economic terms. (It's not *all* Greek.)

The Language of Economics

In the following chapters, you'll encounter a number of important economic terms again and again. Becoming familiar with these terms is a necessary step in learning economics—you have to learn to speak the language. Here we provide a brief introduction to a few of these terms. We will discuss them all in greater detail later in the book.

- **Production.** *Production* is the process of making goods and services, often undertaken by entrepreneurs.

- **Entrepreneur.** An *entrepreneur* is someone who operates a business. In a market system, entrepreneurs decide what goods and services to produce and how to produce them. An entrepreneur starting a new business often puts his or her own money at risk. If an entrepreneur is wrong about what consumers want or about the best way to produce goods or services, the money he or she puts up to start the business can be lost. This is not an unusual occurrence: About half of all new businesses close within a few years. Without entrepreneurs willing to take on the risk of starting and running businesses, economic progress would be impossible.

- **Innovation.** There is a difference between *invention* and *innovation*. An invention is the development of a new good or a new process for making a good. An innovation is the practical application of an invention. (*Innovation* may also be used to refer to any significant improvement in a good or way of making a good.) A lot of time can pass between the appearance of a new idea and its development for widespread use. The first digital electronic computer, the ENIAC—which was the size of a small house (167 m^2)—was developed in 1945. ENIAC can be thought of as an invention. However, the first personal computer (an innovation) wasn't introduced until 1981, and it has only been since the 1990s that computers (which experience continual innovations) have become common in workplaces and homes.

- **Technology.** A firm's *technology* is the processes it uses to turn inputs into outputs (i.e., goods and services). In an economic sense, a firm's technology depends on many factors, such as the skill of its managers, the education of its workers, and the quality of its equipment.

- **Firm, company, or business.** A *firm* is an organization that produces a good or service. Most firms produce goods or services in order to earn profit, but there are also non-profit firms, such as universities. Economists tend to use the terms *firm, company,* and *business* interchangeably.

- **Goods.** *Goods* are tangible items that people want, such as books, computers, clothing, etc.

- **Services.** *Services* are activities done for others, such as cutting hair, cleaning houses, or conducting banking transactions.

- **Revenue.** A firm's *revenue* is all the money it receives when it sells goods or services. It is calculated by multiplying the price per unit by the number of units sold.

- **Profit.** A firm's *profit* is the difference between its revenue and its costs. Economists distinguish between *accounting profit* and *economic profit*. In calculating accounting profit, the costs of some economic resources the firm doesn't explicitly pay for are left out—accounting profit only worries about *explicit costs*. Economic profit includes all the costs associated with operating a firm, including *implicit costs* (particularly opportunity costs). When we use the term *profit* in this book, we're referring to *economic profit*. It is very important that you don't confuse profit with revenue.

- **Household.** A *household* consists of all the people occupying a home that make decisions together. Households are the suppliers of all the factors of production (particularly labour) used by firms to make goods and services. Households are also the consumers of all the goods and services produced in an economy.

- **Factors of production or economic resources.** Firms use *factors of production* to produce goods and services. The main factors of production are labour, capital, natural resources—including land—and entrepreneurial ability. Households earn income by supplying firms with these factors of production.

- **Capital.** The word *capital* can refer to *financial capital* or to *physical capital*. Financial capital includes stocks and bonds issued by firms, bank accounts, and holdings of money. However, in economics, *capital* refers to physical capital, which is any manufactured good that is used to make other goods. Examples of physical capital are computers, factory buildings, tools, and trucks. The total amount of physical capital available in a country is referred to as the country's *capital stock*.

- **Human capital.** *Human capital* is the accumulated training, skills, and knowledge that a person has. For example, university-educated workers generally have more skills and are more productive than workers with only a high school education. Therefore, people with a university degree are said to have more human capital than people with only a high school diploma.

Economics in Your Life

How Much Will You Pay for a Cup of Coffee?

At the start of the chapter, we asked you "How much will you be paying for a cup of coffee?" Some information that will help you think about the answer to this question appears in *Making the Connection* on page 11. The price of a good is determined by how much someone, like you, is willing to pay for it and how much someone else is willing to sell it for. The costs of producing a cup of coffee, including the opportunity costs, play a very important role in how much you have to lay out for that all important first cup of the day. As the minimum wage increases, coffee-growing lands become increasingly scarce, and more people want to have a cup, the price of coffee will increase. As the price goes up, people will also change their behaviour, and some people might stop drinking coffee all together.

Conclusion

The best way to think of economics is as a group of useful ideas about how individuals make choices. Economists have put these ideas into practice by developing economic models. Consumers, business managers, and government policymakers use these models every day to help make choices. In this book, we explore many key economic models and give examples of how to apply them in the real world. Most students taking an introductory economics course do not major in economics or become professional economists. Whatever your major or career path, the economic principles you'll learn in this book will improve your ability to make choices in many aspects of your life. These principles will also improve your understanding of how decisions are made in business and government.

Chapter Summary and Problems

Key Terms

Allocative efficiency, p. 8	Economics, p. 2	Market economy, p. 7	Positive analysis, p. 10
Centrally planned economy, p. 6	Equity, p. 8	Microeconomics, p. 12	Productive efficiency, p. 8
Economic model, p. 2	Macroeconomics, p. 12	Mixed economy, p. 7	Scarcity, p. 2
Economic variable, p. 9	Marginal analysis, p. 4	Normative analysis, p. 10	Trade-off, p. 5
	Market, p. 3	Opportunity cost, p. 5	Voluntary exchange, p. 8

Summary

LO **1.1** *Economics* is the study of the choices consumers, business managers, and government officials make to attain their goals, given their scarce resources. We must make choices because of *scarcity*, which means that although our wants are unlimited, the resources available to fulfill those wants are limited. Economists assume that people are rational in the sense that consumers and firms use all available information as they take actions intended to achieve their goals. Rational individuals weigh the benefits and costs of each action and choose an action only if the benefits outweigh the costs. Although people act from a variety of motives, ample evidence indicates that they respond to economic incentives. Economists use the word *marginal* to mean extra or additional. The optimal decision is to continue any activity up to the point where the marginal benefit equals the marginal cost.

LO 1.2 Society faces *trade-offs*: Producing more of one good or service means producing less of another good or service. The *opportunity cost* of any activity—such as producing a good or service—is the highest-valued alternative that must be given up to engage in that activity. The choices of consumers, firms, and governments determine what goods and services will be produced. Firms choose how to produce the goods and services they sell. In Canada, who receives the goods and services produced depends largely on how income is distributed in the marketplace. In a *centrally planned economy*, most economic decisions are made by the government. In a *market economy*, most economic decisions are made by consumers and firms. Most economies, including Canada's, are *mixed economies* in which most economic decisions are made by consumers and firms but in which the government also plays a significant role. There are two types of efficiency: productive efficiency and allocative efficiency. *Productive efficiency* occurs when a good or service is produced at the lowest possible cost. *Allocative efficiency* occurs when production is in accordance with consumer preferences. *Voluntary exchange* is a situation that occurs in markets when both the buyer and seller of a product are made

better off by the transaction. *Equity* is more difficult to define than efficiency, but it usually involves a fair distribution of economic benefits. Government policymakers often face a trade-off between equity and efficiency.

LO 1.3 An *economic variable* is something measurable that can have different values, such as the wages of software programmers. Economists rely on economic models when they apply economic ideas to real-world problems. *Economic variables* are simplified versions of reality used to analyze real-world economic situations. Economists accept and use an economic model if it leads to hypotheses that are confirmed by statistical analysis. In many cases, the acceptance is tentative, however, pending the gathering of new data or further statistical analysis. Economics is a social science because it applies the scientific method to the study of the interactions among individuals. Economics is concerned with positive analysis rather than normative analysis. *Positive analysis* is concerned with what is. *Normative analysis* is concerned with what ought to be. Because economics is based on studying the actions of individuals, it is a social science. As a social science, economics considers human behaviour in every context of decision making, not just in business.

LO 1.4 *Microeconomics* is the study of how households and firms make choices, how they interact in markets, and how the government attempts to influence their choices. *Macroeconomics* is the study of the economy as a whole, including topics such as inflation, unemployment, and economic growth.

LO 1.5 Becoming familiar with important terms is a necessary step in learning economics. These important economic terms include *capital, entrepreneur, factors of production, firm, goods, household, human capital, innovation, production, profit, revenue, services,* and *technology*.

MyEconLab   Log in to MyEconLab to complete these exercises and get instant feedback.

Review Questions

LO 1.1
1.1 Briefly discuss each of the following economic ideas: People are rational; people respond to incentives; and optimal decisions are made at the margin.
1.2 What is scarcity? Why is scarcity central to the study of economics?

LO 1.2
2.1 Why does scarcity imply that every society and every individual face trade-offs?
2.2 What are the three economic questions that every society must answer? Briefly discuss the differences in how centrally planned, market, and mixed economies answer these questions.

LO 1.3
3.1 Why do economists use models? How are economic data used to test models?
3.2 Describe the five steps by which economists arrive at a useful economic model.
3.3 What is the difference between normative analysis and positive analysis? Is economics concerned mainly with normative analysis or with positive analysis? Briefly explain.

LO 1.4
4.1 Briefly discuss the difference between microeconomics and macroeconomics.

* "Learning Objective" is abbreviated to "LO" in the end-of-chapter material.

Problems and Applications

1.1 Bank robberies are on the rise in New Jersey, and according to the FBI, this increase has little to do with the economic downturn. The FBI claims that banks have allowed themselves to become easy targets by refusing to install clear acrylic partitions, called "bandit barriers," which separate bank tellers from the public. Of the 193 banks robbed in New Jersey in 2008, only 23 had these barriers, and of the 40 banks robbed in the first 10 weeks of 2009, only one had a bandit barrier. According to a special agent with the FBI, "Bandit barriers are a great deterrent. We've talked to guys who rob banks, and as soon as they see a bandit barrier, they go find another bank." Despite this finding, many banks have been reluctant to install these barriers. Wouldn't banks have a strong incentive to install bandit barriers to deter robberies? Why, then, do so many banks not do so?

Based on Richard Cowen, "FBI: Banks Are to Blame for Rise in Robberies," NorthJersey.com, March 10, 2009.

1.2 The grading system is a powerful resource for teachers. In their book *Effective Grading: A Tool for Learning and Assessment*, Barbara Walvoord and Virginia Anderson state that "teachers must manage the power and complexity of the grading system" and that "teachers must consider grading in their first deliberations about a course."

   a. How could the grading system a teacher uses affect the incentives of students to learn the course material?

   b. If teachers put too little weight in the grading scale on a certain part of the course, such as readings outside the textbook, how might students respond?

   c. Teachers often wish that students came to class prepared, having read the upcoming material. How could a teacher design the grading system to motivate students to come to class prepared?

Based on Barbara E. Walvoord and Virginia Johnson Anderson, *Effective Grading: A Tool for Learning and Assessment*, Jossey-Bass: San Francisco,1998, pp. xvii–xviii.

1.3 Most provincial governments and the federal government in Canada offer programs and payments to encourage Canadians to have more children. The federal government currently pays all parents $160 per month for every child under six years old and $60 per month for every child between 6 and 18 years old (this is the Universal Child Care Benefit). Why would the Government of Canada make a cash payment to people with small children? How do you think most people respond to this program?

1.4 **[Related to Making the Connection on page 3]** Lizzy Pope and Jean Harvey found that offering first-year university students money to go to the gym on a regular basis increased gym attendance in the fall semester by between 49 and 51 percent and by 36 percent in the spring semester. They also found that the impact of the monetary incentive decreased when the number of trips required to get paid increased from 2 per week to 5 per week.

   a. Why might a monetary payment affect whether or not people go the gym when the health benefits of physical activity are so well documented?

   b. Why might a payment not cause some people to go the gym?

Based on Lizzy Pope and Jean Harvey (2015) The Impact of Incentives on Intrinsic and Extrinsic Motives for Fitness-Center Attendance in College First-Year Students. *American Journal of Health Promotion*: January/February 2015, Vol. 29, No. 3, pp. 192–199.

1.5 **[Related to Solved Problem 1.1 on page 4]** Two students are discussing *Solved Problem 1.1*:

   Joe: "I think the key additional information you need to know in deciding whether or not you should watch another episode is the grade you're currently getting and the grade you would get if you watched the extra episode. Then we can compare the grade earned before watching the episode and after watching the episode. This information is more important than the change in someone's grade from watching one more episode."

   Jill: "Actually, Joe, knowing the grade before and after watching the extra episode is exactly the same as knowing the change in someone's grade."

   Briefly evaluate their arguments.

1.6 **[Related to Solved Problem 1.1 on page 4]** Late in the semester, a friend tells you, "I was going to drop my psychology course so I could concentrate on my other courses, but I had already put so much time into the course that I decided not to drop it." What do you think of your friend's reasoning? Would it make a difference to your answer if your friend has to pass the psychology course at some point to graduate? Briefly explain.

2.1 Why does Bill Gates, one of the richest people in the world, face scarcity? Does everyone face scarcity? Are there any exceptions?

2.2 Centrally planned economies have been less efficient than market economies.

   a. Has this difference in efficiency happened by chance, or is there some underlying reason?

   b. If market economies are more economically efficient than centrally planned economies, would there ever be a reason to prefer having a centrally planned economy rather than a market economy?

2.3 In a paper, economists Patricia M. Flynn and Michael A. Quinn state the following:

> We find evidence that Economics is a good choice of major for those aspiring to become a CEO [chief executive officer]. When adjusting for size of the pool of graduates, those with undergraduate degrees in Economics are shown to have had a greater likelihood of becoming an S&P 500 CEO than any other major.

A list of famous economics majors published by McMaster University includes business leaders Steve Ballmer (former CEO of Microsoft), Warren Buffet, Sam Walton (Founder of Walmart), and Scott McNealy (CEO of SUN Microsystems). The list also includes politicians Ronald Reagan (former US president), Stephen Harper (former Prime Minister of Canada), Manmohan Singh (former Prime Minister of India), and Kofi Annan (former Secretary-General of the United Nations). Why might studying economics be particularly good preparation for being the top manager of a corporation or a leader in government?

Based on Patricia M. Flynn and Michael A. Quinn, "Economics: A Good Choice of Major for Future CEOs," Social Science Research Network, November 28, 2006; and Famous Economics Majors,

McMaster University; http://www.economics.mcmaster.ca/documents/Famous_Econ.pdf, accessed Feb. 12, 2012.

2.4 Suppose that a local radio station has decided to give away 100 tickets to a Nicki Minaj performance it's promoting. It announces that tickets will be given away at 7:00 A.M. on Monday at the radio station's studio.

   a. What groups of people will be most likely to try to get the tickets? Think of specific examples and then generalize.

   b. What is the opportunity cost of distributing tickets in this way?

   c. Productive efficiency occurs when a good or service, such as the distribution of tickets, is produced at the lowest possible cost. Is this an efficient way to distribute the tickets? If possible, think of a more efficient method of distributing the tickets.

   d. Is this an equitable way to distribute the tickets? Explain.

LO 1.3

3.1 Do you agree with the following assertion: "The problem with economics is that it assumes that consumers and firms always make the correct decision. But we know everyone's human, and we all make mistakes."

3.2 Dr. Strangelove's theory is that the price of mushrooms is determined by the activity of subatomic particles that exist in another universe parallel to ours. When the subatomic particles are emitted in profusion, the price of mushrooms is high. When subatomic particle emissions are low, the price of mushrooms is also low. How would you go about testing Dr. Strangelove's theory? Discuss whether this theory is useful.

3.3 [**Related to Making the Connection on page 11**] *Making the Connection* explains that there are both positive and normative elements to the debate over raising the minimum wage. What economic statistics would be most useful in evaluating the positive elements of the debate? Assuming that these statistics are available or could be gathered, are they likely to resolve the normative issues in this debate?

3.4 [**Related to the Chapter Opener on page 1**] In every El Niño year, coffee crops are likely to be damaged, reducing the amount of coffee available.

   a. How might a company, like Tim Hortons, that is part of a market economy deal with the fact there was less coffee available?

   b. How might a reduction in the amount of coffee available be dealt with if the economy was centrally planned?

3.5 [**Related to Don't Let This Happen to You on page 11**] Explain which of the following statements represent positive analysis and which represent normative analysis:

   a. The legalization of marijuana will lead to an increase in marijuana use by teenagers.

   b. The federal government should spend more on AIDS research.

   c. Rising paper prices will increase textbook prices.

   d. The price of coffee at Starbucks is too high.

LO 1.4

4.1 Briefly explain whether each of the following is primarily a microeconomic issue or a macroeconomic issue:

   a. The effect of higher cigarette taxes on the quantity of cigarettes sold

   b. The effect of higher income taxes on the total amount of consumer spending

   c. The reasons for the economies of East Asian countries growing faster than the economies of sub-Saharan African countries

   d. The reasons for low rates of profit in the airline industry

4.2 Briefly explain whether you agree with the following assertion: "Microeconomics is concerned with things that happen in one particular place, such as the unemployment rate in one city. In contrast, macroeconomics is concerned with things that affect the country as a whole, such as how the rate of underage drinking in Canada would be affected by an increase in the taxes on alcohol."

MyEconLab   MyEconLab is an online tool designed to help you master the concepts covered in your course. It will create a personalized study plan to stimulate and measure your learning. Log in to take advantage of this powerful study aid, and to access quizzes and other valuable course-related material.

Appendix A

Using Graphs and Formulas

Graphs are used to illustrate key economic ideas. Graphs appear not just in economics textbooks but also on websites and in newspaper and magazine articles that discuss events in business and economics. Why the heavy use of graphs? Because they serve two useful purposes: (1) They simplify economic ideas, and (2) they make the ideas more concrete so they can be applied to real-world problems. Economic and business issues can be complicated, but a graph can help cut through complications and highlight the key relationships needed to understand the issue. In that sense, a graph can be like a street map.

For example, suppose you take a bus to Toronto to see the CN Tower. After arriving at the downtown bus station, you will probably use a map similar to the one shown below to find your way to the CN Tower.

Maps are very familiar to just about everyone, so we don't usually think of them as being simplified versions of reality, but they are. This map does not show much more than the streets in this part of Toronto and some of the most important places. The names, addresses, and telephone numbers of the people who live and work in the area aren't given. Almost none of the stores and buildings those people work and live in are shown either. The map doesn't indicate which streets allow curbside parking and which don't. In fact, the map shows almost nothing about the messy reality of life in this section of Toronto except how the streets are laid out, which is the essential information you need to get from the bus station to the CN Tower.

Think about someone who says, "I know how to get around in the city, but I just can't figure out how to read a map." It certainly is possible to find your destination in a city without a map, but it's a lot easier with one. The same is true of using graphs in economics. It is possible to arrive at a solution to a real-world problem in economics and business without using graphs, but it is usually a lot easier if you do use them.

Often, the difficulty students have with graphs and formulas is a lack of familiarity. With practice, all the graphs and formulas in this text will become familiar to you. Once you are familiar with them, you will be able to use them to analyze problems that would otherwise seem very difficult. What follows is a brief review of how graphs and formulas are used.

Valentino Visentini/Alamy Stock Photo

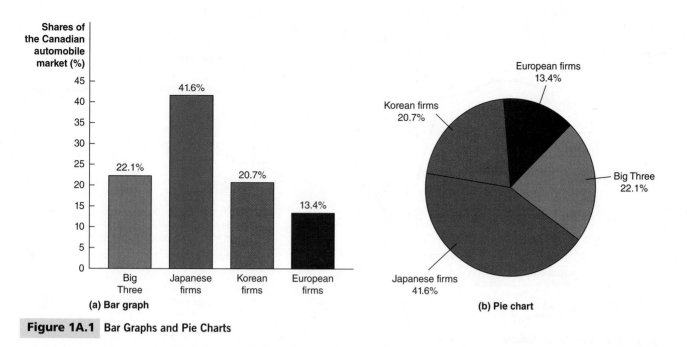

Figure 1A.1 Bar Graphs and Pie Charts

Values for an economic variable are often displayed as a bar graph or as a pie chart. In this case, panel (a) shows market share data for the Canadian automobile industry as a *bar graph*, where the market share of each group of firms is represented by the height of its bar. Panel (b) displays the same information as a *pie chart*, with the market share of each group of firms represented by the size of its slice of the pie.

Source: Data from Global Economic Research, Global Auto Report, Oct. 4, 2012. http://www.gbm.scotiabank.com/English/bns_econ/bns_auto.pdf

Graphs of One Variable

Figure 1A.1 displays values for market shares in the Canadian automobile market using two common types of graphs. Market shares show the percentage of industry sales accounted for by different firms. In this case, the information is for groups of firms: the "Big Three"—Ford, General Motors, and Chrysler—as well as Japanese firms, European firms, and Korean firms.

Information on economic variables is also often displayed in time-series graphs. Time-series graphs are displayed on a coordinate grid. In a coordinate grid, we can measure the value of one variable along the vertical axis (or *y*-axis) and the value of another variable along the horizontal axis (or *x*-axis). The point where the vertical axis intersects the horizontal axis is called the *origin*. At the origin, the value of both variables is zero. The points on a coordinate grid represent values of the two variables. In Figure 1A.2, we measure the number of automobiles and trucks sold worldwide by Ford Motor Company on the vertical axis, and we measure time on the horizontal axis. In time-series graphs, the height of the line at each date shows the value of the variable measured on the vertical axis. Both panels of Figure 1A.2 show Ford's worldwide sales during each year from 2001 to 2010. The difference between panel (a) and panel (b) illustrates the importance of the scale used in a time-series graph. In panel (a), the scale on the vertical axis is truncated, which means it does not start with zero. The slashes (//) near the bottom of the axis indicate that the scale is truncated. In panel (b), the scale is not truncated. In panel (b), the decline in Ford's sales during 2008 and 2009 appears smaller than in panel (a). (Technically, the horizontal axis is also truncated because we start with the year 2001, not the first year Ford sold any trucks.)

Graphs of Two Variables

We often use graphs to show the relationship between two variables. For example, suppose you are interested in the relationship between the price of a pepperoni pizza and the quantity of pizzas sold per week in the small town of Sackville, New Brunswick. A graph showing the relationship between the price of a good and the quantity of the

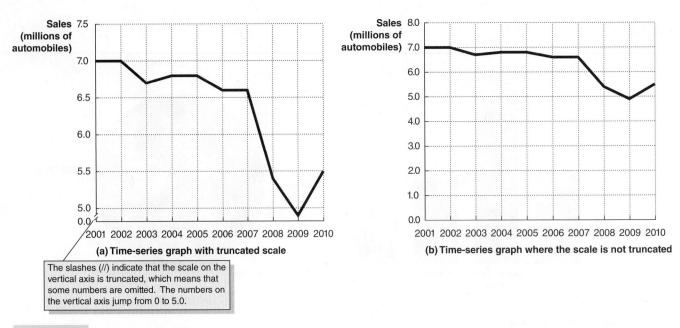

(a) Time-series graph with truncated scale

The slashes (//) indicate that the scale on the vertical axis is truncated, which means that some numbers are omitted. The numbers on the vertical axis jump from 0 to 5.0.

(b) Time-series graph where the scale is not truncated

Figure 1A.2   Time-Series Graphs

Both panels present time-series graphs of Ford Motor Company's worldwide sales during each year from 2001 to 2010. Panel (a) has a truncated scale on the vertical axis, and panel (b) does not. As a result, the fluctuations in Ford's sales appear smaller in panel (b) than in panel (a).
Source: Data from Ford Motor Company, Annual Report, various years.

good demanded at each price is called a *demand curve*. (As we will discuss later, in drawing a demand curve for a good, we have to hold constant any variables other than price that might affect the willingness of consumers to buy the good.) Figure 1A.3 shows the data collected on price and quantity. The figure shows a two-dimensional grid on which we measure the price of pizza along the y-axis and the quantity of pizzas sold per week along the x-axis. Each point on the grid represents one of the price and quantity combinations listed in the table. We can connect the points to form the demand curve for pizza in Sackville, NB. Notice that the scales on both axes in the graph are truncated. In this case, truncating the axes allows the graph to illustrate more clearly the relationship between price and quantity by excluding low prices and quantities.

Slopes of Lines

Once you have plotted the data in Figure 1A.3, you may be interested in how much the quantity of pizzas sold increases as the price decreases. The slope of a line tells us how much the variable we are measuring on the y-axis changes as the variable we are measuring on the x-axis changes. We can use the Greek letter delta (Δ) to stand for the change in a variable. The slope is sometimes referred to as the *rise* over the *run*. So, we have several ways of expressing slope:

$$\text{Slope} = \frac{\text{Change in value on the vertical axis}}{\text{Change in value on the horizontal axis}} = \frac{\Delta y}{\Delta x} = \frac{\text{Rise}}{\text{Run}}.$$

Figure 1A.4 reproduces the graph from Figure 1A.3. Because the slope of a straight line is the same at any point, we can use any two points in the figure to calculate the slope of the line. For example, when the price of pizza decreases from $14 to $12, the quantity of pizzas sold increases from 55 per week to 65 per week. Therefore, the slope is:

$$\text{Slope} = \frac{\Delta \text{Price of pizza}}{\Delta \text{Quantity of pizzas}} = \frac{(\$12 - \$14)}{(65 - 55)} = \frac{-2}{10} = -0.2.$$

Price (dollars per pizza)	Quantity (pizzas per week)	Points
$15	50	A
14	55	B
13	60	C
12	65	D
11	70	E

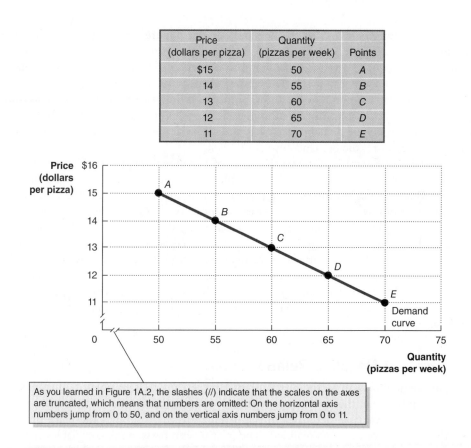

As you learned in Figure 1A.2, the slashes (//) indicate that the scales on the axes are truncated, which means that numbers are omitted: On the horizontal axis numbers jump from 0 to 50, and on the vertical axis numbers jump from 0 to 11.

Figure 1A.3

Plotting Price and Quantity Points in a Graph

The figure shows a two-dimensional grid on which we measure the price of pizza along the vertical axis (or y-axis) and the quantity of pizzas sold per week along the horizontal axis (or x-axis). Each point on the grid represents one of the price and quantity combinations listed in the table. By connecting the points with a line, we can better illustrate the relationship between the two variables.

The slope of this line gives us some insight into how responsive consumers in Sackville are to changes in the price of pizza. The larger the value of the slope (ignoring the negative sign), the steeper the line will be, which indicates that not many additional pizzas are sold when the price falls. The smaller the value of the slope, the flatter the line will be, which indicates a greater increase in pizzas sold when the price falls.

Taking into Account More than Two Variables on a Graph

The demand curve graph in Figure 1A.4 shows the relationship between the price of pizza and the quantity of pizzas demanded, but we know that the quantity of any good demanded depends on more than just the price of the good. For example, the quantity of pizzas demanded in a given week in Sackville can be affected by other variables, such as the price of hamburgers, whether an advertising campaign by local pizza parlours has begun that week, and so on. Allowing the values of any other variables to change will cause the position of the demand curve in the graph to change.

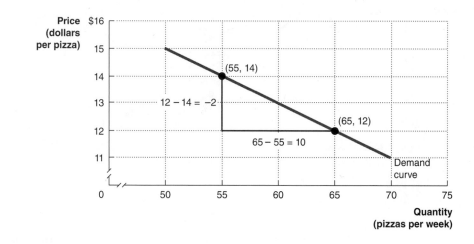

Figure 1A.4

Calculating the Slope of a Line

We can calculate the slope of a line as the change in the value of the variable on the y-axis divided by the change in the value of the variable on the x-axis. Because the slope of a straight line is constant, we can use any two points in the figure to calculate the slope of the line. For example, when the price of pizza decreases from $14 to $12, the quantity of pizzas demanded increases from 55 per week to 65 per week. So, the slope of this line equals −2 divided by 10, or −0.2.

Suppose, for example, that the demand curve in Figure 1A.4 were drawn holding the price of hamburgers constant, at $1.50. If the price of hamburgers rises to $2.00, some consumers will switch from buying hamburgers to buying pizza, and more pizzas will be demanded at every price. The result on the graph will be to shift the line representing the demand curve to the right. Similarly, if the price of hamburgers falls from $1.50 to $1.00, some consumers will switch from buying pizzas to buying hamburgers, and fewer pizzas will be demanded at every price. The result on the graph will be to shift the line representing the demand curve to the left.

The table in Figure 1A.5 shows the effect of a change in the price of hamburgers on the quantity of pizzas demanded. For example, suppose that at first we are on the line labelled *Demand curve₁*. If the price of pizza is $14 (point *A*), an increase in the price of hamburgers from $1.50 to $2.00 increases the quantity of pizzas demanded from 55 to 60 per week (point *B*) and shifts us to *Demand curve₂*. Or, if we start on *Demand curve₁* and the price of pizza is $12 (point *C*), a decrease in the price of hamburgers from $1.50 to $1.00 decreases the quantity of pizzas demanded from 65 to 60 per week (point *D*) and shifts us to *Demand curve₃*. By shifting the demand curve, we have taken into account the effect of changes in the value of a third variable—the price of hamburgers. We will use this technique of shifting curves to allow for the effects of additional variables many times in this book.

Positive and Negative Relationships

We can use graphs to show the relationships between any two variables. Sometimes the relationship between the variables is negative, meaning that as one variable increases in value, the other variable decreases in value. This was the case with the price of pizza and the quantity of pizzas demanded. The relationship between two variables can also be positive, meaning that the values of both variables increase or decrease together. For example, when the level of total income—or personal disposable income—received by households in Canada increases, the level of total consumption spending, which is

Figure 1A.5

Showing Three Variables on a Graph

The demand curve for pizza shows the relationship between the price of pizza and the quantity of pizzas demanded, holding constant other factors that might affect the willingness of consumers to buy pizza. If the price of pizza is $14 (point *A*), an increase in the price of hamburgers from $1.50 to $2.00 increases the quantity of pizzas demanded from 55 to 60 per week (point *B*) and shifts us to *Demand curve₂*. Or, if we start on *Demand curve₁* and the price of pizza is $12 (point *C*), a decrease in the price of hamburgers from $1.50 to $1.00 decreases the quantity of pizza demanded from 65 to 60 per week (point *D*) and shifts us to *Demand curve₃*.

Price (dollars per pizza)	Quantity (pizzas per week)		
	When the Price of Hamburgers = $1.00	When the Price of Hamburgers = $1.50	When the Price of Hamburgers = $2.00
$15	45	50	55
14	50	55	60
13	55	60	65
12	60	65	70
11	65	70	75

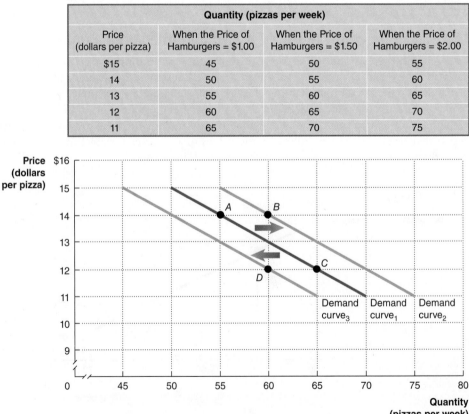

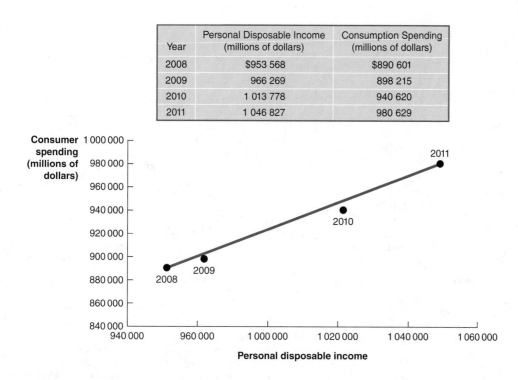

Year	Personal Disposable Income (millions of dollars)	Consumption Spending (millions of dollars)
2008	$953 568	$890 601
2009	966 269	898 215
2010	1 013 778	940 620
2011	1 046 827	980 629

Figure 1A.6

Graphing the Positive Relationship between Income and Consumption

In a positive relationship between two economic variables, as one variable increases, the other variable also increases. This figure shows the positive relationship between personal disposable income and consumption spending. As personal disposable income in Canada has increased, so has consumption spending.
Source: Data from Statistics Canada.

spending by households on goods and services, also increases. The table in Figure 1A.6 shows the values (in millions of dollars) for income and consumption spending for the years 2008–2011. The graph plots the data from the table, with personal disposable income measured along the horizontal axis and consumption spending measured along the vertical axis. Notice that the four points do not all fall exactly on the line. This is often the case with real-world data. To examine the relationship between two variables, economists often use the straight line that best fits the data.

Determining Cause and Effect

When we graph the relationship between two variables, we often want to draw conclusions about whether changes in one variable are causing changes in the other variable. Doing so, however, can lead to incorrect conclusions. For example, suppose you graph the number of homes in a neighbourhood that have a fire burning in the fireplace and the number of leaves on trees in the neighbourhood. You would get a relationship like that shown in panel (a) of Figure 1A.7: The more fires burning in the neighbourhood, the fewer leaves the trees have. Can we draw the conclusion from this graph that using a fireplace causes trees to lose their leaves? We know, of course, that such a conclusion would be incorrect. In spring and summer, there are relatively few fireplaces being used, and the trees are full of leaves. In the fall, as trees begin to lose their leaves, fireplaces are used more frequently. And in winter, many fireplaces are being used and many trees have lost all their leaves. The reason that the graph in Figure 1A.7 is misleading about cause and effect is that there is obviously an omitted variable in the analysis—the season of the year. An omitted variable is one that affects other variables, and its omission can lead to false conclusions about cause and effect.

Although in our example the omitted variable is obvious, there are many debates about cause and effect where the existence of an omitted variable has not been clear. For instance, it has been known for many years that people who smoke cigarettes suffer from higher rates of lung cancer than do nonsmokers. For some time, tobacco companies and some scientists argued that there was an omitted variable—perhaps a failure to exercise or a poor diet—that made some people more likely to smoke and more likely to develop lung cancer. If this omitted variable existed, then the finding that smokers were more likely to develop lung cancer would not have been evidence that smoking caused lung cancer. In this case, however, nearly all scientists eventually concluded that an omitted variable did not exist and that, in fact, smoking does cause lung cancer.

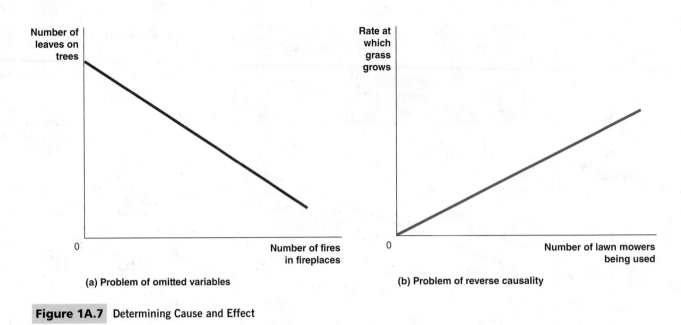

Figure 1A.7 Determining Cause and Effect

Using graphs to draw conclusions about cause and effect can be hazardous. In panel (a), we see that there are fewer leaves on the trees in a neighbourhood when many homes have fires burning in their fireplaces. We cannot draw the conclusion that the fires cause the leaves to fall because we have an *omitted variable*—the season of the year.

In panel (b), we see that more lawn mowers are used in a neighbourhood during times when the grass grows rapidly and fewer lawn mowers are used when the grass grows slowly. Concluding that using lawn mowers causes the grass to grow faster would be making the error of *reverse causality*.

A related problem in determining cause and effect is known as *reverse causality*. The error of reverse causality occurs when we conclude that changes in variable X cause changes in variable Y when, in fact, it is actually changes in variable Y that cause changes in variable X. For example, panel (b) of Figure 1A.7 plots the number of lawn mowers being used in a neighbourhood against the rate at which grass on lawns in the neighbourhood is growing. We could conclude from this graph that using lawn mowers causes the grass to grow faster. We know, however, that in reality, the causality is in the other direction: Rapidly growing grass during the spring and summer causes the increased use of lawn mowers. Slowly growing grass in the fall or winter or during periods of low rainfall causes decreased use of lawn mowers.

Once again, in our example, the potential error of reverse causality is obvious. In many economic debates, however, cause and effect can be more difficult to determine. For example, changes in the money supply, or the total amount of money in the economy, tend to occur at the same time as changes in the total amount of income people in the economy earn. A famous debate in economics was about whether the changes in the money supply caused the changes in total income or whether the changes in total income caused the changes in the money supply. Each side in the debate accused the other side of committing the error of reverse causality.

Are Graphs of Economic Relationships Always Straight Lines?

The graphs of relationships between two economic variables that we have drawn so far have been straight lines. The relationship between two variables is linear when it can be represented by a straight line. Few economic relationships are actually linear. For example, if we carefully plot data on the price of a product and the quantity demanded at each price, holding constant other variables that affect the quantity demanded, we will usually find a curved—or nonlinear—relationship rather than a linear relationship. In practice, however, it is often useful to approximate a nonlinear relationship with a linear relationship. If the relationship is reasonably close to being linear, the analysis is not significantly affected. In addition, it is easier to calculate the slope of a straight line, and it also is easier to calculate the area under a straight line. So, in this book, we often assume that the relationship between two economic variables is linear, even when we know that this assumption is not precisely correct.

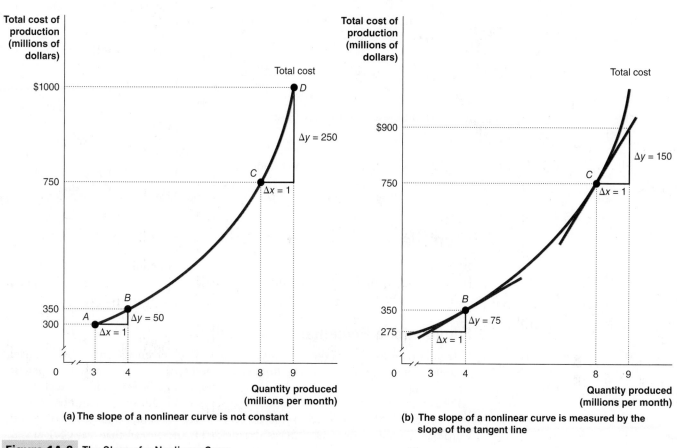

Figure 1A.8   The Slope of a Nonlinear Curve

The relationship between the quantity of iPhones produced and the total cost of production is curved rather than linear. In panel (a), in moving from point A to point B, the quantity produced increases by 1 million iPhones, while the total cost of production increases by $50 million. Farther up the curve, as we move from point C to point D, the change in quantity is the same—1 million iPhones—but the change in the total cost of production is now much larger: $250 million.

Because the change in the y variable has increased, while the change in the x variable has remained the same, we know that the slope has increased. In panel (b), we measure the slope of the curve at a particular point by the slope of the tangent line. The slope of the tangent line at point B is 75, and the slope of the tangent line at point C is 150.

Slopes of Nonlinear Curves

In some situations, we need to take into account the nonlinear nature of an economic relationship. For example, panel (a) of Figure 1A.8 shows the hypothetical relationship between Apple's total cost of producing iPhones and the quantity of iPhones produced.

The relationship is curved rather than linear. In this case, the cost of production is increasing at an increasing rate, which often happens in manufacturing. Put a different way, as we move up the curve, its slope becomes larger. (Remember that with a straight line, the slope is always constant.) To see this effect, first remember that we calculate the slope of a curve by dividing the change in the variable on the y-axis by the change in the variable on the x-axis. As we move from point A to point B, the quantity produced increases by 1 million iPhones, while the total cost of production increases by $50 million. Farther up the curve, as we move from point C to point D, the change in quantity is the same—1 million iPhones—but the change in the total cost of production is now much larger: $250 million. Because the change in the y variable has increased, while the change in the x variable has remained the same, we know that the slope has increased.

To measure the slope of a nonlinear curve at a particular point, we must measure the slope of the *tangent line* to the curve at that point. A tangent line will touch the curve only at that point. We can measure the slope of the tangent line just as we would the slope of any other straight line. In panel (b), the tangent line at point B has a slope equal to:

$$\frac{\Delta\text{Cost}}{\Delta\text{Quantity}} = \frac{75}{1} = 75.$$

The tangent line at point C has a slope equal to:

$$\frac{\Delta\text{Cost}}{\Delta\text{Quantity}} = \frac{150}{1} = 150.$$

Once again, we see that the slope of the curve is larger at point C than at point B.

Formulas

We have just seen that graphs are an important economic tool. In this section, we will review several useful formulas and show how to use them to summarize data and to calculate important relationships.

Formula for a Percentage Change

One important formula is the percentage change. The percentage change is the change in some economic variable, usually from one period to the next, expressed as a percentage. An important macroeconomic measure is the real gross domestic product (GDP). GDP is the value of all the final goods and services produced in a country during a year. "Real" GDP is corrected for the effects of inflation. When economists say that the Canadian economy grew 3.0 percent during 2011, they mean that real GDP was 3.0 percent higher in 2011 than it was in 2010. The formula for making this calculation is:

$$\frac{\text{GDP}_{2011} - \text{GDP}_{2010}}{\text{GDP}_{2010}} \times 100$$

or, more generally, for any two periods:

$$\text{Percentage change} = \frac{\text{Value in the second period} - \text{Value in the first period}}{\text{Value in the first period}} \times 100.$$

In this case, real GDP was \$1 279 586 million in 2010 and \$1 316 622 million in 2011. So, the growth rate of the Canadian economy during 2011 was:

$$\left(\frac{\$1\ 316\ 622 - \$1\ 279\ 586}{\$1\ 279\ 586}\right) \times 100 = 2.89\%.$$

Notice that it doesn't matter that in using the formula, we ignored the fact that GDP is measured in millions of dollars. In fact, when calculating percentage changes, *the units don't matter*. The percentage increase from \$1 279 586 million to \$1 316 622 million is exactly the same as the percentage increase from \$1 279 586 to \$1 316 622.

Formulas for the Areas of a Rectangle and a Triangle

Areas that form rectangles and triangles on graphs can have important economic meaning. For example, Figure 1A.9 shows the demand curve for Pepsi. Suppose that the price is currently \$2.00 and that 125 000 bottles of Pepsi are sold at that price. A firm's total revenue is equal to the amount it receives from selling its product, or the quantity sold multiplied by the price. In this case, total revenue will equal 125 000 bottles times \$2.00 per bottle, or \$250 000.

The formula for the area of a rectangle is:

$$\text{Area of a rectangle} = \text{Base} \times \text{Height}.$$

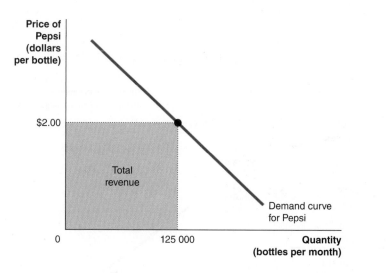

Figure 1A.9

Showing a Firm's Total Revenue on a Graph

The area of a rectangle is equal to its base multiplied by its height. Total revenue is equal to quantity multiplied by price. Here, total revenue is equal to the quantity of 125 000 bottles times the price of $2.00 per bottle, or $250 000. The area of the green-shaded rectangle shows the firm's total revenue.

In Figure 1A.9, the green-shaded rectangle also represents the firm's total revenue because its area is given by the base of 125 000 bottles multiplied by the price of $2.00 per bottle.

We will see in later chapters that areas that are triangles can also have economic significance. The formula for the area of a triangle is:

$$\text{Area of a triangle} = \frac{1}{2} \times \text{Base} \times \text{Height}.$$

The blue-shaded area in Figure 1A.10 is a triangle. The base equals 150 000 – 125 000, or 25 000. Its height equals $2.00 – $1.50, or $0.50. Therefore, its area equals 1/2 × 25 000 × $0.50, or $6250. Notice that the blue area is a triangle only if the demand curve is a straight line, or linear. Not all demand curves are linear. However, the formula for the area of a triangle will usually still give a good approximation, even if the demand curve is not linear.

Summary of Using Formulas

You will encounter several other formulas in this book. Whenever you must use a formula, you should follow these steps:

1. Make sure you understand the economic concept the formula represents.

2. Make sure you are using the correct formula for the problem you are solving.

3. Make sure the number you calculate using the formula is economically reasonable. For example, if you are using a formula to calculate a firm's revenue and your answer is a negative number, you know you made a mistake somewhere.

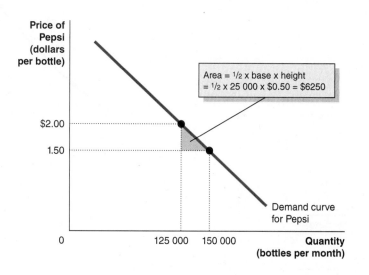

Figure 1A.10

The Area of a Triangle

The area of a triangle is equal to 1/2 multiplied by its base multiplied by its height. The area of the blue-shaded triangle has a base equal to 150 000 – 125 000, or 25 000, and a height equal to $2.00 – $1.50, or $0.50. Therefore, its area equals 1/2 × 25 000 × $0.50, or $6250.

Problems and Applications

LO Review the use of graphs and formulas.

1A.1 The following table shows the relationship between the price of custard pies and the number of pies Jacob buys per week:

Price	Quantity of Pies	Week
$3.00	6	July 2
2.00	7	July 9
5.00	4	July 16
6.00	3	July 23
1.00	8	July 30
4.00	5	August 6

a. Is the relationship between the price of pies and the number of pies Jacob buys a positive relationship or a negative relationship?

b. Plot the data from the table on a graph similar to Figure 1A.3 on page 21. Draw a straight line that best fits the points.

c. Calculate the slope of the line.

1A.2 The following table gives information on the quantity of glasses of lemonade demanded on sunny and overcast days:

Price (dollars per glass)	Quantity (glasses of lemonade per day)	Weather
$0.80	30	Sunny
0.80	10	Overcast
0.70	40	Sunny
0.70	20	Overcast
0.60	50	Sunny
0.60	30	Overcast
0.50	60	Sunny
0.50	40	Overcast

Plot the data from the table on a graph similar to Figure 1A.5 on page 22. Draw two straight lines representing the two demand curves—one for sunny days and one for overcast days.

1A.3 Using the information in Figure 1A.2 on page 20, calculate the percentage change in auto sales from one year to the next. Between which years did sales fall at the fastest rate?

1A.4 Real GDP in 2008 was $13 162 billion. Real GDP in 2009 was $12 703 billion. What was the percentage change in real GDP from 2008 to 2009? What do economists call the percentage change in real GDP from one year to the next?

1A.5 Assume that the demand curve for Pepsi passes through the following two points:

Price per Bottle of Pepsi	Number of Bottles Demanded
$2.50	100 000
1.25	200 000

a. Draw a graph with a linear demand curve that passes through these two points.

b. Show on the graph the areas representing total revenue at each price. Give the value for total revenue at each price.

1A.6 What is the area of the blue triangle shown in the following figure?

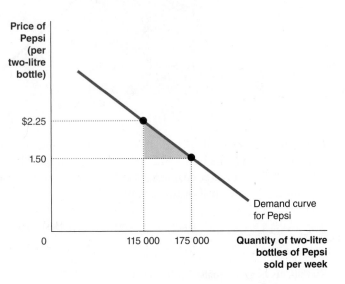

1A.7 Calculate the slope of the total cost curve at point *A* and at point *B* in the following figure.

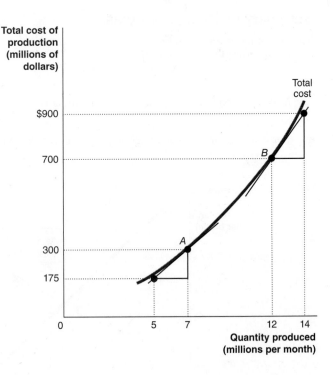

Trade-offs, Comparative Advantage, and the Market System

Dick Loek/Toronto Star/
ZUMAPRESS/Newscom

Managers Make Choices at Toyota

When you think of major automakers, Toyota is likely one of the first companies that comes to mind. Founded in Japan in 1937, Toyota is the largest automaker in the world, selling 10.8 million vehicles in 2015. To compete in the automotive market, the managers of Toyota must make many decisions, such as whether to introduce new car models. Toyota doesn't just sell gasoline-powered cars; it also sells diesel-powered cars and hybrids, and is developing all-electric vehicles.

Toyota's managers must also decide whether to concentrate production in Japanese facilities or build new ones in overseas markets. Keeping production in Japan makes it easier for Toyota's managers to supervise production and to employ Japanese workers, who generally have high skill levels and few labour disputes. By building plants in the countries in which it sells its vehicles, Toyota can benefit from paying lower wages, lower transportation costs, and the reduced political friction that results from investing in local economies. Toyota has assembly plants in Cambridge and Woodstock, Ontario, in which it builds the Toyota Corolla, Matrix, RAV4, the Lexus RX 350, and the Lexus RX 450h (hybrid).

Managers also face smaller-scale business decisions. For instance, they must decide how many Toyota Corolla sedans and Lexus RX 450h SUVs to build in the company's Cambridge plant each month. Like other decisions people make, this one involves a trade-off: Producing more Corolla sedans means making fewer RX 450h SUVs.

Chapter Outline and Learning Objectives

2.1 **Production Possibilities Frontiers and Opportunity Costs,** page 30
Use a production possibilities frontier to analyze opportunity costs and trade-offs.

2.2 **Comparative Advantage and Trade,** page 36
Understand comparative advantage and explain how it is the basis for trade.

2.3 **The Market System,** page 42
Explain the basic idea of how a market system works.

Economics in Your Life

The Trade-offs When You Buy a Car

When you buy a car, you probably consider features such as safety, fuel efficiency, and, of course, cost. Most newer cars are more fuel-efficient than older cars. Fuel-efficiency standards have been improving almost continuously over the last 40 years. Of course, newer cars are more expensive than older ones. Very old, inefficient cars can sometimes be bought for very little. Under what circumstances would you be better off buying an older, less fuel-efficient car than a new highly efficient one? Who do you think is most likely to want a car with high fuel efficiency? As you read this chapter, see if you can answer these questions. You can check your answers against those we provide on page 46 at the end of this chapter.

Scarcity A situation in which unlimited wants exceed the limited resources available to fulfill those wants.

Factors of production The inputs used to make goods and services.

All economics starts with the recognition of **scarcity**. Scarcity exists because we have unlimited wants but only limited resources available to fulfill those wants. *Scarcity requires trade-offs.* When resources are scarce, having more of one thing means having less of something else. The economic resources, or **factors of production**—the inputs used to make goods and services, such as workers, capital, natural resources, and entrepreneurial ability—are scarce. This means goods and services are scarce. Your time is scarce, which means that you face trade-offs: If you spend an hour studying for an economics exam, you have one less hour to spend playing video games. If your university decides to use some of its scarce budget to buy new computers for the computer labs, those funds will not be available to expand parking lots. In a market system, managers at all firms must make decisions like those made by Toyota's managers. If Toyota decides to devote some of the scarce workers and machinery in its Cambridge plant to producing more RX 450h SUVs, those resources will not be available to produce more Corolla sedans.

Canadian households and firms make many of their decision in markets. Trade is a key activity that takes place in markets. Trade involves the decisions of millions of households and firms spread all over the world. By engaging in trade, people can raise their standard of living. In this chapter, we provide an overview of how the market system coordinates the independent decisions of millions of people. We begin our analysis of the economic consequences of scarcity, the benefits of trade, and the workings of the market system by introducing an important economic model: the *production possibilities frontier*.

2.1 LEARNING OBJECTIVE

Use a production possibilities frontier to analyze opportunity costs and trade-offs.

Production possibilities frontier (PPF) A curve showing the maximum attainable combinations of two products that may be produced with available resources and current technology.

Production Possibilities Frontiers and Opportunity Costs

As we saw in the chapter opener, Toyota operates plants in Cambridge and Woodstock, Ontario, where it assembles Toyota sedans and Lexus RX 450h SUVs. Because the firm's resources—workers, machinery, materials, and entrepreneurial skills—are limited, Toyota faces a trade-off: For example, resources devoted to building sedans can't be used to build RX 450h SUVs, and vice versa. Chapter 1 explained that economic models can be useful to analyze a number of questions. We can use a simple model called the *production possibilities frontier* to analyze the trade-offs Toyota faces in its Cambridge plant. **A production possibilities frontier (PPF)** is a curve showing the maximum attainable combinations of two products that may be produced with available resources and technology. For our purposes, let's assume that Toyota produces only Corolla sedans and RX 450h SUVs at its Cambridge plant, using workers, robots, materials, and other machinery.

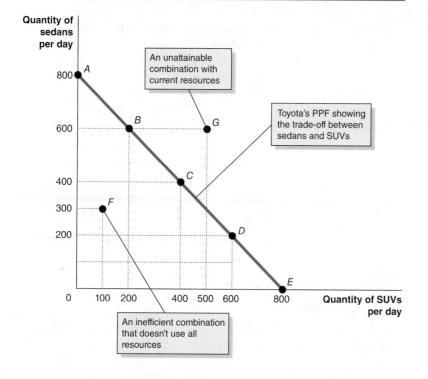

Toyota's Production Possibilities at Its Cambridge Plant		
Choice	Quantity of Corolla Sedans Produced	Quantity of RX 450h SUVs Produced
A	800	0
B	600	200
C	400	400
D	200	600
E	0	800
F	300	100
G	600	500

Figure 2.1

Toyota's Production Possibilities Frontier

Toyota faces a trade-off: To build one more sedan, it must build one less SUV. The production possibilities frontier illustrates the trade-off Toyota faces. Combinations on the production possibilities frontier—such as points A, B, C, D, and E—are *productively efficient* because the maximum output is being obtained from the available resources. Combinations inside the frontier—such as point F—are *inefficient* because some resources are not being used. Combinations outside the frontier—such as point G—are *unattainable* with current resources.

Graphing the Production Possibilities Frontier

Figure 2.1 uses a production possibilities frontier to illustrate the trade-offs that Toyota faces. The numbers on the table are plotted on the graph. The line in the graph is Toyota's production possibilities frontier. If Toyota uses all its resources to produce Corolla sedans, it can make 800 per day—point A at one end of the production possibilities frontier. If Toyota uses all its resources to produce RX 450h SUVs, it can produce 800 per day—point E at the other end of the production possibilities frontier. If Toyota devotes resources to producing both types of vehicles, it could be at a point like B where it produces 600 Corolla sedans and 200 RX 450h SUVs.

All the combinations on the frontier (such as A, B, C, D, and E) or inside it (such as point F) are *attainable* with the resources and technology Toyota currently has. Combinations on the frontier are (productively) *efficient* because all available resources are being fully used, and the fewest possible resources are being used to produce a given amount of output. Toyota is getting the most it can. Combinations inside the frontier, such as point F, are inefficient because maximum output is not being obtained from the available resources. We can tell F is inefficient because Toyota could make 500 SUVs at this factory and still make 300 sedans, instead of only making 100 SUVs and 300 sedans. This would happen if the managers decided to hire a number of workers, but didn't give them anything to do.

Toyota, like most firms, would like to be beyond the frontier—at a point like G, where it would be producing 600 sedans and 500 SUVs—but points outside the

Opportunity cost The highest-valued alternative that must be given up to engage in an activity.

Allocative efficiency A state of the economy in which production is in accordance with consumer preferences; in particular, every good or service is produced up to the point where the last unit provides a marginal benefit to society equal to the marginal cost of producing it.

production possibilities frontier are unattainable with the workers, equipment, materials, and technology currently in use. To be able to produce 600 sedans and 500 SUVs, Toyota would have to hire more resources.

Notice that if Toyota is producing efficiently and is on the production possibilities frontier, the only way to produce more of one type of vehicle is to produce fewer of another type. Recall from Chapter 1 that the **opportunity cost** of any activity is the highest-valued alternative that must be given up to engage in that activity. For Toyota, the opportunity cost of producing one more SUV is the number of sedans it will not be able to produce because it has shifted those resources to making SUVs. For example, in moving from point *B* to point *C*, the opportunity cost of producing 200 more SUVs per day is the 200 fewer sedans that can be made.

Being on the production possibilities frontier is a good idea, but what point on the production possibilities frontier is best? Choosing the best point on the production possibilities frontier is called **allocative efficiency**. Allocative efficiency occurs when a society is making the combination of goods and services that are most valued by consumers. For example, if consumers want SUVs more than they do sedans (as they did in the 1990s and 2000s), then the allocatively efficient point is likely a point like *E*. If consumers want sedans more than they do SUVs (as they tend to when the price of gas is high) the allocatively efficient point is more likely a point like point *A*.

Solved Problem **2.1**

Drawing a Production Possibilities Frontier for Pat's Pizza Pit

Pat's Pizza Pit makes both root beer and pizza. Pat has 5 hours a day to spend on making either pizzas or root beer. In 1 hour, Pat can make 2 pizzas or 1 litre of root beer.

a. Use the information given to complete the table below.

	Hours Spent Making		Quantity Made	
Choice	Root Beer	Pizza	Root Beer (litres)	Pizza
A	5	0		
B	4	1		
C	3	2		
D	2	3		
E	1	4		
F	0	5		

b. Use the data from the table you just completed to draw a production possibilities frontier graph illustrating Pat's trade-offs between making pizza and making root beer. Label the vertical axis "Quantity of pizzas made" and the horizontal axis "Quantity of root beer made." Make sure to label the values where Pat's PPF intersects the vertical and horizontal axes.

c. Label the points representing choice *B* and choice *C*. If Pat is at choice *B*, what is her opportunity cost of making more root beer?

Solving the Problem

Step 1: Review the chapter material. This problem is about using production possibilities frontiers to analyze trade-offs, so you may want to review the section "Graphing the Production Possibilities Frontier," which begins on page 31.

Step 2: Answer part (a) by filling in the table. If Pat can produce 1 litre of root beer in one hour, then with choice *A*, she will make 5 litres of root beer and no pizza. Because she can produce 2 pizzas in 1 hour, with choice *B*, she will make 4 litres of root beer and 2 pizzas. Using similar reasoning, you can fill in the remaining cells of the table as follows:

	Hours Spent Making		Quantity Made	
Choice	Root Beer	Pizza	Root Beer (litres)	Pizza
A	5	0	5	0
B	4	1	4	2
C	3	2	3	4
D	2	3	2	6
E	1	4	1	8
F	0	5	0	10

Step 3: **Answer part (b) by drawing the production possibilities frontier graph.**
Using the data in the table shown in Step 2, you should have a graph that looks
something like this:

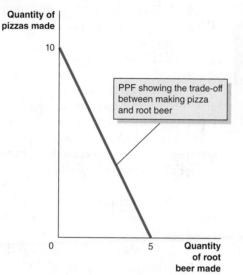

If Pat devotes all 5 hours to making pizza, she will have 10 pizzas. Therefore,
her production possibilities frontier will intersect the vertical axis at 10. If she
spends all her time making root beer, she will have 5 litres. Therefore, her production possibilities frontier will intersect the horizontal axis at 5.

Step 4: **Answer part (c) by showing choices *B* and *C* on your graph.** The
points for choices *B* and *C* can be plotted using the information in the table,
which gives you the following:

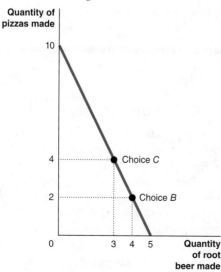

Moving from choice *B* to choice *C* increases Pat's production of pizza from 2
to 4, but lowers her production of root beer by 1 litre (from 4 to 3).

Your Turn: For more practice, do related problem 1.4 on page 48 at the end of this chapter.   MyEconLab

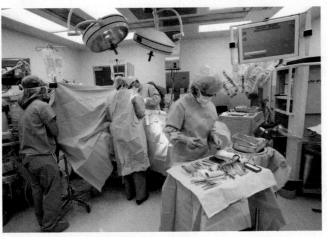

Jim West/ImageBROKER/Glow Images

Spending more on health care means spending less on other goods and services.

| **Making** the **Connection** | **Facing the Trade-offs of Health Care Spending** |

Governments have to deal with scarcity. If your provincial government spends more on health care, say by paying doctors or nurses more, it has less to spend on other areas such as education. Health care expenditures are the single biggest item in the budgets of all provincial governments, accounting for about 40 percent of spending. The federal government also supports health care spending through the Canada Health Transfer, which is the single biggest transfer of funds from the federal government to provincial governments. In 2015–2016, the federal government transferred about $34 billion dollars to provincial governments to pay for health care.

Canada's population is aging; the number of people who are over 65 is greater than ever before and that number is growing. As the population ages, two things will happen. First, older people need more health care than younger adults, which means governments will be asked to provide more money for health care spending. Second, there will be fewer people of working age to pay the taxes that support health care spending. As a result, the money to pay for all government spending will become even scarcer than it is now.

Spending more on health care would mean that less funding is available for all the other government programs, such as education, housing, infrastructure, and so on. If governments increase taxes to fund higher health care costs (instead of cutting spending in other areas), people will have less money for the purchases they want to make. Very soon governments will have to make real and meaningful choices about the areas that will receive funding. If doctors and nurses are paid more or if more doctors and nurses are hired, who are we going to pay less or what services will receive less funding? Will there be fewer teachers? Fewer police officers? More roads in disrepair? Will we have less money to spend on ourselves? Scarcity of resources means that these sorts of trade-offs have to be made.

Department of Finance Canada, Federal Support to Provinces and Territories, https://www.fin.gc.ca/fedprov/mtp-eng.asp; Geddes, John, "The health care time bomb," *McLean's Magazine*, April 12, 2010.

MyEconLab **Your Turn:** Test your understanding by doing related problems 1.5 and 1.6 on page 48 at the end of this chapter.

Increasing Marginal Opportunity Costs

We can use the production possibilities frontier to explore issues concerning the economy as a whole. For example, suppose we divide all the goods and services produced in the economy into just two types: government-provided goods and privately provided goods. In Figure 2.2, we let operations represent government-provided goods and cars represent privately provided goods. If all the country's resources were devoted to producing government-provided goods, 400 operations could be performed in one year. If all the country's resources were devoted to producing privately provided goods, 500 cars could be produced in one year. Devoting resources to producing both types of goods results in the economy being at other points along the production possibilities frontier.

Notice that this production possibilities frontier looks different from the one in Figure 2.1. This PPF is bowed outward rather than a straight line. The fact that the PPF

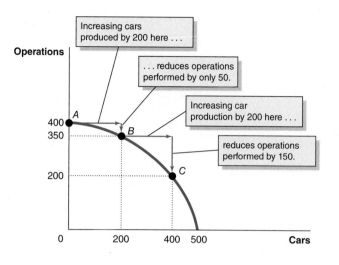

Figure 2.2

**Increasing Marginal
Opportunity Costs**

As the economy moves down the production possibilities frontier, it experiences *increasing marginal opportunity costs* because increasing car production by a given quantity requires larger and larger decreases in the number of operations performed. For example, to increase car production from 0 to 200—moving from point *A* to point *B*—the economy has to give up only 50 operations. But to increase production of cars by another 200 vehicles—moving from point *B* to point *C*—the economy has to give up 150 operations.

is bowed outward tells us that the opportunity cost of producing more cars depends on where the economy currently is on the production possibilities frontier. For example, to increase the production of cars from 0 to 200—moving from point *A* to point *B*—the economy has to give up only 50 operations. To increase the number of cars by another 200 (for a total of 400)—moving from point *B* to point *C*—the economy has to give up another 150 operations.

As the economy moves down the production possibilities frontier, it experiences *increasing marginal opportunity costs*. Marginal opportunity costs increase because some workers, machines, and other resources are better suited to some uses than to others. At point *A*, some resources that are best suited to making cars are used to perform operations. To move from point *A* to point *B*, the resources best suited to producing cars (and worst suited to performing operations) are shifted to car production. The result is a large gain in cars made while giving up few operations. As more cars are produced, resources that are better suited to performing operations are switched into car production. As a result, an increasing number of operations must be given up to get the same increase in the production of cars. Economists generally think that production possibilities frontiers are bowed outward (as in this example) rather than linear (as in the Toyota example earlier in the chapter).

The idea of increasing marginal opportunity costs illustrates an important economic concept: *The more resources already devoted to an activity, the smaller the payoff to devoting additional resources to that activity.* For example, the more hours you have already spent studying economics, the smaller the increase in your test grade from each additional hour you spend studying—and the greater the opportunity cost of using the hour in that way. The more funds a firm devotes to research and development during a given year, the smaller the amount of useful knowledge it receives from each additional dollar—and the greater the opportunity cost of using funds in that way. The more money the federal government spends cleaning up the environment during a given year, the smaller the reduction in pollution from each additional dollar—and, once again, the greater the opportunity cost of using the money in that way.

Economic Growth

At any given time, the total resources available to an economy are fixed. Therefore, if Canada produces more cars, it must produce less of something else, operations in our example. Over time the resources available to an economy may increase. For example, both the labour force and the capital stock—the amount of physical capital available to a country—may increase. The increase in the available labour force and the capital stock shifts the production possibilities frontier outward for the Canadian economy and makes

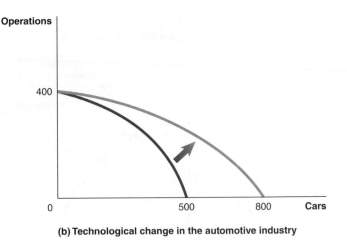
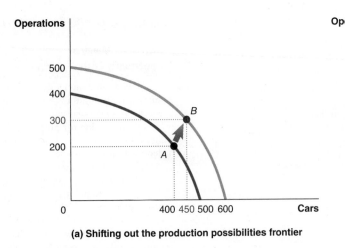

(a) Shifting out the production possibilities frontier

(b) Technological change in the automotive industry

Figure 2.3 Economic Growth

Panel (a) shows that as more economic resources become available and technological change occurs, the economy can move from point *A* to point *B*, performing more operations and producing more cars. Panel (b) shows the results of technological change in the automobile industry that increases the quantity of cars workers can produce per year while leaving unchanged the maximum quantity of operations that can be performed. Shifts in the production possibilities frontier represent *economic growth.*

it possible to produce more of *both* operations and cars. Panel (a) of Figure 2.3 shows that when an economy gets more resources, it can move from point *A* to point *B*, producing more cars *and* performing more operations.

Similarly, technological change makes it possible to produce more goods with the same number of workers and the same amount of machinery, which also shifts the production possibilities frontier outward. Technological progress doesn't necessarily affect all sectors of the economy. Panel (b) of Figure 2.3 shows the results of technological progress in the automotive industry—for example, the invention of a better welding robot—that increases the number of cars produced per year but leaves the number of operations performed per year unchanged.

Economic growth The ability of an economy to produce increasing quantities of goods and services.

Shifts in the production possibilities frontier represent **economic growth** because they allow the economy to increase the production of goods and services, which ultimately raises the standard of living. In Canada and other higher income countries, the market system has aided the process of economic growth, which over the past 200 years has greatly increased the well-being of the average person.

2.2 LEARNING OBJECTIVE

Understand comparative advantage and explain how it is the basis for trade.

Trade The act of buying and selling.

Comparative Advantage and Trade

In Chapter 1 we talked about all the steps and people involved in getting you a cup of coffee. All of these steps and people rely on *trade*. We can use the ideas of production possibilities frontiers and opportunity costs to understand the basic economic activity of **trade**, which is the act of buying and selling. Markets are fundamentally about trade. Sometimes we trade directly, as when children trade one hockey card for another, or you help your friend with her economics homework in exchange for help with your chemistry homework. We often trade indirectly: We sell our labour services as, say, an economist, salesperson, or nurse, for money, and then we use the money to buy goods and services. Although in these cases trade takes place indirectly, ultimately the economist, salesperson, and nurse are trading their services for food, clothing, or video games. One of the great benefits of trade is that it makes it possible for people to become better off by increasing both their production and consumption.

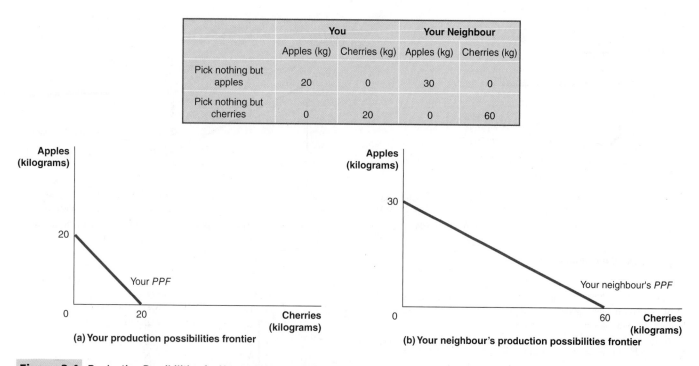

	You		Your Neighbour	
	Apples (kg)	Cherries (kg)	Apples (kg)	Cherries (kg)
Pick nothing but apples	20	0	30	0
Pick nothing but cherries	0	20	0	60

(a) Your production possibilities frontier

(b) Your neighbour's production possibilities frontier

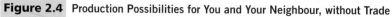

Figure 2.4 Production Possibilities for You and Your Neighbour, without Trade

The table in this figure shows how many kilograms of apples and how many kilograms of cherries you and your neighbour can each pick in one week. The graphs in the figure use the data from the table to construct production possibilities frontiers (PPFs) for you and your neighbour. Panel (a) shows your PPF. If you devote all your time to picking apples and none of it to picking cherries, you can pick 20 kilograms. If you devote all your time to picking cherries, you can pick 20 kilograms. Panel (b) shows that if your neighbour devotes all her time to picking apples, she can pick 30 kilograms. If she devotes all her time to picking cherries, she can pick 60 kilograms.

Specialization and Gains from Trade

Consider the following situation: You and your neighbour both have fruit trees on your properties. Initially, suppose you have only apple trees and your neighbour only has cherry trees. In this situation, if you both like apples and cherries, there is an obvious opportunity for you both to gain from trade: You give your neighbour some apples and she gives you some cherries, making you both better off.

What if you both had apple and cherry trees in your yards? In that case, there could still be gains from trade. For example, if your neighbour was really good at picking cherries and you were really good at picking apples, it would make sense for each of you to focus on picking just one kind of fruit and trading after you were done. Things get a little more complicated if your neighbour is better at picking both apples and cherries than you are, but as we will see there are still gains from trade.

We can use production possibilities frontiers to show how you and your neighbour can benefit from trading *even if she is better at picking both apples and cherries*. (For simplicity, and because it doesn't change the conclusions, we assume that the PPFs are straight lines.) The table in Figure 2.4 shows how many apples and how many cherries you and your neighbour can pick in one week. The graph in the figure uses the same data to draw PPFs. Panel (a) shows your PPF and Panel (b) shows your neighbour's PPF. If you spend all week picking apples you'll end up with 20 kilograms of apples and no cherries. If you spend all week picking cherries you'll get 20 kilograms of cherries and no apples. If your neighbour spends all week picking apples she will have 30 kilograms of apples and no cherries, while if she spends the week picking nothing but cherries she will have 60 kilograms of cherries and no apples.

The PPFs in Figure 2.4 show how many apples and cherries you and your neighbour can *consume* if you do not trade. Suppose that when you don't trade with your neighbour you decide to pick and eat 8 kilograms of apples and 12 kilograms of cherries

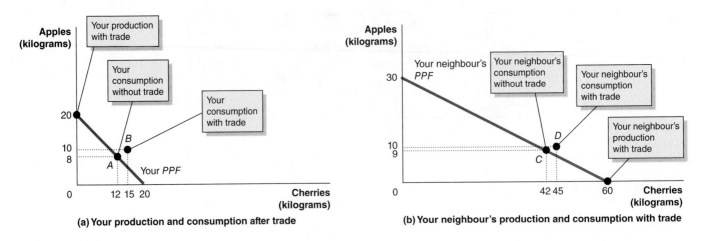

Figure 2.5 Gains from Trade

When you don't trade with your neighbour, you pick and consume 8 kilograms of apples and 12 kilograms of cherries per week—point A in panel (a). When you neighbour doesn't trade with you, she picks and consumes 9 kilograms of apples and 42 kilograms of cherries per week—point C in panel (b). If you specialize in picking apples, you can pick 20 kilograms. If your neighbour specializes in picking cherries, she can pick 60 kilograms.

If you trade 10 kilograms of apples for 15 kilograms of your neighbour's cherries, you will be able to consume 10 kilograms of apples and 15 kilograms of cherries—point B in panel (a). You neighbour can now consume 10 kilograms of apples and 45 kilograms of cherries—point D in panel (b). You and your neighbour are both better off as a result of the trade.

a week. This combination of apples and cherries is represented by point A in panel (a) of Figure 2.5. When your neighbour doesn't trade with you, she picks and consumes 9 kilograms of apples and 42 kilograms of cherries. This combination of apples and cherries is point C in panel (b) of Figure 2.5.

After years of ignoring each other—picking and eating apples and cherries independently—suppose your neighbour comes to you with the following proposal: She offers to trade you 15 kilograms of her cherries for 10 kilograms of your apples next week. Should you accept this offer? Yes! You should accept because you will end up with more apples and more cherries to consume. To take advantage of her proposal, you should specialize in picking only apples rather than splitting your time between picking apples and cherries. This will allow you to pick 20 kilograms of apples. You can then trade 10 kilograms of your apples for 15 kilograms of cherries. As a result of this trading, you end up with 10 kilograms of apples and 15 kilograms of cherries (point B in panel (a) of Figure 2.5), 2 kilograms of apples, and 3 kilograms of cherries more than you had last week. You now get to consume a combination of apples and cherries that was unattainable (outside your PPF) to you before!

It might seem like you've got the better of your neighbour, but she is better off too. By specializing in picking cherries, she can pick 60 kilograms. She trades 15 kilograms of cherries to you for 10 kilograms of apples. She ends up with 10 kilograms of apples and 45 kilograms of cherries (point D in panel (b) of Figure 2.5), which is 1 kilogram more apples and 3 kilograms more cherries than she had before trading with you. She too can now consume a combination of apples and cherries that was unattainable last week. Table 2.1 summarizes the changes in production and consumption that results from trading with your neighbour. (In this example, we chose one specific rate of trading cherries for apples—15 kilograms of cherries for 10 kilograms of apples. There are, however, many other rates of trading cherries for apples that would also make you and your neighbour both better off.)

Absolute Advantage versus Comparative Advantage

Absolute advantage The ability of an individual, a firm, or a country to produce more of a good or service than potential trading partners, using the same amount of resources.

One of the most remarkable aspects of the previous example is that both you and your neighbour benefit from trading, even though your neighbour is better than you at picking both apples and cherries. **Absolute advantage** is the ability of an individual, a firm,

Table 2.1

A Summary of the Gains from Trade

	You		Your Neighbour	
	Apples (kg)	Cherries (kg)	Apples (kg)	Cherries (kg)
Production and consumption *without* trade	8	12	9	42
Production *with* trade	20	0	0	60
Consumption *with* trade	10	15	10	45
Increased consumption (gains from trade)	2	3	1	3

or a country to produce more of a good or service than potential trading partners, using the same amount of resources. Your neighbour has an absolute advantage over you in producing both apples and cherries because she can pick more of each fruit than you can with the same amount of time. Although it seems like you have nothing to offer and she should pick her own apples and cherries, we have already seen that she is (and you are too) better off specializing in cherry picking and leaving the apple picking to you.

We can consider why both you and your neighbour benefit from specializing in picking only one fruit in more detail. First, think about the opportunity cost to each of you of picking each type of fruit. We saw from the PPF in Figure 2.4 that if you devoted all your time to picking apples, you would be able to pick 20 kilograms of apples per week. As you move down your PPF and shift time away from picking apples to picking cherries, you have to give up 1 kilogram of apples for each kilogram of cherries you pick (the slope of your PPF is -1). (For a refresher on calculating slopes, see Appendix A, which follows Chapter 1.) Therefore, your opportunity cost of picking 1 kilogram of cherries is 1 kilogram of apples. Put slightly differently, for every kilogram of cherries you pick, you have to give up 1 kilogram of apples. If you were to start off picking nothing but cherries and were thinking about picking some apples, every kilogram of apples you picked would cost you 1 kilogram of cherries. Your opportunity cost of picking apples is 1 kilogram of cherries per kilogram of apples.

Your neighbour's PPF has a different slope, so she faces a different trade-off: As she shifts time from picking apples to picking cherries, she has to give up 0.5 kilograms of apples for every kilogram of cherries she picks (the slope of your neighbour's PPF is -0.5). Her opportunity cost of picking cherries is 0.5 kilograms of apples per kilogram of cherries. If she were going the other way, shifting time from picking cherries to picking apples, she would have to give up 2 kilograms of cherries in order to pick 1 kilogram of apples. Your neighbour's opportunity cost of picking apples is 2 kilograms of cherries per kilogram of apples.

Table 2.2 summarizes the opportunity costs for you and your neighbour of picking apples and cherries. Note that even though your neighbour can pick more of both apples and cherries than you can, the *opportunity cost* of picking apples is higher for her than it is for you, meaning that it costs you less to pick apples than it costs her. Even though she has an absolute advantage in picking both apples and cherries, you have a *comparative advantage* in picking apples. **Comparative advantage** is the ability of an individual, a firm, or a country to produce a good or service at a lower opportunity cost than potential trading partners. In our example, your neighbour has an absolute advantage in picking apples, while you have the comparative advantage in apple picking. At the same time, your neighbour has both the absolute and comparative advantage in picking cherries. As we demonstrated, you are better off specializing in picking apples, and your neighbour is better off specializing in picking cherries. Determining whether a specific trade will lead to gains requires that we know the *exchange ratio*—in this case, the number of kilograms of cherries you would get for each kilogram of apples (or, more often, a price in terms of dollars).

Comparative advantage The ability of an individual, a firm, or a country to produce a good or service at a lower opportunity cost than potential trading partners.

Table 2.2

Opportunity Costs of Picking Apples and Cherries

	Opportunity Cost of Apples	Opportunity Cost of Cherries
You	1 kg of cherries	1 kg of apples
Your neighbour	2 kg of cherries	0.5 kg of apples

Comparative Advantage and the Gains from Trade

We have just derived an important economic principle: *The basis for trade is comparative advantage, not absolute advantage.* The fastest apple pickers do not necessarily do much apple picking. If the fastest apple pickers have a comparative advantage in something else—for example, picking cherries, playing hockey, or being economists—they are better off specializing in that other activity *and so is everyone else.* Individuals, firms, and countries are better off if they specialize in producing goods and services in which they have a comparative advantage and trade to get the other goods and services they aren't producing.

Don't Let This Happen to You

Don't Confuse Absolute Advantage and Comparative Advantage

First, make sure you know the definitions:

- **Absolute advantage.** The ability of an individual, a firm, or a country to produce more of a good or service than potential trading partners using the same amount of resources. In our example, your neighbour has an absolute advantage over you in both picking apples and picking cherries.

- **Comparative advantage.** The ability of an individual, a firm, or a country to produce a good or service at a lower opportunity cost than potential trading partners. In our example, your neighbour has a comparative advantage in picking cherries,

while you have the comparative advantage in picking apples.

Keep these two key points in mind:

1. It is possible to have an absolute advantage in producing something without having a comparative advantage. This is the case with your neighbour and picking apples.

2. It is possible to have a comparative advantage without having an absolute advantage. In our example, you have the comparative advantage in picking apples, even though your neighbour can pick more than you.

MyEconLab

Your Turn: Test your understanding by doing related problem 2.2 on page 48 at the end of this chapter.

Solved Problem **2.2**

Comparative Advantage and the Gains from Trade

Suppose that Canada and the United States both produce video games and nacho chips. These are the combination of the two goods that each country can produce in one day:

Canada		United States	
Video Games (titles)	Nacho Chips (tonnes)	Video Games (titles)	Nacho Chips (tonnes)
0	60	0	200
10	45	10	160
20	30	20	120
30	15	30	80
40	0	40	40
		50	0

a. Who has the comparative advantage in producing nacho chips? Who has the comparative advantage in producing video games?

b. Suppose that Canada is currently producing (and consuming) 30 video games and 15 tonnes of nacho chips, while the United States is currently producing (and consuming) 10 video games and 160 tonnes of nachos. Demonstrate that Canada and the United States can both be better off if they specialize in producing only one good and engage in trade.

c. Illustrate your answer to question (b) by drawing a PPF for Canada and a PPF for the United States. Show on your PPFs the combinations of video games and nachos produced and consumed in each country before and after trade.

Solving the Problem

Step 1: **Review the chapter material.** This problem is about comparative advantage, so you may want to review the section "Absolute Advantage versus Comparative Advantage," which begins on page 38.

Step 2: **Answer part (a) by calculating the opportunity costs of each activity for each country and comparing your results to see who has the comparative advantage.** Remember that a country has a comparative advantage when it can produce something at a lower opportunity cost. When Canada produces 1 more video game title, it produces 1.5 tonnes fewer nacho chips. When the United States produces 1 more video game title, it produces 4 tonnes fewer nacho chips. Therefore, Canada's opportunity cost of producing video game titles—1.5 tonnes of nacho chips per video game title—is lower than that of the United States—4 tonnes of nacho chips per video game title. When Canada produces 1 more tonne of nacho chips, it produces 0.67 fewer video game titles. When the United States produces 1 more tonne of nacho chips, it produces 0.25 fewer video game titles. Therefore, the United States' opportunity cost of producing nacho chips—0.25 video game titles per tonne of nacho chips—is lower than Canada's—0.67 video game titles per tonne of nacho chips. We can conclude that Canada has the comparative advantage in producing video game titles and the United States has the comparative advantage in producing nacho chips.

Step 3: **Answer part (b) by showing that specialization makes both Canada and the United States better off.** We know that Canada should specialize where it has a comparative advantage, and so should the United States. This means that Canada should produce video games and the United States should produce nacho chips. If both countries specialize completely, Canada will produce 40 video game titles and 0 tonnes of nacho chips, while the United States will produce 0 video game titles and 200 tonnes of nacho chips. After both countries specialize, Canada could then trade 10 video game titles to the United States in exchange for 20 tonnes of nacho chips. (You should be aware that a lot of other mutually beneficial trades are possible as well.) We can summarize the results in a table:

	Before Trade		After Trade	
	Video Games (titles)	Nacho Chips (tonnes)	Video Games (titles)	Nacho Chips (tonnes)
Canada	30	15	30	20
United States	10	160	10	180

Canadians are better off after trade because they can consume the same number of video games and 5 *more* tonnes of nachos than they could before trade. Americans are better off after trade because they can consume the same amount of video games and 20 *more* tonnes of nacho chips.

Step 4: **Answer part (c) by drawing the PPFs.**

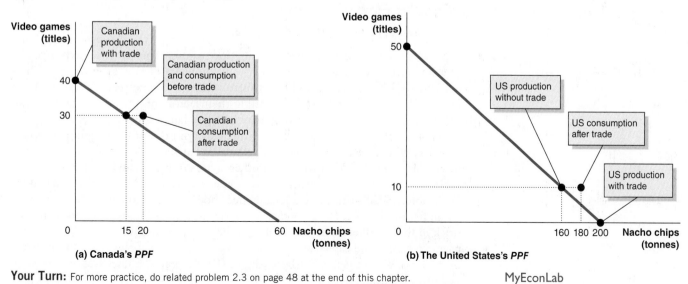

(a) Canada's PPF

(b) The United States's PPF

Your Turn: For more practice, do related problem 2.3 on page 48 at the end of this chapter.   MyEconLab

The Market System

We have seen that households, firms, and the government face trade-offs and incur opportunity costs because resources are scarce. We have also seen that trade allows people to specialize according to their comparative advantage. By engaging in trade, people can raise their material standard of living—the amount of goods and services that they get to consume. Of course, trade in the modern world is a lot more complicated than it was in the examples we have considered so far. Trade today involves the decisions of billions of people around the world. But how does an economy make trade possible, and how are the decisions of these billions of people coordinated? In Canada and most other countries, trade is carried out in markets. It is also through markets that these billions of people determine the answers to the three fundamental questions discussed in Chapter 1: What goods and services will be produced? How will the goods and services be produced? Who will receive the goods and services produced?

Recall that the definition of **market** is a group of buyers and sellers of a good or service and the institutions or arrangements by which they come together to trade. Markets take many forms: They can be physical places, such as a farmers' market, a grocery store, or even the Toronto Stock Exchange, or virtual places such as eBay. In a market, the buyers are the people that demand goods or services (consumers), and the sellers are the people willing to supply them (suppliers). Households and firms interact in two types of markets: *product markets* and *factor markets*. **Product markets** are markets for goods—such as computers—or services—such as haircuts. In product markets, households demand the goods and services supplied by firms. **Factor markets** are markets for the *factors of production*. As mentioned earlier, *factors of production* are the inputs used to make goods and services; they are divided into four broad categories:

Market A group of buyers and sellers of a good or service and the institutions or arrangements by which they come together to trade.

Product market A market for goods—such as computers—or services—such as haircuts.

Factor market A market for the factors of production, such as labour, capital, natural resources, and entrepreneurial ability.

- *Labour* includes all types of work, from the part-time labour of teens working at McDonald's to the work of CEOs of large corporations.

- *Capital* refers to physical capital, such as computers, machines, and buildings that are used to make other goods.

- *Natural resources* include land, water, oil, iron ore, and other raw materials (or "gifts of nature") that are used in producing goods.

- An **entrepreneur** is someone who operates a business. *Entrepreneurial ability* is the ability to bring the other factors of production together to successfully produce and sell goods and services.

Entrepreneur Someone who operates a business, bringing together factors of production—labour, capital, and natural resources—to produce goods and services.

The Circular Flow of Income

Two key groups of people participate in markets:

- A *household* consists of all the people living and making economic decisions together in a home. Households are the owners and suppliers of factors of production—particularly labour—employed by firms to make goods and services. Households use the income they receive from selling their factors of production to purchase the goods and services produced by firms. We are familiar with households as suppliers of labour because the majority of people earn most of their money by going to work, which means they are selling their labour services to firms in the labour market. Households also own all the other factors of production, either directly or indirectly, by owning the firms that have these resources. All firms are owned by households. Small firms, like a local coffee shop, might be owned by one person. Large firms, like Toyota, are owned by millions of households that own shares of stock in them. When firms pay profits to the people who own them, the firms are paying for using the capital and natural resources that are supplied to them by those owners. So, we can generalize by saying in factor markets, households are suppliers and firms are demanders.

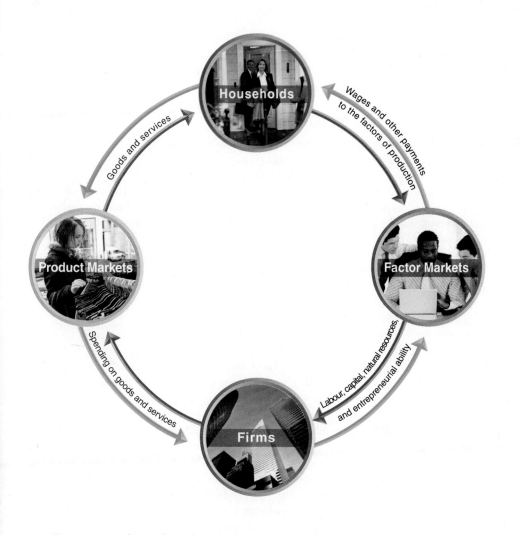

Figure 2.6

A Simple Circular-Flow Diagram

Households and firms are linked together in a circular flow of production, income, and spending. The blue arrows show the flow of the factors of production. In factor markets, households supply labour, entrepreneurial ability, and other factors of production to firms. Firms use these factors of production to make goods and services that they supply to households in product markets. The red arrows show the flow of goods and services from firms to households. The green arrows show the flow of funds. In factor markets, households receive wages and other payments from firms in exchange for supplying the factors of production. Households use these wages and other payments to purchase goods and services from firms in product markets. Firms sell goods and services to households in product markets, and they use the funds to purchase the factors of production from households in factor markets.

Photo credits: (Clockwise from top) JupiterImages; Alamy; Mikael Damkier/Alamy; Elena Elisseeva/Shutterstock

- *Firms* are suppliers of goods and services. Firms use the funds they receive from selling goods and services to buy the factors of production needed to make the goods and services they sell.

We can use a simple economic model called the **circular-flow diagram** to see how participants in markets are linked. Figure 2.6 shows that in factor markets, households supply labour and other factors of production in exchange for wages and other payments from firms. In product markets, households use the payments they earn in factor markets to purchase the goods and services supplied by firms. Firms produce these goods and services using the factors of production supplied by households. In the figure, the blue arrows show the flow of factors of production from households through factor markets to firms. The red arrows show the flow of goods and services from firms through product markets to households. The green arrows show the flow of funds from firms through factor markets to households and the flow of spending from households through product markets to firms.

Like all models, the circular-flow diagram is a simplified version of reality. For example, Figure 2.6 leaves out the important role of government in buying goods from firms and in making payments, such as employment insurance, to households. The figure also leaves out the roles played by banks, the stock and bond markets, and other parts of the financial system in aiding the flow of funds from lenders to borrowers. Finally, the figure does not show that some goods and services purchased by Canadian households are produced in other countries and some goods and services produced by Canadian firms are sold to households in foreign countries.(The government, financial systems, and international sector are explored in later chapters.) Despite its simplifications, the version of the circular flow model in Figure 2.6 shows us how product markets and factor markets link firms and households together. Households depend on firms for their incomes and for

Circular-flow diagram A model that illustrates how participants in markets are linked.

the goods they consume. Firms depend on households to buy the products they produce and to supply the factors of production needed to make those products. It is this interdependence that leads to one of the great wonders of the market system—it manages to successfully coordinate the independent activities of many different people.

The Gains from Free Markets

Free market A market with few government restrictions on how goods or services can be produced or sold, on who can buy or sell goods or services, or on how factors of production can be employed.

A **free market** exists when the government places few restrictions on how goods or services can be produced or sold, on who can buy or sell goods or services, or on how factors of production can be employed. Governments in all modern economies intervene in markets, so no market in the world is completely free. In that sense, we can think of the free market as being a theoretical benchmark against which we can judge actual markets. There are relatively few government restrictions on economic activity in Canada, the United States, Western Europe, Japan, and many other countries. So these countries come fairly close to the free-market benchmark. In countries such as Cuba and North Korea, the free-market system has been rejected in favour of centrally planned economies with extensive government control of product and factor markets. Countries that come closest to the free-market benchmark have much higher standards of living than those with centrally planned economies.

Scottish philosopher Adam Smith is considered the father of modern economics because his book *An Inquiry into the Nature and Causes of the Wealth of Nations*, published in 1776, was an early and very influential argument for the free-market system. Smith was writing at a time when extensive government restrictions on markets were very common. In many parts of Europe, the *guild system* still prevailed. Under this system, governments would give guilds (organizations of producers) the authority to control the production of a good. For example, the shoemakers' guild controlled who was allowed to produce shoes, how many shoes they could produce, and what price they could charge. In France, the cloth makers' guild even dictated the number of threads in cloth.

Smith argued that such restrictions reduced the income, or wealth, of a country and its people by restricting the quantity of goods produced. Some people at the time supported the restrictions of the guild system because it was in their financial interest to do so. If you were a member of a guild, the restrictions served to reduce the competition you faced. But other people sincerely believed that the alternative to the guild system was economic chaos. Smith argued that these people were wrong and that a country could enjoy a smoothly functioning economic system if firms were freed from guild restrictions.

The Legal Basis of a Successful Market System

As noted earlier, in a free market, government imposes few restrictions. However, the market system cannot work without government, as you can see if you look at some of the failed states around the world. Government must take active steps to provide a *legal environment* that will allow the market system to succeed.

Protection of Private Property For the market system to work well, individuals must be willing to take risks. Someone with $250 000 can be cautious and keep it safely in a bank—or even as cash. But the market system won't work unless a lot of people are willing to risk their savings by investing them in businesses. Investing in businesses is risky in any country. Many businesses fail every year in Canada and other high-income countries. But in high-income countries, someone who starts a new business or invests in an existing business doesn't have to worry that the government, the military, or a criminal gang might decide to seize the business or demand payments for not destroying the business. Unfortunately, in many poor countries, owners of businesses are not well protected from having their businesses seized by government or from having their profits taken by criminals. Where these problems exist, opening a business can be extremely risky. Cash can be concealed easily, but a business is a lot harder to hide and difficult to move.

Property rights The rights individuals or firms have to the exclusive use of their property, including the right to buy or sell it.

Property rights are the rights individuals or firms have to the exclusive use of their property, including the right to buy or sell it. Property can be tangible, physical property such as a house, store, or factory. Property can also be intangible, such as the rights to an idea, image, or process.

Property rights in Canada are based on the system of common law that was in effect when Canada was a British colony (with the exception of Quebec, where matters of provincial jurisdiction are based on the civil code system). Both the federal and provincial governments play a role in property rights. The federal government is responsible for intellectual property rights, while provincial governments are responsible for personal and real property. Provincial property rights legislation that concerns goods and services other than land generally has the same name in each province—the Sale of Goods Act. Specifically, this set of acts outlines the obligations of people entering into contracts to buy and sell goods and services. The sale and purchase of land is governed by each province's real estate law, as well as common law (or the civil code, in the case of Quebec). Although seldom used, the federal government has the power to require people to sell their land, which is called *expropriation*. Expropriation law requires that the government "fairly" compensate those from whom it takes land. Unfortunately, many developing countries do not provide the same protection of land property rights.

Enforcement of Contracts and Property Rights Business activity often involves someone agreeing to carry out some action in the future. For example, you borrow $20 000 to buy a car and promise the bank—by signing a loan contract—that you will pay back the money (with interest) over the next five years. BlackBerry might also sign a contract with Qualcomm agreeing to buy 10 000 CPUs for smartphones at a specific price. Usually these agreements take the form of legal contracts. For the market system to work, businesses and individuals have to rely on these contracts being honoured. If one party to a legal contract does not fulfill its obligations—perhaps Qualcomm doesn't deliver the CPUs on time—the other party to the contract can take Qualcomm to court to have the deal enforced. Similarly, if one company believes that another has violated a patent or copyright, a lawsuit is likely to follow.

Making the Connection	**Too Little of a Good Thing**

After reading about the failures of central planning in the former Soviet Union, Cuba, North Korea, and many other countries, it can be easy to get the impression that economists think that we shouldn't have any government at all, but this is not the case. Government plays a central role in allowing markets to generate the high standard of living Canadians enjoy. In fact, having no effective government at all can be one of the worst possible things for an economy.

Consider the case of South Sudan. It became an independent country after a referendum split it from Sudan in 2011. Ever since independence, South Sudan has suffered internal conflict and now ranks atop the Fragile States Index (compiled by the Fund for Peace), which measures the likelihood of total government collapse.

Due to the lack of effective government, economic activity within the country is falling rapidly. *Global Finance* reports that average incomes in South Sudan fell from $2206 in 2011, shortly after independence, to just $1324 in 2013 (the latest year for which data was available). By way of comparison, average incomes in Canada rose from $41 690 in 2011 to $43 593 over the same period.

In South Sudan, the lack of effective government means it is almost impossible to ensure property rights are respected or to ensure that a business deal is honoured. This makes it virtually impossible for people to engage in the type of specialization and trade that makes countries with effective and stable governance, like Canada, so wealthy. So while government cannot replace the market's ability to generate wealth through trade, trade cannot flourish without a government to enforce property rights.

Based on Valentina Pasquali, The Richest Countries in the World, https://www.gfmag.com/global-data/economic-data/richest-countries-in-the-world; Fund for Peace Fragile States Index, http://fsi.fundforpeace.org/

Going to court to enforce a contract or private property rights will be successful only if the court system is independent and judges are able to make impartial decisions on the basis of the law. In Canada and other high-income countries, the court systems have enough independence from other parts of the government and enough protection from threats from outside forces—such as criminals—that they are able to make decisions based on the law. In many developing countries, the court systems lack this independence and will not provide a remedy if the government violates private property rights or if a person with powerful political allies decides to violate a business contract.

If property rights are not well enforced, fewer goods and services will be produced. This reduces economic efficiency, leaving the economy inside its production possibilities frontier and people worse off.

Economics in Your Life

The Trade-offs When You Buy a Car

At the beginning of the chapter, we asked you to think about two questions: Under what circumstances would you be better off buying an older, less fuel-efficient car than a new highly efficient one? Who do you think is most likely to want a car with high fuel efficiency? To answer the first question, you have to think about the trade-off between fuel efficiency and current price. If you buy an older car, you will have to pay less now, but you will have to pay more (in gas) when you drive somewhere. The trade-off is between paying now or paying later. This trade-off would look a lot like the relationship in Figure 2.1 on page 31. What you decide will likely depend on how far or often you plan to drive. If you don't think you will drive much, a cheaper car is probably better for you. That is, you might find you are willing to give up fuel efficiency (future savings) for a lower price (savings now). To have a cheaper and more fuel-efficient car, automakers would have to discover new technologies for making cars. This would shift the PPF out, as in panel (a) of Figure 2.3 on page 36.

To answer the second question, think about the trade-off between purchase price and fuel efficiency. The people most likely to want a fuel-efficient car are people who drive a lot. For them, the savings in gasoline expenses would be more important than the initial purchase price.

Conclusion

We have seen that by trading in markets, people are able to specialize and pursue their comparative advantage. Trading on the basis of comparative advantage makes all participants in trade better off. The key role of markets is to facilitate trade. In fact, the market system is a very effective way of coordinating the decisions of billions of consumers, workers, and firms. At the centre of the market system is the consumer. To be successful, firms must respond to the desires of consumers. These desires are communicated to firms through prices. To explore how markets work, we must study the behaviour of consumers and firms. We continue this exploration of markets in Chapter 3, where we develop the model of demand and supply.

Chapter Summary and Problems

Key Terms

Absolute advantage, p. 38

Allocative efficiency, p. 32

Circular-flow diagram, p. 43

Comparative advantage, p. 39

Economic growth, p. 36

Entrepreneur, p. 42

Factor market, p. 42

Factors of production, p. 30

Free market, p. 44

Market, p. 42

Opportunity cost, p. 32

Product market, p. 42

Production possibilities frontier (PPF), p. 30

Property rights, p. 44

Scarcity, p. 30

Trade, p. 36

Summary

LO 2.1 The *production possibilities frontier (PPF)* is a curve that shows the maximum attainable combinations of two products that may be produced with available resources. The PPF is used to illustrate the trade-offs that arise from scarcity. Points on the frontier are technically efficient. Points inside the frontier are inefficient, and points outside the frontier are unattainable. The *opportunity cost* of any activity is the highest-valued alternative that must be given up to engage in that activity. Because of increasing marginal opportunity costs, production possibilities frontiers are usually bowed out rather than straight lines. This illustrates the important economic concept that the more resources that are already devoted to any activity, the smaller the payoff from devoting additional resources to that activity is likely to be. *Economic growth* is illustrated by shifting a production possibilities frontier outward.

LO 2.2 Fundamentally, markets are about *trade*, which is the act of buying or selling. People trade on the basis of *comparative advantage*. An individual, a firm, or a country has a comparative advantage in producing a good or service if it can produce the good or service at the lowest opportunity cost. People are usually better off specializing in the activity for which they have a comparative advantage and trading for the other goods and services they need. It is important not to confuse comparative advantage with absolute advantage. An individual, a firm, or a country has an *absolute*

advantage in producing a good or service if it can produce more of that good or service using the same amount of resources. It is possible to have an absolute advantage in producing a good or service without having a comparative advantage.

LO 2.3 A *market* is a group of buyers and sellers of a good or service and the institutions or arrangements by which they come together to trade. *Product markets* are markets for goods and services, such as computers and haircuts. *Factor markets* are markets for the *factors of production*, such as labour, capital, natural resources, and entrepreneurial ability. A *circular-flow diagram* shows how participants in product markets and factor markets are linked. Adam Smith argued in his 1776 book *The Wealth of Nations* that in a *free market*, where the government does not control the production of goods and services, changes in prices lead firms to produce the goods and services most desired by consumers. If consumers demand more of a good, its price will rise. Firms respond to rising prices by increasing production. If consumers demand less of a good, its price will fall. Firms respond to falling prices by producing less of a good. An *entrepreneur* is someone who operates a business. In the market system, entrepreneurs are responsible for organizing the production of goods and services. The market system will work well only if there is protection for *property rights*, which are the rights of individuals and firms to use their property.

MyEconLab   Log in to MyEconLab to complete these exercises and get instant feedback.

Review Questions

LO 2.1

1.1 What is a production possibilities frontier? How can we show economic efficiency on a production possibilities frontier? How can we show inefficiency? What causes a production possibilities frontier to shift outward?

1.2 What does *increasing marginal opportunity costs* mean? What are the implications of this idea for the shape of the production possibilities frontier?

LO 2.2

2.1 What is absolute advantage? What is comparative advantage? Is it possible for a country to have a comparative

advantage in producing a good without also having an absolute advantage? Briefly explain.

2.2 What is the basis for trade: absolute advantage or comparative advantage? How can an individual or a country gain from specialization and trade?

LO 2.3

3.1 What is a circular-flow diagram, and what does it demonstrate?

3.2 What is a free market? In what ways does a free market economy differ from a centrally planned economy?

3.3 What are private property rights? What role do they play in the working of a market system? Why are independent courts important for a well-functioning economy?

Problems and Applications

LO 2.1

1.1 Draw a production possibilities frontier that shows the trade-off between the production of cotton and the production of soybeans.

  a. Show the effect that a prolonged drought would have on the initial production possibilities frontier.

  b. Suppose genetic modification makes soybeans resistant to insects, allowing yields to double. Show the effect of

this technological change on the initial production possibilities frontier.

1.2 **[Related to the Chapter Opener on page 29]** One of the trade-offs Toyota faces is between safety and gas mileage. For example, adding steel to a car makes it safer but also heavier, which results in lower gas mileage. Draw a hypothetical production possibilities frontier that Toyota engineers face that shows this trade-off.

---

*"Learning Objective" is abbreviated to "LO" in the end-of-chapter material.

1.3 Suppose you win free tickets to a movie plus all you can eat at the snack bar for free. Would there be a cost to you to attend this movie? Explain.

1.4 **[Related to Solved Problem 2.1 on page 32]** You have exams in economics and chemistry coming up, and you have five hours available for studying. The following table shows the trade-offs you face in allocating the time you will spend in studying each subject:

	Hours Spent Studying		Midterm Score	
Choice	Economics	Chemistry	Economics	Chemistry
A	5	0	95	70
B	4	1	93	78
C	3	2	90	84
D	2	3	86	88
E	1	4	81	90
F	0	5	75	91

a. Use the data in the table to draw a production possibilities frontier graph. Label the vertical axis "Score on economics exam," and label the horizontal axis "Score on chemistry exam." Make sure to label the values where your production possibilities frontier intersects the vertical and horizontal axes.

b. Label the points representing choice C and choice D. If you are at choice C, what is your opportunity cost of increasing your chemistry score?

c. Under what circumstances would choice A be a sensible choice?

1.5 **[Related to Making the Connection on page 34]** Suppose the minister responsible for Health Canada is trying to decide whether the federal government should spend more on research to find a cure for heart disease. She asks you, one of her economic advisers, to prepare a report discussing the relevant factors she should consider. Use the concepts of opportunity cost and trade-offs to discuss some of the main issues you would deal with in your report.

1.6 **[Related to Making the Connection on page 34]** Suppose your provincial government is deciding which of two sports programs it will pay for (assuming that only one program will be funded). The choices are Sport A, which will allow 24 students to play for 8 months and costs $37 500 per year, and Sport B, which will allow 20 students to play for 8 months and costs $15 000 per year. What factors should the provincial government take into account in making this decision?

LO 2.2

2.1 Look again at the information in Figure 2.4 on page 37. Choose a rate of trading cherries for apples different from the rate used in the text (15 kilograms of cherries for 10 kilograms of apples) that will allow you and your neighbour to benefit from trading apples and cherries. Prepare a table like Table 2.1 on page 39 to illustrate your answer.

2.2 **[Related to Don't Let This Happen to You on page 40]** In 2015, one of the largest multilateral trade deals in history was struck (but not ratified at the time of writing) by negotiators representing 12 countries (Australia, Brunei Darussalam, Canada, Chile, Japan, Malaysia, New Zealand, Peru, Singapore, the United States, and Vietnam).

The TransPacific Partnership, or TPP, will dramatically reduce trade barriers between countries accounting for about 40 percent of the world's economy. Some opponents of the deal argue that there is no way for Canada to benefit from trade with developing countries like Vietnam, as Canada is more productive (has an absolute advantage). Is there any way for Canada to gain from trading with a country over which we have an absolute advantage in virtually everything?

2.3 **[Related to Solved Problem 2.2 on page 40]** Suppose that France and Germany both produce schnitzel and wine. The following table shows combinations of the goods that each country can produce in a day:

France		Germany	
Wine (bottles)	Schnitzel (kilograms)	Wine (bottles)	Schnitzel (kilograms)
0	8	0	15
1	6	1	12
2	4	2	9
3	2	3	6
4	0	4	3
		5	0

a. Who has a comparative advantage in producing wine? Who has a comparative advantage in producing schnitzel?

b. Suppose that France is currently producing 1 bottle of wine and 6 kilograms of schnitzel, and Germany is currently producing 3 bottles of wine and 6 kilograms of schnitzel. Demonstrate that France and Germany can both be better off if each specializes in producing only one good and then they engage in trade.

2.4 Can an individual or a country produce beyond its production possibilities frontier? Can an individual or a country consume beyond its production possibilities frontier? Explain.

2.5 Are specialization and trade between individuals and countries more about having a job or about obtaining a higher standard of living? Individually, if you go from a situation of not trading with others (you produce everything yourself) to a situation of trading with others, do you still have a job? Does your standard of living increase? Likewise, if a country goes from not trading with other countries to trading with other countries, does it still have jobs? Does its standard of living increase?

2.6 Some people argue that Canada should import only products that could not be produced here. Do you believe that this would be a good policy? Explain.

LO 2.3

3.1 Identify whether each of the following transactions will take place in the factor market or in the product market and whether households or firms are supplying the good or service or demanding the good or service:

a. George buys a Toyota Camry hybrid.

b. Toyota increases employment at its Cambridge plant.

c. George works 20 hours per week at McDonald's.

d. George sells land he owns to McDonald's so it can build a new restaurant.

3.2 [**Related to Making the Connection on page 45**] In *The Wealth of Nations*, Adam Smith wrote the following (Book I, Chapter II): "It is not from the benevolence of the butcher, the brewer, or the baker, that we expect our dinner, but from their regard to their own interest." Briefly discuss what he meant by this.

3.3 Evaluate the following argument: "Adam Smith's analysis is based on a fundamental flaw: He assumes that people are motivated by self-interest. But this isn't true. I'm not selfish, and most people I know aren't selfish."

3.4 Some economists have been puzzled that although entrepreneurs take on the risk of losing time and money by starting new businesses, on average their incomes are lower than those of people with similar characteristics who go to work at large firms. Economist William Baumol believes part of the explanation for this puzzle may be that entrepreneurs are like people who buy lottery tickets. On average, people who don't buy lottery tickets are left with more money than people who buy tickets because lotteries take in more money than they give out. Baumol argues that "the masses of purchasers who grab up the [lottery] tickets are not irrational if they receive an adequate payment in another currency: psychic rewards."

William J. Baumol, *The Microtheory of Innovative Entrepreneurship*, (Princeton, NJ: Princeton University Press, 2010).

a. What are "psychic rewards"?

b. What psychic rewards might an entrepreneur receive?

c. Do you agree with Baumol that an entrepreneur is like someone buying a lottery ticket? Briefly explain.

3.5 The 2014 International Property Rights Index examines the relationship between the protection of property rights in a country and that country's economic output. The authors of this report found that countries with the strongest protection of property rights are also the countries with the highest standard of living. They also report that countries with the weakest protections of property rights have very low standards of living. How would the creation of stronger property rights be likely to affect the economic opportunities available to citizens of countries ranking lowest in property rights protections?

Based on International Property Rights Index Annual report executive summary. https://s3.amazonaws.com/ATR/IPRI+Executive+Summary_REVISED2.pdf accessed October 14, 2015.

MyEconLab   MyEconLab is an online tool designed to help you master the concepts covered in your course. It will create a personalized study plan to stimulate and measure your learning. Log in to take advantage of this powerful study aid, and to access quizzes and other valuable course-related material.

CHAPTER

3

Where Prices Come From: The Interaction of Supply and Demand

Chapter Outline and Learning Objectives

Red Bull and the Market for Energy Drinks

Markets for some products suddenly explode. This was the case in the market for energy drinks. Red Bull was developed in Austria by Dietrich Mateschitz, who based it on a drink he discovered being sold in pharmacies in Thailand. Before Red Bull entered the market, few soft drinks included caffeine. Red Bull didn't enter the Canadian market until 2004, likely due to soft drink regulations. In Canada, caffeine may not be added to a traditional soft drink other than a cola. For example, Mountain Dew sold in the United States has a relatively high amount of caffeine, but the version sold in Canada contains none. Red Bull and other energy drinks are sold in Canada as natural health products, and are therefore subject to different regulations. Despite not being available in Canada before 2004, the retail sales of sports and energy drinks was expected to top $950 billion in 2016. The market for energy drinks has found a particularly valuable niche with students wanting an extra boost of energy for sports, gaming, or studying. Some people have speculated that energy drinks might replace coffee as the morning drink for the current generation.

The success of Red Bull, Monster Energy, and Rockstar Energy Drink has attracted the attention of huge multi-national beverage corporations as well as entrepreneurs looking to introduce new products into a hot market. Coca-Cola signed an agreement to distribute Monster Energy in Canada, 20 US states, and 6 Western European countries, and Pepsi struck a similar deal with Rockstar Energy Drink. A Canadian company, DD Beverage Company, produces Beaver Buzz Energy and other energy and sports beverages. Well over 200 energy drinks are now available in the North American marketplace.

The intense competition among firms selling energy drinks is a striking example of how the market responds to changes in consumer tastes. Although intense competition is not always good news for firms trying to sell products, it is great news for consumers. Competition among firms increases the variety of products available and reduces the price consumers pay for those products.

Economics in Your Life

Red Bull or Beaver Buzz Energy: What's Your Beverage?

Suppose you are about to buy an energy drink and you are choosing between a Red Bull and a Beaver Buzz Energy. As the more established, well-known brand, Red Bull has many advantages over a smaller competitor like Beaver Buzz Energy. One strategy DD Beverage Company can use to overcome Red Bull's advantages is to have Beaver Buzz Energy compete based on price and value. Would you choose to buy a can of Beaver Buzz Energy if it had a lower price than a can of Red Bull? Would you be less likely to drink Beaver Buzz Energy if your income dropped? As you read this chapter, see if you can answer these questions. You can check your answers against those we provide on page 71 at the end of this chapter.

I n Chapter 1, we explored how economists use models to predict human behaviour. In Chapter 2, we used the production possibilities frontier model to analyze scarcity and trade-offs. In this chapter, we explore the model of demand and supply, which is the most powerful tool in economics, and use it to explain how prices are determined.

Recall from Chapter 1 that because economic models rely on assumptions, they are simplifications of reality. In some cases, the assumptions of the model may not seem to match the economic situation being analyzed. For example, the model of demand and supply assumes that we are analyzing a *perfectly competitive market*. In a **perfectly competitive market**, there are many buyers and sellers, all the products sold are identical to consumers, and there are no barriers to new firms entering the market. These assumptions are very restrictive and only describe a very small number of real world markets, such as the global market for wheat or a few other agricultural products. Experience has shown, however, that the model of demand and supply can be very useful in analyzing markets where competition among sellers is intense, even if there are relatively few sellers and the products being sold are not identical. In fact, in recent studies, the model of demand and supply has been successful analyzing markets with as few as four buyers and four sellers. In the end, the usefulness of a model depends on how well it can predict outcomes in a market. As we will see in this chapter, the model of demand and supply is often very useful in predicting changes in quantities and prices in many markets.

Perfectly competitive market A market that meets the conditions of (1) many buyers and sellers, (2) all firms selling identical products, and (3) no barriers to new firms entering the market.

We begin exploring the model of demand and supply by discussing consumers and the demand side of the market, before turning to firms and the supply side. As you will see, we will apply this model throughout this book to understand prices, the economy, and economic policy.

The Demand Side of the Market

Chapter 2 explained that, in a market system, consumers ultimately determine which goods and services will be produced. The most successful businesses are those that respond best to consumer demand. But what determines consumer demand for a

3.1 LEARNING OBJECTIVE

Discuss the variables that influence demand.

product? Demand is determined by the wants and needs of consumers. It is the choices of consumers like you and how those choices change that determine market demand. But what factors determine how much of a product consumers want and are able to buy? Many, many things influence the willingness of consumers to buy a particular product. For example, consumers who are considering buying an energy drink, such as Red Bull or Beaver Buzz Energy, will make their decisions based on, among other factors, the amount of money they can spend (income) and the effectiveness of advertising campaigns. The main factor in consumer decisions, however, will be the price. So, it makes sense to begin with price when analyzing the decision of consumers to buy a product. It is important to note that when we discuss demand, we are considering not what a consumer *wants* to buy, but what the consumer is both willing and *able* to buy.

Demand Schedules and Demand Curves

Tables that show the relationship between the price of a product and the quantity of the product demanded are called **demand schedules**. The table in Figure 3.1 shows the number of cans of energy drinks consumers would be willing to buy over the course of a month at five different prices. The amount of a good or service that a consumer is willing and able to purchase at a given price is the **quantity demanded**. The graph in Figure 3.1 plots the numbers from the table as a **demand curve**, a curve that shows the relationship between the price of a product and the quantity of the product demanded. (Note that for convenience, we made the demand curve in Figure 3.1 a straight line, or linear. There is no reason to believe that all demand curves are straight lines.) The demand curve in Figure 3.1 shows the **market demand**, or the demand by all the consumers of a given good or service. The market for a product, such as restaurant meals, that is purchased locally would include all the consumers in a city or a relatively small area. The market for a product that is sold internationally, such as energy drinks, would include all the consumers in the world.

The demand curve in Figure 3.1 slopes downward because consumers will buy more cans over the same time period when the price falls. When the price is $3.00 per can, consumers buy 60 million cans per month. If the price is $2.50 per can, consumers buy 70 million cans per month. Buyers demand a larger quantity of a product as the price falls because the product becomes less expensive relative to other products and because they can afford to buy more at a lower price.

The Law of Demand

The inverse relationship between the price of a product and the quantity of the product demanded is known as the **law of demand**: Holding *everything else* constant, when the price of a product falls, the quantity demanded of the product will increase, and when

Demand schedule A table that shows the relationship between the price of a product and the quantity of the product demanded.

Quantity demanded The amount of a good or service that a consumer is willing and able to purchase at a given price.

Demand curve A curve that shows the relationship between the price of a product and the quantity of the product demanded.

Market demand The demand by all the consumers of a given good or service.

Law of demand The rule that, holding *everything else* constant, when the price of a product falls, the quantity demanded of the product will increase, and when the price of a product rises, the quantity demanded of the product will decrease.

Figure 3.1

A Demand Schedule and Demand Curve

As the price changes, consumers change the quantity of energy drinks they are willing to buy. We can show this as a *demand schedule* in a table or as a *demand curve* on a graph. The table and graph both show that as the price of energy drinks falls, the quantity demanded increases. When the price of an energy drink is $3.00, consumers buy 60 million cans per month. When the price drops to $2.50, consumers buy 70 million cans per month. Therefore, the demand curve for energy drinks is downward sloping.

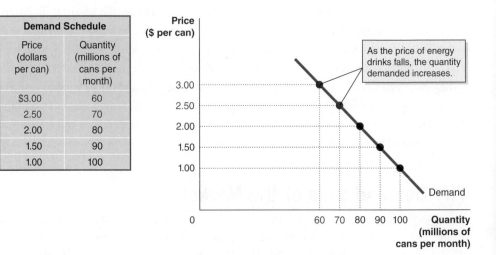

Demand Schedule	
Price (dollars per can)	Quantity (millions of cans per month)
$3.00	60
2.50	70
2.00	80
1.50	90
1.00	100

the price of a product rises, the quantity demanded of the product will decrease. The law of demand holds for any market demand curve. Economists have found only a very few exceptions (after more than 100 years of research).

What Explains the Law of Demand?

It makes intuitive sense that consumers will buy more of something when its price falls (and less when the price rises), but understanding why in more detail can be helpful in understanding why this effect is bigger for some goods than for others. The impact of a price change can be broken up into two different effects, the *substitution effect* and the *income effect*.

The Substitution Effect. When the price of a good rises in comparison to other goods, consumers will start buying those other goods instead. When the price of energy drinks falls relative to the price of coffee, at least some consumers will start drinking energy drinks instead of coffee. The result is an increase in the quantity of energy drinks that people want to buy when the price falls. Put another way, when the price of a good falls relative to the price of another similar product, consumers *substitute* the newly cheaper product for the now more expensive one. The more goods there are that can serve as a substitute for a product, the more important price is in determining the amount people want to buy. (See the definition in the margin for the more technical definition of the **substitution effect**.)

> **Substitution effect** The change in the quantity demanded of a good that results from a change in price, making the good more or less expensive relative to other goods, holding constant the effect of the price change on consumer purchasing power.

The Income Effect. When the price of a good falls, consumers can afford to buy more of everything—the *purchasing power* of their income has increased. *Purchasing* power is the quantity of goods and services that consumers can buy with a fixed income. Imagine you have $10 to spend on drinks as you get ready to study. When the price of energy drinks falls from $5 per can to $2.50 per can, you can now afford four cans instead of just two. You are able to purchase more because of the lower price. (See the definition in the margin for a more technical definition of the **income effect**).

Note that although we can analyze them separately, the substitution effect and the income effect happen simultaneously whenever a price changes. Thus, a fall in the price of energy drinks leads consumers to buy more energy drinks, both because the cans are now less expensive relative to substitute products (such as coffee) and because the consumers in that household can afford to buy more of everything, including energy drinks.

> **Income effect** The change in the quantity demanded of a good that results from the effect of a change in the good's price on consumers' purchasing power.

That Magic Latin Phrase *Ceteris Paribus*

You likely noticed that the definition of the law of demand contains the phrase *holding everything else constant*. In constructing the market demand curve for energy drinks, we focused only on the effect that changes in the price of energy drinks would have on how many cans consumers would be willing and able to buy. We were holding constant all other variables that might affect the willingness of consumers to buy energy drinks. Economists refer to the necessity of holding all other variables constant in constructing a demand curve (or any other model) as the ***ceteris paribus* condition**: *ceteris paribus* is Latin for "all else equal."

What would happen if we allowed a change in a variable—other than price—that might affect the willingness of consumers to buy energy drinks? Consumers would then change the quantity they demanded at each price. We can illustrate this effect by shifting the market demand curve. A shift of a demand curve is *an increase or a decrease in demand*. A movement along a demand curve is *an increase or a decrease in the quantity demanded*. As Figure 3.2 shows, we shift the demand curve to the right if consumers decide to buy more of the good even when the price doesn't change, and we shift the demand curve to the left when consumers decide to buy less of a good even if the price doesn't change.

> ***Ceteris paribus* ("all else equal") condition** The requirement that when analyzing the relationship between two variables—such as price and quantity demanded—other variables must be held constant.

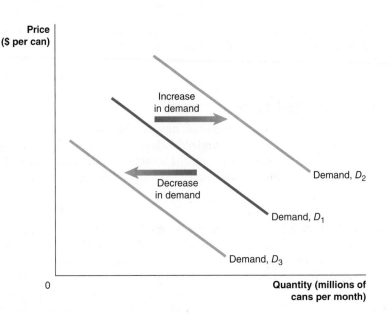

Figure 3.2

Shifting the Demand Curve

When consumers increase the quantity of a product they want to buy at a given price, the market demand curve shifts to the right, from D_1 to D_2. When consumers decrease the quantity of a product they want to buy at a given price, the demand curve shifts to the left from D_1 to D_3.

Variables that Shift Market Demand

Many variables other than price can influence how much of a product consumers are willing and able to buy. These five are the most important:

- Income

- Prices of related goods

- Tastes

- Population and demographics

- Expectations

We next discuss how changes in each of these variables affect the market demand curve.

Income. The income that consumers have available to spend affects their willingness and ability to buy a good. Suppose the market demand curve in Figure 3.1 on page 52 represents the willingness of consumers to buy energy drinks when average household income is $60 000. If household income rises to $65 000, the demand for energy drinks will increase, which we show by shifting the demand curve to the right. A good is a **normal good** when demand increases following a rise in income and decreases following a fall in income. Most goods are normal goods, but the demand for some goods falls when income rises and rises when income falls. For instance, when your income rises, you might buy fewer hot dogs and more steak. A good is an **inferior good** when demand decreases following a rise in income and increases following a fall in income. So, for you, hot dogs would be an example of an inferior good. Remember, when economists say a good is inferior, they aren't saying anything about the quality of the good, just that the amount people buy falls when income rises.

Normal good A good for which the demand increases as income rises and decreases as income falls.

Inferior good A good for which the demand increases as income falls and decreases as income rises.

Prices of Related Goods. The price of other goods can also affect consumers' demand for a product. Goods and services that can be used for the same purpose—such as energy drinks and coffee—are **substitutes**. Two goods are substitutes of one another if, when you buy more of one, you buy less of the other. A decrease in the price of a substitute causes the demand curve for a good to shift to the left. An increase in the price of a substitute causes the demand curve for a good to shift to the right.

Suppose that the market demand curve in Figure 3.1 represents the willingness and ability of consumers to buy energy drinks during a week when the average price of coffee is $2.00. If the average price of coffee falls to $1.50, how will the market for energy

Substitutes Goods and services that can be used for the same purpose.

| Making the Connection | ## The Transformation of Lobster from Inferior to Normal Good |

When economists describe a product as being inferior they aren't saying it is poor quality, they're just saying that consumers buy less of it when their incomes rise. The same product can be an inferior good to some and a normal good to others. It all depends on the attitudes of people in a given time and place and these attitudes can change.

A lobster dinner in Toronto or Calgary can easily cost $50 or more. In many fancy restaurants, a lobster dinner is the most expensive item on the menu. The high price and honoured place on the menu would suggest that lobster is a normal good—when incomes rise, demand for lobster will rise.

This isn't always the case. In many parts of the Maritimes where lobster is caught, it is considered something you eat only if you can't afford anything better—an inferior good. Historically, in these regions, lobster was fed to prisoners and apprentices as a cheap source of protein, rather than as a fancy meal for the wealthy. Maritimers generally won't brag about having a lobster sandwich for lunch.

Whether a good is normal or inferior depends on social attitudes, tastes, and preferences. The only way to know for sure if a good is normal or inferior is to observe how consumers' behaviour changes as their incomes change.

Despite it's high cost in many restaurants, lobster can still be an inferior good.

MyEconLab

Your Turn: Test your understanding by doing related problem 1.4 on page 73 at the end of this chapter.

All Canada Photos/Alamy Stock Photo

---

drinks change? Consumers will demand fewer cans of energy drinks at every price. We show this impact by shifting the demand curve for energy drinks to the left.

Goods and services that are used together—like hamburgers and buns—are **complements**. When two goods are complements, the more consumers buy of one, the more they will buy of the other. A decrease in the price of a complement causes the demand curve for a good to shift to the right. An increase in the price of a complement causes the demand curve to shift to the left.

Complements Goods and services that are used together.

Many people drink Red Bull, Monster Energy, or Beaver Buzz Energy when working out. So, for these people, energy drinks and gym memberships are complements. Suppose that the market demand curve in Figure 3.1 represents the willingness of consumers to buy energy drinks when the average price of a gym membership is $40 per month. If the price of gym memberships drops to $30 per month, consumers will buy more gym memberships *and* more energy drinks, making the demand curve for energy drinks shift to the right.

Tastes. Consumers can be influenced by an advertising campaign for a product. If the firms making Red Bull, Monster Energy, Beaver Buzz Energy, or other energy drinks begin to advertise heavily online, consumers are more likely to buy cans at every price, and the demand curve will shift to the right. An economist would say that the advertising campaign has affected consumers' *taste* for energy drinks. Taste is a catchall category that refers to the many subjective elements that can enter into a consumer's decision to buy a product. A consumer's taste for a product can change for many reasons. Sometimes trends play a substantial role. For example, the popularity of low-carbohydrate diets caused a decline in demand for some goods, such as bread and doughnuts, and an increase in the demand for meat. In general, when consumers' taste for a product increases, the demand curve will shift to the right, and when consumers' taste for a product decreases, the demand curve for the product will shift to the left.

Population and Demographics. Population and demographics can affect the demand for a product. Population determines the total number of consumers who could demand a product. As population increases, the number of consumers grows and so does demand. An increase in population will shift the demand curve to the right.

Making the Connection | **The Aging Baby Boomers**

The average age of Canadians is increasing. After World War II ended in 1945, Canada experienced a "baby boom," as birth rates rose and remained high through the early 1960s. Falling birth rates after 1965 mean that the baby boom generation is larger than the generation before it or those after it. The figure below uses data from Statistics Canada to show how people over the age of 64 have become a significant portion of the population.

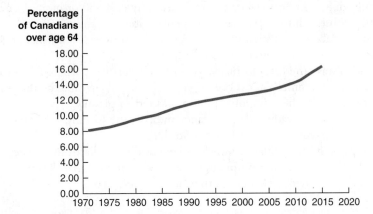

Source: Statistics Canada. Table 051-0001 - Estimates of population, by age group and sex for July 1, Canada, provinces and territories, annual (persons unless otherwise noted) (table), CANSIM (database), Using E-STAT (distributor). Reproduced and distributed on an "as is" basis with the permission of Statistics Canada.

What effects will the aging of the baby boom generation have on the economy? Older people need more medical care than younger adults, which means that there will be greater demand for doctors, nurses, and hospital facilities in the future. In Canada, a growing number of foreign-trained nurses and doctors are being recruited to help meet the growing demand for health care services.

Aging baby boomers will also have an impact on the housing market. Older folks often "downsize" their housing by moving from large, single-family homes with high maintenance costs to smaller homes, condominiums, or apartments. Hence, in the coming years, demand for smaller homes may increase, while demand for large homes falls.

Based on Kaleigh Rogers, "Foreign physician Recruits Helping Meet City's Growing Need for Doctors," *CBC.ca*, March 21, 2013, http://www.cbc.ca/hamilton/news/story/2013/03/20/hamilton-foreign-doctors.html.

MyEconLab   **Your Turn:** Test your understanding by doing related problem 1.5 on page 73 at the end of this chapter.

Demographics The characteristics of a population with respect to age, race, and gender.

Demographics refers to the different types of people that make up a population. The portion of young people in the population is part of demographics. So too is the portion of the population from a given culture. Changes in demographics can change demand for certain products. Halal meat is one example. Halal meat is processed in accordance with Islamic practices. In areas of the country with very small Islamic populations, it is rare to see products labelled as compliant with Halal practice. In a growing number of major grocery store chains, including Superstore, Halal products are displayed prominently. This is a result of the increase in demand for these products due to changing demographics.

Expectations. Consumers choose not only which products to buy but also when to buy them. For instance, if enough consumers become convinced that houses will be selling for lower prices in three months, the demand for houses will decrease now, as some consumers delay their purchases to wait for prices to fall. Alternatively, if enough consumers become convinced that house prices will rise over the next three months, the demand for houses will rise now as some people try to avoid the expected increase in prices.

Expected future prices aren't the only important expectations that affect consumer demand. Consumers also change their purchasing habits when their expected income changes. Most of you are probably consuming more now than your income would suggest. This is because you expect that your income will be higher in the future, meaning that you believe you can afford to consume more now. When the economy slows down and people expect their incomes to be lower in the future, they often put off major purchases or buy different things. How an expected income change affects the demand for a product depends on whether the product is a normal or an inferior good. When incomes are generally falling (e.g., when the economy is doing poorly), people tend to buy more inferior goods, even if their incomes haven't actually changed.

Table 3.1 summarizes the most important variables that cause market demand curves to shift. Note that the table shows the shift in the demand curve that results from an

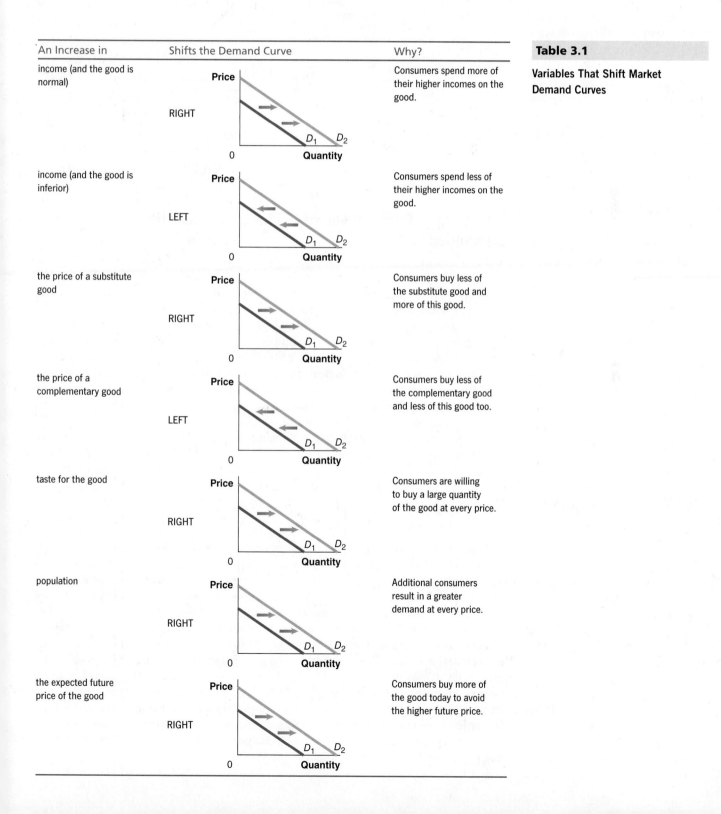

An Increase in	Shifts the Demand Curve	Why?
income (and the good is normal)	RIGHT	Consumers spend more of their higher incomes on the good.
income (and the good is inferior)	LEFT	Consumers spend less of their higher incomes on the good.
the price of a substitute good	RIGHT	Consumers buy less of the substitute good and more of this good.
the price of a complementary good	LEFT	Consumers buy less of the complementary good and less of this good too.
taste for the good	RIGHT	Consumers are willing to buy a large quantity of the good at every price.
population	RIGHT	Additional consumers result in a greater demand at every price.
the expected future price of the good	RIGHT	Consumers buy more of the good today to avoid the higher future price.

Table 3.1

Variables That Shift Market Demand Curves

Figure 3.3

A Change in Demand versus a Change in Quantity Demanded

If the price of energy drinks falls from $3.00 to $2.50, the result will be a movement along the demand curve from point A to point B—an increase in quantity demanded from 60 million cans to 70 million cans. If consumers' incomes increase, or if another factor changes that makes consumers want more energy drinks at every price, the demand curve will shift to the right—an increase in demand. In this case, the increase in demand from D_1 to D_2 causes the quantity of energy drinks demanded at a price of $3.00 to increase from 60 million cans at point A to 80 million cans at point C.

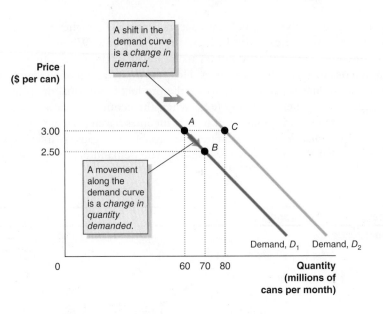

increase in each of the variables. A *decrease* in these variables would cause the demand curve to shift in the opposite direction.

A Change in Demand versus a Change in Quantity Demanded

It is important to understand the difference between a *change in demand* and a *change in quantity demanded*. A change in demand refers to a shift of the demand curve. A shift occurs if there is a change in one of the variables, *other than the price of the product,* that affects the willingness of consumers to buy the product. A change in quantity demanded refers to a movement along the demand curve as a result of a change in the product's price. Figure 3.3 illustrates this important distinction. If the price of energy drinks falls from $3.00 to $2.50 per can, the result will be a movement along the demand curve from point A to point B—an increase in quantity demanded from 60 million to 70 million. If consumers' incomes increase, or if another factor changes that makes consumers want more energy drinks *even if the price doesn't change,* the demand curve will shift to the right—an increase in demand. In this case, the increase in demand from curve D_1 to D_2 causes the quantity of energy drinks demanded at a price of $3.00 to increase from 60 million at point A to 80 million at point C.

3.2 LEARNING OBJECTIVE

Discuss the variables that influence supply.

Quantity supplied The amount of a good or service that a firm is willing and able to supply at a given price.

The Supply Side of the Market

Just as many variables influence the willingness and ability of consumers to buy a good or service, many variables also influence the willingness and ability of firms to sell a good or service. The most important of these variables is price. The amount of a good or service that a firm is willing and able to supply at a given price is the **quantity supplied**. Holding all other variables constant (recall the Latin phrase *ceteris paribus*), when the price of a good rises, producing (and selling) that good is more profitable, and the quantity supplied will increase. When the price of a good falls, the good is less profitable to produce, and the quantity supplied will decrease. In addition, as we saw in Chapter 2, devoting more and more resources to the production of a specific good results in increasing marginal costs. If, for example, Red Bull, Monster Energy, and DD Beverage Company increase production of their energy drinks during a given time period, they are likely to find that the cost of producing additional cans increases as they run existing factories for longer hours and pay higher prices for ingredients and higher wages for workers. As the marginal costs of making a product rises as output increases, a firm will supply more of that product only if the price is higher.

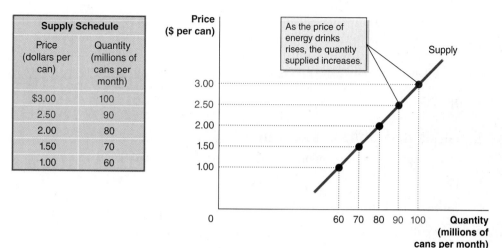

Supply Schedule	
Price (dollars per can)	Quantity (millions of cans per month)
$3.00	100
2.50	90
2.00	80
1.50	70
1.00	60

As the price of energy drinks rises, the quantity supplied increases.

Figure 3.4

A Supply Schedule and Supply Curve

As the price changes, Red Bull, Monster Energy, DD Beverage Company, and other firms producing energy drinks change the quantity they are willing to supply. We can show this as a *supply schedule* in a table or a *supply curve* on a graph. The supply schedule and supply curve both show that as the price of energy drinks rises, firms will increase the quantity they supply. At a price of $2.50 per can, firms will supply 90 million cans. At a price of $3.00 per can, firms will supply 100 million cans.

Supply Schedules and Supply Curves

A **supply schedule** is a table that shows the relationship between the price of a product and the quantity of the product supplied. The table in Figure 3.4 is a supply schedule showing the quantity of energy drinks that firms would be willing to supply per month at different prices. The graph in Figure 3.4 plots the numbers from the supply schedule as a *supply curve*. A **supply curve** shows the relationship between the price of a product and the quantity of the product supplied. The supply schedule and the supply curve both show that as the price of energy drinks rises, firms will increase the quantity they supply. At a price of $2.50 per can, firms will supply 90 million cans per month. At the higher price of $3.00, firms will supply 100 million. (Once again, we are assuming that the relationship is linear—even though most supply curves are not actually straight lines.)

Supply schedule A table that shows the relationship between the price of a product and the quantity of the product supplied.

Supply curve A curve that shows the relationship between the price of a product and the quantity of the product supplied.

The Law of Supply

The *market supply curve* in Figure 3.4 is upward sloping. We expect most supply curves to be upward sloping based on the **law of supply**, which states that, holding everything else constant, increases in price cause increases in the quantity supplied, and decreases in price result in decreases in the quantity supplied. Notice that the definition of the law of supply—just like the definition of the law of demand—contains the phrase *holding everything else constant*. If only the price of the product changes, there is a movement along the supply curve, which is *an increase or a decrease in the quantity supplied*. As Figure 3.5 shows,

Law of supply The rule that, holding everything else constant, increases in price cause increases in the quantity supplied, and decreases in price cause decreases in the quantity supplied.

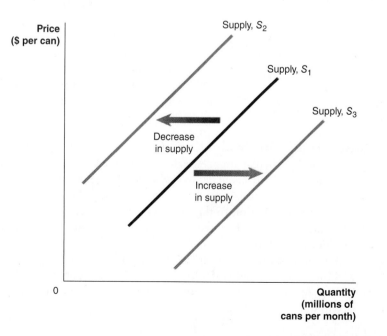

Figure 3.5

Shifting the Supply Curve

When firms increase the quantity of a product they want to sell at a given price, the supply curve shifts to the right. The shift from S_1 to S_3 represents *an increase in supply*. When firms decrease the quantity of a product they want to sell at a given price, the supply curve shifts to the left. The shift from S_1 to S_2 represents *a decrease in supply*.

if any other variable that affects the willingness of firms to supply a good changes, the supply curve will shift, which is *an increase or a decrease in supply*. When firms increase the quantity of a product they would like to sell at a given price, the supply curve shifts to the right. The shift from S_1 to S_3 represents *an increase in supply*. When firms decrease the quantity of a product they would like to sell at a given price, the supply curve shifts to the left. The shift from S_1 to S_2 represents *a decrease in supply*.

Variables that Shift Market Supply

The following are the most important variables that shift the market supply curve:

- Price of inputs
- Technological change
- Prices of substitutes in production
- Number of firms in the market
- Expected future prices

We next discuss how each of these variables affects the market supply curve.

Prices of Inputs.
The factor most likely to cause the supply curve for a product to shift is a change in the price of an *input*. An input is anything used in the making of a good or service. For instance, if the price of guarana (a stimulant in many energy drinks) rises, the cost of producing energy drinks will increase, and energy drinks will be less profitable at every price. The supply of energy drinks will decline, and the market supply curve for energy drinks will shift to the left. Similarly, if the price of an input falls, the supply of energy drinks will increase, and the market supply curve for energy drinks will shift to the right. Any time something like wages or interest rates (the price of labour and capital) change, the market supply curve will shift.

Technological Change.
A second factor that causes a change in supply is *technological change*. **Technological change** is a positive or negative change in the ability of a firm to produce a given level of output from a given quantity of inputs. Positive technological change occurs when a firm is able to produce *more* output with the same amount of inputs. This change will happen when the *productivity* of workers or machines increases. If a firm can produce more output with the same amount of inputs, each unit will cost less and the good will be more profitable to produce at any given price. As a result, when positive technological change occurs, a firm will want to sell more of its product at every given price, making the market supply curve shift to the right. Normally, we expect technological change to have a positive impact on a firm's willingness to supply a product.

Negative technological change is rare, although it might be caused by a natural disaster or a war that reduces a firm's ability to supply as much output with a given amount of inputs. Negative technological change will raise a firm's costs, and the good will be less profitable to produce. Therefore, negative technological change causes the market supply curve to shift to the left.

Prices of Substitutes in Production.
Firms often have to choose which goods they will produce at a particular time. Alternative products that a firm could produce with the same inputs are called *substitutes in production*. A number of companies produce both energy drinks and traditional soft drinks. For instance, the Coca-Cola Company produces Full Throttle in addition to the many varieties of Coke it sells. PepsiCo produces Amp in addition to Pepsi, Mountain Dew, and other drinks. If the price of colas falls, producing Pepsi and Coke will be less profitable, and Coca-Cola, PepsiCo, and other soft drink manufacturers will shift some of their productive capacity out of cola production and into making energy drinks. As a result, each company will offer more energy drinks for sale, even if the price doesn't change, so the market supply curve for energy drinks will shift to the right.

Technological change A change in the quantity of output a firm can produce using a given quantity of inputs.

Table 3.2

Variables That Shift Market Supply Curves

An Increase in	Shifts the Supply Curve		Why?
the price of an input	LEFT		The costs of producing the good rise.
productivity	RIGHT		The costs of producing the good fall.
the price of a substitute in production	LEFT		More of the substitute is produced, and less of the good is produced.
the number of firms in the market	RIGHT		Additional firms result in a greater quantity supplied at every price.
the expected future price of the product	LEFT		Less of the good will be offered for sale today as firms wait to take advantage of the higher price expected in the future.

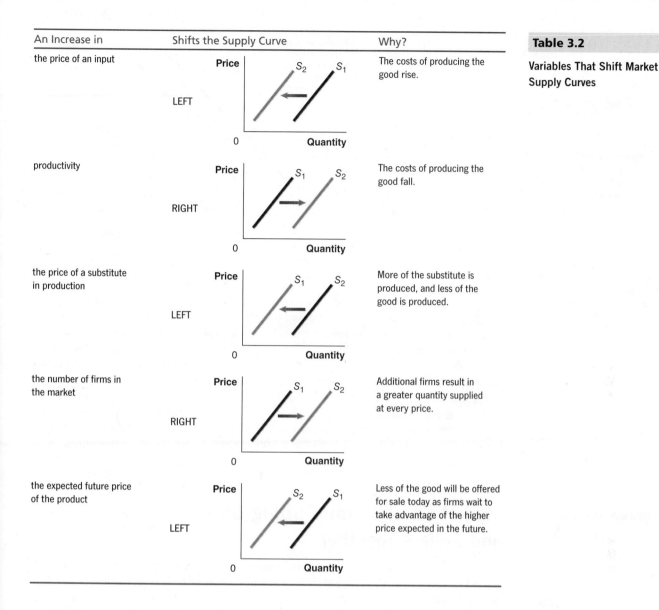

Number of Firms in the Market. A change in the number of firms in the market will change supply. When new firms *enter* a market, the supply curve shifts to the right, and when existing firms leave, or *exit*, a market, the supply curve shifts to the left. For example, when Beaver Buzz Energy was introduced, the market supply curve for energy drinks shifted to the right.

Expected Future Prices. If a firm expects that the price of its product will be higher in the future than it is today, it has an incentive to decrease supply now and increase supply in the future. For example, if Red Bull believes that prices for energy drinks are temporarily low—perhaps due to low incomes of consumers—it may store some of its product today to sell later on, when it expects prices to be higher.

Table 3.2 summarizes the most important variables that cause market supply curves to shift. Note that the table shows the shift in the supply curve that results from an *increase* in each of the variables. A *decrease* in these variables would cause the supply curve to shift in the opposite direction.

A Change in Supply versus a Change in Quantity Supplied

We noted earlier the important difference between a change in demand and a change in quantity demanded. There is a similar difference between a *change in supply* and a *change in quantity supplied*. A change in supply refers to a shift in the supply curve. The

A Change in Supply versus a Change in Quantity Supplied

If the price of energy drinks rises from $1.50 to $2.00 per can, the result will be a movement up the supply curve from point *A* to point *B*—an increase in quantity supplied of Red Bull, Monster Energy, Beaver Buzz Energy, and other energy drinks from 70 million to 80 million cans. If the price of an input decreases or another factor changes that causes sellers to supply more of the product at every price, the supply curve will shift to the right—an increase in supply. In this case, the increase in supply from S_1 to S_2 causes the quantity of energy drinks supplied at a price of $2.00 to increase from 80 million cans to 100 million cans.

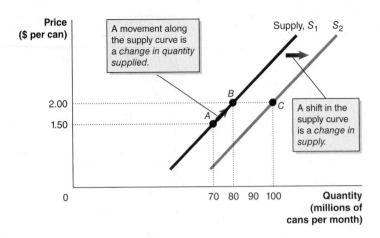

supply curve will shift when there is a change in one of the variables, *other than the price of the product*, that affects the willingness of firms to sell the product. A change in quantity supplied refers to a movement along the supply curve as a result of a change in the product's price. Figure 3.6 illustrates this important distinction. If the price of energy drinks rises from $1.50 to $2.00 per can, the result will be a movement up the supply curve from point *A* to point *B*—an increase in quantity supplied from 70 million cans per month to 80 million cans per month. If the price of an input decreases (or another factor makes sellers supply more of the product at every price), the supply curve will shift to the right—an increase in supply. In this case, the increase in supply from S_1 to S_2 causes the quantity of energy drinks supplied to increase from 80 million to 100 million per month even if the price remains at $2.00 per can (note the move from point *B* to point *C* in the figure).

Use a graph to illustrate market equilibrium.

Market Equilibrium: Putting Buyers and Sellers Together

The purpose of markets is to bring buyers and sellers together. As we saw in Chapter 2, instead of being chaotic and disorderly, the interaction of buyers and sellers in markets ultimately results in firms being led to produce the goods and services that consumers want. To understand how this happens, we first need to see how markets work to reconcile the plans of buyers and sellers.

In Figure 3.7, we bring the market demand curve and the market supply curve together. Notice that the demand curve crosses the supply curve at only one point.

Market Equilibrium

Where the demand curve crosses the supply curve determines market equilibrium. In this case, the demand curve for energy drinks crosses the supply curve at a price of $2.00 and a quantity of 80 million cans. Only at this point is the quantity of energy drinks consumers want to buy equal to the quantity of energy drinks suppliers are willing to sell: The quantity demanded is equal to the quantity supplied.

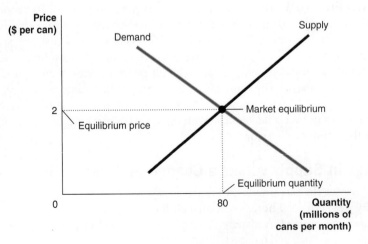

This point represents the price of $2.00 and a quantity of 80 million cans. Only at this point is the quantity of energy drinks consumers are willing to buy equal to the quantity of energy drinks firms are willing to sell. This is the point of **market equilibrium**. Only at market equilibrium will the quantity demanded equal the quantity supplied. In this case, the *equilibrium price* is $2.00 and the *equilibrium quantity* is 80 million. As we noted at the beginning of the chapter, markets that have many buyers and many sellers are competitive markets, and equilibrium in these markets is a **competitive market equilibrium**. In the market for energy drinks, there are many buyers but only about 80 firms. Whether 80 firms are enough for our model of demand and supply to apply to this market is a matter of judgment. In this chapter, we are assuming that the market for energy drinks has enough sellers to be treated as competitive.

> **Market equilibrium** A situation in which quantity demanded equals quantity supplied.

> **Competitive market equilibrium** A market equilibrium with many buyers and many sellers.

How Markets Eliminate Surpluses and Shortages: Getting to Equilibrium

A market that is not in equilibrium moves toward equilibrium. Once a market is in equilibrium, it remains in equilibrium. To see why, consider what happens if the market is not in equilibrium. For instance, suppose that the price in the market for energy drinks is $3.00, rather than the equilibrium price of $2.00. As Figure 3.8 shows, at a price of $3.00 the quantity of energy drinks demanded would be 60 million cans per month, while the quantity supplied would be 100 million cans per month. The quantity supplied is 40 million more than the quantity demanded (100 million − 60 million). When the quantity supplied is greater than the quantity demanded, there is a **surplus** in the market. A surplus means that firms will be unable to sell all the goods they would like and the goods they're producing start piling up. Fortunately, firms have a handy method of getting rid of unwanted inventory—they put it on sale. Remember a sale is just a reduction in price. Cutting the price will simultaneously increase the quantity demanded and decrease the quantity supplied. This adjustment will reduce the surplus, but as long as the price remains above the equilibrium of $2.00, there will be unsold energy drinks and downward pressure on the price. Only when the price has fallen to $2.00 will firms have a reason to stop reducing the price.

> **Surplus** A situation in which the quantity supplied is greater than the quantity demanded.

What if the price were below market equilibrium, say $0.50? If this were the case, the quantity demanded would be 110 million and the quantity supplied would be only 50 million, as shown in Figure 3.8. When the quantity demanded is greater than the quantity supplied, there is a **shortage** in the market. In this case, the shortage is 60 million cans (110 million − 50 million). When a shortage occurs, some consumers will be unable to buy energy drinks at the current price. When this happens, firms will realize they can raise the price without losing sales. A higher price means a decrease in the quantity demanded and an increase in the quantity supplied. The increase in price will reduce the size of the shortage, but as long as the price remains below the equilibrium price of $2.00 there will be a shortage and firms will have an incentive to increase the prices they charge. Only when the price has risen to $2.00 will the market be in equilibrium.

> **Shortage** A situation in which the quantity demanded is greater than the quantity supplied.

At a competitive equilibrium, all consumers willing to pay the market price will be able to buy as much of the product as they want, and all firms willing to accept the market price will be able to sell as much as they want. As a result, neither consumers nor suppliers will have a reason to do anything differently. This means that the price of energy drinks will stay at $2.00, unless the demand curve, the supply curve, or both shift.

Demand and Supply Both Count

Keep in mind that the interaction of demand and supply determines the equilibrium price. Neither consumers nor firms can dictate what the equilibrium price will be. No firm can sell anything, at any price, unless it can find a willing buyer, and no consumer can buy anything, at any price, without finding a willing seller.

Figure 3.8

The Effect of Surpluses and Shortages on the Market

When the market price is above equilibrium, there will be a *surplus*. In the figure, a price of $3.00 per energy drink results in 100 million cans being supplied but only 60 million cans being demanded, or a surplus of 40 million cans. As the firms that produce Red Bull, Monster Energy, Beaver Buzz Energy, and other drinks cut the price to dispose of the surplus, the price will fall to the equilibrium of $2.00. When the market price is below equilibrium, there will be a *shortage*. A price of $0.50 results in 110 million cans being demanded, but only 50 million cans being supplied, or a shortage of 60 million cans. As firms find that consumers who are unable to find energy drinks for sale are willing to pay more for them, the price will rise to the equilibrium of $2.00.

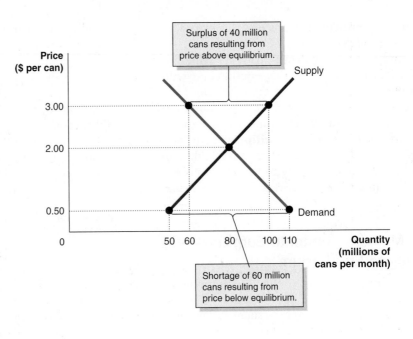

Solved Problem **3.1**

Demand and Supply Both Count: A Tale of Two Cards

Which hockey card do you think is worth more: Sidney Crosby's rookie card or one of Jacques Plante's distributed free in a box of Quaker Oats? Sidney Crosby is one of the most popular hockey players in recent memory; his jersey sells exceptionally well even though he has missed many games due to concussions and other injuries. Jacques Plante was a goaltender from 1946 to 1975 and played for a number of NHL teams, including the Montreal Canadiens and the St. Louis Blues. The demand for Sidney Crosby's rookie card is much higher than the demand for Jacques

Plante's cereal-box card. However, at auction, a Sidney Crosby rookie card can be expected to sell for about $5000, while a Jacques Plante cereal-box card can be expected to fetch about $12 000. Use a demand and supply graph to explain how it is that a card of a player from 50 years ago that was distributed free in a box of cereal has a higher price than a card of one of the most popular modern players that was sold in a sealed foil pack, even though the demand for Sidney Crosby's card is certain to be greater than the demand for Jacques Plante's card.

Solving the Problem

Step 1: Review the chapter material. This problem is about prices being determined at market equilibrium, so you may want to review the section "Market Equilibrium: Putting Buyers and Sellers Together."

Step 2: Draw demand curves that illustrate the greater demand for Sidney Crosby's card. Begin by drawing two demand curves. Label one "Demand for Crosby's card" and the other "Demand for Plante's card." Make sure that the Crosby demand curve is much farther to the right than the Plante demand curve. Make sure you label your axes.

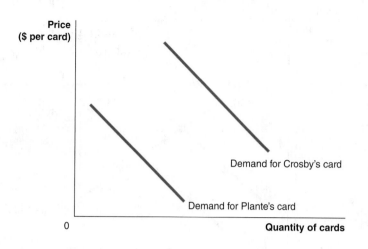

Step 3: **Draw supply curves that illustrate the equilibrium price of Plante's card being higher than the equilibrium price of Crosby's card.** Based on the demand curves you have just drawn, think about how it might be possible for the market price of Crosby's card to be lower than the market price of Plante's card. The only way this can be true is if the supply of Crosby's card is much greater than the supply of Plante's card. (Plante's card was distributed in a cereal box and therefore easily damaged.) In your graph, draw a supply curve for Crosby's card and a supply curve for Plante's card that will result in an equilibrium price of Plante's card of $12 000 and an equilibrium price of Crosby's card of $5000. You have now solved the problem.

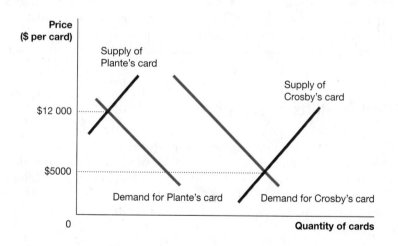

Extra credit: The explanation for this puzzle is that both demand and supply count when determining market price. The demand for Crosby's card is much greater than the demand for Plante's card, but the supply of Crosby's card is also much greater. (Note that the supply curves for the cards of Plante and Crosby are upward sloping, even though only a fixed number of each of these types of cards is available and no more can be produced. The supply curves slope upwards because a higher price will induce more cards to be offered for sale by their current owners.) Try and come up with your own examples of goods with very low demand but very high prices and goods with high demand and very low prices.

Based on http://bleacherreport.com/articles/812055–nhl-the-15-most-valuable-hockey-cards-of-all-time/page/8 and http://bleacherreport.com/articles/812055–nhl-the-15-most-valuable-hockey-cards-of-all-time/page/5.

Your Turn: For more practice, do related problem 3.2 on page 74 at the end of this chapter.   MyEconLab

Figure 3.9

The Effect of an Increase in Supply on Equilibrium

If a firm enters a market, as Coca-Cola Company did when it introduced Full Throttle, the equilibrium price will fall, and the equilibrium quantity will rise:

1. As Coke enters the market for energy drinks, a larger quantity of energy drinks will be supplied at every price, so the market supply curve shifts to the right, from S_1 to S_2, which causes a surplus of energy drinks at the original price, P_1.

2. The equilibrium price falls from P_1 to P_2.

3. The equilibrium quantity rises from Q_1 to Q_2.

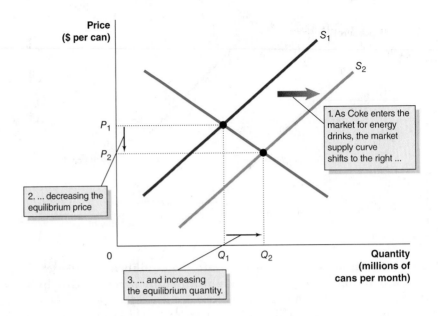

Use demand and supply graphs to predict changes in prices and quantities.

The Effect of Demand and Supply Shifts on Equilibrium

We have seen that the interaction of demand and supply in markets determines the quantity of a good that is produced and the price at which it sells. We have also seen that several variables cause demand curves to shift, and other variables cause supply curves to shift. As a result, demand and supply curves in most markets are constantly moving around, and the prices and quantities that represent equilibrium are constantly changing. In this section, we look at how shifts in demand and supply curves affect equilibrium price and quantity.

The Effect of Shifts in Supply on Equilibrium

When Coke started selling the energy drink Full Throttle, the market supply curve for energy drinks shifted to the right. Figure 3.9 shows the supply curve shifting from S_1 to S_2. When the supply curve shifts to the right, there will be a surplus at the original equilibrium price, P_1. The surplus is eliminated as the equilibrium price falls to P_2, and the equilibrium quantity rises from Q_1 to Q_2. If existing firms exit the market, the supply curve will shift to the left, causing the equilibrium price to rise and the equilibrium quantity to fall.

Making the Connection | **Invisible Solar Cells**

Research on producing clean energy from the sun has been going on for more than 170 years. Alexandre Becquerel first observed the photovoltaic effect in 1839 and a lot of research since then has gone into figuring out how to produce effective solar panels for turning sunlight into electricity.

One of the major problems with current solar panels is finding enough space to install them. Typically, solar panels require a large area dedicated to nothing else and will throw everything underneath them into darkness. A common place for solar panels in major cities is the rooftops of large buildings. This requirement for space has helped increase the cost of the solar power to the point where it still accounts for a relatively small portion of the electricity we consume.

This may change if companies like Ubiquitous Energy and Solar Wind Technologies have their way. These firms are working on developing a new solar energy technology—a transparent solar panel. These panels would replace windows in buildings, so you could still look at the view while the window generates some of the electricity you needed to power your laptop. By producing solar panels that can be installed without taking up extra space, this new technology will reduce the cost of solar power. The figure below shows how the new technology can change the market and drive the price of solar power down.

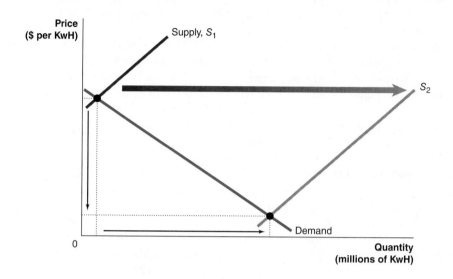

Based on Marianne Lavelle, See-Through Solar Could Turn Windows, Phones Into Power Sources, 2015, *National Geographic* Society. http://news.nationalgeographic.com/energy/2015/08/150805-transparent-solar-could-turn-window-phones-into-power-generators/.

Your Turn: Test your understanding by doing related problem 4.2 on page 75 at the end of this chapter.

MyEconLab

The Effect of Shifts in Demand on Equilibrium

Because energy drinks are generally a normal good, when incomes increase, the market demand for energy drinks shifts to the right. Figure 3.10 shows the effect of a demand curve shifting to the right, from D_1 to D_2. This shift causes a shortage at the original equilibrium price, P_1. To eliminate this new shortage, equilibrium price rises to P_2, and

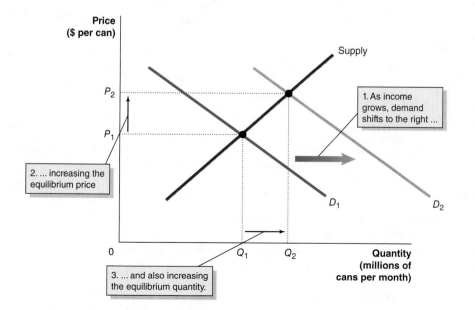

Figure 3.10

The Effect of an Increase in Demand on Equilibrium

Increases in income will cause equilibrium price and quantity to rise:

1. Because energy drinks are a normal good, as income grows, the quantity demanded increases at every price, and the market demand curve shifts to the right, from D_1 to D_2, which causes a shortage of energy drinks at the original price, P_1.

2. The equilibrium price rises from P_1 to P_2.

3. The equilibrium quantity rises from Q_1 to Q_2.

the equilibrium quantity rises from Q_1 to Q_2. In contrast, if the price of a substitute good, such as coffee, were to fall, the demand for energy drinks would decrease, shifting the demand curve for energy drinks to the left. When the demand curve shifts to the left, the equilibrium price and quantity both decrease.

The Effect of Shifts in Demand and Supply over Time

Whenever only demand or only supply shifts, we can easily predict the effect on equilibrium price and quantity. Things are more complicated when *both* supply and demand shift at the same time. For instance, in many markets, the demand curve shifts to the right over time as populations and incomes grow. The supply often shifts to the right over time too, as new firms enter the market or technology improves. Whether the equilibrium price rises or falls over time depends on which shift is bigger. If the shift in the demand curve is bigger than the shift in the supply curve, the price will rise. If the shift in the supply curve is bigger than the shift in the demand curve, the price will fall. Panel (a) of Figure 3.11 shows that when demand shifts to the right more than supply, the equilibrium price rises. But as panel (b) shows, when supply shifts to the right more than demand, the equilibrium price falls.

Table 3.3 summarizes all possible combinations of shifts in demand and supply over time and the effects of the shifts on equilibrium price (P) and quantity (Q). For example, the entry in red in the table shows that if the demand curve shifts to the right and the supply curve also shifts to the right, the equilibrium quantity will increase, while the equilibrium price may increase, decrease, or remain unchanged. To be sure you understand each entry in the table, draw demand and supply graphs to check whether you can reproduce the predicted changes in equilibrium price and quantity. If the entry in the table says the predicted change in equilibrium price or quantity can be either an increase or a decrease, draw two graphs similar to panels (a) and (b) of Figure 3.11—one showing the equilibrium price or quantity increasing and the other showing it decreasing. Note also that in the ambiguous cases where either price or quantity might increase or decrease, it is also possible that price or quantity might remain unchanged. Be sure you understand why.

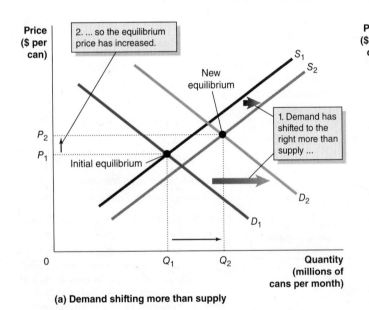

(a) Demand shifting more than supply

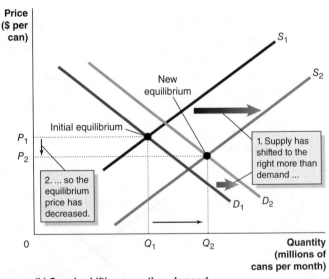

(b) Supply shifting more than demand

Figure 3.11 Shifts in Demand and Supply

Whether the price of a product rises or falls over time depends on whether demand shifts to the right more than supply. In panel (a), demand shifts to the right more than supply, and the equilibrium price rises:

1. Demand shifts to the right more than supply.
2. The equilibrium price rises from P_1 to P_2.

In panel (b), supply shifts to the right more than demand, and the equilibrium price falls:

1. Supply shifts to the right more than demand.
2. The equilibrium price falls from P_1 to P_2.

Table 3.3

How Shifts in Demand and Supply Affect Equilibrium Price (*P*) and Quantity (*Q*)

	Supply Curve Unchanged	Supply Curve Shifts Right	Supply Curve Shifts Left
Demand Curve Unchanged	Q unchanged	Q increases	Q decreases
	P unchanged	P decreases	P increases
Demand Curve Shifts Right	Q increases	Q increases	Q increases or decreases
	P increases	P increases or decreases	P increases
Demand Curve Shifts Left	Q decreases	Q increases or decreases	Q decreases
	P decreases	P decreases	P increases or decreases

Solved Problem **3.2**

High Demand and Low Prices in the Lobster Market

For many communities in the Maritimes, the lobster fishery is an essential part of the local economy. Lobster is fished only in season, and different communities are allowed to fish at different times of the year. For example, the fishing season for the area of Yarmouth, Nova Scotia, is from late November to the end of May. It isn't uncommon for the price of lobster to fluctuate during the season. In some cases, it can change from below $5 per pound to $8 or $9 per pound. A patch of really bad weather can drive up the price quickly, but so does Christmas (lobster tends to be a popular part of winter festivities in Canada, Europe, and other parts of the world).

What would happen if the weather just before Christmas were particularly good, allowing fishers to spend more time on the water and catch more lobster?

Solving the Problem

Step 1: **Review the chapter material.** This problem is about how shifts in demand and supply curves affect the equilibrium price, so you may want to review the section "The Effect of Shifts in Demand and Supply over Time."

Step 2: **Draw the demand and supply graph.** Draw a demand and supply graph, showing the market equilibrium before the Christmas rush and with normal weather. Label the equilibrium price $6.00. Label both the demand and supply curves "Typical."

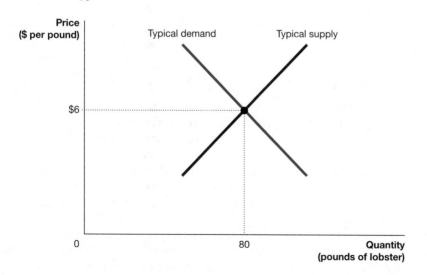

Step 3: **Add a demand and supply curve.** Add a demand curve to account for the increase in the demand for lobster from Europe. Add a supply curve to account for the nicer-than-usual weather.

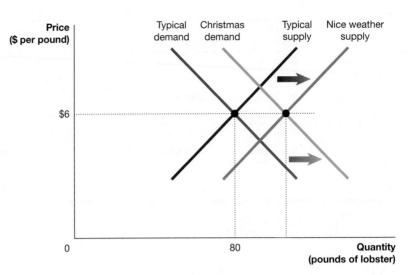

Step 4: **Explain the graph.** After studying the graph, you should see how the two events of increased demand from Europe and the nicer-than-usual weather combine to move the equilibrium price. The increase in supply due to the nicer-than-usual weather is offset by some of the increase in demand from Europeans. We can't say for sure which way the price will go. The price of lobster will rise if the shift in demand is greater than the shift in supply. If the shift in supply is greater than the shift in demand, prices will actually fall. All that we can say for certain is that the quantity of lobster sold (and eaten) will go up.

Based on Province of Nova Scotia, "Lobster Fishing Seasons in Atlantic Canada," *Nova Scotia Fisheries and Aquaculture*, May 17, 2012, http://www.gov.ns.ca/fi sh/marine/map/lobarea.shtml.

MyEconLab **Your Turn:** For more practice, do related problems 4.3 and 4.4 on page 74 at the end of this chapter.

Don't Let This Happen to You

Remember: A Change in a Good's Price Does *Not* Cause the Demand or Supply Curve to Shift

Suppose a student is asked to draw a demand and supply graph to illustrate how an increase in the price of oranges would affect the market for apples, other variables being constant. He draws the graph on the left below and explains it as follows: "Because apples and oranges are substitutes, an increase in the price of oranges will cause an initial shift to the right in the demand curve for apples, from D_1 to D_2. However, because this initial shift in the demand curve for apples results in a higher price for apples, P_2, consumers will find apples less desirable, and the demand curve will shift to the left, from D_2 to D_3, resulting in a final equilibrium price of P_3." Do you agree or disagree with the student's analysis?

You should disagree. The student has correctly understood that an increase in the price of oranges will cause the demand curve for apples to shift to the right. But the second demand curve shift the student describes, from D_2 to D_3, will not take place. Changes in the price of a product do not result in shifts in the product's demand curve. Changes in the price of a product result only in movements along a demand curve.

The graph on the right on the next page shows the correct analysis. The increase in the price of oranges causes the demand curve for apples to increase from D_1 to D_2. At the original price, P_1, the increase in demand initially results in a shortage of apples equal to $Q_3 - Q_1$. But, as we have seen, a shortage causes the price to increase until the shortage is eliminated. In this case, the price will rise to P_2, where the quantity demanded and the quantity supplied are both equal to

Q_2. Notice that the increase in price causes a decrease in the *quantity demanded*, from Q_3 to Q_2, but does not cause a decrease in demand.

MyEconLab

Your Turn: Test your understanding by doing related problems 4.6 and 4.7 on page 77 at the end of this chapter.

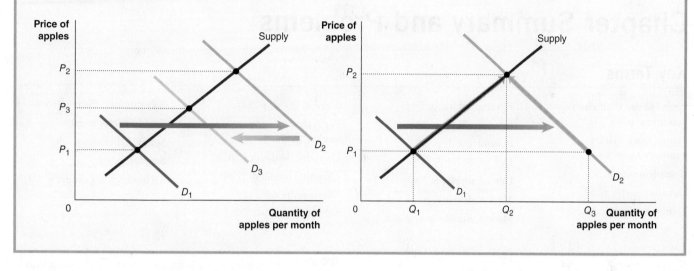

Shifts in a Curve versus Movements along a Curve

When analyzing markets using demand and supply curves, it is important to remember that *when a shift in a demand or supply curve causes a change in equilibrium price, the change in price does not cause a further shift in demand or supply.* For instance, suppose an increase in supply causes the price of a good to fall, while everything else that affects the willingness of consumers to buy the good is constant. The result will be an increase in the quantity demanded, but not an increase in demand. For demand to increase, the whole curve must shift. The point is the same for supply: If the price of the good falls but everything else that affects the willingness of sellers to supply the good is constant, the quantity supplied decreases, but the supply does not. For supply to decrease, the whole curve must shift.

Economics in Your Life

Red Bull or Beaver Buzz Energy: What's Your Beverage?

At the beginning of the chapter, we asked you to consider two questions: Would you choose to buy a can of Beaver Buzz Energy if it had a lower price than a can of Red Bull? Would you be less likely to drink Beaver Buzz Energy if your income dropped? To determine the answer to the first question, you have to recognize that Beaver Buzz Energy and Red Bull are substitutes. If you consider the two drinks to be very close substitutes, then you are likely to buy the one with the lower price. In the market, if consumers generally believe that Beaver Buzz Energy and Red Bull are close substitutes, a fall in the price of Beaver Buzz Energy will increase the quantity of Beaver Buzz Energy demanded and decrease the demand for Red Bull. Suppose that you are currently leaning toward buying Red Bull because you believe that it is better tasting than Beaver Buzz Energy. If a decrease in your income made you more likely to buy Beaver Buzz Energy, then you consider Beaver Buzz Energy an inferior good.

Conclusion

The interaction of demand and supply determines market equilibrium. The model of demand and supply is a powerful tool for predicting how changes in the actions of consumers and firms will cause changes in equilibrium prices and quantities. As we have seen in this chapter, we can use the model to analyze markets that do not meet all of the requirements for being perfectly competitive. As long as there is intense competition among sellers, the model of demand and supply can often successfully predict changes in prices and quantities.

Chapter Summary and Problems

Key Terms

Ceteris paribus ("all else equal") condition, p. 53

Competitive market equilibrium, p. 63

Complements, p. 55

Demand curve, p. 52

Demand schedule, p. 52

Demographics, p. 56

Income effect, p. 53

Inferior good, p. 54

Law of demand, p. 52

Law of supply, p. 59

Market demand, p. 52

Market equilibrium, p. 63

Normal good, p. 54

Perfectly competitive market, p. 51

Quantity demanded, p. 52

Quantity supplied, p. 58

Shortage, p. 63

Substitutes, p. 54

Substitution effect, p. 53

Supply curve, p. 59

Supply schedule, p. 59

Surplus, p. 63

Technological change, p. 60

Summary

*LO 3.1 The model of demand and supply is the most powerful tool in economics. The model applies exactly only to *perfectly competitive markets*, where there are many buyers and sellers, all the products sold are identical, and there are no barriers to new sellers entering the market. But the model can also be useful in analyzing markets that don't meet all these requirements. The *quantity demanded* is the amount of a good or service that a consumer is willing and able to purchase at a given price. A *demand schedule* is a table that shows the relationship between the price of a product and the quantity of the product demanded. A *demand curve* is a graph that shows the relationship between the price of a good and the quantity of the good demanded. *Market demand* is the demand by all consumers of a given good or service. The *law of demand* states that *ceteris paribus*—holding everything else constant—the quantity of a product demanded increases when the price falls and decreases when the price rises. Demand curves slope downward because of the *substitution effect*, which is the change in quantity demanded that results from a price change that makes one good more or less expensive relative to another good, and the *income effect*, which is the change in quantity demanded of a good that results from the effect of a change in the good's price on consumer purchasing power. Changes in income, the prices of related goods, tastes, population and demographics, and expectations all cause the demand curve to shift. *Substitutes* are goods that can be used for the same purpose. *Complements* are goods that are used together. A *normal good* is a good for which demand increases as income increases. An *inferior good* is a good for which demand decreases as income increases. *Demographics* refers to the characteristics of a population with respect to age, race, and gender. A change in demand refers to a shift of the demand curve. A change in quantity demanded refers to a movement along the demand curve as a result of a change in the product's price.

LO 3.2 The *quantity supplied* is the amount of a good that a firm is willing and able to supply at a given price. A *supply schedule* is a table that shows the relationship between the price of a product and the quantity of the product supplied. A *supply curve* shows on a graph the relationship between the price of a product and the quantity of the product supplied. When the price of a product rises, producing the product is more profitable, and a greater amount will be supplied. The *law of supply* states that, holding everything else constant, the quantity of a product supplied increases when the price rises and decreases when the price falls. Changes in the prices of inputs, technology, the prices of substitutes in production, expected future prices, and the number of firms in a market all cause the supply curve to shift. *Technological change* is a positive or negative change in the ability of a firm to produce a given level of output with a given quantity of inputs. A change in supply refers to a shift of the supply curve. A change in quantity supplied refers to a movement along the supply curve as a result of a change in the product's price.

LO 3.3 *Market equilibrium* occurs where the demand curve intersects the supply curve. A *competitive market equilibrium* has a market equilibrium with many buyers and many sellers. Only at this point is the quantity demanded equal to the quantity supplied. Prices above equilibrium result in *surpluses*, with the quantity supplied being greater than the quantity demanded. Surpluses cause the market price to fall. Prices below equilibrium result in *shortages*, with the quantity demanded being greater than the quantity supplied. Shortages cause the market price to rise.

LO 3.4 In most markets, demand and supply curves shift frequently, causing changes in equilibrium prices and quantities. Over time, if demand increases more than supply, equilibrium price will rise. If supply increases more than demand, equilibrium price will fall.

MyEconLab   Log in to MyEconLab to complete these exercises and get instant feedback.

---

*"Learning Objective" is abbreviated to "LO" in the end-of-chapter material.

Review Questions

LO 3.1

1.1 What is a demand schedule? What is a demand curve?

1.2 What is the difference between a change in demand and a change in the quantity demanded?

1.3 What are the main variables that will cause the demand curve to shift? Give an example of each.

LO 3.2

2.1 What is a supply schedule? What is a supply curve?

2.2 What is the difference between a change in supply and a change in the quantity supplied?

2.3 What is the law of supply? What are the main variables that will cause a supply curve to shift? Give an example of each.

LO 3.3

3.1 What do economists mean by *market equilibrium*?

3.2 What do economists mean by a *shortage*? By a *surplus*?

3.3 What happens in a market if the current price is above the equilibrium price? What happens if the current price is below the equilibrium price?

LO 3.4

4.1 Draw a demand and supply graph to show the effect on the equilibrium price in a market in the following two situations:
a. The demand curve shifts to the right.
b. The supply curve shifts to the left.

4.2 If, over time, the demand curve for a product shifts to the right more than the supply curve does, what will happen to the equilibrium price? What will happen to the equilibrium price if the supply curve shifts to the right more than the demand curve? For each case, draw a demand and supply graph to illustrate your answer.

Problems and Applications

LO 3.1

1.1 For each of the following pairs of products, state which are complements, which are substitutes, and which are unrelated.
a. Gasoline and electric car batteries
b. Houses and household appliances
c. UGG boots and Kindle e-readers
d. iPads and Kindle e-readers

1.2 **[Related to the Chapter Opener on page 50]** Many people are concerned about the health effects of consuming large quantities of energy drinks. A recent study by Anna Svatikova and her team asked people who were over 18, non-smokers, and healthy to drink either a can of Rockstar Energy Drink or a similar tasting beverage that did not contain any caffeine or stimulants. Those who took the energy drink experienced increases in their blood pressure and levels of a stress hormone (Norepinephrine). Both of these responses increase your cardiovascular risk. What impact do you think this (and studies like it) will have on the market for energy drinks? What do you think will happen to the price of energy drinks as a result?

1.3 Imagine that the table below shows the quantity demanded of UGG boots at five different prices in 2015 and in 2016:

Quantity Demanded		
Price	2015	2016
$160	5000	4000
170	4500	3500
180	4000	3000
190	3500	2500
200	3000	2000

Name two different variables that could cause the quantity demanded of UGG boots to change as indicated from 2015 to 2016.

1.4 **[Related to Making the Connection on page 55]** A student makes the following argument:

> The chapter says that people in Ontario and other parts of Canada far from the ocean treat lobster as a normal good. I can't stand the stuff—they look like alien bugs and they take too much work to eat. For me, lobster is an inferior good.

Do you agree with the student's reasoning? Briefly explain.

1.5 **[Related to the Making the Connection on page 56]** Name three products whose demand is likely to increase rapidly if the following demographic groups increase at a faster rate than the population as a whole:
a. Teenagers
b. Children under age five
c. Recent immigrants

1.6 Suppose the following table shows the price of a base model Toyota Prius hybrid and the quantity of Priuses sold for three years. Do these data indicate that the demand curve for Priuses is upward sloping? Explain.

Year	Price	Quantity
2015	$24 880	35 265
2016	24 550	33 250
2017	25 250	36 466

1.7 Richard Posner is a US federal court judge who also writes on economic topics. A newspaper reporter summarized Posner's view on the effect of online bookstores and e-books on the demand for books:

> Posner's [argument] is that the disappearance of bookstores is to be celebrated and not mourned, partly because e-books and online stores will reduce the cost of books and thus drive up demand for them.

Do you agree with Posner's statements as given by the reporter? Briefly explain.

Christopher Shea, "Judge Posner Hails the Demise of Bookstores," *Wall Street Journal*, January 13, 2011.

LO 3.2

2.1 Briefly explain whether each of the following statements describes a change in supply or a change in the quantity supplied:

a. To take advantage of high prices for snow shovels during a snowy winter, Alexander Shovels, Inc., decides to increase output.

b. The success of the Apple iPad leads more firms to begin producing tablet computers.

c. In January, 2015, much of Eastern Canada and the Northeastern United States suffered through massive blizzards and incredible snowfall that approached 2 metres in some places. As a result, output of cars from Ontario automakers fell by 10%.

2.2 Suppose that the following table shows the quantity supplied of UGG boots at five different prices in 2015 and in 2016:

	Quantity Supplied	
Price	2015	2016
$160	300 000	200 000
170	350 000	250 000
180	400 000	300 000
190	450 000	350 000
200	500 000	400 000

Name two different variables that would cause the quantity supplied of UGG boots to change as indicated in the table from 2015 to 2016.

2.3 Will each firm in the tablet computer industry always supply the same quantity as every other firm at each price? What factors might cause the quantity of tablet computers supplied by different firms to be different at a particular price?

2.4 If the price of a good increases, is the increase in the quantity of the good supplied likely to be smaller or larger, the longer the time period being considered? Briefly explain.

LO 3.3

3.1 Briefly explain whether you agree with the following statement: "When there is a shortage of a good, consumers eventually give up trying to buy it, so the demand for the good declines, and the price falls until the market is finally in equilibrium."

3.2 **[Related to Solved Problem 3.1 on page 64]** In *The Wealth of Nations*, Adam Smith discussed what has come to be known as the "diamond and water paradox":

Nothing is more useful than water: but it will purchase scarce anything; scarce anything can be had in exchange for it. A diamond, on the contrary, has scarce any value in use; but a very great quantity of other goods may frequently be had in exchange for it.

Graph the market for diamonds and the market for water. Show how it is possible for the price of water to be much lower than the price of diamonds, even though the demand for water is much greater than the demand for diamonds.

Adam Smith, *An Inquiry into the Nature and Causes of the Wealth of Nations, Vol. I*, (Oxford, UK: Oxford University Press, 1976 original edition, 1776).

3.3 If a market is in equilibrium, is it necessarily true that all buyers and all sellers are satisfied with the market price? Briefly explain.

LO 3.4

4.1 As oil prices rose during 2006, the demand for alternative fuels increased. Ethanol, one alternative fuel, is made from corn. According to an article in the *Wall Street Journal*, the price of tortillas, which are made from corn, also rose during 2006: "The price spike [in tortillas] is part of a ripple effect from the ethanol boom."

a. Draw a demand and supply graph for the corn market and use it to show the effect on this market of an increase in the demand for ethanol. Be sure to indicate the equilibrium price and quantity before and after the increase in the demand for ethanol.

b. Draw a demand and supply graph for the tortilla market and use it to show the effect on this market of an increase in the price of corn. Once again, be sure to indicate the equilibrium price and quantity before and after the increase in the demand for ethanol.

c. By 2015, the price of oil had fallen, which reduced the price of gasoline. The demand for ethanol fell along with the price of gasoline. What impact would the fall in the demand for ethanol have on the market for tortillas?

4.2 **[Related to Making the Connection on page 66]** During 2015, the price of oil was near record lows, trading as low as $40 a barrel. This low price of oil reduced the demand for solar energy. At the same time, some speculated that a number of existing makers of solar panels might exit the market. Use a demand and supply graph to analyze the effect of these factors on the equilibrium price and quantity of solar panels. Clearly show on your graph the old equilibrium price and quantity and the new equilibrium price and quantity. Can you tell for certain whether the new equilibrium price will be higher or lower than the old equilibrium price? Briefly explain.

4.3 **[Related to Solved Problem 3.2 on page 69]** The demand for watermelons is highest during summer and lowest during winter. Yet watermelon prices are normally lower in summer than in winter. Use a demand and supply graph to demonstrate how this is possible. Be sure to carefully label the curves in your graph and to clearly indicate the equilibrium summer price and the equilibrium winter price.

4.4 **[Related to Solved Problem 3.2 on page 69]** Tourism is an important part of the economies of the Maritime provinces. The tourist season is generally the summer months, with June, July, and August the most popular. Shediac, New Brunswick, and Prince Edward Island as a whole are particularly popular with tourists. The lobster fishing season in Shediac doesn't begin until mid-August and ends in mid-October. Use a demand and supply graph to explain whether lobster prices would be higher or lower if the lobster fishing season were to begin in June and end in August.

4.5 An article in the *Wall Street Journal* noted that the demand for Internet advertising was declining at the same time that the number of websites accepting advertising was increasing. After reading the article, a student argues: "From this information, we know that the price of Internet ads should fall, but we don't know whether the total quantity of Internet ads will increase or decrease." Is the student's analysis correct? Illustrate your answer with a demand and supply graph.

Based on Martin Peers, "Future Shock for Internet Ads?" *Wall Street Journal*, February 17, 2009.

4.6 [Related to Don't Let This Happen to You on page 70] A student writes the following: "Increased production leads to a lower price, which in turn increases demand." Do you agree with the student's reasoning? Briefly explain.

4.7 [Related to Don't Let This Happen to You on page 70] A student was asked to draw a demand and supply graph to illustrate the effect on the tablet computers market of a fall in the price of displays used in tablet computers, holding everything else constant. She drew the graph below and explained it as follows:

> Displays are an input to tablet computers, so a fall in the price of displays will cause the supply curve for tablets to shift to the right (from S_1 to S_2). Because this shift in the supply curve results in a lower price (P_2), consumers will want to buy more tablets, and the demand curve will shift to the right (from D_1 to D_2). We know that more tablets will be sold, but we can't be sure whether the price of tablets will rise or fall. That depends on whether the supply curve or the demand curve has shifted farther to the right. I assume that the effect on supply is greater than the effect on demand, so I show the final equilibrium price (P_3) as being lower than the initial equilibrium price (P_1).

Explain whether you agree or disagree with the student's analysis. Be careful to explain exactly what—if anything—you find wrong with her analysis.

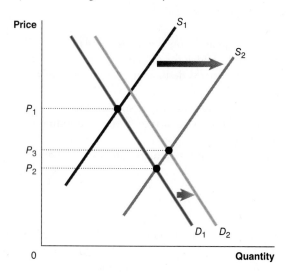

4.8. Proposals have been made to increase government regulation of firms providing child-care services by, for instance, setting education requirements for child-care workers. Suppose that these regulations increase the quality of child-care and cause the demand for child-care services to increase. At the same time, assume that complying with the new government regulations increases the costs of firms providing child-care services. Draw a demand and supply graph to illustrate the effects of these changes in the market for child-care services. Briefly explain whether the total quantity of child-care services purchased will increase or decrease as a result of regulation.

4.9. The following graphs show the supply and demand curves for two markets. One of the markets is for BMW automobiles, and the other is for a cancer-fighting drug, without which lung cancer patients will die. Briefly explain which graph most likely represents which market.

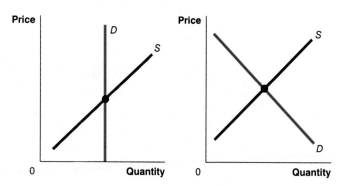

Appendix B

LO
Use quantitative demand and supply analysis.

Quantitative Demand and Supply Analysis

Graphs help us understand economic change *quantitatively*. For instance, a demand and supply graph can tell us that if household incomes rise, the demand curve for a normal good will shift to the right, and its price will rise. Often, though, economists, business managers, and policymakers want to know more than the qualitative direction of change; they want a *quantitative estimate* of the size of the change.

In this chapter, we carried out qualitative analyses of market equilibriums. We saw that an increase in demand would increase the market price and an increase in supply would decrease the market price. To better understand how different shifts in the market impact price and quantity, we need to know how large the effects are. A quantitative analysis of market equilibrium will tell us how much prices and quantities change after a demand or supply curve shifts.

Demand and Supply Equations

The first step in a quantitative analysis is to supplement our use of demand and supply curves with demand and supply *equations*. We noted briefly in this chapter that economists often statistically estimate equations for demand curves. Supply curves can also be statistically estimated. For example, suppose that economists have estimated that the demand for apartments in Toronto is:

$$Q^D = 3\,000\,000 - 1000P$$

and the supply of apartments is:

$$Q^S = -450\,000 + 1300P.$$

We have used Q^D for the quantity of apartments demanded per month, Q^S for the quantity of apartments supplied per month, and P for the apartment rent, in dollars per month. In reality, both the quantity of apartments demanded and quantity of apartments supplied will depend on more than just the rental price of apartments in Toronto. For instance, the demand for apartments in Toronto will also depend on the average incomes of families in the Toronto area and on the rents of apartments in surrounding cities. For simplicity, we will ignore these other factors.

The competitive market equilibrium occurs when the quantity demanded equals the quantity supplied, or:

$$Q^D = Q^S.$$

We can use this equation, which is called an *equilibrium condition*, to solve for the equilibrium monthly apartment rent by setting the quantity demanded from the demand equation equal to the quantity demanded from the supply equation:

$$3\,000\,000 - 1000P = -450\,000 + 1300P$$

$$3\,450\,000 = 2300P$$

$$P = \frac{3\,450\,000}{2300} = \$1500.$$

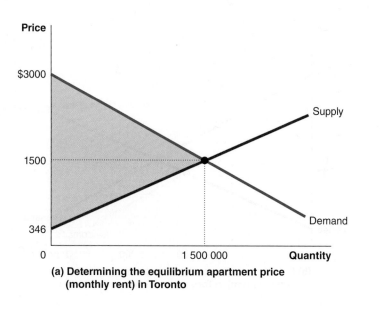

(a) Determining the equilibrium apartment price (monthly rent) in Toronto

Figure 3B.1a

Graphing Supply and Demand Equations

After statistically estimating supply and demand equations, we can use the equations to draw supply and demand curves. In this case, as panel (a) shows, the equilibrium rent for apartments is $1500 per month, and the equilibrium quantity of apartments rented is 1 500 000. The supply equation tells us that at a rent of $346, the quantity of apartments supplied will be zero. The demand equation tells us that at a rent of $3000, the quantity of apartments demanded will be zero. Panel (b), on the next page, shows the shift in the equilibrium price from $1500 to $1283 when the demand for apartments decreases.

We can then substitute this price back into either the demand equation or the supply equation to find the equilibrium quantity of apartments rented:

$$Q^D = 3\,000\,000 - 1000P = 3\,000\,000 - 1000(1500) = 1\,500\,000$$

$$Q^S = -450\,000 + 1300P = -450\,000 + 1300(1500) = 1\,500\,000.$$

Panel (a) of Figure 3B.1 shows in a graph *the same information as we just found using algebra.*

If the economy of Toronto is not performing as well as it has in the past, fewer people are likely to want to live in Toronto, all else being equal. We can represent this idea by reducing the number of apartments that would be rented at every price. This makes the new demand equation:

$$Q^D = 2\,500\,000 - 1000P$$

and the supply equation remains unchanged:

$$Q^S = -450\,000 + 1300P.$$

The new equilibrium price is:

$$2\,500\,000 - 1000P = -450\,000 + 1300P$$

$$2\,950\,000 = 2300P$$

$$P = \frac{2\,950\,000}{2300} = \$1283.$$

The new quantity of apartments rented can be found by substituting this price into either the demand equation or the supply equation:

$$Q^D = 2\,500\,000 - 1000P = 2\,500\,000 - 1000(1283) = 1\,217\,000$$

$$Q^S = -450\,000 + 1300P = -450\,000 + 1300(1283) = 1\,217\,000.$$

When the demand for apartments decreases, the equilibrium price falls from $1500 to $1283, and the equilibrium number of apartments rented falls from 1 500 000 to 1 217 000. Panel (b) of Figure 3B.1 illustrates the result of this shift. Notice that the qualitative results (a decrease in price and quantity) match the quantitative results we just found.

Figure 3B.1b

Graphing Supply and Demand Equations

The process of finding the new equilibrium remains the same no matter whether the demand curve, the supply curve, or both shifts. You set the quantity demanded equal to the quantity supplied and solve for price. Then you substitute the price you found into either the demand equation or the supply equation.

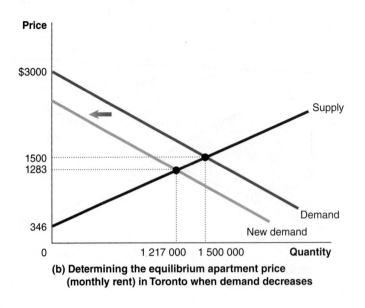

(b) Determining the equilibrium apartment price (monthly rent) in Toronto when demand decreases

Review Questions

LO Use quantitative demand and supply analysis.

3B.1 In a linear demand equation, what economic information is conveyed by the intercept on the price axis? Similarly, what information is conveyed by the intercept on the price axis in a linear supply equation?

Problems and Applications

3B.2 Suppose that you have been hired to analyze wages in a simple market. The demand for labour and supply of labour can be represented by the following equations:

$$\text{Demand:}\quad L^D = 100 - 4W$$
$$\text{Supply:}\quad L^S = 6W$$

a. Calculate the equilibrium wage (price) and quantity of labour employed in this market.
b. A new employer enters the market causing labour demand to become:

$$\text{New Demand: } L_D = 120 - 4W$$

Calculate the new equilibrium wage (price) and quantity of workers employed in this market.

3B.3 Suppose the demand and supply of leather shoes can be represented by the following equations:

$$Q^D = 200 - 2P$$
$$Q^S = 2P$$

a. Calculate the equilibrium price and quantity in this market.
b. Assume that an increase in the cost of leather causes the supply of shoes to change to:

$$Q^S = -50 + 2P$$

Calculate the new equilibrium price and quantity in this market.
c. Assume that in addition to the increase in the price of leather, the demand for leather shoes falls due to a change in fashion and is now as follows:

$$150 - 2P$$

Calculate the equilibrium price and quantity in this market. Remember to use the same supply curve as in part (b).

As Canadians buy record number of pickups and SUVs, new fuel-economy rules may prove hard to meet

AN INSIDE LOOK

(a) Canadians continued to snap up record numbers of SUVs and pickup trucks in July, a trend that will make it very difficult for automakers to meet new fuel-efficiency standards outlined by the government last week.

Auto sales hit another all-time monthly high in July, inching up 0.4 per cent to 177 844 units. But the growth was concentrated in light trucks—a category that includes sport utility vehicles, crossovers, and pickups—which gained 8.2 per cent while car sales declined 10.3 per cent, according to data compiled by DesRosiers Automotive Consultants.

FCA Canada Inc. epitomized the trend, with Jeep sales soaring 21 per cent and Ram pickup sales jumping 17 per cent while car sales plunged 46 per cent.

If low gas prices continue to spur consumer demand for light trucks at the expense of more fuel-efficient cars, it will be virtually impossible for manufacturers to meet new fuel-economy regulations that aim to cut fleet-wide fuel consumption in half by 2025 from 2008 levels.

"It's been shocking the rate at which buyers have migrated to trucks in place of cars," said Tony Faria, co-director of the University of Windsor's Office of Automotive and Vehicle Research.

"At the rate at which we're moving at this point, there's no way the standards for 2025 are going to be met."

(b) The regulations, announced last week, aim to harmonize Canada's fuel-economy standards with the U.S., where automakers have been told to increase fleet-wide fuel economy to 54.5 miles per gallon—approximately 4.3 litres per 100 kilometres—by 2025.

In July, the average fuel economy of new vehicles sold in the US was 25.4 miles per gallon, according to the University of Michigan's Transportation Research Institute.

The trend towards larger vehicles is hammering sales of hybrid and electric vehicles particularly hard. In the US, sales of those vehicles fell 22 percent in the first six months of the year, according to industry site Edmunds.com.

"There's been a complete reversal in the market where hybrids are barely holding their own," said Phil Edmonston, founder of the Automobile Protection Association and author of the Lemon-Aid guides to new and used vehicles.

"We're probably going to have to have some stiffer, more effective and more enforceable regulations in order to keep this buying attitude from changing too much."

(c) Edmonston and Faria said Ottawa will have to consider raising gasoline taxes if it really wants to encourage fuel efficiency, but both doubt there's the political will to do that.

"If the price we were paying per litre was $2.12 versus $1.12, a lot more people would be buying smaller vehicles, no doubt about it," Faria said. "Government officials just don't want to take the hard route."

The US Environmental Protection Agency will review the fuel-economy standards in 2017 and will probably consider revising them downwards at that point, Faria said. If that happens, Canada will almost certainly follow suit.

"I would bet almost anything on it unless we have a major, major breakthrough in technology," he said.

Source: Material republished with the express permission of: National Post, a division of Postmedia Network Inc.

Key Points in the Article

This article discusses some of the trade-offs that consumers, regulators, and car makers face when it comes to fuel efficiency and the size of vehicles. It also makes clear how markets are affected by a change in the price of a complement. North American consumers prefer larger vehicles to smaller ones—opting for light trucks (SUVs and pickup trucks mostly) over smaller sedans and two-door cars when gas prices are low, but choosing more fuel-efficient cars when gas prices are high. Manufacturers also face this sort of trade-off in trying to satisfy the desires of consumers while meeting the requirements of regulators. North American regulators (in Canada and the US) place restrictions on the average fuel economy of cars produced for the North American market. Finally, government regulators face trade-offs in using regulations and policies to ensure that harmful emissions from cars are reduced over time.

Analyzing the News

(a) Gas is a complement for the vast majority of cars on the road. Lower gas prices make larger, less fuel-efficient cars more appealing to consumers. Larger cars tend to be more comfortable, make people feel safer, and have better performance and more features than smaller cars. In choosing a car, people face a trade-off between these features and the cost of keeping the gas tank full.

Between May 2014 and January 2016 the price of gasoline at the pump fell by 50 percent or more across the country. As a result of these lower gas prices, consumers opted for SUVs and pickup trucks instead of sedans and hybrids. When the price of gas (a complement) falls and is expected to stay low, the demand for SUVs and pickup trucks shifts to the right.

(b) Environmental regulators determine the average fuel efficiency for all the cars an automaker produces for the Canadian market. This creates a trade-off for manufacturers. They can make their entire lineup of vehicles more fuel efficient or they can focus their efforts on the fuel efficiency on just a few models. In order to meet a fuel efficiency target of 4.3 litres per hundred kilometres, automakers can ensure that all their vehicles meet this standard or they can produce two models, one with a fuel efficiency of 2.0 litres per hundred kilometres and another that gets just 6.6 litres per hundred kilometres. Virtually all North American manufacturers have opted to produce a range of models—some with very high fuel efficiency and others that consume a lot of fuel but are larger and have more features.

This approach can cause problems if demand for one type of vehicle shifts unexpectedly. Switching production lines from one model to another or finding alternative ways to meet fuel efficiency standards will increase the cost of producing extra vehicles—giving the supply curve an upward slope.

(c) Regulators also face trade-offs in choosing which types of regulations they impose on markets in their efforts to protect the environment. While Canadians already pay more taxes on gasoline than Americans do, the difference isn't large enough to guarantee that the majority of Canadians will trade size and comfort for fuel efficiency—the increased price of the complement isn't enough to shift the demand curve for SUVs and pickups very far to the left. A larger increase in gas taxes (and therefore prices) would shift demand for these types of vehicle further to left, but higher gas prices are unpopular with consumers—who are also voters.

Thinking Critically about Policy

1. In the article Tony Faria, co-director at the Office of Automotive and Vehicle Research at the University of Windsor, said that new fuel-efficiency standards targets for the future will have to be lowered without an improvement in technology. Show the production possibility frontier for fuel efficiency and vehicle size. Assuming Faria's statement is correct, where does the current combination of fuel efficiency and desired vehicle size lie on your graph? Finally, show the improvement in technology required to allow this target to be achieved on your graph.

2. Show the impact of a sudden increase in gasoline prices on the market for SUVs and pickup trucks in a demand and supply graph. How could a government use gasoline prices to encourage people to make more environmentally friendly vehicle choices?

GDP: Measuring Total Production and Income

CHAPTER

4

The Health of the Canadian Economy

Many different factors influence the state of the Canadian economy. One of those factors is exports to other countries. The price of oil fell from over $100 a barrel in January of 2014 to under $38 a barrel in December of 2015. Over the same period, demand for many of the other natural resources that Canada exports fell as economic activity in China slowed. Oil and natural resources account for a significant portion of Canadian exports, so it was not a surprise to most people when the Canadian economy shrank in the first half of 2015.

Canadian exporters were feeling the effects of the *business cycle*, which refers to the alternating periods of economic expansion and recession that occur in all economies. Production and employment increase during expansions and decrease during recessions. Whether the general level of economic activity in a country is increasing is important to all kinds of firms; it is also important to workers wondering if they will be able to keep their jobs and to college and university students wondering if they will be able to find jobs after they graduate.

One US study found that college students who graduate during a recession have to spend more time looking for a job and end up accepting jobs that pay 10 percent less (on average) than the jobs accepted by those who graduate during economic expansions. What makes this even worse is the authors of the study found that students who graduate during recessions will continue to earn less for as long as 15 years after graduation. A similar Canadian study found that people who completed university

Chapter Outline and Learning Objectives

during a recession had lower average earnings for 10 years or more after graduation. Some people try to avoid graduating in a recession by applying to graduate school. The overall state of the economy is important to you!

Based on Lisa B. Kahn, "The Long-Term Labour Market Consequences of Graduating from College in a Bad Economy," *Labour Economics*, Vol. 17, No. 2, April 2010, pp.303-316; Oreopoulos, P., von Wachter, T., & Heisz, A. (2012). The short- and long-term career effects of graduating in a recession. *American Economic Journal*: 4(1), 1-29.

Economics in Your Life

What's the Best Country for You to Work In?

Suppose that a tech firm offers you a job after graduation in 2017. The firm has offices in the United Kingdom and China, and because you are fluent in both English and Mandarin, you get to choose the country in which you will work and live. Gross domestic product (GDP) is a measure of an economy's total production of goods and services, so one factor in your decision is likely to be the growth rate of GDP in each country. Based on the forecasts for 2017, GDP will grow by 1 percent in the United Kingdom and 6 percent in China. What effects do these very different growth rates have on your decision to work and live in one country or the other? If China's much larger growth rate does not necessarily lead you to decide to live and work in China, why not? As you read this chapter, see if you can answer these questions. You can check your answers against those we provide on page 101 at the end of this chapter.

Microeconomics The study of how households and firms make choices, how they interact in markets, and how the government attempts to influence their choices.

Macroeconomics The study of the economy as a whole, including topics such as inflation, unemployment, and economic growth.

Business cycle Alternating periods of economic expansion and economic recession.

Expansion The period of a business cycle during which total production and total employment are increasing.

Recession The period of a business cycle during which total production and total employment are decreasing.

Economic growth The ability of an economy to produce increasing quantities of goods and services.

As we saw in Chapter 1, we can divide economics into the subfields of microeconomics and macroeconomics. **Microeconomics** is the study of how households and firms make choices, how they interact in markets, and how the government attempts to influence their choices. **Macroeconomics** is the study of the economy as a whole, including topics such as inflation, unemployment, and economic growth. In microeconomic analysis, economists generally study individual markets, such as the market for tablet computers. In macroeconomic analysis, economists study factors that affect many markets at the same time. As we saw in the chapter opener, one important macroeconomic issue is the business cycle. The **business cycle** refers to the alternating periods of expansion and recession that the Canadian economy has experienced since Canada became a country. A business cycle **expansion** is a period during which total production and total employment are increasing. A business cycle **recession** is a period during which total production and total employment are decreasing. In the following chapters, we will discuss the factors that influence the business cycle and policies the government may use to reduce its effects.

Another important macroeconomic topic is **economic growth**, which refers to the ability of an economy to produce increasing quantities of goods and services. Economic growth is important because an economy that grows very slowly fails to raise living standards. In some countries in Africa, very little economic growth occurred from the 1950s to 2010, and as a result many people remain in severe poverty. Macroeconomics analyzes both what determines a country's rate of economic growth and the reasons growth rates differ so much among countries.

Macroeconomics also analyzes what determines the total level of employment in an economy. As we will see, in the short run, the level of employment is significantly affected by the business cycle, but in the long run, the effects of the business cycle disappear, and other factors determine the level of employment. A related issue is why some economies are more successful than others in maintaining high levels of employment over time. Yet another important macroeconomic issue is what determines the **inflation rate**, or the percentage increase in the average level of prices from one year to the next. As with employment, inflation is affected both by the business cycle and by other long-run factors. Finally, macroeconomics is concerned with the linkages among economies: international trade and international finance.

Macroeconomic analysis provides information that consumers and firms need in order to understand current economic conditions and to help predict future conditions. A family may be reluctant to buy a house if employment is declining, as declining employment makes it more likely that someone in that family will lose his or her job. Similarly, firms may be reluctant to invest in building new factories or to hire new workers if they expect that future sales may be weak.

In this chapter and in Chapter 5, we begin our study of macroeconomics by considering how best to measure key macroeconomic variables. As we will see, there are important issues to think about when deciding how to measure macroeconomic variables. We start by considering the most common measure of total production and total income in an economy.

Inflation rate The percentage increase in the price level from one year to the next.

Gross Domestic Product Measures Total Production

4.1 LEARNING OBJECTIVE

Explain how total production is measured.

There are few days in which *gross domestic product (GDP)* is *not* in the news. In this section, we explore what GDP is and how it is measured. We also explore why knowledge of GDP is important to consumers, firms, and government policymakers.

Measuring Total Production: Gross Domestic Product

Economists measure total production by **gross domestic product (GDP)**. GDP is the market *value* of all *final* goods and services produced in a geographic area (a country, typically) during a period of time. In Canada, Statistics Canada produces estimates of GDP data, which are released every three months. GDP is a central concept in macroeconomics, so we need to consider its definition carefully.

Gross domestic product (GDP) The market value of all final goods and services produced in a geographic area (country) during a period of time, typically one year.

GDP Is Measured Using Market Values, Not Quantities. The word *value* is important in the definition of GDP. In microeconomics, we tend to think about production in terms of quantity: the number of cups of coffee sold per day, the number of barrels of oil pumped, the number of cars made by automakers, and so on. When we measure total production in an economy, we can't just add together the quantities of every good and service because the result would be a meaningless mess. Barrels of oil would be added to cans of energy drinks, the number of cars, and so on. This would literally be adding apples to oranges. Instead of making a list of all the different goods and services produced (or trying to add apples and oranges), we measure production by taking the *value*, in dollar terms, of all the goods and services produced.

GDP Includes Only the Market Value of Final Goods and Services. In measuring GDP, we include only the value of *final goods and services*. A **final good or service** is one that is purchased by its final user and is not included in the production of any other good or service. Examples of final goods are things like a hamburger you buy to eat for lunch or a computer purchased by a business. Some goods and services, though, become part of other goods and services. Let's consider the car seats made by Magna International in London, Ontario, for Toyota cars. These car seats are considered **intermediate goods**, while the Toyota cars they're installed in are

Final good or service A good or service purchased by a final user.

Intermediate good or service A good or service that is an input into another good or service, such as car seats.

considered final goods. In calculating GDP, we include the value of the car, but not the separate value of the car seats. If we included the value of the car seats, we would be *double counting*: The value of a car seat would be counted once when it was sold to Toyota and a second time when Toyota sold the car, with the seat installed, to a consumer.

GDP Includes Only Current Production. GDP includes only production that takes place during the indicated time period. For example, GDP in 2016 includes only the goods and services made during that year. In particular, GDP does *not* include the value of used goods. If you buy a new copy of this text for your winter class, the purchase is included in GDP; if you then sell your copy to a friend who is taking the class in the fall, that transaction is not included in GDP.

Solved Problem **4.1**

Calculating GDP

Suppose that a very simple economy produces only four goods and services: energy drinks, pizzas, textbooks, and paper. Assume that all paper in this economy is used to make either textbooks or pizza boxes. Use the information in the following table to compute GDP for 2016.

Production and Price Statistics for 2016		
Product	Quantity	Price per Unit
Energy drinks (24 cans)	100	$ 50.00
Pizzas	80	10.00
Textbooks	20	100.00
Paper	2000	0.10

Solving the Problem

Step 1: Review the chapter material. This problem is about gross domestic product, so you may want to review the section "Measuring Total Production: Gross Domestic Product" on page 83.

Step 2: Determine which goods and services listed in the table should be included in the calculation of GDP. GDP is the value of all final goods and services. Therefore, we need to calculate the value of all the final goods and services listed in the table. Energy drinks, pizzas, and textbooks are final goods. Paper would be a final good if a consumer bought it to use in a printer. Here we assumed that all paper is purchased by publishers and pizza producers as an intermediate good. The value of intermediate goods (paper, in this case) is not included in GDP.

Step 3: Calculate the value of the three final goods and services listed in the table. Value is equal to the quantity produced multiplied by the price per unit, so we multiply the numbers in the quantity column by the numbers in the price-per-unit column.

Product	Quantity	Price per Unit	Value
Energy drinks	100	$ 50	$5000
Pizzas	80	10	800
Textbooks	20	100	2000

Step 4: Add the value for each of the three final goods and services to find GDP. GDP = Value of energy drinks produced + Value of pizzas produced + Value of textbooks produced = $5000 + $800 + $2000 = $7800.

MyEconLab **Your Turn:** For more practice, do related problem 1.5 on page 103 at the end of this chapter.

Production, Income, and the Circular-Flow Diagram

When we measure the value of total production in the economy by calculating GDP, we are simultaneously measuring the value of total income. To see why the value of total production is equal to the value of total income, consider what happens to the money you spend on a single product. Suppose you buy an iPad for $450 at Best Buy. *All* of that $450 must end up as someone's income. Apple and Best Buy will receive some of the $450 as profits, workers at Apple will receive some as wages, the salesperson who sold you the iPad will receive some as salary, the firms that sell parts to Apple will receive some as profits, the workers of those firms will receive some as wages, and so on. Every penny must end up as someone's income. (Note, however, that any sales tax—such as the GST or HST—on the iPad will be collected by the store and sent to the government, without ending up as anyone's income until the government spends it.) Therefore, if we add up the value of every good and service sold in the economy (expenditures), we must get a total that is equal to the value of all the income in the economy.

The circular-flow diagram in Figure 4.1 was introduced in Chapter 2 to illustrate the interaction of firms and households in markets. We use it here to illustrate the flow of spending and income in the economy. Firms sell goods and services to three groups: domestic households, foreign firms and households, and the government. Expenditures by foreign firms and households (shown as "Rest of the World" in the diagram) on domestically produced goods and services are called *exports*. For example, Air Canada sells many tickets to passengers in Europe and Asia. As we note at the bottom of Figure 4.1, we can measure GDP by adding up the total expenditures of these three groups on goods and services.

Firms use the *factors of production*—labour, capital, natural resources, and entrepreneurship—to produce goods and services. Households supply the factors of production to firms in exchange for income. We divide income into four categories: wages, interest, rent, and profit. Firms pay wages to households in exchange for the services of labour, interest for the use of capital, and rent for natural resources such as land. Profit is the income that remains after a firm has paid wages, interest, and rent. Profit is the return to entrepreneurs for organizing the other factors of production and for taking on the risk of producing and selling goods and services.

As Figure 4.1 shows, federal, provincial, and local governments make payments of wages and interest to households in exchange for hiring workers and for other factors of production. Governments also make *transfer payments* to households. **Transfer payments** include social program payments (e.g., Old Age Security and Guaranteed Income Supplement) and unemployment insurance payments. These payments are not included in GDP because they are not received in exchange for producing a new good or service. The sum of wages, interest, rent, and profit is the total income in the economy. As we note at the top of Figure 4.1, we can measure GDP as the total income received by households.

Transfer payments Payments by the government to households for which the government does not receive a new good or service in return.

The diagram also allows us to trace the ways that households use their income. Households spend some of their income on goods and services. Some of this spending is on domestically produced goods and services and some is on foreign-produced goods and services. Spending on foreign-produced goods and services is known as *imports*. Households also use some of their income to pay taxes to the government. (Note that firms also pay taxes to the government.) Even after paying taxes to the government, households don't spend all of their income on goods and services; some income is deposited in chequing or savings accounts in banks or used to buy stocks and/or bonds. Banks, as well as stock and bond markets, make up the *financial system*, which allows firms to borrow the money needed to expand and adopt new technologies. In fact, as we will discuss in Chapter 6, no country without a well-developed financial system has been able to sustain high levels of economic growth.

The circular-flow diagram shows that we can measure GDP either by calculating the total value of expenditures on final goods and services or by calculating the value of total income. We get the same dollar amount of GDP using either approach.

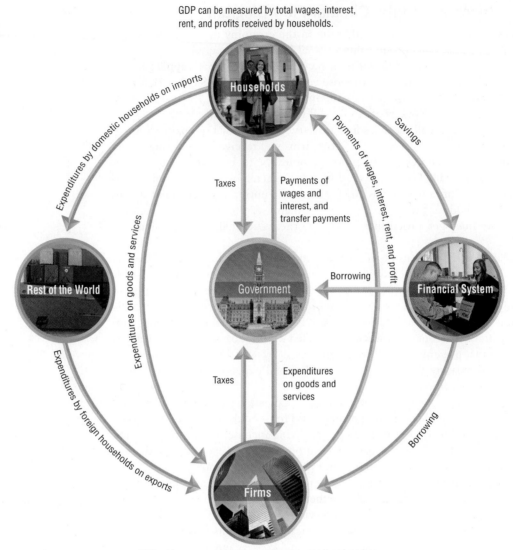

GDP can be measured by total wages, interest, rent, and profits received by households.

GDP can be measured by total expenditures on goods and services by households, firms, government, and the rest of the world.

Figure 4.1 **The Circular Flow and the Measurement of GDP**

The circular flow diagram illustrates the flow of spending and money in the economy. Firms sell goods and services to three groups: domestic households, foreign firms and households, and the government. To produce goods and services, firms use factors of production: labour, capital, natural resources, and entrepreneurship. Households supply the factors of production to firms in exchange for income in the form of wages, interest, profit, and rent. Firms make payments of wages and interest to households in exchange for hiring workers and other factors of production. The sum of wages, interest, rent, and profit is total income in the economy. We can measure GDP as the total income received by households. The diagram also shows that households use their income to purchase goods and services, pay taxes, and save. Firms and the government borrow the funds that flow from households into the financial system. We can measure GDP either by calculating the total value of expenditures on final goods and services or by calculating the value of total income.

Sources: (top) Jupiter Images; (left) Bill Aron/PhotoEdit; (bottom) Mikael Damkier/Alamy; (right) Eric Gevaert/Shutterstock; (centre) jiawangkun/Shutterstock

It may be easier for you to understand the model if you think in terms of inflows and outflows. Exports, government spending, and borrowing are all inflows as money to pay for goods and services flows into households and firms. Imports, savings, and taxes are all outflows as the money involved in these flows does not move from households to firms (and then back to households). Money included in such outflows does not ultimately become part of a Canadian's income.

Don't Let This Happen to You

Remember What Economists Mean by *Investment*

Notice that the definition of *investment* in this chapter is narrower than in everyday use. For example, people often say they are investing in the stock market or in rare coins. As we have seen, economists reserve the word *investment* for purchases of machinery, factories, and houses. Economists don't include purchases of stocks or rare coins or deposits in savings accounts in the definition of investment because these activities don't result in the production of new goods. For example, a share of Microsoft stock represents part ownership of that company. When you buy a share of Microsoft stock, nothing new is produced; there is just a transfer of that small piece of ownership of Microsoft. Similarly, buying a rare coin or putting $1000 into a savings account does not result in an increase in production. GDP is not affected by any of these activities, so they are not included in the economic definition of investment.

MyEconLab

Your Turn: Test your understanding by doing related problem 1.6 on page 103 at the end of this chapter.

Measuring GDP

As we have seen from the circular flow model, total income and total expenditure will both be equal to GDP. This means that there are two ways to measure GDP based on the circular flow, the **expenditure approach** and the **income approach**. In the expenditure approach, all the spending on domestically produced goods and services is added up. In the income approach, all the income received by Canadians as the result of production that takes place in Canada is added up. Statistics Canada uses both the expenditure approach and the income approach to measure GDP. While we focus on the expenditure approach in modelling GDP throughout the text, the income approach can be useful. Figure 4.2 shows the components of both approaches to measuring GDP.

Expenditure approach Measuring GDP by adding up all the different types of expenditure in the economy.

Income approach Measuring GDP by adding up all the income received by the owners of factors of production.

Income Approach

The circular flow model indicates that GDP can be measured by adding up all the income in the economy. Statistics Canada breaks income down into four categories based on the type of the income: compensation of employees, gross operating surplus, gross mixed income, and taxes minus subsidies. We go through each of these categories in turn.

Compensation of Employees.
Compensation of employees covers all the benefits workers receive from providing their labour to firms. This makes up the single largest element of GDP in the income approach at 51.6 percent of GDP.

Compensation of employees is broken down into two components—wages and salaries, and employers' social contributions. Wages and salaries are the pay workers receive in exchange for their efforts at their jobs. Wages and salaries accounted for 86.1 percent of employee compensation and 44.4 percent of GDP in 2015.

Employers' social contributions cover all the payments made by employers to social programs on behalf of their employees. This includes things like payments to the Canada Pension Plan, Employment Insurance, and any health care premiums paid to the government or a private health plan provider. Social contributions amounted to 13.9 percent of employee compensation and 7.2 percent of GDP.

Figure 4.2 **Components of GDP**

Statistics Canada uses both the income and expenditure approaches to calculate GDP. Final consumption spending accounts for 79 percent of GDP in the expenditure approach. Compensation of employees accounts for 52 percent of GDP in the income approach.

Source: Statistics Canada, Table 380-0064 – Gross domestic product, expenditure-based, quarterly (dollars unless otherwise noted), CANSIM (database). Reproduced and distributed on an "as is" basis with the permission of Statistics Canada.

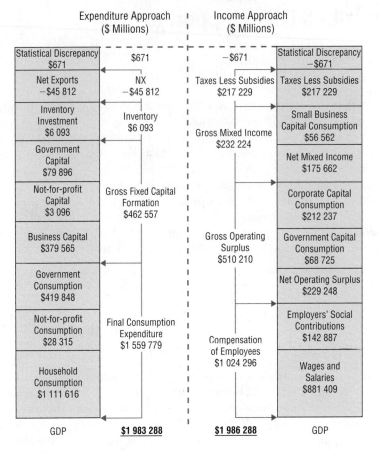

Gross Domestic Product (2015)

Gross operating surplus Payments made to the owners of capital.

Net operating surplus Payments to the owners of capital in excess of depreciation.

Consumption of capital The amount of capital that wears out (depreciates) during use.

Gross Operating Surplus. **Gross operating surplus** means the payments made to the owners of capital by firms and government for the use of their capital in producing goods and services. In 2015, gross operating surplus was 25.9 percent of GDP.

Gross operating surplus is broken down into three elements: net operating surplus of corporations, consumption of fixed capital by corporations, and consumption of fixed capital by governments or non–profit organizations.

Net operating surplus refers to the payments to the owners of capital over and above compensation for the consumption of their capital. **Consumption of capital** essentially refers to depreciation. Capital, machines, buildings, etc., wear out a little bit with each use. Every time you drive a car, the gears and the brakes wear down a little bit. If you let someone else use your capital, you have to be paid for this wear and tear. Net operating surplus is what the owners of capital get paid over and above compensation for the depreciation of their capital. In 2015, net operating surplus was 45 percent of gross operating surplus and 11.6 percent of GDP.

Consumption of fixed capital by corporations refers to the depreciation of capital that occurs while that capital was being used by firms. This accounted for 41.6 percent of gross operating surplus and 10.8 percent of GDP.

Consumption of fixed capital by government, not-for-profit organizations, and households is the depreciation of capital that happens when capital is used by government or other non-business organizations. This was 13.4 percent of gross operating surplus and 3.5 percent of GDP.

Gross Mixed Income. **Gross mixed income** covers the income generated by small businesses. The owners of these businesses often work there as well. This makes it very hard to break their income down into payments as an employee and payments because they own the capital. These payments get "mixed" together as the payments to owners of a small business, hence gross mixed income. Gross mixed income was 11.7 percent of GDP.

Statistics Canada breaks gross mixed income down into consumption of fixed capital by small businesses and net mixed income. Consumption of fixed capital covers the depreciation of the capital used by small businesses. This amounted to 24.3 percent of gross mixed income and 2.8 percent of GDP. Net mixed income is the payment to owners of small businesses over and above compensation for the depreciation of the capital owned by the business. Net mixed income was 75.7 percent of gross mixed income and 8.8 percent of GDP.

> **Gross mixed income** Paid to the owners of small business, this includes payments for labour and capital.

Taxes Less Subsidies. The government levies a variety of taxes on production, products, and imports. These taxes add to the prices of the products and therefore increase spending. Alternatively, you might think of these taxes as the income received by government as the result of production. At the same time, governments often support firms and production with money collected from other taxes (subsidies). **Taxes less subsidies** represent the payment to government that mimics income received by the owners of other inputs. Taxes less subsidies accounted for 10.9 percent of GDP.

> **Taxes less subsidies** Payments to government by businesses net of transfers from government to businesses.

Expenditure Approach

Statistics Canada groups expenditures into four broad categories based on the motivation for the spending when measuring GDP: final consumption, gross fixed capital formation, investment in inventories, and net exports.

Final Consumption. **Final consumption expenditure** captures all the domestic purchases of goods and services used to satisfy individual or community needs and wants. This is the largest single component of the expenditure approach, accounting for 78.6 percent of GDP. Final consumption is broken down by who is doing the consuming. Statistics Canada reports final consumption expenditures of households, not-for-profit organizations that serve households, and government. Household consumption, spending on food, clothing, and so on, is by far the largest component, accounting for 71 percent of final expenditure and 56 percent of GDP. Government final consumption accounts for the second largest portion at 26.9 percent of final consumption expenditure and 21 percent of GDP. Final consumption by not-for-profit organizations is comparatively tiny, accounting for just 1.8 percent of final consumption and 1.4 percent of GDP.

> **Final consumption expenditure** Purchases of goods or services that will be used to satisfy individual or community needs and wants.

Gross Fixed Capital Formation. **Gross fixed capital formation** is the purchases of fixed assets (capital) by firms, governments, and households. Fixed assets are tangible goods that will provide benefits over a long period of time and cannot be easily converted into cash. Fixed assets are typically things like buildings (including residential houses) and machinery that will be used by firms to make products or to provide services. Gross fixed capital formation accounted for 23.5 percent of GDP. Businesses accounted for 82 percent of all fixed capital formation and 19.3 percent of GDP. Gross fixed capital formation undertaken by government accounted for 17.1 percent of fixed capital formation and 4 percent of GDP.

> **Gross fixed capital formation** Purchases of capital by firms, governments, and households.

Investment in Inventories. Businesses don't just need fixed capital to make products and provide services. They also need inventory, finished products kept on hand to sell or inputs kept on hand to turn into finished products. Inventory investment accounted for less than 0.4 percent of GDP in 2015.

Net exports Exports minus imports.

Exports Goods and services produced in Canada that will be consumed by people in other countries.

Imports Goods and services produced by other countries that will be consumed in Canada.

Statistical discrepancy One-half of the difference between the estimates of GDP generated by the expenditure approach and the income approach.

Consumption (C) spending by households on goods and services.

Investment (I) The purchase of capital by firms.

Government spending (G) Spending on consumption goods and capital undertaken by government.

Net Exports of Goods and Services. Net exports are the value of a country's total exports minus its imports. **Exports** are goods and services produced domestically but sold to foreign firms, governments, and households. We add exports to our other categories of expenditure because otherwise we would not be including all the spending on Canadian made goods and services that takes place. For example, if a farmer in Saskatchewan sells wheat to China, the value of the wheat is added to GDP because it represents Canadian production. In 2015, exports accounted for 31.4 percent of GDP.

Imports are goods and services produced in foreign countries and purchased by Canadian firms, governments, and households. We subtract imports from total expenditures because otherwise we would be including spending that does not represent the production of new goods and services in Canada. For example, when you buy a new bookshelf from IKEA that was manufactured in Sweden, that spending is included in Canadian consumption spending, but does not represent Canadian production. Therefore, to avoid including foreign production in GDP, we subtract imports from expenditures. Imports amounted to 33.8 percent of GDP in 2015.

Net exports came to -2.4 percent of GDP in 2015. The negative sign means that we imported more than we exported.

Statistical Discrepancy

Statistics Canada's GDP breakdown includes a **statistical discrepancy**. Differences between the expenditure approach and the income approach to calculating GDP arise due to small errors in the original data and different estimation techniques. To make the two approaches balance, Statistics Canada takes the difference between the estimates based on the expenditure approach and the income approach, divides it in half, and adds one half to the lower of the two estimates and subtracts the other half from the greater of the two estimates. The gap between the two estimates is typically very small. The statistical discrepancy amounts to just 0.03 percent of GDP.

Gross Domestic Product—Income or Expenditure

While the two approaches to measuring GDP provide comparable estimates of the economic activity taking place in a country, the different methods provide different information on the breakdown of what types of economic activity are taking place. The income approach focuses on how much each factor of production is receiving. For example, the income approach makes it clear that labour receives more income than any other factor of production. The expenditure approach focuses on what the output produced in a country is being used for. For example, the expenditure approach reveals that the vast majority of what is produced goes to final consumption, with just over half of GDP (56 percent) ending up as household consumption.

The Expenditure Approach in Macroeconomic Models

A variation on the expenditure approach of measuring GDP is the basis for the models we build throughout the remainder of this text. This variant is based on an older version of the expenditure approach and divides spending based on who is doing the spending rather than the purpose of the expenditure. In the older model, the final consumption expenditure done by households is simply **consumption (C)**. The money spent by firms on fixed capital formation and inventories is called **investment (I)**. Both the final consumption spending and fixed capital formation done by government is called **government spending (G)**. *Net exports (Nx)* are identical in the newer method and the traditional approach.

This older method of adding up expenditures gives us the model:

$$Y = C + I + G + Nx$$

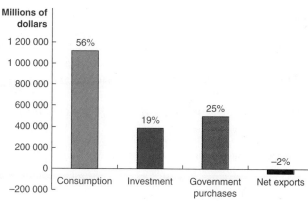

Millions of dollars

56% Consumption
19% Investment
25% Government purchases
−2% Net exports

Figure 4.3

Household consumption accounts for 56 percent of GDP, far more than any of the other components. In recent years, net exports have typically been negative, which reduces GDP. Note that subtotals may not sum to the totals for each category due to rounding.

Source: Statistics Canada, Table 380-0064 - Gross domestic product, expenditure-based, quarterly (dollars unless otherwise noted), CANSIM (database). Reproduced and distributed on an "as is" basis with the permission of Statistics Canada.

Making the Connection | Do Canadians Spend Too Much?

We see in Figure 4.3 that, in 2015, consumption was 56 percent of GDP in Canada. In comparison, as the figure on the next page shows, American consumption accounts for a much greater share of GDP—over 70 percent! The role that consumption plays in the American economy is larger than that of any other rich country in the Organisation for Economic Cooperation and Development (OECD). Comparing the role of consumption in the American economy to its role in other developed economies can be somewhat misleading. The United States is the only developed economy in which citizens have to pay for most of their health care directly. This means that some of the spending that is categorized as "consumption" in the United States is categorized as "government spending" in countries such as Canada. A comparison of Canadian consumption spending to UK consumption spending is somewhat more telling, as both have socialized health care systems.

Consumption spending in the United Kingdom accounts for almost two-thirds of GDP even though that country's health care system is similar to Canada's. In fact, as you can see in the graph above, the role that consumption plays in the Canadian economy, while slightly below average, is far from the highest or lowest in the group.

Consumer spending plays a key role in the Canadian economy.

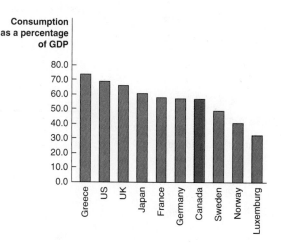

Consumption as a percentage of GDP

Greece, US, UK, Japan, France, Germany, Canada, Sweden, Norway, Luxemburg

Source: Data from OECD National Accounts at a Glance, OECD (2013), National Accounts of OECD Countries, OECD Publishing, Paris, http://dx.doi.org/10.1787/2221433x.

Yun Wang/Alamy Stock Photo

Does this mean that Canadians should not be concerned about the role consumption spending plays in the economy? Not necessarily. Demographics are going to play a role in the sustainability of the Canadian economy. For this level of consumption spending to be sustainable, older Canadians have to have sufficient savings to see them through their retirement years. This isn't generally the case. As a result, it seems likely that Canadians will have to spend less in the future, causing consumer spending to account for less of Canadian GDP. The same applies to virtually all developed countries, particularly the United States.

MyEconLab

Your Turn: Test your understanding by doing related problem 1.7 on page 103 at the end of this chapter.

Measuring GDP Using the Value-Added Method

We have seen that GDP can be calculated by adding together all expenditures on final goods and services. An alternative way of calculating GDP is the *value-added method*. **Value added** refers to the additional market value a firm gives a product and is equal to the difference between the price the firm paid for intermediate goods and the price for which it sells the finished product. Table 4.1 gives a hypothetical example of the value added by each firm involved in the production of a diamond ring—from the diamond's extraction from a diamond mine in the Northwest Territories to the ring's sale at a local jewellery store.

Value added The market value a firm adds to a product.

Suppose Diavik Diamond Mine sells a diamond it has just extracted to a gem cutter for $500. If, for simplicity, we ignore any inputs the mining company purchased from other firms—such as drilling equipment, trucks, and so on—then the mining company's value added is $500. The gem cutter then cuts the diamond into the familiar diamond shape and sells the stone to a jewellery designer for $700; the gem cutter has added $200 in value to the stone. The jewellery designer then designs and makes a ring for the diamond and sets the diamond in the ring. This ring is then sold to your local jewellery store for $1000. The jewellery designer has added $300 in the value to the ring. The jewellery store cleans and displays the ring and helps you pick it out. In selling you the diamond ring for $1500, the jewellery store added another $500 to the value of the ring. Notice that *the price of the diamond ring at the jewellery store is exactly equal to the sum of the value added by each firm involved in the production of the ring.* Similarly, we can calculate GDP by adding up the market value of every final good and service produced during a particular period. Or, we can arrive at the same value for GDP by adding the value added of every firm involved in producing those final goods and services.

Table 4.1	Firm	Value of Product	Value Added	
Calculating Value Added	Diavik Diamond Mine	Value of raw diamond = $500	Value added by diamond miner	= $500
	Gem cutter	Value of cut diamond = $700	Value added by diamond cutter = ($700 − $500)	= $200
	Jewellery designer	Value of set diamond = $1000	Value added by jewellery designer = ($1000 − $700)	= $300
	Jewellery store	Value of diamond ring = $1500	Value added by jewellery store = ($1500 − $1000)	= $500
		Total Value Added		= $1500

Does GDP Measure What We Want It to Measure?

4.2 LEARNING OBJECTIVE
Discuss whether GDP is a good measure of well-being.

Economists use GDP to measure total production in the economy. For that purpose, we would like GDP to be as comprehensive as possible, not overlooking any significant production that takes place in the economy. Most economists believe that GDP does a good—but not flawless—job of measuring production. GDP is also sometimes used as a measure of well-being. Although it is generally true that the more goods and services people have, the better off they are, we will see that GDP provides only a rough measure of well-being.

Shortcomings of GDP as a Measure of Total Production

When Statistics Canada calculates GDP, it does not include two types of production: production in the home and production in the underground economy.

Household Production. With very few exceptions, Statistics Canada does not attempt to estimate the value of goods and services that are not bought and sold in markets. If a carpenter makes and sells bookcases, the value of those bookcases will be counted in GDP. If you make the bookcases yourself, this is **household production**. *Household production* refers to goods and services people produce for themselves. The most important type of household production is the services a homemaker provides to the family. If a person has been looking after children, cleaning, and preparing family meals, the value of these services is not included in GDP. If the person decides to work outside the home, enrols the children in daycare, hires a cleaning service, and chooses to have the family eat all their meals at restaurants, the value of all these services will be included in GDP, even though the production of these services has not really changed.

Household production Goods and services people produce for themselves.

The Underground Economy. Individuals and firms sometimes conceal the buying and selling of goods and services, in which case their production isn't counted in GDP. Individuals and firms hide these transactions for three basic reasons: They are dealing in illegal goods and services—such as drugs or prostitution; they want to avoid paying taxes on the income they earn; or they want to avoid government regulation. These concealed transactions are referred to as the **underground economy**. Estimates of the size of the underground economy are very difficult to make because the people involved want to avoid detection. An estimate by Statistics Canada puts the size of the underground economy at $42.4 billion dollars, or about 2.3 percent of GDP. This is relatively small compared to other countries. Estimates of the American underground economy vary a great deal, but it is likely no more than 10 percent of GDP ($1.6 trillion). The underground economy in some low-income countries, such as Zimbabwe or Peru, may be as much as half of measured GDP.[1]

Underground economy Buying and selling of goods and services that is concealed from the government to avoid taxes or regulations or because the goods and services are illegal.

Is not counting household production or production in the underground economy a serious shortcoming of GDP? Most economists would say "no" because the most important use of GDP is to measure changes in how the economy is performing over short periods of time, such as from one year to the next. For this purpose, omitting household production or production in the underground economy won't have much effect, as these forms of production are unlikely to change quickly.

We also use GDP statistics to measure how production of goods and services grows over fairly long periods of a decade or more. For this purpose, omitting household production and production in the underground economy may be more important. For example, in the 1960s, the proportion of women working outside the home was much smaller, so the production of most women was not included in GDP. Since the 1960s

---

[1]Statistics Canada Study on the Underground Economy in Canada, 1992-2012, http://www.cra-arc.gc.ca/nwsrm/fctshts/2015/m05/fs150501-eng.html, accessed Dec. 7, 2015.

the proportion of women working outside the home has increased dramatically and the products of their labour are now included in GDP.

Shortcomings of GDP as a Measure of Well-Being

The main purpose of GDP is to measure a country's total production. GDP is also used by some people as a measure of well-being. For example, news articles often include tables that show the levels of *real* GDP per person in different countries. Real GDP per capita is calculated by dividing the value of real GDP in a country by that country's population. (We'll discuss how real GDP is calculated in the next section.) These articles imply that people in countries with higher levels of real GDP per capita are better off. Although increases in GDP often do lead to increases in the well-being of the population, it is important to be aware that GDP is not a perfect measure of well-being for several reasons.

The Value of Leisure Is Not Included in GDP.
If an economics professor decides to retire, GDP will decline even though the professor may value increased leisure more than the income earned teaching undergraduate economics courses. The professor's well-being has increased, but GDP has decreased. In the 1800s, it was not uncommon for someone to work 60 hours a week. Today, most Canadians work less than 40 hours per week. If Canadians still worked 60 hours per week, GDP would be much higher, but it isn't hard to imagine that well-being would be much lower, as we would have less time for leisure activities.

GDP Does Not Consider the State of the Environment.
When you get your clothes cleaned at a dry cleaner, the value of that service is included in GDP. If the chemicals used to clean your shirt pollute the air or water, GDP is not adjusted to compensate for the costs of the pollution. Similarly, the value of cigarettes produced is included in GDP, but the cost of lung cancer that some smokers develop is not included in GDP.

We should note, however, that increasing GDP often leads countries to devote more resources to protecting the environment. Canada, the United States, and European countries have tougher emissions standards than many developing countries. Environmental regulation is expensive to enforce, and developing countries may be reluctant to spend scarce resources on pollution reduction rather than on health care or education. China is an excellent example of this; levels of pollution in China are much higher than in Western countries. According to the World Health Organization, 7 of the 10 most polluted cities in the world are in China, but as Chinese GDP continues to rise, the Chinese government is likely to devote more resources to protecting and cleaning up the environment.

GDP Is Not Adjusted for Changes in Crime and Other Social Problems.
An increase in crime reduces well-being but may actually increase GDP if it leads to greater spending on police, security guards, and alarm systems. GDP is also not adjusted for changes in divorce rates, drug addiction, or other factors that may affect people's well-being.

GDP Measures the Size of the Pie but Not How the Pie Is Divided.
When a country's GDP increases, the country has more goods and services, but those goods and services may be very unequally distributed. Therefore, GDP per person may not provide a good description of what the typical person consumes.

To summarize, we can say that a person's well-being depends on many factors that are not considered when calculating GDP. We have to remember that GDP is designed to measure the size of the economy (total production), and it should not be a surprise that GDP is an imperfect measure of well-being.

Making the Connection | GDP and Happiness

As we have seen, GDP has limitations as a measure of the well-being of the people who live in a country. Although GDP was not designed to measure the well-being of a country's people, it isn't uncommon for people to compare countries based on GDP and conclude that people in one country are better off than those in another because their GDP is higher. It turns out that this approach isn't entirely unreasonable.

The OECD (an international organization that conducts research on a variety of issues related to economic performance, education, well-being, and other issues) has developed a way of measuring well-being that does not simply compare GDP per person. The OECD Better Life Index takes into consideration the categories of housing, income, jobs, community, education, environment, governance, health, life satisfaction, safety, and work-life balance.

When you give equal weight to all of the different categories (you can explore the index and change the weights given to each category by going to **www.oecdbetterlifeindex.org**), a very clear relationship emerges between GDP per person and well-being. Countries with relatively low GDP per person such as Mexico and Chile also have low Better Life Index scores. Countries such as Canada, Australia, and the United States have high Better Life Index scores. You can see this relationship in the graph on the next page.

Why might a country like New Zealand score so much higher on the Better Life Index than its GDP would suggest? A lot of factors can influence how content people are. One of these factors is climate. New Zealand has a comfortable climate (compared with Canada, Sweden, and Australia), great scenery, and, unlike other countries in the region, not much of the wildlife is likely to kill you. New Zealanders may also have more trust in one another and their government.

Well-being and Wealth

OECD Better Life Index (10 = best) and GDP per person, 2014*

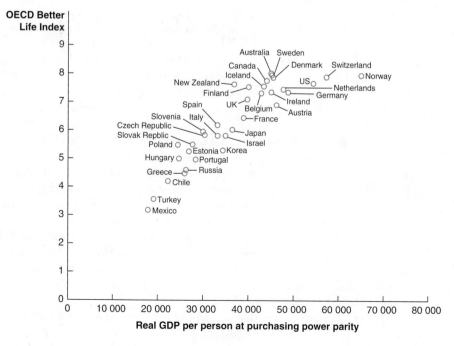

*or latest available year

Source: Data from Well-being and wealth: OECD Better Life index (10=best) and GDP per person, 2014, The Organisation for Economic Cooperation and Development.

So while GDP per person isn't a perfect measure of well-being, it actually performs pretty well.

Sources: OECD Better Life Index, http://www.oecdbetterlifeindex.org/#/11111111111, GDP per capita http://stats.oecd.org/Index.aspx?DataSetCode=PDB_LV, accessed Dec. 7, 2015.

MyEconLab **Your Turn:** Test your understanding by doing related problem 2.3 on page 104 at the end of this chapter.

related problem 2.3 on page 104

4.3 LEARNING OBJECTIVE

Discuss the difference between real GDP and nominal GDP.

Real GDP versus Nominal GDP

GDP is measured in value terms, so we have to be careful about interpreting changes over time. To see why, consider interpreting an increase in the total value of pickup truck production from $40 billion in 2016 to $44 billion in 2017. Can we be sure that because $44 billion is 10 percent more than $40 billion, the number of trucks produced in 2017 is also 10 percent more than in 2016? We can draw this conclusion only if the average price of a truck hasn't changed between 2016 and 2017. In fact, when GDP increases from one year to the next, the increase is due in part to increases in production of goods and services and partly due to increases in prices. Given that we're mainly interested in GDP as a measure of production, we need a way of separating the price changes from the quantity changes.

Calculating Real GDP

Nominal GDP The value of final goods and services evaluated at current-year prices.

Real GDP The value of final goods and services evaluated at base-year prices.

We can separate the price changes from the quantity changes by calculating a measure of production called *real GDP*. **Nominal GDP** is calculated by summing the *current* values of final goods and services. **Real GDP** is calculated by designating a particular year as the *base year* and then using the prices of goods and services in the base year to calculate the value of goods and services in all other years. For instance, if the base year is 2007, real GDP for 2017 would be calculated by using the price of goods and services from 2007. By always using the same prices, we know that changes in real GDP represent changes in the quantity of goods and not changes in prices.

One drawback of calculating real GDP using base-year prices is that, over time, prices may change relative to each other. For example the price of cellphones has fallen dramatically over the last 10 years relative to the price of pizzas. Because this change is not reflected in base-year prices, real GDP is somewhat distorted. The further away from the base year we are, the bigger this problem becomes. To address this problem, Statistics Canada began to use *chain-weighted prices*, and it now publishes real GDP statistics in both 2007 base-year prices and as "chained (2007) dollars."

The details of calculating real GDP using chain-weighted prices are more complicated than we need to discuss here, but the basic idea is straightforward. Starting with the base year, take the average of prices in that year and prices in the following year. Then use this average to calculate real GDP in the year after the base year (2008 if the base year is 2007). For the next year—two years after the base year (2009)—calculate real GDP by taking an average of prices in that year and the previous year. In this way, prices in each year are "chained" to prices from the previous year, and the distortion from changes in relative prices is minimized. Essentially, chain-weighting involves using an average price for goods rather than just the base year price.

Holding prices constant means that the *purchasing power* of a dollar remains the same from one year to the next. Ordinarily, the purchasing power of a dollar falls over the years, as price increases reduce the amount of goods and services that a dollar can buy.

Solved Problem **4.2**

Calculating Real GDP

Suppose that a very simple economy only produces the following three final goods and services: energy drinks, pizzas, and textbooks. Use the information in the table below to compute real GDP for the year 2017. Assume that the base year is 2007.

		2007		2017	
Product	Quantity	Price	Quantity	Price
Energy drinks	80	$ 40	100	$ 50
Pizza	90	11	80	10
Textbooks	15	90	20	100

Solving the Problem

Step 1: **Review the chapter material.** This problem is about calculating real GDP, so you may want to review the section "Calculating Real GDP."

Step 2: **Calculate the value of the three goods and services listed in the table, using the quantities for 2017 and the prices for 2007.** The definition above tells us that real GDP is the value of all final goods and services, evaluated at base-year prices. In this case, the base year is 2007, and we are given information on the price of each product in that year:

Product	2017 Quantity	2007 Price	Value
Energy drinks	100	$40	$4000
Pizzas	80	11	880
Textbooks	20	90	1800

Step 3: **Add up the values for the three products to find real GDP.** Real GDP for 2017 equals the sum of:

Quantity of energy drinks in 2017 × Price of energy drinks in 2007 = $4000 +
Quantity of pizzas in 2017 × Price of pizzas in 2007   = $880 +
Quantity of textbooks in 2017 × Price of textbooks in 2007   = $1800
For a real GDP of $6680.

Extra credit: Notice that the quantities of each good produced in 2007 were irrelevant for calculating real GDP in 2017. Notice also that the value of $6680 for real GDP in 2017 is lower than the value of nominal GDP, $7800, which we calculated in *Solved Problem 4.1* on page 84.

Your Turn: For more practice, do related problem 3.1 on page 104 at the end of this chapter.   MyEconLab

Comparing Real GDP and Nominal GDP

Real GDP holds prices constant, which makes it a better measure than nominal GDP of changes in the production of goods and services from one year to the next. In fact, growth in the economy is almost always measured as growth in real GDP. If a headline in the *Globe and Mail* states "Canadian Economy Grew at 1% Last Year," the article will report that real GDP is 1 percent higher than it was last year.

Figure 4.4

Nominal GDP and Real GDP

Currently, the base year for calculating real GDP is 2007. In the years before 2007, prices were, on average, lower than in 2007, so nominal GDP was lower than real GDP. In 2007, nominal and real GDP were equal. Since 2007, prices have been, on average, higher than in 2007, so nominal GDP is higher than real GDP.

Data from Statistics Canada. Table 380-0064 – Gross domestic product, expenditure-based, quarterly (dollars unless otherwise noted), CANSIM (database).

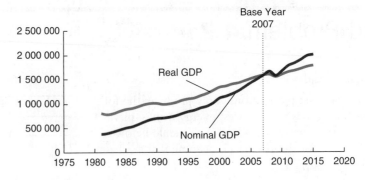

We describe real GDP as being measured in "base year dollars." For example, with a base year of 2007, nominal GDP in 2015 was $1997 billion in 2015 dollars and real GDP in 2015 was $1773 billion in 2007 dollars. Real GDP is smaller than nominal GDP in years after the base year because prices tend to rise over time. In the base year, nominal GDP and real GDP are the same because both are being calculated using the same set of prices. In years before the base year, real GDP will be larger than nominal GDP because prices in year prior to the base year are lower. Figure 4.4 shows movements in real and nominal GDP over time using 2007 as the base year. As you can see, before 2007 nominal GDP is lower than real GDP. In 2007, they are the same, and after 2007 nominal GDP is larger than real GDP.

The GDP Deflator

Price level A measure of the average prices of goods and services in the economy.

GDP deflator A measure of the price level, calculated by dividing nominal GDP by real GDP and multiplying by 100.

Economists and policymakers are not just interested in the level of total production, as measured by real GDP, but also in the *price level*. The **price level** measures the average prices of goods and services in the economy. One of the goals of economic policy is a stable price level. We can use values for nominal GDP and real GDP to compute a measure of the price level called the *GDP deflator*. We calculate the **GDP deflator** by using this formula:

$$\text{GDP Deflator} = \frac{\text{Nominal GDP}}{\text{Real GDP}} \times 100.$$

To see why the GDP deflator is a measure of the price level, think about what would happen if prices of goods and services rose while production remained the same. In that case, nominal GDP would increase, but real GDP would remain constant, so the GDP deflator would increase. In reality, both prices and production increase in most years, but the more prices increase relative to the increase in production, the more nominal GDP increases relative to real GDP, and the higher the value for the GDP deflator. Increases in the GDP deflator allow economists and policymakers to track increases in the price level over time.

Remember that in the base year (currently 2007) nominal GDP and real GDP are the same number. This means that the GDP deflator will always be 100 in the base year. The following table gives the values of nominal and real GDP in 2014 and 2015.

	2014	2015
Nominal GDP	$1 892 billion	$1 973 billion
Real GDP	$1 706 billion	$1 748 billion

We can use this information to calculate the value for the GDP deflator in 2014 and 2015.

For 2014, we get:

$$GDP\ Deflator = \frac{Nominal\ GDP}{Real\ GDP} \times 100 = \frac{\$1892}{\$1706} \times 100 = 110.9$$

For 2015, we get:

$$GDP\ Deflator = \frac{Nominal\ GDP}{Real\ GDP} \times 100 = \frac{\$1973}{\$1748} \times 100 = 112.9$$

From these values for the GDP deflator, we can calculate that the price level rose by 1.76 percent between 2013 and 2014.

$$\frac{112.9 - 110.9}{110.9} \times 100\% = 1.8\%$$

In Chapter 5, we will see that economists and policymakers also rely on another measure of the price level, known as the *consumer price index*. In addition, we will discuss the strengths and weaknesses of different measures of the price level.

Other Measures of Total Production and Total Income

4.4 LEARNING OBJECTIVE

Become familiar with other measures of total production and total income.

National income accounting refers to the methods government agencies use to track total production and total income in the economy. In Canada, the statistical tables containing this information are called the National Economic Accounts. Every quarter, Statistics Canada releases the National Economic Accounts containing data on several measures of total production and total income. We have already discussed the most commonly used measure of total production and total income: gross domestic product (GDP). In addition to GDP, Statistics Canada also calculates the following measures of production and income: gross national income, net national income, household income, and household disposable income.

Gross National Income (GNI)

We have seen that GDP is the value of final goods and services produced within Canada's borders. *Gross national income* (GNI) is the value of incomes received by Canadians for the use of their factors of production no matter where in the world those factors of production are used, including outside Canada. Canadian firms have facilities in other countries and foreign firms have facilities in Canada. Many Canadian mining companies operate mines all around the world, while foreign companies operate mines in Canada. GDP excludes the production of Canadian firms that takes place outside Canada even though Canadians receive a lot of the benefit of that production. At the same time, GDP includes production done in Canada by foreign firms even though a significant portion of the benefit of that production is received by foreigners. For Canada, GNI and GDP are very similar. In 2014, for example, Canadian GDP at market prices was $1973 billion and GNI at market prices was $1943 billion, a difference of only 1.5 percent.

Net National Income (NNI)

In producing goods and services, some machinery, equipment, and buildings wear out and have to be replaced. The value of this worn-out machinery, equipment, and buildings is *depreciation*. In the National Income Account tables, depreciation is often referred to as the *consumption of fixed capital*. If we subtract this value from GNI, we are left with NNI.

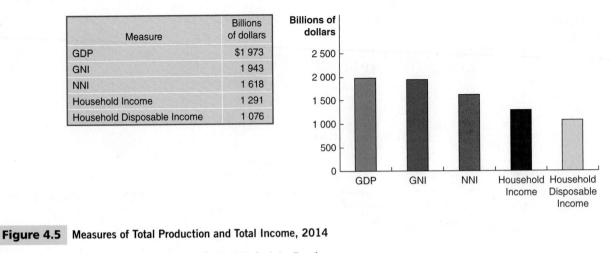

Measure	Billions of dollars
GDP	$1 973
GNI	1 943
NNI	1 618
Household Income	1 291
Household Disposable Income	1 076

Figure 4.5 Measures of Total Production and Total Income, 2014

Data from Cansim Tables 380-0064, 380-0083 and 384-0040, Statistics Canada.

Previously in this chapter, we stressed that the value of total production is equal to the value of total income. This point is not strictly true if by "value of total production" we mean GDP or GNI and by "value of total income" we mean NNI, because national income will always be smaller than GDP or GNI by an amount equal to depreciation. In practice, the difference between the value of GDP and NNI doesn't change the predictions made by macroeconomic models.

Household Income

Household income is income received by households. To calculate household income, we subtract the earnings that corporations retain rather than pay to shareholders in the form of dividends. We also add in the payments received by households from the government in the form of transfer payments or interest payments on government bonds.

Household Disposable Income

Household disposable income is equal to household income minus personal tax payments, such as federal income tax. It is the best measure of the income households actually have to spend.

Figure 4.5 shows the values of these measures for 2014 in a table and a graph.

The Division of Income

Figure 4.1 illustrates the important fact that we can measure GDP in terms of total expenditure or as the total income received by households. GDP calculated as the sum of income payments to households is sometimes referred to as *gross domestic income*. Figure 4.6 shows the division of income among labour income, corporate operating surplus, small business income, and taxes on production and imports (but not income taxes) in both 2004 and 2014. Labour income is the payments that households receive from supplying labour to firms (that they don't own) and government. This accounted for 49 percent of all income in 2004 and 51 percent in 2014. Corporate operating surplus accounted for 28 percent of income in 2004 and 27 percent in 2014. Corporate operating surplus includes the profits that get paid to households that own shares in these corporations. Small business income, also called mixed income, made up 12 percent of income in 2004 and 11 percent in 2014. This category covers the wages and profits earned by owners of unincorporated businesses. Finally, taxes on production and imports accounted for 11 percent of all income in both 2004 and 2014.

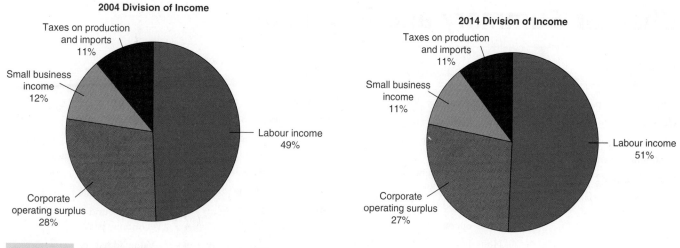

Figure 4.6   The Division of Income, 2004 and 2014

We can measure GDP in terms of total expenditure or as the total income received by households. The largest component of income is labour income. Labour income accounts for more of GDP than the operating surplus of corporations and small business combined.

Source: Statistics Canada, Table 380-0063 – Gross domestic product, income-based, annual (dollars). Reproduced and distributed on an "as is" basis with the permission of Statistics Canada.

These taxes are included in the calculation because they are included in the market price of the goods and services that Canadians buy. By comparing the division in 2004 and 2014, we see that there hasn't been a lot of change in these categories over the past 10 years. The biggest change was in labour income, whose share rose from 49 percent to 51 percent.

Economics in Your Life

What's the Best Country for You to Work In?

At the beginning of the chapter we posed two questions: What effect should the United Kingdom's and China's two very different GDP growth rates have on your decision to live and work in one country or the other? And if China's much higher growth rate does not necessarily lead you to decide to live and work in China, why not? This chapter has shown that although it is generally true that the more goods and services people have, the better off they are, GDP provides only a rough measure of well-being. GDP does not include the value of leisure; nor is it adjusted for pollution and other negative effects of production, crime, or any other social problems. So, in deciding where to live and work, you would need to balance China's much higher growth rate of GDP against these other considerations. You would also need to take into account that although China's *growth rate* is higher than the United Kingdom's, the United Kingdom's current *level* of real GDP per person is much higher than China's.

Conclusion

In this chapter, we have begun the study of macroeconomics by examining an important concept: how a nation's total production and income can be measured. Understanding GDP is important for understanding the business cycle and the process of long-run economic growth. In Chapter 5, we discuss the issues involved in measuring two other key economic variables: the unemployment rate and the inflation rate.

Chapter Summary and Problems

Key Terms

Business cycle, p. 82	GDP deflator, p. 98	Income approach, p. 87	Price level, p. 98
Consumption (c), p. 90	Government spending (g), p. 90	Inflation rate, p. 83	Real GDP, p. 96
Consumption of capital, p. 88	Gross domestic product (GDP), p. 83	Intermediate good or service, p. 83	Recession, p. 82
Economic growth, p. 82			Statistical discrepancy, p. 90
Expansion, p. 82	Gross fixed capital formation, p. 89	Investment (i), p. 90	Taxes less subsidies, p. 89
Expenditure approach, p. 87		Macroeconomics, p. 82	Transfer payments, p. 85
Exports, p. 90	Gross mixed income, p. 89	Microeconomics, p. 82	Underground economy, p. 93
Final consumption expenditure, p. 89	Gross operating surplus, p. 88	Net exports, p. 90	
	Household production, p. 93	Net operating surplus, p. 88	Value added, p. 92
Final good or service, p. 83	Imports, p. 90	Nominal GDP, p. 96	

Summary

*LO 4.1 Economics is divided into the subfields of *microeconomics*—which studies how households and firms make choices—and *macroeconomics*—which studies the economy as a whole. An important macroeconomic issue is the *business cycle*, which refers to alternating periods of economic expansion and economic recession. An *expansion* is a period during which production and employment are increasing. A *recession* is a period during which production and employment are decreasing. Another important macroeconomic topic is *economic growth*, which refers to the ability of the economy to produce increasing quantities of goods and services. Macroeconomics also studies the *inflation rate*, or the percentage increase in the price level from one year to the next. Economists measure total production by *gross domestic product (GDP)*, which is the value of all final goods and services produced in an economy during a period of time. A *final good or service* is purchased by a final user. An *intermediate good or service* is an input into another good or service and is not included in GDP. When we measure the value of total production in the economy by calculating GDP, we are simultaneously measuring the value of total income. GDP is divided into four major categories of expenditures: final consumption, gross fixed capital formation, inventories, and net exports. Government transfer payments are not included in GDP because they are payments to individuals for which the government does not receive a good or service in return. We can also calculate GDP by adding up the value added of every firm involved in producing final goods and services.

LO 4.2 GDP does not include household production, which refers to goods and services people produce for themselves, nor

does it include production in the *underground economy*, which consists of concealed buying and selling. The underground economy in some developing countries may be more than half of measured GDP. GDP is not a perfect measure of well-being because it does not include the value of leisure, it is not adjusted for pollution or other negative effects of production, and it is not adjusted for changes in crime and other social problems.

LO 4.3 *Nominal GDP* is the value of final goods and services evaluated at current-year prices. *Real GDP* is the value of final goods and services evaluated at *base-year* prices. By keeping prices constant, we know that changes in real GDP represent changes in the quantity of goods and services produced in the economy. When the *price level*, the average prices of goods and services in the economy, is increasing, real GDP is greater than nominal GDP in years before the base year and less than nominal GDP for years after the base year. The *GDP deflator* is a measure of the price level and is calculated by dividing nominal GDP by real GDP and multiplying by 100.

LO 4.4 The most important measure of total production and total income is gross domestic product (GDP). As we will see in later chapters, for some purposes, the other measures of total production and total income shown in Figure 4.5 are actually more useful than GDP. These measures are gross national product (GNP), national income, household income, and household disposable income.

MyEconLab Log in to MyEconLab to complete these exercises and get instant feedback.

Review Questions

LO 4.1

1.1 Why in microeconomics do we measure production in terms of quantity, but in macroeconomics we measure production in terms of market value?

1.2 If Statistics Canada added up the values of every good and service sold during the year, would the total be larger or smaller than GDP?

1.3 In the circular flow of income, why must the value of total production in an economy equal the value of total income?

*"Learning Objective" is abbreviated to "LO" in the end-of-chapter material.

1.4 Describe the four major categories of expenditures in GDP and write the equation used to represent the relationship between GDP and the four expenditure categories.

LO 4.2

2.1 Why does the size of a country's GDP matter? How does it affect the quality of life of the country's people?

2.2 Why is GDP an imperfect measure of economic well-being? What types of production does GDP not measure? Even if GDP included these types of production, why would it still be an imperfect measure of economic well-being?

LO 4.3

3.1 Why does inflation make nominal GDP a poor measure of the increase in total production from one year to the next? How does Statistics Canada deal with the problem inflation causes with nominal GDP?

3.2 What is the GDP deflator, and how is it calculated?

LO 4.4

4.1 What is the difference between GDP and GNP? Briefly explain whether the difference is important for Canada.

4.2 What are the differences between national income, household income, and household disposable income?

Problems and Applications

LO 4.1

1.1 A student remarks: "It doesn't make sense that intermediate goods are not counted in GDP. A computer chip is an intermediate good, and without it a PC won't work. So why don't we count the computer chip in GDP?" Provide an answer for the student's question.

1.2 Briefly explain whether each of the following transactions represents the purchase of a final good.
   a. The purchase of wheat from a wheat farmer by a bakery
   b. The purchase of a frigate by the federal government
   c. The purchase of a French wine by a Canadian consumer
   d. The purchase of a new airliner by WestJet

1.3 **[Related to the Chapter Opener on page 81]** Which component of GDP will be affected by each of the following transactions involving Ford Motor Company? If you believe that none of the components of GDP will be affected by the transactions, briefly explain why.
   a. You purchase a new Ford Edge (built in Oakville, Ontario) from a Ford dealer.
   b. You purchase a 2010 Ford Edge from a friend.
   c. Ford purchases seats for the Ford Edge from Magna International, located in London, Ontario.
   d. Ford purchases new machine tools to use in its Oakville plant.

1.4 Is the value of a house built in 2010 and resold in 2017 included in the GDP of 2017? Briefly explain. Would the services of the real estate agent who helped sell (or buy) the house in 2017 be counted in GDP for 2017? Briefly explain.

1.5 **[Related to Solved Problem 4.1 on page 84]** Suppose that a simple economy produces only four goods: textbooks, hamburgers, shirts, and cotton. Assume that all the cotton is used in the production of shirts. Use the information in the following table to calculate nominal GDP for 2017:

Production and Price Statistics for 2017		
Product	Quantity	Price
Textbooks	100	$60.00
Hamburgers	100	2.00
Shirts	50	25.00
Cotton	80	0.60

1.6 **[Related to Don't Let This Happen to You on page 87]** Briefly explain whether you agree with the following statement: "In years when people buy many shares of stock, investment will be high and, therefore, so will GDP."

1.7 **[Related to Making the Connection on page 91]** Household debt is becoming an ever more serious concern for the Canadian economy. In September 2015, Canadians' debt-to-income ratio was 164.6 percent—meaning the average Canadian was carrying debt equal to 1.6 times their income. At the turn of the century, the debt-to-income ratio was much lower at 110 per cent. This debt is identified by nearly all economists as posing a danger to future growth of the Canadian economy. The problem is that Canadians will have to cut debt and build up savings in the near future. Why does cutting debt and increasing personal savings affect consumer spending? What would happen to GDP and incomes if the majority of consumers decided to reduce their spending at the same time?

Based on Barbara Shecter, Debt load has many Canadians 'living on the edge,' with high housing prices largely to blame: report, 2015. http://business.financialpost.com/news/economy/debt-load-has-many-canadians-living-on-the-edge-with-high-housing-prices-largely-to-blame-report.

1.8 For the total value of expenditures on final goods and services to equal the total value of income generated from producing those final goods and services, all the money that a business receives from the sale of its product must be paid out as income to the owners of the factors of production. How can a business make a profit if it pays out as income all the money it receives?

LO 4.2

2.1 Which of the following are likely to increase measured GDP, and which are likely to reduce it?
   a. The fraction of women working outside the home increases.
   b. There is a sharp increase in the crime rate.
   c. Higher tax rates cause some people to hide more of the income they earn.

2.2 Does the fact that the typical Canadian works less than 40 hours per week today and worked 60 hours per week in 1890 indicate whether the economic well-being of Canadians today versus 1890 is higher or lower? Or, can we use the difference between real GDP per capita today and in 1890 alone to measure differences in economic well-being? Briefly explain.

2.3 **[Related to Making the Connection on page 95]** Each year, the United Nations publishes the Human Development Report, which provides information on the standard of living in nearly every country in the world. The report includes data on real GDP per person and also contains a broader measure of the standard of living called the Human Development Index (HDI). The HDI combines data on gross national income (GNI) per person with data on life expectancy at birth, average years of schooling, and expected years of schooling. (GNI is a measure of the total income per person in a country.) The following table shows values for GNI per person and the HDIs for several countries. Prepare one list that ranks countries from highest GNI per person to lowest and another list that ranks countries from highest HDI to lowest. Briefly discuss possible reasons for any differences in the rankings of countries in your two lists. (All values in the table are for the year 2012.)

Country	Real GNI per Person (2012 PPP)	HDI
Australia	41 524	0.933
Greece	24 658	0.853
China	11 477	0.719
Iran	13 451	0.749
Norway	63 909	0.944
Canada	41 887	0.902
Singapore	72 371	0.901
South Korea	30 345	0.891
United Arab Emirates	56 068	0.827
United States	52 308	0.914
Venezuela	17 067	0.764
Zimbabwe	1307	0.492

Data from United Nations Development Programme, "The Human Development Index," (http:/hdr.undp.org/en/statistics/hdi/). Retrieved December 15, 2015.

LO 4.3

3.1 **[Related to Solved Problem 4.2 on page 97]** Suppose the information in the table below is for a simple economy that produces only four goods and services: textbooks, hamburgers, shirts, and cotton. Assume that all the cotton is used in the production of shirts.

Product	2007 Quantity	2007 Price	2016 Quantity	2016 Price	2017 Quantity	2017 Price
Textbooks	90	$50.00	100	$60.00	100	$65.00
Hamburgers	75	2.00	100	2.00	120	2.25
Shirts	50	30.00	50	25.00	65	25.00
Cotton	100	0.80	800	0.60	120	0.70

a. Use the information in the table to calculate real GDP for 2016 and 2017, assuming that the base year is 2007.

b. What is the growth rate of real GDP from 2016?

LO 4.4

4.1 Suppose a country has many of its citizens temporarily working in other countries, and many of its firms have facilities in other countries. Furthermore, relatively few citizens of foreign countries are working in this country, and relatively few foreign firms have facilities in this country. In these circumstances, which would you expect to be larger for this country, GDP or GNP? Briefly explain.

4.2 Suppose the amount the federal government collects in personal income taxes increases, while the level of GDP remains the same. What will happen to the values of national income, household income, and household disposable income?

4.3 If you were attempting to forecast the level of consumption spending by households, which measure of total production or total income might be most helpful to you in making your forecast? Briefly explain.

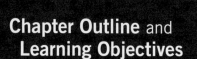

Unemployment and Inflation

Canadian Manufacturers Grow While Others Shrink

When we study macroeconomics, we are looking at the big picture: total production, total employment, and the price level. Of course, the big picture is made up of millions of consumers, workers, and firms. The actions of all these individuals come together to determine how many people will find jobs and how many will lose them.

One sector of the economy that receives a great deal of media and political attention is the manufacturing sector. Manufacturing firms make goods (rather than provide services), and their hiring decisions can have a major impact on the entire economy. As such, economists, policymakers, and other firms would all like to know when manufacturing firms are planning to expand or contract as early as possible to understand how employment and the economy overall will be affected.

One way to assess the coming employment picture is the Purchasing Managers' Index (PMI). Produced in more than 40 countries, the PMI is a monthly survey of firms' plans to purchase goods and services as well as their assessment of how they feel the economy will do over the next few months (i.e., "better than before," "worse than before," or "the same"). Think about the PMI index as a continuum: If all firms surveyed report that they were going to lay off workers and shut down operations, the PMI would be 0; if most firms surveyed reported that they were likely to cut back operations (indicating a negative economic outlook), the PMI would be below 50; if all firms surveyed reported that they were going to keep production the same as in previous months, the PMI would be 50; if most firms surveyed reported that

Chapter Outline and Learning Objectives

they expected to expand operations (indicating a positive economic outlook), the PMI would be above 50; and if all firms surveyed reported that they expected to hire more employees and expected the economy to improve, the PMI would be 100.

In November of 2015, the PMI for Canada's manufacturing sector was 48.6, indicating that Canadian manufacturers were likely to reduce the number of workers they employ and decrease production. Canada's outlook was very different from that of Germany, whose November PMI for the manufacturing sector stood at 52.9, which meant that the German manufacturing sector was likely to expand rather than contract. Keep in mind that forecasting the number of jobs that will be created or destroyed in any economy is exceptionally difficult, but the PMI gives us a starting point.

In this chapter, we will focus on measuring changes in unemployment as well as changes in the price level, or inflation. Both unemployment and inflation are major economic and political problems, so it is important to understand how they are measured.

Based on Germany Manufacturing PMI, http://www.tradingeconomics.com/germany/manufacturing-pmi; RBC Purchasing Managers' Index, http://www.rbc.com/newsroom/reports/rbc-purchasing-managers-index.html.

Economics in Your Life

Should You Change Your Career Plans if You Graduate during a Recession?

Suppose you are in the second year of your degree, majoring in economics and geology. You plan to find a job in the energy industry after graduation. The energy industry, particularly the oil and gas sector, has seen much less growth since 2014 and unemployment in the entire economy is still quite high. After meeting with some older students, you learn that many of them already have jobs in the finance industry. Should you switch your major to economics and finance? As you read this chapter, see if you can answer this question. You can check your answer against the one we provide on page 124 at the end of this chapter.

Unemployment and inflation are the macroeconomic problems most discussed in the media and during political campaigns. For many people, the state of the economy can be described by just two measures: the unemployment rate and the inflation rate. In the 1960s, Arthur Okun, an American economist, coined the term *misery index*, which adds the inflation rate and the unemployment rate together to give a rough measure of the state of the economy. As we will see in later chapters, although inflation and unemployment are important problems, the long-run success of an economy is generally judged by its ability to generate high levels of real GDP per person. We devote this chapter to discussing how unemployment and inflation rates are measured. In particular, we'll look closely at the measures produced by Statistics Canada on a monthly basis.

Unemployment rate The percentage of the labour force that is unemployed.

5.1 LEARNING OBJECTIVE

Define the unemployment rate and the labour force participation rate, and understand how they are computed.

Measuring the Unemployment Rate and the Labour Force Participation Rate

On the first or second Friday of every month at 7:00 A.M., Statistics Canada (also called StatsCan) reports its estimate of the previous month's **unemployment rate**. The estimates are widely reported in newspapers, radio, TV, and on blogs. If the unemployment rate is higher or lower than expected, investors and firms are likely to change their views on the health of the economy. The unemployment rate can also have a major impact on the outcome of elections. In many provincial and federal elections, the party in power does well if the unemployment rate has been steady or falling. If the unemployment rate is rising, a change in government is much more likely.

The unemployment rate is one of the key macroeconomic statistics, but how does Statistics Canada prepare its estimates, and how accurate are these estimates? We explore the answers to these questions in this section.

The Labour Force Survey

Each month, Statistics Canada conducts the Labour Force Survey (LFS) to collect the data needed to compute the unemployment rate. The LFS involves interviewing about 56 000 (on a monthly basis) households to gain information on people's labour market activities as well as the demographic makeup of the people living in the household. The LFS focuses only on the **working age population**, people 15 years of age and older who are legally entitled to work in Canada.

Working age population People 15 years of age and older who are legally entitled to work in Canada.

Participants in the survey are put into one of three categories: *employed*, *unemployed*, or *not in the labour force*.

- **Employed:** Anyone who did paid work, unpaid work for a family business, or worked for themselves is considered "employed." Also considered employed is anyone who would normally have worked but did not due to illness, disability, family crisis, vacation, or labour dispute (strike or lockout). Essentially, anyone with a job is classified as employed.

- **Unemployed:** People who don't have a job but are willing and able to work and have looked for work in the last four weeks are considered "unemployed." This category includes people who have been temporarily laid off, or will be starting a new job within four weeks. The most important part of the definition of *unemployed* is the requirement that an individual must have looked for work in the last four weeks. If someone doesn't have a job and hasn't looked for one in the last four weeks, that person is placed in the category that is described next.

- **Not in the labour force:** People who were unable or unwilling to do paid work are considered to be outside the labour force. This category includes people who would like to have a job, but have given up looking for one.

We need one more definition before we can show you how to calculate the unemployment rate and the participation rate. We need to define *labour force* clearly. The **labour force** is all the people who are working or actively looking for work. Essentially, the labour force is all the people who could be working on very short notice. Statistics Canada calculates the size of the labour force by adding up all the people who were classified as employed and all the people who were classified as unemployed. Figure 5.1 shows

Labour force The sum of employed and unemployed workers in the economy.

Figure 5.1

The Employment Status of the Working Age Population, November 2015

In November 2015, the working age population of Canada was 29.4 million. The working age population is divided into those in the labour force (19.4 million) and those not in the labour force (10 million). The labour force is divided into the employed (18 million) and the unemployed (1.4 million). Those not in the labour force are further divided into different groups. The most important of these groups from an economic standpoint are the discouraged workers (19 400). These are people who would like to have a job but who have given up looking for work.

Source: Data from CANSIM Tables 282-0085 and 282-0087.

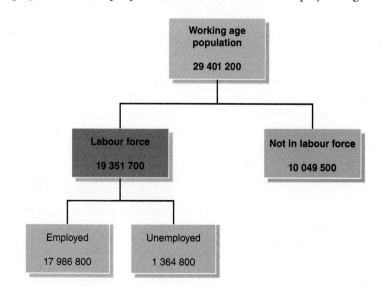

how the population is broken down into the different categories we discussed. The numbers in the figure are taken from the November 2015 estimates.

The unemployment rate is calculated as follows:

$$\text{Unemployment rate} = \frac{\text{Number of unemployed}}{\text{Labour force}} \times 100.$$

Using the numbers from Figure 5.1, we can see that the unemployment rate for November 2015 was:

$$\text{Unemployment Rate} = \frac{1\,364\,800}{19\,351\,700} \times 100 = 7.1\%.$$

Labour force participation rate
The percentage of the working age population in the labour force.

The **labour force participation rate**, or simply the *participation rate*, is calculated as follows:

$$\text{Participation rate} = \frac{\text{Labour force}}{\text{Working age population}} \times 100.$$

For November 2015 the participation rate was:

$$\text{Participation rate} = \frac{19\,351\,700}{29\,401\,200} \times 100 = 65.8\%.$$

Employment–population ratio
A measure of the portion of the population engaged in paid work.

Another measure of the state of the economy is the **employment–population ratio**. The employment–population ratio measures the portion of the population engaged in paid work. It is calculated as follows:

$$\text{Employment–population ratio} = \frac{\text{Number of employed}}{\text{Working age population}} \times 100$$

For November 2015, the employment–population ratio was:

$$\text{Employment–population ratio} = \frac{17\,986\,800}{29\,401\,200} \times 100 = 61.2\%.$$

Problems with Measuring the Unemployment Rate

Although Statistics Canada reports the unemployment rate measured to a tenth of a percentage point, it is not a perfect measure of the current state of joblessness in the economy. One problem that Statistics Canada faces is distinguishing between people who are not in the labour force. During a recession, some unemployed people who are having a hard time finding a job will stop looking for work. Remember that only people who have actively looked for work in the last four weeks are counted as "unemployed" by Statistics Canada. So, even though these **discouraged workers** are willing and able to work, they are counted as "not in the labour force."

Discouraged workers People who are available for work but have not looked for a job during the previous four weeks because they believe no jobs are available for them.

Another problem with the unemployment rate is that everyone with a job is considered "employed," even if they are only working a few hours a week. The "employed" category includes everyone with a full-time or a part-time job. Some part-time workers would like to have a full-time job, but they can only find part-time work. The unemployment rate doesn't tell us how many people are in this situation. Both of these issues mean that the unemployment rate *understates* problems in the labour market.

There are other measurement problems, however, that cause the measured unemployment rate to *overstate* the extent of joblessness. These problems arise because the LFS doesn't verify the responses of people included in the survey. Some people who claim to be unemployed and actively looking for work may not be looking. A person might claim to be actively looking for a job to remain eligible for Employment Insurance. In this case, a person who is actually not in the labour force is counted as unemployed. Other people might be employed but not in a legal activity—such as selling drugs—or might want to conceal a legitimate job to avoid paying taxes. In these cases, individuals who are actually working are counted as unemployed. These inaccurate responses to the LFS bias the unemployment rate upward. We can conclude that, although the unemployment

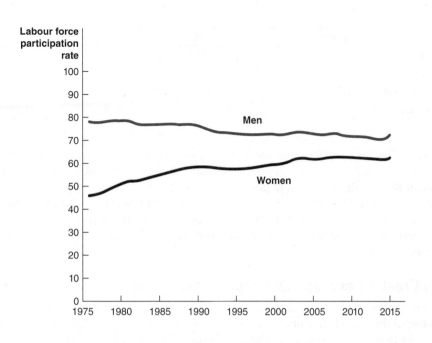

Figure 5.2

Trends in the Labour Force Participation Rate of Men and Women, 1976 to 2015

The labour force participation rate of men declined gradually from 1976 to 2014, while the participation rate of women increased significantly over the same period. In 2015 (the last year in which data were available when writing), labour force participation for both men and women had increased over 2014 levels. The total labour force participation rate remains higher today than it was 1976.

Source: Statistics Canada, Table 282-0001 - Labour force survey estimates (LFS), by sex and detailed age group, unadjusted for seasonality, annual (persons unless otherwise noted). Reproduced and distributed on an "as is" basis with the permission of Statistics Canada.

rate provides useful information about the employment situation in the country, it is far from an exact measure of joblessness.

Trends in Labour Force Participation

The labour force participation rate is important because it determines the amount of labour that will be available to the economy from a given population. The higher the labour force participation rate, the more labour is available and the higher a country's levels of GDP and GDP per person. Figure 5.2 highlights two important trends in labour force participation rates of adults over 15 years old since 1976—the rising participation of women and the falling participation of men.

The labour force participation rate of males over 15 years old has fallen from 78.4 percent in 1981 to 69 percent in January 2015. Some of this decline is due to older men retiring earlier and younger men staying in school longer. There has also been a decline in the participation of males who are not in school but are too young to retire.

The decline in labour force participation by men has been offset by the increase in participation by women. The labour force participation rate for women in Canada rose from 45.7 per cent in 1976 to a peak of 62.4 per cent in 2010. As a result, the overall labour force participation increased from 61.5 per cent to a high of 62.7 per cent in 2008. The increase in the labour force participation rate for women has several explanations, including changing social attitudes, federal and provincial legislation, increasing wages, and families in general having fewer children.

How Long Are People Typically Unemployed?

The longer a person is unemployed, the more hardship they endure. During the Great Depression, some people were unemployed for years at a time. In the modern Canadian economy, the typical person remains unemployed for only a few months. Table 5.1 shows the breakdown of the unemployment spells (a spell of unemployment is the length of time someone is unemployed) for 2006, 2010, and 2014. In 2006, the Canadian economy was growing steadily and jobs were relatively easy to get. In 2010, the Canadian economy was beginning to recover from the recession caused by the 2007–2008 US financial crisis and jobs were hard to find. Many people who were unemployed for long periods in 2010 had lost their jobs or tried to enter the work force during the recession of 2008–2009. In 2014, most regions of Canada had recovered from the recession, but many people were still spending much longer unemployed than before the recession.

In an economic boom, the length of time a person is unemployed tends to be quite short. In a boom, many new firms are started and existing firms expand, increasing the

Table 5.1

Length of Unemployment Before, During, and After a Recession

When the economy is shrinking, as in a recession, it is much harder for people to find new jobs. This makes the length of time people are unemployed a good indicator of the state of joblessness in the economy.

Source: Statistics Canada, Table 282-0048 - Labour force survey estimates (LFS), duration of unemployment by sex and age group, annual (persons unless otherwise noted), CANSIM (database). Reproduced and distributed on an "as is" basis with the permission of Statistics Canada.

Length of Time Unemployed	2006	2010	2014
Less than 4 weeks	37.5%	31.7%	33.2%
5 to 13 weeks	27.4%	26.5%	26.9%
14 to 25 weeks	12.7%	13.1%	14.6%
26 weeks or more	15.2%	22.3%	21.3%

opportunities for people to find work. In a recession, on the other hand, few firms are started and many reduce the number of workers they employ, making it exceptionally difficult for people to find new jobs. We can see by the portion of people who were unemployed for 26 weeks or longer in 2010 and 2014 that the Canadian economy still had not fully recovered from the recession caused by the financial crisis. In 2014, 21.3 percent of those who were unemployed were still without a job for more than six months.

Job Creation and Job Destruction over Time

One important fact about employment is little known: Thousands of jobs are created and lost in the Canadian economy every year. In November 2015, 124 000 more people had jobs than at the same time the year before. This means that there were at least 124 000 jobs more than just a year earlier. In fact, the number of jobs created over the period of time was much larger than 124 000, as some firms cut workers and went out of business altogether during the same period. In fact, the number of jobs in the economy fell by 36 000 between October and November of 2015. The really good news is that there was an increase in the number of full-time jobs between November 2014 and November 2015 (192 400) and a drop in part-time work (−68 400). Some provinces gained jobs and others lost them. Ontario gained 34 100 employees from November 2014 to November 2015. Over the same period of time, Newfoundland saw employment drop by 4500 jobs.

Different industries saw different changes as well. The professional, scientific, and technical services industry did well year over year, adding 56 000 jobs. The natural resource sector of the economy shrank from November 2014 to November 2015, with 26 400 fewer people working in that industry. Many other industries, like public administration (government), wholesale, and manufacturing remained essentially the same as one year earlier.[1]

Changes in the overall unemployment rate don't show you the whole picture of what is happening in the economy. Even when the unemployment rate is rising, some firms are hiring new employees and creating jobs. By the same token, even when the unemployment rate is falling, some firms are laying off workers or are going out of business entirely.

5.2   LEARNING OBJECTIVE

Identify the four types of unemployment.

Types of Unemployment

As Figure 5.3 illustrates, the unemployment rate follows the business cycle, rising during recessions and falling during expansions. Notice, though, that the unemployment rate never falls to zero. To understand why this is true, we need to discuss the four types of unemployment:

- Frictional unemployment

- Structural unemployment

- Cyclical unemployment

- Seasonal unemployment

---

[1]*Source:* Data from Statistics Canada – The Daily for December 4, 2015.

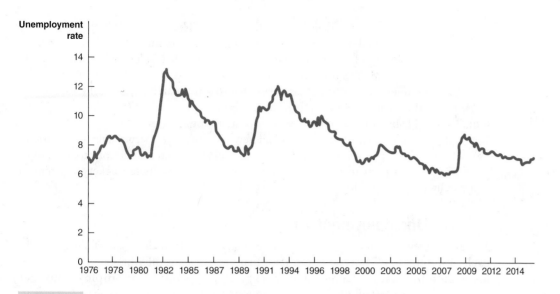

Figure 5.3 The Unemployment Rate in Canada, January 1976 to October 2015

The unemployment rate rises during recessions and falls during expansions. It's not hard to tell when the Canadian economy was performing poorly by looking at the unemployment rate. There were recessions in 1981–1982, early 1991–1992, and again in 2008–2009.

Source: Statistics Canada, Table 282-0087 - Labour force survey estimates (LFS), by sex and age group, seasonally adjusted and unadjusted, monthly (persons unless otherwise noted). Reproduced and distributed on an "as is" basis with the permission of Statistics Canada.

Frictional Unemployment and Job Search

Workers have different skills, interests, and abilities. Jobs have different skill requirements, working conditions, and pay levels. As a result, a new worker entering the labour force or a worker who has lost a job probably will not find an acceptable job right away. Most workers spend at least some time engaging in *job search*, just as most firms spend time searching for a new person to fill a job opening. **Frictional unemployment** is short-term unemployment that arises from the process of matching workers with jobs. Some frictional unemployment is unavoidable. As we have seen, the Canadian economy creates and destroys jobs all the time. The process of job search takes time, so there will always be some workers who are frictionally unemployed because they are between jobs and in the process of finding new ones.

Frictional unemployment Short-term unemployment that arises from the process of matching workers with jobs.

Would eliminating all frictional unemployment be good for the economy? No, because some frictional unemployment actually increases economic efficiency. Frictional unemployment occurs because workers and firms take the time necessary to ensure a good match between the attributes of workers and the characteristics of jobs. By devoting time to job search, workers end up with jobs they find more satisfying and in which they can be more productive. Of course, having more productive and better-satisfied workers is also in the best interest of firms.

Structural Unemployment

By 2015, computer-generated imagery (CGI), used in movies such as the Hobbit trilogy, many of the Marvel Universe movies, and just about every other popular action movie, had replaced most traditional or "practical" special effects. *Star Wars: The Force Awakens* was something of an exception. Many highly skilled make-up artists or model builders lost their jobs at movie studios due to this change. To become employed again, these workers either had to become skilled in computer-generated imagery or find new occupations. In the meantime, they were unemployed. Economists refer to these people as *structurally unemployed*. **Structural unemployment** arises from a persistent mismatch between the skills or attributes of workers and the requirements of jobs. While frictional unemployment is short term, structural unemployment can last for longer periods because workers need time to learn new skills. As the price of oil fell dramatically in 2014 and 2015, firms

Structural unemployment Unemployment that arises from a persistent mismatch between the skills and attributes of workers and the requirements of jobs.

in Alberta and Saskatchewan drilled many fewer wells. The drop in drilling meant many people who had worked on these provinces' oil rigs became unemployed. Some people previously employed working on the rigs found work in other industries. However, those with highly specialized skills had a difficult time finding new work without retraining.

Structural unemployment can also arise due to a mismatch between the location of workers and the location of new jobs. Those who have lost jobs in the fisheries of Newfoundland and Labrador have often had to relocate to the Prairies to find jobs as labourers. Before these people decided to move to find new jobs, they were structurally unemployed.

Workers that lack even basic skills, such as literacy, or have addictions to alcohol or other drugs find it particularly difficult to train for new jobs. These workers may remain structurally unemployed for years.

Cyclical Unemployment

Cyclical unemployment
Unemployment caused by a business cycle recession.

When the economy moves into recession, many firms find their sales falling and cut back on production. As production falls, firms start laying off workers. Workers who lose their jobs because of a recession are experiencing **cyclical unemployment**. For example, in February of 2009, Chrysler announced that it would temporarily close its assembly plant in Brampton, Ontario, due to low sales. Chrysler and other automakers have low sales when the economy is in a recession. The laid-off Chrysler employees experienced cyclical unemployment.

Seasonal Unemployment

Seasonal unemployment
Unemployment that is due to seasonal factors, such as weather or the fluctuation in demand for some products during different times of the year.

Some unemployment is due to seasonal factors, such as weather or the fluctuation in demand for some products during different times of the year. For example, ski resorts typically reduce their hiring during the summer months. Department stores increase their hiring in November and December and reduce their hiring after New Year's Day. In the fisheries, employment increases when the season opens and is much lower for the rest of the year. Construction workers often experience **seasonal unemployment** during the winter. Seasonal unemployment can make unemployment rates seem artificially high during some months and artificially low in others. As a result, Statistics Canada publishes two sets of unemployment figures each month: one that is *seasonally adjusted* and another that is not seasonally adjusted. The seasonally adjusted data eliminate the effects of seasonal unemployment. Economists and policymakers use the seasonally adjusted unemployment statistics as a more accurate reflection of the state of the labour market. From this point forward, when we talk about the unemployment rate, you can assume that we are discussing the seasonally adjusted unemployment rate.

Full Employment

As the economy moves through the expansion phase of the business cycle, cyclical unemployment eventually drops to zero. The unemployment rate will not be zero, however, because of frictional and structural unemployment. As Figure 5.3 shows, the unemployment rate in Canada hasn't been below 6 percent in the last 35 years. When the only remaining unemployment is structural and frictional unemployment, the economy is said to be at *full employment*.

Natural rate of unemployment
The normal rate of unemployment, consisting of frictional unemployment plus structural unemployment.

Economists consider frictional and structural unemployment as the normal underlying level of unemployment in the economy. The sum of frictional and structural unemployment is referred to as the **natural rate of unemployment**. The fluctuations of the rate of unemployment, which we see in Figure 5.3, are mainly due to changes in cyclical unemployment. Unfortunately, economists disagree on the exact value of the natural rate of unemployment, and there is good reason to believe it varies over time. Many estimate that the natural rate of unemployment for Canada is between 6.5 percent and 7.5 percent. The natural rate of unemployment is also sometimes called the *full-employment rate of unemployment*.

You will notice that the official rate of unemployment as reported by Statistics Canada is different from the natural rate of employment most of the time. The natural rate is a theoretical concept that represents the portion of the labour force that would be unemployed if everything in the economy was going well and only structural and frictional unemployment occur. The official rate of unemployment reported by Statistics Canada is a measure of what is actually happening in the economy, and includes cyclical unemployment in addition to structural and frictional unemployment. The official rate of unemployment is equal to the natural rate of unemployment only when cyclical unemployment is zero.

Making	**How Should We Categorize the**
the	**Unemployment of Laid-off TV News**
Connection	**Employees?**

The people who lost their jobs at CHCH TV fit into more than one category of unemployment.

In December 2015, CHCH TV, an independent broadcaster based in Hamilton, Ontario, announced it had cut at least 129 full-time employees in its local news division, potentially leaving only one independent TV news broadcaster in Canada. These job losses were a consequence of falling advertising revenue from national advertisers. As more and more people get their news from online sources rather than television, firms are spending more on online ads. The low level of economic growth taking place adds to the problem as firms look to make cost savings everywhere—including in their advertising budget.

We can categorize the unemployment caused by CHCH's decision in three ways: cyclical unemployment, frictional unemployment, or structural unemployment. To know which type of unemployment applies in this case, we have to consider the situation more carefully.

Workers who lose their jobs due to the state of the economy are classified as *cyclically unemployed*. CHCH TV's news division was supported by both local and national advertising. Demand for this sort of advertising is sensitive to the business cycle. If CHCH TV's layoffs were in response to the businesses cutting back on advertising during a recession, the laid-off workers would be classified as *cyclically unemployed*.

Frictional unemployment occurs when new entrants to the labour force or displaced workers search for a new job. In Ontario, there are a number of television stations that produce news programs. If the laid-off workers are able to find work at one of these other stations fairly quickly, they would be classified as *frictionally unemployed*.

Structural unemployment occurs when a new technology or production process leads to a mismatch between the skills workers have and the requirements of jobs. In this case, CHCH TV's news service has been replaced by Internet news. Writing Internet news/blog posts or running a website requires a different set of skills than doing the hair and make-up of a TV news anchor. If the laid-off workers are unable to find work at another TV station and must learn new skills to find other work, they would be classified as *structurally unemployed*.

Based on CHCH TV announces massive layoffs as part of restructuring plan, http://www.thestar.com/news/gta/2015/12/11/chch-tv-cancels-friday-night-newscast-causing-speculation-on-stations-future.html.

Your Turn: Test your understanding by doing related problem 2.3 on page 127 at the end of this chapter.

MyEconLab

Explaining Unemployment

5.3 LEARNING OBJECTIVE
Explain what factors determine the unemployment rate.

We have seen that some unemployment is a result of the business cycle. In later chapters, we will explore the causes of the business cycle, which will help us understand the causes of cyclical unemployment. In this section, we will look at the factors that determine the levels of frictional and structural unemployment.

Government Policies and the Unemployment Rate

Workers generally search for jobs by sending out resumés, registering with Internet job sites such as Monster.ca, and getting referrals from friends and relatives. Firms fill job openings by advertising in newspapers, listing openings online, participating in job fairs, and recruiting on university campuses. Government policy can aid these private efforts. Governments can help reduce the level of frictional unemployment by pursuing policies that speed up the process of matching employees with employers. Governments can reduce structural unemployment by implementing policies that aid worker retraining.

Some government policies, however, can add to the level of frictional and structural unemployment. These government policies increase the unemployment rate either by increasing the time workers devote to searching for jobs, by providing disincentives for firms to hire workers, or by keeping wages above the market-clearing wage (or *equilibrium wage*).

Employment Insurance. Suppose that you have been in the labour force for a few years, but have just lost your job. You could probably find a low-wage job immediately if you needed to—perhaps at Walmart or McDonald's. Instead, you decide to search for a better, higher-paying job by sending out resumés and responding to want ads and online job postings. Remember from Chapter 1 that the *opportunity cost* of any activity is the highest-valued alternative that you must give up to engage in that activity. In this case, the opportunity cost of continuing to search for a job is the salary you are giving up at the job you didn't take (say, at McDonald's). The longer you search, the greater your chances of finding a better, higher-paying job, but the longer you search, the more salary you have given up by not working, so the greater the total cost of searching.

In Canada and most other industrial countries, people are eligible for payments from the government if they become unemployed. The Canadian program for supporting unemployed workers is called *Employment Insurance (EI)*. While conditions and payments vary by region, EI will replace 55 percent of your earnings up to a maximum of $537 per week (in 2016). The unemployed receiving EI payments spend more time searching for jobs because the opportunity cost of job search is lower. The additional time people spend searching for a job raises the unemployment rate (recall the definition of *unemployed* that appears on page 107). Does this mean that EI is a bad idea? Most economists would say it is a good idea. If not for the EI program, unemployed workers would suffer very large declines in their income, which would lead them to greatly reduce spending, which would make any recession worse. EI helps the unemployed maintain their incomes and spending, which also reduces the personal hardship of being unemployed. Finally, EI helps both workers and firms make "good matches." Allowing unemployed people to spend more time searching for an appropriate job means more people find jobs that are appropriate to their skills and tastes. The better the match between employer and employee, the more productive the economy will be.

Minimum Wage Laws, Each province and territory in Canada sets the lowest legal wage that firms can pay workers. As of October 2016, the highest minimum wage was $13 in Nunavut, and the lowest was $10.65 in New Brunswick. If the minimum wage is set above the market-clearing wage (determined by the demand and supply of labour), the quantity of labour supplied will be greater than the quantity of labour demanded. Some workers will be unemployed who would have been employed if there were no minimum wage. As a result, the unemployment rate will be higher than it would be without a minimum wage. Economists agree that the current minimum wage is above the market-clearing wage for some workers, but they disagree on the amount of unemployment that minimum wages cause. Teenagers, with relatively few job-related skills, are one of the groups most likely to receive the minimum wage. Some studies have estimated that a 10 percent increase in the minimum wage reduces teenage employment by about 2 percent. Despite this impact on teenagers, most economists agree that current minimum wages have only a small impact on the overall unemployment rate.

Labour Unions

Labour unions are organizations of workers that bargain with employers for higher wages and better working conditions for their members. In unionized industries, the wage is usually above the market-clearing wage. This higher wage results in employers in unionized industries hiring fewer workers. Does this reduction in hiring by unionized firms significantly increase the unemployment rate? Most economists would say the answer is no. By the end of 2015, the last year for which data was available, about 28.6 percent of Canadian workers belonged to a union. The vast majority of government employees, 72.4 percent, are members of a union. In the private sector, only 15 percent of workers are unionized.[2] This means that most of the workers not able to find jobs in unionized industries are able to find jobs in other areas.

Efficiency Wages

Many firms pay wages that are higher than the market-clearing wage, not because the government requires them to or because a union has negotiated a contract, but because they believe doing so will increase their profits. This may seem strange at first: Wages are the largest cost for many employers, so paying higher wages seems like a good way for firms to reduce profits rather than increase them. The key to understanding why firms might want to pay higher wages is that the level of wages can influence worker productivity. Many studies have shown that workers are motivated to work harder by higher wages. An **efficiency wage** is a higher-than-market wage that a firm pays to motivate workers to be more productive. Can't firms ensure that workers work hard by supervising them? In some cases, they can. For example, when you phone a call centre, you often hear this message: "This call may be monitored for quality assurance and training purposes." In many situations, however, it is much harder to monitor workers. Many firms must rely on workers being motivated enough to work hard. By paying a wage above the market-clearing wage, a firm raises the cost to workers of losing their jobs because many other available jobs pay less. The increase in productivity that results from paying a higher wage can more than offset the extra cost of the wage, meaning that the firm's costs of production actually falls.

Efficiency wage A higher-than-market wage that a firm pays to increase worker productivity.

When firms pay efficiency wages, the quantity of labour supplied will exceed the quantity of labour demanded. As with minimum wage laws or unions, a supply of labour larger than the demand for labour leads to unemployment. Efficiency wages are another reason we don't see an unemployment rate of zero, even in an economic boom.

Making the **Connection**	**Why Does Costco Pay Its Workers More than Walmart?**

The concept of efficiency wages raises the possibility that firms might find it more profitable to pay higher wages even when they don't have to. We might expect that a firm would maximize profits by paying the lowest wages at which it was possible to hire all the workers the firm needs. But if low wages significantly reduce worker productivity, then paying higher wages can actually reduce costs and increase profits. Walmart and Costco are international competitors in the discount department store industry, but the two have taken different approaches to compensating their employees.

Walmart employs about 95 000 people in Canada and about 2.1 million employees worldwide. Costco employs thousands of people in Canada and almost 150 000 employees around the world. While Walmart generally pays new employees the minimum wage, Costco pays new employees well above the minimum wage—$2 or $3 above, in some cases.

---

[2]*Source:* Statistics Canada. Table 282-0223 - Labour Force Survey estimates (LFS), employees by union status, North American Industry Classification System (NAICS) and sex, Canada (table), CANSIM (database), Using E-STAT (distributor). Reproduced and distributed on an "as is" basis with the permission of Statistics Canada.

Why does Costco pay so much more to its employees than Walmart does? Costco's chief executive officer, Jim Sinegal, argues that paying higher wages reduces employee turnover, and raises morale and productivity: "Paying good wages and keeping your people working for you is very good business . . . Imagine that you have 120 000 loyal ambassadors out there who are constantly saying good things about Costco. It has to be a significant advantage for you." However, it is likely that the higher wages Costco pays are not entirely due to an efficiency wage strategy. Unlike Walmart, Costco charges a fee of at least $50 per year to shop in its stores. The typical Costco store stocks only about 4000 items, as opposed to the 100 000 items carried by the average Walmart store. Costco stores also sell more big-ticket items, such as higher-priced jewellery and consumer electronics. As a result, the average income of Costco customers is a lot higher than the average income of Walmart customers. One observer concludes that Costco pays higher wages than Walmart "because it requires higher-skilled workers to sell higher-end products to its more affluent customers." So, even if Costco were not pursuing a strategy of paying efficiency wages, it is likely that it would still have to pay higher wages than Walmart.

Based on Alan B. Goldberg and Bill Ritter. "Costco CEO Finds Pro-Worker Means Profitability," ABCNews.com, August 2, 2006; Lori Montgomery, "Maverick CEO Joins Push to Raise Minimum Wage," *Washington Post*, January 30, 2007; and John Tierney, "The Good Goliath," *New York Times*, November 29, 2005.

MyEconLab

Your Turn: Test your understanding by doing related problem 2.4 on page 127 at the end of this chapter.

5.4 **LEARNING** OBJECTIVE

Define price level and inflation rate, and understand how they are computed.

Inflation A general increase in the prices of goods and services over time.

Price level A measure of the average prices of goods and services in the economy.

Inflation rate The percentage increase in the price level from one year to the next.

Measuring Inflation

One of the facts of economic life is that the prices of most goods and services rise over time, a process known as **inflation**. As a result, the cost of living continually rises. In 1914, in the United States, Henry Ford famously began paying his workers $5 a day, more than twice what Ford's competitors were paying. While it would be illegal for anyone in Canada to work for as little as $5 an *hour* today, at the time, Ford's $5 workday meant his employees could enjoy a comfortable middle-class lifestyle. In 1914, you could buy a number of goods with just a nickel or even a penny. Today, even dollar stores charge more than a dollar for most things.

Knowing how employment and unemployment statistics are compiled is important in understanding what they mean. The same is true of the statistics on the cost of living. As we saw in Chapter 4, the **price level** measures the average prices of goods and services in the economy. The **inflation rate** is the percentage increase in the price level from one year to the next. In Chapter 4, we introduced the *GDP deflator* as a measure of the price level. The GDP deflator is the broadest measure we have of the price level because it includes the price of every final good and service produced in the country. Recall that the GDP deflator is calculated as the ratio of Nominal GDP to Real GDP times 100.

The GDP deflator isn't the best measure of price level in every circumstance, as it includes goods and services that households don't consume (like large-scale electric generators) and does not include many of the goods and services that households consume. In particular, the GDP deflator excludes the price of imports and includes the price of goods made for export. In this chapter we introduce you to another measure of price level that better reflects the cost of living, called the *consumer price index*. We also briefly discuss a third measure of the price level, called the *producer price index*.

The Consumer Price Index

The idea behind the *consumer price index (CPI)* is to measure changes in the prices faced by the average household. To figure out what goods and services the average household buys, Statistics Canada conducts the Survey of Household Spending each year. The survey asks 16 758 Canadian households about their purchasing habits, including what they buy, how much they buy, and where they buy it. Based on the results of the survey,

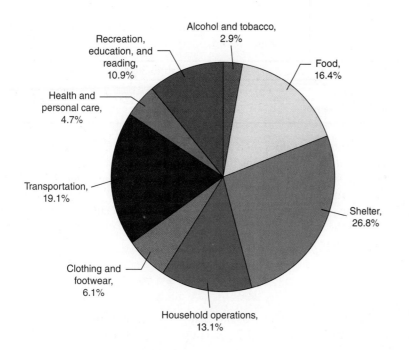

Figure 5.4

The CPI Basket, 2015

Statistics Canada surveys 16 758 Canadian households on their spending habits. The results are used to construct a basket of goods and services purchased by a typical household. The chart shows these goods and services, grouped into eight broad categories. The percentages represent the expenditure shares of the categories within the basket. The categories of shelter, transportation, and food account for about two-thirds of the basket.

Data from Canadian CPI Basket of Goods and Services, http://inflationcalculator.ca/cpi-basket/

Statistics Canada constructs a shopping list, or basket of goods and services, that the average household buys. The types of goods and services that are included in the basket are updated every few years to reflect changing purchasing habits. The most recent basket of goods and services is based on what consumers bought in 2015. The prices of the goods and services in the basket are researched in stores in various cities across the country each month to ensure they are up to date.

The weight of each good and service in the basket (somewhat like the amount of each item put into a shopping basket) is based on the results of the Survey of Household Spending. Figure 5.4 shows the goods and services included in the basket grouped into eight broad categories.

The **consumer price index (CPI)** is an average of the prices of the goods and services in the basket. One year is chosen as the base year, and the value of the CPI is set equal to 100 for that year. In any year other than the base year, the CPI is equal to the ratio of the dollar amount necessary to buy the basket of goods and services in that year to the dollar amount required to purchase the same basket of goods and services in the base year, multiplied by 100. Because the CPI measures the price of the goods and services that the average household buys, it is a fairly good indicator of the cost of living.

A simple example can clarify how the CPI is constructed. For the purposes of this example, we assume that the basket has only three products in it: root beer, pizzas, and movies:

Consumer price index (CPI) An average of the prices of the goods and services purchased by a typical household.

Product	Quantity	Base Year (2002) Price	Base Year (2002) Expenditures	2014 Price	2014 Expenditures (on base-year quantities)	2015 Price	2015 Expenditures (on base-year quantities)
Root beer	1	$50.00	$50.00	$100.00	$100.00	$85.00	$85.00
Pizzas	20	10.00	200.00	15.00	300.00	14.00	280.00
Movies	20	25.00	500.00	25.00	500.00	27.50	550.00
TOTAL			$750.00		$900.00		$915.00

Suppose that during the base year of 2002, a survey determines that each month the typical family purchases 1 case of root beer, 20 pizzas, and 20 movies. At 2002 prices, the typical family must spend $750.00 to purchase this basket of goods and services. The CPI for every year after the base year is determined by dividing the amount necessary to purchase the basket in that year by the amount required in the base year, multiplied by 100. Notice that the quantities of the products purchased in 2014 and 2015 are irrelevant in calculating the CPI because *we are assuming that households buy exactly the same basket of goods every month*. Using the numbers in the table, we can calculate the CPI for 2014 and 2015:

Formula		Applied to 2014	Applied to 2015
$CPI = \dfrac{\text{Expenditures now}}{\text{Expenditures in base year}} \times 100$		$\dfrac{\$900}{\$750} \times 100 = 120$	$\dfrac{\$915}{\$750} \times 100 = 122$

How do we interpret values such as 120 or 122? The first thing to recognize is that they are *index numbers*, which means that they are not measured in dollars or any other units. *The CPI is intended to measure changes in the price level over time.* We can't use the CPI to tell us in an absolute sense how high the price level is—only how much it has changed over time. We measure the inflation rate as the percentage increase in the CPI from one year to the next. For our simple example, the inflation rate in 2015 would be the percentage change in the CPI from 2014 to 2015:

$$\frac{122 - 120}{120} \times 100 = 1.7\%$$

Because the CPI is a measure of the changes in the cost of living, we can also say that the cost of living increased by 1.7 percent between 2014 and 2015.

Making the Connection | Prices Will Rise

That prices rise over time is something that economists take for granted. If you talk to someone much older than you for a while, often you end up hearing stories about how things were so much cheaper when they were young—and how young folks respected their elders back then too. There is a problem with simply comparing the prices of something now to prices many years ago. Just because something cost a lot less in 1915 doesn't mean it was really cheaper. In 1915, a lot of Canadians received their purchases through the mail, just like more and more people are doing today, but ordering was done through printed catalogues rather than webpages. One of the most common catalogues in Canada was produced by Eaton's, which sold pretty much everything from farm equipment and houses to children's toys. While many of these goods have changed beyond recognition, socks haven't changed that much over the last 100 years. It is still possible to purchase socks that look pretty much the same as they would have in 1915. Consider the cashmere socks in the Fall/Winter 1915 Eaton's Catalogue.

In 1915, cashmere socks were selling for 35 cents a pair. Today, you are lucky if you can find anything to buy with just 35 cents. In fact, cashmere socks that look very similar are available on Amazon.ca for $39—more than 100 times as much as they cost in 1915. Does this mean that socks are really more expensive now than they were in 1915? Not necessarily. In 1915, Canada's output per person was $337 while today it $55 500. The average income in 1915 would buy 963 pairs of cashmere socks, while the average income in 2015 would buy 1423 pairs of socks. Put differently, the price of a nice pair of socks increased 111 times between 1915 and 2015, while output per person increased 165 time over the same period.

The CPI tells a very similar story. In 1915 the CPI was 6.1 and in 2015 the CPI was 127.1, an increase of 20 times. Using the CPI to convert into modern day prices, that 35-cent pair of socks would cost $72.93 rather than $39. Socks were actually more expensive in 1915 than they are today!

Based on GNP from New Estimates of Gross National Product, Canada 1870-1926: Some implications for Canadian Development. M.C. Urquhart. In *Long-Term Factors in American Economic Growth*. S. Engerman and R. Gallman, eds. NBER, University of Chicago Press. 1986.

Is the CPI Accurate?

The CPI is the most widely reported measure of inflation. Policymakers use the CPI to track the state of the economy. Businesses use it to help set the prices they charge and the wages they pay their employees. Each year, the federal government increases payments to seniors based on the CPI over the previous year.

It is important that the CPI be as accurate as possible, but there are four biases that cause changes in the CPI to overstate the true rate of inflation experienced by households:

- **Substitution bias.** In constructing the CPI, Statistics Canada assumes that each month, households purchase exactly the same amount of each product in the basket. In fact, households are likely to buy less of a product when its price increases relative to other goods. For example, if apple prices rise rapidly while orange prices fall, households will reduce their apple purchases and increase their orange purchases. Therefore, the prices of the basket households actually buy will rise less than the prices of the basket Statistics Canada uses to compute the CPI.

- **Increase in quality bias.** Over time, most products included in the CPI improve in quality: Cars become safer and more fuel efficient, computers become faster and have more memory, and so on. Increases in the prices of these products partly reflect their improved quality and partly are pure inflation.

- **New product bias.** The CPI shopping list isn't updated every time a new product comes out (or an existing product becomes unpopular). This means that new products introduced between updates are not included in the basket. For example, iPads weren't available when the basket was last updated, so any change in the price of iPads won't be captured by the CPI (if iPads largely replace other, more expensive devices such as desktop computers, that wouldn't be captured either). This bias applies to all new products that become popular quickly.

- **Outlet bias.** During the 1990s, consumers began to increase their purchases from discount stores such as Walmart and Costco. Over the past decade, the Internet has also become a significant retail source for Canadians. If the CPI basket is not updated to reflect changes in where people buy things, the CPI will overstate inflation.

Most economists believe these biases cause changes in the CPI to overstate the true rate of inflation from 0.5 percentage point to 1 percentage point. That is, if the CPI indicates that the inflation rate was 3 percent, the true inflation rate is probably between 2 and 2.5 percent.

Don't Let This Happen to You

Don't Miscalculate the Inflation Rate

Suppose you are given the data in the following table and are asked to calculate the inflation rate for 2018:

Year	CPI
2017	216
2018	219

It is tempting to avoid calculations and simply to report that the inflation rate in 2018 was 119 percent because 219 is a 119 percent increase from 100. But 119 would be the wrong inflation rate. A value for the CPI of 219 in 2018 tells us that the price level in 2018 was 119 percent higher than in the base year, but the inflation rate is the percentage increase from the previous year, not from the base year. The correct calculation of the inflation rate for 2018 is:

$$\left(\frac{219 - 216}{216} \right) \times 100 = 1.4\%$$

MyEconLab

Your Turn: Test your understanding by doing related problem 4.1 on page 127 at the end of this chapter.

The Producer Price Index

Producer price index (PPI) An average of the prices received by producers of goods and services at all stages of production.

In addition to the GDP deflator and the CPI, Statistics Canada also computes the **producer price index (PPI)**. Like the CPI, the PPI tracks the prices of a basket of goods and services. However, unlike the CPI, the PPI tracks the prices that firms receive for goods and services at all stages of production. The PPI includes the prices of intermediate goods (such as flour, cotton, yarn, steel, and lumber) and raw materials (such as coal and crude oil). If the prices of these goods rise, the cost to firms of producing final goods and services will rise, which may lead firms to increase the prices of the goods and services they sell to consumers. Changes in the PPI can give an early warning of future movements in the CPI.

5.5   LEARNING OBJECTIVE

Use price indexes to adjust data for the effects of inflation.

Using Price Indexes to Adjust for the Effects of Inflation

You are likely to receive a much higher salary after graduation than your parents or professor did when they started their first job, say 25 years ago. On the other hand, prices were much lower 25 years ago than they are today. Put another way, the purchasing power of a dollar was much higher 25 years ago because the prices of most goods were much lower. Price indexes such as the CPI give us a way of adjusting for the effects of inflation so that we can compare dollar values from different years. For example, suppose your mother received a salary of $30 000 in 1990. By using the CPI, we can calculate what $30 000 in 1990 would be equivalent to 2015. The CPI in 1990 was 79.5 and 127.2 in 2015. As 127.2/79.5 = 1.6, we know that on average prices were 1.6 time as high in 2015 as they were in 1990. We can use this result to inflate a salary of $30 000 received in 1990 to its value in terms of 2015 purchasing power.

$$Value\ in\ 2015\ dollars = Value\ in\ 1990\ dollars \times \frac{CPI\ in\ 2015}{CPI\ in\ 1990}$$

$$= \$30\,000 \times \frac{127.2}{79.5} = \$48\,000$$

Our calculation shows that if you were paid a salary of $48 000 in 2015, you would be able to purchase roughly the same amount of goods and services that your mother could have purchased with a salary of $30 000 in 1990. Economic variables that are calculated in current year prices are referred to as *nominal variables*. The calculation we have just made uses a price index to adjust a nominal variable—your mother's starting salary—for the effects of inflation.

For some purposes, we are interested in tracking changes in an economic variable over time rather than seeing what its value would be in today's dollars. In that case, to correct for the effects of inflation, we can divide the nominal variable by a price index and multiply by 100 to obtain a *real variable*. The real variable will be measured in dollars of the base year for the price index. In 2016 the base year for the CPI was 2002.

Solved Problem 5.1

Calculating Real Hourly Wages

Suppose your economics professor is complaining about how lucky students have it today compared with when your professor was an undergraduate student. In those days, while working through an undergraduate degree, your professor had to take a part-time job that paid the minimum wage of $5 an hour, way back in 1992. Your professor moans that the minimum wage where you live is $11 an hour. You can make twice as much today! Is your professor right in complaining about "how easy young folks have it today"?

Solving the Problem

Step 1: **Review the chapter material.** This problem is about using price indexes to correct for inflation, so you may want to review the section "Using Price Indexes to Adjust for the Effects of Inflation" on the previous page.

Step 2: **Calculate the real hourly wage for each year.** To calculate the real hourly wage for each year, divide the nominal hourly wage by the CPI and multiply by 100. In this case:

Real 1992 Wage	Real 2015 Wage
$\frac{\$5}{84} \times 100 = \$5.95$	$\frac{\$11}{127.2} \times 100 = \$8.65$

We can conclude that someone earning minimum wage today is in fact earning more than your professor did as an undergraduate student.

Your Turn: For more practice, do related problems 5.1 and 5.2 on page 127 at the end of this chapter.

MyEconLab

Real versus Nominal Interest Rates

5.6 LEARNING OBJECTIVE

Distinguish between the nominal interest rate and the real interest rate.

The difference between real and nominal values is important when borrowing and lending money. The *interest rate* is the cost of borrowing money expressed as a percentage of the amount borrowed. If a firm borrowed $1000 from you for a year and charge an interest rate of 6 percent, the firm will have to pay back $1060, or 6 percent more than you lent them. But is $1060 received a year from now really 6 percent more than $1000 today? If prices rise during the year, you will not be able to buy as much with the $1060 you receive at the end of the year than you would have if you had $1060 at the beginning of the year. Your true return from lending the $1000 is equal to the percentage change in your purchasing power after taking into account the effects of inflation.

The stated interest rate on a loan is the **nominal interest rate**. The **real interest rate** corrects the nominal interest rate for the effect of inflation on the purchasing power of money. Essentially, the real interest rate is the amount of extra buying power you pay back (or get, if you're the lender) when a loan is repaid. As a simple example, suppose that the only good you purchase is coffee, and at the beginning of the year a cup of coffee costs $2.00. With $1000, you can buy 500 cups of coffee. If you lend the $1000 out for one year at an interest rate of 6 percent, you will receive $1060 at the end of the year. Suppose the inflation rate during the year is 2.5 percent, so the price of coffee has risen to $2.05 by the end of the year. How has your purchasing power increased as a result of making the loan? At the beginning of the year, your $1000 could have bought 500 cups of coffee. At the end of the year, your $1060 can buy $1060/$2.05 = 517 cups of coffee. In other words, you can purchase 3.4 percent more coffee than you could at the beginning of the year. In this case, the real interest rate you received from lending was 3.4 percent. For low rates of inflation, a convenient approximation of the real interest rate is:

Real interest rate = Nominal interest rate − Inflation rate.

Nominal interest rate The stated interest rate on a loan.

Real interest rate The nominal interest rate minus the inflation rate.

In our example, we can calculate the real interest rate by using this formula as 6 percent − 2.5 percent = 3.5 percent, which is close to the 3.4 percent we calculated above (this result would be even closer if we included the 0.0731707 of a cup of coffee you could have bought with the $1060 you had at the end of the year that we left out due to rounding). Holding the nominal interest rate constant, the higher the inflation rate, the lower the real interest rate. Notice that if the inflation rate turns out to be higher than expected, borrowers pay and lenders receive a lower real interest rate than either of them expected. For example, if the actual inflation rate is 5 percent instead of the 2.5 both you and the borrower expected, the real interest rate will be 1 percent instead of the 3.5 percent you thought you were going to get. This is bad news for you, but good news for your borrower.

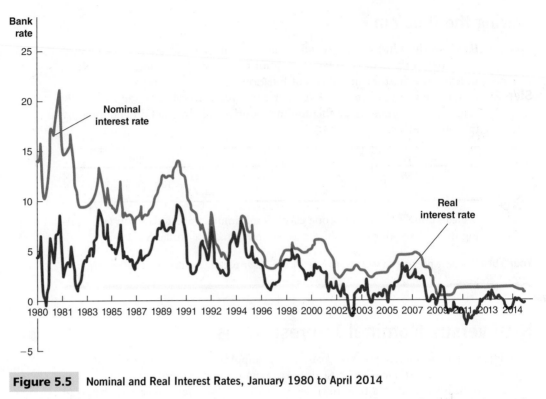

Figure 5.5 Nominal and Real Interest Rates, January 1980 to April 2014

The real interest rate is equal to the nominal interest rate minus the inflation rate. The real interest rate provides a better measure of the true cost of borrowing and the true return to lending than does the nominal interest rate. The nominal interest rate in the figure is the bank rate. The inflation rate is measured by the percentage change in the CPI from the same month one year earlier.

Data from Table 326-0020 - Consumer Price Index, monthly (2002=100 unless otherwise noted), Statistics Canada.

You have likely heard people talk about a number of different interest rates. The *prime rate* is the rate at which the most credit-worthy businesses can borrow. The *conventional mortgage rate* is the rate at which the most credit-worthy individuals can borrow to purchase a house. The *overnight rate* is the rate at which banks can borrow from other banks for a period of 24 hours. The *bank rate* is the rate at which the Bank of Canada (our central bank) will lend to commercial banks. In general, all of the interest rates tend to move up when the bank rate increases and down when the bank rate falls. Figure 5.5 shows the key nominal interest rate in the Canadian economy and an estimate of the real interest rate. In periods when inflation is high, as was the case in the early 1980s, the nominal interest rate is high and the gap between the nominal interest rate and the real interest rate is large. When inflation is low, as was the case in the recession of 2008 to 2009, the nominal interest rate is low and the gap between the nominal interest rate and the real interest rate is quite small.

It is difficult to know whether a particular nominal interest rate involves a high cost of borrowing or a low cost of borrowing. In August 1980, the nominal interest rate was 10.45 percent, which seems fairly high, but once we account for inflation, the real interest rate was actually *negative* 0.5 percent. A negative real interest rate means that the total amount you pay back from your loan can buy *less* than the amount you borrowed in the first place. By the same token, a low nominal interest rate doesn't always mean that borrowing is cheap. In June 1994, the nominal interest rate was almost 7 percent, but inflation was effectively zero at that time. This means that the real interest rate was actually 7 percent.

5.7 LEARNING OBJECTIVE

Discuss the problems inflation can cause.

Does Inflation Impose Costs on the Economy?

Imagine waking up tomorrow and finding that the price of everything has doubled. The prices of food, gas, computers, movies, pizzas, and beer have all doubled. But suppose that all wages and salaries have also doubled. Will this doubling of prices and wages matter? Think about walking into Best Buy, expecting to spend $800 on a new iPhone. Instead you find that iPhones now cost $1600. Will you leave without one? Probably not, because you know that you're now getting paid $50 000 a year instead of the $25 000 per year you were making yesterday. Even though prices have doubled, your purchasing power has stayed exactly the same.

This fantasy situation makes an important point: Nominal income generally increases with inflation. Remember from Chapter 4 that we can think of the $800 price of the iPhone as representing either the value of the product or the value of all the income generated in producing the product. The two amounts are the same, whether the iPhone sells for $800 or $1600. When the price of the iPhone rises from $800 to $1600, that extra $800 ends up as income that goes to the workers at Apple, Foxconn (the manufacturers of the iPhone), sales staff at Best Buy, and the stockholders of Apple, just like the first $800 did.

It's tempting to think that the problem with inflation is that, as prices rise, consumers can no longer afford to buy as many goods and services, but our example shows that this isn't always the case. Rising prices don't always mean we can afford less (ask your grandparents what they could afford when they were your age). An expected inflation rate of 10 percent will raise the average price of goods and services by 10 percent, but it will also rise average incomes by 10 percent. Goods and services will be as affordable to the average consumer as they were before inflation.

Inflation Affects the Distribution of Income

If inflation doesn't reduce the affordability of goods and services to the average consumer, why do people dislike inflation? One reason is that there are very few *average people*. Some people will find their incomes rising faster than the rate of inflation, and so their purchasing power will rise. Other people will find their incomes rising more slowly than the rate of inflation, causing their purchasing power to fall. People on fixed incomes are particularly likely to be hurt by inflation. If a retired worker receives a fixed pension of $3000 per month, over time, inflation will reduce the purchasing power of that payment. In this way, inflation can change the distribution of income in a way that strikes many as being unfair.

The extent to which inflation redistributes income depends in part on whether the inflation is *anticipated*—in which case consumers, workers, and firms can see it coming and can prepare for it—or *unanticipated*—in which case they do not see it coming and do not prepare for it.

The Problem with Anticipated Inflation

Like many of life's problems, inflation is easier to deal with if you see it coming. Suppose that everyone knows that the inflation rate for the next 10 years will be 10 percent per year. Workers know that unless their wages go up by at least 10 percent per year, the real purchasing power of their wages will fall. Businesses will be willing to increase workers' wages enough to compensate for inflation because they know that the prices they can charge for their products will also increase. Lenders will realize that the loans they make will be paid back with dollars that are worth less than they were a year before, so they charge higher interest rates to compensate for this fact. Borrowers are willing to pay the higher interest rates because they also know the dollars they pay back will buy less than the ones they borrowed. So far, there do not seem to be any costs to anticipated inflation.

Even when inflation is perfectly anticipated, some individuals will experience a cost. Inevitably, there will be a redistribution of income, as some people's incomes do not grow at the same rate as anticipated inflation. In addition, firms and consumers have to hold some paper money to facilitate their buying and selling. Anyone holding paper money will find its purchasing power decreasing every year by the rate of inflation. To avoid this cost, firms and workers will try to hold as little paper money as possible, but they will have to hold some. In addition, to keep up with inflation, firms will have to change the price stickers on products and on shelves, which means paying someone to

Menu costs The costs to firms of changing prices.

do it. Restaurants will have to reprint their menus more often to make sure their prices keep up with inflation. The costs to firms of changing the prices they charge for their products are called **menu costs**. At moderate levels of anticipated inflation, menu costs are relatively small, but when anticipated inflation is high, menu costs and the costs of holding paper money can be substantial. Finally, even anticipated inflation acts to raise the taxes paid by investors and raises the cost of capital for business investment. These effects arise because investors are taxed on the nominal interest payments they receive rather than on the real interest payments.

The Problem with Unanticipated Inflation

In any advanced economy—such as Canada's—households, workers, and firms routinely enter into contracts that commit them to make or receive payments for years in the future. For example, your university will have negotiated a contract with your professors, which commits the university to pay them a specific wage or salary for the duration of the contract (usually three to four years). When people buy houses, they usually borrow most of the amount they need from a bank. These loans, called *mortgages*, commit a borrower to make fixed monthly payments for the length of the loan. Most mortgage loans are for periods of 25 years but must be renewed several times over the length of the loan.

To make these long-term commitments, households and firms must forecast the rate of inflation. If a firm believes the inflation rate over the next three years will be 6 percent per year, signing a three-year contract with a union that calls for wage increases of 8 percent per year may seem reasonable because the firm may be able to raise its prices by at least the rate of inflation each year. If the firm believes that inflation will only be 2 percent per year, paying wages that increase by 8 percent per year may significantly reduce profits or even force the firm out of business.

When people borrow or lend money, they must forecast the rate of inflation so they can calculate the real rate of interest. In the 1980s, it was not uncommon for banks to charge interest rates of 18 percent or more on a mortgage. This seems really high by today's standards, seeing that the interest rates on mortgages are generally 4 or 5 percent. However, inflation rates in the 1980s were 10 percent or so compared with the 2 to 3 percent we see today.

When the actual inflation rate turns out to be very different from the expected inflation rate, some people gain and some people lose. This outcome seems unfair to most people because they are either winning or losing only because something they did not expect has happened. This apparently unfair redistribution is a key reason why people dislike unanticipated inflation.

Economics in Your Life

Should You Change Your Career Plans If You Graduate during a Recession?

At the beginning of the chapter, we asked if layoffs in the energy industry should cause you to change your major and give up your plans to work for an energy company and switch your major to economics and finance instead. We have learned in this chapter that unemployment rates are higher and layoffs more common in a recession than in an economic expansion. Because you're only in the second year of your degree, you have a few years before you graduate, and by then the recession is likely to have ended and the unemployment rate will have fallen. You should probably investigate whether the layoffs in the energy sector represent a permanent contraction in the size of the industry or a short-term decline due to the recession. If the reduction in the size of the energy sector appears to be mostly related to the current recession, then you probably don't need to change your career path. If you believe the industry will be permanently smaller, then a change might be in your best interest.

Conclusion

Inflation and unemployment are key macroeconomic problems. Elections are often won and lost on the basis of which candidate and party is able to convince the public that they can best deal with these problems. Many economists, however, would argue that, in the long run, maintaining high rates of growth of real GDP per person is the most important macroeconomic concern. Only when real GDP per person is increasing will a country's standard of living increase. In Chapter 6, we discuss the important issue of economic growth.

Chapter Summary and Problems

Key Terms

Consumer price index (CPI), p. 117

Cyclical unemployment, p. 112

Discouraged workers, p. 108

Efficiency wage, p. 115

Employment–population ratio, p. 108

Frictional unemployment, p. 111

Inflation, p. 116

Inflation rate, p. 116

Labour force, p. 107

Labour force participation rate, p. 108

Menu costs, p. 124

Natural rate of unemployment, p. 112

Nominal interest rate, p. 121

Price level, p. 116

Producer price index (PPI), p. 120

Real interest rate, p. 121

Seasonal unemployment, p. 112

Structural unemployment, p. 111

Unemployment rate, p. 106

Working age population, p. 107

Summary

*LO 5.1 Statistics Canada uses the results of the Labour Force Survey to calculate the *unemployment rate*, the *labour force participation rate*, and the *employment-population ratio*. The *labour force* is the total number of people who have jobs plus the number of people who do not have jobs but are actively looking for them. The *unemployment rate* is the percentage of the labour force that is unemployed. *Discouraged workers* are people who are available for work but who are not actively looking for a job because they believe no jobs are available for them. Discouraged workers are not counted as unemployed. The *labour force participation rate* is the percentage of the working age population in the labour force. Since the 1970s, the participation rate of women has been rising, while the labour force participation of men has been falling. The *employment–population ratio* measures the portion of the working age population that is employed. Except for severe recessions, the typical unemployed person finds a new job or returns to his or her previous job within a few months. Each year, thousands of jobs are created in Canada, and thousands of jobs are destroyed.

LO 5.2 There are four types of unemployment: frictional, structural, cyclical, and seasonal. *Frictional unemployment* is short-term unemployment that arises from the process of matching workers with jobs. *Structural unemployment* arises from a persistent mismatch between the job skills or attributes of workers and the requirements of jobs. *Cyclical unemployment* is caused by a business cycle recession. *Seasonal unemployment* is due to factors such as weather, variations in tourism, legislation that restricts activities to certain times of year, and other calendar-related events. The *natural rate of unemployment* is the normal rate of unemployment, consisting of frictional unemployment plus structural unemployment. The

natural rate of unemployment is also sometimes called the *full-employment rate of unemployment*.

LO 5.3 Government policies can reduce the level of frictional and structural unemployment by aiding in the search for jobs and the retraining of workers. Some government policies, however, can add to the level of frictional, structural, and seasonal unemployment. Employment Insurance payments can raise the unemployment rate by extending the time that unemployed workers search for jobs and can reduce the incentive for seasonal workers to look for off-season work. Government policies in Canada (and most high-income countries) have led to unemployment rates that are historically higher than in the United States. Wages above market levels can also increase unemployment. Wages may be above market levels because of minimum wage laws, labour unions, and efficiency wages. An *efficiency wage* is a higher-than-market wage that a firm pays to increase worker productivity.

LO 5.4 The *price level* measures the average prices of goods and services in the economy. The *inflation rate* is equal to the percentage change in the price level from one year to the next. Statistics Canada compiles data on three different measures of the price level: the consumer price index (CPI), the GDP deflator, and the producer price index (PPI). The *consumer price index (CPI)* is an average of the prices of goods and services purchased by a typical household. Changes in the CPI are the best measure of changes in the cost of living as experienced by the typical household. Biases in the construction of the CPI cause changes in it to overstate the true inflation rate from between 0.5 percentage point to 1 percentage point. The *producer price index (PPI)* is an average of prices received by producers of goods and services at all stages of production.

*"Learning Objective" is abbreviated to "LO" in the end-of-chapter material.

LO 5.5 Price indexes are designed to measure changes in the price level over time, not the absolute level of prices. To correct for the effects of inflation, we can divide a *nominal variable* by a price index and multiply by 100 to obtain a *real variable*. The real variable will be measured in dollars of the base year for the price index.

LO 5.6 The stated interest rate on a loan is the *nominal interest rate*. The *real interest rate* is the nominal interest rate minus the inflation rate. Because it is corrected for the effects of inflation, the real interest rate provides a better measure of the true cost of borrowing and the true return from lending than does the nominal interest rate.

LO 5.7 Inflation does not reduce the affordability of goods and services to the average consumer, but it does impose costs on the economy. When inflation is anticipated, its main costs are that paper money loses some of its value and firms incur *menu costs*. *Menu costs* include the costs of changing prices on products and printing new catalogues. When inflation is unanticipated, the actual inflation rate can turn out to be different from the expected inflation rate. As a result, income is redistributed as some people gain and some people lose.

MyEconLab Log in to MyEconLab to complete these exercises and get instant feedback.

Review Questions

LO 5.1

1.1 How is the unemployment rate measured? What are the three conditions someone needs to meet to be counted as unemployed?

1.2 What are the problems in measuring the unemployment rate? In what ways does the official Statistics Canada measure of the unemployment rate *overstate* the true degree of unemployment? In what ways does the official Statistics Canada measure of the unemployment rate *understate* the true degree of unemployment?

LO 5.2

2.1 What are the four types of unemployment?

2.2 What is the natural rate of unemployment? What is the relationship between the natural rate of unemployment and full employment? Would it be better for economists to define full employment as being an unemployment rate equal to zero?

LO 5.3

3.1 What effect does the payment of Employment Insurance have on the unemployment rate? On the severity of recessions?

3.2 Discuss the effect of each of the following on the unemployment rate.
   a. Provincial minimum wage laws
   b. Labour unions
   c. Efficiency wages

LO 5.4

4.1 Briefly describe the three major measures of the price level.

4.2 What potential biases exist in calculating the consumer price index?

LO 5.5

5.1 What is the difference between a nominal variable and a real variable?

5.2 Briefly explain how you can use data on nominal wages for 2004 to 2016 and data on the consumer price index for the same years to calculate the real wage for these years.

LO 5.6

6.1 What is the difference between the nominal interest rate and the real interest rate?

6.2 The chapter explains that it is impossible to know whether a particular nominal interest rate is "high" or "low." Briefly explain why.

LO 5.7

7.1 Why do nominal incomes generally increase with inflation? If nominal incomes increase with inflation, does inflation reduce the purchasing power of the average consumer? Briefly explain.

7.2 How can inflation affect the distribution of income?

Problems and Applications

LO 5.1

1.1 Fill in the missing values in the following table of data collected in the Labour Force Survey in October 2015:

Working Age Population	
Employment	19 374 800
Unemployment	
Unemployment rate	7.0%
Labour force	
Labour force participation rate	66.0%
Employment–population ratio	

Based on CANSIM Table 282-0001 Series v2091030, v2091051, v2091072, v2091135, v2091177, v2091198, v2091219. Statistics Canada.

1.2 Is it possible for the total number of people who are unemployed to increase while the unemployment rate decreases? Briefly explain.

1.3 In February 2012, the unemployment rate fell to 7.7 percent, despite the fact that Statistics Canada reported that 2800 jobs were lost. How could the unemployment rate fall when the number of jobs in the economy is also decreasing? Further, the same report identifies that 9100 full-time jobs were created during the month. How is it possible to have the same report saying that the economy lost 2800 jobs at the same time 9100 new full-time jobs were created?

LO 5.2

2.1 Macroeconomic conditions affect the decisions firms and families make. Why, for example, might a student graduating from college enter the job market during an economic expansion but apply for graduate school during a recession?

2.2 A politician makes the following argument: "The economy would operate more efficiently if frictional unemployment were eliminated. Therefore, a goal of government policy should be to reduce the frictional rate of unemployment to the lowest possible level." Briefly explain whether you agree with this argument.

2.3 **[Related to Making the Connection on page 113]** What advice for finding a job would you give someone who is frictionally unemployed? What advice would you give someone who is structurally unemployed? What advice would you give someone who is cyclically unemployed?

2.4 **[Related to Making the Connection on page 115]** Describe the advantages and disadvantages of efficiency wages.

LO 5.3

3.1 If Parliament eliminated the Employment Insurance system, what would be the effect on the level of frictional unemployment? What would be the effect on the level of real GDP? Would well-being in the economy be increased? Briefly explain.

3.2 Why do you think the minimum wage in Newfoundland and Labrador was set at only $0.50 per hour in 1965? Wouldn't this wage have been well below the equilibrium wage?

3.3 Costco typically pays its workers higher wages than does Walmart. One analyst argues that Costco pays higher wages "because it requires higher-skilled workers to sell higher-cost products to more affluent customers." If this analyst is correct, can we conclude that Costco is paying efficiency wages and Walmart is not? Briefly explain.

Based on Lori Montgomery, "Maverick Costco CEO Joins Push to Raise Minimum Wage," *Washington Post*, January 30, 2007.

LO 5.4

4.1 **[Related to Don't Let This Happen to You on page 119]** Briefly explain whether you agree or disagree with the following statement: "I don't believe the government price statistics. The CPI for 2010 was 218, but I know that the inflation rate couldn't have been as high as 118 percent in 2010."

4.2 In calculating the consumer price index for the year, why does Statistics Canada use the quantities in the basket of goods and services rather than the quantities purchased during the current year?

4.3 The new house price index issued by Statistics Canada is an indicator of housing price trends in Canada. The base for the index is June 2007. The following table lists index numbers for October 2014 and October 2015 for seven cities.

City	October 2014	October 2015
Halifax	118.0	118.9
Montreal	116.9	117.7
Toronto	123.0	127.9
Winnipeg	137.9	140.1
Regina	159.7	157.1
Calgary	110.9	110.2
Vancouver	96.2	97.7

a. Calculate the percentage change in housing prices from October 2014 to October 2015 for each of these seven cities. In which city did housing prices change the most? The least?

b. Can you determine on the basis of these numbers which city had the most expensive homes in October 2015? Briefly explain.

Data from CANSIM Table 327-0046.

LO 5.5

5.1 **[Related to Solved Problem 5.1 on page 120]** Use the information in the following table to determine the percentage changes in the US and French *real* minimum wages between 1957 and 2010. Does it matter for your answer that you have not been told the base year for the US CPI or the French CPI? Was the percentage increase in the price level greater in the United States or in France during these years?

Year	United States Minimum Wage (dollars per hour)	CPI	France Minimum Wage (euros per hour)	CPI
1957	$1.00	27	€0.19	10
2010	7.25	215	8.86	128

Based on John M. Abowd, Francis Kramarz, Thomas Lemieux, and David N. Margolis, "Minimum Wages and Youth Employment in France and the United States," in D. Blanchflower and R. Freeman, eds., *Youth Employment and Joblessness in Advanced Countries*, (Chicago: University of Chicago Press, 1999), pp. 427–472 (the value for the minimum wage is given in francs; it was converted to euros at a conversion rate of 1 euro = 6.55957 francs); Insee online data bank, www.insee.fr; U.S. Department of Labor; and U.S. Bureau of Labor Statistics.

5.2 **[Related to Solved Problem 5.1 on page 120]** The recession that began in 2008 was one of the most important economic events for the G7 countries of the last 70 years. Canada's performance during the recession was one of the best in the developed world. Use the data in the table below to calculate the percentage decline in real GDP between 2007 and 2009.

CANSIM Series v3260022 and v464937. Reproduced and distributed on an "as is" basis with the permission of Statistics Canada.

Year	Nominal GDP (billions of dollars)	Consumer Price Index (2002 = 100)
2007	$1529.6	111.45
2009	1529.0	114.45

Data from Statistics Canada, CANSIM Tables 380-0064 and 176-0043.

LO 5.6

6.1 Suppose you were borrowing money to buy a car. Which of these situations would you prefer: The interest rate on your car loan is 20 percent and the inflation rate is 19 percent OR the interest rate on your car loan is 5 percent and the inflation rate is 2 percent? Briefly explain.

6.2 Suppose that the only good you purchase is hamburgers and that at the beginning of the year, the price of a hamburger is

$2.00. Suppose you lend $1000 for one year at an interest rate of 5 percent. At the end of the year, a hamburger costs $2.08. What is the real rate of interest you earned on your loan?

6.3 During the 1990s, Japan experienced periods of deflation (negative inflation) and low nominal interest rates that approached zero percent. Why would lenders of funds agree to a nominal interest rate of almost zero percent? (Hint: Were real interest rates in Japan also low during this period?)

LO 5.7

7.1 What are menu costs? What effect has the Internet had on the size of menu costs?

7.2 Suppose that the inflation rate turns out to be much higher than most people expected. In that case, would you rather have been a borrower or a lender? Briefly explain.

MyEconLab MyEconLab is an online tool designed to help you master the concepts covered in your course. It will create a personalized study plan to stimulate and measure your learning. Log in to take advantage of this powerful study aid, and to access quizzes and other valuable course-related material.

Economic Growth, the Financial System, and Business Cycles

Doug Steakley/Lonely Planet
Images/Getty Images

Chapter Outline and Learning Objectives

Economic Growth and the Business Cycle at Bombardier

In 1937, Joseph-Armand Bombardier invented a snowmobile to help people navigate snowy roads in Quebec. In 1942, he founded L'Auto-Neige Bombardier Limitée and began manufacturing 12-passenger snowmobiles. Bombardier also developed a personal snowmobile, the Ski-Doo, in 1959. Short-run changes in the state of the economy can dramatically change the opportunities facing firms. When the oil crisis of 1973 hit, the demand for Ski-Doos fell by half and Bombardier had to look for new markets and new products, eventually finding a new niche, making train cars for subways and mass-transit systems.

Long-run economic growth provides firms with new opportunities as people's incomes grow. In 1986, Bombardier added another product line to its manufacturing business: the Canadair Regional Jet (CRJ), a 50-seat short-haul passenger aircraft. Today, the CRJ line of regional jets is the world's most successful regional aircraft program. Bombardier now employs more than 70 000 people worldwide and produces aerospace and transportation products.

Despite a long history as a maker of regional passenger aircraft, Bombardier is still vulnerable to the business cycle. When global demand falls, demand for Bombardier's products falls as well. In October 2015, Bombardier received a $1 billion bailout from the government of Quebec. Bombardier's C-Series jets, designed to serve the growing global short-haul air travel market, have been hit with two problems. The first is the C-Series project has encountered delays and cost overruns, which means Bombardier hasn't been able to deliver the planes yet. The second problem is the global recession that took place in 2007–2009 and its aftermath significantly reduced demand for the types of planes Bombardier makes. As a result, the company has had to ask the provincial government for support while it waits for the market to improve.

In this chapter, we provide an overview of long-run growth and the business cycle and their importance for firms, consumers, and the economy as a whole.

Economics in Your Life

Do You Help the Economy More If You Spend or If You Save?

Suppose that you have received an income tax refund cheque from the federal government. You are not sure what to do with the money, so you ask your two roommates for advice. One roommate tells you that if you want to help the economy, you should save all the money because a country's economic growth depends on the amount of saving by households. The other roommate disagrees and advises you to spend all the money because consumer spending is a major component of gross domestic product (GDP), and your spending would help increase production and create more jobs. Which of your two roommates is right? As you read this chapter, see if you can answer this question. You can check your answer against the one we provide on page 147 at the end of this chapter.

A successful economy is capable of increasing production of goods and services faster than the growth in population. Increasing production faster than population growth is the only way that the standard of living of the average person in a country can increase. Unfortunately, some economies around the world are not growing at all or are growing slowly compared with their rate of population growth. In some countries of sub-Saharan Africa, living standards are barely higher, or in a few cases are even lower, than they were 50 years ago. Most people in these low-growth countries live in the same poverty their ancestors did. In Canada and most developed countries, however, living standards are much higher than they were 50 years ago. An important topic in macroeconomics is why some countries grow much faster than others.

As we will see, one determinant of economic growth is the ability of firms to expand their operations, buy additional equipment, train workers, and adopt new technologies. To carry out these activities, firms must acquire funds from households, either directly through financial markets—such as the stock and bond markets—or indirectly through financial intermediaries—such as banks. Financial markets and financial intermediaries together make up the *financial system*. In this chapter, we will present an overview of the financial system and see how funds flow from households to firms through the *market for loanable funds*.

Dating back to at least the early nineteenth century, the Canadian economy has experienced periods of expanding production and employment followed by periods of recession, during which production and employment fall. As we noted in Chapter 4, these alternating periods of **expansion** and **recession** are called the **business cycle**. The business cycle is not uniform: Each period of expansion is not the same length, nor is each period of recession, but every period of expansion in Canadian history has been followed by a period of recession, and every recession has been followed by a period of expansion.

In this chapter, we begin to explore two key aspects of macroeconomics: the long-run growth that has steadily raised living standards in Canada and the short-run fluctuations of the business cycle.

Expansion The period of a business cycle during which total production and total employment are increasing.

Recession The period of a business cycle during which total production and total employment are decreasing.

Business cycle Alternating periods of economic expansion and economic recession.

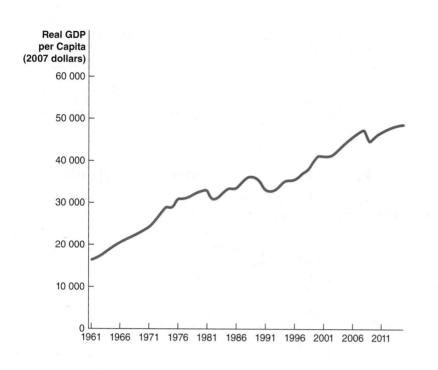

Figure 6.1

Real GDP per Capita 1961–2012

Measured in 2007 dollars, real GDP per capita grew from about $16 000 per person in 1961 to $48 500 per person in 2015. The average Canadian could buy 3.02 times as many goods and services in 2015 as the average Canadian could in 1961.

Based on Cansim series v3862688, v3860248, v62305752, v466668, D892580. Statistics Canada.

Long-Run Economic Growth

6.1 LEARNING OBJECTIVE

Discuss the importance of long-run economic growth.

Most people in Canada, the United States, Western Europe, Japan, and other advanced countries expect that over time their standard of living will improve. They expect that year after year, firms will introduce new and improved products; new prescription drugs and better medical techniques will allow them to be healthier and live longer; and their ability to afford the goods and services they desire will increase. For most people, these are reasonable expectations.

Figure 6.1 illustrates two important points about GDP per capita. First, GDP per capita has been rising over the last 55-plus years; this is what we mean when we talk about "economic growth." Second, GDP per capita fluctuates from year to year; economic growth hasn't been smooth. In fact, since 1961, GDP per capita in Canada has fallen during three periods. These drops and rises over the short run are due to the business cycle.

The process of **long-run economic growth** brought the typical Canadian from the standard of living of 1961 to the standard of living we see today. The best measure of standard of living is real GDP per person, which is usually referred to as *real GDP per capita*. So we measure long-run economic growth by increases in real GDP per capita over long periods of time, generally decades or more. We use real GDP rather than nominal GDP to adjust for changes in the price level over time. Figure 6.1 shows the real GDP per capita for Canada from 1961 to 2015.

In 1961, Canada enjoyed one of the highest living standards in the world with real GDP per capita of about $16 000 (in 2007 dollars). Even though Canada was one of the wealthiest countries in the world, most households had one television with only a few channels, household air conditioning was unheard of, and long-distance calls were very expensive. In 2015, real GDP per capita was about $48 500 (again in 2007 dollars). The purchasing power of the average Canadian today is more than three times as much as the average Canadian's in 1961. As big as the increase in real GDP per capita is, it actually understates the true increase in the standard of living that Canadians enjoy today. Many of the products we now take for granted, such as small passenger jets, mobile phones, and solar-powered anything were the realm of science fiction in 1961. If you were attending university in 1961, there's no way you would be able to purchase a reasonably sized computer, no matter your income.

Long-run economic growth The process by which rising productivity increases the average standard of living.

Of course, the quantity of goods and services you can purchase is not a perfect indicator of how happy or content you might be. The level of crime, spiritual well-being, pollution, and many other factors ignored in calculating GDP contribute to a person's happiness. Nevertheless, economists rely heavily on comparisons of real GDP per capita because it is the best means of comparing the performance of one economy over time or the performance of different economies at any one particular time.

Making the Connection | Economic Prosperity and Health

We can see the direct impact of economic growth on living standards by looking at health in high-income countries over the past 50 years. The research of Robert Fogel, winner of the Nobel Prize in Economics, highlights the close connection between economic growth, improvements in technology, and improvements in human physiology. One important measure of health is life expectancy at birth. As the graph below shows, life expectancy since 1960 has increased. Men born in 1960 could expect to live 68.2 years, while women born in the same year could expect to live 74.2 years. A man born in 2013 could expect to live to 80, and a woman with the same birth year can expect to reach 84 years of age.

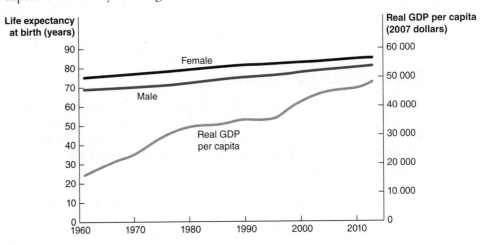

There is a similar relationship between life expectancy at birth and real GDP per capita when we compare different countries. Countries with high real GDP per capita, such as Canada, Sweden, and Switzerland, also have high life expectancies. Countries with very low real GDP per capita, such as Chad, Zimbabwe, and Togo, also have very low life expectancies.

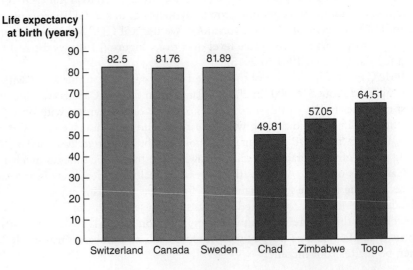

When countries produce more goods and services, more of those goods and services can be devoted to providing health care to people. Higher real GDP per capita is also linked to access to more and better-quality food.

Data from Canadian Mortality Data Base, WHO, and CIA World Fact Book.

Your Turn: Test your understanding by doing related problem 1.2 on page 149 at the end of this chapter.   MyEconLab

Calculating Growth Rates and the Rule of 70

The growth rate of real GDP or real GDP per capita during a particular year is equal to the percentage change from the previous year. For example, measured in prices of the year 2007, real GDP was $1 747 709 million in 2014 and rose to $1 766 706 million in 2015. We calculate the growth in real GDP between 2014 and 2015 as follows:

$$\frac{\$1\ 766\ 706\ \text{million} - \$1\ 747\ 709\ \text{million}}{\$1\ 747\ 709\ \text{million}} \times 100\% = 1.1\%$$

For longer periods of time, we can use the *average annual growth rate*. For example, the real GDP in Canada was $966 112 million in 1990 and $1 553 488 million in 2010. To find the average annual growth rate during this 20-year period, we compute the annual growth rate that would result in $966 112 million increasing to $1 553 488 million over 20 years. In this case, the growth rate is 2.4 percent. That is, if $966 112 million grows at an average rate of 2.4 percent per year, after 20 years, it will have grown to $1 553 488 million.

For shorter periods of time, we get approximately the same answer by averaging the growth rate for each year. For example, real GDP in Canada shrank by 0.2 percent in 2008 (which is the same as growing at −0.2 percent per year), shrank again by 2 percent in 2009, and grew by 2.9 percent in 2010. So the average annual growth rate for the period 2008 to 2010 was 0.23 percent, which is the average of the three annual growth rates:

$$\frac{-0.2\% - 2\% + 2.9\%}{3} = 0.23\%.$$

Note that when discussing long-run economic growth, we usually shorten "average annual growth rate" to "growth rate."

We can judge how rapidly an economic variable is growing by calculating the number of years it would take to double. For example, if real GDP per capita in a country doubles, say, every 20 years, most people in the country will experience significant increases in their standard of living over the course of their lives. If real GDP per capita doubles only every 100 years, increases in the standard of living will occur too slowly to be noticed. One easy way to calculate approximately how many years it will take real GDP per capita to double is to use the *rule of 70*. The formula for the rule of 70 is as follows:

$$\text{Number of years to double} = \frac{70}{\text{Growth rate}}$$

For example, if real GDP per capita is growing at a rate of 5 percent per year, it will take 70/5 = 14 years to double. If real GDP per capita is growing at a rate of 2 percent per year, it will double in 70/2 = 35 years to double. These examples illustrate an important point that we will discuss further in Chapter 7: Small differences in growth rates can have large effects on how rapidly the standard of living in a country increases. Finally, notice that the rule of 70 applies not only to growth in real GDP per capita but also to growth in any variable. For example, if you invest $1000 in the stock market and your investment grows at an average annual rate of 7 percent, your investment will double to $2000 in 10 years.

What Determines the Rate of Long-Run Growth?

In Chapter 7, we explore the sources of economic growth in more detail and discuss why growth in Canada and other high-income countries has been so much faster than

Labour productivity The quantity of goods and services that can be produced by one worker or by one hour of work.

in poorer countries (until fairly recently). For now, we will focus on the basic point that *increases in real GDP per capita depend on increases in labour productivity*. **Labour productivity** is the quantity of goods and services that can be produced by one worker or by one hour of work. In analyzing long-run growth, economists usually measure labour productivity as output per hour of work to avoid the effects of fluctuations in the length of the workday or in the fraction of the population employed. If the quantity of goods and services consumed by the average person is to increase, the quantity of goods and services produced per hour of work must also increase. Why in 2015 was the average Canadian able to consume three times as much as the average Canadian in 1961? The simple answer is because the average Canadian worker was three times more productive in 2015 than the average Canadian worker was in 1961.

If increases in labour productivity are the key to long-run economic growth, what causes labour productivity to increase? Economists believe two key factors determine labour productivity: the quantity of capital per hour worked and the level of technology. Therefore, economic growth occurs if the quantity of capital per hour worked increases and if technological change occurs.

Increases in Capital per Hour Worked. Workers today in high-income countries, such as Canada, have more physical capital available than workers in low-income countries. Canadian workers today have much more capital than did Canadian workers in 1961. **Capital** refers to manufactured goods that are used to produce other goods and services. Examples of capital are computers, factories, buildings, machines and tools, warehouses, and trucks. The total amount of physical capital available in a country is known as the country's *capital stock*.

Capital Manufactured goods that are used to produce other goods and services.

As the capital stock per hour worked increases, worker productivity increases. A secretary with a personal computer can produce more documents per day than a secretary with a manual typewriter. A worker with a backhoe can dig a bigger hole in a day than a worker equipped with just a shovel.

Human capital refers to the accumulated knowledge and skills workers acquire from education, training, or from life experience. For example, workers with a university education generally have more skills and are more productive than workers who have only a high school degree. Increases in human capital are particularly important in stimulating economic growth.

Technological Change. Economic growth depends more on technological change than on increases in capital per hour worked. *Technology* refers to the processes a firm uses to turn inputs into outputs of goods and services. Technological change is an increase in the quantity of output firms can produce using a given quantity of inputs. Technological change can come from many sources. For example, a firm's managers may rearrange a factory floor or the layout of a retail store to increase production and sales. Most technological change, however, is embodied in new machinery, equipment, or software.

A very important point is that just accumulating more inputs—such as labour, capital, or natural resources—will not ensure that an economy experiences economic growth unless technological change also occurs. For example, the Soviet Union failed to maintain a high rate of economic growth, even though it continued to increase the quantity of capital available per hour worked. The Soviet system experienced little technological change.

In implementing technological change, *entrepreneurs* are critical. Recall from Chapter 2 that an entrepreneur is someone who operates a business, bringing together the factors of production—labour, capital, and natural resources—to produce goods and services. In a market economy, entrepreneurs make crucial decisions about whether to introduce new technology to produce better or lower-cost products. Entrepreneurs also decide whether to allocate the firm's resources to research and development that can result in new technologies. One of the difficulties centrally planned economies have in sustaining economic growth is that managers employed by the government are typically much slower to develop and adopt new technologies than are entrepreneurs in a market system.

Property Rights. Finally, an additional requirement for economic growth is that the government must provide secure rights to private property. As we saw in Chapter 2, a market system cannot function unless rights to private property are secure. In addition, the government can help the market system work and aid economic growth by establishing an independent court system that enforces contracts between private individuals. Many economists would also say that the government has a role in facilitating the development of an efficient financial system, as well as systems of education, transportation, and communication.

Making the Connection | Can India Sustain Its Rapid Growth?

When you have a computer problem and need technical support, the person who answers your call and helps you may well be in India. In addition to information technology, Indian firms have also made gains in the global markets for steel, oil, and automobiles—just to name a few sectors.

To many people in Canada and other rich countries, the rapid economic growth of India has been a surprise. As the figure below shows, Indian real GDP per capita increased very slowly up to the time India gained independence from Britain in 1947. India's GDP in 1950 was less than $1000 per person (measured in 2015 dollars), or less than 8 per cent of Canada's real GDP per capita at the time. During the first 40 years of independence, India's growth rate increased but was still too slow to reduce the country's poverty. Recent years have been much different, however. In 1991, the Indian government decided to scale back central planning, reduce regulations, and introduce market-based reforms. The result was that the growth rate doubled over the following decade. In the most recent period, India has been growing even more quickly.

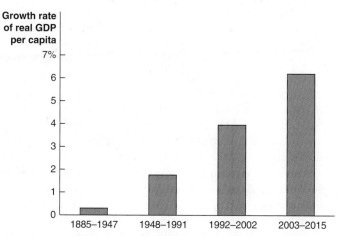

Still, India remains a very poor country, with many people struggling to find enough to eat. Nearly half of its 1.3 billion people are employed in agriculture, and many cannot produce enough to feed themselves. Infant mortality rates are still 10 times higher than in high-income countries, and about 40 percent of adult women and 20 percent of adult men cannot read or write. The rapid economic growth that began in 1991 will have to continue for decades if the average person in India is eventually to enjoy a standard of living equal to what Canadians take for granted. But can India maintain its rapid growth?

Some economists and policymakers worry that India's growth rates may begin to decline, leaving hundreds of millions of people trapped in deep poverty. These economists point to several problems facing the Indian economy. The public education system struggles to provide basic instruction, particularly in rural and poorer urban areas. India's spending on education ranks 134th of 173 countries and is much lower than in the most successful developing countries. As a result, many Indians never get the opportunity to develop the basic skills needed to be part of a modern economy. Despite producing some brilliant economists and scientists, many Indian high school and university graduates lack the skills to work for firms that compete in global markets. Only 60 percent of urban residents have access to modern sewage systems, and less than one-quarter of rural residents do. In general, India has struggled to meet its infrastructure needs, as highways, bridges, and the train system—which dates back to the British colonial period—have deteriorated.

India also suffers from political problems, with ethnic, religious, cultural, and geographic divisions—it has 15 official languages compared with Canada's 2. These divisions make policy reforms very difficult for government to implement. Reform is also hindered by corruption, estimated at 50 percent of GDP. It also remains difficult for firms, both from India and abroad, to make large investments in setting up new manufacturing facilities in India. Ever more investment will be needed to allow the financial, retail, and manufacturing sectors to continue to increase productivity.

The economic progress India has made in the past 25 years has already lifted hundreds of millions of people out of poverty. In order for this progress to continue, many economists believe the Indian government will have to upgrade infrastructure, improve the provision of education and health services, and renew its commitment to the rule of law and to market-based reforms.

Based on "Ready, Steady, Go," *Economist*, April 18, 2015; Ellen Barry, "After a Year of Outsize Expectations, Narendra Modi Adjusts His Plan for India," *New York Times*, May 25, 2015; Amartya Sen, "Why India Trails China," *New York Times*, June 19, 2013; Geeta Anand, "India Graduates Millions, but Too Few Are Fit to Hire," *Wall Street Journal*, April 5, 2011; data in graph are authors' calculations from the Maddison Project database, www.ggdc.net/maddison/maddison-project/home.htm; and International Monetary Fund, *World Economic Outlook Database*.

MyEconLab **Your Turn:** Test your understanding by doing related problem 1.6 on page 149 at the end of this chapter.

Potential GDP

Potential GDP The level of real GDP attained when all firms are producing at capacity.

In thinking about long-run economic growth, the concept of *potential GDP* is useful. **Potential GDP** is the level of real GDP attained when all firms are producing at capacity. The capacity of a firm is *not* the maximum output the firm is capable of producing. A Bombardier assembly plant could operate 24 hours per day for 365 days per year and would be at its maximum production level. The plant's capacity, however, is measured by its production when operating on normal hours, using a normal workforce. If all firms in the economy were operating at capacity, the level of total production of final goods and services would equal potential GDP. Potential GDP will increase over time as the labour force grows, new factories are built, new machinery and equipment are installed, and technological change takes place.

In Canada, the Bank of Canada estimates and reports the "output gap," which is the percentage difference between *actual* GDP and *potential* GDP. Sometimes the output gap is negative, and at other times it is positive. When the output gap is negative, actual real GDP is below potential real GDP and the economy is not making full use of its resources. When the output gap is positive, real GDP is above potential GDP and the economy is using its resources in an unsustainable way or, more accurately, the economy is using resources in a way that will lead to inflation. Figure 6.2 shows the output gap

Figure 6.2

The Output Gap

The Bank of Canada measures the output gap as the difference between actual GDP and potential GDP as a percentage of potential GDP. When the output gap is positive, actual GDP is larger than potential GDP; when the output gap is negative, actual GDP is smaller than potential GDP. A negative output gap is associated with a recession.

Source: Data from Bank of Canada. http://www.bankofcanada.ca/rates/indicators/capacity-and-inflation-pressures/product-market-definitions/product-market-historical-data/.

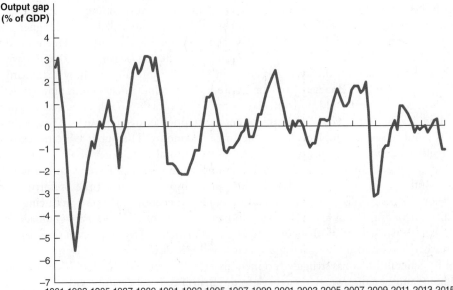

for the Canadian economy since 1981. You can see that actual GDP was below potential GDP quite a few times in the last 30 years. The major deviations of actual GDP from potential GDP correspond to recessions. The Canadian economy experienced recessions in the early 1980s, early 1990s, and late 2000s.

Saving, Investment, and the Financial System

6.2 LEARNING OBJECTIVE

Discuss the role of the financial system in facilitating long-run economic growth.

The process of economic growth depends on the ability of firms to expand their operations, buy additional equipment, train workers, and adopt new technologies. Firms can pay for some of these activities from *retained earnings*, which are profits that are reinvested in the firm rather than paid to the firm's owners. For many firms, retained earnings are not sufficient to finance the rapid expansion required in economies with high rates of economic growth. Firms can also get funds from households, either directly through financial markets—such as stock and bond markets—or indirectly through financial intermediaries—such as banks. Financial markets and financial intermediaries together make up the **financial system**. Without a well-functioning financial system, economic growth is almost impossible because firms will be unable to expand and adopt new technologies. As we noted earlier, no country without a well-developed financial system has been able to sustain high levels of economic growth.

Financial system The system of financial markets and financial intermediaries through which firms acquire funds from households.

An Overview of the Financial System

The financial system channels funds from savers to borrowers and channels the returns on borrowed funds back to savers. Through **financial markets**, such as the stock market or the bond market, firms raise funds by selling financial securities directly to savers. A *financial security* is a document—sometimes an electronic one—that states the terms under which funds pass from the buyer of the security (the lender) to the seller (the borrower). *Stocks* are financial securities that represent partial ownership of a firm. If you buy one share of Bell Canada, you will own relatively close to a billionth of the company (specifically, you will own one share out of 869.51 million shares). *Bonds* are financial securities that represent promises to repay a fixed amount in the future. When Bell Canada sells a bond, the firm promises to pay the purchaser of the bond an interest payment each year for the term of the bond, as well as a final payment that includes the original amount borrowed.

Financial markets Markets where financial securities, such as stocks and bonds, are bought and sold.

Financial intermediaries, such as banks, mutual funds, pension funds, and insurance companies, act as go-betweens for borrowers and lenders. In effect, financial intermediaries borrow funds from savers and lend them to borrowers. When you deposit funds in your chequing account, you are lending that money to the bank. The bank may then lend your funds (along with money from other savers) to an entrepreneur who wants to start a business. Suppose Lena wants to open a laundry. Rather than Lena having to ask 100 people to each lend her $100, the bank acts as a go-between. The bank pools the funds from 100 people, each who deposited $100 in their accounts, and makes a single loan of $10 000 to Lena. Intermediaries, such as the bank in this example, pay interest to savers in exchange for the use of their funds and earn profit by lending money to borrowers and charging borrowers a higher rate of interest on loans. For example, a bank might pay 2 percent interest on a savings account, but charge you 6 percent on your student loan.

Financial intermediaries Firms, such as banks, mutual funds, pension funds, and insurance companies, that borrow funds from savers and lend them to borrowers.

Banks, mutual funds, pension funds, and insurance companies also make investments in stocks and bonds on behalf of savers. For example, *mutual funds* sell shares to savers and then use the funds to buy a portfolio of stocks, bonds, mortgages, and other financial securities. Banks, for example, offer many alternative stock and bond funds. Some funds hold a wide range of stocks or bonds, while others specialize in securities issued by firms in a particular industry or sector of the economy, such as mining or manufacturing. Other funds invest as an index fund in a fixed market basket of securities, such as shares of the S&P/TSX 60, which includes the stocks of 60 companies in 10 sectors of the economy ("S&P" stands for "Standard & Poor's," and "TSX" stands for "Toronto Stock Exchange"). Over the last 30 years, the role of mutual funds in the financial system has increased dramatically. Today, hundreds of mutual funds are offered by banks and other firms competing for savers' funds.

In addition to matching households wanting to save with firms that want to borrow, the financial system provides three key services for savers and borrowers: risk sharing, liquidity, and information. *Risk* is the chance that the value of a financial asset will change relative to what you expect. For example, you may buy that share of Bell Canada at a price of $58, only to have the price fall to $40. Most individual savers are not gamblers and seek a steady return on their savings, rather than erratic swings between high and low (negative) earnings. The financial system provides risk sharing by allowing savers to spread their money among many financial assets. For example, you can divide your money among a bank certificate of deposit, individual bonds, and a mutual fund.

Liquidity is the ease with which one asset can be converted into a different asset. Generally, when talking about liquidity, we think in terms of exchanging a financial asset for money. The financial system provides the service of liquidity by providing savers with markets in which they can sell their financial assets. For example, you can easily sell your share of Bell Canada stock at the Toronto Stock Exchange. You don't have to ask everyone you meet if they want to buy a small piece of the company.

A third service that the financial system provides to savers is the collection and communication of *information*, or facts about borrowers and expectations about returns on financial securities. For example, Lena's Laundry may want to borrow $10 000 from you. Finding out what Lena intends to do with the funds and how likely she is to pay you back is likely costly and time-consuming. By depositing $100 in the bank, you are, in effect, allowing the bank to gather this information for you. Because banks specialize in gathering information on borrowers, they are often able to do it faster and at a lower cost than individual savers. The financial system plays an important role in communicating information. If you read a news story announcing that an automaker has invented a car with an engine that runs on water, how would you determine the effect of that discovery on the firm's profits? Financial markets do some of the job for you by incorporating information into the prices of stocks, bonds, and other financial securities. In this example, the expectation of higher future profits for that automaker would boost the prices of their stocks and bonds.

The Macroeconomics of Saving and Investment

We've seen that the funds available to firms through the financial system come from saving. When firms use funds to purchase machinery or build new factories, they are engaging in investment. In this section, we explore the macroeconomics of saving and investment. A key point we will develop is that the *total value of saving in the economy must equal the total value of investment*. We saw in Chapter 4 that *national income accounting* refers to the methods government agencies use to track total production and total income in the economy. We can use some relationships from national income accounting to understand why total saving must equal total investment.

We begin with the relationship between GDP (Y) and its components, consumption (C), investment (I), government purchases (G), and net exports (NX):

$$Y = C + I + G + NX$$

Remember that GDP is a measure of both total production in the economy and total income.

In an *open economy*, there is interaction with other economies in terms of trading goods and services as well as borrowing and lending. Virtually all economies today are open economies, although a lot of variation exists in the degree of openness. In a *closed economy*, there is no trading, borrowing, or lending with other economies. For simplicity, we will develop the relationship between saving and investment in a closed economy. This allows us to focus on the most important points in a simpler framework. We will consider the case for an open economy in Chapter 14.

In a closed economy, net exports are zero, so we can rewrite the relationship between GDP and its components as follows:

$$Y = C + I + G$$

If we rearrange this relationship, we have an expression for investment in terms of the other variables:

$$I = Y - C - G$$

This expression tells us that in a closed economy, investment spending is equal to total income minus consumption spending and minus government purchases.

We can also derive an expression for total saving. *Private saving* is equal to what households retain from their income after purchasing goods and services (C) and paying taxes (T). Households receive income in two ways; by supplying the factors of production to firms (Y) and as transfers from government (TR). Recall that transfer payments include social program payments and employment insurance payments. We can write the resulting relationship between private savings ($S_{Private}$) as follows:

$$S_{Private} = Y + TR - C - T$$

The government also engages in saving. *Public saving* (S_{Public}) equals the amount of tax revenue the government retains after paying for government purchases and making transfer payments to households:

$$S_{Public} = T - G - TR$$

So, total savings in the economy (S) is equal to the sum of private saving and public saving:

$$S = S_{Private} + S_{Public}$$

or:

$$S = (Y + TR - C - T) + (T - G - TR)$$

or:

$$S = Y - C - G$$

The right side of this expression is identical to the expression we derived earlier for investment spending. So, we conclude that total saving must equal total investment:

$$S = I$$

When the government spends the same amount as it collects in taxes, there is a *balanced budget*. When the government spends more than it collects in taxes, there is a *budget deficit*. When there is a budget deficit, T is less than $G + TR$, which means that public savings is negative. Negative savings is sometimes referred to as *dissaving*. How can public saving be negative? When the federal government runs a budget deficit, the government must sell bonds to borrow the money needed to fund the spending not paid for with taxes. In this case, rather than adding to the total amount of saving in the economy, the federal government subtracts from it. Put slightly differently, the government is using up some of the savings that would have otherwise been used to finance investment. We can conclude that, holding all other factors constant (*ceteris paribus*), there is a lower level of investment spending in the economy when there is a budget deficit than when the government has a balanced budget.

When the government spends less than it collects in taxes, there is a *budget surplus*. A budget surplus increases public saving and thus increases the total level of saving in the economy. A higher level of saving results in a higher level of investment spending. Therefore, holding everything else constant (*ceteris paribus*, again), investment spending is higher when the government runs a surplus than when the government has a balanced budget.

The Market for Loanable Funds

We have seen that the value of total saving must equal the value of total investment, but we have not yet discussed how this equality is actually brought about in the financial

Market for loanable funds The interaction of borrowers and lenders that determines the market interest rate and the quantity of loanable funds exchanged.

system. We can think of the financial system as being composed of many markets through which funds flow from lenders to borrowers: the market for certificates of deposit at banks, the market for stocks, the market for bonds, the market for mutual fund shares, and so on. For simplicity, we can think of all these different markets as making up the market for *loanable funds*. In the model of the **market for loanable funds**, the interaction between borrowers and lenders determines the market interest rate and the quantity of loanable funds exchanged. As we will discuss in Chapter 14, firms can also borrow from savers in other countries. For the remainder of this chapter, we will assume that there are no interactions between households and firms in Canada and those in other countries.

Demand and Supply in the Loanable Funds Market. The demand for loanable funds is determined by the willingness of firms to borrow money to engage in new investment projects, such as building new factories or buying new equipment. In determining whether to borrow funds, firms compare the return they expect to make on an investment with the interest rate they must pay to borrow the needed funds. For example, if Sobey's is considering opening several new stores and expects to earn a return of 15 percent on its investment, the investment will only be profitable if Sobey's can borrow at an interest rate of less than 15 percent. If Sobey's could only borrow at an interest rate of 20 percent, it would pay more for its investment than it would get, so opening the new stores would not be a good idea. If Sobey's could borrow at an interest rate of 10 percent, it would get more from its investment than it would pay, so opening the new stores would be a good idea.

In Figure 6.3, the demand for loanable funds is downward sloping because the lower the interest rate, the more investment projects firms can profitably undertake, and the greater the quantity of loanable funds they will demand.

The supply of loanable funds is determined by the willingness of households to save and by the extent of government saving or dissaving. When households save, they reduce the amount of goods and services they can consume and enjoy right now. The willingness of households to save rather than consume their incomes today will be determined in part by the interest rate they receive when they lend their savings. The higher the interest rate, the greater the reward for saving and the larger the amount of funds households will save. Therefore, the supply curve for loanable funds in Figure 6.3 is upward sloping: The greater the interest rate, the bigger the reward for saving, and households will save (lend) more of their income.

In Chapter 5, we discussed the distinction between the *nominal interest rate* and the *real interest rate*. The nominal interest rate is the stated interest rate on a loan. The real interest rate corrects the nominal interest rate for the impact of inflation and is equal to the nominal interest rate minus the inflation rate. Because both borrowers and lenders are concerned with the real interest rate they receive or pay, equilibrium in the market for loanable funds determines the real interest rate rather than the nominal interest rate.

Figure 6.3

The Market for Loanable Funds

The demand for loanable funds is determined by the willingness of firms to borrow money to engage in new investment projects. The supply of loanable funds is determined by the willingness of households to save and by the extent of government saving or dissaving. Equilibrium in the market for loanable funds determines the real interest rates and the quantity of loanable funds exchanged.

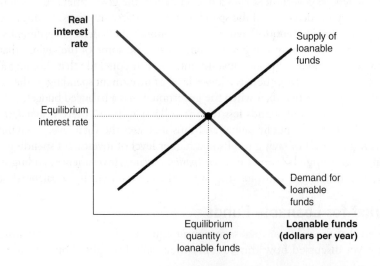

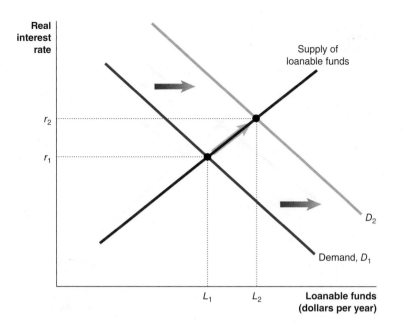

Figure 6.4

An Increase in the Demand for Loanable Funds

An increase in the demand for loanable funds increases the equilibrium interest rate from r_1 to r_2, and it increases the equilibrium quantity of loanable funds from L_1 to L_2. As a result, saving and investment both increase.

Explaining Movements in Saving, Investment, and Interest Rates.

Equilibrium in the market for loanable funds determines the quantity of loanable funds that will flow from lenders to borrowers each period. It also determines the real interest rate that lenders will receive and that borrowers must pay. We draw the demand curve for loanable funds the same way we draw any demand curve, by holding everything but the real interest rate (i.e., the price of loanable funds) constant. A number of factors can influence how much firms want to borrow, and a change in any of those factors will cause the demand curve to shift.

If the profitability of new investments increases dues to technological change, for example, firms will increase their demand for loanable funds at all real interest rates. Figure 6.4 shows the impact of an increase in demand in the market for loanable funds. As with the markets we discussed in Chapter 3, an increase in demand in the market for loanable funds shifts the demand curve to the right. In the new equilibrium, the interest rate increases from r_1 to r_2, and the equilibrium quantity of funds loaned increases from L_1 to L_2. Notice that an increase in the quantity of funds loaned means that both the quantity of saving by households and the quantity of investment by firms have increased. Increasing investment increases the capital stock and helps increase economic growth.

We also assume that everything other than the real interest rate that might have an impact on the supply of loanable funds is held constant when we draw the supply curve in Figure 6.3. If something other than the real interest rate changes how much people want to save, the supply of loanable funds will shift. If households change their beliefs so that saving is more important to them, they will save more at every real interest rate, causing the supply of loanable funds to shift to the right. You can see this change in Figure 6.5.

We can also use the market for loanable funds to examine the impact of a government budget deficit. Putting aside the effects of foreign saving—which we will consider in Chapter 14—recall that if the government begins running a budget deficit, it reduces the total amount of saving in the economy. Suppose the government increases spending, which results in a budget deficit. We illustrate the effects of the budget deficit in Figure 6.6 by shifting the supply of loanable funds to the left. In the new equilibrium, the interest rate is higher, and the equilibrium quantity of loanable funds is lower. Running a deficit has reduced the level of total saving in the economy and, by increasing the interest rate, has also reduced the level of investment spending by firms. By borrowing to finance its budget deficit, the government will have *crowded out* some firms that would have otherwise borrowed to finance investment. **Crowding out** refers to a decline in

Crowding out A decline in private investment expenditures as a result of an increase in government purchases.

Figure 6.5

An Increase in the Supply of Loanable Funds

An increase in the supply of loanable funds decreases the interest rate from r_1 to r_2, and it increases the equilibrium quantity of loanable funds from L_1 to L_2. As a result, both saving and investment increase.

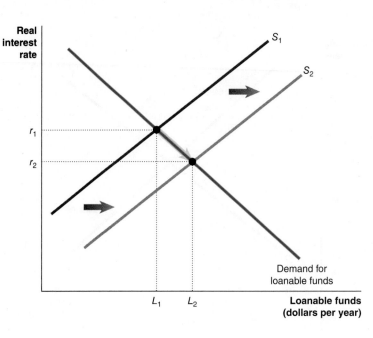

investment spending as a result of an increase in government purchases. In Figure 6.6, the decline in investment spending due to crowding out is shown by the movement from L_1 to L_2 on the demand for loanable funds curve. Lower investment spending means that capital stock and the quantity of capital per worker will not be as high as it would have been without the government budget deficit.

A government budget surplus has the opposite effect of a deficit. A budget surplus increases the total amount of saving in the economy, shifting the supply of loanable funds to the right. In the new equilibrium, the interest rate will be lower, and the quantity of loanable funds will be higher. We can conclude that a budget surplus increases the level of saving and investment.

In practice, however, the impact of government budget deficits and surpluses on the equilibrium interest rate is relatively small. (This finding reflects in part the importance of global saving in determining the interest rate.) Small does not mean non-existent, of course. Further, paying off government debt in the future may require higher taxes, which can depress economic growth.

Figure 6.6

The Effect of a Budget Deficit on the Market for Loanable Funds

When the government begins running a budget deficit, the supply of loanable funds shifts to the left. The equilibrium interest rate increases from r_1 to r_2, and the equilibrium quantity of loanable funds falls from L_1 to L_2. As a result, saving and investment both decline.

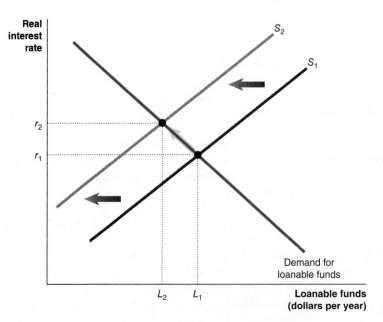

Solved Problem **6.2**

How Does a Consumption Tax Affect Saving, Investment, the Interest Rate, and Economic Growth?

Some economists and policymakers have suggested that governments should rely less on income taxes and rely more on consumption taxes (such as the GST and HST) to generate revenue. Under an income tax, households pay taxes on all income earned. Under a consumption tax, households pay taxes only on the income they spend. Households would pay taxes on saved income only if they spent the money later on. Use the market for loanable funds model to analyze the effect on saving, investment, the interest rate, and economic growth of switching from an income tax to a consumption tax as the primary source of government revenue.

Solving the Problem

Step 1: **Review the chapter material.** This problem is about applying the market for loanable funds model, so you may want to review the section "Explaining Movements in Saving, Investment, and Interest Rates" on page 141.

Step 2: **Explain the effect of switching from an income tax to a consumption tax.** Households are interested in the return they receive from saving after they have paid their taxes. For example, consider someone who puts savings in a certificate of deposit at an interest rate of 4 percent and whose tax rate is 25 percent. Under an income tax, this person's after-tax return to saving is 3 percent [$4 \times (1 - 0.25)$]. Under a consumption tax, income that is saved is not taxed, so the return rises to 4 percent. We can conclude that moving from an income tax to a consumption tax would increase the return to saving, causing the supply of loanable funds to increase.

Step 3: **Draw a graph of the market for loanable funds to illustrate your answer.** The supply curve for loanable funds will shift to the right as the after-tax return to saving increases under the consumption tax. The equilibrium interest rate will fall, and the levels of saving and investment will both increase. As a result of the increase in investment, the capital stock and the capital per worker will rise, which means that the rate of economic growth should increase. Note that the size of the fall in the interest rate and the size of the increase in loanable funds shown in the graph are both larger than the effects that most economists would expect from the replacement of the income tax with a consumption tax.

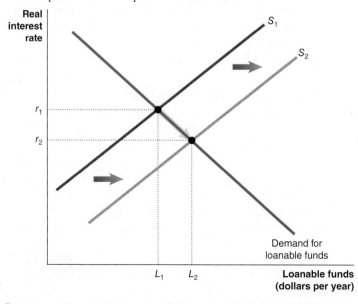

Your Turn: For more practice, do related problem 2.10 on page 150 at the end of this chapter.   MyEconLab

The Business Cycle

Figure 6.1 illustrates the massive increase in the standard of living Canadians have enjoyed over the last 50-plus years. But close inspection of the figure reveals that real GDP per capita did not increase every year during the last 50 years. For example, GDP per capita actually fell in the early 1980s, the early 1990s, and again in 2008. What accounts for these deviations from the long-run upward trend?

Some Basic Business Cycle Definitions

The fluctuations in real GDP per capita shown in Figure 6.1 reflect the underlying fluctuations in real GDP. Dating back as long as Canada has been a country, the economy has experienced a business cycle that consists of alternating periods of expanding and contracting economic activity. Given that real GDP is our best measure of economic activity, the business cycle is usually illustrated using movements in real GDP.

During the *expansion phase* of the business cycle, production, employment, and income are increasing. The period of expansion ends with a *business cycle peak*. Following the business cycle peak, production, employment, and income decline as the economy enters the *recession phase* of the business cycle. The recession comes to an end with a *business cycle trough*, after which another period of expansion begins. Figure 6.7 illustrates the phases of the business cycle. Panel (a) shows an idealized business cycle, with real GDP increasing smoothly in an expansion to a business cycle peak and then decreasing smoothly in a recession to a business cycle trough, which is followed by another expansion. Panel (b) shows the somewhat messier reality of an actual business cycle by plotting fluctuations in real GDP from 2001 to 2015. The figure shows that the expansion that began in the 1990s (not shown on the graph) continued through the early 2000s until the business cycle peak in 2008. The economy then entered a recession from 2008 to 2009, when the trough of the business cycle was reached, and the next period of expansion began in 2009. Using yearly data disguises some of the movement in real GDP around the actual business cycle. GDP is typically reported in quarters, and it is not uncommon to have real GDP slow down for a single quarter and then continue rising, even though the period in question is generally thought of as an expansion. This inconsistency in real GDP movements can make the exact beginning of a recession (or peaks and troughs for that matter) difficult to identify.

How Do We Know When the Economy Is in a Recession?

Statistics Canada produces many statistics that make it possible to monitor the economy. Statistics Canada does not officially decide when a recession begins or when it ends. In Canada, there is no official beginning or end to a recession. However, elaborating on our earlier definition, there is general agreement that a recession is defined as two consecutive quarters of negative real GDP growth. That is six months of falling real GDP.

What Happens during the Business Cycle

Each business cycle is different. The lengths of the expansion and recession phases and which sectors of the economy are most affected are rarely the same in any two cycles. Most business cycles share certain characteristics. As the economy nears the end of an expansion, interest rates are usually rising, and the wages of workers are usually rising faster than prices. As a result of rising interest rates and wages, the profits of firms will be falling. Typically, toward the end of an expansion, both households and firms will have substantially increased their debts. These debts are the result of the borrowing firms and households undertake to help finance their spending during the expansion.

A recession will often begin with a decline in spending by firms on capital goods, such as machinery, equipment, new factories, and new office buildings, or by households on new houses and consumer durables, such as furniture and automobiles. As spending declines, firms selling capital goods and consumer durables will find their sales

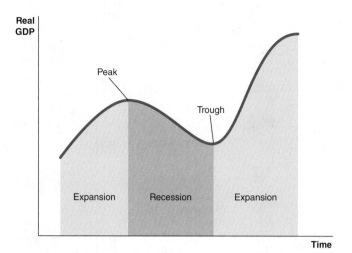

(a) An idealized business cycle

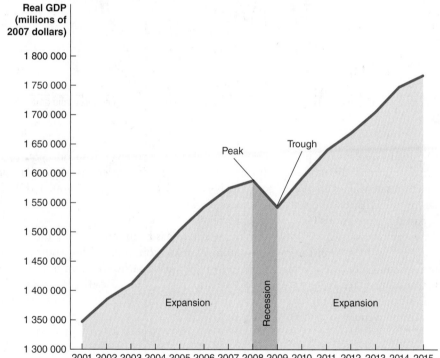

Figure 6.7

The Business Cycle

Panel (a) shows an idealized business cycle with real GDP increasing smoothly in an expansion to a business cycle peak and then decreasing smoothly in a recession to a business cycle trough, which is followed by another expansion. The periods of expansion are shown in green, and the period of recession is shown in red. Panel (b) shows the actual movements in real GDP from 2001 to 2012. The recession that began in 2008 was a particularly deep recession.
(b) CANSIM Table 380-0064.

Source: Statistics Canada, Table 380-0064 – Gross domestic product, expenditure-based, quarterly (dollars unless otherwise noted), CANSIM (database). Reproduced and distributed on an "as is" basis with the permission of Statistics Canada.

declining. As sales decline, firms cut back on production and begin to lay off workers. Rising unemployment and falling profits reduce income, which leads to further declines in spending.

As the recession continues, economic conditions gradually begin to improve. The declines in spending eventually come to an end; households and firms begin to reduce their debt, thereby increasing their ability to spend; and interest rates decline, making it more likely that households and firms will borrow to finance new spending. Firms begin to increase their spending on capital goods as they anticipate the need for additional production during the next expansion. Increased spending by households on consumer durables and by businesses on capital goods will finally bring the recession to an end and start the next expansion.

The Effect of the Business Cycle on the Inflation Rate.

In Chapter 5 we saw that the *price level* measures the average prices of goods and services in the economy

Figure 6.8

The Effect of Recessions on the Inflation Rate

Toward the end of a typical expansion, the inflation rate begins to rise; these times are marked with blue shading. Recessions, marked by red shading, cause the inflation rate to fall. By the end of a recession, the inflation rate is below what it had been at the beginning of the recession.

Source: Statistics Canada, Consumer Price Index, monthly (2002=100 unless otherwise noted), CANSIM (database). (accessed: December 28, 2015). Reproduced and distributed on an "as is" basis with the permission of Statistics Canada.

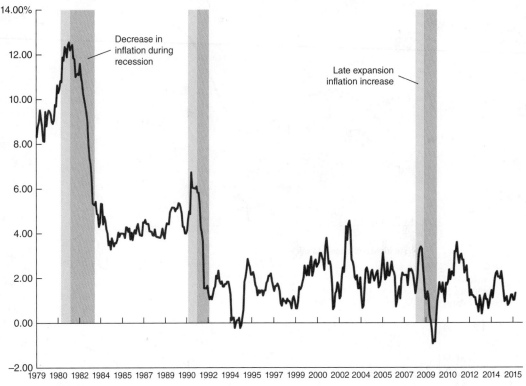

and the *inflation rate* is the percentage increase in the price level from one year to the next. An important fact about the business cycle is that during economic expansions, the inflation rate usually increases, particularly near the end of the expansion, and during recessions, the inflation rate usually decreases. Figure 6.8 illustrates that this has been true of the last three recessions Canada has experienced.

In every recession since 1980, the inflation rate has been lower in the months following a recession than in the months before the recession began. This result isn't surprising. During a business cycle expansion, spending by businesses and households is strong, and producers of goods and services find it easy to raise prices. As spending declines during a recession, firms have a harder time selling their goods and services and are less likely to increase prices.

Don't Let This Happen to You

Don't Confuse the Price Level with the Inflation Rate

Do you agree with the following statement: "The consumer price index is a widely used measure of the inflation rate"? This statement sounds like it might be correct, but it's wrong. As we saw in Chapter 5, the consumer price index is a measure of the *price level*, not of the inflation rate. We can measure the inflation rate as the *percentage change* in the consumer price index from

one year to the next. In macroeconomics, it is important not to confuse the level of a variable with the change in the variable. To give another example, real GDP does not measure economic growth. Economic growth is measured by the percentage change in real GDP from one year to the next.

MyEconLab

Your Turn: Test your understanding by doing related problem 3.4 on page 150 at the end of this chapter.

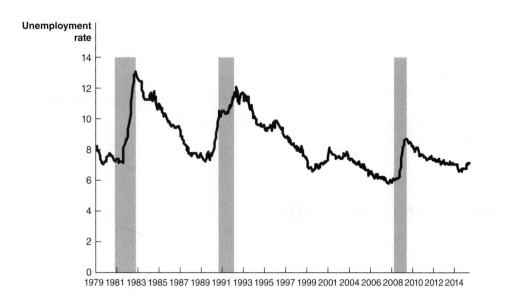

Figure 6.9

How Recessions Affect the Unemployment Rate

Unemployment rises during recessions and falls during expansions. The reluctance of firms to hire new employees as well as the re-entry of discouraged workers into the labour force during the early stages of a recovery mean that the unemployment rate usually continues to rise even after the recession has ended.

Source: Statistics Canada. Table 282-0087 - Labour force survey estimates (LFS), by sex and age group, seasonally adjusted and unadjusted, monthly (persons unless otherwise noted), CANSIM (database). (accessed: December 28, 2015). Reproduced and distributed on an "as is" basis with the permission of Statistics Canada.

The Effect of the Business Cycle on the Unemployment Rate. Recessions cause the inflation rate to fall, but they cause the unemployment rate to increase. As firms see their sales decline, they begin to reduce production and lay off workers. Figure 6.9 shows that this has been true of the recessions since 1980. Notice in the figure that large increases in the unemployment rate correspond to recessions and decreases in the inflation rate.

You should also notice that the unemployment rate continues to rise even after most economists believe that a particular recession has ended. This is typical, and is caused by two factors. First, even though employment begins to increase as a recession ends, it may increase more slowly than the growth in the labour force that results from population growth. If employment grows more slowly than the labour force, the unemployment rate will rise. Further, some workers who became discouraged during the recession and stopped looking for work (and therefore aren't classified as *unemployed*) re-enter the labour force once the economy begins to recover. These returning workers increase the number of people in the labour force. Second, not all firms expand at the same rate after a recession. Some firms that laid off workers during a recession may be particularly slow to call workers back even after a recession is over.

Economics in Your Life

Do You Help the Economy More If You Spend or If You Save?

At the beginning of the chapter we posed a question: Which of your two roommates is right: The one who argues that you would help the economy more by saving your income tax refund cheque, or the one who argues that you should spend it? In this chapter, we have seen that consumption spending promotes the production of more consumption goods and services—such as coffee and doughnuts—and fewer investment goods and services—such as physical capital and education. Saving—not consuming—is necessary to fund investment expenditure. So, saving your refund cheque will help the economy grow over the long run. But if the economy is in a recession, spending your refund cheque will spur more production of consumption goods. In a sense, then, both of your roommates are correct: Spending your cheque will help stimulate the economy during a recession, while saving it will help the economy grow over time.

Conclusion

The Canadian economy remains a remarkable engine for improving the well-being of Canadians. The standard of living we enjoy today is much higher than it was 100 years ago or even 50 years ago. But households and firms still have to deal with the ups and downs of the business cycle. In the following chapters, we will continue our analysis of this basic fact of macroeconomics: Ever-increasing long-run prosperity is achieved in the context of short-run stability.

Chapter Summary and Problems

Key Terms

Business cycle, p. 130

Capital, p. 134

Crowding out, p. 141

Expansion, p. 130

Financial intermediaries, p. 137

Financial markets, p. 137

Financial system, p. 137

Labour productivity, p. 134

Long-run economic growth, p. 131

Market for loanable funds, p. 140

Potential GDP, p. 136

Recession, p. 130

Summary

*LO 6.1 The Canadian economy has experienced both *long-run economic growth* and the *business cycle*. The *business cycle* refers to alternating periods of economic expansion and economic recession. *Long-run economic growth* is the process by which rising productivity increases the standard of living of the typical person. Because of economic growth, the typical Canadian today can buy almost three times as much as the typical Canadian could in 1961. Long-run growth is measured by increases in real GDP per capita. Increases in real GDP per capita depend on increases in labour productivity. *Labour productivity* is the quantity of goods and services that can be produced by one worker or by one hour of work. Economists believe that two key factors determine labour productivity: the quantity of capital per hour worked and the level of technology. *Capital* refers to manufactured goods that are used to produce other goods and services. *Human capital* is the accumulated knowledge and skills workers acquire from education, training, or their life experiences. Economic growth occurs if the quantity of capital per hour worked increases and if technological change occurs. Economists often discuss economic growth in terms of growth in *potential GDP*, which is the level of GDP attained when all firms are producing at capacity.

LO 6.2 Financial markets and financial intermediaries together comprise the *financial system*. A well-functioning financial system is an important determinant of economic growth. Firms acquire funds from households, either directly through *financial markets*—such as

the stock and bond markets—or indirectly through *financial intermediaries*—such as banks. The funds available to firms come from saving. There are two categories of saving in the economy: private saving by households and public saving by the government. The value of total saving in the economy is always equal to the value of total investment spending. In the model of the *market for loanable funds*, the interaction of borrowers and lenders determines the market interest rate and the quantity of loanable funds exchanged.

LO 6.3 During the *expansion* phase of the business cycle, production, employment, and income are increasing. The period of expansion ends with a business cycle peak. Following the business cycle peak, production, employment, and income decline during the *recession* phase of the cycle. The recession comes to an end with a business cycle trough, after which another period of expansion begins. The inflation rate usually rises near the end of a business cycle expansion and then falls during a recession. The unemployment rate declines during the later part of an expansion and increases during a recession. The unemployment rate often continues to increase even after an expansion has begun. Economists have not found a method to predict when recessions will begin and end. Recessions are difficult to predict because they are due to more than one cause. Until the recession of 2008, the Canadian economy had not experienced a recession since the early 1990s.

MyEconLab   Log in to MyEconLab to complete these exercises and get instant feedback.

★"Learning Objective" is abbreviated to "LO" in the end-of-chapter material.

Review Questions

LO 6.1

1.1 By how much did real GDP per capita in Canada increase between 1961 and 2015? Discuss whether the increase in real GDP per capita is likely to be greater or less than the true increase in living standards.

1.2 What is the rule of 70? If real GDP per capita grows at a rate of 7 percent per year, how many years will it take to double?

1.3 What is the most important factor in explaining increases in real GDP per capita in the long run?

1.4 What is potential real GDP? Does potential real GDP remain constant over time?

LO 6.2

2.1 Why is the financial system of a country important for long-run economic growth? Why is it essential for economic growth that firms have access to adequate sources of funds?

2.2 Briefly explain why the total value of saving in the economy must equal the total value of investment.

2.3 What are loanable funds? Why do businesses demand loanable funds? Why do households supply loanable funds?

LO 6.3

3.1 What are the names of the following events that occur during a business cycle?
 a. The high point of economic activity
 b. The low point of economic activity
 c. The period between the high point of economic activity and the following low point
 d. The period between the low point of economic activity and the following high point

Problems and Applications

LO 6.1

1.1 Briefly discuss whether you would rather live in Canada in 1900 with an income of $1 000 000 or Canada in 2017 with an income of $50 000. Assume that the incomes for both years are in 2017 dollars.

1.2 [**Related to Making the Connection on page 132**] Think about the relationship between economic prosperity and life expectancy. What implications does this relationship have for the size of the health care sector of the economy? In particular, is this sector likely to expand or contract in coming years?

1.3 A question from Chapter 5 asked about the relationship between real GDP and the standard of living in a country. Based on what you read about economic growth in this chapter, elaborate on the importance of growth in GDP, particularly real GDP per capita, to the quality of life of a country's citizens.

1.4 Use the table to answer the following questions.

Year	Real GDP (billions of 2005 dollars)
1990	$8034
1991	8015
1992	8287
1993	8523
1994	8871

 a. Calculate the growth rate of real GDP for each year from 1991 to 1994.
 b. Calculate the average annual growth rate of real GDP for the period from 1991 to 1994.

1.5 Real GDP per capita in Canada, as mentioned in the chapter, grew from about $16 000 per person in 1961 to about $48 500 per person in 2015, which represents an annual growth rate of 2.4 percent. If Canada continues to grow at this rate, how many years will it take for real GDP per capita to double? If government attempts to balance the budget and reduce the annual growth rate to 1.8 percent, how many years will it take for real GDP per capita to double?

1.6 [**Related to Making the Connection on page 135**] The steps that economists say India needs to take to maintain its current fast rate of economic growth sound relatively simple. What might prevent the government of India from taking these steps?

LO 6.2

2.1 Suppose that you can receive an interest rate of 3 percent on a certificate of deposit at a bank that is charging borrowers 7 percent on new car loans. Why might you be unwilling to loan money directly to someone who wants to borrow from you to buy a new car, even if that person offers to pay you an interest rate higher than 3 percent?

2.2 Consider the following data for a closed economy:
 $Y = \$11$ trillion
 $C = \$8$ trillion
 $I = \$2$ trillion
 $TR = \$1$ trillion
 $T = \$3$ trillion
 Use these data to calculate the following:
 a. Private saving
 b. Public saving
 c. Government purchases
 d. The government budget deficit or budget surplus

2.3 Consider the following data for a closed economy:
 $Y = \$12$ trillion
 $C = \$8$ trillion
 $G = \$2$ trillion
 $S_{Public} = -\$0.5$ trillion
 $T = \$2$ trillion
 Use these data to calculate the following:
 a. Private saving
 b. Investment spending
 c. Transfer payments
 d. The government budget deficit or budget surplus

2.4 In problem 2.3, suppose that government purchases increase from $2 trillion to $2.5 trillion. If the values for Y and C are unchanged, what must happen to the values of S and I? Briefly explain.

2.5 Use the graph below to answer the following questions:
   a. Does the shift from S_1 to S_2 represent an increase or a decrease in the supply of loanable funds?
   b. With the shift in supply, what happens to the equilibrium quantity of loanable funds?
   c. With the change in the equilibrium quantity of loanable funds, what happens to the quantity of saving? What happens to the quantity of investment?

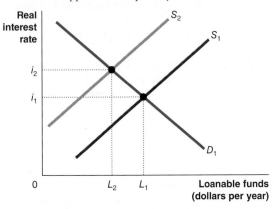

2.6 Use this graph to answer the questions that follow:

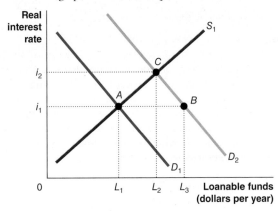

   a. With the shift in the demand for loanable funds, what happens to the equilibrium real interest rate and the equilibrium quantity of loanable funds?
   b. How can the equilibrium quantity of loanable funds increase when the real interest rate increases? Doesn't the quantity of loanable funds demanded decrease when the interest rate increases?

2.7 Suppose the economy is currently in a recession and that economic forecasts indicate that the economy will soon enter an expansion. What is the likely effect of the expansion on the expected profitability of new investment in plant and equipment? In the market for loanable funds, graph and explain the effect of the forecast of an economic expansion, assuming that borrowers and lenders believe the forecast is accurate. What happens to the equilibrium real interest rate and the quantity of loanable funds? What happens to the quantity of saving and investment?

2.8 Firms care about their after-tax rate of return on investment projects. In the market for loanable funds, graph and explain the effect of an increase in taxes on business profits. (For simplicity, assume no change in the federal budget deficit or budget surplus.) What happens to the equilibrium real interest rate and the quantity of loanable funds? What will be the effect on the quantity of investment by firms and the economy's capital stock in the future?

2.9 The federal government has been cutting spending to reduce budget deficits.
   a. Use a market for loanable funds graph to illustrate the effect of shrinking federal budget deficits. What happens to the equilibrium real interest rate and the quantity of loanable funds? What happens to the quantity of saving and investment?
   b. Now suppose that households believe that the return to balanced budgets will lead to lower taxes in the near future, and households decrease their saving in anticipation of paying those lower taxes. Briefly explain how your analysis in part (a) will be affected.

2.10 **[Related to Solved Problem 6.2 on page 143]** Savers are taxed on the nominal interest payments they receive rather than on the real interest payments. Suppose the government shifted from taxing nominal interest payments to taxing only real interest payments. (That is, savers could subtract the inflation rate from the nominal interest rate they received and only pay taxes on the resulting real interest rate.) Use a market for loanable funds graph to analyze the effects of this change in tax policy. What happens to the equilibrium real interest rate and the equilibrium quantity of loanable funds? What happens to the quantity of saving and investment?

LO 6.3

3.1 **[Related to the Chapter Opener on page 129]** Briefly explain whether production of each of the following goods is likely to fluctuate more or less than real GDP does during the business cycle:
   a. Ford F-150 pickup trucks
   b. McDonald's Big Macs
   c. Kenmore refrigerators
   d. Huggies diapers
   e. Bombardier passenger aircraft

3.2 No agency in Canada is responsible for declaring when recessions begin and end. Can you think of reasons why Statistics Canada, which is a federal government agency, might not want to take on this responsibility?

3.3 Some firms actually prosper by expanding during recessions. What risks do firms take when they pursue this strategy? Are there circumstances in particular industries under which a more cautious approach might be advisable? Briefly explain.

3.4 **[Related to Don't Let This Happen to You on page 146]** "Real GDP in 2012 was $1.6 trillion. This value is a large number. Therefore, economic growth must have been high during 2012." Briefly explain whether you agree with this statement.

Sollina Images/Blend
Images/Getty Images

Long-Run Economic Growth: Sources and Policies

Will Economic Reforms in Mexico Boost Growth?

Founded in 1944, Palliser Furniture Upholstery Ltd. is a Canadian firm based in Winnipeg, Manitoba, that makes customized furniture using high-end materials and specialized designs. In recent years, the company has faced strong competition and has sought ways to reduce costs. The firm considered building a factory in China but chose instead to go to Mexico, because it was closer and managers from the company could more easily oversee production. Today, Palliser's manufacturing for the Canadian market takes place in Winnipeg, while its three Mexican plants in the state of Coahuila service markets in Mexico, Latin America, and the United States.

Palliser is not alone in choosing to locate plants in Mexico rather than China. More than 2500 Canadian companies, including Bombardier, Linamar, and Scotiabank, and more than 18 000 US companies, including many Fortune 500 firms, have operations in Mexico. As Christopher Wilson, an economist at the Woodrow Wilson International Center for Scholars in Washington, observed: "Mexico has become the most competitive place to manufacture goods for the North American market." While proximity to the United States and Central and South America is an advantage of doing business in Mexico, rather than China or India, investing in Mexico can be risky. Organized crime and corruption are major concerns. Coca-Cola, for example, suspended its operations in Chilpancingo because of attacks on its employees. Some local Mexican firms have been reluctant to expand because they fear coming to the attention of criminal gangs who might demand payments or government inspectors who might demand bribes.

These problems indicate that the Mexican government has failed to fully establish the rule of law, which is critical for the long-term prospects of the Mexican economy. Without the rule of law, entrepreneurs cannot fulfill their role in the market system of bringing together the factors of production—labour, capital, and natural resources—to produce goods and services. Mexican entrepreneurs also suffer from problems in the banking system that make it difficult to obtain the funding needed to finance expansion.

Although Mexico has experienced some increases in real GDP per capita during the past 30 years, its record of economic growth has been disappointing, particularly in comparison with China and other rapidly growing countries in the developing world. Being able to attain faster rates of growth would benefit people in Mexico—particularly those with low incomes—and the wider world economy.

Based on Damien Cave, "As Ties with China Unravel, U.S. Companies Head to Mexico," *New York Times*, May 31, 2014; Dolia Estevez, "U.S. Warns against Rising Costs of Doing Business in Mexico Due to Criminal Activity," *Forbes*, June 5, 2014; and Laura Dawson, "Canada's Trade with Mexico: Where We've Been, Where We're Going and Why It Matters," *Canadian Council of Chief Executives*, February, 2014.

Economics in Your Life

Would You Be Better Off without China?

For decades, China was a very poor country whose economy was growing very slowly. In 1978, the government introduced economic reforms, which spurred rapid economic growth. Suppose that you could choose to live and work in a world with the Chinese economy growing very rapidly or in a world with the Chinese economy growing as slowly as it did before 1978. Which world would you choose to live in? How does the current high-growth, high-export Chinese economy affect you as a consumer? How does it affect you as someone about to start a career? As you read the chapter, try to answer these questions. You can check your answers against the one we provide on page 180 at the end of this chapter.

E conomic growth is not inevitable. For most of human history, no sustained increases in output per capita occurred, and, in the words of the philosopher Thomas Hobbes, the lives of most people were "poor, nasty, brutish, and short." Sustained economic growth first began with the Industrial Revolution in England in the late eighteenth century. From there, economic growth spread to the United States, Canada, and the countries of Western Europe. Following the end of World War II in 1945, rapid economic growth also began in Japan and, eventually, in several other Asian countries, but the economies of many other countries stagnated, leaving their people trapped in poverty.

Real GDP per capita is the best measure of a country's standard of living because it represents the ability of the average person to buy goods and services. Economic growth occurs when real GDP per capita increases. In this chapter we will develop a *model of economic growth* that will help us answer important questions like these:

- Why have countries such as Canada, the United States, and the United Kingdom, which had high standards of living at the beginning of the twentieth century, continued to grow rapidly?
- Why have countries such as Argentina, which at one time had relatively high standards of living, failed to keep pace?
- Why was the Soviet Union unable to sustain the rapid growth rates of its early years?
- Why are some countries that were very poor at the beginning of the twentieth century still very poor?

- Why have some countries, such as South Korea and Japan, that once were very poor now become much richer?
- What explains China's very rapid recent growth rates?

Economic Growth over Time and around the World

You live in a world that is very different from the world when your grandparents were young. You can listen to music on an iPhone that fits in your pocket; your grandparents played vinyl records on large stereo systems. You can send a text message to someone in another city, province, or country; your grandparents mailed letters that took days or weeks to arrive. More important, you have access to health care and medicines that have prolonged life and improved its quality. In many poorer countries, however, people endure grinding poverty and have only the bare necessities of life, just as their great-grandparents did.

The difference between you and people in poor countries is that you live in a country that has experienced substantial economic growth. A growing economy produces both increasing quantities of goods and services and better goods and services. It is only through economic growth that living standards can increase, but through most of human history, no economic growth took place. Even today, billions of people are living in countries where economic growth is extremely slow.

Economic Growth from 1 000 000 BCE to the Present

In 1 000 000 BCE (Before Common Era), our ancestors survived by hunting animals and gathering edible plants. Farming was many years in the future, and production was limited to food, clothing, shelter, and simple tools. Bradford DeLong, an economist at the University of California, Berkeley, estimates that in those primitive circumstances, GDP per capita was about $145 per year in 2015 dollars, which was the minimum amount necessary to sustain life. DeLong estimates that real GDP per capita worldwide was still $145 in the year 1300 CE (Common Era). In other words, no sustained economic growth occurred between 1 000 000 BCE and 1300 CE.

A peasant toiling on a farm in France in the year 1300 was no better off than his ancestors thousands of years before. In fact, for most of human existence, the typical person had only the bare minimum of food, clothing, and shelter necessary to sustain life. Few people survived beyond age 40, and most people suffered from debilitating illnesses.

Sustained economic growth did not begin until the **Industrial Revolution**, which started in England around the year 1750. The production of cotton cloth in factories using machinery powered by steam engines marked the beginning of the Industrial Revolution. Before that time, production of goods had relied almost exclusively on human or animal power. The use of mechanical power spread to the production of many other goods, greatly increasing the quantity of goods each worker could produce. First England and then other countries, such as Canada, the United States, France, and Germany, experienced *long-run economic growth*, with sustained increases in real GDP per capita that eventually raised living standards in those countries to the high levels of today.

Industrial Revolution The application of mechanical power to the production of goods, beginning in England around 1750.

Making the Connection | Why Did the Industrial Revolution Begin in England?

The Industrial Revolution was a key turning point in human history. Before the Industrial Revolution, economic growth was slow and halting. After the Industrial Revolution, economic growth became rapid and sustained in a number of countries. Although historians and economists agree on the importance of the Industrial Revolution, they have not reached a consensus on why it happened in the time and place that it did. Why the eighteenth century and not the sixteenth century or the twenty-first century? Why England and not China or India or Africa or Japan?

There is always a temptation to read history backward. We know when and where the Industrial Revolution occurred; therefore, it had to happen where it did and when

The British government's guarantee of property rights set the stage for the Industrial Revolution.

it did. But what was so special about England in the eighteenth century? Nobel Laureate Douglass North, of Washington University in St. Louis, has argued that institutions in England differed significantly from those in other countries in ways that greatly aided economic growth. North believes that the Glorious Revolution of 1688 was a key turning point. After that date, the British Parliament, rather than the king, controlled the government. The British court system also became independent of the king. As a result, the British government was credible when it committed to upholding private property rights, protecting wealth, and eliminating arbitrary increases in taxes. These institutional changes gave entrepreneurs incentives to make the investments necessary to use the important technological developments of the second half of the eighteenth century—particularly the spinning jenny and the water frame, which were used in the production of cotton textiles, and the steam engine, which was used in mining and in the manufacture of textiles and other products. Without the institutional changes, entrepreneurs would have been reluctant to risk their property or their wealth by starting new businesses.

Although not all economists agree with North's specific argument about the origins of the Industrial Revolution, we will see that most economists accept the idea that economic growth is not likely to occur unless a country's government provides the type of institutional framework North describes.

Sources: Based on Douglass C. North, *Understanding the Process of Economic Change* (Princeton, NJ: Princeton University Press, 2005); and Douglass C. North and Barry R. Weingast, "Constitutions and Commitment: The Evolution of Institutions Governing Public Choice in Seventeenth-Century England," *Journal of Economic History* Vol. 49, No. 4, December 1989.

MyEconLab   **Your Turn:** Test your understanding by doing related problem 1.1 on page 182 at the end of this chapter.

Figure 7.1 shows how growth rates of real GDP per capita for the entire world have changed over long periods. Prior to 1300 CE, there were no sustained increases in real GDP per capita. Over the next 500 years, to 1800, there was very slow growth. Significant growth began in the nineteenth century, as a result of the Industrial Revolution. A further acceleration in growth occurred during the twentieth century, as the average growth rate increased from 1.3 percent per year to 2.3 percent per year.

Small Differences in Growth Rates Are Important

The difference between 1.3 percent and 2.3 percent may seem trivial, but over long periods, small differences in growth rates can have a large effect. For example, suppose

Figure 7.1

Average Annual Growth Rates for the World Economy

World economic growth was essentially zero in the years before 1300, and it was very slow—an average of only 0.2 percent per year—between 1300 and 1800. The Industrial Revolution made possible the sustained increases in real GDP per capita that have allowed some countries to attain high standards of living.

Source: Data from J. Bradford DeLong, "Estimating World GDP, One Million B.C.–Present," working paper, University of California, Berkeley.

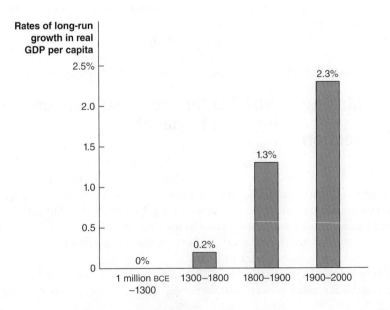

you have $100 in a savings account earning an interest rate of 1.3 percent, which means you will receive an interest payment of $1.30 this year. If the interest rate on the account is 2.3 percent, you will earn $2.30. The difference of an extra $1.00 interest payment seems insignificant. But if you leave the interest as well as the original $100 in your account for another year, the difference becomes greater because now the higher interest rate is applied to a larger amount—$102.30—and the lower interest rate is applied to a smaller amount—$101.30. This process, known as *compounding*, magnifies even small differences in interest rates over long periods of time. Over a period of 50 years, your $100 would grow to $312 at an interest rate of 2.3 percent but to only $191 at an interest rate of 1.3 percent.

The principle of compounding applies to economic growth rates as well as to interest rates. For example, in 1950, real GDP per capita in Argentina was $5474 (measured in 2005 US dollars), which was larger than Italy's real GDP per capita of $5361. Over the next 64 years, the economic growth rate in Italy averaged 2.5 percent per year, while in Argentina, the growth rate was only 1.5 percent per year. Although this difference in growth rates of only 1 percentage point may seem small, in 2014, real GDP per capita in Italy had risen to $26 550, while real GDP per capita in Argentina was only $13 980. In other words, because of a relatively small difference in the growth rates of the two economies, the standard of living of the typical person in Italy went from being a little below that of a typical person in Argentina to being much higher. Here is the key point to keep in mind: *In the long run, small differences in economic growth rates result in big differences in living standards.*

Why Do Growth Rates Matter?

Why should anyone care about growth rates? Growth rates matter because an economy that grows too slowly fails to raise living standards. In some countries in Africa and Asia, very little economic growth has occurred in the past 50 years, so many people remain in severe poverty. In high-income countries, only 4 out of every 1000 babies die before they are 2 year old. In the poorest countries, more than 100 out of every 1000 babies die before they are 2 year old, and millions of children die annually from diseases that could be avoided with access to clean water or cured by using medicines that cost only a few dollars.

Although their problems are less dramatic, countries that experience slow growth have also missed opportunities to improve the lives of their citizens. For example, the failure of Argentina to grow as rapidly as the other countries that had similar levels of GDP per capita in 1950 has left many of its people in poverty. Life expectancy in Argentina is lower than in Canada and other high-income countries, and about 50 percent more babies in Argentina die before the age of 1.

Don't Let This Happen to You

Don't Confuse the Average Annual Percentage Change with the Total Percentage Change

When economists talk about growth rates over a period of more than one year, the numbers are always *average annual percentage changes* and *not* total percentage changes. For example, in Canada, real GDP per capita was $12 931 in 1960 and $38 293 in 2014 (in 2005 US dollars). The percentage change in real GDP per capita between these two years is:

$$\left(\frac{\$38\ 293 - \$12\ 931}{\$12\ 931}\right) \times 100 = 196\%.$$

However, this is *not* the growth rate between the two years. The growth rate between these two years is the rate at which $12 931 in 1960 would have to grow on average *each year* to end up as $38 293 in 2014, which is 2.0 percent.

In general, the average annual growth rate between year 0 (in this case, 1960) and year *t* (in this case, 2014) can be calculated as follows:

$$\text{Average annual growth rate} = \left[\frac{y_t}{y_0}\right]^{1/t} - 1.$$

MyEconLab
Your Turn: Test your understanding by doing related problem 1.4 on page 183 at the end of this chapter.

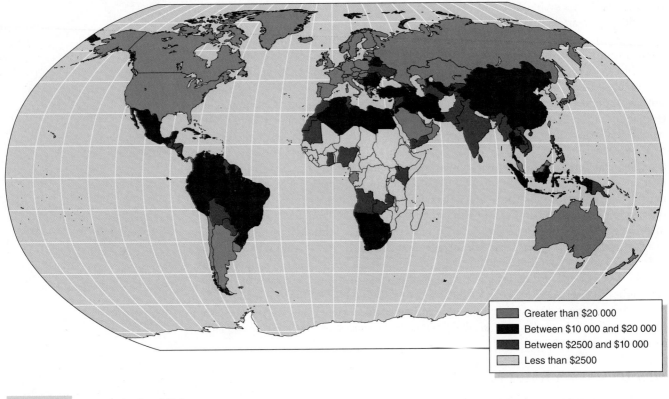

Legend:
- Greater than $20 000
- Between $10 000 and $20 000
- Between $2500 and $10 000
- Less than $2500

Figure 7.2 GDP per Capita, 2014

GDP per capita is measured in US dollars, corrected for differences across countries in the cost of living.

"The Rich Get Richer and..."

We can divide the world's economies into two groups:

1. The *high-income countries*, sometimes also referred to as the *industrial countries* or the *developed countries*, including Australia, Canada, Japan, New Zealand, the United States, and the countries of Western Europe
2. The lower-income countries, or *developing countries*, including most of the countries of Africa, Asia, and Latin America

In the 1980s and 1990s, a small group of countries, mostly East Asian countries such as Singapore, South Korea, and Taiwan, began to experience high rates of growth and are sometimes referred to as the *newly industrializing countries*.

Figure 7.2 shows the levels of GDP per capita around the world in 2014. GDP is measured in US dollars, corrected for differences across countries in the cost of living. In 2014, GDP per capita ranged from a high of $144 400 in the Persian Gulf country of Qatar to a low of $600 in the Central African Republic. To understand why the gap between rich and poor countries exists, we need to look at what causes economies to grow.

Making the Connection | **Is Income All that Matters?**

The more income you have, the more goods and services you can buy. When people are surviving on very low incomes of $2 per day or less, their ability to buy even minimal amounts of food, clothing, and housing is limited. So, most economists argue that unless the incomes of the very poor increase significantly, they will be unable to attain a higher standard of living. In some countries—primarily those coloured in yellow in Figure 7.2—the growth in average income has been very slow, or even negative, over a period of decades. Many economists and policymakers have concluded that the standard of living in these countries has been largely unchanged for many years.

Some economists argue, though, that if we look beyond income to other measures of the standard of living, we can see that even the poorest countries have made significant progress in recent decades. For example, Charles Kenny, an economist with the Center for Global Development, argues that "those countries with the lowest quality of life are making the fastest progress in improving it—across a range of measures including health, education, and civil and political liberties." For example, since 1960, deaths among children declined, often by more than 50 percent, in nearly all countries, including most of those with the lowest incomes. Even in sub-Saharan Africa, where growth in incomes has been very slow, the percentage of children dying before age 5 has decreased by more than 30 percent over the past 50 years. Similarly, the percentage of people able to read and write

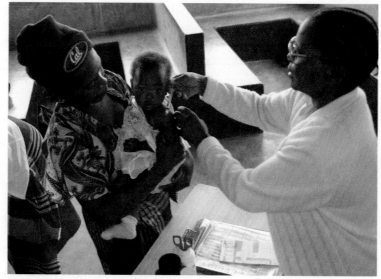

In sub-Saharan Africa and other parts of the world, increases in technology and knowledge are leading to improvements in health care and the standard of living.

has more than doubled in sub-Saharan Africa since 1970. Many more people now live in democracies where basic civil rights are respected than at any other time in world history. Although some countries, such as Somalia, Democratic Republic of the Congo, and Afghanistan, have suffered from civil wars, political instability has also decreased in many countries in recent years, which has reduced the likelihood of dying from violence.

What explains these improvements in health, education, democracy, and political stability? William Easterly, an economist at New York University, has found that, although at any given time countries that have a higher income also have a higher standard of living, over time increases in income *within a particular country* are typically not the main cause of improvements in a country's standard of living in terms of health, education, individual rights, political stability, and similar factors. Kenny's argument and Easterly's finding are connected: Some increases in living standards do not require significant increases in income. The key factors in raising living standards in low-income countries have been increases in technology and knowledge—such as the development of inexpensive vaccines that reduce epidemics or the use of mosquito-resistant netting that reduces the prevalence of malaria—that are inexpensive enough to be widely available. Changes in attitudes, such as placing a greater value on education, particularly for girls, or increasing support for political freedoms, have also played a role in improving conditions in low-income countries.

There are limits, of course, to how much living standards can increase if incomes stagnate. Ultimately, much higher rates of economic growth will be necessary for low-income countries to significantly close the gap in living standards with high-income countries.

Sources: Based on Charles Kenny, *Getting Better* (New York: Basic Books, 2011); Ursula Casabonne and Charles Kenny, "The Best Things in Life Are (Nearly) Free: Technology, Knowledge, and Global Health," Center for Global Development Working Paper No. 252, May 31, 2011; and William Easterly, "Life during Growth," *Journal of Economic Growth*, Vol. 4, No. 3, September 1999, pp. 239-276.

Your Turn: Test your understanding by doing related problems 1.5 and 1.6 on page 183 at the end of this chapter.

Economic growth model A model that explains growth rates in real GDP per capita over the long run.

MyEconLab

What Determines How Fast Economies Grow?

To explain changes in economic growth rates over time within countries and differences in growth rates among countries, we need to develop an *economic growth model*. An **economic growth model** explains growth rates in real GDP per capita over the long

7.2 LEARNING OBJECTIVE

Use the economic growth model to explain why growth rates differ across countries.

Labour productivity The quantity of goods and services that can be produced by one hour of work.

run. As we have seen, the average person can buy more goods and services only if the average worker produces more goods and services. Recall that **labour productivity** is the quantity of goods and services that can be produced by one worker or by one hour of work. Because of the importance of labour productivity in explaining economic growth, the economic growth model focuses on the causes of long-run increases in labour productivity.

How can a country's workers become more productive? Economists believe two key factors determine labour productivity:

1. The quantity of capital available to workers
2. The level of technology

Technological change A change in the quantity of output a firm can produce using a given quantity of inputs.

Therefore, to explain changes in real GDP per capita, the economic growth model focuses on technological change and changes over time in the quantity of capital available to workers. Recall that **technological change** is a change in the quantity of output firms can produce using a given quantity of inputs.

There are three main sources of technological change:

1. **Better machinery and equipment.** Beginning with the steam engine during the Industrial Revolution, the invention of new machinery has been an important source of rising labour productivity. Today, continuing improvements in computers, factory machine tools, electric generators, and many other machines contribute to increases in labour productivity.
2. **Increases in human capital.** Capital refers to *physical capital*, including computers, factory buildings, machine tools, warehouses, and trucks. The more physical capital workers have available, the more output they can produce. **Human capital** is the accumulated knowledge and skills that workers acquire from education and training or from their life experiences. As workers increase their human capital through education or on-the-job training, their productivity also increases. The more educated workers are, the greater is their human capital.
3. **Better means of organizing and managing production.** Labour productivity increases if managers can do a better job of organizing production. For example, the *just-in-time system*, first developed by Toyota Motor Corporation, involves assembling goods from parts that arrive at the factory at exactly the time they are needed. With this system, firms need fewer workers to store and keep track of parts in the factory, so the quantity of goods produced per hour worked increases.

Human capital The accumulated knowledge and skills that workers acquire from education and training or from their life experiences.

Note that technological change is *not* the same thing as more physical capital. New capital can *embody* technological change, as when a faster computer chip is embodied in a new computer. But simply adding more capital that is the same as existing capital is not technological change. To summarize, we can say that a country's standard of living will be higher the more capital workers have available on their jobs, the better the capital, the more human capital workers have, and the better the job managers do in organizing production.

The Per-Worker Production Function

Per-worker production function The relationship between real GDP per hour worked and capital per hour worked, holding the level of technology constant.

Often when analyzing economic growth, we look at increases in real GDP *per hour worked* and increases in capital *per hour worked*. We use measures of GDP per hour and capital per hour rather than per person, so we can analyze changes in the underlying ability of an economy to produce more goods with a given amount of labour without having to worry about changes in the fraction of the population working or in the length of the workday. We can illustrate the economic growth model using the **per-worker production function**, which is the relationship between real GDP per hour worked and capital per hour worked, *holding the level of technology constant*. For simplicity, from now on we will shorten "per-worker production function" to just "production function." Figure 7.3 shows the production function as a graph. In the figure, we measure capital per hour worked along the horizontal axis and real GDP per hour worked

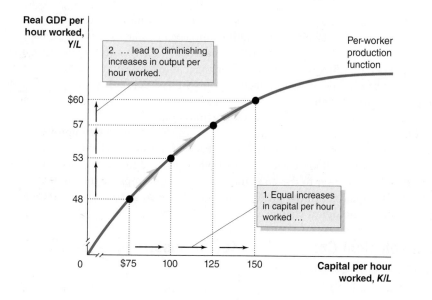

Figure 7.3

The Per-Worker Production Function

The per-worker production function shows the relationship between capital per hour worked and real GDP per hour worked, holding technology constant. Increases in capital per hour worked increase output per hour worked but at a diminishing rate. For example, an increase in capital per hour worked from $75 to $100 increases real GDP per hour worked from $48 to $53. An increase in capital per hour worked from $100 to $125 increases real GDP per hour worked by a smaller amount, from $53 to $57. Each additional $25 increase in capital per hour worked results in a progressively smaller increase in output per hour worked.

along the vertical axis. Letting K stand for capital, L stand for labour, and Y stand for real GDP, real GDP per hour worked is Y/L, and capital per hour worked is K/L. The curve represents the production function. Notice that we do not explicitly show technological change in the figure. We assume that as we move along the production function, the level of technology remains constant. As we will see, we can illustrate technological change using this graph by *shifting up* the curve representing the production function.

The figure shows that increases in the quantity of capital per hour worked result in movements up along the production function, increasing the quantity of output each worker produces. When *we hold technology constant*, however, equal increases in the amount of capital per hour worked lead to *diminishing* increases in output per hour worked. For example, increasing capital per hour worked from $75 to $100 increases real GDP per hour worked from $48 to $53, an increase of $5. Another $25 increase in capital per hour worked, from $100 to $125, increases real GDP per hour worked from $53 to $57, an increase of only $4. Each additional $25 increase in capital per hour worked results in progressively smaller increases in real GDP per hour worked. In fact, at very high levels of capital per hour worked, further increases in capital per hour worked will not result in any increase in real GDP per hour worked. This effect results from the *law of diminishing returns*, which states that as we add more of one input—in this case, capital—to a fixed quantity of another input—in this case, labour—output increases by smaller additional amounts.

Why are there diminishing returns to capital? Consider a simple example in which you own a copy store. At first you have 10 employees but only 1 copy machine, so each of your workers is able to produce relatively few copies per day. When you buy a second copy machine, your employees will be able to produce more copies. Adding additional copy machines will continue to increase your output—but by increasingly smaller amounts. For example, adding a twentieth copy machine to the 19 you already have will not increase the copies each worker is able to make by nearly as much as adding a second copy machine did. Eventually, adding additional copying machines will not increase your output at all.

Which Is More Important for Economic Growth: More Capital or Technological Change?

Technological change helps economies avoid diminishing returns to capital. Let's consider two simple examples of the effects of technological change. First, suppose you have 10 copy machines in your copy store. Each copy machine can produce 10 copies per minute. You don't believe that adding an eleventh machine identical to the 10 you already have will significantly increase the number of copies your employees can produce in a day. Then you find out that a new copy machine has become available that produces 20 copies per minute. If you replace your existing machines with the new machines, the productivity of your workers will increase. The replacement of existing capital with more productive capital is an example of technological change.

Or suppose you realize that the layout of your store could be improved. Maybe the paper for the machines is on shelves at the back of the store, which requires your workers to spend time walking back and forth whenever the machines run out of paper. By placing the paper closer to the copy machines, you can improve the productivity of your workers. Reorganizing how production takes place so as to increase output is also an example of technological change.

Technological Change: The Key to Sustaining Economic Growth

Figure 7.4 shows the effect of technological change on the production function. Technological change shifts up the production function and allows an economy to produce more real GDP per hour worked with the same quantity of capital per hour worked. For example, if the current level of technology puts the economy on Production function$_1$, then when capital per hour worked is $150, real GDP per hour worked is $60. Technological change that shifts the economy to Production function$_2$ makes it possible to produce $65 in goods and services per hour worked with the same level of capital per hour worked. Further increases in technology that shift the economy to higher production functions result in further increases in real GDP per hour worked. Because of diminishing returns to capital, continuing increases in real GDP per hour worked can be sustained only if there is technological change. Remember that a country will experience increases in its standard of living only if it experiences increases in real GDP per hour worked. Therefore, we can draw the following important conclusion: *In the long run, a country will experience an increasing standard of living only if it experiences continuing technological change.*

Figure 7.4

Technological Change Increases Output per Hour Worked

Technological change shifts up the production function and allows more output per hour worked with the same amount of capital per hour worked. For example, along Production function$_1$ with $150 in capital per hour worked, the economy can produce $60 in real GDP per hour worked. However, an increase in technology that shifts the economy to Production function$_2$ makes it possible to produce $65 in real GDP per hour worked with the same level of capital per hour worked.

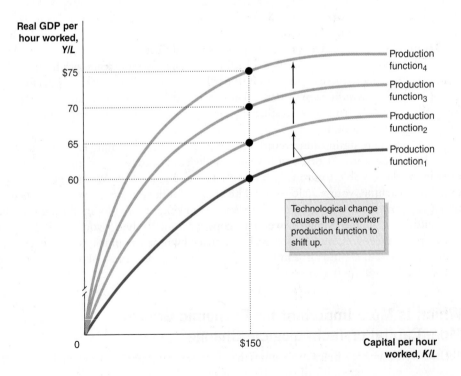

Making the Connection

What Explains the Economic Failure of the Soviet Union?

The economic growth model can help explain one of the most striking events of the twentieth century: the economic collapse of the Soviet Union. The Soviet Union was formed from the old Russian Empire following the Russian Revolution of 1917. Under Communism, the Soviet Union was a centrally planned economy where the government owned nearly every business and made all production and pricing decisions. In 1960, Nikita Khrushchev, the leader of the Soviet Union, addressed the United Nations in New York City. He declared to the United States and the other democracies: "We will bury you. Your grandchildren will live under Communism."

Many people at the time took Khrushchev's boast seriously. Capital per hour worked grew rapidly in the Soviet Union from 1950 through the 1980s. At first, these increases in capital per hour worked also produced rapid increases in real GDP per hour worked. Rapid increases in real GDP per hour worked during the 1950s caused some economists in the United States to predict incorrectly that the Soviet Union would someday surpass the United States economically. In fact, diminishing returns to capital meant that the additional factories the Soviet Union was building resulted in smaller and smaller increases in real GDP per hour worked.

In the former Soviet Union there were frequent shortages, and unhappy consumers often had to wait in long lines to shop for groceries and other goods.

The Soviet Union did experience some technological change—but at a rate much slower than in the United States and other high-income countries. Why did the Soviet Union fail the crucial requirement for growth: implementing new technologies? The key reason is that in a centrally planned economy, the people managing most businesses are government employees and not entrepreneurs or independent businesspeople, as is the case in market economies. Soviet managers had little incentive to adopt new ways of producing goods and services. Their pay depended on producing the quantity of output specified in the government's economic plan, not on discovering new, better, and lower-cost ways to produce goods. In addition, these managers did not have to worry about competition from either domestic or foreign firms.

Entrepreneurs and managers of firms in Canada and the United States, by contrast, are under intense competitive pressure from other firms. They must constantly search for better ways of producing the goods and services they sell. Developing and using new technologies is an important way to gain a competitive edge and earn higher profits. The drive for profit provides an incentive for technological change that centrally planned economies are unable to duplicate. In market economies, entrepreneurs and managers who have their own money on the line make decisions about which investments to make and which technologies to adopt. Nothing concentrates the mind like having your own funds at risk.

In hindsight, it is clear that a centrally planned economy, such as the Soviet Union's, could not, over the long run, grow faster than a market economy. The Soviet Union collapsed in 1991, and contemporary Russia now has a more market-oriented system, although the government continues to play a much larger role in the economy than does the government in Canada.

Your Turn: Test your understanding by doing related problem 2.6 on page 184 at the end of this chapter.

MyEconLab

Solved Problem **7.1**

Using the Economic Growth Model to Analyze the Failure of the Soviet Economy

Use the economic growth model and the information in *Making the Connection* on page 161 to analyze the economic problems the Soviet Union encountered.

Solving the Problem

Step 1: **Review the chapter material.** This problem is about using the economic growth model to explain the failure of the Soviet economy.

Step 2: **Draw a graph like Figure 7.3 on page 159 to illustrate the economic problems of the Soviet Union.** For simplicity, assume that the Soviet Union experienced no technological change.

The Soviet Union experienced rapid increases in capital per hour worked from 1950 through the 1980s, but its failure to implement new technology meant that output per hour worked grew at a slower and slower rate.

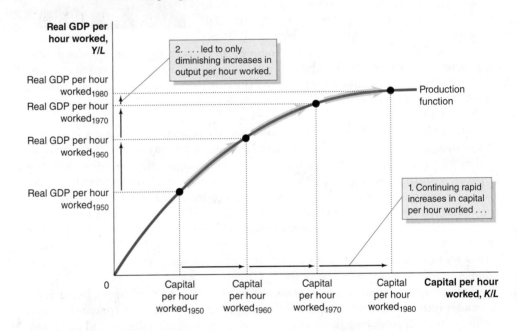

Extra Credit: The Soviet Union hoped to raise the standard of living of its citizens above that enjoyed in the United States and other high-income countries. Its strategy was to make continuous increases in the quantity of capital available to its workers. The economic growth model helps us understand the flaws in this policy for achieving economic growth.

MyEconLab   **Your Turn:** For more practice, do related problems 2.3 and 2.4 on page 184 at the end of this chapter.

New Growth Theory

The economic growth model we have been using was first developed in the 1950s by Nobel Laureate Robert Solow of MIT. According to this model, productivity growth is the key factor in explaining long-run growth in real GDP per capita. In recent years, some economists have become dissatisfied with this model because it does not explain the factors that determine productivity growth. Paul Romer, of New York University, developed the **new growth theory** to provide a better explanation of the sources of technological change. Romer argues that the rate of technological change is influenced by how individuals and firms respond to economic incentives. Earlier accounts of economic growth did not explain technological change or attributed it to factors such as chance scientific discoveries.

Romer argues that the accumulation of *knowledge capital* is a key determinant of economic growth. Firms add to an economy's stock of knowledge capital when they engage in research and development or otherwise contribute to technological change. We have seen that accumulation of physical capital is subject to diminishing returns: Increases in capital per hour worked lead to increases in real GDP per hour worked but at a decreasing rate. Romer argues that the same is true of knowledge capital *at the firm level*. As firms add to their stock of knowledge capital, they increase their output but at a decreasing rate. At the level of the entire economy, however, Romer argues that knowledge capital is subject to *increasing returns*. Increasing returns can exist because knowledge, once discovered, becomes available to everyone. The use of physical capital, such as a computer or machine tool, is *rival* because if one firm uses it, other firms cannot, and it is *excludable* because the firm that owns the capital can keep other firms from using it. The use of knowledge capital, such as the chemical formula for a drug that cures cancer, is nonrival, however, because one firm's using that knowledge does not prevent another firm from using it. Knowledge capital is also nonexcludable because once something like a chemical formula becomes known, it becomes widely available for other firms to use (unless, as we discuss shortly, the government gives the firm that invents a new product the legal right to its exclusive use).

Because knowledge capital is nonrival and nonexcludable, firms can *free ride* on the research and development of other firms. Firms free ride when they benefit from the results of research and development they did not pay for. For example, transistor technology was first developed at Western Electric's Bell Laboratories in the 1950s and served as the basic technology of the information revolution. Bell Laboratories, however, received only a tiny fraction of the immense profits that were eventually made by all the firms that used this technology. Romer points out that firms are unlikely to invest in research and development up to the point where the marginal cost of the research equals the marginal return from the knowledge gained because *other* firms gain much of the marginal return. Therefore, there is likely to be an inefficiently small amount of research and development, slowing the accumulation of knowledge capital and economic growth.

Government policy can help increase the accumulation of knowledge capital in three ways:

1. **Protecting intellectual property with patents and copyrights.** Governments can increase the incentive to engage in research and development by giving firms the exclusive rights to their discoveries for a period of years. The Canadian government grants patents to companies that develop new products or new ways of making existing products. A **patent** gives a firm the exclusive legal right to a new product for a period of 20 years from the date the patent is filed with the government. For example, a pharmaceutical firm that develops a drug that cures cancer can secure a patent on the drug, keeping other firms from manufacturing the drug without permission. The profits earned during the period the patent is in force provide firms with an incentive for undertaking research and development. The patent system has drawbacks, however. In filing for a patent, a firm must disclose information about the product or process. This information enters the public record and may help competing firms develop products or processes that are similar but that do not infringe on the patent. To avoid this problem, a firm may try to keep the results of its research a *trade secret*, without patenting it. (A famous example of a trade secret is the formula for Coca-Cola.) Tension also arises between the government's objectives of providing patent protection that gives firms the incentive to engage in research and development and making sure that the knowledge gained through the research is widely available, which increases the positive effect of the knowledge on the economy. Economists debate the features of an ideal patent system.

New growth theory A model of long-run economic growth that emphasizes that technological change is influenced by economic incentives and so is determined by the working of the market system.

Patent The exclusive right to produce a product for a period of 20 years from the date the patent is applied for.

2. **Supporting research and development.** The government can help increase the quantity of research and development that takes place. In Canada, the federal government conducts some research directly. The government also subsidizes research by providing grants and other payments to researchers in universities through a number of agencies. Finally, the government provides tax benefits to firms that invest in research and development.

3. **Subsidizing education.** People with technical training carry out research and development. If firms are unable to capture all the profits from research and development, they will pay lower wages and salaries to technical workers. These lower wages and salaries reduce the incentive to workers to receive this training. If the government subsidizes education, it can increase the number of workers who have technical training. In Canada, the government subsidizes education by directly providing free education from grades kindergarten through 12 and by providing support for public colleges and universities. The government also provides student loans at reduced interest rates.

These government policies can bring the accumulation of knowledge capital closer to the optimal level.

Joseph Schumpeter and Creative Destruction

The new growth theory has revived interest in the ideas of Joseph Schumpeter. Born in Austria in 1883, Schumpeter served briefly as that country's finance minister. In 1932, he became an economics professor at Harvard University. Schumpeter developed a model of growth that emphasized his view that new products unleash a "gale of creative destruction" that drives older products—and, often, the firms that produced them—out of the market. According to Schumpeter, the key to rising living standards is not small changes to existing products but, rather, new products that meet consumer wants in qualitatively better ways. For example, in the early twentieth century, the automobile displaced the horse-drawn carriage by meeting consumer demand for personal transportation in a way that was qualitatively better. In the early twenty-first century, the DVD and the DVD player displaced the VHS tape and the VCR by better meeting consumer demand for watching films at home. Downloading or streaming movies from the Internet are now in the process of displacing the DVD just as the DVD displaced the VHS tape.

To Schumpeter, the entrepreneur is central to economic growth: "The function of entrepreneurs is to reform or revolutionize the pattern of production by exploiting an invention or, more generally, an untried technological possibility for producing new commodities or producing an old one in a new way."

The profits an entrepreneur hopes to earn provide the incentive for bringing together the factors of production—labour, capital, and natural resources—to start new firms and introduce new goods and services. Successful entrepreneurs can use their profits to finance the development of new products and are better able to attract funds from investors.

7.3 LEARNING OBJECTIVE

Discuss fluctuations in productivity growth in Canada.

Economic Growth in Canada

The economic growth model can help us understand the record of growth in Canada. Figure 7.5 shows average annual growth rates in real GDP per person since 1870. As Canada experienced the Industrial Revolution during the nineteenth century, Canadian firms increased the quantities of capital per hour worked. New technologies such as the steam engine, the railroad, and the telegraph also became available. Together, these factors resulted in an average annual growth rate of real GDP per person of 1.7 percent from 1870 to 1900. At this growth rate, real GDP per capita would double about every 41 years, which means that living standards were growing steadily and relatively fast.

By the twentieth century, technological change had been institutionalized. Many large corporations began to set up research and development facilities to improve the quality of their products and the efficiency with which they produced them. Universities

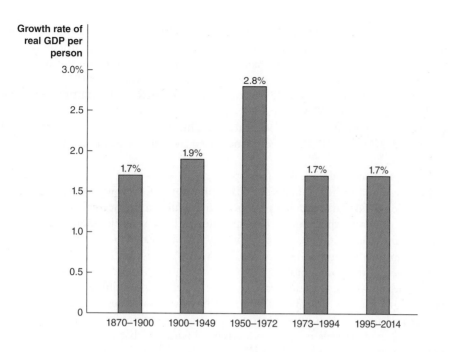

Figure 7.5

Average Annual Growth Rates in Real GDP per Person in Canada

The growth rate in Canada increased from 1870 through the mid-1970s. Then growth slowed considerably.

Sources: Data on nominal GDP and the GDP deflator since 1961 are from Statistics Canada, CANSIM Table II, series V3862688 and V3860248; values from 1870 to 1960 are from M. C. Urquhart, "Canadian Economic Growth 1870–1985" (Discussion paper no. 734, Institute for Economic Research, Queens University, Kingston, ON, 1988); since 1971, the population series is from Statistics Canada, CANSIM Table II, series V466668; from 1921 to 1970, the population series is from Statistics Canada, CANSIM Table I, series D892580; and from 1870 to 1920, the population series is from Urquhart (1988).

also began to conduct research that had business applications. The accelerating rate of technological change led to more rapid growth rates.

Economic Growth in Canada since 1950

Continuing technological change allowed the Canadian economy to avoid the diminishing returns to capital that stifled growth in the Soviet economy. In fact, until the 1970s, growth of the Canadian economy accelerated over time. As Figure 7.5 shows, growth in the first half of the twentieth century was faster than growth during the nineteenth century, and growth in the immediate post–World War II period from 1950 to 1972 was faster yet. Then the unexpected happened: For more than 20 years, from 1973 to 1994, the growth rate of real GDP per person decreased. The growth rate during these years was more than 1 percentage point per year lower than during the 1950 to 1972 period. Beginning in the mid-1990s, the growth rate declined again, although it remained at roughly the same rate as for the 1973 to 1994 period.

Is Canada Headed for a Long Period of Slow Growth?

Economists have not reached a consensus in explaining the swings in Canadian productivity growth. Broadly speaking, economists' views fall into two camps:

- **The optimistic view.** Some economists argue that although productivity has become more difficult to measure for reasons discussed later, in the long run rates of productivity growth will remain high, significantly increasing the standard of living of the average person in the decades ahead.

- **The pessimistic view.** Other economists believe that productivity growth entered a long-run decline in the mid-1970s that was partly overcome only for a brief period of time by the initial effects of the revolution in information technology. These economists argue that future productivity growth rates are likely to remain low and, therefore, the standard of living of the average person in Canada will increase only slowly.

We can briefly discuss some of the key issues involved in this debate.

Measurement Issues Some economists argue that recent productivity growth rates may appear worse than they are because of problems in measuring output. If growth in real GDP understates the true growth rate of output, then measured productivity growth will also understate the true growth rate of productivity. After 1970, services—such as haircuts and financial advice—became a larger fraction of GDP, and goods—such as automobiles and hamburgers—became a smaller fraction. It is more difficult to measure increases in the output of services than to measure increases in the output of goods. For example, before banks began using automated teller machines (ATMs) in the 1980s, you could withdraw money only by going to a bank before closing time—which was usually 3:00 P.M. Once ATMs became available, you could withdraw money at any time of the day or night at a variety of locations. This increased convenience from ATMs does not show up in GDP. If it did, measured output per hour worked would have grown more rapidly.

There may also be a measurement problem in accounting for improvements in the environment and in health and safety. Beginning in 1970, new laws required firms to spend billions of dollars reducing pollution, improving workplace safety, and redesigning products to improve their safety. This spending did not result in additional output that would be included in GDP—although it may have increased overall well-being. If these increases in well-being had been included in GDP, measured output per hour worked would have grown more rapidly.

All the high-income countries have experienced roughly similar movements in productivity growth rates. Because all the high-income economies began producing more services and fewer goods and enacted stricter environmental regulations at about the same time, explanations of the productivity slowdown that emphasize measurement problems become more plausible.

The Role of Information Technology Some economists argue that the development of *information technology* (*IT*) caused the productivity growth that began in the mid-1990s. As computers became less expensive and faster, they made it possible for people and organizations to communicate and process data more efficiently. Today, a single laptop computer has more computing power than all the mainframe computers NASA used to control the *Apollo* spacecrafts that landed on the moon in the late 1960s and early 1970s.

Faster data processing has had a major effect on nearly every firm. Business record keeping, once done laboriously by hand, is now done more quickly and accurately by computers. During the 1990s, firms used the Internet to market and sell products. Smartphones, tablets, laptop computers, and wireless Internet access allow people to work at home and while travelling. These developments in IT have significantly increased labour productivity.

Despite the wonders of IT, productivity growth since 1995 has fallen to the same rate as during the period from the mid-1970s to the mid-1990s. Is IT not a productivity booster, or are the data not capturing some of IT's benefits? What insight do the answers to these questions give us about how rapid growth will be in the coming decades?

Some economists believe that developments in IT have improved the delivery of services to both consumers and firms in ways that the GDP statistics fail to capture. For instance, receiving detailed driving directions using Google Maps or a similar app is much easier than before smartphones were developed. In recent years, the widespread use of apps to arrange for car rides, make short-term room rentals, locate friends, and so on have provided benefits to consumers that are not measured or are only partially measured by GDP. Similarly, a store manager can quickly check on available warehouse inventory using a dedicated smartphone or tablet app.

Economists who believe that IT is having large, but difficult to measure, effects on the economy are usually also optimistic about future growth rates. They believe that continuing advances in semiconductor technology—which underlie progress in IT—will result in substantial gains in labour productivity. The gains will come from higher productivity in the IT sector itself and in other sectors of the economy as the result of progress made possible by advances in IT. For example, ever more rapid and inexpensive computing lowers the cost and speeds the adoption of existing products, such as 3D printers, and helps innovators develop new products, which, in turn, raise productivity growth above its current levels.

Other economists doubt that the unmeasured benefits of the IT revolution are any greater than the unmeasured benefits of earlier innovations. Robert J. Gordon of Northwestern University has argued that productivity increases from the IT revolution were in fact much smaller than increases resulting from earlier innovations, such as the railroad, electrification of homes and businesses, petroleum refining, and the automobile. Moreover, Gordon and some other economists argue that most of the gains from the IT revolution occurred in the 1990s, as a result of the development of the World Wide Web, Windows, and computerized inventory control systems. These innovations raised labour productivity because they changed how businesses operated. By the early 2000s, the IT revolution was having a greater effect on consumer products, such as smartphones and tablets, than on labour productivity. Gordon identifies other factors, such as an aging population, declining educational achievement, and the consequences of increased regulations and higher taxes, that will lead to lower productivity growth rates. Gordon forecasts an extended period of productivity growth rates of 0.5 percent or less.

"Secular Stagnation ... " In the late 1930s, toward the end of the Great Depression, Alvin Hansen of Harvard University predicted that the US economy would experience an extended period of slow growth, or *secular stagnation*. The rapid growth rates the US economy experienced beginning in 1950 indicate that Hansen's analysis was incorrect. Recently, however, Lawrence Summers of Harvard, along with some other economists, has revived the term in arguing that growth rates are likely to remain low in future years. These economists do not focus on potentially slow rates of technological progress. Instead, they believe that real GDP may grow slowly because of insufficient demand for investment spending.

In Chapter 6, we saw that in the loanable funds model, the equilibrium level of saving and investment is determined at the level of the real interest rate, where the quantity of loanable funds demanded equals the quantity of loanable funds supplied. Economists who forecast a future of secular stagnation believe that the demand for loanable funds may be low in coming years for three main reasons:

1. Slowing population growth in Canada will reduce the demand for housing.
2. Modern information technology firms, such as Twitter, Google, and Facebook, require much less capital than older industrial firms, such as General Motors or General Electric.
3. The price of capital, particularly information technology goods such as computers, has been falling relative to the prices of other goods. Accordingly, firms can meet their needs for capital with lower levels of expenditure.

As a result of these factors, the real interest that brings equality to the loanable funds market may be very low—possibly even negative. So, investment spending will be very low. With this component of GDP growing slowly, GDP will itself only grow slowly.

... or a Return to Faster Growth? Critics of the secular stagnation view believe that low rates of investment in recent years have resulted from the severity of the recession of 2007–2009 and the relatively slow recovery from that recession. They argue that as the economic recovery continues, the demand for investment goods will increase. In addition, they argue that economic growth in other countries may increase the demand for Canadian goods, allowing exports to increase, thereby offsetting the effects on GDP of lower production of investment goods.

The debate over future growth rates is an important one. If the optimistic forecasts are correct, then in future decades, the Canadian standard of living will be much higher than if the pessimistic forecasts are correct. A large difference in the standard of living will have an enormous effect on nearly every aspect of Canadian life, including the extent of poverty, the ability of individuals and the government to finance increasing medical costs, and the ability of the country to deal with the effects of an aging population.

Figure 7.6

The Catch-up Predicted by the Economic Growth Model

According to the economic growth model, countries that start with lower levels of real GDP per capita should grow faster (points near the upper-left section of the line) than countries that start with higher levels of real GDP per capita (points near the lower-right section of the line).

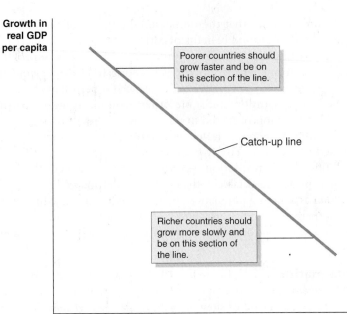

7.4 **LEARNING** OBJECTIVE

Explain economic catch-up and discuss why many poor countries have not experienced rapid economic growth.

Catch-up The prediction that the level of GDP per capita (or income per capita) in poor countries will grow faster than in rich countries.

Why Isn't the Whole World Rich?

The economic growth model tells us that economies grow when the quantity of capital per hour worked increases and when technological change occurs. This model seems to provide a good blueprint for developing countries to become rich:

1. Increase the quantity of capital per hour worked.
2. Use the best available technology.

There are economic incentives for both of these things to happen in poor countries. The profitability of using additional capital or better technology is generally greater in a developing country than in a high-income country. For example, replacing an existing computer with a new, faster computer will generally have a relatively small payoff for a firm in Canada. In contrast, installing a new computer in a Zambian firm where records have been kept by hand is likely to have an enormous payoff.

This observation leads to an important conclusion: *The economic growth model predicts that poor countries will grow faster than rich countries.* If this prediction is correct, we should observe poor countries catching up to rich countries in levels of GDP per capita (or income per capita). Has this **catch-up**—or *convergence*—actually occurred? Here we come to a paradox: If we look only at the countries that currently have high incomes, we see that the lower-income countries have been catching up to the higher-income countries, but the developing countries as a group have not been catching up to the high-income countries as a group.

Catch-up: Sometimes but Not Always

We can construct a graph that makes it easier to see whether catch-up is happening. In Figure 7.6, the horizontal axis shows the initial level of real GDP per capita, and the vertical axis shows the rate at which real GDP per capita is growing. We can then plot points on the graph for rich and poor countries. Each point represents the combination of a country's initial level of real GDP per capita and its growth rate over the following years. The catch-up line in the figure shows the situation where the catch-up prediction holds exactly: Low-income countries should be on the upper-left section of the line because they would have low initial levels of real GDP per capita but fast growth rates. High-income countries should be in the lower-right section of the line because they would have high initial levels of real GDP per capita but slow growth rates. When we plot the actual observations for each country, the closer the points for each country are to the line, the more accurate the catch-up prediction is.

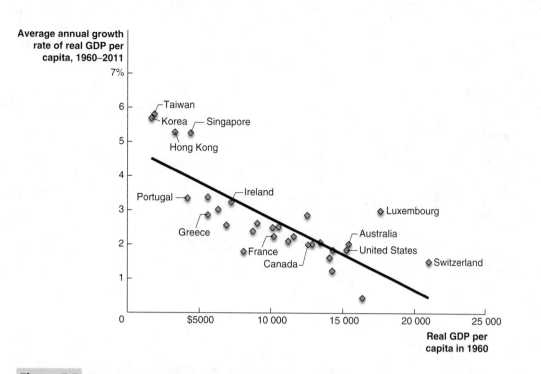

Figure 7.7 There Has Been Catch-up among High-Income Countries

If we look only at countries that currently have high incomes, we see that countries such as Taiwan, Korea, and Singapore that had the lowest incomes in 1960 grew the fastest between 1960 and 2011. Countries such as Switzerland and the United States that had the highest incomes in 1960 grew the slowest.

Note: Data are real GDP per capita in 2005 US dollars. Each point in the figure represents one high-income country.
Source: Authors' calculations from data in *Penn World Table Version 8.1*; Robert C. Feenstra, Robert Inklaar, and Marcel P. Timmer, "The Next Generation of the Penn World Table" www.ggdc.net/pwt, April 2015.

Catch-up among the High-Income Countries. If we look at only the countries that currently have high incomes, we can see the catch-up predicted by the economic growth model. Figure 7.7 shows that the high-income countries that had the lowest incomes in 1960, such as Taiwan, Korea, and Hong Kong, grew the fastest between 1960 and 2011. Countries that had the highest incomes in 1960, such as Switzerland, Australia, and the United States, grew the slowest.

Are the Developing Countries Catching Up to the High-Income Countries? If we expand our analysis to include every country for which statistics are available, it becomes more difficult to find the catch-up predicted by the economic growth model. Figure 7.8 does not show a consistent relationship between the level of real GDP in 1960 and growth from 1960 to 2011. Some countries that had low levels of real GDP per capita in 1960, such as Niger and the Democratic Republic of the Congo, actually experienced *negative* economic growth: They had *lower* levels of real GDP per capita in 2011 than in 1960. Other countries that started with low levels of real GDP per capita, such as Malaysia and China, grew rapidly. Some middle-income countries in 1960, such as Venezuela, grew slowly between 1960 and 2011, while others, such as Ireland, grew much more rapidly.

Solved Problem **7.2**

The Economic Growth Model's Prediction of Catch-up

The economic growth model makes a prediction about an economy's initial level of real GDP per capita relative to

other economies and how fast the economy will grow in the future.

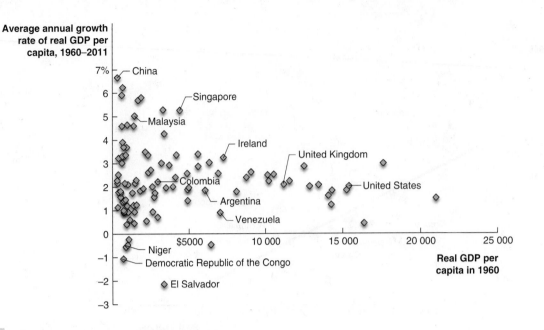

Figure 7.8 **Most of the World Hasn't Been Catching Up**

If we look at all countries for which statistics are available, we do not see the catch-up predicted by the economic growth model. Some countries that had low levels of real GDP per capita in 1960, such as Niger and the Democratic Republic of the Congo, actually experienced *negative* economic growth. Other countries that started with low levels of real GDP per capita, such as Malaysia and China, grew rapidly. Some middle-income countries in 1960, such as Venezuela, hardly grew between 1960 and 2011, while others, such as Ireland, experienced significant growth.

Note: Data are real GDP per capita in 2005 dollars. Each point in the figure represents one country.
Source: Authors' calculations from data in *Penn World Table Version 8.1*; Robert C. Feenstra, Robert Inklaar, and Marcel P. Timmer, "The Next Generation of the Penn World Table" www.ggdc.net/pwt, April 2015.

a. Consider the statistics in the following table:

Country	Real GDP per Capita, 1960 (2005 dollars)	Annual Growth in Real GDP per Capita, 1960–2011
Taiwan	$1861	5.81%
Panama	2120	3.50
Brazil	2483	2.73
Costa Rica	4920	1.42
Venezuela	7015	0.91

Are these statistics consistent with the economic growth model? Briefly explain.

b. Now consider the statistics in the following table:

Country	Real GDP per Capita, 1960 (2005 dollars)	Annual Growth in Real GDP per Capita, 1960–2011
Japan	$5 586	3.39%
Belgium	10 132	2.50
United Kingdom	11 204	2.10
Australia	15 255	1.85

Are these statistics consistent with the economic growth model? Briefly explain.

c. Construct a new table that lists all nine countries, from the lowest real GDP per capita in 1960 to the highest, along with their growth rates. Are the statistics in your new table consistent with the economic growth model?

Solving the Problem

Step 1: **Review the chapter material.** This problem is about catch-up in the economic growth model, so you may want to review the section "Why Isn't the Whole World Rich?" which begins on page 168.

Step 2: **Explain whether the statistics in the table in part (a) are consistent with the economic growth model.** These statistics are consistent with the economic growth model. The countries with the lowest levels of real GDP per capita in 1960 had the fastest growth rates between 1960 and 2011, and the countries with the highest levels of real GDP per capita had the slowest growth rates.

Step 3: **Explain whether the statistics in the table in part (b) are consistent with the economic growth model.** These statistics are also consistent with the economic growth model. Once again, the countries with the lowest levels of real GDP per capita in 1960 had the fastest growth rates between 1960 and 2011, and the countries with the highest levels of real GDP per capita had the slowest growth rates.

Step 4: **Construct a table that includes all nine countries from the tables in parts (a) and (b) and discuss the results.**

Country	Real GDP per Capita, 1960 (2005 dollars)	Annual Growth in Real GDP per Capita, 1960–2011
Taiwan	$1 861	5.81%
Panama	2 120	3.50
Brazil	2 483	2.73
Costa Rica	4 920	1.42
Japan	5 586	3.39
Venezuela	7 015	0.91
Belgium	10 132	2.50
United Kingdom	11 204	2.10
Australia	15 255	1.85

The statistics in the new table are *not* consistent with the predictions of the economic growth model. For example, Australia and the United Kingdom had higher levels of real GDP per capita in 1960 than did Costa Rica and Venezuela. The economic growth model predicts that Australia and the United Kingdom should, therefore, have grown more slowly than Costa Rica and Venezuela. The data in the table show, however, that Australia and the United Kingdom grew faster. Similarly, Belgium grew faster than Costa Rica, even though its real GDP per capita was already much higher than Costa Rica's in 1960.

Extra Credit: The statistics in these tables confirm what we saw in Figures 7.7 and 7.8 on pages 169–170: There has been catch-up among the high-income countries, but there has not been catch-up if we include in the analysis all the countries of the world.

Your Turn: For more practice, do related problems 4.1 and 4.2 on page 185 at the end of this chapter.   MyEconLab

Why Haven't Most Western European Countries, Canada, and Japan Caught Up to the United States?

Figure 7.7 indicates that there has been catch-up among the high-income countries over the past 50 years. If we look at the catch-up of other high-income countries to the United States during the most recent period, we discover a surprising fact: Over the past 25 years, other high-income countries have actually fallen further behind the United States rather than catching up to it. Figure 7.9 shows real GDP per capita in Canada, Japan, and the five largest economies in Western Europe relative to real GDP per capita in the United States. The green bars show real GDP per capita in 1990 relative to the United States, and the blue bars show real GDP per capita in 2014 relative to the United States. In each case, relative levels of real GDP per capita were lower in 2014 than they were in 1990. Each of these countries experienced significant catch-up to the United States between 1960 and 1990, but they have experienced no catch-up since 1990.

Why have other high-income countries had trouble completely closing the gap in real GDP per capita with the United States? Many economists believe there are two main explanations: the greater flexibility of US labour markets and the greater efficiency of the US financial system. US labour markets are more flexible than labour markets in other countries for several reasons. In many European countries, government regulations

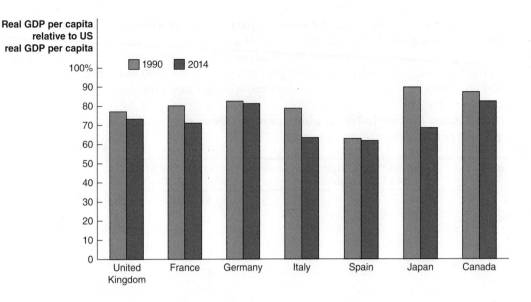

Figure 7.9 Other High-Income Countries Have Stopped Catching Up to the United States

The green bars show real GDP per capita in 1990 relative to the United States, and the blue bars show real GDP per capita in 2014 relative to the United States. In each case, relative levels of real GDP per capita are lower in 2014 than they were in 1990, which means that these countries have ceased catching up to the United States.

Source: Authors' calculations from data in Organization for Economic Co-operation and Development, stat.oecd.org.

make it difficult for firms to fire workers and thereby make firms reluctant to hire workers in the first place. As a result, many younger workers have difficulty finding jobs, and once a job is found, a worker tends to remain in it even if his or her skills and preferences are not a good match for the characteristics of the job. In the United States, by contrast, government regulations are less restrictive, workers have an easier time finding jobs, and workers change jobs fairly frequently. This high rate of job mobility ensures a better match between workers' skills and preferences and the characteristics of jobs, which increases labour productivity. Many European countries also have restrictive work rules that limit the flexibility of firms to implement new technologies. These rules restrict the tasks firms can ask workers to perform and the number of hours they work. So, the rules reduce the ability of firms to use new technologies that may require workers to learn new skills, perform new tasks, or work during the night or early mornings.

Workers in the United States tend to enter the labour force earlier, retire later, and experience fewer long spells of unemployment than do workers in Europe. Unemployed workers in the United States typically receive smaller government payments for a shorter period of time than do unemployed workers in Canada and most of the countries of Western Europe. Because the opportunity cost of being unemployed is lower in those countries, the unemployment rate tends to be higher, and the fraction of the labour force that is unemployed for more than one year also tends to be higher. Studies have shown that workers who are employed for longer periods tend to have greater skills, greater productivity, and higher wages. Many economists believe that the design of the US employment insurance program has contributed to the greater flexibility of US labour markets and to higher rates of growth in labour productivity and real GDP per capita.

As we have seen, technological change is essential for rapid productivity growth. To obtain the funds needed to implement new technologies, firms turn to the financial system. It is important that funds for investment be not only available but also allocated efficiently. Large corporations can raise funds by selling stocks and bonds in financial markets. US corporations benefit from the efficiency of US financial markets. The level of legal protection of investors is relatively high in US financial markets, which encourages both US and foreign investors to buy stocks and bonds issued by US firms. The volume of trading in US financial markets also ensures that investors will be able to quickly sell the stocks and bonds they buy. This *liquidity* serves to attract investors to US markets.

Smaller firms that are unable to issue stocks and bonds often obtain funding from banks. Entrepreneurs founding new firms—startups—particularly firms that are based on new technologies, generally find that investors are unwilling to buy their stocks and bonds because the firms lack records of profitability. Banks are also reluctant to lend to new firms founded to introduce new and unfamiliar technologies. However, some technology startups obtain funds from *venture capital firms*. Venture capital firms raise funds from institutional investors, such as pension funds, and from wealthy individuals. The owners of venture capital firms closely examine the business plans of startup firms, looking for those that appear most likely to succeed. In exchange for providing funding, a venture capital firm often becomes part owner of the startup and may even play a role in managing the firm. A successful venture capital firm is able to attract investors who would not otherwise be willing to provide funds to startups because the investors would lack enough information on the startup. A number of well-known US high-technology firms, such as Google, relied on venture capitals firms to fund their early expansion. The ability of venture capital firms to finance technology-driven startup firms may be giving the United States an advantage in bringing new products and new processes to market.

The US financial system suffered severe problems between 2007 and 2009. But, over the long run, it has succeeded in efficiently allocating investment funds.

Why Don't More Low-Income Countries Experience Rapid Growth?

The economic growth model predicts that the countries that were very poor in 1960 should have grown rapidly over the next 50 years. As we have just seen, some did, but many did not. Why are many low-income countries growing so slowly? There is no single answer, but most economists point to four key factors:

- Failure to enforce the rule of law

- Wars and revolutions

- Poor public education and health

- Low rates of saving and investment

Failure to Enforce the Rule of Law. In the years since 1960, increasing numbers of developing countries, including China, have abandoned centrally planned economies in favour of more market-oriented economies. For entrepreneurs in a market economy to succeed, however, the government must guarantee private **property rights** and enforce contracts. Unless entrepreneurs feel secure in their property, they will not risk starting a business. It is also difficult for businesses to operate successfully in a market economy unless they can use an independent court system to enforce contracts. The **rule of law** refers to the ability of a government to enforce the laws of the country, particularly with respect to protecting private property and enforcing contracts. The failure of many developing countries to guarantee private property rights and to enforce contracts has hindered their economic growth.

Consider, for example, the production of shoes in a developing country. Suppose the owner of a shoe factory signs a contract with a leather tannery to deliver a specific quantity of leather on a particular date for a particular price. On the basis of this contract, the owner of the shoe factory signs a contract to deliver a specific quantity of shoes to a shoe wholesaler. This contract specifies the quantity of shoes to be delivered, the quality of the shoes, the delivery date, and the price. The owner of the leather tannery uses the contract with the shoe factory to enter into a contract with cattle ranchers for the delivery of hides. The shoe wholesaler enters into contracts to deliver shoes to retail stores, where they are sold to consumers. For the flow of goods from cattle ranchers to shoe customers to operate efficiently, each business must carry out the terms of the contract it has signed. In developed countries, such as Canada, businesses know that if they fail to carry out a contract, they may be sued in court and forced to compensate the other party for any economic damages.

Property rights The rights individuals or firms have to the exclusive use of their property, including the right to buy or sell it.

Rule of law The ability of a government to enforce the laws of the country, particularly with respect to protecting private property and enforcing contracts.

Many developing countries do not have functioning, independent court systems. Even if a court system does exist, a case may not be heard for many years. In some countries, bribery of judges and political favouritism in court rulings are common. If firms cannot enforce contracts through the court system, they will insist on carrying out only face-to-face cash transactions. For example, the shoe manufacturer will wait until the leather producer brings the hides to the factory and will then buy them for cash. The wholesaler will wait until the shoes have been produced before making plans for sales to retail stores. Production still takes place, but it is carried out more slowly and inefficiently. With slow and inefficient production, firms have difficulty finding investors willing to provide them with the funds they need to expand.

Making the Connection | ## Why Hasn't Mexico Grown as Fast as China?

Many people consider China *the* great economic growth success story. The decision by Chinese government leaders in the 1970s to turn away from a centrally planned economy and toward a market system unleashed economic growth that has lifted more than a billion people in China out of poverty. As we will discuss in Section 7.5, the Chinese economy still faces significant obstacles to maintaining high growth rates, and the Chinese Communist Party has maintained its dictatorship over the country. Despite these problems, many economists and policymakers see China as an example of the rapid growth that low-income countries can attain.

As we saw in the chapter opener, some Canadian firms have chosen in recent years to locate factories and other facilities in Mexico rather than in China because Mexico is closer to Canada and because labour costs have been increasing more rapidly in China. This trend has been good news for the Mexican economy because it has increased factory employment and given the country easier access to US technology. Overall, though, the growth rates of the Mexican economy have been disappointing. The graph below compares the growth rates of real GDP per capita for the Mexican and Chinese economies over the past 35 years.

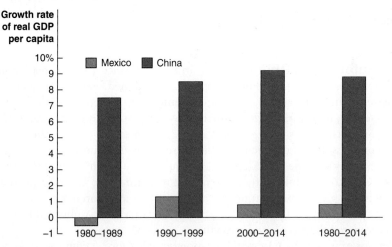

Taking the whole period between 1980 and 2014, the average annual growth rate for the Chinese economy has been 8.8 percent, while the growth rate for the Mexican economy has been a very slow 0.8 percent. In Chapter 6, we saw that if we divide a growth rate into 70, the result is approximately the number of years it will take real GDP per capita to double. When we apply that rule here, we find that it will take real GDP per capita more than 85 years to double in Mexico but only 8 years in China.

What explains the slow growth of the Mexican economy? For most of the period from the Mexican Revolution of 1910 until 2000, the Institutional Revolutionary Party (PRI) dominated the Mexican government. For decades, the party followed a policy of limiting imports and foreign investment, concentrating on building up domestic industry behind high tariff walls. The Mexican government took over, or nationalized, some businesses, including the oil industry. By the 1980s, dissatisfaction with the country's poor economic performance led the PRI, under President Miguel de la Madrid, to institute a series of reforms. The reforms, which were broadened in the 1990s, included allowing banks again to be private businesses; signing the North American Free Trade Agreement (NAFTA) with the United States and Canada, which greatly reduced tariffs on imports; and allowing foreign investment in most sectors of the economy apart from the oil industry. As the graph above shows, though, these reforms have not resulted in high rates of economic growth.

Some economic historians believe that the Spanish colonial background of the nineteenth century and earlier hobbled the Mexican economy. Unlike in the United States, in Mexico and other Spanish and Portuguese colonies, land was often concentrated in very large estates, which led to highly unequal distributions of income and may have made it difficult for a broad-based middle class capable of supporting a large manufacturing base to develop. Other countries in Latin America, though, including Chile and Uruguay, with similar colonial backgrounds have experienced much more rapid growth.

Some economists believe that the financial sector has been an important obstacle to growth. The Mexican legal system makes it difficult for banks to seize a business's assets when the business defaults on a loan. As a result, Mexican banks are reluctant to make loans to businesses. As we noted in the chapter opener, Mexico also suffers from government corruption that makes businesses either reluctant to expand or forces them to operate in the underground economy. In either case, the businesses are unable to take advantage of economies of scale and may be unwilling to make large investments in machinery or buildings. In certain areas of Mexico, criminal gangs have also disrupted business. The educational system in Mexico has failed to provide many students with the skills needed to find work at firms competing in the global marketplace. Finally, infrastructure, including poor roads and inconsistent and expensive provision of electricity—with occasional blackouts—have also hindered business expansion.

Timothy J. Kehoe of the University of Minnesota and Kim J. Ruhl of New York University note that China also suffers from institutional problems, but it has grown much faster than Mexico. China, though, began its rapid growth from very low levels of income, so that in 2014, real GDP per capita in Mexico was still more than twice the level in China. Kehoe and Ruhl argue that, as a middle-income country, Mexico has already taken advantage of many of the relatively easy ways of increasing real GDP—including moving resources out of the low-productivity agricultural sector, accumulating capital in manufacturing, and adopting modern technology. We saw in the discussion of Figure 7.9 that, probably for institutional reasons, many high-income countries have made no progress in closing the gap in real GDP per capita between themselves and the United States during the past 25 years. Mexico may now be in a similar situation of having difficulty growing fast enough to close the gap with higher-income countries. Because Mexico's institutional barriers to growth are more severe than those in European countries, the gap in real GDP per capita between the United States and Mexico may persist at a high level.

Economists and policymakers in Mexico continue to look for ways to increase growth rates. Without an increase in growth, it may be decades before millions of low-income people in Mexico are able to escape poverty.

Based on The 100-Year View," *Economist*, May 8, 2015; Gordon H. Hanson, "Why Isn't Mexico Rich?" *Journal of Economic Literature*, Vol. 48, No. 4, December 2010, pp. 987–1004; Timothy J. Kehoe and Kim J. Ruhl, "Why Have Economic Reforms in Mexico Not Generated Growth?" *Journal of Economic Literature*, Vol. 48, No. 4, December 2010, pp. 98–1004; Nora Lustig, "Mexico's Quest for Stability and Growth," *Journal of Economic Perspectives*, Vol. 15, No. 1, Winter 2001, pp. 85–106; and *Federal Reserve Bank of St. Louis*.

Your Turn: Test your understanding by doing related problems 4.5 and 4.6 on page 186 at the end of this chapter.

MyEconLab

Wars and Revolutions Many of the countries that were very poor in 1960 have experienced extended periods of war or violent changes of government during the years since. These wars have made it impossible for countries such as Afghanistan, Angola, Ethiopia, the Central African Republic, and the Democratic Republic of the Congo to accumulate capital or adopt new technologies. In fact, conducting any kind of business has been very difficult. Ending war has a positive effect on growth, as shown by the case of Mozambique, which suffered through almost two decades of civil war and declining real GDP per capita. With the end of civil war, Mozambique experienced a strong annual growth rate of 8 percent in real GDP per capita from 1990 to 2014.

Poor Public Education and Health.
We have seen that human capital is one of the determinants of labour productivity. Many low-income countries have weak public school systems, so many workers are unable to read and write. Few workers acquire the skills necessary to use the latest technology.

People in many low-income countries suffer from diseases that are either nonexistent or readily treated in high-income countries. For example, few people in developed countries suffer from malaria, but about 500 000 Africans die from it each year. Treatments for AIDS have greatly reduced deaths from this disease in Canada, the United States, and Europe. But millions of people in low-income countries continue to die from AIDS. These countries often lack the resources, and their governments are often too ineffective, to provide even routine medical care, such as childhood vaccinations.

People who are sick work less and are less productive when they do work. Poor nutrition or exposure to certain diseases in childhood can leave people permanently weakened and can affect their intelligence as adults. Poor health has a significant negative effect on the human capital of workers in developing countries.

Low Rates of Saving and Investment.
To invest in factories, machinery, and computers, firms need funds. Some of the funds can come from the owners of the firm and from their friends and families; firms in high-income countries raise most of their funds from bank loans and selling stocks and bonds in financial markets. In most developing countries, stock and bond markets do not exist, and often the banking system is very weak. In high-income countries, the funds that banks lend to businesses come from the savings of households. In high-income countries, many households are able to save a significant fraction of their income. In developing countries, many households barely survive on their incomes and, therefore, have little or no savings.

The low savings rates in developing countries can contribute to a vicious cycle of poverty. Because households have low incomes, they save very little. Because households save very little, few funds are available for firms to borrow. Lacking funds, firms do not invest in the new factories, machinery, and equipment needed for economic growth. Because the economy does not grow, household incomes remain low, as do their savings, and so on.

The Benefits of Globalization

One way for a developing country to break out of the vicious cycle of low saving and investment and low growth is through foreign investment. **Foreign direct investment (FDI)** occurs when corporations build or purchase facilities in foreign countries. **Foreign portfolio investment** occurs when an individual or a firm buys stocks or bonds issued in another country. Foreign direct investment and foreign portfolio investment can give a low-income country access to funds and technology that otherwise would not be available. Until recently, many developing countries were reluctant to take advantage of this opportunity.

From the 1940s through the 1970s, many developing countries closed themselves off from the global economy. They did this for several reasons. During the 1930s and early 1940s, the global trading and financial system collapsed as a result of the Great Depression and World War II. Developing countries that relied on exporting to the high-income countries were hurt economically. Also, many countries in Africa and Asia achieved independence from the colonial powers of Europe during the 1950s and 1960s and were afraid of being dominated by them economically. As a result, many developing countries imposed high tariffs on foreign imports and strongly discouraged or even prohibited foreign investment. These policies made it difficult to break out of the vicious cycle of poverty.

Foreign direct investment (FDI) The purchase or building by a corporation of a facility in a foreign country.

Foreign portfolio investment The purchase by an individual or a firm of stocks or bonds issued in another country.

The policies of erecting high tariff barriers and avoiding foreign investment failed to produce much growth, so by the 1980s, many developing countries began to change policies. The result was **globalization**, which refers to the process of countries becoming more open to foreign trade and investment. Developing countries that are more globalized have grown faster than developing countries that are less globalized. Globalization has benefited developing countries by making it easier for them to obtain technology and investment funds.

Globalization The process of countries becoming more open to foreign trade and investment.

Growth Policies

What can governments do to promote long-run economic growth? We have seen that even small differences in growth rates compounded over the years can lead to major differences in standards of living. Therefore, there is potentially a very high payoff to government policies that increase growth rates. We have already discussed some of these policies in this chapter. In this section, we explore additional policies.

Enhancing Property Rights and the Rule of Law

A market system cannot work well unless property rights are enforced. Entrepreneurs are unlikely to risk their own funds, and investors are unlikely to lend their funds to entrepreneurs, if property is not protected from being arbitrarily seized. We have seen that in many developing countries, the rule of law and property rights are undermined by government *corruption*. In some developing countries, it is impossible for an entrepreneur to obtain a permit to start a business without paying bribes, often to several different government officials. Is it possible for a country to reform a corrupt government bureaucracy?

Property rights are unlikely to be secure in countries that are afflicted by wars and civil strife. For a number of countries, increased political stability is a necessary prerequisite to economic growth.

Making the Connection | **Will China's Standard of Living Ever Exceed that of Canada?**

In 2014, GDP per capita in Canada was more than nine times higher than GDP per capita in China. However, the growth rate of real GDP per capita in Canada has averaged only 1.7 percent per year since 1980, compared to China's average growth rate of 8.8 percent per year over the same time period. If these growth rates were to continue, China's standard of living, as measured by real GDP per capita, would exceed the Canadian standard of living in the year 2036.

For China to maintain its high rates of growth in real GDP per capita, however, it would have to maintain high rates of productivity growth, which is unlikely for several reasons. First, Canada invests more in activities, such as research and development, which result in new technologies and increases in productivity. Although China has been successful in adopting existing technologies developed in other countries, it has been much less successful in developing new technologies. Second, a good part of China's growth is due to the transition from a centrally planned economy to a market economy, so China's growth rate is likely to decrease as the transition is completed. Third, China's economic growth has depended on moving workers from agriculture, where their productivity was low, to manufacturing jobs in cities, where their productivity is much

Some economists argue that China may have overinvested in physical capital, such as bullet trains.

higher. The large supply of low-wage agricultural workers helped to keep manufacturing wages low and provided China with a cost advantage in manufacturing goods compared with Canada and other high-income countries. China has exhausted much of its supply of low-wage agricultural workers, so manufacturing wages have begun to rise, eroding China's cost advantage. As we saw in the chapter opener, some Canadian firms have reacted to rising labour costs in China by moving factories to Mexico—or back to Canada.

Another looming problem is demographic. Because of China's low birth rate, the country will soon experience a decline in its labour force. Over the next two decades, the population of men and women between 15 and 29 years will fall by roughly 100 million, or about 30 percent. China will also experience a large increase in older workers, a group that will on average be less productive and less healthy than younger workers. Given current trends, the US Census Bureau projects fewer people under age 50 in China in 2030 than today, including fewer people in their 20s and early 30s, and many more people in their 60s and older. China still has potential sources for enhancing productivity, including the wider application of technology and the movement of workers into high-productivity industries, such as the manufacture of automobiles and household appliances, provided that domestic demand increases rapidly. These factors can fuel future growth, but at some point, China's demographic problems could slow growth.

Perhaps most troubling for China is the fact that the country remains autocratic, with the Communist Party refusing to allow meaningful elections and continuing to limit freedom of expression. The government has yet to establish secure property rights and the rule of law. Some observers believe that the lack of political freedom in China may ultimately lead to civil unrest, which could slow growth rates. Whether or not civil unrest eventually develops, the lack of democracy in China may already be resulting in problems that could slow growth in the near future. Large, state-owned firms, controlled by Communist Party members, continue to receive government subsidies. The result is that these firms, which typically have low productivity and are not globally competitive, receive funds that otherwise would have allowed high-productivity firms to expand.

Nouriel Roubini, an economist at New York University, argues that China's Communist Party may be repeating some of the mistakes the Soviet Communist Party committed decades ago. He argues that by employing policies that have resulted in investment being 50 percent of GDP, the government may have boosted short-term growth at the expense of the health of the economy in the long term. He notes:

> China is rife with overinvestment in physical capital, infrastructure, and property. To a visitor, this is evident in sleek but empty airports and bullet trains . . . highways to nowhere, thousands of colossal new central and provincial government buildings, ghost towns, and brand-new aluminum smelters kept closed to prevent global prices from plunging.

Growth in China is already showing signs of slowing. Between 2010 and 2014, real GDP per capita grew at an annual rate of 6.0 percent. While still rapid, this growth rate is well below what the Chinese economy had achieved in previous decades. In early 2015, Chinese Premier Li Keqiang noted, "The downward pressure on economic growth continues to increase."

China has been engaged in an economic experiment: Can a country maintain high rates of economic growth in the long run while denying its citizens basic political rights?

Based on Mark Magnier, "China's First-Quarter Growth Slowest in Six Years at 7%," *Wall Street Journal*, April 15, 2015; Pranab Bardhan, "The Slowing of Two Economic Giants," *New York Times*, July 14, 2013; Alex Frangos and Eric Bellman, "China Slump Ripples Globally," *Wall Street Journal*, July 15, 2013; Nicholas Eberstadt, "The Demographic Future," *Foreign Affairs*, Vol. 89, No. 6, November/December 2010, pp. 54–64; and Nouriel Roubini, "Beijing's Empty Bullet Trains," *Slate*, April 14, 2011.

MyEconLab   **Your Turn:** Test your understanding by doing related problem 5.2 on page 186 at the end of this chapter.

Improving Health and Education

Recently, many economists have become convinced that poor health is a major impediment to growth in some countries. The research of Nobel Laureate Robert Fogel emphasizes the important interaction between health and economic growth. As people's health improves and they become stronger and less susceptible to disease, they also become more productive. Recent initiatives in developing countries to increase vaccinations against infectious diseases, to improve access to treated water, and to improve sanitation have begun to reduce rates of illness and death.

We discussed earlier in this chapter Paul Romer's argument that there are increasing returns to knowledge capital. Nobel Laureate Robert Lucas of the University of Chicago similarly argues that there are increasing returns to *human* capital. Lucas argues that productivity increases as the total stock of human capital increases but that these productivity increases are not completely captured by individuals as they decide how much education to purchase. Therefore, the market may produce an inefficiently low level of education and training unless the government subsidizes education. Some researchers have been unable to find evidence of increasing returns to human capital, but many economists believe that government subsidies for education have played an important role in promoting economic growth.

The rising incomes that result from economic growth can help developing countries deal with the *brain drain*, which refers to highly educated and successful individuals leaving developing countries for high-income countries. This migration occurs when successful individuals believe that economic opportunities are very limited in the domestic economy. Rapid economic growth in India and China in recent years has resulted in more entrepreneurs, engineers, and scientists deciding to remain in those countries rather than leave for Canada, the United States, or other high-income countries.

Policies that Promote Technological Change

One of the lessons from the economic growth model is that technological change is more important than increases in capital in explaining long-run growth. Government policies that facilitate access to technology are crucial for low-income countries. The easiest way for developing countries to gain access to technology is through foreign direct investment, where foreign firms are allowed to build new facilities or to buy domestic firms. Recent economic growth in India has been greatly aided by the Indian government's relaxation of regulations on foreign investment. Relaxing these regulations made it possible for India to gain access to the technology of BlackBerry, Dell, Microsoft, and other multinational corporations.

In high-income countries, government policies can aid the growth of technology by subsidizing research and development. As we noted previously, in Canada, the federal government conducts some research and development on its own and also provides grants to researchers in universities. Tax breaks to firms undertaking research and development also facilitate technological change.

Policies that Promote Saving and Investment

Firms turn to the loanable funds market to finance expansion and research and development (see Chapter 6). Policies that increase the incentives to save and invest will increase the equilibrium level of loanable funds and may increase the level of real GDP per capita. For instance, governments can use tax incentives to increase saving. In Canada, many workers are able to save for retirement by placing funds in Registered Retirement Savings Plans (RRSPs). Income placed in these plans is not taxed until it is withdrawn during retirement. Because the funds are allowed to accumulate tax-free, the return is increased, which raises the incentive to save.

Governments also increase incentives for firms to engage in investment in physical capital by using *investment tax credits*. Investment tax credits allow firms to deduct from their taxes some fraction of the funds they have spent on investment. Reductions in the taxes firms pay on their profits also increase the after-tax return on investments.

Is Economic Growth Good or Bad?

Although we didn't state so explicitly, in this chapter we have assumed that economic growth is desirable and that governments should undertake policies that will increase growth rates. It seems undeniable that increasing the growth rates of very low-income countries would help relieve the daily suffering that many people in those countries endure. But some people are unconvinced that, at least in the high-income countries, further economic growth is desirable.

The arguments against further economic growth reflect concern about the effects of growth on the environment or concern about the effects of the globalization process that has accompanied economic growth. In 1973, the Club of Rome published a controversial book titled *The Limits to Growth*, which predicted that economic growth would likely grind to a halt in Canada and other high-income countries because of increasing pollution and the depletion of natural resources, such as oil. Although these dire predictions have not yet come to pass, many people remain concerned that economic growth may be contributing to global warming, destruction of rain forests, and other environmental problems.

Some people believe that globalization has undermined the distinctive cultures of many countries, as imports of food, clothing, movies, and other goods have displaced domestically produced goods. We have seen that allowing foreign direct investment is an important way in which low-income countries can gain access to the latest technology. Some people, however, believe multinational firms behave unethically in low-income countries because, they claim, the firms pay very low wages and fail to follow the same safety and environmental regulations the firms are required to follow in high-income countries.

As with many other normative questions, economic analysis can contribute to the ongoing political debate over the consequences of economic growth, but it cannot settle the issue.

Economics in Your Life

Would You Be Better Off without China?

At the beginning of the chapter, we asked you to imagine that you could choose to live and work in a world with the Chinese economy growing very rapidly or in a world with the Chinese economy as it was before 1978—very poor and growing slowly. Which world would you choose to live in? How does the current high-growth, high-export Chinese economy affect you as a consumer? How does it affect you as someone about to start a career?

It's impossible to walk into stores in Canada without seeing products imported from China. Many of these products were at one time made in Canada. Imports from China replace domestically produced goods when the imports are either priced lower or have higher quality than the domestic goods they replace. Therefore, the rapid economic growth that has enabled Chinese firms to be competitive with firms in Canada has benefited you as a consumer: You have lower-priced goods and better goods available for purchase than you would if China had remained very poor. As you begin your career, there are some Canadian industries that, because of competition from Chinese firms, will have fewer jobs to offer. But, as we saw when discussing international trade, expanding trade changes the types of products each country makes, and, therefore, the types of jobs available, but it does not affect the total number of jobs. So, the economic rise of China will affect the mix of jobs available to you in Canada but will not make finding a job any more difficult.

Conclusion

For much of human history, most people have had to struggle to survive. Even today, more than half of the world's population lives in extreme poverty. The differences in living standards among countries today are a result of many decades of sharply different rates of economic growth. According to the economic growth model, increases in the quantity of capital per hour worked and increases in technology determine the growth in real GDP per hour worked and a country's standard of living. The keys to higher living standards seem straightforward:

1. Establish the rule of law.
2. Provide basic education and health care for the population.
3. Increase the amount of capital per hour worked.
4. Adopt the best technology.
5. Participate in the global economy.

However, for many countries, these policies have proved very difficult to implement.

Having discussed what determines the growth rate of economies, we will turn in the following chapters to the question of why economies experience short-run fluctuations in output, employment, and inflation.

Chapter Summary and Problems

Key Terms

Catch-up, p. 168

Economic growth model, p. 157

Foreign direct investment (FDI), p. 176

Foreign portfolio investment, p. 176

Globalization, p. 177

Human capital, p. 158

Industrial Revolution, p. 153

Labour productivity, p. 158

New growth theory, p. 163

Patent, p. 163

Per-worker production function, p. 158

Property rights, p. 173

Rule of law, p. 173

Technological change, p. 158

Summary

*LO 7.1 For most of history, the average person survived with barely enough food. Living standards began to rise significantly only after the *Industrial Revolution* in England in the 1700s, with the application of mechanical power to the production of goods. The best measure of a country's standard of living is its level of real GDP per capita. Economic growth occurs when real GDP per capita increases, thereby increasing the country's standard of living.

LO 7.2 An *economic growth model* explains changes in real GDP per capita in the long run. *Labour productivity* is the quantity of goods and services that can be produced by one worker or by one hour of work. Economic growth depends on increases in labour productivity. Labour productivity will increase if there is an increase in the amount of *capital* available to each worker or if there is an improvement in *technology*. *Technological change* is a change in the ability of a firm to produce a given level of output with a given quantity of inputs. There are three main sources of technological change: better machinery and equipment, increases in human

capital, and better means of organizing and managing production. *Human capital* is the accumulated knowledge and skills that workers acquire from education and training or from their life experiences. We can say that an economy will have a higher standard of living the more capital it has per hour worked, the more human capital its workers have, the better its capital, and the better the job its business managers do in organizing production.

The *per-worker production function* shows the relationship between capital per hour worked and output per hour worked, holding technology constant. *Diminishing returns to capital* means that increases in the quantity of capital per hour worked will result in diminishing increases in output per hour worked. Technological change shifts up the per-worker production function, resulting in more output per hour worked at every level of capital per hour worked. The economic growth model stresses the importance of changes in capital per hour worked and technological change in explaining growth in output per hour worked. *New growth theory* is a model of long-run economic growth that emphasizes that technological change is influenced by how individuals and firms respond to economic incentives.

---

*"Learning Objective" is abbreviated to "LO" in the end-of-chapter material.

One way governments can promote technological change is by granting *patents*, which are exclusive rights to a product for a period of 20 years from the date the patent is filed with the government. To Joseph Schumpeter, the entrepreneur is central to the "creative destruction" by which the standard of living increases as qualitatively better products replace existing products.

LO 7.3 Productivity in Canada grew rapidly from the end of World War II until the mid-1970s. Growth then slowed down. Economists debate whether this growth slowdown will be long lived or whether the Canadian economy will return to the faster growth rates of previous years.

LO 7.4 The economic growth model predicts that poor countries will grow faster than rich countries, resulting in *catch-up*. In recent decades, some poor countries have grown faster than rich countries, but many have not. Some poor countries have not experienced rapid growth for four main reasons: wars and revolutions, poor public education and health, failure to enforce the rule of law, and low rates of saving and investment. The *rule of law* refers to the ability of a government to enforce the laws of the country, particularly with respect to protecting private property and enforcing contracts. *Globalization* has aided countries that have opened their economies to foreign trade and investment. *Foreign direct investment (FDI)* is the purchase or building by a corporation of a facility in a foreign country. *Foreign portfolio investment* is the purchase by an individual or firm of stocks or bonds issued in another country.

LO 7.5 Governments can attempt to increase economic growth through policies that enhance property rights and the rule of law, improve health and education, subsidize research and development, and provide incentives for savings and investment. Whether continued economic growth is desirable is a normative question that cannot be settled by economic analysis.

MyEconLab   Log in to MyEconLab to complete these exercises and get instant feedback.

Review Questions

LO 7.1

1.1 Why does a country's rate of economic growth matter?

1.2 Explain the difference between the total percentage increase in real GDP between 2005 and 2015 and the average annual growth rate in real GDP between the same years.

LO 7.2

2.1 Using the per-worker production function graph from Figures 7.3 and 7.4 on pages 159–160, show the effect on real GDP per hour worked of an increase in capital per hour worked, holding technology constant. Now, again using the per-worker production function graph, show the effect on real GDP per hour worked of an increase in technology, holding constant the quantity of capital per hour worked.

2.2 What are the consequences for growth of diminishing returns to capital? How are some economies able to maintain high growth rates despite diminishing returns to capital?

2.3 What is the *new growth theory*? How does the new growth theory differ from the growth theory developed by Robert Solow?

2.4 Why are firms likely to underinvest in research and development? Briefly discuss three ways in which government policy can increase the accumulation of knowledge capital.

2.5 Why does knowledge capital experience increasing returns at the economy level while physical capital experiences decreasing returns?

LO 7.3

3.1 Describe the record of productivity growth in Canada from 1800 to the present.

3.2 Briefly describe the debate among economists over how high Canadian productivity growth rates are likely to be in the future.

LO 7.4

4.1 Why does the economic growth model predict that poor countries should catch up to rich countries in income per capita? Have poor countries been catching up to rich countries?

4.2 What are the main reasons many poor countries have experienced slow growth?

4.3 What does *globalization* mean? How have developing countries benefited from globalization?

LO 7.5

5.1 Briefly describe three government policies that can increase economic growth.

5.2 Can economic analysis arrive at the conclusion that economic growth will always improve economic well-being? Briefly explain.

Problems and Applications

LO 7.1

1.1 **[Related to Making the Connection on page 153]** Economists Carol Shiue and Wolfgang Keller of the University of Texas at Austin published a study of "market efficiency" in the eighteenth century in England, other European countries, and China. If the markets in a country are efficient, a product should have the same price wherever in the country it is sold, allowing for the effect of transportation costs. If prices are not the same in two areas within a country, it is possible to make profits by buying the product where its price is low and reselling it where its price is high. This trading will drive prices to equality. Trade is most likely to occur, however, if entrepreneurs feel confident that their gains will not be seized by the government and that contracts to buy and sell can be enforced in the courts. Therefore, in the eighteenth century, the more efficient a country's markets, the more its institutions favoured long-run growth. Shiue and Keller found that in 1770, the efficiency of markets in England was significantly greater than the efficiency of markets elsewhere in Europe and in China. How does this finding relate to Douglass North's argument concerning why the Industrial Revolution occurred in England?

Based on Carol H. Shiue and Wolfgang Keller, "Markets in China and Europe on the Eve of the Industrial Revolution," *American Economic Review*, Vol. 97, No. 4, September 2007, pp. 1189–1216.

1.2 Use the data on real GDP in this table to answer the following questions. The values are measured in each country's domestic currency. The base year for Brazil is 1995; the base year for Mexico is 2008; and the base year for Thailand is 1988.

Country	2011	2012	2013	2014
Brazil	1 192	1 213	1 247	1 248
Mexico	12 774	13 286	13 471	13 757
Thailand	4 600	4 898	5 040	5 076

a. Which country experienced the highest rate of economic growth during 2012 (that is, for which country did real GDP increase the most from 2011 to 2012)?

b. Which country experienced the highest average annual growth rate between 2012 and 2014?

c. Does it matter for your answers to parts (a) and (b) that each country's real GDP is measured in a different currency and uses a different base year? Briefly explain.

Source: International Monetary Fund, *World Economic Outlook Database*, April 2015.

1.3 Andover Bank and Lowell Bank each sell one-year certificates of deposit (CDs). The interest rates on these CDs are given in the following table for a three-year period.

Bank	2016	2017	2018
Andover Bank	5%	5%	5%
Lowell Bank	2%	6%	7%

Suppose you deposit $1000 in a CD in each bank at the beginning of 2016. At the end of 2016, you take your $1000 and any interest earned and invest it in a CD for the following year. You do this again at the end of 2017. At the end of 2018, will you have earned more on your Andover Bank CDs or on your Lowell Bank CDs? Briefly explain.

1.4 **[Related to the Don't Let This Happen to You on page 155]** Use the data for Canada in this table to answer the following questions.

Year	Real GDP per Capita (in 2005 US dollars)
2010	$36 466
2011	37 176
2012	37 442
2013	37 754
2014	38 293

a. What was the percentage change in real GDP per capita between 2010 and 2014?

b. What was the average annual growth rate in real GDP per capita between 2010 and 2014? (*Hint:* Remember that the average annual growth rate for relatively short periods can be approximated by averaging the growth rates for each year during the period [see Chapter 6].)

1.5 **[Related to Making the Connection on page 156]** In his book *The White Man's Burden*, William Easterly reports the following:

> A vaccination campaign in southern Africa virtually eliminated measles as a killer of children. Routine childhood immunization combined with measles vaccination in seven southern Africa nations starting in 1996 virtually eliminated measles in those countries by 2000. A national campaign in Egypt to make parents aware of the use of oral rehydration therapy from 1982 to 1989 cut childhood deaths from diarrhea by 82 percent over that period.

a. Is it likely that real GDP per capita increased significantly in southern Africa and Egypt as a result of the near elimination of measles and the large decrease in childhood deaths from diarrhea? If these events did not increase real GDP per capita, is it still possible that they increased the standard of living in southern Africa and Egypt? Briefly explain.

b. Which seems more achievable for a developing country: the elimination of measles and childhood deaths from diarrhea or sustained increases in real GDP per capita? Briefly explain.

William Easterly, *The White Man's Burden: Why the West's Efforts to Aid the Rest Have Done So Much Ill and So Little Good* (New York: The Penguin Press, 2006), p. 241.

1.6 **[Related to Making the Connection on page 156]** Economist Charles Kenny of the Center for Global Development has argued the following:

> The process technologies—institutions like laws and inventory management systems—that appear central to raising incomes per capita flow less like water and more like bricks. But ideas and inventions—the importance of ABCs and vaccines for DPT—really might flow more easily across borders and over distances.

If Kenny is correct, what are the implications of these facts for the ability of low-income countries to rapidly increase their rates of growth of real GDP per capita in the decades ahead? What are the implications for the ability of these countries to increase their standards of living? Briefly explain.

From Charles Kenny, *Getting Better* (New York: Basic Books, 2011), p. 117.

 7.2

2.1 Which of the following will result in a movement along China's per-worker production function, and which will result in a shift of China's per-worker production function? Briefly explain.

a. Capital per hour worked increases from 200 yuan per hour worked to 250 yuan per hour worked.

b. The Chinese government doubles its spending on support for university research.

c. A reform of the Chinese school system results in more highly trained Chinese workers.

2.2 People who live in rural areas often have less access to capital and, as a result, their productivity is lower on average than the productivity of people who live in cities. An article in the *New York Times* quotes a financial analyst as arguing that "the core driver" of economic growth in China "is the simple process of urbanization."

    a. What does the analyst mean by the "process of urbanization"?

    b. If the analyst is correct that urbanization is the core driver of economic growth in China, would we expect that China will be able to continue to experience high rates of economic growth in the long run? Briefly explain.

Based on Neil Irwin, "China Will Keep Growing. Just Ask the Soviets," *New York Times*, October 24, 2014.

2.3 **[Related to Solved Problem 7.1 on page 162]** Use the graph below to answer the following questions:

    a. True or false: The movement from point *A* to point *B* shows the effects of technological change.

    b. True or false: The economy can move from point *B* to point *C* only if there are no diminishing returns to capital.

    c. True or false: To move from point *A* to point *C*, the economy must increase the amount of capital per hour worked *and* experience technological change.

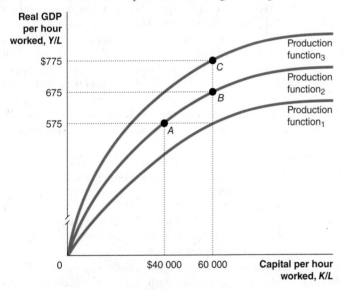

2.4 **[Related to Solved Problem 7.1 on page 162]** Shortly before the fall of the Soviet Union, economist Gur Ofer of Hebrew University of Jerusalem wrote this: "The most outstanding characteristic of Soviet growth strategy is its consistent policy of very high rates of investment, leading to a rapid growth rate of [the] capital stock." Explain why this turned out to be a very poor growth strategy.

Gur Ofer, "Soviet Economic Growth, 1928–1985," *Journal of Economic Literature*, Vol. 25, No. 4, December 1987, p. 1,784.

2.5 Why is the role of the entrepreneur much more important in the new growth theory than in the traditional economic growth model?

2.6 **[Related to Making the Connection on page 161]** *Making the Connection* argues that a key difference between market

economies and centrally planned economies, such as that of the former Soviet Union, is as follows:

> In market economies, decisions about which investments to make and which technologies to adopt are made by entrepreneurs and managers with their own money on the line. In the Soviet system, these decisions were usually made by salaried bureaucrats trying to fulfill a plan formulated in Moscow.

But in large corporations, investment decisions are often made by salaried managers who do not have their own money on the line. These managers are spending the money of the firm's shareholders rather than their own money. Why, then, do the investment decisions of salaried managers in Canada tend to be better for the long-term growth of the Canadian economy than were the decisions of salaried bureaucrats in the Soviet Union?

LO 7.3

3.1 Figure 7.5 shows average annual growth rates in real GDP per person in Canada for various periods from 1870 onward. How might the growth rates in the figure be different if they were calculated for real GDP *per hour worked* instead of per person? (*Hint:* How do you think the number of hours worked per person has changed in Canada since 1870?)

3.2 Some economists argue that the apparent slowdown in productivity growth in Canada and the United States in recent years is a measurement problem resulting from the failure of GDP measures to capture the effects of many recent innovations, such as cloud computing. James Manyika, head of technology at McKinsey & Company, argues that for many of these innovations, "we have all these benefits but we're not paying for them."

    a. Before the arrival of the Internet, people looking for facts, such as the population of France or the salary of the president of the United States, had to go to the library to look them up. Now people can find that information in a few seconds with a Google search. Are the benefits to you of being able to do a Google search included in GDP? Briefly explain.

    b. Does your answer to part (a) indicate that the slowdown in Canadian productivity growth in recent years is just a measurement problem? What other information would you need to arrive at a definite answer?

Based on Timothy Aeppel, "Silicon Valley Doesn't Believe U.S. Productivity Is Down," *Wall Street Journal*, July 16, 2015.

3.3 Economist Robert Gordon of Northwestern University has argued the following:

> My interpretation of the [information] revolution is that it is increasingly burdened by diminishing returns. The push to ever smaller devices runs up against the fixed size of the human finger that must enter information on the device. Most of the innovations since 2000 have been directed to consumer enjoyment rather than business productivity, including video games, DVD players, and iPods. iPhones are nice, but the ability to reschedule business

meetings and look up corporate documents while on the road already existed by 2003.

If Gordon's observations about the information revolution are correct, what are the implications for future labour productivity growth rates?

From Robert J. Gordon, "Revisiting U.S. Productivity Growth over the Past Century with a View of the Future," National Bureau of Economic Research Working Paper 15834, March 2010.

LO 7.4

4.1 **[Related to Solved Problem 7.2 on page 169]** Briefly explain whether the statistics in the following table are consistent with the economic growth model's predictions of catch-up.

Country	Real GDP per Capita, 1960 (2005 US dollars)	Growth in Real GDP per Capita, 1960–2011
China	$331	6.66%
Uganda	657	1.37
Madagascar	1 051	−0.23
Ireland	7 223	3.25
United States	15 398	2.02

Source: Authors' calculations from data in *Penn World Table Version 8.1;* Robert C. Feenstra, Robert Inklaar, and Marcel P. Timmer, "The Next Generation of the Penn World Table" www.ggdc.net/pwt, April 2015.

4.2 **[Related to Solved Problem 7.2 on page 169]** In the following figure, each dot represents a country, with its initial real GDP per capita and its growth rate of real GDP per capita.

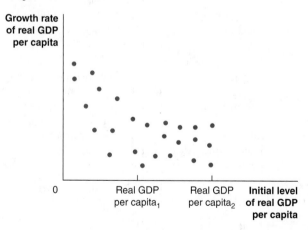

a. For the range of initial GDP per capita from 0 to Real GDP per capita$_2$, does the figure support the economic growth model's prediction of catch-up? Briefly explain.

b. For the range of initial GDP per capita from 0 to Real GDP per capita$_1$, does the figure support the catch-up prediction? Briefly explain.

c. For the range from initial Real GDP per capita$_1$ to Real GDP per capita$_2$, does the figure support the catch-up prediction? Briefly explain.

4.3 Refer to Figures 7.7–7.9 on pages 169, 170, and 172. The lines in the following three graphs show the average

relationship between the initial level of real GDP per capita and the growth rate of real GDP per capita for three groups of countries over a given time period. Match each group of countries with the graph that best depicts the relationship between the initial level of real GDP per capita and the growth rate of real GDP per capita for that group.

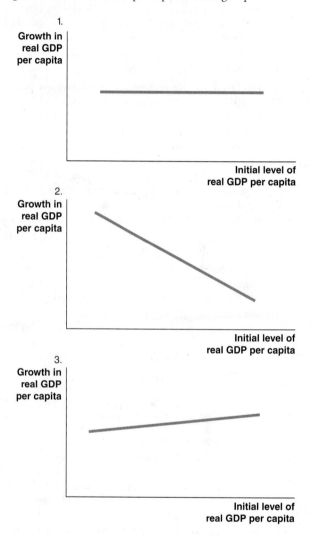

a. All countries for which statistics are available, 1960–2011

b. United States, Western Europe, Canada, and Japan, 1990–2014

c. Current high income countries, 1960–2011

4.4 An article in the *New York Times* notes that since 2001, Italy has had the lowest rate of growth in labour productivity among European countries that use the euro common currency. The article quoted Italy's economy minister as saying, "The real tragedy for Italy is falling productivity." At the time the minister made these remarks, the unemployment rate in Italy was greater than 12 percent—more than twice the rate in Germany, the United Kingdom, Canada, or the United States. Despite the high unemployment rate, why might Italy's economy minister call low productivity growth rates "the real tragedy"?

Based on Reuters, "Italy Economy Minister Warns Deflation Would Be 'Disaster,'" *New York Times,* May 31, 2014.

4.5 [Related to the Making the Connection on page 174]
A study by the McKinsey Global Institute reported that labour productivity increased at an average annual rate of 5.8 percent between 1999 and 2013 in Mexico's large companies, but it fell at an average annual rate of 6.5 percent over the same period for Mexico's smaller firms, such as family-owned stores and bakeries. Briefly explain why productivity growth would be much higher for Mexico's largest companies than for its smaller companies.

Based on Anthony Harrup, "Two Economies Explain Mexico's Productivity Quandary," *Wall Street Journal*, March 27, 2014.

4.6 [Related to the Making the Connection on page 174]
In 2014, real GDP per capita in Mexico increased by 0.9 percent. A Mexican economist was quoted in an article in the *Wall Street Journal* as saying, "It's clearly insufficient if we want to significantly reduce poverty and move Mexico toward a middle-class country."

a. Given that growth rate, how long would it take the standard of living of the average person in Mexico to double?

b. Why isn't the Mexican economy growing more rapidly?

Source: Juan Montes, "Mexican Economy Expanded Modestly in 2014," *Wall Street Journal*, February 20, 2015.

4.7 The Roman Empire lasted from 27 BCE to 476 CE. The empire was wealthy enough to build such monuments as the Roman Colosseum. Roman engineering skill was at a level high enough that aqueducts built during the empire to carry water long distances remained in use for hundreds of years. Yet the empire's growth rate of real GDP per capita was very low, perhaps zero. Why didn't the Roman Empire experience sustained economic growth? What would the world be like today if it had? (*Note:* There are no definite answers to this question; it is intended to get you to think about the preconditions for economic growth.)

LO 7.5

5.1 [Related to the Chapter Opener on page 151] An article on the Mexican economy in the *Economist* notes, "A huge, unproductive informal sector and general lawlessness also drag the economy down." If these factors were the main barriers to more rapid economic growth in Mexico, would that be good news or bad news for the Mexican government's attempts to increase their economy's growth rate? Briefly explain.

Source: "The 100-Year View," *Economist*, May 2, 2015.

5.2 [Related to Making the Connection on page 177] In China, why may a lower birthrate lead to slower growth in real GDP per capita? Why might high levels of spending on investment in China lead to high rates of growth in the short run, but not in the long run?

5.3 Pranab Bardhan, an economist at the University of California, Berkeley, argues: "China may be close to exhausting the possibilities of technological catch-up with the West, particularly in manufacturing."

a. What does Bardhan mean by "technological catch-up"?

b. If Bardhan is correct, what problems might the Chinese economy encounter in the future?

c. Briefly discuss the similarities and differences between the Chinese economy today and the Soviet economy in the 1980s.

Source: Pranab Bardhan, "The Slowing of Two Economic Giants," *New York Times*, July 14, 2013.

5.4 Briefly explain which of the following policies are likely to increase the rate of economic growth in Canada.

a. The government passes an investment tax credit, which reduces a firm's taxes if it installs new machinery and equipment.

b. The government passes a law that allows taxpayers to reduce their income taxes by the amount of provincial sales taxes they pay.

c. The government provides more funds for low-interest loans to college students.

5.5 Economist George Ayittey, in an interview on PBS about economic development in Africa, stated that of the 54 African countries, only 8 had a free press. For Africa's economic development, Ayittey argued strongly for the establishment of a free press. Why would a free press be vital for the enhancement of property rights and the rule of law? How could a free press help reduce corruption?

Based on George Ayittey, Border Jumpers, Anchor Interview Transcript, WideAngle, PBS.org, July 24, 2005.

5.6 More people in high-income countries than in low-income countries tend to believe that rapid rates of economic growth are not desirable. Recall the concept of a "normal good" from Chapter 3. Does this concept provide insight into why some people in high-income countries might be more concerned with certain consequences of rapid economic growth than are people in low-income countries?

MyEconLab MyEconLab is an online tool designed to help you master the concepts covered in your course. It will create a personalized study plan to stimulate and measure your learning. Log in to take advantage of this powerful study aid, and to access quizzes and other valuable course-related material.

The Worries about China's Slowing Growth

On the face of it, this should be a triumphant day for China. It reported that the economy grew by 6.9% last year, just a shade lower than 2014's 7.3% pace. That is some achievement, given the turmoil in emerging markets and the sheer size ($10 trillion) of the economy (6.9% growth now yields more additional output than 14.2% growth did back in 2007). But the plunging Chinese stock market, the global commodity collapse and downward pressure on the yuan have given rise to a prevalent view that reality is grimmer. If the data are so strong, why are so many people so down on China?

The most obvious answer is that no one much believes the numbers. China has long been suspected of massaging data to smooth its growth trend, under-reporting GDP when overheated and over-reporting it during lulls. Judging by the eerie stability of key indicators recently, China's statisticians appear to have been doing just that. In year-on-year terms, growth over the past six quarters has been 7.2%, 7.2%, 7%, 7%, 6.9%, and 6.8%. Such a tight clustering is improbable.

Private surveys suggest that growth was much lumpier last year, with the economy initially soft, then picking up in the final months thanks to stimulus policies. Using a composite of alternative data from electricity usage to car sales, many analysts reckon last year's growth rate was really 5-6%—not bad, though certainly not as buoyant as the government says.

Headline growth is, however, only the first of the concerns. Look under the hood at the composition of Chinese growth, and the picture that emerges is of extreme weakness in certain parts of the economy. Heavy industry is in bad shape, blighted by overcapacity and falling demand. Service sectors from finance to health care are much more robust. But services, by their nature, are mainly delivered locally; China is able to provide more of what it needs by itself, not through imports. That is cold comfort for other countries, especially commodity producers, which had come to count on ever-stronger Chinese demand. Official data are admirably clear on this bifurcation of the economy: services output grew by 11.6% year-on-year in nominal terms in the first nine months of 2015, whereas manufacturing grew by just 1.2%.

The biggest fear about Chinese growth is that much worse is still to come. Total debt has gone from about 150% of GDP before the global financial crisis in 2008 to nearly 250% today. Increases in indebtedness of that magnitude have been a forerunner of financial woes in other countries. Cracks are beginning to appear in China: capital outflows have surged, bankruptcies are occurring more frequently and bad loans in the banking sector are rising. It is all but certain that more pain lies ahead, though quite how much and how it will play out are matters for debate. If there is one thing all can agree on about China's economy, it is that the gap between official data and market perceptions has widened to a chasm.

Key Points in the Article

The Chinese economy has been growing at a rapid pace over the past two decades, due in large part to high levels of investment. From 1996 to 2014, China experienced an annual growth rate of real GDP per capita of close to 9 percent. According to the article, this remarkably high growth performance of the Chinese economy will be unsustainable. Many people believe that China will grow in the future at a much slower rate than it has in the recent past.

Analyzing the News

(a) In a recent article, Robert J. Barro of Harvard University argues that China will grow in the future at a much slower rate than it has in the recent past.* As he puts it, the evidence from long-term data on international experience within a convergence-type framework (as we discussed in Chapter 7) has "generated a pair of '2s'. First, in the long run, each country's growth rate of real per capita GDP is about 2% per year. Second, a country's per capita GDP tends to converge to its long-run path at around 2% per year (dubbed the 'iron law of convergence')." According to Barro, the main reason for China's remarkably high growth rate of real GDP per capita over the past two decades is that China was very poor in this period and the convergence process predicts a response of high growth. The fact that China has gotten a lot

richer leads, through the convergence process, to reduced growth prospects.

(b) As you read in Chapter 7, the quantity of capital available to workers is a source of long-run economic growth. Much of the growth in China over the past two decades came from investment in capital goods. In 2014, gross domestic investment (also known as gross capital formation) accounted for 46 percent of Chinese GDP, a far higher percentage than in other major economies, and household final consumption expenditure was only 36.5 percent. In contrast, household final consumption expenditure was 55.8 percent of GDP in Canada and 68.6% in the United States. Relying on investment as a means of economic growth is not a long-run solution though, as eventually an economy encounters diminishing returns to capital. Because of diminishing returns to capital, further increases in the quantity of capital would result in even smaller increases in real GDP per worker. The production function in the figure below illustrates this point: An increase in capital per hour worked from $(K/L)_{2018}$ to $(K/L)_{2019}$ leads to an increase in output per hour worked from $(Y/L)_{2018}$ to $(Y/L)_{2019}$. This increase in output per hour is much smaller than the increase resulting from the same size increase in capital per hour worked from $(K/L)_{2001}$ to $(K/L)_{2002}$, when the level of capital per hour worked was much smaller.

(c) Analysts are concerned about the increase in the debt-to-GDP ratio in China from about 150% in 2008 to close to 250% today. Such increases in indebtedness have been a forerunner of financial problems in other countries, as they reflect excessive risk taking and the development of asset price bubbles. For example, in China's megacities, Shenzhen, Beijing, Shanghai, and Xiamen, house prices are well above levels that can be justified by the fundamentals. If the housing bubble bursts, it will affect not only house prices, but all prices within China's economy and globally.

Thinking Critically about Policy

1. What policies can the Chinese government pursue to raise the country's long-run economic growth without further increases in investment spending? How would these policies affect China's per-worker production function?

2. According to the article, there are suspicions that China's government is manipulating the data to smooth its growth trend, under-reporting GDP during economic expansions and over-reporting it during economic contractions. Why would China's statisticians massage the national-accounts data?

*Barro, Robert J. "China's growth prospects," VOX EU, 4 February, 2016.

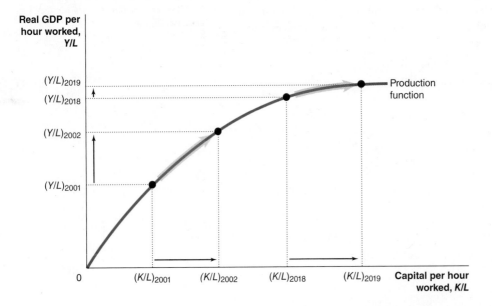

Continuous increases in capital per hour worked lead to smaller and smaller increases in output per hour worked.

Aggregate Expenditure and Output in the Short Run

Fluctuating Demand at Tim Hortons

Tim Hortons coffee is part of Canadian culture. There is a Tim Hortons outlet in just about every small town in the country, and it's hard to go to a rink or a mall and not see someone taking a sip from that famous brown paper cup. Many people seem to need that cup of coffee from "Timmy's" to get through their morning.

Just like most other businesses, Tim Hortons outlets have to worry about the wider economy. When people lose their jobs or are worried about their financial future, they tend to cut back on spending. That morning cup of coffee at the local coffee shop can be one of those things that people decide to do without when times are tight.

In 2014–2015, the Alberta energy sector lost an estimated 40 000 jobs. When firms in any industry are struggling, they reduce output and lay off workers. These laid-off workers will reduce their spending and make fewer purchases in an effort to save money. This often means cutting back on things like restaurant meals and take-out coffee. If people buy fewer cups of coffee, in turn, Tim Hortons may find it necessary to reduce its number of employees and may even cut the hours of the employees it keeps on.

This is just one example of how some firms that cut production can reduce the total spending, or *aggregate expenditure*, of an economy. In this chapter, we will explore how changes in aggregate expenditure affect the level of total production in the economy.

Chapter Outline and Learning Objectives

Economics in Your Life

When Consumer Confidence Falls, Is Your Job at Risk?

Suppose that while taking your degree, you work part time at a local Tim Hortons. One morning you read a local newspaper's story that consumer confidence in the economy has fallen and, as a result, many households expect their future income to be much less than their current income. Should you be concerned about losing your job? What factors should you consider in deciding how likely your boss is to lay you off? As you read the chapter, see if you can answer these questions (pay particular attention to *Making the Connection,* "Do Changes in Consumer Confidence Affect Consumption Spending?" on page 195). You can check your answers against those we provide on page 219 at the end of this chapter.

Aggregate expenditure (*AE*) Total spending in the economy: the sum of consumption, planned investment, government purchases, and net exports.

I n Chapter 7, we analyzed the determinants of long-run economic growth. In the short run, as we saw in Chapter 6, the economy experiences a business cycle around the long-run upward trend in real GDP. In this chapter, we begin by exploring the causes of the business cycle by examining the effect of changes in total spending on real GDP.

During some years, total spending in the economy, or **aggregate expenditure (*AE*)**, and total production of goods and services increase by the same amount. If this happens, most firms will sell what they expected to sell. These firms are not likely to increase or decrease their production. This means there won't be large changes in the total number of workers employed. During other years, total spending in the economy increases more than total production. In these years, firms will increase their production and hire more workers in order to meet the demands of consumers. Sometimes, however, the increase in total spending in the economy is less than total production. As a result, firms reduce their production and potentially lay off a few workers, which can trigger a slowdown in other sectors of the economy—potentially leading to a recession. In this chapter, we will explore why changes in total spending play such an important role in the economy.

Understand how macroeconomic equilibrium is determined in the aggregate expenditure model.

Aggregate expenditure model
A macroeconomic model that focuses on the short-run relationship between total spending and real GDP, assuming that the price level is constant.

The Aggregate Expenditure Model

The business cycle involves the interaction of many different economic variables. A simple model called the *aggregate expenditure model* can help us understand the relationships among some of these variables. Recall from Chapter 6 that nominal GDP is the current market value of all final goods and services produced in a country in a year. Real GDP corrects nominal GDP for the effects of inflation. The **aggregate expenditure model** focuses on the short-run relationship between total spending and real GDP. A central assumption of this model is that the price level doesn't change. This means we don't have to worry about a difference between real GDP and nominal GDP. In Chapter 9, we will develop a more complete model of the business cycle that relaxes the assumption of constant prices.

The key idea of the aggregate expenditure model is that *in any particular year, the level of real GDP is determined mainly by the level of aggregate expenditure.* To understand the relationship between aggregate expenditure and real GDP, we need to look more closely at the components of aggregate expenditure.

Aggregate Expenditure

Economists first began to study the relationship between changes in aggregate expenditure and changes in GDP during the Great Depression of the 1930s. Canada, the United States, the United Kingdom, and other industrial countries suffered declines in real GDP of 25 percent or more during the early part of the 1930s. In 1936, British economist John Maynard Keynes published one of the most important books in economics, *The General Theory of Employment, Interest, and Money*, that systematically analyzed the relationship between changes in aggregate expenditure and changes in GDP. Keynes identified four components of aggregate expenditure (which we discussed in Chapter 4), that together equal GDP: consumption, investment, government purchases, and net exports. The four components that make up planned aggregate expenditure (*AE*) are very similar:

- **Consumption (C):** This is spending by households on goods and services; it includes everything from food to haircuts to snowmobiles.

- **Planned Investment (I_p):** This is the planned spending by firms on capital goods, such as factories, office buildings, and machines, and by households on new homes.

- **Government Purchases (G):** This is spending by local, provincial, and federal governments on goods and services, such as the armed forces, bridges and roads, and the salaries of RCMP officers.

- **Net Exports (NX):** This is spending by foreign firms and households on goods and services produced in Canada minus the spending by Canadian firms and households on goods and services produced in other countries.

In this chapter, we use the term *planned aggregate expenditure* for the most part because we are focusing on the desired (rather than the actual) spending of an economy in a given period, which is represented by the following equation:

Planned aggregate expenditure = Consumption + Planned investment

+ Government purchases + Net exports

or:

$$AE = C + Ip + G + NX.$$

Governments around the world gather statistics on aggregate expenditure based on these four components. Economists and business analysts usually explain changes in GDP in terms of changes in these four components of spending.

The Difference between Planned Investment and Actual Investment

As you likely know, not everything goes as planned. This is true for businesses as well as university students. You likely noticed that we included "planned investment" rather than "investment" in the equation above. How is it that the amount businesses plan to spend on investment can be different from the amount they actually end up spending?

Understanding how the difference can arise begins with thinking about how firms go about selling goods. In many cases, firms don't wait for a customer to purchase something before they produce it. Instead they produce it, and hold it in *inventory*, while waiting for a customer to make a purchase. **Inventories** are simply products that have been produced but not yet sold to the consumer. Changes in inventories are included as part of investment spending, along with spending on machinery, equipment, office buildings, and factories.

Inventories Goods that have been produced but not yet sold.

In the case of Tim Hortons, actual investment would include its bakeries and stores as well as any doughnuts or cans of coffee it hadn't sold yet. For a retailer, all of the products in the store are part of inventory. Businesses need some inventory in order to sell to consumers. A difference between planned and actual investment arises when firms don't sell the amount of a product they were planning to.

For example, Chapters may want to have 5 copies of *The Big Short* on its shelves at all times. Assume that it already has 5 copies. If it expects to sell 95 more copies, it would then order 95 copies of the book. If it sells 95 copies, its inventory remains unchanged at 5 copies of the book. If it only sells 90 copies of the book, it has an unplanned increase in inventory of 5 books, leaving it with a total of 10. In short, changes in inventories often depend on sales of goods, which firms can't usually predict with perfect accuracy.

For the economy as a whole, we can say that actual investment spending will be greater than planned investment spending when there is an unplanned increase in inventories. Actual investment spending will be less than planned investment spending when there is an unplanned decrease in inventories. *Therefore, actual investment will equal planned investment only when there is no unplanned change in inventories.* In this chapter, we use I_p to represent planned investment. We will also assume that the government data on investment spending (not including inventories) compiled by Statistics Canada represent planned spending. This is a simplification because some of the spending on inventories would be planned by firms.

Macroeconomic Equilibrium

Macroeconomic equilibrium is similar to microeconomic equilibrium. In a microeconomic equilibrium, such as in the market for apples, neither buyers nor sellers have any incentive to change their plans. Equilibrium in the market for apples occurs when the quantity of apples demanded is equal to the quantity of apples supplied, and thus neither producers nor consumers have an incentive to change their behaviour. This means apple producers are selling the amount they planned to. When equilibrium in the apple market is achieved, the quantity of apples produced and sold will not change unless the demand for apples or the supply of apples changes. For the economy as a whole, macroeconomic equilibrium occurs where total spending, or planned aggregate expenditure, equals total production, or GDP:[1]

$$\text{Planned aggregate expenditure} = \text{GDP}.$$

As we saw in Chapter 7, in the long run, real GDP in Canada grows, and the standard of living rises over time. In this chapter, we are interested in understanding why GDP fluctuates in the short run. To simplify the analysis of macroeconomic equilibrium, we assume that the economy is not growing. In Chapter 9, we discuss the more realistic case of macroeconomic equilibrium in a growing (or shrinking) economy. If we assume that the economy is not growing, equilibrium GDP will not change unless planned aggregate expenditure changes.

Getting to Macroeconomic Equilibrium

In Chapter 3, where we discussed equilibrium in the market for a single good, we assumed that price would adjust so that the quantity demanded would equal the quantity supplied. In the macroeconomic equilibrium model, we assume that the price level is constant, so price adjustments can't cause the market to move to equilibrium. Instead, firms' responses to unplanned inventory investment will lead to equilibrium.

The easiest way to show that the economy will move toward an output level that is equal to planned aggregate expenditure is to consider what would happen if the two were not equal. As an example, let's look at how a manager at a Chapters store might respond to different levels of sales of *The Big Short*.

If planned aggregate expenditure is greater than GDP, firms have sold more than they expected to sell. For our Chapters example, the store may have planned to sell 95 copies of *The Big Short*, but actually sold 100. It has seen a reduction in its inventories of 5 books. As a result, Chapters has an unplanned investment in inventories of −5 (meaning that inventories have fallen by 5—the minus sign tells you that inventories have decreased). How would the manager respond to such a change in inventories? The manager would likely order more copies of *The Big Short* this time, say 100 copies. If stores and producers in the economy are experiencing similar unplanned drops in inventories,

---

[1]Another way to think of this idea is to make planned aggregate expenditure equal to actual aggregate expenditure. Macroeconomic equilibrium occurs when the plans of producers such as Tim Hortons are realized, or when most firms get production "right."

If ...	then ...	and ...
planned aggregate expenditure equals GDP,	inventories don't change	the economy is in macroeconomic equilibrium.
planned aggregate expenditure is less than GDP,	inventories rise	GDP and employment decrease.
planned aggregate expenditure is greater than GDP,	inventories fall	GDP and employment increase.

Table 8.1

The Relationship between Planned Aggregate Expenditure and GDP

everyone will increase their orders, and the output of the economy (GDP) will increase. To increase production, firms have to hire more workers, and employment rises. In summary, *when planned aggregate expenditure is greater than GDP, inventories will decline, and (as a result of firms' reactions to the drop in inventories) GDP and total employment will increase.*

If planned aggregate expenditure is less than GDP, firms have not sold as much as they expected to sell. For our Chapters example, the store may have planned to sell 95 copies of *The Big Short*, but instead only sold 90. It has seen an unplanned increase in its inventories of 5 books (it now has 10 in stock when it wanted only 5). How would the manager respond to such an unplanned increase in inventories? The manager would likely order fewer copies of *The Big Short*, say 85 copies, in hopes of selling all of the copies ordered this time. If many other stores and producers throughout the economy have experienced similar unplanned increases in inventories, they too will decrease their orders. In response to the decrease in orders, firms will cut back production and GDP will decrease. To decrease production, firms generally have to lay off workers, leading to lower employment. Managers of small-town Tim Hortons may have to take such actions when major employers in the area close. In summary, *when planned aggregate expenditure is less than GDP, inventories will increase, and (as a result of firms' reactions to the increase in inventories) GDP and total employment will decrease.*

Only when planned aggregate expenditure is equal to GDP will firms sell what they expected to sell. In that case, their unplanned inventory investments are 0, and they won't have an incentive to increase or decrease their production. The economy will be in macroeconomic equilibrium. Table 8.1 summarizes the relationship between planned aggregate expenditure and GDP.

This process of increasing and decreasing planned aggregate expenditure causes the year-to-year changes we see in GDP. Economists devote a lot of time and energy to forecasting what will happen to each component of planned aggregate expenditure. Those who are really good at it can make a lot of money working for business or government. When economists forecast that planned aggregate expenditure will decline in the future, that is equivalent to forecasting that GDP will decline and that the economy will enter a recession. Individuals and firms closely watch these forecasts because changes in GDP can have dramatic consequences. When GDP increases, wages, profits, and job opportunities also tend to increase. When GDP declines, it can be bad news for a lot of workers, firms, and job seekers.

When economists forecast that planned aggregate expenditure is likely to decline and the economy is headed for a recession, the federal and provincial governments may implement *macroeconomic policies* in an attempt to head off the decrease in expenditure and keep the economy from falling into recession. We discuss macroeconomic policies in Chapters 11 and 12.

Determining the Level of Aggregate Expenditure in the Economy

To better understand how macroeconomic equilibrium is determined in the aggregate expenditure model, we look more closely at the components of planned aggregate expenditure. Table 8.2 lists the four components of aggregate expenditure for 2015. Each component is measured in *real* terms, meaning that it is corrected for inflation by

8.2 LEARNING OBJECTIVE

Discuss the determinants of the four components of aggregate expenditure and define marginal propensity to consume and marginal propensity to save.

Table 8.2

**Components of Aggregate
Expenditure, 2015**

Source: Statistics Canada. Table 380-0064 –
Gross domestic product, expenditure-
based, quarterly (dollars unless otherwise
noted), CANSIM (database). Reproduced
and distributed on an "as is" basis with the
permission of Statistics Canada.

Expenditure Category	Real Expenditure (billions of 2007 dollars)
Consumption	996.79
Planned Investment	331.01
Government Spending	410.05
Net Exports	–6.83

being measured in billions of 2007 dollars. Consumption is clearly the largest component of aggregate expenditure. Government purchases, including some items considered
government investment, is the second-largest component, followed closely by planned
investment (not including inventories). Net exports are negative because in 2015, unlike
most years before the mid-2000s, Canada imported more goods and services than it
exported. Next we consider the variables that determine each of the four components of
aggregate expenditure.

Consumption

Figure 8.1 shows real consumption from 1981 to 2015. Notice that consumption generally follows a smooth, upward trend. Only during periods of recession does consumption decline. You can see this as drops in consumption between 1981 and 1982, as well
as between 1991 and 1992, and a plateau between 2008 and 2009 before shrinking
between 2009 and 2010. The Canadian economy was in or recovering from a recession
during these periods.

The following are the five most important variables that determine the level of
consumption:

- Current disposable income

- Household wealth

- Expected future income

- The price level

- The interest rate

We will discuss how changes in each of these variables affect consumption in turn.

Current Disposable Income.   The most important determinant of consumption
is the current disposable income of households. Recall from Chapter 4 that disposable
income is the income remaining to households after they have paid the personal income

Figure 8.1

Real Consumption

Consumption follows a smooth, upward
trend, interrupted only infrequently by
brief recessions.

Source: Statistics Canada. Table 380-0064 –
Gross domestic product, expenditure-based,
quarterly (dollars unless otherwise noted),
CANSIM (database) (accessed: December 30,
2015). Reproduced and distributed on an
"as is" basis with the permission of Statistics
Canada.

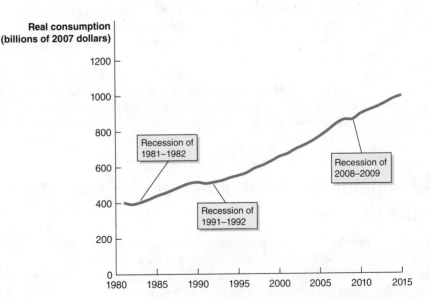

tax and received government *transfer payments,* such as social security payments. For most households, the higher their disposable income the more they spend, and the lower their disposable income the less they spend. Macroeconomic consumption is the total of all consumption by Canadian households. So, we would expect consumption to increase when the current disposable income of households increases and to decrease when current disposable income decreases. As was discussed in Chapter 4, total income in Canada increases in most years. Only during recessions, which have not occurred that often in the last 30 years, does total income decline. The main reason why consumption in Figure 8.1 shows such a strong upward trend is that incomes have been rising over the same period of time.

Household Wealth. Consumption depends in part on the wealth of households. A household's *wealth* is the value of its *assets* minus the value of its *liabilities.* An **asset** is anything of value owned by a person or a firm, and a **liability** is any debt or obligation owed by a person or firm. A household's assets include its home, stock and bond holdings, bank accounts, and cars. A household's liabilities include any loans that must be paid back, such as student loans, mortgages, and car loans. A household with $10 million in wealth is likely to spend more than a household with $10 000 in wealth, even if both have the same disposable income. Therefore, when the wealth of households increases, consumption is likely to increase, and when the wealth of households decreases, consumption is likely to decrease.

Asset Anything of value owned by a person or a firm.

Liability Anything owed by a person or a firm.

The value of stocks held by households is an important indicator of household wealth. When stock prices increase, household wealth increases, and so should consumption. For example, a family whose stock holdings have increased in value from $50 000 to $100 000 may be willing to spend a larger portion of their disposable income because that household will be less concerned with saving for the future. A decline in stock prices is likely to lead to a decline in consumption. Economists who have studied the determinants of consumption have concluded that permanent increases in wealth have a larger impact than temporary increases. A recent estimate of the effect of changes in wealth on consumption spending indicates for a permanent $1 increase in household wealth, consumption spending increases by 4 to 5 cents per year.

Expected Future Income.   Consumption depends in part on expected future income. Most people prefer to keep their consumption fairly stable from year to year, even if their income changes a lot. Some salespeople, for example, earn most of their income from commissions (fixed percentages of the price) on the products they sell. A salesperson might have high income in some years and much lower incomes in other years. Most people in this situation keep their consumption steady and do not increase it much in good years and do not reduce it much in bad years.

The same can be said of most students in Canada. Canadian students generally spend much more of their income than people who are not students with the same income. In fact many students even borrow to improve their consumption possibilities. This may be because students believe their future incomes will be much higher than their current incomes.

If we looked only at the current income of people in the early stages of their lives, we might have difficulty estimating people's current consumption. Instead, we need to take people's expected future income into account.

Making the Connection | **Do Changes in Consumer Confidence Affect Consumption Spending?**

Since 1980, the Conference Board of Canada has conducted surveys of consumers and calculated the *Consumer Confidence Index.* This index is intended to capture the expectations of consumers about the future. The survey is based on the following four questions:

1. Considering everything, would you say that your family is better or worse off financially than six months ago?

2. Again, considering everything, do you think that your family will be better off, the same, or worse off financially six months from now?
3. How do you feel the job situation and overall employment will be in this community six months from now?
4. Do you think that right now is a good or bad time for the average person to make a major outlay for items such as a home, car, or other major item?

The percentages of positive and negative responses for each question are calculated. The index value for each question is:

$$\text{Value} = \frac{\text{Percentage of positive responses}}{\text{Percentage of positive responses } + \text{ Percentage of negative responses}}$$

The index is the average of the values for the four questions, adjusted so that the index is 100 in 2014 (see the graph below).

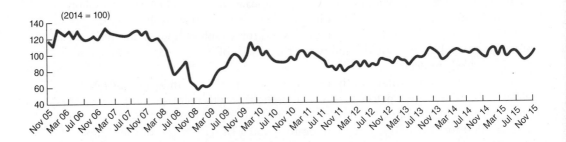

We can see that consumer confidence fell sharply in 2008 as the global recession began to hit Canadians. We can also see falling confidence throughout most of the early part of 2015. Despite this drop, as well as a sluggish economy throughout most of the year, Canadian consumers became more confident in November of 2015 than they had been for most of that year. This may be evidence of the beginning of an economic recovery.

Andy Kwan of Chinese University Hong Kong and John Cotsomitis of Concordia University have studied the relationship between the Consumer Confidence Index and the Canadian economy. It turns out that the Consumer Confidence Index is a good predictor of household spending in Canada. The link between spending and expected future income is supported by their study. They find spending increases when consumers are more confident about the future and falls when they are less confident. Consumer confidence data are also widely reported in the press and on the evening news. You too can use the Consumer Confidence Index to predict what will happen to consumer spending in the near future.

Source: Do Changes in Consumer Confidence Affect Consumption Spending? The Conference Board of Canada. http://www.conferenceboard.ca/topics/economics/Consumer_confidence.aspx. Reprinted with permission.

MyEconLab   **Your Turn:** Test your understanding by doing related problem 2.4 on page 221 at the end of this chapter.

The Price Level Recall from Chapter 5 that the *price level* is a measure of the average prices of goods and services in the economy. Consumption is affected by changes in the price level. It is tempting to assume that an increase in prices will reduce consumption by making goods and services less affordable. In fact, the effect of an increase in the price of one product on the quantity demanded of that product is different from the effect of an increase in the price level on *total* spending by households on goods and services. Changes in the price level affect consumption through the impact on real household wealth. An increase in price level leads to a reduction in the *real* value of wealth. For example, if you have $2000 in a chequing account, the higher the price level, the fewer goods you can buy with that $2000. If the price level falls, the more you can buy. Therefore, as the price level rises, the *real* value of your wealth falls, and so will your consumption. Conversely, if the price level falls, which almost never happens in Canada, your real wealth and thus your consumption will increase.

The Interest Rate Finally, consumption also depends on the interest rate. When the interest rate is high, the reward for saving is increased, and households are likely to save more and spend less. In Chapter 5, we discussed the difference between the *nominal interest rate* and the *real interest rate*. The **nominal interest rate** is the stated interest rate on a loan or a financial asset such as a bond. The **real interest rate** corrects the nominal interest rate for the impact of inflation and is equal to the nominal interest rate minus the expected if ex-ante inflation rate.[2] Households are concerned with the payments they will make or receive after the effects of inflation are taken into account. As a result, consumption spending depends on the real interest rate.

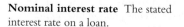

Nominal interest rate The stated interest rate on a loan.

Real interest rate The nominal interest rate minus the inflation rate.

Consumption spending is divided into three categories: spending on *services*, such as education and haircuts; spending on *nondurable goods*, such as food and clothing; and spending on *durable goods*, such as cars and furniture. Spending on durable goods is most likely to be affected by changes in the interest rate because a high real interest rate increases the cost of borrowing to purchase durable goods. The monthly payments on a four-year car loan will be higher if the real interest rate is 4 percent than if the real interest rate is 2 percent. *You can check this out for yourself at* www4.bmo.com/popup/loans/Calculator.html.

The Consumption Function. Panel (a) in Figure 8.2 shows the relationship between consumption spending and disposable income from the years 1981 to 2014, where both consumption and disposable income are measured in billions of 2007 dollars.

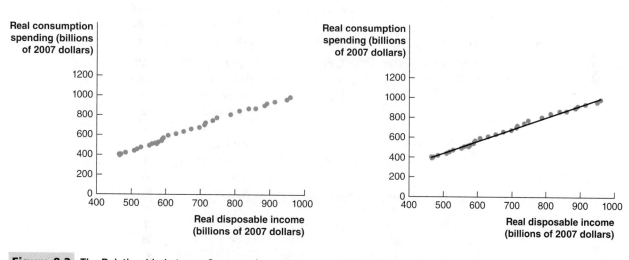

Figure 8.2 The Relationship between Consumption and Income, 1981–2014

Panel (a) shows the relationship between consumption and income. The points represent combinations of real consumption spending and real disposable income for the years 1981–2014. In panel (b), we draw a straight line though the points from panel (a). The line, which represents the relationship between consumption and disposable income, is called the *consumption function*. The slope of the consumption function is the marginal propensity to consume.

Data from CANSIM Table 326-0021, 380-0064, 384-0040.

---

[2]This relationship is sometimes known as the *Fisher equation*, named for the famous economist Irving Fisher. The relationship is often simplified to $r = i -$ inflation, where r is the real interest rate and i is the nominal interest rate.

Consumption function The relationship between consumption spending and disposable income.

Autonomous consumption The level of consumption that occurs no matter what disposable income is.

Marginal propensity to consume (MPC) The slope of the consumption function: The amount by which consumption spending changes when disposable income changes.

Each of the dots represents a combination of consumption spending and disposable income for a given year. The straight line in panel (b) shows the estimated relationship between consumption and disposable income. The fact that most of the points lie almost on the line means we can say *consumption is a function of disposable income*. The relationship between consumption and disposable income is called the **consumption function.**

One of the first things you likely noticed is that consumption will never be zero. Even if disposable income is zero, consumption will be positive. This is because people always have to consume something—even if you have no income, you still need a place to live and food to eat. The consumption that takes place even when disposable income is zero is called **autonomous consumption**. It's called autonomous because it occurs automatically or isn't linked to income at all. Graphically, you can think of autonomous consumption as the intercept of the consumption function.

How is autonomous consumption paid for? It's typically paid for out of past savings. The easiest way to think about this is to think about someone who is out of work or retired. They may not be earning any income right now, but they usually have savings that they can spend to meet their basic needs.

The slope of the consumption function is particularly important. It is called the **marginal propensity to consume (MPC)**. It is calculated as the change in consumption divided by the change in disposable income. Using the Greek letter delta, Δ, to represent "change in," C to represent consumption, and YD to represent disposable income, we can write the formula for MPC as follows:

$$MPC = \frac{\text{Change in consumption}}{\text{Change in disposable income}} = \frac{\Delta C}{\Delta YD}$$

For example, between 2011 and 2012, consumption spending increased by $31.4 billion, while disposable income increased by $39.0 billion. The marginal propensity to consume was, therefore:

$$\frac{\Delta C}{\Delta YD} = \frac{\$31.4 \text{ billion}}{\$39.0 \text{ billion}} = 0.80$$

The value for the MPC tells us the part of an extra dollar of disposable income that households spend. Between 2011 and 2012, households spent 80 cents out of every additional dollar of disposable income. As the relationship is very close to a straight line, we can apply the MPC to determine how consumption will change as disposable income changes. For example, if disposable income were to increase by $10 000, consumption spending would increase by $10 000 × 0.80, or $8000. This can be expressed by the formula:

Change in consumption = MPC × Change in disposable income.

The Relationship between Consumption and National Income

We have seen that consumption spending by households depends on disposable income. We now shift our attention slightly to the similar relationship that exists between consumption spending and GDP. We make this shift because we are interested in using the aggregate expenditure model to explain changes in real GDP rather than changes in disposable income. The first step in examining the relationship between consumption and GDP is to recall from Chapter 4 that the differences between GDP and national income are small and can be ignored without affecting our analysis. In fact, in this and the following chapters, we will use the terms *GDP* and *national income* interchangeably. Also recall that disposable income is equal to national income plus government transfer payments minus taxes. Taxes minus government transfer payments are referred to as *net taxes*. So, we can write the following:

Disposable income = National income − Net taxes.

We can rearrange the equation like this:

National income = GDP = Disposable income + Net taxes.

The table in Figure 8.3 shows hypothetical values for national income (GDP), net taxes, disposable income, and consumption spending. Notice that national income and disposable income differ by a constant amount, which is equal to net taxes of $1000 billion. In reality, net taxes are not a constant amount because they are affected by changes in income. As income rises, net taxes rise because some taxes, such as personal income tax, increase and some government transfer payments, such as employment insurance payments, fall. None of the results presented in this section is dramatically affected by this simplifying assumption.

The graph in Figure 8.3 shows a line similar to the consumption function shown in Figure 8.2. We defined the marginal propensity to consume (*MPC*) as the change in consumption divided by the change in disposable income, which is the slope of the consumption function. In fact, notice that if we calculate the slope of the line in Figure 8.3 between points *A* and *B*, we get a result that will not change whether we use the values for national income or the values for disposable income. Using the values for national income:

$$\frac{\Delta C}{\Delta Y} = \frac{\$5250 \text{ billion} - \$3750 \text{ billion}}{\$7000 \text{ billion} - \$5000 \text{ billion}} = 0.75.$$

Using the corresponding values for disposable income from the table:

$$\frac{\Delta C}{\Delta YD} = \frac{\$5250 \text{ billion} - \$3750 \text{ billion}}{\$6000 \text{ billion} - \$4000 \text{ billion}} = 0.75.$$

National Income or GDP (billions of dollars)	Net Taxes (billions of dollars)	Disposable Income (billions of dollars)	Consumption (billions of dollars)	Change in National Income (billions of dollars)	Change in Disposable Income (billions of dollars)
$ 1000	$1000	$ 0	$ 750	—	—
3000	1000	2000	2250	$2000	$2000
5000	1000	4000	3750	2000	2000
7000	1000	6000	5250	2000	2000
9000	1000	8000	6750	2000	2000
11 000	1000	10 000	8250	2000	2000
13 000	1000	12 000	9750	2000	2000

Figure 8.3

The Relationship between Consumption and National Income

Because national income differs from disposable income only by net taxes—which, for simplicity, we assume are constant—we can graph the consumption function using national income rather than disposable income. We can also calculate the *MPC*, which is the slope of the consumption function, using either the change in national income or the change in disposable income and always get the same value. The slope of the consumption function between point *A* and point *B* is equal to the change in consumption—$1500 billion—divided by the change in national income—$2000 billion—or 0.75.

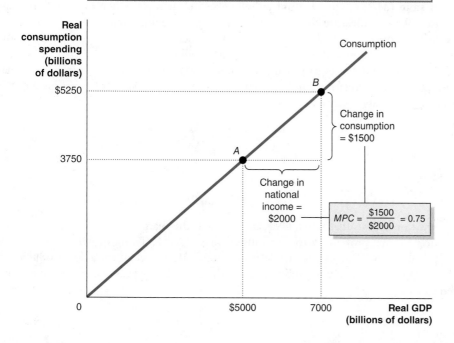

It should not be surprising that we get the same result in either case. National income (real GDP) and disposable income differ by a constant amount, so changes in the two numbers always give the same value, as shown in the last columns of the table in Figure 8.3. Therefore we can graph the consumption function using national income rather than using disposable income. We can also calculate the *MPC* using either the change in real GDP or the change in disposable income and always get the same value.

Income, Consumption, and Saving

To complete our discussion of consumption, we can look briefly at the relationships among income, consumption, and saving. Households either spend their income, save it, or use it to pay taxes. For the economy as a whole, we can write the following:

$$\text{National income} = \text{Consumption} + \text{Saving} + \text{Taxes}$$

When national income increases, there must be some combination of an increase in consumption, an increase in saving, and an increase in taxes:

$$\text{Change in national income} = \text{Change in consumption} + \text{Change in saving}$$
$$+ \text{ Change in taxes}.$$

Using symbols, where Y represents national income (GDP), C represents consumption, S represents saving, and T represents taxes, we can write the following:

$$Y = C + S + T$$

and

$$\Delta Y = \Delta C + \Delta S + \Delta T.$$

To simplify, we can assume that taxes are always a constant amount, in which case $\Delta T = 0$, so the following is also true:

$$\Delta Y = \Delta C + \Delta S.$$

Marginal propensity to save (*MPS*) The amount by which saving changes when disposable income changes.

We have already seen that the marginal propensity to consume equals the change in consumption divided by the change in income. We can define the **marginal propensity to save (*MPS*)** as the amount by which saving increases when disposable income increases. We can measure the *MPS* as the change in saving divided by the change in disposable income. In calculating the *MPS*, as in calculating *MPC*, we can safely ignore the difference between national income and disposable income.

If we divide the last equation above by the change in income, ΔY, we get an equation that shows the relationship between the marginal propensity to consume and the marginal propensity to save:

$$\frac{\Delta Y}{\Delta Y} = \frac{\Delta C}{\Delta Y} + \frac{\Delta S}{\Delta Y}$$

or

$$1 = MPC + MPS.$$

This equation tells us that when taxes are constant, the marginal propensity to consume plus the marginal propensity to save must always equal 1. Think of *MPC* and *MPS* as what people do with an additional dollar of income. If you get an extra dollar of income, and you spend 75 cents, what did you do with the remaining 25 cents? You must have saved it!

Solved Problem **8.1**

Calculating the Marginal Propensity to Consume and the Marginal Propensity to Save

Fill in the blanks in the following table. For simplicity, assume that taxes are zero. Show that MPC plus MPS equals 1.

Real GDP (Y)	Consumption (C)	Saving (S)	Marginal Propensity to Consume (MPC)	Marginal Propensity to Save (MPS)
$900	$800		—	—
1000	800			
1100	900			
1200	900			
1300	1040			

Solving the Problem

Step 1: **Review the chapter material.** This problem is about the relationship among income, consumption, and saving, so you may want to review the section "Income, Consumption, and Saving" on page 200.

Step 2: **Fill in the table.** We know that $Y = C + S + T$. With taxes equal to zero, this equation becomes $Y = C + S$. We can use this equation to fill in the "Saving" column. We can use the equation for MPC and MPS to fill in the other two columns.

$$MPC = \frac{\Delta C}{\Delta Y}$$

$$MPS = \frac{\Delta S}{\Delta Y}$$

For example, to calculate the value of MPC in the second row of the table, we have:

$$MPC = \frac{\Delta C}{\Delta Y} = \frac{\$860 - \$800}{\$1000 - \$900} = \frac{\$60}{\$100} = 0.6.$$

To calculate the value of MPS in the second row of the table, we have:

$$MPS = \frac{\Delta S}{\Delta Y} = \frac{\$140 - \$100}{\$1000 - \$900} = \frac{\$40}{\$100} = 0.4.$$

Real GDP (Y)	Consumption (C)	Saving (S)	Marginal Propensity to Consume (MPC)	Marginal Propensity to Save (MPS)
$900	$800	$100	—	—
1000	860	140	0.6	0.4
1100	920	180	0.6	0.4
1200	980	220	0.6	0.4
1300	1040	260	0.6	0.4

Step 3: **Show that MPC plus MPS equals 1.** At every level of national income, the MPC is 0.6 and MPS is 0.4. Therefore, the MPC plus MPS is always equal to 1.

Your Turn: For more practice, do related problem 2.5 on page 222 at the end of this chapter.   MyEconLab

Planned Investment

Figure 8.4 shows movements in real private-sector investment spending from 1981 to 2014. Notice that while investment generally does have an upward trend, it is not as smooth as consumption. Investment declined significantly in 1982, from 1991 to 1994, and in 2009. As you might have guessed, the Canadian economy was in or recovering from a recession during these periods.

The four most important variables that determine the level of investment are as follows:

- Expectations of future profits

- Interest rate

- Taxes

- Cash flow

Expectations of Future Profits. Investment goods, such as factories, office buildings, and machinery, are long lived. A firm is unlikely to build a new factory unless it believes demand for its product will remain strong for at least several years. When the economy moves into a recession, many firms delay buying investment goods, even if the demand for their own product is strong, because they fear the recession may become worse. During an expansion, some firms may become optimistic and begin to increase spending on investment goods even before the demand for their own product has increased. The key point is this: *The optimism or pessimism of firms is an important determinant of investment spending.*

Residential construction (the building of houses) is included in investment spending. Since 1990, residential construction in Canada has averaged about 32.5 percent of total investment spending. The swings in residential construction can be substantial, ranging from a high of 40 percent to a low of 28 percent of total investment spending. The decline in spending on residential construction in 2008 contributed to the recession, and the increase in spending contributed to the recovery.[3]

Interest Rate. Some business investment is financed by borrowing, which takes the form of issuing corporate bonds or receiving loans from banks. Households also borrow to finance most of their spending on new homes. The higher the interest rate, the more expensive it is for firms and households to borrow. Firms and households are interested in

Figure 8.4

Real Investment

Investment is subject to larger changes than consumption. Investment declined significantly during the recessions of 1981–1982, 1991, and 2008–2009.

Source: Statistics Canada. Table 380-0064 - Gross domestic product, expenditure-based, annual (dollars unless otherwise noted), (accessed: January 01, 2016). Reproduced and distributed on an "as is" basis with the permission of Statistics Canada.

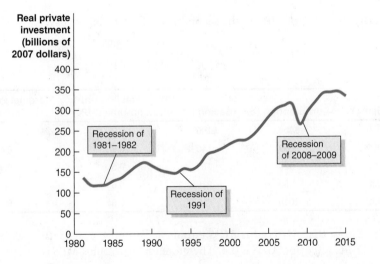

---

[3]*Sources:* Statistics Canada, CANSIM Table 380-0002, and authors' calculations.

the cost of borrowing after taking inflation into account, meaning it is the real interest rate that influences investment spending. The higher the real interest rate, the more interest has to be repaid, which means borrowing is more expensive. Therefore, holding everything else that affects investment constant, there is an inverse relationship between investment spending and the real interest rate. *A higher real interest rate results in less investment spending, while a lower real interest rate results in more investment spending.* As we will discuss in Chapter 12 the ability of households to borrow money at very low real interest rates helps explain the rapid increase in American spending on residential construction from 2002 to 2006.[4]

Taxes. Taxes affect the level of investment spending. Firms focus on the profits that remain after they have paid taxes. Federal and provincial governments impose a *corporate income tax* on the profits of firms. This tax will have an impact on the benefit firms receive, or get to keep, from any investment they make. A reduction in corporate income tax increases the after-tax profitability (the amount of money the firm gets to keep) of investment spending. An increase in the corporate income tax rate decreases the after-tax profitability of investment spending. An *investment tax incentive* provides firms with a tax reduction when they spend on new investment goods, which can increase investment spending.

Cash Flow. Many firms do not borrow to finance spending on new factories, machinery, and other investments. Instead, they use their own funds. **Cash flow** is the difference between the cash revenues received by a firm and the cash spending by the firm. Neither noncash receipts nor noncash spending is included in cash flow. For example, tax laws allow firms to count depreciation to replace worn-out or obsolete machinery as a cost, even when new machinery that has not been purchased would represent noncash spending. The depreciation of existing equipment does not count toward cash flow. The largest contributor to cash flow is profit. The more profitable a firm is, the greater its cash flow and the greater its ability to finance investment. During periods of recession, many firms experience reduced profits, which in turn reduces their ability to finance spending on new factories or machines.

Cash flow The difference between the cash revenues received by a firm and the cash spending by the firm.

<table>
<tr><td>**Making**
the
Connection</td><td>**The Hills and Valleys of Snowmobile Purchases**</td></tr>
</table>

Bombardier Recreational Products (BRP), the first company to mass-manufacture snowmobiles, is facing lower sales of its Ski-Doos in the current economic climate. Snowmobiles are durable goods, and spending on durable goods tends to follow the business cycle. During recessions, households cut back on spending on snowmobiles as they do on other luxury or entertainment items. Firms that use snowmobiles are likely to cut back on new purchases during recessions as well, because they view the machines as an investment, and, as we've seen, investment falls during recessions.

Often households and firms will "make do" with their current machines in a recession rather than buy new ones. As the first graph on the next page shows, snowmobile sales in Canada tend to follow the state of the economy. Sales fell approximately 17.4 percent from 2009 to 2011, more than 12 percent from 1990 to 1991, and by more than 27 percent between 1981 and 1982. Clearly, there are other factors that affect the number of snowmobiles sold—snowfall in a given year, the price of gasoline, the size of the rural population, etc.—but income still plays an important part. The trend has been a decline in snowmobile sales since the mid-1990s. The trend reversed in 2013, when sales grew almost 10 percent over the previous year.

Changes in real GDP even impact snowmobile sales.

© Fotosearch/AGE Fotostock

---

[4]This expansion played a large part in sparking the global recession that began in 2007.

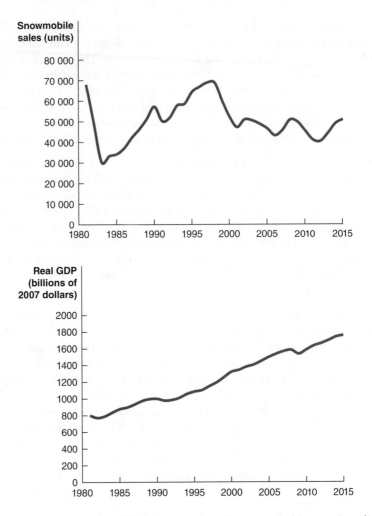

It is interesting to note that BRP has continually expanded its product line into areas other than snowmobiles. In 1968, the Sea-Doo was launched. This small water-craft is in many ways a Ski-Doo for the summer. In 1997, BRP entered the all-terrain vehicle market with a personal "quad," and in 2007, BRP launched its first on-road vehicle called the Spider. BRP is likely expanding its product line for two reasons. First, the potential for periods of declining sales would encourage it to apply its expertise to other areas and products. Second, many firms attempt to diversify their product lines to minimize their exposure to the risk of an economic downturn, as not all products will see their demand reduced by the same amount when the economy enters a recession.

Based on snowmobile.com. http://www.snowmobile.com/events/snowmobile-sales-climb-92-for-2013-2014-1842.html; international snowmobile manufacturers association, http://www.snowmobile.org/snowmobiling-statistics-and-facts.html; Statistics Canada. Table 380-0064 – Gross domestic product, expenditure-based, annual (dollars unless otherwise noted). (accessed: January 01, 2016). Reproduced and distributed on an "as is" basis with the permission of Statistics Canada.

MyEconLab   **Your Turn:** Test your understanding by doing related problem 2.6 on page 222 at the end of the chapter.

Government Purchases

Total government purchases includes all the money spent by federal, provincial, and local governments for goods and services. We include government spending on things that might be classed as investment by government such as construction of new build-ings or roads, as government spending decisions are not made in the same way that private business investment decisions are. Recall from Chapter 4 that government pur-chases do not include transfer payments, such as welfare payments or pension payments to retired civil servants, because the government does not receive a good or service in return for these payments.

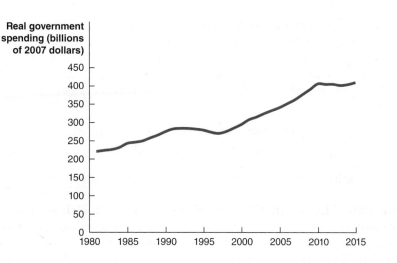

Figure 8.5

Real Government Purchases

Government purchases grew steadily for most of the 1981–2012 period. However, in the mid-1990s, concern about the federal budget deficit caused real government purchases to fall from 1992 to 1997. Real government purchases also grew slowly from 2011 to 2015, while the federal government again focused on reducing the deficit.

Source: Statistics Canada. Table 380-0064 - Gross domestic product, expenditure-based, annual (dollars unless otherwise noted) (accessed: January 01, 2016). Reproduced and distributed on an "as is" basis with the permission of Statistics Canada.

Figure 8.5 shows levels of real government spending from 1981 to 2015. Government purchases grew for most of this period with two notable exceptions. From 1993 to 1997, the federal Liberal government under Jean Chrétien undertook a series of spending cuts to reduce Canada's federal budget deficit. As a result of these cuts, the federal government started to take in more taxes than it spent, and the country's debt started to fall. In 2009, the Conservative government of Steven Harper greatly increased federal government spending to stimulate the economy in the aftermath of the global recession. From 2011 to 2015, the Conservative government held spending relatively constant or cut it, in an effort to return the federal government budget to balance.

Net Exports

Net exports equal exports minus imports. We can calculate net exports by taking the value of spending by foreign firms and households on goods and services produced in Canada and *subtracting* the value of spending by Canadian firms and households on goods and services produced in other countries. Figure 8.6 illustrates movements in real net exports from 1981 through 2015.

For most of this period net exports were positive. This means foreign firms and households bought more from Canada than Canadian firms households bought from them. For Canada, a fall in net exports is often associated with a recession *in the United States!* This is because the United States is Canada's biggest trading partner, with between 70 and 80 percent of our exports going to American firms and households. When the United States enters a recession, the demand for Canadian products and

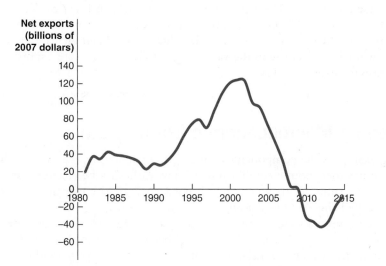

Figure 8.6

Real Net Exports

Net exports were positive for most of the period between 1981 and 2015. Net exports have usually increased when the American economy is booming and decreased when the United States enters a recession.

Source: Statistics Canada. Table 380-0064 - Gross domestic product, expenditure-based, annual (dollars unless otherwise noted) (accessed: January 01, 2016). Reproduced and distributed on an "as is" basis with the permission of Statistics Canada.

services decreases. This lower demand makes it hard for Canadian firms to sell products in the United States, causing our exports to fall. Canadian imports don't follow the same decreasing pattern as exports do when the United States is in recession, so a drop in net exports is the result. We will explore the behaviour of net exports further in Chapter 15.

The following are the three most important variables that determine the level of net exports:

- The price level in Canada relative to the price levels in other countries
- The growth rate of GDP in Canada relative to other countries
- The exchange rate between the Canadian dollar and other currencies

The Price Level in Canada Relative to the Price Level in Other Countries. If inflation in Canada is lower than inflation in other countries, prices of Canadian products increase more slowly than the prices of products in other countries. This slower increase in the Canadian price level increases the demand for Canadian products. The relative rise in prices of foreign-made products makes Canadian demand for foreign products fall. So, Canadian exports increase and Canadian imports decrease, which increases net exports. The reverse happens during periods when the inflation rate in Canada is higher than the inflation rates in other countries: Canadian exports decrease and Canadian imports increase, which decreases net exports.

The Growth Rate of GDP in Canada Relative to Growth Rates in Other Countries. As GDP rises in Canada, the incomes of households rise, leading them to increase their purchases of all goods and services, including goods and services produced in other countries. As a result, imports rise. When incomes in other countries rise, their households will increase their purchases of goods and services, including some goods and services made in Canada. As a result, Canadian exports (which are other country's imports) rise. When incomes in Canada rise faster than in other countries, Canadian imports rise more than exports. As a result, Canada's net exports fall.

The Exchange Rate between the Canadian Dollar and Other Currencies. As the value of the Canadian dollar rises, the foreign currency price of Canadian products sold in other countries rises, and the dollar price of foreign products sold in Canada falls. For example suppose the exchange rate between the Japanese yen and the Canadian dollar is ¥100 Japanese yen for $1 Canadian dollar, or ¥100 = $1. At this exchange rate, someone in Canada could buy ¥100 for $1, or someone in Japan could buy $1 for ¥100. Leaving aside transportation costs, an item that sells for $10 in Canada will sell for ¥1000 in Japan, and a Japanese product that sells for ¥1000 in Japan will sell for $10 in Canada. If the exchange rate changes to ¥150 = $1, the value of the dollar has risen, as it takes more yen to buy $1. Under the new exchange rate, a product that still sells for $10 in Canada will now cost ¥1500 in Japan, reducing the quantity demanded by Japanese consumers. The Japanese product that sells in Japan for ¥1000 will now sell in Canada for $6.67, increasing the quantity demanded by Canadian consumers. An increase in the value of the dollar will reduce exports and increase imports, so net exports will fall. A decrease in the value of the dollar will increase exports and reduce imports, so net exports will rise.

8.3 **LEARNING** OBJECTIVE

Use a 45°-line diagram to illustrate macroeconomic equilibrium.

Graphing Macroeconomic Equilibrium

Having examined the components of aggregate expenditure, we can now look more closely at macroeconomic equilibrium. We saw earlier in the chapter that macroeconomic equilibrium occurs when GDP is equal to aggregate expenditure. We can use a graph called the *45°-line diagram* to illustrate macroeconomic equilibrium. (The 45°-line diagram is also sometimes referred to as the *Keynesian cross* because it is based on the analysis of John Maynard Keynes.) To become familiar with this diagram, consider Figure 8.7, which is a 45°-line diagram that shows the relationship between the

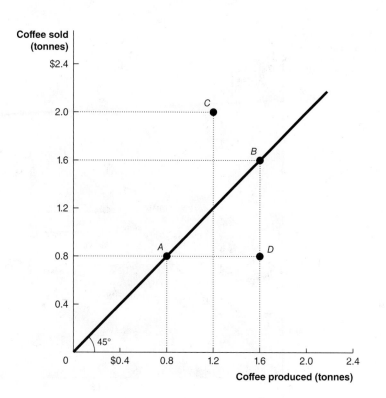

Figure 8.7

An Example of the 45°-Line Diagram

The 45° line shows all the points that are equal distances from both axes. Points such as *A* and *B*, at which the quantity produced equals the quantity sold, are on the 45° line. Points such as *C*, at which the quantity sold is greater than the quantity produced, lie above the line. Points such as *D*, at which the quantity sold is less than the quantity produced, lie below the line.

quantity of cups of coffee sold (on the vertical axis) and the quantity of cups of coffee produced (on the horizontal axis).

The line on the diagram forms an angle of 45° with the horizontal axis. The line represents all the points that are equal distances from both axes. So, points such as *A* and *B*, where the number of cups of coffee sold equals the number of cups of coffee produced, lie on the 45° line. Points such as *C*, where the quantity sold is greater than the quantity produced, lie above the line. Points such as *D*, where the quantity sold is less than the quantity produced, lie below the line.

Figure 8.8 is similar to Figure 8.7, except that it measures real national income, or real GDP (Y),[5] on the horizontal axis and planned real aggregate expenditure (AE) on the vertical axis. Because macroeconomic equilibrium occurs where planned aggregate expenditure equals GDP, *we know that all points of macroeconomic equilibrium must lie along the 45° line.* For all points above the 45° line, planned aggregate expenditure will be greater than GDP. For all points below the 45° line, planned aggregate expenditure will be less than GDP.

The 45° line shows many potential points of macroeconomic equilibrium. During any particular year, only one of these points will represent the actual level of equilibrium real GDP, given the actual level of planned real expenditure. To determine this point, we need to draw a line on the graph to show the *aggregate expenditure function*. The aggregate expenditure function shows us the amount of planned aggregate expenditure that will occur at every level of national income, or GDP.

Changes in GDP have a much greater impact on consumption than on planned investment, government purchases, or net exports. We assume for simplicity that the variables that determine planned investment, government purchases, and net exports all remain constant, as do the variables other than GDP that affect consumption. For example, we assume that a firm's level of planned investment at the beginning of the year will not change during the year, even if the level of GDP changes.

[5]Keep in mind that GDP can be used to represent each of the following: (1) income, (2) actual expenditure, and (3) production.

Figure 8.8

The Relationship between Planned Aggregate Expenditure and GDP in a 45°-Line Diagram

Every point of macroeconomic equilibrium is on the 45° line, where planned aggregate expenditure equals GDP. At points above the line, planned aggregate expenditure is greater than GDP. At points below the line, planned aggregate expenditure is less than GDP.

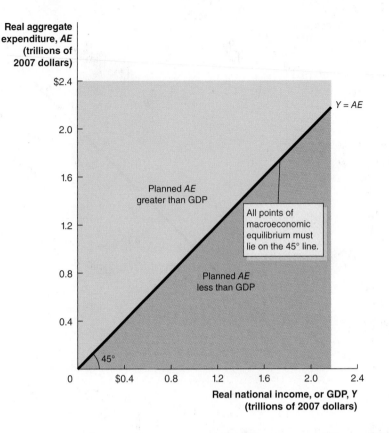

Figure 8.9 shows the aggregate expenditure function on the 45°-line diagram. The lowest upward-sloping line (the dark blue one), C, represents the consumption function, as shown in Figure 8.2. The quantities of planned investment, government purchases, and net exports are constant because we assume the variables they depend on are constant. So, the level of planned aggregate expenditure at any level of GDP is the amount of consumption spending at that level of GDP plus the sum of the constant amounts of planned investment, government purchases, and net exports. In Figure 8.9, we add each

Figure 8.9

Macroeconomic Equilibrium on the 45°-Line Diagram

Macroeconomic equilibrium occurs where the AE line crosses the 45° line. The lowest upward-sloping line, C, represents the consumption function. The quantities of planned investment, government purchases, and net exports are constant because we assume that the variables they depend on are constant. So, the total of planned aggregate expenditure at any level of GDP is the amount of consumption at that level of GDP plus the sum of the constant amounts of planned investment, government purchases, and net exports. We successively add each component of spending to the consumption function line to arrive at the line representing aggregate expenditure.

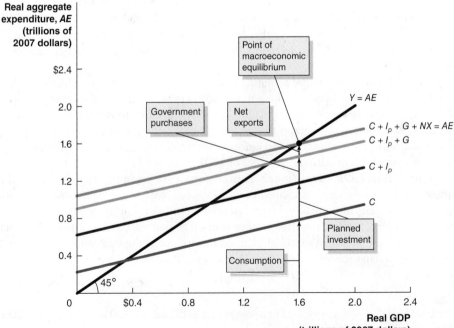

component of spending successively to the consumption function line to arrive at the line representing planned aggregate expenditure (AE). The $C + I_p$ line (the red one) is higher than the C line by the constant amount of planned investment. The $C + I_p + G$ line (the light blue one) is higher than the $C + I_p$ line by the constant amount of government purchases. The $C + I_p + G + NX$ line (the pink one) is higher than the $C + I_p + G$ line by the constant amount of net exports. (In some years, such as 2010, NX is negative and the $C + I_p + G + NX$ will be *lower* than the $C + I_p + G$ line.) The $C + I_p + G + NX$ line shows all four components of expenditure and is the aggregate expenditure (AE) function. At the point where the AE line crosses the 45° line, planned aggregate expenditure is equal to GDP, and the economy is in macroeconomic equilibrium.

Figure 8.10 makes the relationship between planned aggregate expenditure and GDP clearer by showing only the 45° line and the AE line. The figure shows that the AE line intersects the 45° line at a level of GDP of $1.6 trillion. Therefore, $1.6 trillion represents the equilibrium level of real GDP. To see why this is true, consider what would happen if real GDP were only $1.2 trillion. By moving vertically from $1.2 trillion on the horizontal axis up to the AE line, we see that planned aggregate expenditure will be greater than $1.2 trillion at this level of real GDP. Whenever total spending is greater than total production, firms' inventories will fall. The fall in inventories is equal to the vertical distance between the AE line, which shows the level of total spending, and the 45° line, which shows the $1.2 trillion in total production. Unplanned declines in inventories lead firms to increase their production.[6] As real GDP increases from $1.2 trillion, so will total income and, therefore, consumption. The economy will move up the AE line as consumption increases. The gap between total spending and total production will fall, but so long as the AE line is above the 45° line, inventories will continue to decline, and firms will continue to expand production. When real GDP rises to $1.6 trillion, inventories stop falling, and the economy will be in macroeconomic equilibrium.

As Figure 8.10 shows, if GDP is initially $2 trillion, planned aggregate expenditure will be less than GDP, and firms will experience an unplanned increase in inventories. Rising inventories lead firms to decrease production. As GDP falls from $2 trillion,

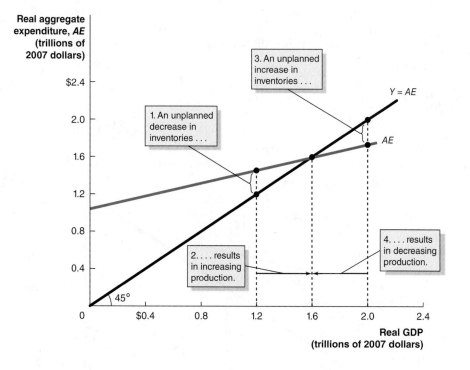

Figure 8.10

Macroeconomic Equilibrium

Macroeconomic equilibrium occurs where the AE line crosses the 45° line. In this case, that occurs at GDP of $1.6 trillion. If GDP is less than $1.6 trillion, the corresponding point on the AE line is above the 45° line, planned aggregate expenditure is greater than total production, firms will experience an unplanned decrease in inventories, and GDP will increase. If GDP is greater than $1.6 trillion, the corresponding point on the AE line is below the 45° line, planned aggregate expenditure is less than total production, firms will experience an unplanned increase in inventories, and GDP will decrease.

---

[6]This is what happened at the Chapters bookstore we discussed earlier, when the manager had ordered 95 copies of *The Big Short* and sold 100.

consumption will also fall, which causes the economy to move down the AE line. The gap between planned aggregate expenditure and GDP will fall, but as long as the AE line is below the 45° line, inventories will continue to rise and firms will continue to cut production. When GDP falls to $1.6 trillion, inventories will stop rising, and the economy will be in macroeconomic equilibrium.

Showing a Recession on the 45°-Line Diagram

Notice that *macroeconomic equilibrium can occur at any point on the 45° line*. Ideally, we would like equilibrium to occur at *potential real GDP*. At potential real GDP, firms will be operating at the normal level of capacity, and the economy will be at the *natural rate of unemployment*. As we saw in Chapter 5, at the natural rate of unemployment, the economy will be at *full employment*: Everyone in the labour force who wants a job will have a job, except the structurally and frictionally unemployed. However, for equilibrium to occur at the level of potential GDP, planned aggregate expenditure must be high enough. As Figure 8.11 shows, if there is insufficient total spending, equilibrium will occur at a lower level of real GDP. Many firms will be operating below their normal capacity, and the unemployment rate will be above the natural rate of unemployment.

Suppose the level of potential real GDP is $2 trillion. As Figure 8.11 shows, when GDP is $2 trillion, planned aggregate expenditure is below $2 trillion, perhaps because firms have become pessimistic about their future profitability and have reduced their investment spending. For example, when firms are worried about future revenues, they might not update their computers as often. The shortfall in planned aggregate expenditure that leads to the recession can be measured as the vertical distance between the AE line and the 45° line at the level of potential real GDP. This shortfall is equal to the unplanned increase in inventories that would occur if the economy was initially at a level of GDP of $2 trillion. The unplanned increase in inventories measures the amount by which current planned aggregate expenditure is too low for the current level of production to be the equilibrium level. Or, put another way, if any of the four components of aggregate expenditure increased by this amount, the AE line would shift upward and intersect the 45° line at a GDP of $2 trillion, and the economy would be in macroeconomic equilibrium at full employment.

Figure 8.11 shows that macroeconomic equilibrium will occur where GDP is $1.6 trillion. This is a full 10 percent below the potential real GDP of $2 trillion. As a

Figure 8.11

Showing a Recession on the 45°-Line Diagram

When the AE line intersects the 45° line at a level of GDP below potential GDP, the economy is in recession. The figure shows that potential GDP is $2 trillion, but because planned aggregate expenditure is too low, the equilibrium level of GDP is only $1.6 trillion, where the AE line intersects the 45° line. As a result, some firms will be operating below their normal capacity, and unemployment will be above the natural rate of unemployment. We can measure the shortfall in planned aggregate expenditure as the vertical distance between the AE line and the 45° line at the level of potential GDP.

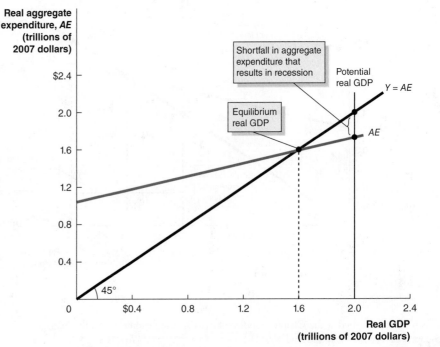

Table 8.3 Macroeconomic Equilibrium

Real GDP (Y)	Consumption (C)	Planned Investment (I_p)	Government Purchases (G)	Net Exports (NX)	Planned Aggregate Expenditure (AE)	Unplanned Inventory Investment	Real GDP Will...
$800	$740	$125	$125	–$30	$960	–$160	increase
1200	1060	125	125	–30	1280	–80	increase
1600	1380	125	125	–30	1600	0	be in equilibrium
2000	1700	125	125	–30	1920	80	decrease
2400	2020	125	125	–30	2240	160	decrease

Note: The values are in billions of 2007 dollars.

result, many firms will be operating below their normal capacity, and the unemployment rate will be well above the natural rate of unemployment. The economy will remain at this level of real GDP until there is an increase in one or more of the components of aggregate expenditure.

The Important Role of Inventories

Whenever planned aggregate expenditure is less than real GDP, some firms will experience unplanned increases in inventories. If firms do not cut back their production promptly when spending declines, they will accumulate inventories. If firms accumulate excess inventories, then even if spending quickly returns to normal levels, firms will have to sell their excess inventories before they can return to producing at normal levels.

A Numerical Example of Macroeconomic Equilibrium

In forecasting real GDP, economists rely on quantitative models of the economy. We can increase our understanding of the causes of changes in real GDP by considering a simple numerical example of macroeconomic equilibrium. Although simplified, this example captures some of the key features contained in the sort of quantitative models that economic forecasters use. Table 8.3 shows several hypothetical combinations of real GDP and planned aggregate expenditure. The first column lists real GDP. The next four columns list levels of the four components of planned aggregate expenditure that occur at the corresponding level of real GDP. We assume that planned investment, government purchases, and net exports do not change as GDP changes. Because consumption depends on GDP, it increases as GDP increases.

In the first row, GDP of $800 billion (or $0.8 trillion) results in consumption of $740 billion. Adding consumption, planned investment, government purchases, and net exports across the row gives planned aggregate expenditure of $960 billion, which is shown in the sixth column. In this row, planned aggregate expenditure is more than GDP so inventories will fall by $160 billion. This unplanned decline in inventories will lead firms to increase production, and GDP will increase. GDP will continue to increase until it reaches $1600 billion. At that level of GDP planned aggregate expenditure is also $1600 billion, unplanned changes in inventories are zero, and the economy has reached a macroeconomic equilibrium.

In the last row of Table 8.3, GDP of $2400 billion results in consumption of $2020 billion and planned aggregate expenditure of $2240 billion. Now planned aggregate expenditure is less than GDP, so inventories increase by $160 billion. This unplanned increase in inventories will lead firms to decrease production, and GDP will decrease. GDP will continue to decrease until it reaches $1600 billion, unplanned inventory investment is zero, and the economy is in a macroeconomic equilibrium.

Only when real GDP equals $1600 billion will the economy be in macroeconomic equilibrium. At other levels of real GDP, planned aggregate expenditure will be higher or lower than GDP, and the economy will be expanding or contracting.

Describe the multiplier effect
and use the multiplier formula to
calculate changes in equilibrium
GDP.

The Multiplier Effect

To this point, we have seen that aggregate expenditure determines real GDP in the short run and we have seen how the economy adjusts if it is not in equilibrium. We have also seen that whenever aggregate expenditure changes, there will be a new level of equilibrium real GDP. In this section, we will look more closely at the effects of changes in aggregate expenditure on equilibrium real GDP. We begin the discussion with Figure 8.12, which illustrates the effects of an increase in planned investment spending. We assume that the economy starts in equilibrium at point A, at which real GDP is $1.6 trillion. Remember that there are no unplanned changes in inventories at this level of output under current conditions. Now assume that firms become more optimistic about their future profitability and increase spending on factories, machinery, and equipment by $80 billion. This increase in planned investment shifts the AE line up by $80 billion from AE_1 to AE_2. (Notice the vertical distance between the two AE curves is $80 billion.) The new equilibrium occurs at point B, at which real GDP is $2 trillion, which is also potential real GDP in this story.

    Notice that the initial $80 billion increase in planned investment results in a $400 billion increase in equilibrium real GDP. The increase in planned investment has had a *multiplied effect* on equilibrium real GDP. It is not only planned investment that will have this multiplied effect; any increase in *autonomous expenditure* will shift the aggregate expenditure function upward and lead to a multiplied increase in equilibrium GDP. **Autonomous expenditure** does not depend on the level of GDP. In the aggregate expenditure model we have been using, planned investment spending, government purchases, and net exports are all autonomous expenditures. Consumption actually has both an autonomous component, which does not depend on the level of GDP, and a nonautonomous (also known as *induced*) component that does depend on the level of GDP. For example, if households decide to spend more of their incomes, which also means saving less, at every level of income, there will be an autonomous increase in consumption spending. The increase in autonomous consumption spending will cause the aggregate expenditure function to shift up, just like the increase in planned investment did. If, however, it is an increase in real GDP that causes households to increase their spending, as indicated in the consumption function, the economy will move up along the aggregate expenditure function, and the increase in consumption spending will be nonautonomous.

Autonomous expenditure An expenditure that does not depend on the level of GDP.

Figure 8.12

The Multiplier Effect

The economy begins at point A, at which equilibrium real GDP is $1.6 trillion. An $80 billion increase in planned investment shifts up aggregate expenditure from AE_1 to AE_2. The new equilibrium is at point B, where real GDP is $2 trillion, which is potential real GDP. Because of the multiplier effect, an $80 billion increase in investment results in a $400 billion increase in equilibrium real GDP.

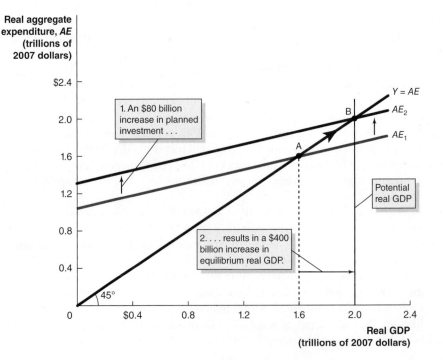

The ratio of the increase in equilibrium real GDP to the increase in autonomous expenditure is called the **multiplier**. The series of induced increases in consumption spending that result from an initial increase in autonomous expenditure is called the **multiplier effect**. The multiplier effect occurs because an initial increase in autonomous expenditure sets off a series of increases in real GDP.

We can look more closely at the multiplier effect shown in Figure 8.12. Suppose the whole $80 billion increase in investment spending shown in the figure consists of firms building additional factories and office buildings. Initially, this additional spending will cause the construction of factories and office buildings to increase by $80 billion, so GDP will also increase by $80 billion. Remember that increases in production result in equal increases in national income. So, this increase in real GDP of $80 billion is also an increase in national income of $80 billion. In this example, the income is received as wages and salaries by the employees of the construction firms, as profits by the owners of the firms, and so on. After receiving this additional income, these workers, managers, and owners will increase their consumption of cars, appliances, furniture, and many other products (such as Tim Hortons coffee). If the marginal propensity to consume (*MPC*) is 0.8, we know the increase in consumption spending will be $64 billion. This additional $64 billion in spending will cause the firms making cars, appliances, coffee, and other products to increase production by $64 billion, so GDP will rise by $64 billion. This increase in GDP means national income will increase by another $64 billion. This increase in income will be received by the workers, managers, and owners of the firms producing the cars, appliances, coffee, and other products. These workers, managers, and owners will, in turn, increase their consumption spending, and the process of increasing production, income, and consumption will continue.

Eventually, the total increase in consumption will be $320 billion (the equilibrium change in real GDP is $400 billion and the marginal propensity to consume is 0.8, so consumer spending is $320 billion higher in the new equilibrium). This $320 billion increase in consumption combined with the initial $80 billion increase in investment spending will result in a total change in equilibrium GDP of $400 billion. We can think of the multiplier effect occurring in rounds of spending. In round 1, there is an increase of $80 billion in autonomous expenditure—the $80 billion in planned investment spending in our example—which causes GDP to rise by $80 billion. In round 2, induced expenditure rises by $64 billion (which equals the $80 billion in increase in real GDP in round 1 multiplied by the *MPC*). The $64 billion in induced expenditure in round 2 causes a $64 billion increase in real GDP, which leads to a $51.2 billion increase in induced expenditure in round 3, and so on. The final column sums up the total increases in expenditure, which equal the total increase in GDP. In each round, the additional induced expenditure becomes smaller because the *MPC* is less than 1. By round 10, additional induced expenditure is only $10.74 billion, and the total increase in GDP from the beginning of the process is $357.05 billion. By round 20, the process is almost complete: Additional induced expenditure is only $1.15 billion, and the total increase in GDP is $395.39 billion. Eventually, the process will be finished, although we can't say precisely how many rounds of spending it will take, so we just label the last round "*n*" instead of giving it a specific number.

We can calculate the value of the multiplier in our example by dividing the increase in equilibrium real GDP by the increase in autonomous expenditure:

$$\frac{\Delta Y}{\Delta I} = \frac{\text{Change in real GDP}}{\text{Change in investment spending}} = \frac{\$400 \text{ billion}}{\$80 \text{ billion}} = 5.$$

With a multiplier of 5, each increase in autonomous expenditure of $1 will result in an increase in equilibrium GDP of $5.

A Formula for the Multiplier

Table 8.4 shows that during the multiplier process, each round of increases in consumption is smaller than the previous round, so, eventually, the increases will come to an end, and we will have a new macroeconomic equilibrium. But how do we know that when

Multiplier The increase in equilibrium real GDP divided by the increase in autonomous expenditure.

Multiplier effect The process by which an increase in autonomous expenditure leads to a larger increase in real GDP.

Table 8.4

The Multiplier Effect in Action

	Additional Autonomous Expenditure	Additional Induced Expenditure (C)	Total Additional Expenditure = Total Additional GDP
Round 1	$80 billion	$0	$80.00 billion
Round 2	0	64.00 billion	144.00 billion
Round 3	0	51.20 billion	195.20 billion
Round 4	0	40.96 billion	236.16 billion
Round 5	0	32.77 billion	268.93 billion
.	.	.	.
.	.	.	.
.	.	.	.
Round 10	0	10.74 billion	357.05 billion
.	.	.	.
.	.	.	.
.	.	.	.
Round 20	.	1.15 billion	395.39 billion
.		.	.
Round n	0	0	400.00 billion

we add all the increases in GDP, the total will be $400 billion? We can show this is true by first writing out the total change in equilibrium GDP:

The total change in equilibrium GDP equals the initial increase in planned investment spending = $80 billion

Plus the first induced increase in consumption = $MPC \times$ $80 billion

Plus the second induced increase in consumption = $MPC \times (MPC \times$ $80 billion)

Plus the third induced increase in consumption = $MPC \times (MPC \times (MPC \times$ $80 billion))

Plus the fourth induced increase in consumption = $MPC \times MPC \times (MPC \times (MPC \times$ $80 billion))

And so on…

Equivalently:

Total change in GDP = $80 billion + $MPC \times$ $80 billion + $MCP^2 \times$ $80 billion + $MPC^3 \times$ $80 billion + $MPC^4 \times$ $80 billion +…

The ellipses (…) indicate the pattern continues on for an infinite number of similar terms. If we factor out the $80 billion from each term in the expression, we have:

Total change in GDP = $80 billion $\times (1 + MPC + MCP^2 + MPC^3 + MPC^4 +…)$

Mathematicians have shown an expression like the one in parentheses above sums to:

$$\frac{1}{1 - MPC}.$$

In this case, the *MPC* is equal to 0.8. So, we can calculate the change in equilibrium GDP = $80 billion $\times [1/(1 - 0.8)] =$ $80 billion $\times 5 =$ $400 billion. We have also arrived at a general formula for the multiplier:

$$\text{Multiplier} = \frac{\text{Change in equilibrium real GDP}}{\text{Change in autonomous expenditure}} = \frac{1}{1 - MPC}.$$

In this case, the multiplier is $1/(1 - 0.8)$, or 5, which means that for each additional $1 of autonomous spending, equilibrium GDP will increase by $5. An $80 billion increase in planned investment spending results in a $400 billion increase in equilibrium GDP. Notice that the value of the multiplier depends on the value of the *MPC*. In particular, the larger the value of the *MPC*, the larger the value of the multiplier will be. For example, if the *MPC* were 0.9 instead of 0.8, the multiplier would increase from 5 to $1/(1 - 0.9) = 10$.

Summarizing the Multiplier Effect

You should note four key points about the multiplier effect:

1. The multiplier effect occurs both when autonomous expenditure increases and when it decreases. For example, with an *MPC* of 0.8, a *decrease* in planned investment of $80 billion will cause a *decrease* in equilibrium income of $400 billion.
2. The multiplier effect makes the economy more sensitive to changes in autonomous expenditure than it would be otherwise. The recent declines in exports have set off a series of declines in production, income, and spending. These declines have caused firms that clearly do not export, like barbers, to experience declines in sales. The multiplier effect means a decline in spending in one sector will cause declines in spending and production in other sectors of the economy.
3. The larger the *MPC* (all else equal), the larger the value of the multiplier. With an *MPC* of 0.8, the multiplier is 5, but with an *MPC* of 0.5, the multiplier is only 2. This direct relationship between the value of the *MPC* and the value of the multiplier holds true because the larger the *MPC*, the more additional consumption takes place after each rise (or fall) in the multiplier process.
4. The formula for the multiplier, $1/(1 - MPC)$, is oversimplified because it ignores many real-world complications, such as the effect of increased GDP on imports, inflation, interest rates, and income taxes. These effects combine to cause the simple formula we've presented to overstate the true value of the multiplier. Beginning in Chapter 12, we will start to take these real-world complications into account.

Solved Problem **8.2**

Using the Multiplier Formula

Use the information in the table to answer the questions on the right.

Real GDP (Y)	Consumption (C)	Planned Investment (I_p)	Government Purchases (G)	Net Exports (NX)
$800	$690	$100	$100	-$50
900	770	100	100	-50
1000	850	100	100	-50
1100	930	100	100	-50
1200	1010	100	100	-50

Note: The values are in billions of 2007 dollars.

a. What is the equilibrium level of real GDP?
b. What is the *MPC*?
c. Suppose government purchases increase by $20 billion. What will the new equilibrium level of real GDP be? Use the multiplier formula to determine your answer.

Solving the Problem

Step 1: Review the chapter material. This problem is about the multiplier process so you may want to review the section "The Multiplier Effect," which begins on page 212.

Step 2: Determine equilibrium GDP. Just as in Solved Problem 8.1, we can find macroeconomic equilibrium by calculating the level of planned aggregate expenditure for each level of real GDP.

Real GDP (Y)	Consumption (C)	Planned Investment (I_p)	Government Purchases (G)	Net Exports (NX)	Planned Aggregate Expenditure (AE)
$800	$690	$100	$100	–$50	$840
900	770	100	100	–50	920
1000	850	100	100	–50	1000
1100	930	100	100	–50	1080
1200	1010	100	100	–50	1160

Note: The values are in billions of 2007 dollars.

Step 3: **Calculate the MPC.**

$$MPC = \frac{\Delta C}{\Delta Y}.$$

In this example:

$$MPC = \frac{\$80 \text{ billion}}{\$100 \text{ billion}} = 0.8.$$

Step 4: **Use the multiplier formula to calculate the new equilibrium level of real GDP.** We could find the new level of equilibrium real GDP by constructing a new table with government purchases at the new ($120 billion) level. This would take a lot more time than the multiplier method, however.

$$\text{Multiplier} = \frac{1}{1 - MPC} = \frac{1}{1 - 0.8} = 5.$$

So:

Change in equilibrium real GDP = Change in autonomous expenditure $\times$ 5.

Or:

Change in equilibrium real GDP = $20 billion $\times$ 5 = $100 billion.

Therefore:

New level of equilibrium GDP = $1000 billion + $100 billion

= $1100 billion.

MyEconLab   **Your Turn:** For more practice, do related problem 4.2 on page 223 at the end of this chapter.

Don't Let This Happen to You

Understand Why Protectionism Doesn't Raise the Multiplier

We have seen that there is a link between net exports and real GDP in this chapter. When net exports increase, autonomous expenditure increases, and the result is an increase in real GDP. As you learned, net exports are equal to exports minus imports. Net exports will increase whenever exports rise or imports fall. Increasing exports can be very difficult; this is what

various trade missions attempt to do. Another way to make net exports rise is to restrict imports, which can be done with the imposition of tariffs. Tariffs are taxes on imports, which increase the cost of imports to domestic consumers. The desired result is an increase in net exports and an increase in real GDP.

Tariffs are a tempting option for governments looking to stimulate an economy in a recession. Instead of increasing government spending (which often means more government borrowing), a government could restrict imports, expecting that GDP will increase as citizens substitute domestically produced goods for imported ones. In this situation, the multiplier tells us that GDP will rise by more than imports fell.

The problem with this strategy is that it only works if your country alone uses it. If other countries impose tariffs on the products your country exports, your net exports will fall. When one country imposes tariffs on the exports of another, the situation usually ends with both countries imposing tariffs. This situation is sometimes called a *trade war*.

For example, the Smoot Hawley Tariff Act, a US tariff law passed in 1930, caused problems for the world economy. The act increased the tariffs on more than 20 000 goods imported into the United States to record levels. Most countries that traded with the United States,

including Canada, responded by imposing their own tariffs on US-produced goods. In fact, Canada acted before the bill was passed, adding tariffs to 16 products that made up about 30 percent of US exports to Canada. The increase in tariffs around the world resulted in a reduction in global trade of about 66 percent. Not only did many economies shrink as a result of the tariffs, but consumers around the world faced much higher prices for many products. Tariffs may seem like a good way to improve the domestic economy at first, but usually lead to a decrease in exports and GDP, as well as imports.

MyEconLab

Your Turn: Test your understanding by doing related problem 4.8 on page 223 at the end of this chapter.

The Paradox of Thrift

We saw in Chapters 6 and 7 that an increase in savings can increase the rate of economic growth in the long run by providing funds for investment. In the short run, if households save more of their income and spend less of it, aggregate expenditure and real GDP will decline. In discussing the aggregate expenditure model, John Maynard Keynes argued that if many households decide at the same time to increase their saving and reduce their spending, they may make themselves worse off by causing aggregate expenditure to fall, thereby pushing the economy into a recession. The lower incomes in the recession might mean that total saving does not increase, despite the attempt by many individuals to increase their own saving. Keynes referred to this outcome as the *paradox of thrift* because what appears to be something favourable for the long-run performance of the economy might be counterproductive in the short run.

The paradox is sometimes observed at the beginning of recessions. Households that expect negative economic times reduce their spending in case they lose their jobs, and thus their incomes. As households switch from spending to saving, the aggregate expenditure in the economy falls. Firms respond to the fall in aggregate spending by reducing their production. A reduction in production means laying off workers. In some cases, people trying to protect themselves from a recession end up contributing to one.

The Aggregate Demand Curve

8.5 LEARNING OBJECTIVE

Understand the relationship between the aggregate demand curve and aggregate expenditure.

When demand for a product increases, firms usually respond by increasing production, but they are also likely to increase prices. Similarly, when demand falls, production falls, but often, prices do as well. We would expect, then, that an increase or a decrease in aggregate expenditure to affect not just real GDP but the *price level* as well. Will a change in price level, in turn, affect the components of aggregate expenditure? In fact, as we will see, increases in the price level cause aggregate expenditure to fall, and decreases in the price level cause aggregate expenditure to rise. There are three main reasons for this relationship. We discussed the first two reasons earlier in this chapter, when considering the factors that determine consumption and net exports:

- A rising price level decreases consumption by decreasing the real value of household wealth; a falling price level has the reverse effect.

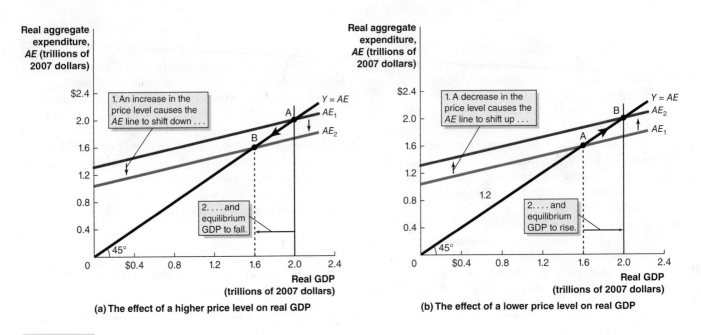

(a) The effect of a higher price level on real GDP

(b) The effect of a lower price level on real GDP

Figure 8.13 The Effect of a Change in the Price Level on Real GDP

In panel (a), an increase in the price level results in declining consumption, planned investment, and net exports and causes the aggregate expenditure line to shift down from AE_1 to AE_2. As a result, equilibrium real GDP declines from \$2 trillion to \$1.6 trillion. In panel (b), a decrease in the price level results in rising consumption, planned investment, and net exports and causes the aggregate expenditure line to shift up from AE_1 to AE_2. As a result, equilibrium real GDP increases from \$1.6 trillion to \$2 trillion.

- If the price level in Canada rises relative to the price levels of other countries, Canadian exports become relatively more expensive, and foreign imports become less expensive, causing net exports to fall. A falling price level in Canada has the opposite effect.

- When prices rise, firms and households need more money to finance buying and selling. If the central bank (the Bank of Canada) does not increase the money supply, the result will be an increase in the interest rate. In Chapter 11 we will analyze this result in more detail. As we discussed earlier in this chapter, a higher rate of interest means lower investment spending, as firms borrow less to finance the building of factories or the purchase of new machines. Even households borrow less to finance the purchase of new homes. A falling price level has the opposite effect: Other things being equal, lower interest rates mean a higher level of investment spending.

We can now incorporate the effect of a change in the price level into the basic aggregate expenditure model, in which equilibrium real GDP is determined by the intersection of the aggregate expenditure (*AE*) line and the 45°-line. Remember that we measure the price level as an index number with a value of 100 in the base year. If the price level rises from say 100 to 103, consumption, planned investment, and net exports will all fall, causing the *AE* line to shift down on the 45°-line diagram. The *AE* line shifts down because with higher prices, less spending will occur in the economy at every level of GDP. Panel (a) of Figure 8.13 shows that the downward shift of the *AE* line results in a lower level of equilibrium real GDP.

If the price level falls from, say, 100 to 97, then planned investment, consumption, and net exports will all rise. As panel (b) of Figure 8.13 shows, the *AE* line will shift up, which will cause equilibrium real GDP to increase.

Figure 8.14 summarizes the effect of changes in the price level on real GDP. The table shows the combinations of price level and real GDP from Figure 8.13. The graph

Price level	Equilibrium real GDP
105	$2.0 trillion
120	1.6 trillion
135	1.2 trillion

Figure 8.14

The Aggregate Demand Curve

The aggregate demand (*AD*) curve shows the relationship between the price level and the level of planned aggregate expenditure in the economy. When the price level is 105, real GDP is $2 trillion. An increase in the price level to 120 causes consumption, planned investment, and net exports to fall, which reduces real GDP to $1.6 trillion.

plots the numbers from the table. In the graph, the price level is measured on the vertical axis, and real GDP is measured on the horizontal axis. The relationship shown in Figure 8.14 between the price level and the level of planned aggregate expenditure is known as the **aggregate demand (*AD*) curve**.

Aggregate demand (*AD*) curve
A curve that shows the relationship between the price level and the level of planned aggregate expenditure in the economy, holding constant all other factors that affect aggregate expenditure.

Economics in Your Life

When Consumer Confidence Falls, Is Your Job at Risk?

At the beginning of this chapter, we asked you to suppose that you work part time at a local Tim Hortons. You have learned that consumer confidence in the economy has fallen and that many households expect their future income to be dramatically lower than their current income. Should you be concerned about losing your job? We have seen that if consumers expect their future incomes to decline (see *Making the Connection*, "Do Changes in Consumer Confidence Affect Consumption Spending?"), they will cut their consumption spending. Consumption spending is about 63 percent of total expenditure in the economy. So if the decline in consumer confidence is correct in forecasting the decline in consumption, then aggregate expenditure and real GDP are likely to decline as well. If the economy moves into a recession, spending at Tim Hortons is likely to fall; this could reduce your location's sales and possibly cost you a job. Before you panic, though, keep in mind surveys of consumer confidence are not always accurate predictors of recessions, so you may not end up in your parents' basement after all.

Conclusion

In this chapter, we examined a key macroeconomic idea: In the short run, the level of GDP is determined mainly by the level of aggregate expenditure. When economists forecast changes in GDP, they do so by forecasting changes in the four components of aggregate expenditure. We constructed an aggregate demand curve by asking what would happen to the level of aggregate expenditure when the price level changes.

But our story is incomplete. In the next chapter, we will analyze the aggregate supply curve. Then, we will use the aggregate demand curve *and* the aggregate supply curve to show how equilibrium real GDP and the equilibrium price level are determined at the same time. We will also need to discuss the roles that the financial system and government policy play in determining real GDP in the short run. We will cover these important topics in the next three chapters.

Chapter Summary and Problems

Key Terms

Aggregate demand (*AD*) curve, p. 219

Aggregate expenditure (*AE*), p. 190

Aggregate expenditure model, p. 190

Asset, p. 195

Autonomous consumption, p. 198

Autonomous expenditure, p. 212

Cash flow, p. 203

Consumption function, p. 198

Inventories, p. 191

Liability, p. 195

Marginal propensity to consume (MPC), p. 198

Marginal propensity to save (MPS), p. 200

Multiplier, p. 213

Multiplier effect, p. 213

Nominal interest rate, p. 197

Real interest rate, p. 197

Summary

*LO 8.1 *Aggregate expenditure (AE)* is the total amount of spending in the economy. The *aggregate expenditure model* focuses on the relationship between total spending and real GDP in the short run, assuming that the price level is constant. In any particular year, the level of GDP is determined by the level of total spending, or aggregate expenditure, in the economy. The four components of aggregate expenditure are consumption (*C*), planned investment (*I*ₚ), government purchases (*G*), and net exports (*NX*). When aggregate expenditure is greater than GDP, there is an unplanned decrease in *inventories*, which are goods that have been produced but not yet sold, and GDP and total employment will increase. When aggregate expenditure is less than GDP, there is an unplanned increase in inventories, and GDP and total employment will decline. When aggregate expenditure is equal to GDP, firms will sell what they expected to sell, production and employment will be unchanged, and the economy will be in macroeconomic equilibrium.

LO 8.2 The five determinants of consumption are current disposable income, household wealth, expected future income, the price level, and the interest rate. The *consumption function* is the relationship between consumption and disposable income. The *marginal propensity to consume (MPC)* is the change in consumption divided by the change in disposable income. The *marginal propensity to save (MPS)* is the change in saving divided by the change in disposable income. The determinants of planned investment are expectations of future profitability, real interest rate, taxes, and *cash flow*, which is the difference between the cash revenues received by a firm and the cash spending by the firm. Government purchases include spending by the federal government, provincial governments, and local governments for goods and services. Government purchases do not include transfer payments, such as social security payments by the federal government or pension payments by local governments to retired police officers and firefighters. The three determinants of net exports are changes in the price level in Canada relative to changes in the price levels in other countries, the growth rate of GDP in Canada relative to the growth rates of GDP in other countries, and the exchange rate between the Canadian dollar and other currencies.

LO 8.3 The 45°-line diagram shows all the points where aggregate expenditure equals real GDP. On the 45°-line diagram, macroeconomic equilibrium occurs where the line representing the aggregate expenditure function crosses the 45° line. The economy is in recession when the aggregate expenditure line intersects the 45° line at a level of GDP that is below potential GDP. Numerically, macroeconomic equilibrium occurs when:

Consumption + Planned investment + Government purchases + Net Exports = GDP.

LO 8.4 *Autonomous expenditure* is expenditure that does not depend on the level of GDP. An autonomous change is a change in expenditure not caused by a change in income. An induced change is a change in aggregate expenditure caused by a change in income. An autonomous change in expenditure will cause rounds of induced changes in expenditure. Therefore, an autonomous change in expenditure will have a multiplier effect on equilibrium GDP. The *multiplier effect* is the process by which an increase in autonomous expenditure leads to a larger increase in real GDP. The *multiplier* is the ratio of the change in equilibrium GDP to the change in autonomous expenditure. The formula for the multiplier is

$$\frac{1}{1 - MPC}.$$

Because of the paradox of thrift, an attempt by many individuals to increase their saving may lead to a reduction in aggregate expenditure and a recession.

LO 8.5 Increases in the price level cause a reduction in consumption, investment, and net exports. This causes the aggregate expenditure function to shift down on the 45°-line diagram, leading to a lower equilibrium real GDP. A decrease in the price level leads to a higher equilibrium real GDP. The *aggregate demand (AD) curve* shows the relationship between the price level and the level of aggregate expenditure, holding constant all factors other than the price level that affect aggregate expenditure.

MyEconLab   Log in to MyEconLab to complete these exercises and get instant feedback.

---

* "Learning Objective" is abbreviated to "LO" in the end-of-chapter material.

Review Questions

LO 8.1

1.1 What is the key idea in the aggregate expenditure macroeconomic model?

1.2 What are inventories? What usually happens to inventories at the beginning of a recession? At the beginning of an expansion?

1.3 Which of the following does the aggregate expenditure model seek to explain: long-run economic growth, the business cycle, inflation, or cyclical unemployment?

LO 8.2

2.1 In the aggregate expenditure model, why is it important to know the factors that determine consumption spending, investment spending, government purchases, and net exports?

2.2 Give an example of each of the four categories of aggregate expenditure.

2.3 What are the four main determinants of investment? How would a change in interest rates affect investment?

2.4 What are the three main determinants of net exports? How would an increase in the growth rate of GDP in the BRIC nations (Brazil, Russia, India, and China) affect Canadian net exports?

LO 8.3

3.1 What is the meaning of the 45° line in the 45°-line diagram?

3.2 Use a 45°-line diagram to illustrate macroeconomic equilibrium. Make sure your diagram shows the aggregate expenditure function and the level of equilibrium real GDP and that your axes are properly labelled.

3.3 What does the slope of the aggregate expenditure line equal? How is the slope of the aggregate expenditure line related to the slope of the consumption function?

3.4 What is the difference between aggregate expenditure and consumption spending?

LO 8.4

4.1 What is the multiplier effect? Use a 45°-line diagram to illustrate the multiplier effect of a decrease in government purchases.

4.2 What is the formula for the multiplier? Explain why this formula is considered to be too simple.

LO 8.5

5.1 Briefly explain the difference between aggregate expenditure and aggregate demand.

5.2 Briefly explain which components of aggregate expenditure are affected by a change in the price level.

Problems and Applications

LO 8.1

1.1 Into which category of aggregate expenditure would each of the following transactions fall?
   a. The Jones family buys a new car.
   b. The Toronto District School Board buys 12 new school buses.
   c. The Jones family buys a newly constructed house from the Garcia Construction Co.

1.2 Suppose Apple plans to produce 2.2 million iPhones in Canada this year. The company expects to sell 2.1 million and add 100 000 to the inventories in its stores.
   a. Suppose that at the end of the year, Apple has sold 1.9 million iPhones. What was Apple's planned investment? What was Apple's actual investment?
   b. Now suppose that at the end of the year, Apple has sold 2.3 million iPhones. What was Apple's planned investment? What was Apple's actual investment?

1.3 Between January and October of 2015, manufacturing inventories increased by $1.75 billion. Can we tell from this information whether aggregate expenditure was higher or lower than GDP for these nine months of 2015? If not, what other information would you need?

Data from Statistics Canada CANSIM Table 304-0014.

LO 8.2

2.1 **[Related to the Chapter Opener on page 189]** Suppose Tim Hortons is forecasting demand for its products during the next year. How will the forecast be affected by each of the following?
   a. A survey shows a sharp rise in consumer confidence that income growth will be increasing.
   b. Real interest rates are expected to increase.
   c. The exchange rate value of the Canadian dollar is expected to increase.
   d. Planned investment spending in the economy is expected to decrease.

2.2 Draw the consumption function and label each axis. Show the effect of an increase in income on consumption spending. Does the change in income cause a movement along the consumption function or a shift of the consumption function? How would an increase in expected future income or an increase in household wealth affect the consumption function? Would these increases cause a movement along the consumption function or a shift of the consumption function?

2.3 Unemployed workers receive Employment Insurance payments from the government. Does the existence of Employment Insurance make it likely that consumption will fluctuate more or fluctuate less over the business cycle than it would in the absence of Employment Insurance? Briefly explain.

2.4 **[Related to Making the Connection on page 195]** Why might a small business owner be willing to pay for the detailed consumer confidence data of the Consumer Confidence Index?

2.5 [**Related to Solved Problem 8.1 on page 201**] Fill in the blanks in the following table. Assume for simplicity that taxes are zero. Also assume that the values represent billions of 2007 dollars.

Real GDP (Y)	Consumption (C)	Saving (S)	Marginal Propensity to Consume (MPC)	Marginal Propensity to Save (MPS)
$900	$800		—	—
1000	875			
1100	950			
1200	1025			
1300	1100			

2.6 [**Related to Making the Connection on page 203**] We saw that sales of snowmobiles are linked to changes in the economy. Based on this linkage, do you think BRP pays attention to the Consumer Confidence Index? Why or why not?

3.1 At point *A* in the following graph, is planned aggregate expenditure greater than, equal to, or less than GDP? What about at point *B*? At point *C*? For points *A* and *C*, indicate the vertical distance that measures the unintended change in inventories.

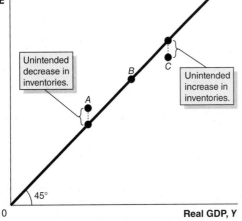

3.2 Suppose we drop the assumption that net exports do not depend on real GDP. Draw a graph with the value of net exports on the vertical axis and the value of real GDP on the horizontal axis. Now, add a line representing the relationship between net exports and real GDP. Does your net exports line have a positive or negative slope? Briefly explain.

3.3 Consider the following table, which shows business investment in inventories for each quarter from the first quarter of 2007 to the first quarter of 2012, measured in millions of 2007 dollars. Provide a macroeconomic explanation for this pattern. (Hint: When did the recession during this period begin and end?)

Year	Quarter	Inventory Investment (millions of 2007 dollars)
2007	Q1	$ 3360
	Q2	−2822
	Q3	15 570
	Q4	19 644
2008	Q1	6061
	Q2	9512
	Q3	11 856
	Q4	4699
2009	Q1	−2364
	Q2	−7779
	Q3	−4807
	Q4	−4807
2010	Q1	2663
	Q2	−2508
	Q3	4841
	Q4	−6805
2011	Q1	8965
	Q2	12 153
	Q3	6462
	Q4	2179
2012	Q1	2061
	Q2	7298
	Q3	14 091
	Q4	3875
2013	Q1	6031

Data from Statistics Canada, CANSIM Table 380-0064.

3.4 Fill in the missing values in the following table. Assume that the value of the *MPC* does not change as real GDP changes. Also assume that the values represent billions of 2007 dollars.
a. What is the value of the *MPC*?
b. What is the value of equilibrium real GDP?

Real GDP (Y)	Consumption (C)	Planned Investment (I_p)	Government Purchases (G)	Net Exports (NX)	Planned Aggregate Expenditures (AE)	Unplanned Change in Inventories
$900	$760	$120	$120	−$40		
1000	840	120	120	−40		
1100		120	120	−40		
1200		120	120	−40		
1300		120	120	−40		

LO 8.4

4.1 In Figure 8.12, the economy is initially in equilibrium at point *A*. Aggregate expenditure and real GDP both equal $6 trillion. The increase in investment of $1 trillion increases aggregate expenditure to $7 trillion. If real GDP increases to $7 trillion, will the economy be in equilibrium? Briefly explain. What happens to aggregate expenditure when real GDP increases to $7 trillion?

4.2 **[Related to Solved Problem 8.2 on page 215]** Use the information in the following table to answer the following questions. Assume that the values represent billions of 2007 dollars.

Real GDP (Y)	Consumption (C)	Planned Investment (I_p)	Government Purchases (G)	Net Exports (NX)
$800	$730	$100	$100	−$50
900	790	100	100	−50
1000	850	100	100	−50
1100	910	100	100	−50
1200	970	100	100	−50

   a. What is the equilibrium level of real GDP?

   b. What is the *MPC*?

   c. Suppose net exports increase by $40 billion. What will be the new equilibrium level of real GDP? Use the multiplier formula to determine your answer.

4.3 If the marginal propensity to consume is 0.75, by how much will an increase in planned investment spending of $40 billion shift up the aggregate expenditure line? By how much will it increase equilibrium real GDP?

4.4 Explain whether each of the following would cause the value of the multiplier to be larger or smaller.

   a. An increase in real GDP increases imports.

   b. An increase in real GDP increases interest rates.

   c. An increase in real GDP increases the marginal propensity to consume.

   d. An increase in real GDP causes the average tax rate paid by households to decrease.

   e. An increase in real GDP increases the price level.

4.5 Suppose booming economies in the BRIC nations (Brazil, Russia, India, and China) cause net exports to rise by $75 billion in Canada. If the *MPC* is 0.8, what will be the change in equilibrium GDP?

4.6 Would a larger multiplier lead to longer and more severe recessions or shorter and less severe recessions? Briefly explain.

4.7 Use the following graph to answer the questions.

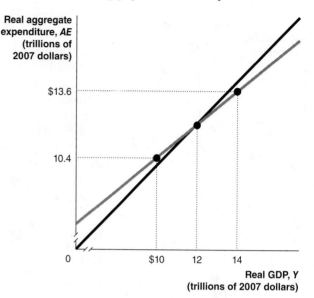

   a. What is the value of equilibrium real GDP?

   b. What is the value of the *MPC*?

   c. What is the value of the multiplier?

4.8 **[Related to Don't Let This Happen to You on page 216]** Statistics Canada estimates that the multiplier for nonresidential construction projects in Quebec is 1.52, but only 1.07 for construction projects in Nunavut. Why might this be the case?

Based on Statistics Canada, *Provincial Input-Output Multipliers, 2009*, Catalogue No. 15F0046XDB.

LO 8.5

5.1 Briefly explain why the aggregate expenditure line is upward sloping, while the aggregate demand curve is downward sloping.

5.2 Briefly explain whether you agree with the following statement: "The reason the aggregate demand curve slopes downward is that when the price level is higher, people cannot afford to buy as many goods and services."

Appendix C

LO

Apply the algebra of macroeconomic equilibrium.

The Algebra of Macroeconomic Equilibrium

In this chapter, we relied primarily on graphs and tables to illustrate the aggregate expenditure model of short-run real GDP. Graphs help us understand economic change *qualitatively*. When we write an economic model using equations, we make it easier to make *quantitative estimates*. When economists forecast future movements in GDP, they often rely on *econometric models*. An econometric model is an economic model written in the form of equations, where each equation has been statistically estimated, using methods similar to the methods used in estimating demand curves that we briefly described in Chapter 3. We can use equations to represent the aggregate expenditure model described in this chapter.

The following equations are based on the example shown in Table 8.3 on page 211. Y stands for real GDP, and the numbers (with the exception of the *MPC*) represent billions of dollars.

1. $C = 100 + 0.8Y$ Consumption function

2. $I_p = 125$ Planned investment function

3. $G = 125$ Government spending function

4. $NX = -30$ Net export function

5. $Y = C + I_p + G + NX$ Equilibrium condition

The first equation is the consumption function. The *MPC* is 0.8, and 100 is autonomous consumption, which is the level of consumption that does not depend on income. If we think of the consumption function as a line on the 45°-line diagram, 100 would be the intercept, and 0.8 would be the slope. The "functions" for the other three components of planned aggregate expenditure are very simple because we have assumed that these components are not affected by GDP and, therefore, are constant. Economists who use this type of model to forecast GDP would, of course, use more realistic investment, government, and net export functions. The *parameters* of the functions—such as the value of autonomous consumption and the value of the *MPC* in the consumption function—would be estimated statistically, using data on the values of each variable over a period of years.

In this model, GDP is in equilibrium when it equals planned aggregate expenditure. Equation 5—the equilibrium condition—shows us how to calculate equilibrium in the model: We need to substitute equations 1 through 4 into equation 5. Doing so gives us the following:

$$Y = 100 + 0.8Y + 125 + 125 - 30.$$

We need to solve this expression for Y to find equilibrium GDP. The first step is to subtract $0.8Y$ from both sides of the equation:

$$Y - 0.8Y = 100 + 125 + 125 - 30.$$

Then, we solve for Y:

$$0.2Y = 320.$$

Or:

$$Y = \frac{320}{0.2} = 1600.$$

To make this result more general, we can replace particular values with general values represented by letters:

1. $C = \overline{C} + MPC(Y)$ Consumption function

2. $I_p = \overline{I}_p$ Planned investment function

3. $G = \overline{G}$ Government spending function

4. $NX = \overline{NX}$ Net export function

5. $Y = C + I_p + G + NX$ Equilibrium condition

The letters with bars over them represent fixed, or autonomous, values. So, for example, $\overline{C}$ represents autonomous consumption, which had a value of 100 in our original example. Now, solving for equilibrium, we get

$$Y = \overline{C} + MPC(Y) + \overline{I} + \overline{G} + \overline{NX},$$

or

$$Y - MPC(Y) = \overline{C} + \overline{I} + \overline{G} + \overline{NX},$$

or

$$Y(1 - MPC) = \overline{C} + \overline{I} + \overline{G} + \overline{NX},$$

or

$$Y = \frac{\overline{C} + \overline{I} + \overline{G} + \overline{NX}}{1 - MPC}.$$

Remember that $1/(1 - MPC)$ is the multiplier, and all four variables in the numerator of the equation represent autonomous expenditure. Therefore, an alternative expression for equilibrium GDP is:

Equilibrium GDP = Autonomous expenditure Multiplier.

MyEconLab   Log in to MyEconLab to complete these exercises and get instant feedback.

LO Apply the algebra of macroeconomic equilibrium.

Review Questions

8A.1 Write a general expression for the aggregate expenditure function. If you think of the aggregate expenditure function as a line on the 45°-line diagram, what would be the intercept and what would be the slope, using the general values represented by letters?

8A.2 Find equilibrium GDP using the following macroeconomic model (where the numbers, with the exception of the *MPC*, represent billions of dollars).

   1. $C = 150 + 0.75Y$ Consumption function

   2. $I_p = 100$ Planned investment function

   3. $G = 100$ Government spending function

   4. $NX = 25$ Net export function

   5. $Y = C + I_p + G + NX$ Equilibrium condition

8A.3 For the macroeconomic model in problem 8A.2, write the aggregate expenditure function. For GDP of $1600, what is the value of aggregate expenditure, and what is the value of the unintended change in inventories? For GDP of $1200, what is the value of aggregate expenditure, and what is the value of the unintended change in inventories?

8A.4 Suppose that autonomous consumption is 50, government purchases are 100, planned investment spending is 125, net exports are −25, and the *MPC* is 0.9. What is equilibrium GDP?

© David Buzzard / Alamy

CHAPTER

9

Aggregate Demand and Aggregate Supply Analysis

Chapter Outline and Learning Objectives

Canadian National Railway and the Business Cycle

In terms of land area, Canada is the second-largest country in the world. As you can imagine, businesses involved in moving goods around a country this large are an important part of the economy.

Canadian National Railway (CN) was formed in 1919 by the federal government from the remains of several failed Canadian railway companies. CN was returned to the private sector in 1995. Since it was privatized, CN has expanded to the United States. It is now Canada's largest freight railway—operating in eight provinces and one territory—as well as the only transcontinental rail network in North America. In 2015, CN alone moved more than 300 million tons of cargo worth over $250 billion.

Despite its size, CN is subject to the business cycle just like other firms. During recessions, as demand for goods falls, CN handles less cargo on its network. When the economy is expanding, CN handles more cargo and longer trains more often. When the price of oil or labour rises, CN often has to increase its prices, and firms find it more expensive to get their goods to market. Increases in the price of a key good or service, such as transportation, tend to reduce the supply of goods and services in all parts of the economy.

To understand the relationship between the business cycle and firms such as CN, we need to explore how production, employment, and prices interact throughout the business cycle.

Sources: Canadian National Railway, 2015 Annual Report.

Economics in Your Life

Is an Employer Likely to Cut Your Pay during a Recession?

Suppose that you have worked as a barista for a local coffeehouse for two years. From on-the-job training and experience, you have honed your coffee-making skills and mastered the perfect latte. Then the economy moves into a recession, and sales at the coffeehouse decline. Is the owner of the coffeehouse likely to cut the prices of lattes and other drinks? Suppose the owner asks to meet with you to discuss your wages for the next year. Is the owner likely to cut your pay? As you read this chapter, see if you can answer these questions. You can check your answers against those we provide on page 248 at the end of this chapter.

We saw in Chapter 6 that the Canadian economy has experienced a long-run upward trend in real gross domestic product (GDP). This upward trend has resulted in the standard of living in Canada being much higher today than it was just 50 years ago. In the short run, however, real GDP fluctuates around the long-run upward trend because of the business cycle. Fluctuations in GDP lead to fluctuations in employment. These fluctuations in real GDP and employment are the most visible and dramatic part of the business cycle. During recessions, we are more likely to see factories close, businesses declare bankruptcy, and workers lose their jobs. During expansions, we are more likely to see new businesses open and new jobs created. In addition to these changes in output and employment, the business cycle causes changes in wages and prices. Some firms react to a decline in sales by cutting back on production, but they may also cut the prices they charge and the wages they pay. Other firms respond to a recession by raising prices and workers' wages by less than they would have in an expansion.

In this chapter, we expand our story of the business cycle by developing the aggregate demand and aggregate supply model. This model will help us analyze the effects of recessions and expansions on production, employment, and prices.

Aggregate Demand

To understand what happens during the business cycle, we need an explanation of why real GDP, the unemployment rate, and the inflation rate fluctuate. We have already seen that fluctuations in the unemployment rate are caused mainly by fluctuations in real GDP. In this chapter, we use the **aggregate demand and aggregate supply model** to explain fluctuations in real GDP and the **price level**. As Figure 9.1 shows, real GDP and the price level in this model are determined in the short run by the intersection of the *aggregate demand curve* and the *aggregate supply curve*. Fluctuations in real GDP and the price level are caused by shifts in the aggregate demand curve, the aggregate supply curve, or both.

The **aggregate demand (*AD*) curve** shows the relationship between the price level and the quantity of real GDP demanded by households, firms, and the government. The **short-run aggregate supply (*SRAS*) curve** shows the relationship between the price level and the quantity of real GDP supplied by firms *in the short run*. The aggregate demand and short-run aggregate supply curves in Figure 9.1 should seem familiar. They are similar to the individual market demand and supply curves we explored in Chapter 3. However, because these curves apply to the whole economy, rather than to a single market, the aggregate demand and aggregate supply model is quite different from the model of demand and supply in individual markets. Because we're dealing with the economy as a whole, we need *macroeconomic* explanations of why the aggregate demand curve is downward sloping, why the short-run aggregate supply curve is upward sloping, and why the curves shift. We begin by explaining why the aggregate demand curve is downward sloping.

Aggregate demand and aggregate supply model A model that explains short-run fluctuations in real GDP and the price level.

9.1 LEARNING OBJECTIVE

Identify the determinants of aggregate demand and distinguish between a movement along the aggregate demand curve and a shift of the curve.

Price level A measure of the average prices of goods and services in the economy.

Aggregate demand (*AD*) curve A curve that shows the relationship between the price level and the quantity of real GDP demanded by households, firms, and the government.

Short-run aggregate supply (*SRAS*) curve A curve that shows the relationship in the short run between the price level and the quantity of real GDP supplied by firms.

Figure 9.1

Aggregate Demand and Aggregate Supply

In the short run, real GDP and the price level are determined by the intersection of the aggregate demand curve and the short-run aggregate supply curve. In the figure, real GDP is measured on the horizontal axis, and the price level is measured on the vertical axis by the CPI. In this example, the equilibrium real GDP is $1.8 trillion and the equilibrium price level is 125.

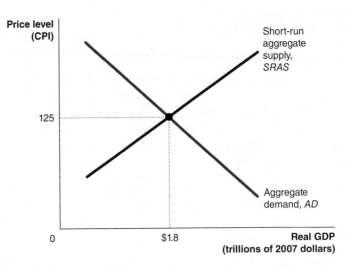

Why Is the Aggregate Demand Curve Downward Sloping?

We saw in Chapter 5 that GDP has four components: consumption (C), investment (I), government purchases (G), and net exports (NX). If we let Y stand for real GDP, we can write the following:

$$Y = C + I + G + NX.$$

The aggregate demand curve is downward sloping because a fall in the price level increases the quantity of real GDP demanded. To understand why this is true, we need to look at how changes in the price level affect each of the components of aggregate demand. We begin with the assumption that government purchases are determined by the policy decisions of lawmakers and are not influenced by changes in the price level. We can then consider the effect of changes in the price level on each of the three remaining components of real GDP: consumption, investment, and net exports.

The Wealth Effect: How a Change in the Price Level Affects Consumption Current income is the most important variable determining the consumption of households. As income rises, consumption will rise, and as income falls, consumption will fall. But consumption also depends on household wealth. A household's wealth is the difference between the value of its assets and the value of its debts. Consider two households, both with incomes of $80 000 per year. The first household has wealth of $5 million, while the second has wealth of $50 000. The first household is likely to spend a lot more of its income than the second household. So, as total household wealth rises, consumption will rise. Some household wealth is held in cash or other *nominal assets* that lose value as the price level rises and gain value as the price level falls. For instance, if you have $10 000 in cash, a 10 percent increase in the price level will reduce the purchasing power of that cash by 10 percent. When the price level rises, the *real value* of household wealth falls, meaning higher price levels lead to lower consumption spending by households. When the price level falls, the real value of household wealth rises, and so consumption goes up. The impact of the price level on consumption is called the *wealth effect*, and is one reason the aggregate demand curve is downward sloping.

The Interest-Rate Effect: How a Change in the Price Level Affects Investment When prices rise, households and firms need more money to finance buying and selling. Therefore, when the price level rises, households and firms will try to increase the amount of money they hold by withdrawing funds from banks, borrowing from banks, or selling financial assets, such as stocks or bonds. These actions tend to drive up the interest rate charged on bank loans and the interest rate on bonds. (In Chapter 11, we analyze in more detail the relationship between money and interest rates.) A higher interest rate raises the cost of borrowing for firms and households. As a result, firms will borrow less to build new factories or install new machinery and equipment, and households will borrow less to buy new houses. To a smaller extent, consumption will also fall as households borrow less to finance spending on cars, furniture, and other durable goods. So, because a higher price level increases the interest rate and reduces investment spending, it also reduces the quantity of goods and services demanded. A lower price level will decrease the interest rate and increase investment spending, thereby increasing the quantity of goods and services demanded. This impact of the price level is known as the *interest-rate effect*, and is a second reason the aggregate demand curve is downward sloping.

The International-Trade Effect: How a Change in the Price Level Affects Net Exports *Net exports* equals spending by foreign households and firms on goods and services produced in Canada minus spending by Canadian households and firms on goods and services produced in other countries. If the price level in Canada increases relative to the price levels in other countries, Canadian exports will become relatively more expensive, and foreign-made products (i.e., imports) will become relatively less expensive. Some consumers in foreign countries will shift from buying Canadian products to buying domestic products, and some Canadian consumers will also shift from buying Canadian products to buying imported products. Canadian exports will fall, and Canadian imports will rise, causing net exports to fall, thereby reducing the quantity of goods and services demanded. A lower price level in Canada relative to other countries has the reverse effect, causing net exports to rise, increasing the quantity of goods and services demanded. This impact of the price level on net exports is known as the *international-trade effect*, and is a third reason the aggregate demand curve is downward sloping.

Shifts of the Aggregate Demand Curve versus Movements along It

An important point to remember is that the aggregate demand curve tells us the relationship between the price level and the quantity of real GDP demanded, *holding everything else constant*. If the price level changes but other variables that affect the willingness of households, firms, and the government to spend are unchanged, the economy will move along a stationary aggregate demand curve. If any variable other than the price level changes, the aggregate demand curve will shift. For example, if government purchases increase and the price level remains the same, the aggregate demand curve will shift to the right at every price level. Or, if firms become pessimistic about the future profitability of investment and cut back spending on factories and equipment, the aggregate demand curve will shift to the left. There is a simple way to tell if a change causes a movement along a curve or a shift of the curve. If the variable that changed is on either the *x*-axis or *y*-axis, you're dealing with a *movement* along the curve. If the variable that changed isn't on either of the axes, you're dealing with a *shift* of the curve.

Variables That Shift the Aggregate Demand Curve

The variables that cause the aggregate demand curve to shift fall into three categories:

- Changes in government policy
- Changes in the expectations of households and firms
- Changes in foreign variables

Changes in Government Policy As we will discuss further in Chapters 11 and 12, the federal government uses monetary and fiscal policy to shift the aggregate demand curve. **Monetary policy** involves actions that the Bank of Canada—the nation's central bank—takes to manage the money supply and interest rates and to ensure the flow of funds from lenders to borrowers. The Bank of Canada takes these actions to achieve its inflation target. For example, by lowering interest rates, the Bank of Canada can lower the cost to firms and households of borrowing. Lower borrowing costs increase consumption and investment spending, which shifts the aggregate demand curve to the right. Higher interest rates shift the aggregate demand curve to the left. **Fiscal policy** involves changes in federal taxes and purchases that are intended to achieve macroeconomic policy

Monetary policy The actions the Bank of Canada takes to manage the money supply and interest rates to pursue macroeconomic policy goals.

Fiscal policy Changes in federal taxes and purchases that are intended to achieve macroeconomic policy objectives.

Don't Let This Happen to You

Understand Why the Aggregate Demand Curve Is Downward Sloping

The aggregate demand curve and the demand curve for a single product are both downward sloping—but for different reasons. When we draw a demand curve for a single product, such as apples, we know that it will slope downward because as the price of apples rises, apples become more expensive relative to other products—such as oranges—and consumers will buy fewer apples and more of the other products. In other words, consumers substitute other products for apples. When the overall price level rises, the prices of all domestically

produced goods and services are rising, so consumers have no other domestic products to which they can switch. The aggregate demand curve slopes downward for the reasons given on pages 229–230: A lower price level raises the real value of household wealth (which increases consumption), lowers interest rates (which increases investment and consumption), and makes Canadian exports less expensive and foreign imports more expensive (which increases net exports).

MyEconLab

Your Turn: Test your understanding by doing related problem 1.2 on page 250 at the end of this chapter.

objectives. As government purchases are one component of aggregate demand, an increase in government purchases shifts the aggregate demand curve to the right, and a decrease in government purchases shifts the aggregate demand curve to the left. An increase in personal income taxes reduces the amount of disposable income for households. Higher personal income taxes reduce consumption spending and shift the aggregate demand curve to the left. Lower personal income taxes increase consumption spending and shift the aggregate demand curve to the right. Increases in business taxes reduce the profitability of investment and shift the aggregate demand curve to the left. Lower business taxes make investments more appealing to firms and shift the aggregate demand curve to the right.

Changes in Expectations of Households and Firms. If households become more optimistic about their future incomes, they are likely to increase their current consumption. This increased consumption will shift the aggregate demand curve to the right. If households become more pessimistic about their future incomes, the aggregate demand curve will shift to the left. Similarly, if firms become more optimistic about the future profitability of investment spending, the aggregate demand curve will shift to the right. If firms become more pessimistic, the aggregate demand curve will shift to the left.

Changes in Foreign Variables. If firms and households in other countries buy fewer Canadian goods or if firms and households in Canada buy more foreign goods, net exports will fall, and the aggregate demand curve will shift to the left. As we saw in Chapter 5, when real GDP increases, so does the income available for consumers to spend. If real GDP in Canada increases faster than real GDP in other countries, Canadian imports will increase faster than Canadian exports, making net exports fall. Net exports will also fall if the *exchange rate* between the Canadian dollar and foreign currencies rises because the price in a foreign currency of Canadian products sold in other countries will rise, and the dollar price of foreign products sold in Canada will fall. For example, if the current exchange rate between the dollar and the euro is $1 = €1, then a $3000 Ski-Doo exported from Canada to France will cost €3000 in France, and a €50 bottle of French wine will cost $50 in Canada. If the exchange rate rises to $1 = €1.50, then the Ski-Doo will increase to €4500 (1.50 × 3000) in France, causing its sales to fall. At the same time, the $1 = €1.50 exchange rate will make the cost of the French wine fall from $50 to $33.33 (50 ÷ 1.5) per bottle in Canada, causing its sales to increase. Canadian exports will fall, Canadian imports will rise, and the aggregate demand curve will shift to the left.

An increase in net exports at every price level will shift the aggregate demand curve to the right. Net exports will increase if real GDP grows more slowly in Canada than in other countries or if the value of the dollar falls against other currencies. A change in net exports that results from a change in the price level in Canada will result in a movement along the aggregate demand curve, *not* a shift of the aggregate demand curve.

Making the Connection

Canada's Mini Recession

The first half of 2015 saw the Canadian economy meet the basic definition of a recession—two consecutive quarters of negative GDP growth. Canada's GDP shrank in both the first and second quarters of 2015. The drop in GDP coupled with little or no inflation tells us that the aggregate demand (*AD*) curve shifted to the left during this period. This tells us the what, but not the why. We need to look at different components of aggregate demand over this period to see which element caused the *AD* curve to shift to the left, keeping in mind that a decrease in any of the four elements of *AD* can cause the curve to shift to the left.

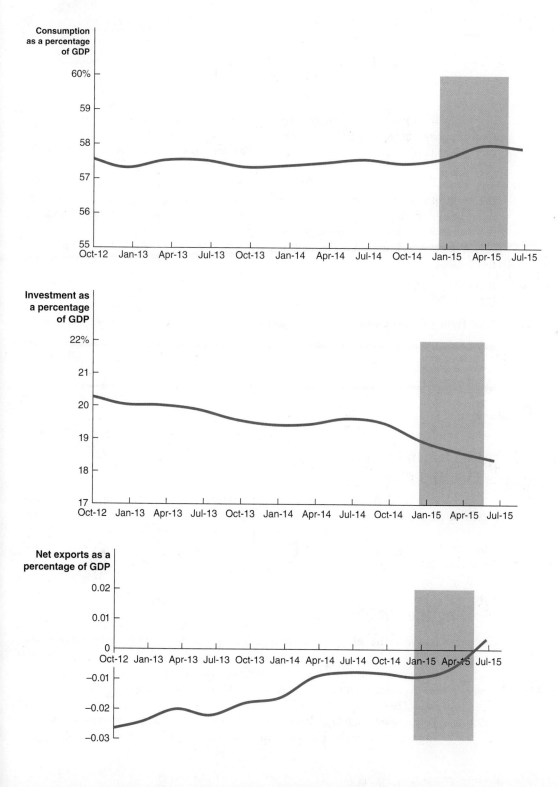

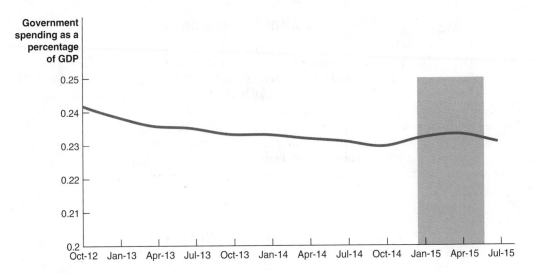

From the figures it is clear that the only significant decrease was in investment. Consumption grew slightly, government spending was about the same at the start of 2015 as it was at the end of the second quarter, and net exports rose during the recession.

This tells us that the leftward shift in the *AD* curve during the first half of 2015 was the result of falling investment spending by firms. A lot of this drop was due to energy companies reducing their investment in oil extraction in Alberta and Saskatchewan in reaction to plummeting crude oil prices.

Whenever a drop in one element of GDP is not offset by the other elements, we're likely to see a recession.

Based on Table 380-0064 – Gross domestic product, expenditure-based, quarterly (dollars unless otherwise noted). (accessed: January 02, 2016). Statistics Canada.

MyEconLab   **Your Turn:** Test your understanding by doing related problem 1.3 on page 250 at the end of this chapter.

Solved Problem 9.1

Movements along the Aggregate Demand Curve versus Shifts of the Aggregate Demand Curve

Suppose the current price level is 123, and the current level of real GDP is $1.6 trillion. Illustrate each of the following situations on a graph.

The price level rises to 127, while everything else remains exactly the same.

Firms become more pessimistic and reduce their investment spending. Assume that the price level remains constant.

Solving the Problem

Step 1: **Review the chapter material.** This problem is about understanding the difference between movements along an aggregate demand curve and shifts of an aggregate demand curve, so you may want to review the section "Shifts of the Aggregate Demand Curve versus Movements along It," which begins on page 229.

Step 2: **To answer part (a), draw a graph that shows a movement along the aggregate demand curve.** Because there will be a movement along the aggregate demand curve but no shift of the aggregate demand curve, your graph should look like this:

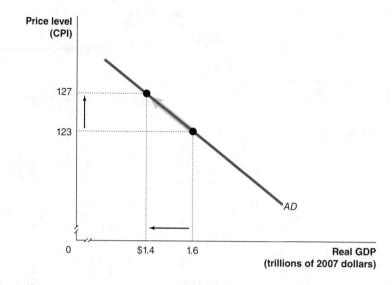

We don't have enough information to be certain what the new level of real GDP demanded will be. We only know that it has to be less than the initial $1.6 trillion; the graph shows this value as $1.4 trillion. **To answer part (b), draw a graph that shows a leftward shift of the aggregate demand curve.** We know that the aggregate demand curve will shift left, but we don't have enough information to determine how far left it will shift. Let's assume that the shift is $200 billion (or $0.2 trillion). In that case, your graph should look like this:

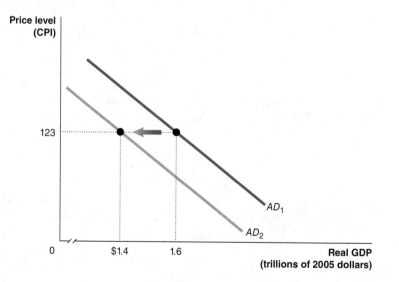

The graph shows a parallel shift in the aggregate demand curve so that at every price level, the quantity of real GDP demanded declines by $200 billion. For example, if the price level remains at 123, the quantity of real GDP demanded will fall from $1.6 trillion to $1.4 trillion.

Your Turn: For more practice, do related problem 1.4 on page 250 at the end of this chapter.

MyEconLab

Table 9.1 summarizes the most important variables that cause the aggregate demand curve to shift. The table shows the shift in the aggregate demand curve that results from an *increase* in each of the variables. A *decrease* in these variables would cause the aggregate demand curve to shift in the opposite direction.

Table 9.1

Variables that Shift the
Aggregate Demand Curve

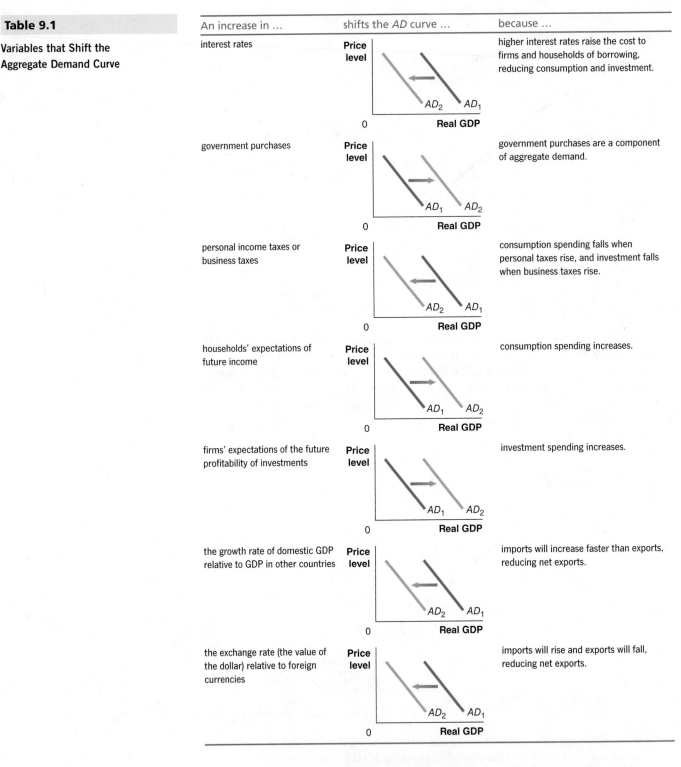

An increase in ...	shifts the *AD* curve ...	because ...
interest rates		higher interest rates raise the cost to firms and households of borrowing, reducing consumption and investment.
government purchases		government purchases are a component of aggregate demand.
personal income taxes or business taxes		consumption spending falls when personal taxes rise, and investment falls when business taxes rise.
households' expectations of future income		consumption spending increases.
firms' expectations of the future profitability of investments		investment spending increases.
the growth rate of domestic GDP relative to GDP in other countries		imports will increase faster than exports, reducing net exports.
the exchange rate (the value of the dollar) relative to foreign currencies		imports will rise and exports will fall, reducing net exports.

Making the Connection

Predicting Shifts of the Aggregate Demand Curve

Predicting the state of the economy is a multimillion-dollar business, and people have been developing methods for predicting the future of the economy for centuries. These efforts range from the basic and intuitive to the downright quirky.

On the logical side of the spectrum are the Conference Board of Canada's Index of Consumer Confidence and the Ivey Business School's Ivey Purchasing Managers Index; the former measures the plans of consumers, and the latter measures the activities of producers. The Index of Consumer Confidence is based on the views of households about current and expected economic conditions, including whether now is a good time to make a major purchase (such as a house); the index is issued monthly. The Ivey Purchasing Managers Index measures the change in the value of purchases made by purchasing managers across the country each month. An increase in the Index of Consumer Confidence indicates that consumers are planning to spend more, and an increase in the Purchasing Managers Index indicates that firms are spending more than they did in the previous month. Increases in either index suggest that the economy is growing.

On the quirky side of the spectrum, there is no shortage of economic indicators. For example, in the 1920s, economist George Taylor noted a relationship between stock market prices and the length of women's skirts. According to Taylor's Hemline Index, as the economy improves, skirts get shorter, and as the economy worsens, skirts get longer. This fashion trend is still reported in the media as an economic indicator.

Leonard Lauder, CEO of Estée Lauder, created the Lipstick Index, which proposes that lipstick sales tend to increase as the economy declines. The rise in lipstick sales is likely due to people substituting a relatively cheap luxury for a more expensive one, such as new clothing. Meanwhile, the Skinny Tie Width indicator proposes two points: (1) necktie sales go up during tough economic times because men want to show their bosses that they are serious and working hard, and (2) during economic downturns, neckties get skinnier, while as the economy improves, neckties get wider and more colourful.

All of these indicators have one thing in common: they reflect the state of aggregate demand in the economy. The state of aggregate demand, as we shall see, plays a key role in determining the phase of the business cycle of the economy.

Based on Conference Board of Canada, Consumer Confidence Index: http://www2.conferenceboard.ca/weblinx/ica/Default.htm, Richard Ivey School of Business and the Purchasing Management Association of Canada, Ivey Purchasing Manager's Index: http://iveypmi.uwo.ca/English/Welcomeeng.htm, *New York Times*, The Hemline Index, Updated: http://www.nytimes.com/2008/10/19/business/worldbusiness/19iht-19lewin.17068071.html?_r=1, *The Economist*, Lip Service: What lipstick sales tell you about the economy: http://www.economist.com/displaystory. cfm?story_id=12998233, *Financial Times*, The Information: The Tie Index: http://www.ft.com/cms/s/2/15f88980-e695-11dd-8e4f-0000779fd2ac.html.

Your Turn: Test your understanding by doing related problem 1.5 on page 251 at the end of this chapter.

MyEconLab

Aggregate Supply

The aggregate demand curve is only half of the aggregate demand and aggregate supply model. Now we turn to aggregate supply, which shows the effect of changes in the price level on the quantity of goods and services that firms are willing and able to provide. Because the impact of changes in the price level on aggregate supply is very different in the short run as compared with the long run, we use two aggregate supply curves: one for the long run and one for the short run. We start by discussing the long-run aggregate supply curve.

The Long-Run Aggregate Supply Curve

In the long run, the level of real GDP is determined by the supply of inputs—the labour force and the capital stock—and the available technology. The labour force is the number of workers available to be employed. The capital stock is the amount of physical capital (e.g., factories, office buildings, machinery, and equipment) available. The supply of both factors is determined by the decisions people have made in the past. The current labour force is based on people's decisions to have children or immigrate, made years ago. The current capital stock is based on firm's investment decisions made in previous years. This leads to a level of output the economy can produce when markets clear. The level of real GDP in the long run is referred to as **potential GDP**, or *full-employment GDP*. At potential GDP, firms will operate at their normal level of capacity, and the only unemployment we will observe will be structural and frictional. Because potential GDP is determined by decisions made in the past, it is not influenced by changes in the price level. The **long-run aggregate supply (*LRAS*) curve** shows the relationship between the price level and the quantity of real GDP supplied. As Figure 9.2 shows, whether the price level is 119, 123, or 127, potential GDP remains the same. Therefore, the long-run aggregate supply (*LRAS*) curve is a vertical line at potential GDP.

9.2 LEARNING OBJECTIVE

Identify the determinants of aggregate supply and distinguish between a movement along the short-run aggregate supply curve and a shift of the curve.

Potential GDP The level of real GDP attained when all firms are producing at capacity.

Long-run aggregate supply (*LRAS*) curve A curve that shows the relationship in the long run between the price level and the quantity of real GDP supplied.

Figure 9.2

The Long-Run Aggregate Supply Curve

Changes in the price level do not affect the level of aggregate supply in the long run. Therefore, the long-run aggregate supply (LRAS) curve is a vertical line at potential GDP. For instance, the price level was 127 in 2015, and potential GDP was $1.77 trillion. If the price level had been 131, or if it had been 125, long-run aggregate supply would still have been a constant $1.77 trillion. Each year, the long-run aggregate supply curve shifts to the right as the number of workers in the economy increases, more machinery and equipment are accumulated, and technological change occurs.

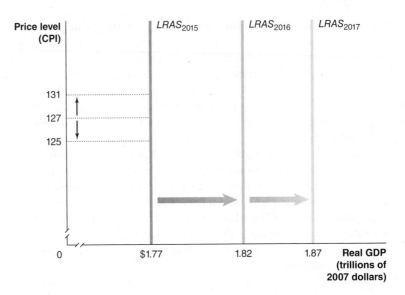

Figure 9.2 also shows that the *LRAS* curve shifts to the right each year. This shift occurs because potential GDP increases almost every year, as we accumulate more machinery, the labour force grows, and technology improves. Figure 9.2 shows real potential GDP increasing from $1.77 trillion in 2015 to $1.82 trillion in 2016 to $1.87 trillion in 2017.

The Short-Run Aggregate Supply Curve

While the *LRAS* curve is vertical, the short-run aggregate supply curve (*SRAS*) is upward sloping. The *SRAS* curve is upward sloping because, over the short run, as the price level increases, the quantity of goods and services firms are willing to supply will increase. The main reason firms behave this way is that, *as prices of final goods and services rise, prices of inputs— such as the wages of workers or the price of natural resources—rise more slowly.* Profits increase when the prices of the goods and services that firms sell rise faster than the prices they pay for inputs. Therefore, a higher price level leads to higher profits and increases the willingness of firms to supply more goods and services. A secondary reason the *SRAS* curve slopes upward is that, as the price level rises or falls, some firms are slow to adjust their prices. A firm that is slow to raise its prices when the price level is increasing may find its sales increase and, therefore, will increase production. A firm that is slow to reduce its prices when the price level is decreasing may find its sales falling and cut production as a result.

Why do some firms adjust prices more slowly than others, and why might the wages of workers and the prices of other inputs change more slowly than the prices of final goods and services? Most economists believe the explanation is that *some firms and workers fail to accurately predict changes in the price level.* If firms and workers could predict the future price level exactly, the short-run aggregate supply curve would be the same as the long-run aggregate supply curve.

But how does the failure of workers and firms to perfectly predict the price level result in an upward sloping *SRAS* curve? Economists are not in complete agreement on this point, but we can briefly discuss the three most common explanations:

1. Contracts make some wages and prices "sticky."
2. Firms are often slow to adjust wages.
3. Menu costs make some prices sticky.

Contracts Make Some Wages and Prices "Sticky." Prices or wages are said to be "sticky" when they do not respond quickly to changes in demand or supply. Contracts can make wages or prices sticky. For example, suppose Purolator Courier negotiates a three-year contract with Teamsters Canada (the union for truck drivers, package handlers, and other employees) during a time when the economy is in recession and the volume of packages being shipped is falling. Suppose that after the union signs the contract, the economy begins to expand rapidly, and the volume of packages shipped increases, so that Purolator can raise the rates it charges. Purolator will find that shipping more packages will be profitable because the prices it charges are rising while the wages it pays its workers are fixed by contract. Or a steel mill might have signed a multi-year contract to buy coal, which is used to make steel, at a time when the demand for steel was stagnant. If the demand for steel (and thus the price of steel) begins to rise rapidly, producing additional steel will be profitable because the cost of coal to the steel firm will remain fixed by contract. In both of these examples, rising prices lead to higher output. If these examples are representative of enough firms in the economy, a rising price level should lead to a greater quantity of goods and services supplied. In other words, the short-run aggregate supply curve will be upward sloping.

Notice, though, that if the workers at Purolator or the managers of the coal companies had accurately predicted what would happen to prices, this prediction would have been reflected in the contracts, and Purolator and the steel mill would not have earned greater profits when prices rose. In that case, rising prices would not lead to higher output.

Firms Are Often Slow to Adjust Wages. We just noted that the wages of union workers remain fixed by contract for several years. Many non-union workers also have their wages or salaries adjusted only once a year. For instance, suppose that you accept a job at a management consulting firm in June at a salary of $65 000 per year. The firm probably will not adjust your salary until the following June, even if the prices it can charge for its services rise after you are first hired. If firms are slow to adjust wages, a rise in the price level will increase the profitability of hiring more workers and producing more output. Similarly, a fall in the price level will decrease the profitability of hiring more workers and producing more output. Once again, we have an explanation for why the short-run aggregate supply curve slopes upward.

It is worth noting that firms are often slower to *cut* wages than to increase them. Cutting wages can have a negative effect on the morale and productivity of workers and can also cause some of a firm's best workers to quit and look for jobs elsewhere.

Menu Costs Make Some Prices Sticky. Firms base their prices today partly on what they expect future prices to be. For instance, before printing its menus, a restaurant has to decide the prices it will charge for meals. Some firms still print catalogues that list the prices of their products. If demand for their products is higher or lower than the firms had expected, they may want to charge different prices from those printed in their menus or catalogues. Changing prices would be costly, however, because it would involve printing new menus or catalogues. The costs to firms of changing prices are called **menu costs**. To see why menu costs can lead to an upward-sloping short-run aggregate supply curve, consider the effect of an unexpected increase in the price level. In this case, firms will want to increase the prices they charge. Some firms, however, may not be willing to increase prices because of menu costs. The firms that don't increase their prices will find their sales increasing (because their prices are lower than those of other firms), which will cause them to increase output. Once again, we have an explanation for a higher price level leading to a larger quantity of goods and services supplied.

Menu costs The costs to firms of changing prices.

Shifts of the Short-Run Aggregate Supply Curve versus Movements along It

It is important to remember the difference between a shift in a curve and a movement along it. The short-run aggregate supply curve tells us the short-run relationship between the price level and the quantity of goods and services firms are willing to supply, *holding everything else that can affect the willingness of firms to supply goods and services constant.* If the price level changes, but nothing else does, the economy will move up or down a stationary aggregate supply curve. If any variable other than the price level changes, the aggregate supply curve will shift.

Variables that Shift the Short-Run Aggregate Supply Curve

We now briefly discuss the five most important variables that cause the short-run aggregate supply curve to shift.

Increases in the Labour Force and in the Capital Stock.

A firm will supply more output at every price if it has more workers and more physical capital. The same is true of the economy as a whole. So, as the labour force and the capital stock grow, firms will supply more output at every price level, and the short-run aggregate supply curve will shift to the right. In Japan, for example, the population is aging and the labour force is shrinking. Holding other things constant, this decrease in the labour force causes the short-run aggregate supply curve in Japan to shift to the left.

Technological Change.

As positive technological change takes place, the productivity of workers and machinery increases, which means firms can produce more goods and services with the same amount of labour and machinery. This increase in productivity reduces firms' costs of production and, thus, allows them to produce more output at every price level. As a result, the short-run aggregate supply curve shifts to the right.

Expected Changes in the Future Price Level.

If workers and firms believe that the price level is going to increase by 3 percent during the next year, they will try to adjust their wages and prices accordingly. For instance, if a labour union believes there will be 3 percent inflation next year, it knows that wages must rise by 3 percent to preserve the purchasing power of those wages. Similar adjustments by other workers and firms will result in costs increasing throughout the economy by 3 percent. The result, shown in Figure 9.3, is that the short-run aggregate supply curve shifts to the left, so that any level of real GDP is associated with a price level that is 3 percent higher. In general, *if workers and firms expect the price level to increase by a certain percentage, the SRAS curve will shift by that amount,* holding constant all other variables that can shift the *SRAS* curve.

Adjustments of Workers and Firms to Errors in Past Expectations about the Price Level.

Workers and firms sometimes make incorrect predictions about the price level. As time passes, they will attempt to compensate for these errors. Suppose, for example, that Teamsters Canada signs a contract with Purolator Courier that provides for only small wage increases because the company and the union both expect only small increases in the price level. If increases in the price level turn out to be unexpectedly large, the union will take this into account when negotiating the next contract. The higher wages Purolator workers receive under the new contract will increase Purolator's costs and result in Purolator needing to receive higher prices to produce the same level of output. If workers and firms across the economy are adjusting to the price level being higher than expected, the *SRAS* curve will shift to the left. If they are adjusting to the price level being lower than expected, the *SRAS* curve will shift to the right.

Unexpected Changes in the Price of an Important Natural Resource.

An unexpected event that causes the short-run aggregate to shift to the left is called a **supply shock**. Supply shocks are often caused by unexpected increases or decreases

Supply shock An unexpected event that causes the short-run aggregate supply curve to shift.

Figure 9.3

How Expectations of the Future Price Level Affect the Short-Run Aggregate Supply Curve

The *SRAS* curve shifts to reflect worker and firm expectations of future prices.
1. If workers and firms expect that the price level will rise by 3 percent, from 127 to 130.9, they will adjust their wages and prices by that amount.
2. Holding constant all other variables that affect aggregate supply, the short-run aggregate supply curve will shift to the left.

If workers and firms expect that the price level will be lower in the future, the short-run aggregate supply curve will shift to the right.

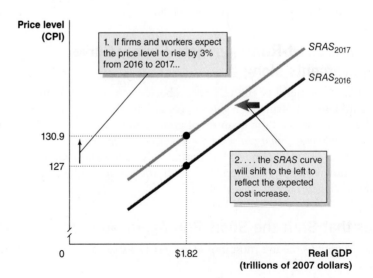

1. If firms and workers expect the price level to rise by 3% from 2016 to 2017...

2. ... the *SRAS* curve will shift to the left to reflect the expected cost increase.

in the prices of important natural resources. For example, an unexpected increase or decrease in the price of a key natural resource can cause firms' costs to be different from what they had expected. Oil prices can be particularly volatile. Some firms use oil in the production process. Other firms use products, such as plastics, that are made from oil. If oil prices rise unexpectedly, the costs of production will rise for these firms. Some utilities also burn oil to generate electricity, so electricity prices will rise. Rising oil prices lead to rising gasoline prices, which raise transportation costs for firms. Because firms face rising costs, they will supply the same level of output only if they receive higher prices, and the short-run aggregate supply curve will shift to the left.

Because the Canadian economy has experienced at least some inflation in virtually every year since the 1930s, workers and firms always expect next year's price level to be higher than this year's price level. Holding everything else constant, expectations of a higher price level will cause the *SRAS* curve to shift to the left. But everything else is never constant because the Canadian labour force and the Canadian capital stock are also increasing, and technology is always changing—factors that shift the *SRAS* curve to the right. The direction in which the *SRAS* curve shifts in a particular year depends on how large an impact these variables have during that year.

Table 9.2 summarizes the most important variables that cause the *SRAS* curve to shift. The table shows the shift in the *SRAS* curve that results from an *increase* in each of the variables. A *decrease* in these variables would cause the *SRAS* curve to shift in the opposite direction.

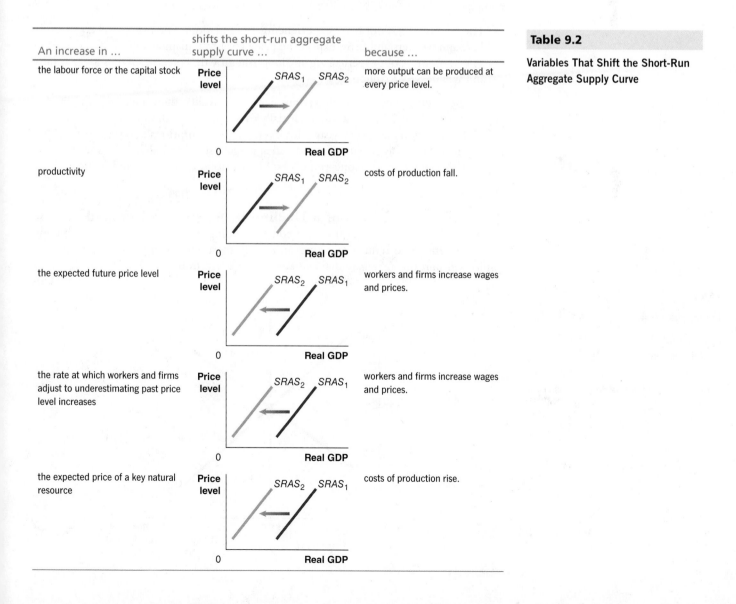

Table 9.2

Variables That Shift the Short-Run Aggregate Supply Curve

9.3 LEARNING OBJECTIVE

Use the aggregate demand and aggregate supply model to illustrate the difference between short-run and long-run macroeconomic equilibrium.

Macroeconomic Equilibrium in the Long Run and the Short Run

Now that we have discussed the components of the aggregate demand and aggregate supply model, we can use it to analyze changes in real GDP and the price level. In Figure 9.4, we bring the aggregate demand curve, the short-run aggregate supply curve, and the long-run aggregate supply curve together in one graph, to show the *long-run macroeconomic equilibrium* for the economy. In the figure, equilibrium occurs at real GDP of $1.77 trillion and a price level of 127. Notice that in the long-run equilibrium, the short-run aggregate supply curve, and the aggregate demand curve intersect at a point on the long-run aggregate supply curve. Because equilibrium occurs at a point on the long-run aggregate supply curve, we know the economy is at potential GDP: Firms will be operating at their normal capacity, and everyone who wants a job will have one—except for the structurally and frictionally unemployed. We know, however, that the economy is often not in long-run macroeconomic equilibrium. In the following section, we discuss the economic forces that can push the economy out of its long-run macroeconomic equilibrium.

Recessions, Expansions, and Supply Shocks

Because the full analysis of the aggregate demand and aggregate supply model can be complex, we begin with a simplified case, using two assumptions:

1. The economy has not been experiencing any inflation. The price level is currently 127, and workers and firms expect the price level to remain at 127.
2. The economy is not experiencing any long-run growth. Potential GDP is $1.77 trillion and will be $1.77 trillion in the future.

These assumptions are simplifications because in reality, the Canadian economy has experienced at least some inflation in virtually every year since the 1930s, and the potential GDP also increases every year. However, these assumptions allow us to focus on the key ideas of the aggregate demand and aggregate supply model. In this section, we examine the short-run and long-run effects of recessions, expansions, and supply shocks.

Recession

The Short-Run Effect of a Decline in Aggregate Demand
Suppose that rising interest rates cause firms to reduce spending on factories and equipment and cause households to reduce spending on new homes. The decline in investment that results will shift the aggregate demand curve to the left, from AD_1 to AD_2, as shown in

Figure 9.4

Long-Run Macroeconomic Equilibrium

In long-run macroeconomic equilibrium, the *AD* and *SRAS* curves intersect at a point on the *LRAS* curve. In this case, equilibrium occurs at real GDP of $1.77 trillion and a price level of 127.

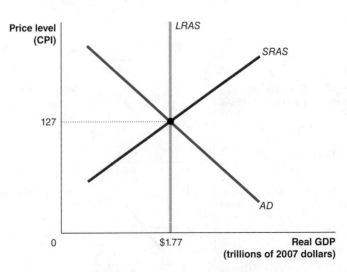

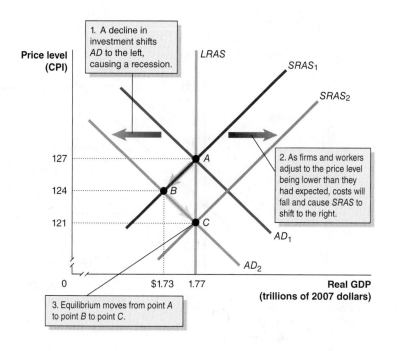

1. A decline in investment shifts *AD* to the left, causing a recession.

2. As firms and workers adjust to the price level being lower than they had expected, costs will fall and cause *SRAS* to shift to the right.

3. Equilibrium moves from point *A* to point *B* to point *C*.

Figure 9.5

The Short-Run and Long-Run Effects of a Decrease in Aggregate Demand

In the short run, a decrease in aggregate demand causes a recession. In the long run, it causes only a decrease in the price level.

Figure 9.5. The economy moves from point *A* to a new *short-run macroeconomic equilibrium*, where the AD_2 curve intersects the *SRAS* curve at point *B*. In the new short-run equilibrium, real GDP has declined from $1.77 trillion to $1.73 trillion and is below potential GDP. This lower level of GDP will result in declining profitability for many firms and layoffs for some workers—in short, the economy will be in recession.

Adjustment Back to Potential GDP in the Long Run.
We know that the recession will eventually end because there are forces at work that push the economy back to potential GDP in the long run. Figure 9.5 shows how the economy moves from recession back to potential GDP. The shift from AD_1 to AD_2 initially leads to a short-run equilibrium, with the price level having fallen from 127 to 124 (point *B*). Firms will be willing to accept lower prices due to lower sales. In addition, the unemployment resulting from the recession will make workers more willing to accept lower wages. As a result, the *SRAS* curve will shift to the right, from $SRAS_1$ to $SRAS_2$. At this point, the economy will be back in long-run equilibrium (point *C*). The shift from $SRAS_1$ to $SRAS_2$ will not happen instantly. It may take the economy several years to return to potential GDP. The important conclusion is that a decline in aggregate demand causes a recession in the short run, but in the long run it causes only a decline in the price level.

Economists refer to the process of adjustment back to potential GDP just described as an *automatic mechanism* because it occurs without any actions by the government. An alternative to waiting for the automatic mechanism to end a recession is for the government to use monetary or fiscal policy to shift the *AD* curve to the right and restore potential GDP more quickly. We will discuss monetary and fiscal policy in Chapters 11 and 12. Economists debate whether it is better to wait for the automatic mechanism to end a recession or whether government intervention is a better solution.

Expansion

The Short-Run Effect of an Increase in Aggregate Demand.
Suppose that instead of becoming pessimistic, many firms become optimistic about the future profitability of new investment, as happened during the information and telecommunication boom of the late 1990s and the real-estate boom of the 2000s. The resulting increase in investment will shift the *AD* curve to the right, as shown in Figure 9.6. Equilibrium moves from point *A* to point *B*. Real GDP rises from $1.77 trillion to $1.85 trillion, and the price level rises from 127 to 131. The economy will be operating above potential GDP: Firms are operating beyond their normal capacity, and some

Figure 9.6

The Short-Run and Long-Run Effects of an Increase in Aggregate Demand

In the short run, an increase in aggregate demand causes an increase in real GDP. In the long run, it causes only an increase in the price level.

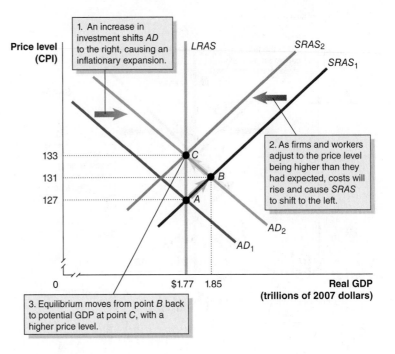

workers who would ordinarily be structurally or frictionally unemployed or who would normally not be in the labour force are employed.

Adjustment Back to Potential GDP in the Long Run. Just as an automatic mechanism brings the economy back to potential GDP from a recession, an automatic mechanism brings the economy back from a short-run equilibrium beyond potential GDP. Figure 9.6 illustrates this mechanism. The shift from AD_1 to AD_2 initially leads to a short-run equilibrium, with the price level rising from 127 to 131 (point *B*). Workers and firms will begin to adjust to the price level being higher than they had expected. Workers will push for higher wages—because each dollar of wages is able to buy fewer goods and services than before—and firms will charge higher prices. In addition, the low level of unemployment resulting from the expansion will make it easier for workers to negotiate for higher wages, and the increase in demand will make it easier for firms to increase their prices. As a result, the *SRAS* will shift to the left, from $SRAS_1$ to $SRAS_2$. At this point, the economy will be back in long-run equilibrium. Once again, the shift from $SRAS_1$ to $SRAS_2$ will not happen instantly. The process of returning to potential GDP may stretch out for more than a year.

Supply Shock

The Short-Run Effect of a Supply Shock. Suppose oil prices increase substantially. This supply shock will increase costs for many firms and cause the *SRAS* curve to shift to the left, as shown in panel (a) of Figure 9.7. Notice that the price level is higher in the new short-run equilibrium (131 rather than 127), but real GDP is lower ($1.72 trillion rather than $1.77 trillion). This unpleasant combination of inflation and recession is called **stagflation**.

Stagflation A combination of inflation and recession, usually resulting from a supply shock.

Adjustment Back to Potential GDP in the Long Run. The recession caused by a supply shock increases unemployment and reduces output. This eventually results in workers being willing to accept lower wages and firms being willing to accept lower prices. In panel (b) of Figure 9.7, the short-run aggregate supply curve shifts from $SRAS_2$ to $SRAS_1$, moving the economy from point *B* to point *A*. The economy is back to potential GDP at the original price level. It may take several years for this process to be completed. An alternative would be to use monetary or fiscal policy to shift the aggregate demand curve to the right. Using policy in this way would bring the economy back to potential GDP more quickly but would result in a permanently higher price level.

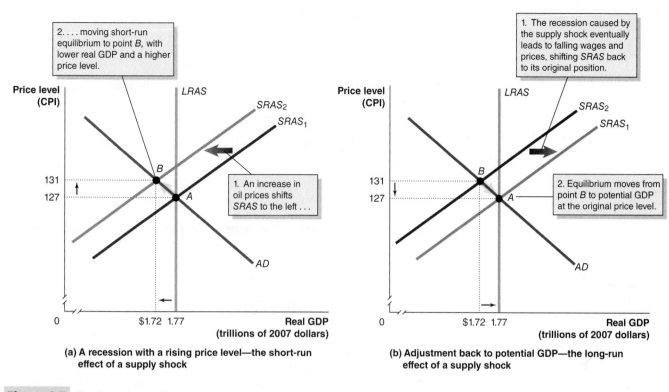

2. . . . moving short-run equilibrium to point *B*, with lower real GDP and a higher price level.

1. The recession caused by the supply shock eventually leads to falling wages and prices, shifting *SRAS* back to its original position.

1. An increase in oil prices shifts *SRAS* to the left . . .

2. Equilibrium moves from point *B* to potential GDP at the original price level.

(a) A recession with a rising price level—the short-run effect of a supply shock

(b) Adjustment back to potential GDP—the long-run effect of a supply shock

Figure 9.7 The Short-Run and Long-Run Effects of a Supply Shock

Panel (a) shows that a supply shock, such as a large increase in oil prices, will cause a recession and a higher price level in the short run. The recession caused by the supply shock increases unemployment and reduces output. In panel (b), rising unemployment and falling output result in workers being willing to accept lower wages and firms being willing to accept lower prices. The short-run aggregate supply curve shifts from $SRAS_2$ to $SRAS_1$. Equilibrium moves from point *B* back to potential GDP and the original price level at point *A*.

Making the Connection

Does Government Intervention Help Fight a Recession?

The federal government is engaging in large increases in spending in an effort to stimulate the economy. While economists generally agree that automatic mechanisms bring the economy back to potential GDP in the long run, there is a lot less agreement over how effective the kind of government stimulus currently underway will be. The best chance to observe the impact of government spending on GDP is during recessions.

The global recession led to a Canadian recession in late 2008. As a result of the global recession, Canadian net exports and domestic spending decreased, causing the aggregate demand curve to shift to the left, moving the economy into a recession. The federal government responded to the recession by introducing the politically named "Economic Action Plan." The Economic Action Plan, introduced in the 2009 federal budget, greatly increased government spending in a wide variety of areas and introduced some income tax breaks as well. The purpose of the increased spending and reduced taxes was to off-set the leftward shift in the aggregate demand curve, thus reducing the length and intensity of the recession for Canadians.

During recessions, governments often increase their spending to stimulate the economy.

In 2009, as the Canadian economy made the transition from recession to growth once more, debate began over the effectiveness of the government's stimulus efforts to limit the impact of the recession. In particular, Niels Veldhuis, president of the Fraser Institute, and Charles Lammam, an associate director at the Fraser Institute, argue that the government's actions did little to spur the recovery of the Canadian economy. They believe that the recovery was driven by increases in private spending and investment instead of the increase in government spending and reduced taxation. While their analysis ignores the impact of the government's stimulus efforts on consumer and investor confidence, the evidence they present against a direct link between government intervention and Canada's economic turnaround is fairly strong.

The debate over the effectiveness of government spending in stimulating the economy will likely continue for years to come. Why do economists vary in their economic forecasts and policy advice? A key reason is that economists don't always agree on the specific assumptions they should use in building models. One thing economists can agree on is that the aggregate demand and aggregate supply model plays an important role in economic policymaking.

Source: Based on "The Stimulus Didn't Work: Government stimulus spending had virtually no effect on Canada's economic recovery." Neils Veldhuis and Charles Lammam in *Fraser Forum*, May 2010, p.17 to 19. http://www.fraserinstitute.org/commerce.web/product_files/fraserforum-may2010.pdf

---

9.4 LEARNING OBJECTIVE

Use the dynamic aggregate demand and aggregate supply model to analyze macroeconomic conditions.

A Dynamic Aggregate Demand and Aggregate Supply Model

The basic aggregate demand and aggregate supply model used so far in this chapter provides important insights into how short-run macroeconomic equilibrium is determined. Unfortunately, the model also provides some misleading results. For instance, it incorrectly predicts that a recession caused by the aggregate demand curve shifting to the left will cause the price level to fall, which has not happened for an entire year since the 1930s. The difficulty with the basic model arises from the following two assumptions we made: (1) The economy does not experience continuing inflation, and (2) the economy does not experience long-run growth. We can develop a more useful aggregate demand and aggregate supply model by dropping these assumptions. The result will be a model that takes into account that the economy is not *static*, with an unchanging level of potential GDP and no continuing inflation, but *dynamic*, with potential GDP that grows over time and inflation that continues every year. We can create a *dynamic aggregate demand aggregate supply model* by making changes to the basic model that incorporates the following important macroeconomic facts:

- Potential GDP increases continually, shifting the long-run aggregate supply curve to the right.

- During most years, the aggregate demand curve shifts to the right.

- Except during periods when workers and firms expect high rates of inflation, the short-run aggregate supply curve shifts to the right.

Figure 9.8 illustrates how incorporating these macroeconomic facts changes the basic aggregate demand and aggregate supply model. We start in panel (a), in which $SRAS_1$ and AD_1 intersect at point A, at a price level of 127 and real GDP of $1.77 trillion. Because this intersection occurs at a point on $LRAS_1$, we know the economy is in long-run equilibrium. As panel (b) shows, the long-run aggregate supply curve shifts to the right, from $LRAS_1$ to $LRAS_2$. This shift occurs because during the year, potential GDP increases as the Canadian labour force and the Canadian capital stock increase and technological progress occurs. The short-run aggregate supply curve shifts from $SRAS_1$ to $SRAS_2$. This shift occurs because the same variables that cause the long-run aggregate supply curve to shift to the right will also increase the quantity of goods and services that firms are willing to supply in the short run. Finally, as panel (c) shows, the aggregate demand curve shifts to the right, from AD_1 to AD_2. The aggregate demand curve shifts for several reasons: As the population grows and incomes rise, consumption will increase over time. As the economy grows, firms will expand capacity, and new firms will be formed, increasing investment. An expanding population and expanding economy require increased government services, such as more police officers and teachers, so government purchases will increase.

The new equilibrium in panel (c) of Figure 9.8 occurs at point B, where AD_2 intersects $SRAS_2$ on $LRAS_2$. In the new equilibrium, the price level is 129, while real GDP increases to $1.81 trillion. Notice that the price level has risen in this example. Inflation has occurred because the aggregate demand curve shifted to the right by a

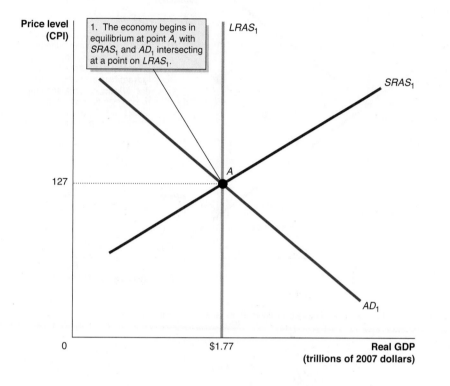

1. The economy begins in equilibrium at point A, with $SRAS_1$ and AD_1 intersecting at a point on $LRAS_1$.

(a) The basic aggregate demand and aggregate supply model.

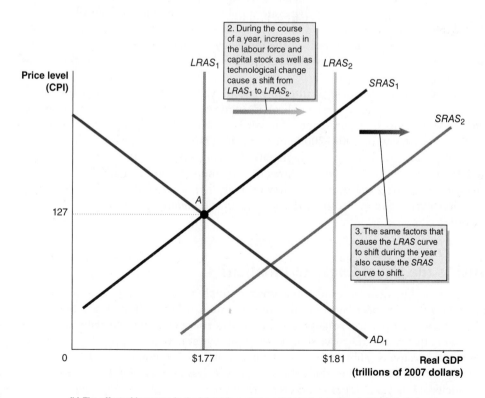

2. During the course of a year, increases in the labour force and capital stock as well as technological change cause a shift from $LRAS_1$ to $LRAS_2$.

3. The same factors that cause the $LRAS$ curve to shift during the year also cause the $SRAS$ curve to shift.

(b) The effect of increases in the labour force and capital stock as well as technological change.

Figure 9.8

A Dynamic Aggregate Demand and Aggregate Supply Model

We start with the basic aggregate demand and aggregate supply model in panel (a). In the dynamic model, increases in the labour force and capital stock as well as technological change cause the long-run aggregate supply to shift over the course of a year from $LRAS_1$ to $LRAS_2$. Typically, these same factors cause the short-run aggregate supply curve to shift from $SRAS_1$ to $SRAS_2$ as in panel (b). Aggregate demand will shift from AD_1 to AD_2 if, as is usually the case, spending by consumers, firms, and the government increases during the year. The shift in the aggregate demand curve is added to the model in panel (c).

(*Continued*)

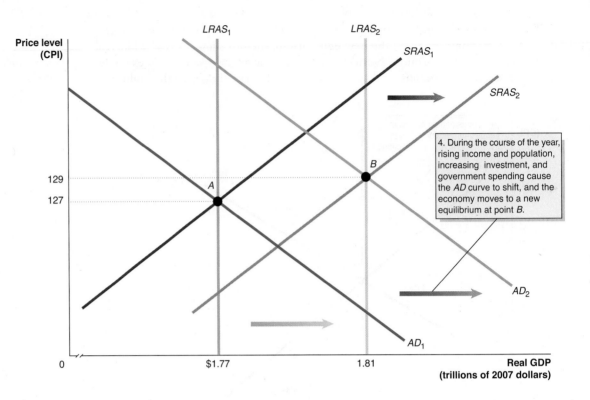

4. During the course of the year, rising income and population, increasing investment, and government spending cause the AD curve to shift, and the economy moves to a new equilibrium at point B.

(c) The effect of increased spending by consumers, firms, and the government.

Figure 9.8   (*Continued*)

greater amount than the short-run aggregate supply curve. This is fairly typical. The rightward shifts in the short-run aggregate supply curve are tempered by workers' and firms' expectations about inflation and supply shocks. These variables offset some (or in extreme cases more than offset) of the tendency for the short-run aggregate supply curve to shift to the right as new workers enter the labour force and new technologies are adopted.

Price increases are not guaranteed. In some years the aggregate demand curve may not shift to the right very much or it might even shift to the left. Consumers, firms, governments, and foreigners may cut back on their spending over the course of a year. As we saw in 2008–2009 and again in 2015, a significant drop in any one of the elements that determines aggregate demand will cause the curve to shift to the left. A large enough leftward aggregate demand shift will actually lead to *falling* prices. Falling prices are quite rare, however. In fact, as we will see shortly, *changes in the price level and in real GDP in the short run are determined by shifts in the* SRAS *and* AD *curves.*

What Is the Usual Cause of Inflation?

The dynamic aggregate demand and aggregate supply model provides a more accurate explanation than the basic model of the source of most inflation. If total spending in the economy grows faster than total production, prices rise. Figure 9.9 illustrates this point by showing that if the *AD* curve shifts to the right by more than the *LRAS* curve, inflation results because equilibrium occurs at a higher price level, point *B*. In the new equilibrium, the *SRAS* curve has shifted to the right by less than the *LRAS* curve because the anticipated increase in prices offsets some of the technological change and increases the labour force and capital stock that occur during the year. Although inflation generally results from total spending growing faster than total production, a shift to the left of

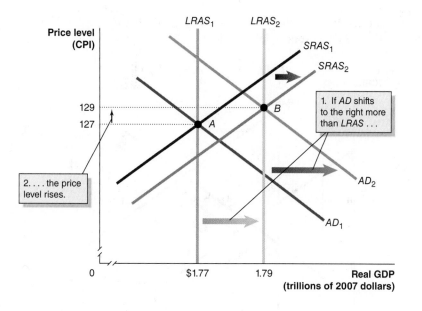

Figure 9.9

Using Dynamic Aggregate Demand and Aggregate Supply to Understand Inflation

The most common cause of inflation is total spending increasing faster than total production.

1. The economy begins at point A, with real GDP of $1.77 trillion and a price level of 127. An increase in full-employment real GDP from $1.77 trillion to $1.79 trillion causes long-run aggregate supply to shift from $LRAS_1$ to $LRAS_2$. Aggregate demand shifts from AD_1 to AD_2.
2. Because AD shifts to the right by more than the $LRAS$ curve, the price level in the equilibrium rises from 127 to 129.

the short-run aggregate supply curve can also cause an increase in the price level, as we saw earlier, in the discussion of supply shocks.

As we saw in Figure 9.8, if aggregate demand increases by the same amount as short-run and long-run aggregate supply, the price level will not change. In this case, the economy experiences economic growth without inflation.

Solved Problem **9.2**

Showing the Millennium Economic Boom on a Dynamic Aggregate Demand and Aggregate Supply Graph

The booming economy of 2000–2001 clearly shows how a demand shock affects the economy. Throughout 2000 and into 2001, the value of the Canadian dollar was low and falling compared with the American dollar. The low value of the Canadian dollar combined with growing economies in the United States and much of the world meant that demand for Canadian products was high. Based on this information and the statistics in the following table, draw a dynamic aggregate demand and aggregate supply graph showing

macroeconomic equilibrium for 2000 and 2001. Provide a brief explanation of your graph and predict what is likely to happen to the price level in the future.

	Actual Real GDP (trillions of 2007 dollars)	Potential GDP (trillions of 2007 dollars)	Price Level (CPI)
2000	$1.32	$1.30	95.4
2001	$1.34	$1.35	97.8

Solving the Problem

Step 1: Review the chapter material. This problem is about using the dynamic aggregate demand and aggregate supply model, so you may want to review the section "A Dynamic Aggregate Demand and Aggregate Supply Model," which begins on page 244.

Step 2: Use the information in the table to draw the graph. You need to draw six curves: $SRAS_{2000}$, $SRAS_{2001}$, $LRAS_{2000}$, $LRAS_{2001}$, AD_{2000}, and AD_{2001}. You know the two $LRAS$ curves will be vertical lines at the values given for potential GDP in the table. Because of the large aggregate demand shock, the AD curve has shifted to the right significantly. While the $SRAS$ will have shifted to the left, this shift needs to be relatively small to get the results we see from the data. Your graph should look like this:

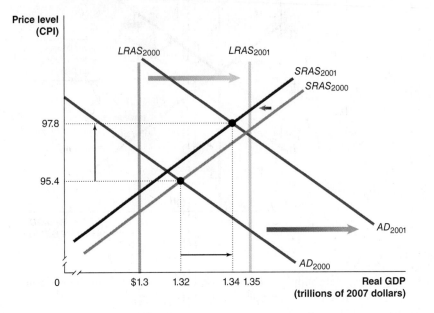

Step 3: **Explain your graph.** $LRAS_{2000}$ and $LRAS_{2001}$ are at the levels of potential GDP for each year. Macroeconomic equilibrium for 2000 occurs where the AD_{2000} curve intersects the $SRAS_{2000}$ curve with a real GDP of $1.32 trillion dollars and a price level of 95.4. Macroeconomic equilibrium for 2001 occurs where AD_{2001} intersects the $SRAS_{2001}$ curve with real GDP equal to $1.34 trillion and a price level of 97.8. The rightward shift of the AD curve was much larger than the leftward shift of the $SRAS$ curve. The result is an increase in real GDP as well as an increase in the price level.

Based on CANSIM Tables 380-0064 and 326-0020; and Bank of Canada, *Indicators of Capacity and Inflation Pressures for Canada* (Output Gap).

MyEconLab   **Your Turn:** For more practice, do related problem 4.3 on page 252 at the end of this chapter.

Economics in Your Life

Is an Employer Likely to Cut Your Pay during a Recession?

At the beginning of this chapter, we asked you to consider whether during a recession your employer is likely to reduce your pay and cut the prices of the products he or she sells. In this chapter, we saw that even during a recession, the price level rarely falls. Although some firms reduced prices during the Canadian recession of 2008–2009, most firms did not. So, the owner of the coffeehouse where you work will probably not cut the price of lattes unless sales have declined drastically. We also saw that most firms are more reluctant to cut wages than to increase them because wage cuts can have a negative effect on worker morale and productivity. Some firms did cut wages in response to the recession, but given that you are a highly skilled barista, your employer is unlikely to cut your wages for fear that you might quit and work for a competitor.

Conclusion

Chapter 3 demonstrated the power of the microeconomic model of demand and supply in explaining how the prices and quantities of individual products are determined. This chapter showed that we need a different model to explain the behaviour of the whole economy. We saw that the macroeconomic model of aggregate demand and aggregate supply explains fluctuations in real GDP and the price level. Fluctuations in real GDP, employment, and the price level have led the federal government to implement macroeconomic policies. We will explore these policies in Chapter 12 and Chapter 13, but first, in Chapter 11, we consider the role money plays in the economy.

Chapter Summary and Problems

Key Terms

Aggregate demand (*AD*) curve, p. 227

Aggregate demand and aggregate supply model, p. 227

Fiscal policy, p. 229

Long-run aggregate supply (*LRAS*) curve, p. 235

Menu costs, p. 237

Monetary policy, p. 229

Potential GDP, p. 235

Price level, p. 227

Short-run aggregate supply (*SRAS*) curve, p. 227

Stagflation, p. 242

Supply shock, p. 238

Summary

★LO 9.1 The *aggregate demand and aggregate supply model* enables us to explain short-run fluctuations in real GDP and price level. The *aggregate demand curve* shows the relationship between the *price level* and the level of planned aggregate expenditures by households, firms, and the government. The *short-run aggregate supply curve* shows the relationship in the short run between the price level and the quantity of real GDP supplied by firms. *The long-run aggregate supply curve* shows the relationship in the long run between the price level and the quantity of real GDP supplied. The four components of aggregate demand are consumption (*C*), investment (*I*), government purchases (*G*), and net exports (*NX*). The aggregate demand curve is downward sloping because a decline in the price level causes consumption, investment, and net exports to increase. If the price level changes but all else remains constant, the economy will move up or down a stationary aggregate demand curve. If any variable other than the price level changes, the aggregate demand curve will shift. The variables that cause the aggregate demand curve to shift are divided into three categories: changes in government policy, changes in the expectations of households and firms, and changes in foreign variables. For example, *monetary policy* involves the actions the Bank of Canada takes to manage the money supply and interest rates to pursue macroeconomic policy objectives. When the Bank of Canada takes actions to change interest rates, consumption and investment spending will change, shifting the aggregate demand curve. *Fiscal policy* involves changes in taxes and purchases that are intended to achieve macroeconomic policy objectives. Changes in federal taxes and purchases shift the aggregate demand curve.

LO 9.2 The *long-run aggregate supply curve* is a vertical line because in the long run, real GDP is always at its potential level and is unaffected by the price level. The short-run aggregate supply curve slopes upward because workers and firms fail to predict accurately the future price level. The three main explanations of why this

failure results in an upward-sloping aggregate supply curve are that (1) contracts make some wages and prices "sticky"; (2) firms are often slow to adjust wages; and (3) menu costs make some prices sticky. *Menu costs* are the costs to firms of changing prices on menus or in catalogues. If the price level changes but all else remains constant, the economy will move up or down a stationary aggregate supply curve. If any variable other than the price level changes, the aggregate supply curve will shift. The aggregate supply curve shifts as a result of increases in the labour force and capital stock, technological change, expected increases or decreases in the future price level, adjustments of workers and firms to errors in past expectations about the price level, and unexpected increases or decreases in the price of an important raw material. A *supply shock* is an unexpected event that causes the short-run aggregate supply curve to shift.

LO 9.3 In long-run macroeconomic equilibrium, the aggregate demand and short-run aggregate supply curves intersect at a point on the long-run aggregate supply curve. In short-run macroeconomic equilibrium, the aggregate demand and short-run aggregate supply curves often intersect at a point off the long-run aggregate supply curve. An automatic mechanism drives the economy to long-run equilibrium. If short-run equilibrium occurs at a point below potential GDP, wages and prices will fall, and the short-run aggregate supply curve will shift to the right until potential GDP is restored. If short-run equilibrium occurs at a point beyond potential GDP, wages and prices will rise, and the short-run aggregate supply curve will shift to the left until potential GDP is restored. Real GDP can be temporarily above or below its potential level, either because of shifts in the aggregate demand curve or because supply shocks lead to shifts in the aggregate supply curve. *Stagflation* is a combination of inflation and recession, usually resulting from a supply shock.

LO 9.4 To make the aggregate demand and aggregate supply model more realistic, we need to make it dynamic by incorporating

---

★"Learning Objective" is abbreviated to "LO" in the end-of-chapter material.

three facts that were left out of the basic model: (1) Potential GDP increases continually, shifting the long-run aggregate supply curve to the right; (2) during most years, aggregate demand shifts to the right; and (3) except during periods when workers and firms expect high rates of inflation, the aggregate supply curve shifts to

the right. The dynamic aggregate demand and aggregate supply model allows us to analyze macroeconomy.

MyEconLab   Log in to MyEconLab to complete these exercises and get instant feedback.

Review Questions

LO 9.1

1.1 Explain the three reasons the aggregate demand curve slopes downward.

1.2 What variables cause the *AD* curve to shift? For each variable, identify whether an increase in that variable will cause the *AD* curve to shift to the right or to the left.

LO 9.2

2.1 Explain why the long-run aggregate supply curve is vertical.

2.2 What variables cause the long-run aggregate supply curve to shift? For each variable, identify whether an increase in that variable will cause the long-run aggregate supply curve to shift to the right or to the left.

2.3 Why does the short-run aggregate supply curve slope upward?

2.4 What variables cause the short-run aggregate supply curve to shift? For each variable, identify whether an increase

in that variable will cause the short-run aggregate supply curve to shift to the right or to the left.

LO 9.3

3.1 What is the relationship among the *AD*, *SRAS*, and *LRAS* curves when the economy is in long-run macroeconomic equilibrium?

3.2 Why are the long-run effects of an increase in aggregate demand on price and output different from the short-run effects?

LO 9.4

4.1 What are the key differences between the basic aggregate demand and aggregate supply model and the dynamic aggregate demand and aggregate supply model?

4.2 In the dynamic aggregate demand and aggregate supply model, what is the result of aggregate demand increasing more quickly than potential GDP? What is the result of aggregate demand increasing more slowly than potential GDP?

Problems and Applications

LO 9.1

1.1 Explain how each of the following events would affect the aggregate demand curve.
   a. An increase in the price level
   b. Higher provincial income taxes
   c. Higher interest rates

1.2 **[Related to Don't Let This Happen to You on page 230]** A student was asked to draw an aggregate demand and aggregate supply graph to illustrate the effect of an increase in aggregate supply. The student drew the following graph:

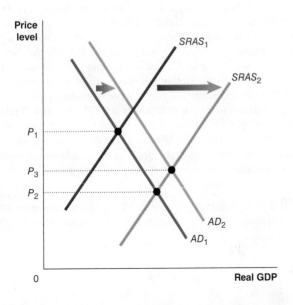

The student explains the graph as follows:

> An increase in aggregate supply causes a shift from $SRAS_1$ to $SRAS_2$. Because this shift in the aggregate supply curve results in a lower price level, there will be an increase in consumption, investment, and net exports. This change causes the aggregate demand curve to shift to the right, from AD_1 to AD_2. We know that real GDP will increase, but we can't be sure whether the price level will rise or fall because that depends on whether the aggregate supply curve or the aggregate demand curve has shifted farther to the right. I assume that aggregate supply shifts out farther than aggregate demand, so I show the final price level, P_3, as being lower than the initial price level, P_1.

Explain whether you agree with the student's analysis. Be careful to explain exactly what—if anything—you find wrong with this analysis.

1.3 **[Related to Making the Connection on page 231]** It is not uncommon for some elements of GDP to rise while others fall. How would you determine what happens to the aggregate demand curve if investment rises while consumption falls? Give an example of what might cause investment to rise while consumption falls.

1.4 **[Related to Solved Problem 9.1 on page 232]** Explain whether the following will cause a shift of the *AD* curve or a movement along the *AD* curve:
   a. Firms become more optimistic about future sales and increase their spending on machinery and equipment.
   b. The Canadian economy experiences 6 percent inflation.

1.5 **[Related to Making the Connection on page 234]** (a) What do you think is likely to happen to the economy if you notice a lot of long skirts and skinny neckties? (b) Give an example of something that you think could be a leading indicator of the current state and future health of the Canadian economy.

1.6 In early 2016, the global economy was hit by a series of shocks, many of which traced their origins to decisions being made in China. Not all sectors of the economy were affected by these shocks in the same ways. Why might some sectors be more harmed by changes in China than others?

LO 9.2

2.1 Explain how each of the following events would affect the long-run aggregate supply curve.
a. A higher price level
b. An increase in the quantity of capital goods
c. Technological change

2.2 An article in the *Economist* noted that "the economy's potential to supply goods and services [is] determined by such things as the labour force and capital stock, as well as inflation expectations." Do you agree with this list of the determinants of potential GDP? Briefly explain.

Based on "Money's Muddled Message," *Economist*, May 19, 2009.

2.3 Explain how each of the following events would affect the short-run aggregate supply curve.
a. An increase in the price level
b. An increase in what the price level is expected to be in the future
c. An unexpected increase in the price of an important raw material
d. An increase in the labour force participation rate

2.4 Workers and firms often enter into contracts that fix prices or wages, sometimes for years at a time. If the price level turns out to be higher or lower than was expected when the contract was signed, one party to the contract will lose out. Briefly explain why, despite knowing this, workers and firms still sign long-term contracts.

LO 9.3

3.1 Draw a basic aggregate demand and aggregate supply graph (with *LRAS* constant) that shows the economy in long-run equilibrium.
a. Assume that there is a large increase in demand for Canadian exports. Show the resulting short-run equilibrium on your graph. In this short-run equilibrium, is the unemployment rate likely to be higher or lower than it was before the increase in exports? Briefly explain. Explain how the economy adjusts back to long-run equilibrium. When the economy has adjusted back to long-run equilibrium, how have the values of each of the following changed relative to what they were before the increase in exports:
    i.   Real GDP
    ii. The price level
    iii. The unemployment rate
b. Assume that there is an unexpected increase in the price of oil. Show the resulting short-run equilibrium on your graph. Explain how the economy adjusts back to long-run equilibrium. In this short-run equilibrium, is the unemployment rate likely to be higher or lower than it was before the increase in exports? Briefly explain. When the economy has adjusted back to long-run equilibrium,

how have the values of each of the following changed relative to what they were before the increase in exports:
   i.   Real GDP
   ii. The price level
   iii. The unemployment rate

3.2 List four variables that would cause a decrease in real GDP (if large enough, a recession). Indicate whether changes in each variable increase or decrease aggregate demand or short-run aggregate supply. Next, state four variables that would cause an increase in the price level (short-run inflation). Indicate whether changes in the variable increase or decrease aggregate demand or short-run aggregate supply.

3.3 Many economists viewed the improvement in the American economy in 2016 as excellent news for Canada. In the United States, unemployment fell and average wages rose. Why would strong employment data from the United States bode well for the Canadian economy?

3.4 Use the graph below to answer the following questions:
a. Which of the points *A*, *B*, *C*, or *D* can represent a long-run equilibrium?
b. Suppose that initially the economy is at point *A*. If aggregate demand increases from AD_1 to AD_2, which point represents the economy's short-run equilibrium? Which point represents the eventual long-run equilibrium? Briefly explain how the economy adjusts from the short-run to the long-run equilibrium.

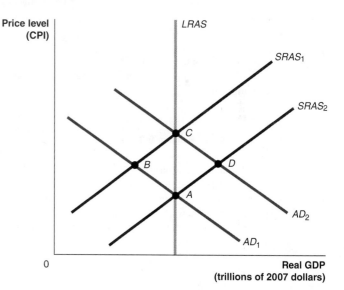

3.5 In the chapter, we saw that goods such as lipstick, neckties, and hemlines could be used as indicators of future developments in the economy. Why do these goods work as economic indicators? What other goods or services can you think of that could also play a similar role in forecasting the economy?

3.6 Consider the data in the following table for the years 2000 and 2001:

Year	Actual Real GDP (millions of 2007 dollars)	Potential GDP (millions of 2007 dollars)	Unemployment Rate (annual average)
2000	$1 319 435	$1 304 921	6.8%
2001	$1 341 712	$1 341 712	7.2%

a. In 2000, actual real GDP was greater than potential GDP. Explain how this is possible.

b. Even though real GDP in 2001 was greater than that in 2000, the unemployment rate increased between 2000 and 2001. Why did this increase in unemployment occur?

c. Was the inflation rate in 2001 likely to have been higher or lower than the inflation rate in 2000? Does your answer depend on whether the slowdown was caused by a change in a component of aggregate demand or by a supply shock?

Data from StatsCan tables 282-0002 and 380-0017, Bank of Canada Potential GDP estimates from Office of the Parliamentary Budget Officer, Estimates of Canada's Potential GDP and Output Gap – A Comparative Analysis, April 28, 2010 http://www2.parl.gc.ca/sites/pbo-dpb/documents/Potential_GDP.pdf

LO 9.4

4.1 Draw a dynamic aggregate demand and aggregate supply graph showing the economy moving from potential GDP in 2015 to potential GDP in 2016, with no inflation. Your graph should contain the *AD*, *SRAS*, and *LRAS* curves for both 2015 and 2016 and should indicate the short-run macroeconomic equilibrium for each year and the directions in which the curves have shifted. Identify what must happen to have growth during 2016 without inflation.

4.2 According to the Bank of Canada, the only sustained period of deflation in Canada occurred in the 1930s as a result of the Great Depression. "Deflation can be particularly harmful when caused by a protracted sharp contraction in spending (as in the 1930s), which triggers a persistent fall in the general level of prices." Why is this type of deflation so harmful? (*Hint:* Think about which curve will shift in this case and think about how consumers might react to consistently falling prices.)

Bank of Canada Fact Sheet: Disinflation and Deflation, http://www.bankofcanada.ca/en/backgrounders/bg-i6.html

4.3 **[Related to Solved Problem 9.2 on page 247]** Look at the table in *Solved Problem 9.2*. The price level for 2000 is given as 95.4, and the price level for 2001 is given as 97.8. The values for the price level are just below 100. What does this indicate about inflation during these years? Briefly explain.

4.4 In the graph that follows, suppose that the economy moves from point A in year 1 to point B in year 2. Using the graph, briefly explain your answer to each of the questions.

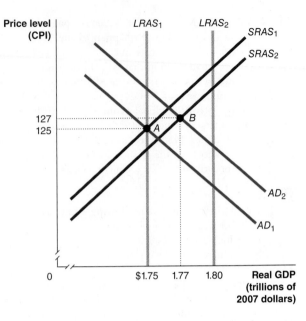

a. What is the growth rate in potential GDP from year 1 to year 2?

b. Is the unemployment rate in year 2 higher or lower than in year 1?

c. What is the inflation rate in year 2?

d. What is the growth rate of real GDP in year 2?

4.5 Throughout much of the period between 2009 and 2015 demand for new workers grew but starting salaries were not growing. How is it that can be strong evidence that the economy was recovering?

4.6 Canadian National (the rail company) is often thought of as an economic "bellwether."

a. What is an economic bellwether?

b. Briefly compare how sensitive CN's sales are likely to be to changes in the business cycle to how sensitive the following firms' sales are likely to be to changes in the business cycle. (In other words, explain whether CN's sales are likely to fluctuate more or less than the sales of each of these other firms as the economy moves from recession to expansion and back to recession.)

• Tim Hortons (a chain of restaurants specialized in coffee and baked goods)

• Kent Homes (a home builder)

• Harlequin Romance Ltd. (a novel publisher)

MyEconLab   MyEconLab is an online tool designed to help you master the concepts covered in your course. It will create a personalized study plan to stimulate and measure your learning. Log in to take advantage of this powerful study aid, and to access quizzes and other valuable course-related material.

Appendix D

Macroeconomic Schools of Thought

Macroeconomics became a separate field of economics in 1936 with the publication of John Maynard Keynes's book *The General Theory of Employment, Interest, and Money*. Keynes, an economist at the University of Cambridge in England, was attempting to explain the devastating Great Depression of the 1930s. As we discussed in Chapter 8, real GDP in Canada and other industrial countries fell by more than 25 percent between 1929 and the mid-1930s. In 1930, the unemployment rate in Canada was estimated at 30 percent. The Canadian economy did not truly recover until the start of World War II in 1939. To explain what Canada and other industrial countries were experiencing, Keynes developed a version of the aggregate demand and aggregate supply model. The widespread acceptance during the 1930s and 1940s of Keynes's model became known as the **Keynesian revolution**.

In fact, using the aggregate demand and aggregate supply model remains the most widely accepted approach to analyzing macroeconomic issues. Because the model has been modified significantly from Keynes's day, many economists who use the model today refer to themselves as *new Keynesians*. The new Keynesians emphasize the importance of the stickiness of wages and prices in explaining fluctuations in real GDP. A significant number of economists, however, dispute whether using the aggregate demand and aggregate supply model, as we have discussed it in this chapter, is the best way to analyze macroeconomic issues. These alternative *schools of thought* use models that differ significantly from the standard aggregate demand and aggregate supply model. We can briefly consider each of the three major alternative models:

1. The monetarist model
2. The new classical model
3. The real business cycle model

Keynesian revolution The name given to the widespread acceptance during the 1930s and 1940s of John Maynard Keynes's macroeconomic model.

The Monetarist Model

The monetarist model—also known as the *neo-Quantity Theory of Money model*—was developed beginning in the 1940s by Milton Friedman, an economist at the University of Chicago who was awarded the Nobel Prize in Economics in 1976. Friedman argued that the Keynesian approach overstates the amount of macroeconomic instability in an economy. In particular, he argued that an economy will ordinarily be at potential real GDP. In the book *A Monetary History of the United States: 1867–1960*, written with Anna Jacobson Schwartz, Friedman argued that most fluctuations in real output were caused by fluctuations in the money supply rather than by fluctuations in consumption spending or investment spending. Friedman and Schwartz argued that the severity of the Great Depression in the United States was caused by the central banks, particularly the American central bank, allowing the quantity of money to fall dramatically.

Central banks are responsible for managing the amount of money circulating in the economy. As we will discuss further in Chapter 11, central banks historically focused more on controlling interest rates than on controlling the money supply. Friedman argued that central banks should change their practices and adopt a **monetary growth rule**, which is a plan for increasing the quantity of money at a fixed rate. Friedman believed that adopting a monetary growth rule would reduce fluctuations in real GDP, employment, and inflation.

Friedman's ideas, which are referred to as **monetarism**, attracted significant support during the 1970s and early 1980s, when developed economies experienced high rates of unemployment and inflation. The support for monetarism declined during the late

Monetary growth rule A plan for increasing the quantity of money at a fixed rate that does not respond to changes in economic conditions.

Monetarism The macroeconomic theories of Milton Friedman and his followers, particularly the idea that the quantity of money should be increased at a constant rate.

1980s and 1990s, when the unemployment and inflation rates in developed economies were relatively low. In Chapter 10, we will discuss the *quantity theory of money*, which underlies the monetarist model.

The New Classical Model

The new classical model was developed in the mid-1970s by a group of economists including Nobel Laureate Robert Lucas of the University of Chicago, Nobel Laureate Thomas Sargent of New York University, and Robert Barro of Harvard University. Some of the views held by the new classical macroeconomists are similar to those held by economists before the Great Depression. Keynes referred to the economists before the Great Depression as "classical economists." Like the classical economists, the new classical macroeconomists believe that the economy normally will be at potential real GDP. They also believe that wages and prices adjust quickly to changes in demand and supply. Put another way, they believe the stickiness in wages and prices emphasized by the new Keynesians is unimportant.

New classical macroeconomics
The macroeconomic theories of Robert Lucas and others, particularly the idea that workers and firms have rational expectations.

Lucas argues that workers and firms have *rational expectations*, meaning that they form their expectations of the future values of economic variables, such as the inflation rate, by making use of all available information, including information on variables—such as changes in the quantity of money—that might affect aggregate demand. If the actual inflation rate is lower than the expected inflation rate, the actual real wage will be higher than the expected real wage. These higher real wages will lead to a recession because they will cause firms to hire fewer workers and cut back on production. As workers and firms adjust their expectations to the lower inflation rate, the real wage will decline, and employment and production will expand, bringing the economy out of recession. The ideas of Lucas and his followers are referred to as the **new classical macroeconomics**. Supporters of the new classical model agree with supporters of the monetarist model that central banks should adopt a monetary growth rule. They argue that a monetary growth rule will make it easier for workers and firms to accurately forecast the price level, thereby reducing fluctuations in real GDP.

The Real Business Cycle Model

Beginning in the 1980s, some economists, including Nobel Laureates Finn Kydland of Carnegie Mellon University and Edward Prescott of Arizona State University, began to argue that Lucas was correct in assuming that workers and firms formed their expectations rationally and that wages and prices adjust quickly to supply and demand but was wrong about the source of fluctuations in real GDP. They argue that fluctuations in real GDP are caused by temporary shocks to productivity. These shocks can be negative, such as a decline in the availability of oil or other raw materials, or positive, such as technological change that makes it possible to produce more output with the same quantity of inputs.

Real business cycle model A macroeconomic model that focuses on real, rather than monetary, causes of the business cycle.

According to this school of thought, shifts in the aggregate demand curve have no impact on real GDP because the short-run aggregate supply curve is vertical. Other schools of thought believe that the short-run aggregate supply curve is upward sloping and that only the *long-run* aggregate supply curve is vertical. Fluctuations in real GDP occur when a negative productivity shock causes the short-run aggregate supply curve to shift to the left—reducing real GDP—or a positive productivity shock causes the short-run aggregate supply curve to shift to the right—increasing real GDP. Because this model focuses on "real" factors—productivity shocks—rather than changes in the quantity of money to explain fluctuations in real GDP, it is known as the **real business cycle model**.

Making	**Karl Marx: Capitalism's Severest Critic**
the	
Connection	

The schools of macroeconomic thought we have discussed in this appendix are considered part of mainstream economic theory because of their acceptance of the market system as the best means of raising living standards in the long run. One quite influential critic of mainstream economic theory was Karl Marx. Marx was born in Trier, Germany, in 1818. After graduating from the University of Berlin in 1841, he began a career as a political journalist and agitator. His political activities caused him to be expelled first from Germany and then from France and Belgium. In 1849, he moved to London, where he spent the remainder of his life.

In 1867, Marx published the first volume of his greatest work, *Das Kapital*. Marx read closely the most prominent mainstream economists, including Adam Smith, David Ricardo, and John Stuart Mill. But Marx believed that he understood how market systems would evolve in the long run much better than those earlier authors. Marx argued that the market system would eventually be replaced by a Communist economy, in which the workers would control production. He believed in the *labour theory of value*, which attributed all of the value of a good or service to the labour embodied in it. According to Marx, the owners of businesses—capitalists—did not earn profits by contributing anything of value to the production of goods or services. Instead, capitalists earned profits because their "monopoly of the means of production"—their ownership of factories and machinery—allowed them to exploit workers by paying them wages that were much lower than the value of workers' contribution to production.

Marx argued that the wages of workers would be driven to levels that allowed only bare survival. He also argued that small firms would eventually be driven out of business by larger firms, forcing owners of small firms into the working class. Control of production would ultimately be concentrated in the hands of a few firms, which would have difficulty selling the goods they produced to the impoverished masses. A final economic crisis would lead the working classes to rise up, seize control of the economy, and establish Communism. Marx died in 1883, without having provided a detailed explanation of how the Communist economy would operate.

Marx had relatively little influence on mainstream thinking in the United States, but several political parties in Europe were guided by his ideas. In 1917, the Bolshevik party seized control of Russia and established the Soviet Union, the first Communist state. Although the Soviet Union was a vicious dictatorship under Vladimir Lenin and his successor, Joseph Stalin, its prestige rose when it avoided the macroeconomic difficulties that plagued the market economies during the 1930s. By the late 1940s, Communist parties had also come to power in China and the countries of Eastern Europe. Poor economic performance contributed to the eventual collapse of the Soviet Union and its replacement by a market system, although one in which government intervention is still widespread. The Communist Party remains in power in China, but the economy is evolving toward a market system. Today, only North Korea and Cuba have economies that claim to be based on the ideas of Karl Marx.

Karl Marx predicted that a final economic crisis would lead to the collapse of the market system.

Lebrecht/Alamy

Key Terms

CIBC downgrades its 2016 Canadian economic outlook for the second time in a month

The spike in financial market volatility around the world will not leave Canada unscathed, said CIBC World Markets as it downgraded its outlook for the country's economic growth this year.

(a) The bank's chief economist said Thursday that he now sees gross domestic product expanding by just 1.3 per cent this year, compared with a forecast of 1.7 per cent made at the start of the year.

CIBC acknowledged the downgrade, hitting just a month after it issued its 2016 forecast, is unusual.

(b) "But then again, these are unusual times," said Avery Shenfeld, chief economist of CIBC World Markets. "Oil's further plunge, and a similar malaise across most of the resource space, continues to push back the timetable for reaching a bottom in related capital spending in Canada."

The downgrade brings CIBC even further below consensus calls for economic growth this year which, based on a survey of economists by Bloomberg, currently sits at 1.8 per cent.

(c) It also adds to the concerns voiced by both economists and central banks this week about the volatility in global markets. On Wednesday, the U.S. Federal Reserve issued a dovish statement that said it was closely monitoring the steep selloff in stock markets this month.

Shenfeld said even his 1.3 per cent growth call might be optimistic, as it factors in the federal government spending $10 billion more on stimulus this year than originally envisioned, a $30-billion federal deficit and the Canadian dollar going even lower.

The forecast weighs the positive effects of a lower loonie for exporters versus the negative effects of the oil price crash. Shenfeld notes that the latter is still filtering into the economy, adding to the downside pressure.

"While the country's GDP is less heavily weighted to resource sector spending than it was a year ago, we're only in the early stages of the negative spillover effects on other sectors," he said.

(d) With that shock still hurting business confidence and leading to layoffs,

Canada's one economic bright spot will also be under assault this year: job creation. The Canadian economy managed to produce 158,000 new jobs last year despite the layoffs in the energy sector, a growth rate of 0.9 per cent. Stronger than the growth rate of 0.7 per cent in both 2013 and 2014.

But it will be hard to repeat that feat this year, said Shenfeld.

"It's only because employment grew that we didn't record an official recession, since real GDP fell slightly in the year to October 2015," he said. "That employment trend looks vulnerable in the affected provinces given signs of accelerating layoffs in the resource sector, and the fact that job creation has been leaning so heavily on self-employment rather than business hiring."

Key Points in the Article

This article examines the outlook for the Canadian economy in early 2016, as well as brief look back at the shocks that hit the economy in 2015. Economic forecasters regularly predict the level of output at which the aggregate demand curve will intersect the short run aggregate supply curve. The number of factors that affect the Canadian economy in different ways and in different regions make predicting the future state of the economy difficult.

Analyzing the News

a CIBC (a major bank) is predicting that GDP in 2016 will be 1.3 percent larger than it was in 2015. This growth is based on movements of the aggregate demand curve and the short-run aggregate supply curve. The aggregate demand curve will shift to the right as Canadian consumers demand more goods and services, firms undertake new investment projects, government increases spending, and foreign consumers demand more goods made in Canada.

CIBC's new forecast is for less growth than they originally thought. See the figure below.

b Even though all six major Canadian banks and other institutions employ highly trained professional economists with access to a lot of data about the economy, they seldom agree on what exactly will happen to the Canadian economy. CIBC's forecast of 1.3 percent economic growth is a lot lower than the average forecast of 1.8 percent growth. CIBC's economists see the low price of oil and the impact it has on aggregate demand for oil from the western oil-producing provinces as likely to slow economic growth more than they originally expected. Not only does the low price of oil reduce Canada's net exports, it also reduces the amount energy firms are willing to spend on investment.

c In creating their forecasts, economists also have to try and guess what the federal government and other economic agents will do in response to the current economic situation. In early 2016, CIBC's forecasters expected the federal government to run much larger deficits than they promised during the election.

The wealth and perceived wealth of consumers also plays an important role in the state of the economy. When general stock prices fall, households feel that their past savings and pension plans (often part of which are stocks) fall in value. This can cause consumer spending to fall, shifting the aggregate demand curve to the left.

Forecasters also have to predict how foreign consumers and firms will react to changes in the Canadian economy. When Canada goes into recession or performs poorly while the US economy is stable, the value of the Canadian dollar tends to fall.

d There is a difference between the economy growing more slowly than expected and a recession. While there is no official definition of a recession in Canada (Mr. Shenfeld misspoke), the most commonly used one is two consecutive quarters of negative GDP growth. Strangely enough, a recession does not guarantee that employment will fall. If firms have a positive outlook about the future, they will hire more workers even though GDP is shrinking.

Thinking Critically about Policy

1. Based on CIBC's forecast, what do you think will happen to the number of Canadian workers who are unemployed in 2016? What about the unemployment rate?

2. Based on the dynamic AD-AS model and CIBC's forecast what do you think will happen to the price level in 2016? Do you think the inflation rate will be higher or lower than in 2015?

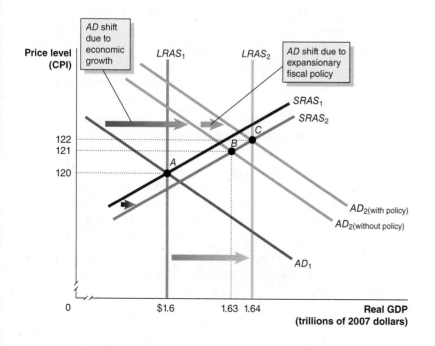

Laurence Geai/SIPA/
Newscom

CHAPTER

10

Money, Banks, and the Bank of Canada

Chapter Outline and Learning Objectives

Can Greece Function without Banks?

How often do you use a bank? If you are like most people, you withdraw cash from an ATM a couple of times per week and occasionally deposit cheques. You may have visited a bank to apply for a student loan or a car loan. Suppose you own your own business. Then you will have had many more interactions with banks. For example, you may have taken out a long-term loan to finance expanding your business. And you probably will also have borrowed money for shorter periods to help pay for inventories and to bridge the gap between when you receive revenue from sales and when you have to pay your workers or suppliers.

Individuals and businesses in most countries would consider it difficult to function without banks. But that's the situation people in Greece faced in 2015. In 2001, Greece and most other European countries abandoned their individual currencies in favor of the euro. (Greece's currency had been the drachma.) Following the 2007–2009 financial crisis, the Greek government had trouble paying interest on the bonds it had issued. Many people feared that Greece might leave the euro and resume using the drachma. If that happened, the drachma might be worth less than the euro, which gave people in Greece an incentive to hold as many euros as they could. In 2015, Greece appeared to be in danger of defaulting on its debts. People responded by withdrawing large amounts of euros from Greek banks. To keep the banks from losing all their funds, the Greek government decided to close the banks for three weeks and limit withdrawals from ATM machines to 60 euros (about $90) per day.

Closing the banks dealt a heavy blow to the Greek economy. With the banks closed, many businesses insisted on being paid in cash. Consumers had trouble finding cash, though, because many ATMs had been emptied of currency. Pharmacies and some grocery stores began accepting promises to pay later from customers who had no cash. One pharmacist noted: "I have countless i.o.u.s behind my counter." Nikos Manisoitis & Son is a Greek firm that imports spices, pasta, and other products. Like other firms that relied on importing goods, the firm had no way to pay for them. The owner complained: "We feel like hostages. We can't move our money from the banks, and we fear that we are about to lose everything." Some importers loaded suitcases with euros and flew to other countries to pay their suppliers.

As we saw in Chapter 6, a country needs a well-functioning financial system if its economy is to prosper and grow. Greece's situation in the summer of 2015 shows what can happen when a country's banking system breaks down. In this chapter, we will study the role banks play in the financial system. We will also discuss the link between changes in the money supply and the inflation rate, as well as provide an overview of the operations of the Bank of Canada, which is Canada's central bank.

Based on Suzanne Daley, Greeks Spend in Droves, Afraid of Losing Savings to a Bailout, New York Times, July 8, 2015; Liz Alderman, Greek Economy under Siege, with Fears That the Worst Is Coming, New York Times, July 9, 2015; and When Banks Die, Economist, July 5, 2015.

Economics in Your Life

What If Money Became Increasingly Valuable?

Most people are used to the fact that as prices rise each year, the purchasing power of money falls. You will be able to buy fewer goods and services with $1000 one year from now, and you will be able to buy even fewer goods and services the year after that. In fact, with an inflation rate of just 3 percent, in 25 years, $1000 will buy only what $475 can buy today. Suppose that you could live in an economy where the purchasing power of money rose each year. What would be the advantages and disadvantages of living in such an economy? As you read this chapter, try to answer these questions. You can check your answers against those we provide on page 286 at the end of this chapter.

In this chapter, we will explore the role of money in the economy. We will see how the banking system creates money and what policy tools the Bank of Canada uses to manage the quantity of money in Canada. We will also examine the crisis in the global banking system during and after the 2007–2009 recession. At the end of the chapter, we will explore the link between changes in the quantity of money and changes in the price level. What you learn in this chapter will serve as an important foundation for understanding monetary policy and fiscal policy, which we study in the next three chapters.

What Is Money, and Why Do We Need It?

Could an economy function without money? There are historical examples of economies in which people traded goods for other goods rather than use money. For example, Canada's indigenous people historically traded furs for European products without using money. Most economies, though, use money. What is money? The economic definition of **money** is any asset that people are generally willing to accept in exchange for goods and services or for payment of debts. Recall that an **asset** is anything of value owned by a person or a firm. There are many possible kinds of money: In West Africa, at one time, cowrie shells served as money. During World War II, prisoners of war used cigarettes as money.

10.1 LEARNING OBJECTIVE

Define money and discuss the four functions of money.

Money Assets that people are generally willing to accept in exchange for goods and services or for payment of debts.

Asset Anything of value owned by a person or a firm.

Barter and the Invention of Money

To understand the importance of money, let's consider further the situation in economies that do not use money. Economies where goods and services are traded directly for other goods and services are called *barter economies*. Barter economies have a major shortcoming. To illustrate this shortcoming, consider a farmer on the recently settled prairies. Suppose the farmer needed another cow and proposed trading a spare plough to a neighbour for one of the neighbour's cows. If the neighbour did not want the plough, the trade would not happen. For a barter trade to take place between two people, each person must want what the other one has. Economists refer to this requirement as a *double coincidence of wants*. The farmer who wants the cow might eventually be able to obtain one if he first trades with some other neighbour for something the neighbour with the cow wants. However, it may take several trades before the farmer is ultimately able to trade for what the neighbour with the cow wants. Locating several trading partners and making several intermediate trades can take considerable time and energy.

To avoid the problems with barter, societies have an incentive to identify a product that most people will accept in exchange for what they have to trade. For example, in colonial times, animal skins were very useful in making clothing. The European demand for beaver fur meant that beaver pelts often traded as money among settlers and indigenous groups. A good used as money that also has value independent of its use as money is called **commodity money**. Historically, once a good became widely accepted as money, people who did not have an immediate use for it would be willing to accept it. Early settlers or members of an indigenous group might not really want a beaver pelt, but would take it knowing that it could be traded for something they really did want.

Trading goods and services is much easier when money becomes available. People only need to sell what they have for money and then use the money to buy what they want. If our fictitious farmer could find someone to buy his plough, he could use the money to buy the cow he wanted. The family with the cow would accept the money because they would know they could use it to buy what they wanted. When money is available, families are more likely to specialize and less likely to produce everything or nearly everything they need themselves.

Most people in modern economies are highly specialized. They do only one thing—work as a nurse, an accountant, or an engineer—and use the money they earn to buy everything else they need. As we discussed in Chapter 2, people become much more productive by specializing because they can pursue their *comparative advantage*. The high income levels in modern economies are based on the specialization that money makes possible. We can now answer the question, "Why do we need money?" *By making exchange easier, money allows people to specialize and become more productive.*

Commodity money A good used as money that also has value independent of its use as money.

The Functions of Money

Anything used as money—whether a deerskin, a cowrie seashell, cigarettes, or a dollar bill—must serve four key functions in the economy.

- It must act as a medium of exchange.
- It must serve as a unit of account.
- It must serve as a store of value.
- It must offer a standard of deferred payment.

Medium of Exchange. Money serves as a medium of exchange when sellers are willing to accept it in exchange for goods or services. When the local supermarket accepts your $5 bill in exchange for bread and milk, the $5 bill is serving as a medium of exchange. With a medium of exchange, people can sell goods and services for money and use the money to buy what they want. An economy is more efficient when a single good is recognized as a medium of exchange.

Unit of Account. In a barter system, each good has many prices. A cow may be worth two ploughs, twenty bushels of wheat, or six axes. Once a single good is used as money, each good has a single price rather than many prices. This function of money gives buyers and sellers a *unit of account*, a way of measuring value in the economy in terms of money. Because the Canadian economy uses dollars as money, each good has a price in terms of dollars.

Store of Value. Money allows people to easily store value. If you do not use all your dollars to buy goods and services today, you can hold the rest to use in the future. Money is not the only store of value, however. Any asset—shares of Facebook stock, Canada bonds, real estate, or Renoir paintings, for example—represents a store of value. Financial assets, such as stocks and bonds, offer an important benefit relative to holding money because they pay a higher rate of interest or may increase in value in the future. Other assets also have advantages relative to money because they provide services. A house, for example, offers you a place to sleep.

Why, then, do people hold any money? The answer has to do with *liquidity*, or the ease with which an asset can be converted into the medium of exchange. Because money is the medium of exchange, it is the most liquid asset. If you want to buy something and you need to sell an asset to do so, you are likely to incur a cost. For example, if you want to buy a car and need to sell bonds or stocks in order to do so, you will need to pay a commission to your broker. To avoid such costs, people are willing to hold some of their wealth in the form of money, even though other assets offer a greater return as stores of value.

Standard of Deferred Payment. Money is useful because it can serve as a standard of deferred payment in borrowing and lending. Money can facilitate exchange at a *given point in time* by providing a medium of exchange and unit of account. Money can facilitate exchange *over time* by providing a store of value and a standard of deferred payment. For example, a computer manufacturer may buy hard drives from another firm in exchange for the promise of making payment in 60 days.

How important is it that money be a reliable store of value and standard of deferred payment? People care about how much food, clothing, and other goods and services their dollars will buy. The value of money depends on its *purchasing power*, which refers to its ability to buy goods and services. Inflation causes a decline in purchasing power because with rising prices, a given amount of money can purchase fewer goods and services. When inflation reaches very high levels, money is no longer a reliable store of value or standard of deferred payment.

What Can Serve as Money?

Having a medium of exchange helps to make transactions easier, which allows the economy to work more efficiently. The next question to consider is: What can serve as money? That is, which assets can be used as the medium of exchange? We saw earlier that an asset must, at a minimum, be generally accepted as payment to serve as money. In practical terms, however, it must be even more.

Five criteria make an asset suitable for use as a medium of exchange:

1. The asset must be *acceptable* to (that is, usable by) most people.
2. It should be of *standardized quality* so that any two units are identical.
3. It should be *durable* so that value is not lost by its quickly wearing out.
4. It should be *valuable* relative to its weight so that amounts large enough to be useful in trade can be easily transported.
5. It should be *divisible* so that it can be used in purchases of both low-priced and high-priced goods.

Dollar bills meet all these criteria. What determines the acceptability of dollar bills as a medium of exchange? Basically, it is through self-fulfilling expectations: You value something as money only if you believe that others will accept it from you as payment. A society's willingness to use paper dollars as money makes dollars an acceptable medium of exchange.

Commodity Money. Commodity money has value independent of its use as money. Gold, for example, was a common form of money in the nineteenth and early twentieth centuries because it was a medium of exchange, a unit of account, a store of value, and a standard of deferred payment. But commodity money has a significant problem: Its value depends on its purity. Therefore, someone who wanted to cheat could mix a low-value metal, like iron, with a precious metal, like gold or silver. Another problem with using gold as money was that the money supply was difficult to control because it depended partly on unpredictable discoveries of new gold fields.

Fiat Money. It can be inefficient for an economy to rely on only gold or other precious metals for its money supply. What if you had to transport bars of gold to settle your transactions? Not only would doing so be difficult and costly, but you would run the risk of being robbed. To get around this problem, private institutions or governments began to store gold and issue paper certificates that could be redeemed for gold. In modern economies, paper currency is generally issued by a *central bank*, which is an agency of the government that regulates the money supply. The **Bank of Canada** is the central bank of Canada. Today, no government in the world issues paper currency that can be redeemed for gold. Paper currency has no value unless it is used as money, and it is therefore not a commodity money. Instead, paper currency is a **fiat money**, which has no value except as money. If paper currency has no value except as money, why do consumers and firms use it?

Canadian currency is fiat money, which means the Bank of Canada is not required to give you gold, silver, or even beaver pelts for your five dollar bills. Currency is *legal tender* in Canada, which means the federal government requires that it be accepted in payment of debts and requires that cash or cheques denominated in dollars be used in payment of taxes. Despite being legal tender, dollar bills would not be a good medium of exchange and could not serve as money if they weren't widely accepted by people. The key to this acceptance is that *households and firms have confidence that if they accept paper dollars in exchange for goods and services, the dollars will not lose much value during the time they hold them.* Without this confidence, dollar bills would not serve as a medium of exchange.

Bank of Canada The central bank of Canada.

Fiat money Money, such as paper currency, that is authorized by a central bank or governmental body and that does not have to be exchanged by the central bank for gold or some other commodity money.

Making the Connection

Apple Didn't Want My Cash!

If currency (paper money and coins) is legal tender, doesn't that mean that everyone in the country, including every business, has to accept paper money and coins? The answer to this question is "no," as a woman in California found out when she went to an Apple store in Palo Alto and tried to buy an iPad using $600 in currency. The store refused to sell her the iPad for cash. At that time, the iPad had just been released, and Apple did not want to sell large numbers to people who were buying them to resell on eBay, Craigslist, or elsewhere. So, a customer wanting to buy an iPad had to pay with either a credit card or a debit card, which would make it easier for Apple to keep track of anyone attempting to buy more than the limit of two per customer.

Because currency is legal tender, creditors must accept it in payment of debts, and the government will accept it in payment of taxes. However, as this incident demonstrates, firms do not have to accept cash as payment for goods and services.

The woman who tried to buy an iPad for cash was disabled and on a limited income, so the incident led to negative publicity for Apple. As a result, Apple decided to lift its ban on paying for iPads with cash, provided that the customer was willing to set up an Apple account at the time of purchase. In addition, Apple presented a free iPad to the customer who was originally turned down when she tried to pay with cash.

The law doesn't stop Apple from requiring customers to use a credit card rather than cash, but the company decided to lift its ban on paying for iPads with cash after bad publicity.

Based on Michael Winter, "Apple Ends No-Cash Policy and California Woman Gets Free iPad," www.usatoday.com, May 20, 2010; and U.S. Treasury, "FAQs: Currency," www.treasury.gov/resource-center/faqs/Currency/Pages/edu_faq_currency_index2.aspx.

MyEconLab   **Your Turn:** Test your understanding by doing related problem 1.5 on page 288 at the end of this chapter.

How Is Money Measured in Canada Today?

Discuss the definitions of the money supply used in Canada today.

People are interested in the money supply because, as we will see, changes in the money supply can affect other economic variables, including employment, gross domestic product (GDP), and inflation. If the only function of money were to serve as a medium of exchange, then a narrow definition of the money supply should include only currency, chequing account deposits, and traveller's cheque, because households and firms can easily use these assets to buy goods and services. A broader definition of the money supply would include other assets that can be used as a medium of exchange even though they are not as liquid as currency or chequing account deposits. For example, you can't directly buy goods or services with funds in a bank savings (non-chequable) account, but it is easy to withdraw funds from your savings account and then use these funds to buy goods and services.

The Bank of Canada has conducted several studies to determine the appropriate definition of *money*. The job of defining the money supply has become more difficult during the past two decades, as innovation in financial markets and institutions has created new substitutes for traditional chequing account deposits. The Bank of Canada uses six different definitions of the money supply: M1+, M1++, M2, M2+, M2++, and M3.

Next, we will look more closely at the Bank of Canada's definitions of the money supply. Central banks outside of Canada use similar measures.

The M1+ and M1++ Definitions of the Money Supply

Panel (a) of Figure 10.1 illustrates the narrow definitions of the money supply in Canada. The narrowest definition is called **M1+**. It includes the following:

1. *Currency,* which is all the paper money and coins held by households and firms (not including currency held by banks)
2. The value of all chequable deposits at chartered banks, trust and mortgage loan companies (TMLs), and credit unions and *caisses populaires* (CUCPs)

These assets are all extremely liquid because they can be turned into cash quickly at very little cost. A broader definition of the money supply is **M1++**. As panel (a) of Figure 10.1 shows, M1++ includes everything that is in M1+ as well as all non-chequable deposits at chartered banks, TMLs, and CUCPs.

The M2, M2+, and M2++ Definitions of the Money Supply

As panel (b) of Figure 10.1 shows, the **M2** money supply includes currency, personal deposits at chartered banks, non-personal demand and notice deposits at chartered banks, and fixed-term deposits. The **M2+** money supply includes everything that is in M2 plus deposits at TMLs, deposits at CUCPs, life insurance company individual annuities, personal deposits at government-owned savings institutions, and money market mutual funds. **M2++** is the broadest definition of the money supply in Canada and includes everything that is in M2+ as well as Canada Savings Bonds and other retail instruments, and non-money market mutual funds.

The M3 Definition of the Money Supply

Another definition of the money supply is *M3*. As panel (c) of Figure 10.1 shows, **M3** includes everything that is in M2 plus non-personal term deposits at chartered banks, and foreign currency deposits of residents at chartered banks.

In the discussion that follows, we will use the M1+ definition of the money supply because it corresponds most closely to money as a medium of exchange. However, there are two key points to keep in mind about the money supply:

1. The money supply consists of *both* currency and chequing and non-chequing account deposits.
2. Because balances in chequing and non-chequing account deposits are included in the money supply, banks play an important role in the way the money supply increases and decreases.

We will discuss this second point further in the next section.

M1+ The narrowest definition of the money supply: It includes currency and other assets that have cheque-writing features—all chequable deposits at chartered banks, TMLs, and CUCPs.

M1++ This broader definition of the money supply includes everything that is in M1+ as well as all non-chequable deposits at chartered banks, TMLs, and CUCPs.

M2 A monetary aggregate that includes currency outside banks and personal deposits at chartered banks, non-personal demand and notice deposits at chartered banks, and fixed-term deposits.

M2+ A broader monetary aggregate that includes everything that is in M2 plus deposits at TMLs, deposits at CUCPs, life insurance company individual annuities, personal deposits at government-owned savings institutions, and money market mutual funds.

M2++ The broadest definition of the money supply: It includes everything that is in M2+ as well as Canada Savings Bonds and other retail instruments, and non-money market mutual funds.

M3 A category within the money supply that includes everything that is in M2 plus non-personal term deposits at chartered banks and foreign currency deposits of residents at chartered banks.

Figure 10.1

Components of the Money Supply

The Bank of Canada uses six different definitions of the money supply: M1+, M1++, M2, M2+, M2++, and M3. M1+ is the narrowest definition of the money supply and M2++ is the broadest.

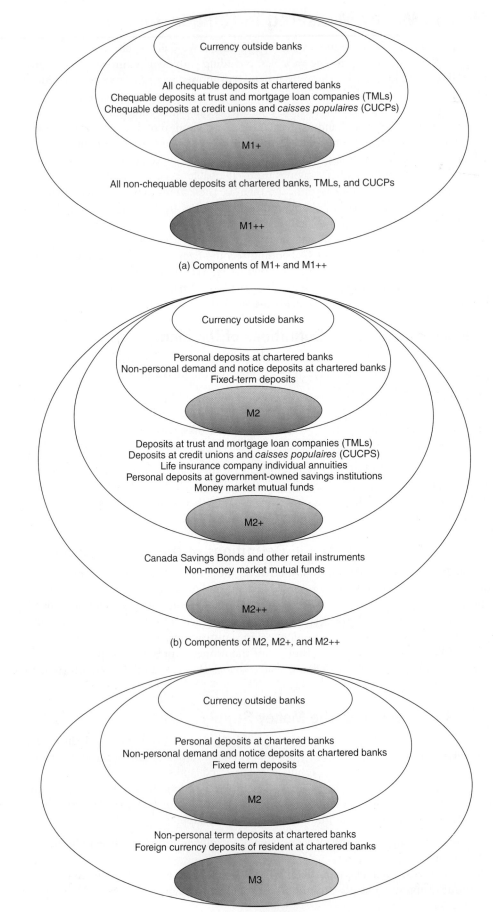

Currency outside banks

All chequable deposits at chartered banks
Chequable deposits at trust and mortgage loan companies (TMLs)
Chequable deposits at credit unions and *caisses populaires* (CUCPs)

M1+

All non-chequable deposits at chartered banks, TMLs, and CUCPs

M1++

(a) Components of M1+ and M1++

Currency outside banks

Personal deposits at chartered banks
Non-personal demand and notice deposits at chartered banks
Fixed-term deposits

M2

Deposits at trust and mortgage loan companies (TMLs)
Deposits at credit unions and *caisses populaires* (CUCPS)
Life insurance company individual annuities
Personal deposits at government-owned savings institutions
Money market mutual funds

M2+

Canada Savings Bonds and other retail instruments
Non-money market mutual funds

M2++

(b) Components of M2, M2+, and M2++

Currency outside banks

Personal deposits at chartered banks
Non-personal demand and notice deposits at chartered banks
Fixed term deposits

M2

Non-personal term deposits at chartered banks
Foreign currency deposits of resident at chartered banks

M3

(c) Component of M3

Making the Connection

Are Bitcoins Money?

Typically, when we think of "money," we think of currency issued by a government. But currency represents only a small part of the Canadian money supply, whether measured as M1+ or M1++. The non-currency components of M1+ or M1++, although not issued by the government, are familiar financial assets such as chequing or savings accounts. Some households and firms have shifted away from M1+ or M1++ to finance their buying and selling of goods and services and are instead using e-money, or digital funds. The best-known form of e-money is PayPal, which until 2015 was owned by eBay, the online auction site. An individual or a firm can set up a PayPal account by transferring funds from a chequing account or credit card. As long as a seller is willing to accept funds from a buyer's PayPal (or other e-money) account, e-money functions like conventional government-issued money.

Bitcoins are created by computer calculations, not by central banks.

Recently, journalists, economists, and policymakers have been debating the merits of bitcoin, a new form of e-money. Unlike PayPal and other similar services for transferring money electronically, bitcoin is not owned by a firm but is instead the product of a decentralized system of linked computers. Bitcoin was founded in 2009 by "Satoshi Nakamoto," which is likely an assumed name taken by bitcoin's founder or founders. Bitcoins are produced by people performing the complicated calculations necessary to ensure that online purchases made with bitcoins are legitimate—that is, that someone doesn't try to spend the same bitcoin multiple times. People who successfully complete these calculations are awarded a fixed amount of bitcoins—typically 25. This process of bitcoin "mining" will continue until a maximum of 21 million bitcoins are produced—a total expected to be reached in 2030.

People can buy and sell bitcoins in exchange for dollars and other currencies on websites, so some people refer to it as a "cryptocurrency." You can buy bitcoins and store them in a "digital wallet" on a smartphone. You can then buy something in a store that accepts bitcoins by scanning a bar code with your phone. A number of websites, such as BitPay, which is based in Atlanta, allow merchants to process purchases made with bitcoins in a way similar to how they process credit card payments.

Why would buyers and sellers prefer to use bitcoins rather than cash or a credit card? The popularity of bitcoins with some buyers may be due to its being a new and fashionable way to make purchases and because of the convenience of using a smartphone to make a purchase. In addition, some people are afraid that because central banks in most countries greatly increased the money supply during and after the recession of 2007–2009, the result will eventually be high rates of inflation. These people hope that because the total amount of bitcoins is limited, inflation will not undermine their value. Finally, when you buy something with a credit card, the credit card company has a permanent record of your transaction. Bitcoin transactions are more private because no such record of your transaction exists.

Some retailers prefer bitcoins to credit card purchases because the retailers pay only about 1 percent of the sale in processing costs, as opposed to about 3 percent for a credit card purchase. In addition, a bitcoin sale is final, just as if the purchase were made with cash, unlike credit card sales, where the buyer can dispute the purchase even months after it was made.

Despite these possible benefits to using bitcoin, by 2015 it had not yet been widely adopted. The introduction of Apple Pay and Google Wallet provided consumers with a way to use their smartphones linked to a credit card to make payments, which undercut one of bitcoin's advantages. Some firms also questioned whether the software underlying bitcoin was capable of dealing with a large number of transactions, which would be a barrier to the cryptocurrency being widely used. The collapse of Mt. Gox, based in Japan, which had been the most popular online bitcoin exchange, also reduced confidence in the cryptocurrency. At the time of its collapse, the firm's CEO said that software problems had allowed hackers to withdraw more than $500 million worth of bitcoins investors had stored on the exchange. The Japanese police later arrested the CEO.

Some policymakers are concerned that investors on exchanges might manipulate the prices of bitcoins and other virtual currencies. The value of bitcoins in exchange for U.S. dollars rose from $5 per bitcoin in June 2012 to $266 per bitcoin in April 2013, before falling to $94 per bitcoin in July 2013 and then rising to $287 in July 2015. Whether these swings in value represented underlying movements in demand and supply for bitcoins or manipulation of their values was not clear.

Should the Bank of Canada include bitcoins and other virtual or cryptocurrencies in its measures of the money supply? So far, the volume of transactions in these currencies has been small, which makes the question of little practical importance. At this point, the Bank of Canada treats virtual currencies as being the equivalent of credit or debit cards, rather than currency or chequing account balances, and does not include them in its definitions of the money supply.

Based on Paul Vigna, "Bitcoiners Decamp to Bretton Woods, Assess the Future of Bitcoin," *Wall Street Journal*, July 30, 2015; Takashi Mochizuki, Japanese Police Arrest Mark Karpelès of Collapsed Bitcoin Exchange Mt. Gox, *Wall Street Journal*, August 1, 2015; Lingling Wei, Fed Studying Risk at Online Payment Providers, *Wall Street Journal*, June 3, 2013; and How Does Bitcoin Work? *Economist*, April 11, 2013.

MyEconLab   **Your Turn:** Test your understanding by doing related problem 2.9 on page 289 at the end of this chapter.

Don't Let This Happen to You

Don't Confuse Money with Income or Wealth

According to *Forbes* magazine, Bill Gates's wealth of US$79 billion makes him the richest person in the world. He also has a very large income, but how much money does he have? Your *wealth* is equal to the value of your assets minus the value of any debts you have. Your *income* is equal to your earnings during the year. Bill Gates's earnings as chairman of Microsoft and from his investments are very large. But his *money* is just equal to what he has in currency and in chequing accounts. Only a small proportion of Gates's US$79 billion in wealth is likely to be in currency or chequing accounts. Most of his wealth is invested in stocks and bonds and other financial assets that are not included in the definition of money.

In everyday conversation, we often describe someone who is wealthy or who has a high income as "having a lot of money." But when economists use the word *money*, they are usually referring to currency plus chequing account deposits. It is important to keep straight the differences between wealth, income, and money.

Just as money and income are not the same for a person, they are not the same for the whole economy. National income in Canada was equal to $1.78 trillion in 2014. The money supply in 2014 was $730 billion (using the M1+ measure). There is no reason why national income in a country should be equal to the country's money supply, nor will an increase in a country's money supply necessarily increase the country's national income.

Source: Based on "The World's Billionaires," *Forbes*, March 2, 2015.

MyEconLab
Your Turn: Test your understanding by doing related problems 2.4 and 2.5 on page 289 at the end of this chapter.

Solved Problem **10.1**

The Definitions of M1+ and M2++

Suppose that you decide to withdraw $2000 from your chequing account and use the money to buy Canada Savings Bonds. Briefly explain how this will affect M1+ and M2++.

Solving the Problem

Step 1: **Review the chapter material.** This problem is about the definitions of the money supply, so you may want to review the section "How Is Money Measured in Canada Today?" which begins on page 263.

Step 2: **Use the definitions of M1+ and M2++ to answer the problem.** Funds in chequable deposit accounts are included in both M1+ and M2++. Funds in non-chequable deposit accounts are included only in M2++. It is tempting to answer this problem by saying that shifting $2000 from a chequable deposit account to a non-chequable deposit account reduces M1+ by $2000 and increases M2++ by $2000, but the $2000 in your chequable deposit account was already counted in M2++. So, the correct answer is that your action reduces M1+ by $2000 but leaves M2++ unchanged.

Your Turn: For more practice, do related problems 2.2 and 2.3 on page 289 at the end of this chapter.

MyEconLab

What about Credit Cards and Debit Cards?

Many people buy goods and services with credit cards, yet credit cards are not included in definitions of the money supply. The reason is that when you buy something with a credit card, you are in effect taking out a loan from the bank that issued the credit card. The transaction is complete only when you pay your credit card bill at the end of the month—often with a cheque or an electronic transfer from your chequing account. In contrast, with a debit card, the funds to make the purchase are taken directly from your chequing account. In either case, the cards themselves do not represent money.

How Do Banks Create Money?

We have seen that the most important component of the money supply is chequing accounts in banks. To understand the role money plays in the economy, we need to look more closely at how banks operate. Banks are profit-making private businesses, just like department stores and supermarkets. Some banks are quite small, with just a few branches, and they do business in a limited area. Others are among the largest corporations in Canada, with thousands of branches spread across many provinces. Banks play an important role in the economy by accepting deposits and making loans. By taking these actions, banks fulfill a key function in the *money supply process* by which central banks control the money supply.

Bank Balance Sheets

To understand how banks create money, we need to briefly examine a typical bank balance sheet. On a balance sheet, a firm's assets are listed on the left, and its liabilities and shareholders' equity are listed on the right. Assets are the value of anything owned by the firm, liabilities are the value of anything the firm owes, and shareholders' equity is the difference between the total value of assets and the total value of liabilities. Shareholders' equity represents the value of the firm if it had to be closed, all its assets were sold, and all its liabilities were paid off. A corporation's shareholders' equity is also called its *net worth*. A bank's shareholders' equity or net worth is also called its *capital*.

Figure 10.2 shows a typical balance sheet for a large bank. The key assets on a bank's balance sheet are its *reserves*, *loans*, and *securities*, such as Canada bonds.

Reserves are deposits that a bank has retained rather than loaned out or invested. Banks keep reserves either physically within the bank, as *vault cash*, or on deposit with the Bank of Canada. Banks desire to keep a fraction of their deposits as reserves: in 2015, banks kept about 5 percent of their deposits as reserves. These reserves are called **desired reserves**. The minimum fraction of deposits that banks desire to keep as reserves is called the **desired reserve ratio**. We can abbreviate the desired reserve ratio as r_d.

Reserves Deposits that a bank keeps as cash in its vault or on deposit with the Bank of Canada.

Desired reserves Reserves that a bank desires to hold, based on its chequing account deposits.

Desired reserve ratio The minimum fraction of deposits banks desire to keep as reserves.

Figure 10.2

Balance Sheet for Royal Bank, July 31, 2015

The items on a bank's balance sheet of greatest economic importance are its reserves, loans, and deposits. Notice that the difference between the value of this bank's total assets and its total liabilities is equal to its shareholders' equity. As a consequence, the left side of the balance sheet always equals the right side.

Note: Some entries have been combined to simplify the balance sheet.

Source: Data from the Office of the Superintendent of Financial Institutions. (Accessed on October 10, 2015.)

Asset (in millions of dollars)		Liabilities and Stockholders' Equity (in millions of dollars)	
Reserves	31 319	Deposits	647 433
Loans	814 959	Borrowing	12 761
Securities	235 515	Other liabilities	363 080
Other assets	3 379		
		Total liabilities	1 023 274
		Stockholders' equity	61 898
Total assets	1 085 172	Total liabilities and stockholders' equity	1 085 172

Source: http://www.osfi-bsif.gc.ca/Eng/Pages/default.aspx (accessed on October 10, 2015).

Excess reserves Reserves that banks hold over and above the desired amounts.

Any reserves that banks hold over and above the desired amounts are called **excess reserves**. The balance sheet in Figure 10.2 shows that loans are this bank's largest asset, which is true of most banks.

Banks make *consumer loans* to households and *commercial loans* to businesses. A loan is an asset to a bank because it represents a promise by the person taking out the loan to make certain specified payments to the bank. A bank's reserves and its holdings of securities are also assets because they are things of value owned by the bank.

Deposits are a typical bank's largest liability. Deposits include chequing accounts, savings accounts, and certificates of deposit. Deposits are liabilities to banks because they are owed to the households or firms that have deposited the funds. If you deposit $100 in your chequing account, the bank owes you the $100, and you can ask for it back at any time. So, your chequing account is an asset to you, and it is a liability to the bank. Banks also borrow short term from other banks and from the Federal Reserve and borrow long term by selling bonds to investors. These *borrowings* are also liabilities.

Making the Connection

Would You Borrow from an Online Peer-to-Peer Lender?

The basic business of banks is taking in deposits from savers and using those funds to make loans to households and firms. Banks often require *collateral* before making a loan, which means that if the borrower stops making payments on the loan, the bank can seize the asset pledged by the borrower as collateral. For example, if you take out a loan to buy a car and stop making payments on the loan, the bank can repossess your car and sell it to get its money back.

In addition to collateral, banks rely on a borrower's *credit score* in deciding whether to make a loan. The higher the credit score, the less likely the borrower is to default. Credit scores are determined by a variety of factors, including whether the buyer has been on time with payments on other loans and on credit cards; how long the borrower has lived at his current residence; how long the buyer has held her current job; and how much other debt the buyer has. Borrowers with high scores are called *prime borrowers*, and borrowers with low scores are called *subprime borrowers*. A bank will typically charge a prime borrower a lower interest rate than it will charge a subprime

Air Images/Shutterstock

Some people with low credit scores who can't get a bank loan turn to peer-to-peer lending to borrow the funds to meet needs such as buying furniture.

borrower. The higher interest rate on a *subprime loan* compensates the bank for the greater risk that the borrower will default.

During the housing bubble of the early 2000s in the United States, many banks and other lenders made mortgage loans to subprime borrowers buying houses. High default rates on these mortgages following the bursting of the housing bubble in 2006 contributed to the 2007–2009 financial crisis and led policymakers in the United States and other countries to tighten regulations on banks granting subprime loans. Some consumer advocates also criticize these loans because they believe that the high interest rates exploit borrowers. To avoid both the new regulations and the criticism, many banks have cut back on subprime loans, particularly subprime *personal loans*, which are made to individuals who do not provide collateral for the loan. In past years, after getting a job, many new university graduates would take out a personal loan from a bank to buy the furniture or small appliances needed to set up an apartment. You may have a low credit score if you were late with a couple of credit card payments, have only a short work history, or have just moved into a new apartment. A bank may then consider you a subprime borrower and be unwilling to lend you money.

You could borrow on your credit card by taking a cash advance, but the interest rate is likely to be high—typically more than 20 percent. When banks cut back on subprime personal loans, it left a hole in the financial system. In the past few years, some new businesses have developed to fill that hole. For example, Lending Club and FreedomPlus in the United States and Grouplend and FundThrough in Canada facilitate peer-to-peer lending on the Internet. These businesses gather information on borrowers, determine the interest rate on the loan, and then post the loan online. Individual investors can then fund the loans. Some loans are funded by a single investor, while others are funded by several investors. The loans can be as short as a few weeks or as long as several years and have interest rates from 7 percent to more than 20 percent, with the typical interest rate being around 14 percent. These firms are part of what is sometimes called the "sharing economy," which also includes the car-ride firm Uber and short-term apartment rental firm Airbnb. In this case, it's money that is being shared.

By 2015, peer-to-peer lending sites were making $10 billion worth of loans. While this amount has been growing rapidly, it still far less than the trillions of dollars in loans of all types made by banks. It remains to be seen whether the peer-to-peer lending sites will end up becoming a major source of credit to households and firms.

Based on Ianthe Jeanne Dugan and Telis Demos, New Lenders Spring Up to Cater to Subprime Sector, *Wall Street Journal*, March 5, 2014; and From the People, for the People, *Economist*, May 9, 2015. Sonya Bell, Alternative lending bubbles up into Canadian mainstream, gains traction among entrepreneurs, *Financial Post*, July 7, 2015.

Your Turn: Test your understanding by doing related problem 3.6 on page 290 at the end of this chapter.

MyEconLab

Using T-Accounts to Show How a Bank Can Create Money

It is easier to show how banks create money by using a T-account than by using a balance sheet. A T-account is a stripped-down version of a balance sheet that shows only how a transaction *changes* a bank's balance sheet. Suppose you deposit $1000 in currency into an account at Bank of Montreal. This transaction raises the total deposits at Bank of Montreal by $1000 and also raises its reserves by $1000. We show this result on the following T-account:

Assets		Liabilities	
Reserves	+$1000	Deposits	+$1000

Your deposit of $1000 into your chequing account increases Bank of Montreal's assets and liabilities by the same amount.

Remember that because the total value of all the entries on the right side of a balance sheet must always be equal to the total value of all the entries on the left side of a balance sheet, any transaction that increases (or decreases) one side of the balance sheet must also increase (or decrease) the other side of the balance sheet. In this case, the T-account shows that we increased both sides of the balance sheet by $1000.

Initially, this transaction does not increase the money supply. The currency component of the money supply declines by $1000 because the $1000 you deposited is no longer in circulation and, therefore, is not counted in the money supply. But the decrease in currency is offset by a $1000 increase in the chequing account deposit component of the money supply.

This initial change is not the end of the story, however. To simplify the analysis, assume that banks keep 10 percent of deposits as reserves. Because the Bank of Canada pays banks only a low rate of interest on their reserves, the bank rate less 50 basis points, banks have an incentive to loan out or buy securities with the other 90 percent. In this case, Bank of Montreal can keep $100 as desired reserves and loan out the other $900, which represents excess reserves. Assume that Bank of Montreal loans out the $900 to someone to buy a very inexpensive used car. Bank of Montreal could give the $900 to the borrower in currency, but usually banks make loans by increasing the borrower's chequing account. We can show this transaction with another T-account:

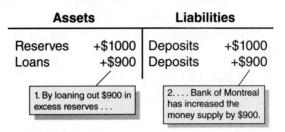

Notice that *by making this $900 loan, Bank of Montreal has increased the money supply by $900.* The initial $1000 in currency you deposited into your chequing account has been turned into $1900 in chequing account deposits—a net increase in the money supply of $900.

But the story does not end here. The person who took out the $900 loan did so to buy a used car. To keep things simple, let's suppose he buys the car for exactly $900 and pays by writing a cheque on his account at Bank of Montreal. The seller of the used car will now deposit the cheque in her bank. That bank may also be a branch of Bank of Montreal, but in most cities, there are many banks, so let's assume that the seller of the car has her account at a branch of Royal Bank. Once she deposits the cheque, Royal Bank will send it to Bank of Montreal to *clear* the cheque and collect the $900. We show the result in the following T-accounts:

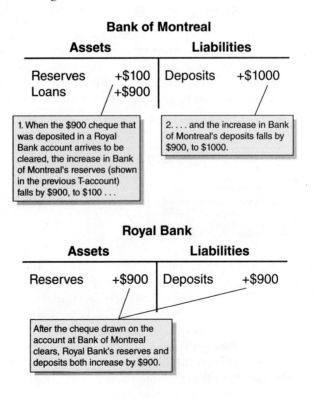

After the car buyer's cheque clears, Bank of Montreal has lost $900 in deposits—the amount loaned to the car buyer—and $900 in reserves—the amount it had to pay Royal Bank when Royal Bank sent Bank of Montreal the car buyer's cheque. Royal Bank has an increase in chequing account deposits of $900—the deposit of the car seller—and an increase in reserves of $900—the amount it received from Bank of Montreal.

Royal Bank has 100 percent reserves against this new $900 deposit, but it needs only 10 percent reserves. The bank has an incentive to keep $90 as reserves and to loan out the other $810, which are excess reserves. If Royal Bank does this, we can show the change in its balance sheet by using another T-account:

Royal Bank

Assets		Liabilities	
Reserves	+$900	Deposits	+$900
Loans	+$810	Deposits	+$810

By making an $810 loan, Royal Bank has increased both its loans and its deposits by $810.

In loaning out the $810 in excess reserves, Royal Bank creates a new chequing account deposit of $810. The initial deposit of $1000 in currency into Bank of Montreal has now resulted in the creation of $1000 + $900 + $810 = $2710 in chequing account deposits. The money supply has increased by $2710 − $1000 = $1710.

The process is still not finished. The person who borrows the $810 will spend it by writing a cheque against his account. Whoever receives the $810 will deposit it in her bank, which could be a Bank of Montreal branch or a Royal Bank branch or a branch of some other bank. That new bank—if it's not Royal Bank—will send the cheque to Royal Bank and will receive $810 in new reserves. That new bank will have an incentive to loan out 90 percent of these reserves—keeping 10 percent to meet the desired reserves—and the process will go on. At each stage, the additional loans being made and the additional deposits being created are shrinking by 10 percent, as each bank wants to withhold that amount as desired reserves. We can use a table to show the total increase in chequing account deposits set off by your initial deposit of $1000. The dots in the table represent additional rounds in the money creation process:

Bank	Increase in Chequing Account Deposits
Bank of Montreal	$1000
Royal Bank	+ 900 (= 0.9 × $1000)
Third Bank	+ 810 (= 0.9 × $ 900)
Fourth Bank	+ 729 (= 0.9 × $ 810)
•	+ •
•	+ •
•	+ •
Total change in chequing account deposits	= $10 000

The Simple Deposit Multiplier

Your initial deposit of $1000 increased the reserves of the banking system by $1000 and led to a total increase in chequing account deposits of $10 000. The ratio of the amount of deposits created by banks to the amount of new reserves is called the **simple deposit multiplier**. In this case, the simple deposit multiplier is equal to $10 000/$1000 = 10. Why 10? How do we know that your initial $1000 deposit ultimately leads to a total increase in deposits of $10 000?

There are two ways to answer this question. First, each bank in the process is keeping desired reserves equal to 10 percent of its deposits. For the banking system as a whole, the total increase in reserves is $1000—the amount of your original currency deposit.

Simple deposit multiplier The ratio of the amount of deposits created by banks to the amount of new reserves.

Therefore, the system as a whole will end up with $10 000 in deposits because $1000 is 10 percent of $10 000.

A second way to answer the question is by deriving an expression for the simple deposit multiplier. The total increase in deposits equals:

$$\$1000 + [0.9 \times \$1000] + [(0.9 \times 0.9) \times \$1000] + [(0.9 \times 0.9 \times 0.9) \times \$1000] + \ldots$$

or

$$\$1000 + [0.9 \times \$1000] + [0.9^2 \times \$1000] + [0.9^3 \times \$1000] + \ldots$$

or

$$\$1000 \times (1 + 0.9 + 0.9^2 + 0.9^3 + \ldots).$$

The rules of algebra tell us that an expression like the one in the parentheses sums to

$$\frac{1}{1 - 0.9}$$

Simplifying further, we have

$$\frac{1}{0.10} = 10.$$

So

$$\text{Total increase in deposit} = \$1000 \times 10 = \$10\ 000$$

Note that 10 is equal to 1 divided by the desired reserve ratio, r_d, which in this case is 10 percent, or 0.10. So, we have another way of expressing the simple deposit multiplier:

$$\text{Simple deposit multiplier} = \frac{1}{r_d}$$

This formula makes it clear that the higher the desired reserve ratio, the smaller the simple deposit multiplier. With a desired reserve ratio of 10 percent, the simple deposit multiplier is 10. If the desired reserve ratio were 20 percent, the simple deposit multiplier would fall to 1/0.20, or 5.

We can use this formula to calculate the total increase in chequing account deposits from an increase in bank reserves due to, for instance, currency being deposited in a bank:

$$\text{Change in chequing account deposits} = \text{Change in bank reserves} \times \frac{1}{r_d}$$

For example, if $100 000 in currency is deposited in a bank and the desired reserve ratio is 10 percent, then:

$$\text{Change in chequing account deposits} = \$100\ 000 \times \frac{1}{0.10}$$

$$= \$100\ 000 \times 10 = \$1\ 000\ 000$$

Don't Let This Happen to You

Don't Confuse Assets and Liabilities

Consider the following reasoning: "How can chequing account deposits be a liability to a bank? After all, they are something of value that is in the bank. Therefore, chequing account deposits should be counted as a bank *asset* rather than as a bank liability."

This statement is incorrect. The balance in a chequing account represents something the bank *owes* to the owner of the account. Therefore, it is a liability to the bank, although it is an asset to the owner of the account. Similarly, your car loan is a liability to you—because it is a debt you owe to the bank—but it is an asset to the bank.

MyEconLab
Your Turn: Test your understanding by doing related problem 3.5 on page 289 at the end of this chapter.

Solved Problem **10.2**

Showing How Banks Create Money

Suppose that you deposit $5000 in currency into your chequing account at a branch of Royal Bank, which we will assume has no excess reserves at the time you make your deposit. Also assume that the desired reserve ratio is 0.10.

a. Use a T-account to show the initial effect of this transaction on Royal Bank's balance sheet.

b. Suppose that Royal Bank makes the maximum loan it can from the funds you deposited. Use a T-account to show the initial effect on Royal Bank's balance sheet from granting the loan. Also include in this T-account the transaction from question (a).

c. Now suppose that whoever took out the loan in question (b) writes a cheque for this amount and that the person receiving the cheque deposits it in Bank of Montreal. Show the effect of these transactions on the balance sheets of Royal Bank and Bank of Montreal *after the cheque has cleared*. On the T-account for Royal Bank, include the transactions from questions (a) and (b).

d. What is the maximum increase in chequing account deposits that can result from your $5000 deposit? What is the maximum increase in the money supply that can result from your deposit? Explain.

Solving the Problem

Step 1: **Review the chapter material.** This problem is about how banks create chequing account deposits, so you may want to review the section "Using T-Accounts to Show How a Bank Can Create Money," which begins on page 269.

Step 2: **Answer part (a) by using a T-account to show the effect of the deposit.** Keeping in mind that T-accounts show only the changes in a balance sheet that result from the relevant transaction and that assets are on the left side of the account and liabilities are on the right side, we have:

Royal Bank

Assets		Liabilities	
Reserves	+$5000	Deposits	+$5000

Because the bank now has your $5000 in currency in its vault, its reserves (and, therefore, its assets) have risen by $5000. But this transaction also increases your chequing account balance by $5000. Because the bank owes you this money, the bank's liabilities have also risen by $5000.

Step 3: **Answer part (b) by using a T-account to show the effect of the loan.** The problem tells you to assume that Royal Bank currently has no excess reserves and that the desired reserve ratio is 10 percent. This means that if the bank's chequing account deposits go up by $5000, the bank wants to keep $500 as reserves and can loan out the remaining $4500. Remembering that new loans usually take the form of setting up, or increasing, a chequing account for the borrower, we have:

Royal Bank

Assets		Liabilities	
Reserves	+$5000	Deposits	+$5000
Loans	+$4500	Deposits	+$4500

The first line of the T-account shows the transaction from question (a). The second line shows that Royal Bank has loaned out $4500 by increasing the chequing account of the borrower by $4500. The loan is an asset to Royal Bank because it represents a promise by the borrower to make certain payments spelled out in the loan agreement.

Step 4: **Answer part (c) by using T-accounts for Royal Bank and Bank of Montreal to show the effect of the cheque clearing.** We now show the effect of the borrower having spent the $4500 he received as a loan from Royal Bank. The person who received the $4500 cheque deposits it in her account at Bank of Montreal. We need two T-accounts to show this activity:

Royal Bank

Assets		Liabilities	
Reserves	+$500	Deposits	+$5000
Loans	+$4500		

Bank of Montreal

Assets		Liabilities	
Reserves	+$4500	Deposits	+$4500

Look first at the T-account for Royal Bank. Once Bank of Montreal sends the cheque written by the borrower to Royal Bank, Royal Bank loses $4500 in reserves, and Bank of Montreal gains $4500 in reserves. The $4500 is also deducted from the account of the borrower. Royal Bank is now satisfied with the result. It received a $5000 deposit in currency from you. When that money was sitting in the bank vault, it wasn't earning any interest for Royal Bank. Now $4500 of the $5000 has been loaned out and is earning interest. These interest payments allow Royal Bank to cover its costs and earn a profit, which it has to do to remain in business.

Bank of Montreal now has an increase in deposits of $4500, resulting from the cheque being deposited, and an increase in reserves of $4500. Bank of Montreal is in the same situation as Royal Bank was in question (a): It has excess reserves as a result of this transaction and a strong incentive to lend them out.

Step 5: **Answer part (d) by using the simple deposit multiplier formula to calculate the maximum increase in chequing account deposits and the maximum increase in the money supply.** The simple deposit multiplier expression is (remember that r_d is the desired reserve ratio):

$$\text{Change in chequing account deposits} = \text{Change in bank reserves} \frac{1}{r_d}$$

In this case, bank reserves rose by $5000 as a result of your initial deposit, and the desired reserve ratio is 0.10, so:

$$\text{Change in chequing account deposits} = \$5000 \times \frac{1}{0.10}$$

$$= \$5000 \times 10 = \$50\ 000$$

Because chequing account deposits are part of the money supply, it is tempting to say that the money supply has also increased by $50 000. Remember, though, that your $5000 in currency was counted as part of the money supply while you had it, but it is not included when it is sitting in a bank vault. Therefore:

$$\text{Increase in chequing account deposits} - \text{Decline in currency in} \\ \text{circulation} = \text{Change in the money supply}$$

or

$$\$50\ 000 - \$5000 = \$45\ 000.$$

MyEconLab **Your Turn:** For more practice, do related problem 3.3 on page 289 at the end of the chapter.

The Simple Deposit Multiplier versus the Real-World Deposit Multiplier

The story we have just told of the money supply process has been simplified in two ways. First, we assumed that banks do not keep any excess reserves. That is, we assumed that when you deposited $1000 in currency into your chequing account at Bank of Montreal, it loaned out $900, keeping only the $100 in desired reserves. In fact, banks often, and especially during anxious times, keep some excess reserves to guard against the possibility that many depositors may simultaneously make withdrawals from their accounts. During the financial crisis that began in 2007, banks kept substantial excess reserves. The more excess reserves banks keep, the smaller the deposit multiplier. Imagine an extreme case in which Bank of Montreal keeps your entire $1000 as reserves. If Bank of Montreal does not loan out any of your deposit, the process described earlier—loans leading to the creation of new deposits, leading to the making of additional loans, and so on—will not take place. The $1000 increase in reserves will lead to a total increase of $1000 in deposits, and the deposit multiplier will be only 1, not 10.

Second, we assumed that the whole amount of every cheque is deposited in a bank; no one takes any of it out as currency. In reality, households and firms keep roughly constant the amount of currency they hold relative to the value of their chequing account balances. So, we would expect to see people increasing the amount of currency they hold as the balances in their chequing accounts rise. Once again, think of the extreme case. Suppose that when Bank of Montreal makes the initial $900 loan to the borrower who wants to buy a used car, the seller of the car cashes the cheque instead of depositing it. In that case, Royal Bank does not receive any new reserves and does not make any new loans. Once again, the $1000 increase in your chequing account at Bank of Montreal is the only increase in deposits, and the deposit multiplier is 1.

The effect of these two simplifications is to reduce the real-world deposit multiplier. However, the key point to bear in mind is that the most important part of the money supply is the chequing account balance component. When banks make loans, they increase chequing account balances, and the money supply expands. Banks make new loans whenever they gain reserves. The whole process can also work in reverse: If banks lose reserves, they reduce their outstanding loans and deposits, and the money supply contracts.

We can summarize these important conclusions:

1. When banks gain reserves, they make new loans, and the money supply expands.
2. When banks lose reserves, they reduce their loans, and the money supply contracts.

The Bank of Canada

10.4 LEARNING OBJECTIVE

Discuss the policy tools the Bank of Canada uses to manage the money supply.

Many people are surprised to learn that banks do not keep locked away in their vaults all the funds that are deposited in chequing accounts. Canada, like nearly all other countries, has a **fractional reserve banking system**, which means that banks keep less than 100 percent of deposits as reserves. When people deposit money in a bank, the bank loans most of the money to someone else. What happens if depositors want their money back? Depositors withdrawing money would seem to be a problem because banks have loaned out most of the money and can't easily get it back.

Fractional reserve banking system A banking system in which banks keep less than 100 percent of deposits as reserves.

In practice, withdrawals are usually not a problem for banks. On a typical day, about as much money is deposited as is withdrawn. If a small amount more is withdrawn than deposited, banks can cover the difference from their excess reserves or by borrowing from other banks. Sometimes depositors lose confidence in a bank when they question the value of the bank's underlying assets, particularly its loans. Often, the reason for a loss of confidence is bad news, whether true or false. When many depositors simultaneously decide to withdraw their money from a bank, there is a **bank run**. If many banks experience runs at the same time, the result is a **bank panic**. It is possible for one bank to handle a run by borrowing from other banks, but if many banks simultaneously experience runs, the banking system may be in trouble.

Bank run A situation in which many depositors simultaneously decide to withdraw money from a bank.

Bank panic A situation in which many banks experience runs at the same time.

A *central bank*, like the Bank of Canada, can help stop a bank panic by acting as a *lender of last resort*. In acting as a lender of last resort, a central bank makes loans to banks that cannot borrow funds elsewhere. The banks can use these loans to pay off depositors. When the panic ends and the depositors put their money back in their accounts, the banks can repay the loans to the central bank.

The Establishment of the Bank of Canada

The Bank of Canada plays a central role in the Canadian economy. It conducts monetary policy, designs and issues currency, promotes a stable financial system, manages the funds of the federal government, and even engages in important economic research. Given its important role in the Canadian economy, you might be surprised to learn that the Bank of Canada is less than 100 years old. It was created after a Royal Commission in 1933 and came into being in 1934.

Board of directors (of the Bank of Canada) A board with 15 members (including the governor) that is responsible for the management of the Bank of Canada.

The overall responsibility for the operation of the Bank of Canada rests with a **board of directors**, which consists of 15 members—the governor, the senior deputy governor, the deputy minister of finance, and 12 outside directors. The board appoints the governor and senior deputy governor, with the government's approval, for a renewable term of seven years. The outside directors are appointed by the minister of finance, with Cabinet approval, for a three-year term, and they are required to come from all regions of Canada and represent a variety of occupations with the exception of banking. The governor of the Bank of Canada is the chief executive officer and chair of the board of directors. Currently, the governor of the Bank of Canada is Stephen Poloz, appointed in May 2013 for a term of seven years.

Governing council (of the Bank of Canada) A council with six members (including the governor) that is responsible for the management of the Bank of Canada.

In 1994 the board of directors made some changes to the internal organization of the Bank of Canada. The most prominent change was the establishment of a new senior decision-making authority within the Bank of Canada called the **governing council**. The governing council is chaired by the governor and is composed of the senior deputy governor and four deputy governors. Since this change, the six members of the governing council collectively assume responsibility for the Bank of Canada's quarterly *Monetary Policy Report* that presents the Bank of Canada's projections for inflation and growth and its assessment of risks in the Canadian economy. This system of "collective responsibility" ensures that the Bank of Canada's governor is not personally identified with the Bank of Canada's policy.

Monetary policy The actions the Bank of Canada takes to manage the money supply and interest rates to pursue macroeconomic policy objectives.

The Bank of Canada is responsible for **monetary policy** in Canada, but the objectives of monetary policy are determined jointly by the Bank of Canada and the minister of finance, with the latter acting on behalf of the federal government. In fact, the governor of the Bank of Canada and the minister of finance consult regularly and, in the event of a serious disagreement over the conduct of monetary policy, the government has the right to override the Bank of Canada's decisions. In particular, the minister of finance can issue a directive to the Bank of Canada indicating the specific policy changes that the Bank of Canada must follow. However, the directive must be published, indicating not only the new policy that the Bank of Canada is supposed to undertake but also the period during which it is to apply.

Hence, ultimate responsibility for monetary policy rests with the democratically elected government, with the Bank of Canada having instrumental independence but not goal independence. However, because of the consequences of issuing a directive, it is unlikely that such a directive would be issued, and none has been issued to date. (For more information on monetary policy, see Chapter 11.)

The Bank of Canada's Operating Band for the Overnight Interest Rate

Overnight interest rate The interest rate banks charge each other for overnight loans.

Key policy rate The Bank of Canada's target for the overnight interest rate.

Collateralized transactions Transactions that involve property being pledged to the lender to guarantee payment in the event that the borrower is unable to make debt payments.

The Bank of Canada signals its stance on monetary policy by announcing a target for the **overnight interest rate**. The target for the overnight interest rate, known as the **key policy rate** (or *policy rate*, for short), is the Bank of Canada's main tool for conducting monetary policy. This rate refers to **collateralized transactions** in the overnight interbank market. (For more information on the overnight interest rate, see Chapter 11.)

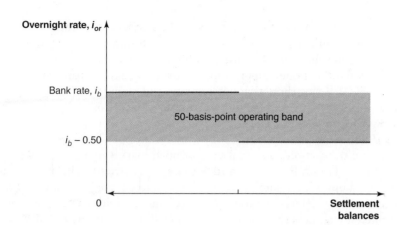

Figure 10.3

Operating Band for the Overnight Interest Rate

The upper limit of the operating band for the overnight interest rate defines the bank rate (or lending rate), and the lower limit of the operating band defines the deposit rate.

In normal times, the Bank of Canada's operational objective is to keep the overnight interest rate within an **operating band** (also known as a *channel* or *corridor*) of 50 basis points (half of 1 percent). This channel/corridor system for setting the overnight interest rate is also used by the Reserve Bank of Australia, the Bank of England, the European Central Bank, the Bank of Japan, the Reserve Bank of New Zealand, Norges Bank of Norway, and the Riksbank of Sweden.

As Figure 10.3 shows, the upper limit of the operating band defines the **bank rate**, i_b. The bank rate is the interest rate the Bank of Canada charges financial institutions that require an overdraft loan to cover negative **settlement balances** on the Bank of Canada's books at the end of the banking day. Loans that the Bank of Canada makes to banks are referred to as **advances to banks**. The lower limit of the operating band is the rate the Bank of Canada pays to financial institutions with positive settlement balances at the end of the day. The midpoint of the operating band is the Bank of Canada's target for the overnight interest rate. For example, when the operating band is from 0.75 percent to 1.25 percent, the bank rate is 1.25 percent, the rate the Bank of Canada pays on deposits to financial institutions is 0.75 percent, and the Bank of Canada's target for the overnight interest rate is 1 percent.

Since December 2000, the Bank of Canada has been operating under a system where any changes to the target and the operating band for the overnight interest rate are announced on eight "fixed" dates throughout the year, and the Bank of Canada has the option of acting between the fixed dates in "extraordinary circumstances." The Bank of Canada implements the operating band for the overnight interest rate by using its **standing liquidity facilities**, lending to and taking deposits from financial institutions. In particular, if the overnight interest rate increases toward the upper limit of the operating band, then the Bank of Canada will lend at the bank rate, i_b, to put a ceiling on the overnight interest rate, i_{or}. If the overnight interest rate declines toward the lower limit of the operating band, then the Bank of Canada will accept deposits from financial institutions at the bank rate less 50 basis points, i_b-0.50, to put a floor on the overnight interest rate.

How the Bank of Canada Implements Monetary Policy

The Bank of Canada is responsible for managing interest rates and the money supply. As we will see in Chapter 11, managing interest rates and the money supply is part of monetary policy, which the Bank of Canada undertakes to pursue macroeconomic objectives (mainly price stability). To manage interest rates and the money supply, the Bank of Canada mainly uses the following two monetary policy tools:

1. Open market buyback operations
2. Lending to financial institutions

Remember that the most important component of the money supply is chequing accounts in banks. Not surprisingly, both of the Bank of Canada's monetary policy tools are aimed at influencing interest rates and bank reserves.

Operating band The Bank of Canada's 50-basis-point range for the overnight interest rate.

Bank rate The interest rate the Bank of Canada charges on loans (advances) to banks.

Settlement balances Deposits held by banks in their accounts at the Bank of Canada.

Advances to banks Loans the Bank of Canada makes to banks.

Standing liquidity facilities The Bank of Canada's readiness to lend to or borrow from a bank.

Open market buyback operations Agreements in which the Bank of Canada, or another party, purchase securities with the understanding that the seller will repurchase them in a short period of time, usually less than a week.

Open market operations The buying and selling of government securities by the Bank of Canada in order to control the money supply.

Monetary base The sum of the Bank of Canada's monetary liabilities (i.e., paper money in circulation and bank settlement balances) and the Canadian Mint's coins outstanding (i.e., coins in circulation).

Purchase and Resale Agreements (PRAs) The Bank of Canada's purchase of government securities from primary dealers (i.e., banks or securities brokers/dealers), with an agreement to resell them later.

Sale and Repurchase Agreements (SRAs) The Bank of Canada's sale of government securities to primary dealers (i.e., banks or securities brokers/dealers), with an agreement to repurchase them later.

Open Market Buyback Operations. **Open market operations** (the buying and selling of government securities) are an important monetary policy tool for many central banks around the world because they are the primary determinants of changes in interest rates and the money supply. Open market purchases expand bank settlement balances, thereby lowering short-term interest rates and raising the money supply. Open market sales shrink bank reserves and the **monetary base**, raising short-term interest rates and lowering the money supply.

Since 1994, the Bank of Canada's most common open market operations have been repurchase transactions, a special type of open market operations. In particular, the Bank of Canada uses **Purchase and Resale Agreements (PRAs)** as a tool to reduce undesired upward pressure on the overnight interest rate, and **Sale and Repurchase Agreements (SRAs)** as a tool to reduce undesired downward pressure on the overnight interest rate. Let's see how the Bank of Canada uses PRAs and SRAs in order to reinforce the target for the overnight interest rate during the course of a day and to manage the money supply.

Assume that the operating band for the overnight interest rate is 0.75 percent to 1.25 percent and that the Bank of Canada is targeting the overnight interest rate at the midpoint of the band, at 1 percent. If overnight funds are traded at a rate higher than the target rate of 1 percent, then the Bank of Canada enters into PRAs at a price that works out to a 1 percent interest rate, the midpoint of the operating band. That is, the Bank of Canada purchases government of Canada Treasury bills and bonds, with an agreement that the sellers will repurchase those Treasury bills and bonds at a specified time in the future. When the sellers of the Canada securities deposit the funds in their banks, the settlement balance of the banks rise. This increase in reserves starts the process of increasing loans and chequing account deposits that increases the money supply.

If, on the other hand, overnight funds are traded at a rate below the target rate of 1 percent, then the Bank of Canada enters into SRAs, in which the Bank of Canada sells government securities and the buyer agrees to sell them back to the Bank of Canada a number of business days later. When the buyers pay for the securities with cheques, the reserves of their banks fall. This decrease in bank reserves starts a contraction of loans and chequing account deposits that reduces the money supply.

The Bank of Canada conducts monetary policy principally through open market buyback operations for three reasons. First, because the Bank of Canada initiates open market buyback operations, it completely controls their volume. Second, the Bank of Canada can make both large and small open market buyback operations. Third, the Bank of Canada can implement its open market buyback operations quickly, with no administrative delay or required changes in regulations. Many other central banks, including the US Federal Reserve, the European Central Bank, and the Bank of Japan, also use open market operations to conduct monetary policy.

The Bank of Canada is responsible for putting the paper currency of Canada into circulation. Recall that if you look at a Canadian bill, you see the words "Bank of Canada: This Note Is Legal Tender." When the Bank of Canada takes actions to increase the money supply, commentators sometimes say that it is "printing more money." The main way the Bank of Canada increases the money supply, however, is not by printing more paper dollars but by buying government securities. Similarly, to reduce the money supply, the Bank of Canada does not set fire to stacks of paper dollars. Instead, it sells government securities. We will spend more time discussing how and why the Bank of Canada manages the money supply in Chapter 11, in which we discuss monetary policy.

Lending to Financial Institutions. As we have seen, the Bank of Canada is operating its standing liquidity facilities to reinforce the operating band for the overnight interest rate. When a bank borrows money from the Bank of Canada by taking out a loan, the interest rate the bank pays is the bank rate, i_b, which is typically higher than the target overnight interest rate by 25 basis points. However, the bank's reserves increase, and with more reserves, the bank will make more loans to households and firms, which will increase chequing account deposits and the money supply.

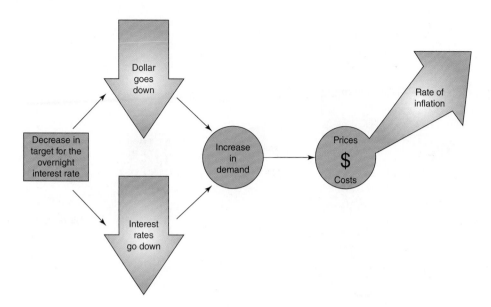

Figure 10.4

How the Bank of Canada Keeps the Rate of Inflation from Falling Below the Target Range

If the Bank of Canada expects the economy to slow down, it lowers the target and operating band for the overnight interest rate. This reduces interest rates and the value of the dollar and leads to an increase in the supply of money, aggregate demand, and the price level, preventing the inflation rate from falling below 1 percent.

Source: From The Bank of Canada. Reprinted with permission.

In addition to its use of standing liquidity facilities to reinforce the operating band for the overnight interest rate, Bank of Canada lending is also important in preventing financial panics. In fact, one of the Bank of Canada's most important roles is to be the lender of last resort in the Canadian economy. It provides emergency lending assistance (against eligible collateral) for a maximum period of six months (which can be extended for periods of up to six months as many times as the Bank of Canada judges necessary) to solvent (but illiquid) deposit-taking institutions to prevent bank failures from spinning further out of control, thereby preventing bank and financial panics.

The Bank of Canada's Approach to Monetary Policy

The goal of the Bank of Canada's current monetary policy is to keep the inflation rate within a target range of 1 to 3 percent, with the midpoint of the inflation target range, 2 percent, being the most desirable outcome. The Bank of Canada implements monetary policy by changing the policy rate in order to influence other short-term interest rates, the exchange rate, and the level of economic activity.

As an example, suppose that the Bank of Canada expects the economy to slow down and wishes to ease monetary conditions. It lowers the target and operating band for the overnight interest rate. As you can see in Figure 10.4, this reduces interest rates and the value of the dollar and leads to an increase in the supply of money, aggregate demand (the total quantity of output demanded in the economy), and the price level, thereby preventing the inflation rate from falling below the target range of 1 to 3 percent.

In the opposite case, if the Bank of Canada expects the economy to exceed its capacity at some point in the future, it raises the operating band in order to prevent inflationary pressures from building. The consequent increase in interest rates and the value of the dollar lead to a decline in the supply of money, aggregate demand, and the inflation rate, thereby preventing the inflation rate from moving above the Bank of Canada's target range of 1 to 3 percent (see Figure 10.5).

The "Shadow Banking System" and the Global Financial Crisis of 2007–2009

The banks we have been discussing in this chapter are *commercial banks*, whose most important economic role is to accept funds from depositors and lend those funds to borrowers. Large firms can sell stocks and bonds on financial markets, but investors are typically unwilling to buy stocks and bonds from small and medium-sized firms because they lack sufficient information on the financial health of smaller firms. So, smaller firms—and households—have traditionally relied on bank loans for their credit needs. In the past 25 years, however, two important developments have occurred in the financial

Figure 10.5

How the Bank of Canada Keeps the Rate of Inflation from Moving Above the Target Range

If the Bank of Canada expects the economy to exceed its capacity, it increases the target and operating band for the overnight interest rate. This increases interest rates and the value of the dollar and leads to a decline in the supply of money, aggregate demand, and the inflation rate, preventing the inflation rate from rising above 1 percent.

Source: From The Bank of Canada. Reprinted with permission.

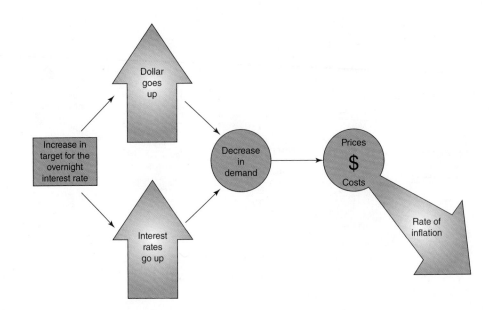

system: (1) Banks have begun to resell many of their loans rather than keeping them until borrowers pay them off, and (2) financial firms other than commercial banks have become sources of credit to businesses.

Securitization Comes to Banking. Traditionally, when a bank made a *residential mortgage loan* to a household to buy a home or made a commercial loan to a business, the bank would keep the loan and collect the payments until the loan was paid off. A financial asset—such as a loan or a stock or a bond—is considered a **security** if it can be bought and sold in a *financial market*. Shares of stock issued by BlackBerry are an example of a security because they can be bought and sold on the Toronto Stock Exchange. When a financial asset is first sold, the sale takes place in the *primary market*. Subsequent sales take place in the *secondary market*. Prior to 1970, most loans were not securities because they could not be resold—there was no secondary market for them. First, residential mortgages and then other loans, including car loans and commercial loans, began to be *securitized*. The process of **securitization** involves creating a secondary market in which loans that have been bundled together can be bought and sold in financial markets, just as corporate or government bonds are. Figure 10.6 outlines the

Security A financial asset—such as a stock or a bond—that can be bought and sold in a financial market.

Securitization The process of transforming loans or other financial assets into securities.

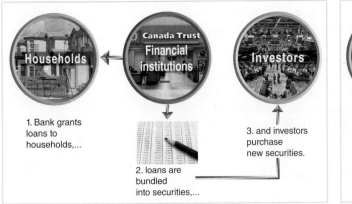

1. Bank grants loans to households,...

2. loans are bundled into securities,...

3. and investors purchase new securities.

(a) Securitizing a loan

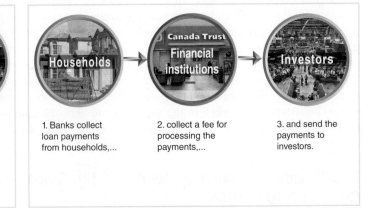

1. Banks collect loan payments from households,...

2. collect a fee for processing the payments,...

3. and send the payments to investors.

(b) The flow of payments on a securitized loan

Figure 10.6 The Process of Securitization

Panel (a) shows how in the securitization process banks grant loans to households and bundle the loans into securities that are then sold to investors. Panel (b) shows that banks collect payments on the original loans and, after taking a fee, send the payments to the investors who bought the securities.

Photo credits : (left to right) AP Photos/Lynne Sladky; Torontonian/Alamy Stock Photo; © EIGHTFISH/Alamy; (bottom) © imagebroker/Alamy

securitization process. We will discuss the process of securitization further in Chapter 11, when we consider monetary policy.

The Shadow Banking System. In addition to the changes resulting from securitization, the financial system was transformed in the 1990s and 2000s by the increasing importance of *nonbank financial firms*. Investment banks, such as BMO Nesbitt Burns and CIBC World Markets in Canada, and Goldman Sachs and Morgan Stanley in the United States, differ from commercial banks in that they do not accept deposits, and they rarely lend directly to households. Instead, investment banks traditionally concentrated on providing advice to firms issuing stocks and bonds or considering mergers with other firms. In the late 1990s, investment banks expanded their buying of mortgages, bundling large numbers of them together as bonds known as *mortgage-backed securities*, and reselling them to investors. Mortgage-backed securities proved very popular with investors because they often paid higher interest rates than other securities with comparable default risk.

Money market mutual funds have also increased their importance in the financial system over time. These funds sell shares to investors and use the money to buy short-term securities such as Treasury bills and commercial paper issued by corporations. Commercial paper represents short-term borrowing corporations use to fund their day-to-day operations. Many corporations that previously met such needs by borrowing from banks began instead to sell commercial paper to money market mutual funds.

Hedge funds raise money from wealthy investors and use sophisticated investment strategies that often involve significant risk. By the mid-2000s, hedge funds had become an important source of demand for securitized loans and an important source of loans to other financial firms.

In 2008, Timothy Geithner, who became Treasury secretary in the Obama administration, used the term the *shadow banking system* to refer to investment banks, money market mutual funds, hedge funds, and other nonbank financial firms engaged in similar activities. By raising money from investors and lending it directly or indirectly to firms and households, these firms carry out a function that at one time was almost exclusively carried out by commercial banks.

The Financial Crisis of 2007–2009. The firms in the shadow banking system differed from commercial banks in two important ways: First, the government agencies—including the Office of the Superintendent of Financial Institutions Canada (OSFI) and the Bank of Canada—that regulated the commercial banking system did not regulate these firms. Second, these firms were more highly *leveraged*—that is, they relied more heavily on borrowed money to finance their operations—than chartered banks. If a firm uses a small amount of its own money and a lot of borrowed money to make an investment, both the firm's potential profits and its potential losses are increased. Suppose a firm invests $100 of its own money. If the investment earns a return of $3, the firm has earned 3 percent ($3/$100) on its funds. But if the firm's investment consists of $10 of its own money and $90 it has borrowed, a return of $3 becomes a return of 30 percent ($3/$10) on the firm's $10 investment. If the investment loses $2, however, the firm's return is −20 percent (−$2/$10). Leveraged investments have a potential for both large gains and large losses.

Chartered banks have rarely experienced bank runs since the federal government established the Canada Deposit Insurance Corporation (CDIC) in 1967 to insure deposits (currently up to $100 000) with all federally chartered banks and near banks. However, beginning in 2007, firms in the shadow banking system were quite vulnerable to runs. As we will discuss further in Chapter 11, the underlying cause of the financial crisis of 2007–2009 was problems in the US housing market. As housing prices began to fall in the United States, a significant number of borrowers began to default on their mortgages, which caused mortgage-backed securities to lose value. Financial firms, including both commercial banks and many firms in the shadow banking system, that had invested in these securities suffered heavy losses. The more leveraged the firm, the larger the losses. Although deposit insurance helped commercial banks avoid runs, investment banks and other financial firms that had borrowed short term and invested the funds long term were in trouble. As lenders refused to renew their short-term loans, many of these firms had to sell their holdings of securities in an attempt to raise cash. But as the prices of these securities continued to fall, the losses to these firms increased.

In the spring of 2008, US investment bank Bear Stearns was saved from bankruptcy only when the Federal Reserve arranged for it to be acquired by JPMorgan Chase. In the fall of 2008, the Federal Reserve and the US Treasury decided not to take action to save the investment bank Lehman Brothers, which failed. The failure of Lehman Brothers echoed throughout the financial system, setting off a panic. The process of securitization—apart from government-guaranteed residential mortgages—ground to a halt. The well-publicized difficulties of a money market mutual fund that had suffered losses on loans to Lehman Brothers led to a wave of withdrawals from these funds. In turn, the funds were no longer able to fulfill their role as buyers of corporate commercial paper. As banks and other financial firms sold assets and cut back on lending to shore up their financial positions, the flow of funds from savers to borrowers was disrupted. The resulting credit crunch significantly worsened the global recession that had begun in December 2007.

10.5 LEARNING OBJECTIVE

Explain the quantity theory of money, and use it to explain how high rates of inflation occur.

The Quantity Theory of Money

People have been aware of the connection between increases in the money supply and inflation for centuries. In the sixteenth century, the Spanish conquered Mexico and Peru and shipped large quantities of gold and silver from those countries back to Spain. The gold and silver were minted into coins and spent across Europe to further the political ambitions of the Spanish kings. Prices in Europe rose steadily during these years, and many observers discussed the relationship between this inflation and the flow of gold and silver into Europe from the Americas.

Connecting Money and Prices: The Quantity Equation

In the early twentieth century, Irving Fisher, an economist at Yale University, formalized the connection between money and prices by using the *quantity equation*:

$$M \times V = P \times Y.$$

Velocity of money The average number of times per year each dollar in the money supply is used to purchase goods and services included in GDP.

The quantity equation states that the money supply (*M*) multiplied by the *velocity of money* (*V*) equals the price level (*P*) multiplied by real output (*Y*). Fisher defined the **velocity of money**, often called simply "velocity," as the average number of times each dollar of the money supply is used to purchase goods and services included in GDP. Rewriting the original equation by dividing both sides by *M*, we have the equation for velocity:

$$V = \frac{P \times Y}{M}$$

If we use M1+ to measure the money supply, the GDP price deflator to measure the price level, and real GDP to measure real output, the value for velocity for 2014 was:

$$V = \frac{1.08 \times \$1747 \text{ billion}}{\$730 \text{ billion}} = 2.6$$

This result tells us that, during 2012, each dollar of M1+ was on average spent about 2.7 times on goods or services included in GDP.

Quantity theory of money A theory about the connection between money and prices that assumes that the velocity of money is constant.

Because velocity is defined to be equal to $(P \times Y)/M$, we know that the quantity equation must always hold true: The left side *must* be equal to the right side. A theory is a statement about the world that might possibly be false. Therefore, the quantity equation is not a theory. Irving Fisher turned the quantity equation into the **quantity theory of money** by asserting that velocity was constant. He argued that the average number of times a dollar is spent depends on how often people get paid, how often they do their grocery shopping, how often businesses mail bills, and other factors that do not change very often. Because this assertion may be true or false, the quantity theory of money is, in fact, a theory.

The Quantity Theory Explanation of Inflation

The quantity equation gives us a way of showing the relationship between changes in the money supply and changes in the price level, or inflation. To see this relationship more clearly, we can use a handy mathematical rule that states that an equation where variables are multiplied together is equal to an equation where the *growth rates* of these variables are *added* together. So, we can transform the quantity equation from:

$$M \times V = P \times Y$$

to:

Growth rate of the money supply + Growth rate of velocity =

Growth rate of the price level (or inflation rate) + Growth rate of real output.

This way of writing the quantity equation is more useful for investigating the effect of changes in the money supply on the inflation rate. Remember that the growth rate for any variable is the percentage change in the variable from one year to the next. The growth rate of the price level is the inflation rate, so we can rewrite the quantity equation to help understand the factors that determine inflation:

Inflation rate = Growth rate of the money supply +

Growth rate of velocity − Growth rate of real output.

If Irving Fisher was correct that velocity is constant, then the growth rate of velocity will be zero. That is, if velocity is, say, always eight, then its percentage change from one year to the next will always be zero. This assumption allows us to rewrite the equation one last time:

Inflation rate = Growth rate of the money supply − Growth rate of real output.

This equation leads to the following predictions:

1. If the money supply grows at a faster rate than real GDP, there will be inflation.
2. If the money supply grows at a slower rate than real GDP, there will be deflation. (Recall that *deflation* is a decline in the price level.)
3. If the money supply grows at the same rate as real GDP, the price level will be stable, and there will be neither inflation nor deflation.

It turns out that Irving Fisher was wrong in asserting that the velocity of money is constant. From year to year, there can be significant fluctuations in velocity. As a result, the predictions of the quantity theory of money do not hold every year, but most economists agree that the quantity theory provides useful insight into the long-run relationship between the money supply and inflation: *In the long run, inflation results from the money supply growing at a faster rate than real GDP.*

How Accurate Are Estimates of Inflation Based on the Quantity Theory?

Note that the accuracy of the quantity theory depends on whether the key assumption that velocity is constant is correct. If velocity is not constant, then there may not be a tight link between increases in the money supply and increases in the price level. For example, an increase in the quantity of money might be offset by a decline in velocity, leaving the price level unaffected. Because velocity can move erratically in the short run, we would not expect the quantity equation to provide good forecasts of inflation in the short run. Over the long run, however, there is a strong link between changes in

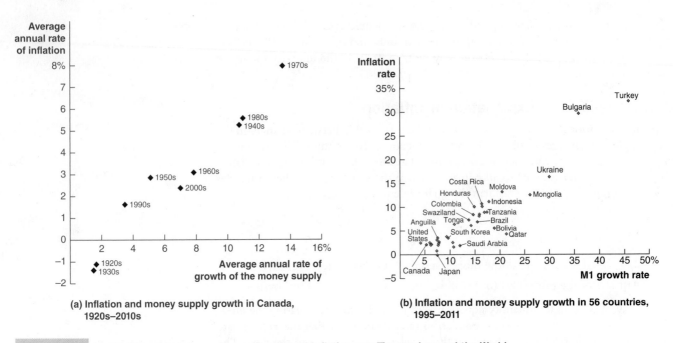

(a) Inflation and money supply growth in Canada, 1920s–2010s

(b) Inflation and money supply growth in 56 countries, 1995–2011

Figure 10.7 The Relationship between Money Growth and Inflation over Time and around the World

Panel (a) shows that, by and large, in Canada, the rate of inflation has been highest during the decades in which the money supply has increased most rapidly, and the rate of inflation has been lowest during the decades in which the money supply has increased least rapidly. Panel (b) shows the relationship between money supply growth and inflation for 56 countries between 1995 and 2011. There is not an exact relationship between money supply growth and inflation, but countries such as Bulgaria, Turkey, and Ukraine that had high rates of money supply growth had high inflation rates, and countries such as the United States and Japan had low rates of money supply growth and low inflation rates.

Sources: Panel (a): Data for 1870 to 1960, M.C. Urquhart, "Canadian Economic Growth 1870-1985," Institute for Economic Research, Queens University: Kingston, Ontario, Discussion Paper No. 734; and since 1961 Statistics Canada CANSIM II series V3860248 and V41552796; Panel (b): International Monetary Fund, *International Monetary Statistics.*

the money supply and inflation. Panel (a) of Figure 10.7 shows the relationship between the growth of the M2 measure of the money supply and the inflation rate by decade in Canada. (We use M2 here because data on M2 are available for a longer period of time.) There is a clear pattern that decades with higher growth rates in the money supply were also decades with higher inflation rates. In other words, most of the variation in inflation rates across decades can be explained by variation in the rates of growth of the money supply.

Panel (b) provides further evidence consistent with the quantity theory by looking at rates of growth of the money supply and rates of inflation across 56 countries for the years 1995–2011. Although there is not an exact relationship between rates of growth of the money supply and rates of inflation across countries, panel (b) shows that countries where the money supply grew rapidly tended to have high inflation rates, while countries where the money supply grew more slowly tended to have much lower inflation rates. Not included in panel (b) are data for Zimbabwe, which may be the most extreme case of inflation in recent years. In some years since 1995, the money supply in Zimbabwe grew by more than 7500 percent. The result was an accelerating rate of inflation that eventually reached 15 billion percent during 2008. Zimbabwe was suffering from *hyperinflation*—that is, a rate of inflation that exceeds 50 percent per month.

High Rates of Inflation

The quantity theory can help us understand the reasons for high rates of inflation. Hyperinflation is caused by central banks increasing the money supply at a rate far in excess of the growth rate of real GDP. A high rate of inflation causes money to lose its value so rapidly that households and firms avoid holding it. If, as happened in

Zimbabwe, the inflation rate becomes high enough, people stop using paper currency, so it no longer serves the important functions of money discussed earlier in this chapter. Economies suffering from high inflation usually also suffer from very slow growth, if not severe recession.

Given the dire consequences that follow from high inflation, why do governments cause it by expanding the money supply so rapidly? The main reason is that governments often want to spend more than they are able to raise through taxes. Developed countries, such as Canada, can usually bridge gaps between spending and taxes by borrowing through selling bonds to the public. Developing countries, such as Zimbabwe, often have difficulty selling bonds because investors are skeptical of their ability to pay back the money. If they are unable to sell bonds to the public, governments in developing countries will force their central banks to purchase them. As we discussed previously, when a central bank buys bonds, the money supply will increase.

Making the Connection | The German Hyperinflation of the Early 1920s

When Germany lost World War I, a revolution broke out that overthrew Kaiser Wilhelm II and installed a new government known as the Weimar Republic. In the peace treaty of 1919, the Allies—the United States, Great Britain, France, and Italy—imposed payments called *reparations* on the new German government. The reparations were meant as compensation to the Allies for the damage Germany had caused during the war. It was very difficult for the German government to use tax revenue to cover both its normal spending and the reparations.

The German government decided to pay for the difference between its spending and its tax revenues by selling bonds to the central bank, the Reichsbank. After a few years, the German government fell far behind in its reparations payments. In January 1923, the French government sent troops into the German industrial area known as the Ruhr to try to collect the payments directly. German workers in the Ruhr went on strike, and the German government decided to support them by paying their salaries. The government raised the funds by selling additional bonds to the Reichsbank, thereby further increasing the money supply.

During the hyperinflation of the 1920s, people in Germany used paper currency to light their stoves.

The inflationary increase in the money supply was very large: The total number of marks—the German currency—in circulation rose from 115 million in January 1922 to 1.3 billion in January 1923 and then to 497 billion *billion*, or 497 000 000 000 000 000 000, in December 1923. Just as the quantity theory predicts, the result was a staggeringly high rate of inflation. The German price index that stood at 100 in 1914 and 1440 in January 1922 had risen to 126 160 000 000 000 in December 1923. The German mark became worthless. The German government ended the hyperinflation by (1) negotiating a new agreement with the Allies that reduced its reparations payments, (2) reducing other government expenditures and raising taxes to balance its budget, and (3) replacing the existing mark with a new mark. Each new mark was worth 1 trillion old marks. The German central bank was also limited to issuing a total of 3.2 billion new marks.

These steps were enough to bring the hyperinflation to an end—but not before the savings of anyone holding the old marks had been wiped out. Most middle-income Germans were extremely resentful of this outcome. Many historians believe that the hyperinflation greatly reduced the allegiance of many Germans to the Weimar Republic and may have helped pave the way for Adolph Hitler and the Nazis to seize power 10 years later.

Source: Based on Thomas Sargent, "The End of Four Big Hyperinflations," Rational Expectations and Inflation (New York: Harper & Row, 1986).

Your Turn: Test your understanding by doing related problem 5.5 on page 290 at the end of this chapter.

MyEconLab

Economics in Your Life

What If Money Became Increasingly Valuable?

At the beginning of this chapter, we asked you to consider whether you would like to live in an economy in which the purchasing power of money rises every year. The first thing to consider when thinking about the advantages and disadvantages of this situation is that the only way for the purchasing power of money to increase is for the price level to fall; in other words, *deflation* must occur. Because the price level in Canada hasn't fallen for an entire year since the 1930s, most people alive today have experienced only rising price levels—and declining purchasing power of money. Would replacing rising prices with falling prices necessarily be a good thing? It might be tempting to say "yes," because if you have a job, your salary will buy more goods and services each year. But, in fact, just as a rising price level results in most wages and salaries rising each year, a falling price level is likely to mean falling wages and salaries each year. So, it is likely that, on average, people would not see the purchasing power of their incomes increase, even if the purchasing power of any currency they hold would increase. There can also be a significant downside to deflation, particularly if the transition from inflation to deflation happens suddenly. Recall that the real interest rate is equal to the nominal interest rate minus the inflation rate. If an economy experiences deflation, then the real interest rate will be greater than the nominal interest rate. A rising real interest rate can be bad news for anyone who has borrowed, including homeowners who may have substantial mortgage loans. So, you are probably better off living in an economy experiencing mild inflation than one experiencing deflation.

Conclusion

Money plays a key role in the functioning of an economy by facilitating trade in goods and services and by making specialization possible. Without specialization, no advanced economy can prosper. Households and firms, banks, and the central bank (such as the Bank of Canada) are participants in the process of creating the money supply. In Chapter 11, we will explore how the Bank of Canada uses monetary policy to promote its economic objectives.

Chapter Summary and Problems

Key Terms

Advances to banks, p. 277

Asset, p. 259

Bank of Canada, p. 262

Bank panic, p. 275

Bank rate, p. 277

Bank run, p. 275

Board of directors (of the Bank of Canada), p. 276

Collateralized transactions, p. 276

Commodity money, p. 260

Desired reserve ratio, p. 267

Desired reserves, p. 267

Excess reserves, p. 268

Fiat money, p. 262

Fractional reserve banking system, p. 275

Governing council (of the Bank of Canada), p. 276

Key policy rate, p. 276

M1+, p. 263

M1++, p. 263

M2, p. 263

M2+, p. 263

M2++, p. 263

M3, p. 263

Monetary base, p. 278

Monetary policy, p. 276

Money, p. 259

Open market buyback operations, p. 277

Open market operations, p. 278

Operating band, p. 277

Overnight interest rate, p. 276

Purchase and Resale Agreements (PRAs), p. 278

Quantity theory of money, p. 282

Reserves, p. 267

Sale and Repurchase Agreements (SRAs), p. 278

Securitization, p. 280

Security, p. 280

Settlement balances, p. 277

Simple deposit multiplier, p. 271

Standing liquidity facilities, p. 277

Velocity of money, p. 282

Summary

*LO 10.1 A *barter economy* is an economy that does not use money and in which people trade goods and services directly for other goods and services. Barter trade occurs only if there is a *double coincidence of wants*, where both parties to the trade want what the other one has. Because barter is inefficient, there is strong incentive to use *money*, which is any *asset* that people are generally willing to accept in exchange for goods or services or in payment of debts. An *asset* is anything of value owned by a person or a firm. A *commodity money* is a good used as money that also has value independent of its use as money. Money has four functions: It is a medium of exchange, a unit of account, a store of value, and a standard of deferred payment. The *gold standard* was a monetary system under which the government produced gold coins and paper currency that were convertible into gold. The gold standard collapsed in the early 1930s. Today, no government in the world issues paper currency that can be redeemed for gold. Instead, paper currency is *fiat money*, which has no value except as money.

LO 10.2 The narrowest definition of the money supply in Canada today is M1+, which includes currency plus all chequable deposits at chartered banks, TMLs, and CUCPs. A broader definition of the money supply is M1++, which includes everything that is in M1+ and all non-chequable deposits at chartered banks, TMLs, and CUCPs. Other definitions of the money supply are M2, M2+, M2++, and M3, with M2++ being the broadest definition of the money supply.

LO 10.3 On a bank's balance sheet, *reserves* and loans are assets, and deposits are liabilities. *Reserves* are deposits that the bank has retained rather than loaned out or invested. *Desired reserves* are reserves that banks desire to hold, based on their chequing account deposits. The fraction of deposits that banks desire to keep as reserves is called the *desired reserve ratio*. Any reserves banks hold over and above the desired reserves are called *excess reserves*. When a bank accepts a deposit, it keeps only a fraction of the funds as reserves and loans out the remainder. In making a loan, a bank increases the chequing account balance of the borrower. When the borrower uses a cheque to buy something with the funds the bank has loaned, the seller deposits the cheque in his or her bank. The seller's bank keeps part of the deposit as reserves and loans out the remainder. This process continues until no banks have excess reserves. In this way, the process of banks making new loans increases the volume of chequing account balances and the money supply. This money creation process can be illustrated with T-accounts, which are stripped-down versions of balance sheets that show only how a transaction changes a bank's balance sheet. The *simple deposit multiplier* is the ratio of the amount of deposits created by banks to the amount of new reserves. An expression for the simple deposit multiplier is $1/r_d$.

LO 10.4 Canada has a *fractional reserve banking system* in which banks keep less than 100 percent of deposits as reserves. In a *bank run*, many depositors decide simultaneously to withdraw money from a bank. In a *bank panic*, many banks experience runs at the same time. The Bank of Canada is the central bank of Canada. It was originally established in 1934. The recession of 2007–2009 put renewed emphasis on the Bank of Canada's goal of financial market stability. *Monetary policy* refers to the actions the Bank of Canada takes to manage the money supply and interest rates to pursue macroeconomic policy objectives. The Bank of Canada's main monetary policy tools are *open market buyback operations* and lending to financial institutions. *Open market operations* are the buying and selling of government securities by the Bank of Canada. The loans the Bank of Canada makes to banks are called *advances to banks*, and the interest rate the Bank of Canada charges on advances to banks is the *bank rate*. In the past 20 years, a "shadow banking system" has developed. During the financial crisis of 2007–2009, the existence of the shadow banking system complicated the policy response of central banks around the world. A *security* is a financial asset—such as a stock or a bond—that can be bought and sold in a financial market. The process of *securitization* involves creating a secondary market in which loans that have been bundled together can be bought and sold in financial markets just as corporate or government bonds are.

LO 10.5 The *quantity equation*, which relates the money supply to the price level, is $M \times V = P \times Y$ where M is the money supply, V is the *velocity of money*, P is the price level, and Y is real output. The *velocity of money* is the average number of times each dollar in the money supply is spent during the year. Economist Irving Fisher developed the *quantity theory of money*, which assumes that the velocity of money is constant. If the quantity theory of money is correct, the inflation rate should equal the rate of growth of the money supply minus the rate of growth of real output. Although the quantity theory of money is not literally correct because the velocity of money is not constant, it is true that in the long run, inflation results from the money supply growing faster than real GDP. When governments attempt to raise revenue by selling large quantities of bonds to the central bank, the money supply will increase rapidly, resulting in a high rate of inflation.

MyEconLab Log in to MyEconLab to complete these exercises and get instant feedback.

Review Questions

LO 10.1

1.1 A baseball fan with a Mike Trout baseball card wants to trade it for a Miguel Cabrera baseball card, but everyone the fan knows who has a Cabrera card doesn't want a Trout card. What do economists call the problem this fan is having?

1.2 What is the difference between commodity money and fiat money?

1.3 What are the four functions of money? Can something be considered money if it does not fulfill all four functions?

1.4 Why do businesses accept paper currency when they know that, unlike a gold coin, the paper the currency is printed on is worth very little?

---

*"Learning Objective" is abbreviated to "LO" in the end-of-chapter material.

LO 10.2

2.1 What is the main difference between the M1+ and M1++ definitions of the money supply?

2.2 Why does the Bank of Canada use six definitions of the money supply rather than one?

2.3 Distinguish among money, income, and wealth. Which one of the three does the central bank of a country control?

LO 10.3

3.1 What are the largest asset and the largest liability of a typical bank?

3.2 Suppose you decide to withdraw $100 in cash from your chequing account. Draw a T-account showing the effect of this transaction on your bank's balance sheet.

3.3 What does it mean to say that banks "create money"?

3.4 Give the formula for the simple deposit multiplier. If the desired reserve ratio is 20 percent, what is the maximum increase in chequing account deposits that will result from an increase in bank reserves of $20 000?

3.5 What causes the real-world money multiplier to be smaller than the simple deposit multiplier?

LO 10.4

4.1 Why did the government decide to set up the Bank of Canada in 1934?

4.2 What policy tools does the Bank of Canada use to control the money supply? Which tool is the most important?

4.3 Why does an open market purchase of government securities by the Bank of Canada increase bank reserves? Why does an open market sale of government securities by the Bank of Canada decrease bank reserves?

4.4 What is the "shadow banking system"? Why were the financial firms of the shadow banking system more vulnerable than commercial banks to bank runs?

LO 10.5

5.1 What is the quantity theory of money? What explanation does the quantity theory provide for inflation?

5.2 Is the quantity theory of money better able to explain the inflation rate in the long run or in the short run? Briefly explain.

5.3 What is hyperinflation? Why do governments sometimes allow it to occur?

Problems and Applications

LO 10.1

1.1 The English economist William Stanley Jevons described a world tour during the 1880s by a French singer, Mademoiselle Zélie. One stop on the tour was a theatre in the Society Islands, part of French Polynesia in the South Pacific. She performed for her usual fee, which was one-third of the receipts. This turned out to be three pigs, 23 turkeys, 44 chickens, 5000 coconuts, and "considerable quantities of bananas, lemons, and oranges." She estimated that all of this would have had a value in France of 4000 francs. According to Jevons, "as Mademoiselle could not consume any considerable portion of the receipts herself, it became necessary in the meantime to feed the pigs and poultry with the fruit." Do the goods Mademoiselle Zélie received as payment fulfill the four functions of money described in the chapter? Briefly explain.

Money and the Mechanism of Exchange (New York: D. Appleton and Company, 1889), pp. 1–2.

1.2 **[Related to the Chapter Opener on page 258]** An article in the *New York Times* in 2015 noted, "A rising number of Greeks in rural areas are swapping goods and services in cashless transactions since the government shut down banks on June 28 for three weeks." If Greeks were able to swap goods and services for other goods and services, did it matter that currency was not available because the banks had been closed? Briefly explain.

Based on Reuters, "Hay for Cheese? Barter Booms in Cash-Squeezed Rural Greece," *New York Times*, July 29, 2015.

1.3 In the late 1940s, the Communists under Mao Zedong were defeating the government of China in a civil war. The paper currency issued by the Chinese government was losing much of its value, and most businesses refused to accept it. At the same time, there was a paper shortage in Japan.

During these years, Japan was still under military occupation by the United States, following its defeat in World War II. Some of the US troops in Japan realized that they could use dollars to buy up vast amounts of paper currency in China, ship it to Japan to be recycled into paper, and make a substantial profit. Under these circumstances, was the Chinese paper currency a commodity money or a fiat money? Briefly explain.

1.4 According to Peter Heather, a historian at King's College London, during the time of the Roman Empire, the German tribes east of the Rhine River produced no coins of their own but used Roman coins instead:

> Although no coinage was produced in Germania, Roman coins were in plentiful circulation and could easily have provided a medium of exchange (already in the first century, Tacitus tells us, Germani of the Rhine region were using good-quality Roman silver coins for this purpose).

a. What is a medium of exchange?

b. What does the author mean when he writes that Roman coins could have provided the German tribes with a medium of exchange?

c. Why would any member of a German tribe have been willing to accept a Roman coin from another member of the tribe in exchange for goods or services when the tribes were not part of the Roman Empire and were not governed by Roman law?

Peter Heather, *The Fall of the Roman Empire: A New History of Rome and the Barbarians* (New York: Oxford University Press, 2006), p. 89.

1.5 **[Related to Making the Connection on page 262]** Suppose that the government changes the law to require all firms to accept paper currency in exchange for whatever they are selling. Briefly discuss who would gain and who would lose from this legislation.

LO 10.2

2.1 Briefly explain whether each of the following is counted in M1+.
   a. The coins in your pocket
   b. The funds in your chequing account
   c. The funds in your savings account
   d. The Canada Savings Bonds that you are holding
   e. Your Bank of Montreal Platinum MasterCard

2.2 [Related to Solved Problem 10.1 on page 266] Suppose that you have $2000 in currency in a shoebox in your closet. One day, you decide to deposit the money in a chequing account. Briefly explain how doing so will affect M1+ and M2++.

2.3 [Related to Solved Problem 10.1 on page 266] Suppose that you decide to withdraw $100 in currency from your chequing account. What is the effect on M1+? Ignore any actions the bank may take as a result of your having withdrawn the $100.

2.4 [Related to Don't Let This Happen to You on page 266] Briefly explain whether you agree with the following statement: "I recently read that more than half of the money issued by the government is actually held by people in foreign countries. If that's true, then Canada is less than half as wealthy as government statistics indicate."

2.5 [Related to Don't Let This Happen to You on page 266] A newspaper article contains the statement: "Income is only one way of measuring wealth." Do you agree that income is a way of measuring wealth?

From Sam Roberts, "As the Data Show, There's a Reason the Wall Street Protesters Chose New York," *New York Times*, October 25, 2011.

2.6 The paper currency of Canada is technically called "Bank of Canada Notes." If you took a $20 bill to the Bank of Canada, would the Bank of Canada redeem it with some other type of money?

2.7 In the nineteenth century, the Canadian government had difficulty getting banks and the public to accept the penny, which had been introduced a few years before. As a result, the government offered pennies for sale at a 20 percent discount. One account of this episode describes what the Canadian government did as "negative seigniorage." What is seigniorage? Why might the Canadian government's selling pennies at a 20 percent discount be considered "negative seigniorage"?

Based on Nicholas Kohler, "A Penny Dropped," macleans.ca, January 14, 2011.

2.8 There were several billion Canadian pennies in circulation before the government scrapped the penny in its 2012 budget. Suppose that instead of scrapping the penny, the government followed the proposal of François Velde, an economist at the Federal Reserve Bank of Chicago, and made the penny worth 5 cents. What would be the effect on the value of M1+? Would that change have had much impact on the economy?

François Velde, "What's a Penny (or a Nickel) Really Worth?" Federal Reserve Bank of Chicago, Chicago Fed Letter, No. 235a, February 2007.

2.9 [Related to the Making the Connection on page 265] In 2015, some business startups were offering the service of transferring money in the form of bitcoins among individuals and businesses in developing countries. At the same time, an article in the *Wall Street Journal* noted that in the United States, "Most ordinary consumers remain wary of using an unproven, six-year-old digital currency that many associate with illicit drugs, extreme price fluctuations and security risks." Why might using bitcoins be more attractive to individuals and firms in developing countries than to individuals and firms in the United States?

Based on Michael J. Casey and Paul Vigna, "Interest in Bitcoin Grows on Wall Street," *Wall Street Journal*, March 29, 2015.

LO 10.3

3.1 "Most of the money supply of Canada is created by banks making loans." Briefly explain whether you agree with this statement.

3.2 Would a series of bank runs in a country decrease the total quantity of M1+? Wouldn't a bank run simply move funds in a chequing account to currency in circulation? How could that movement of funds decrease the quantity of money?

3.3 [Related to Solved Problem 10.2 on page 273] Suppose that you deposit $2000 in currency into your chequing account at a branch of Bank of Montreal, which we will assume has no excess reserves at the time you make your deposit. Also assume that the desired reserve ratio is 0.20, or 20 percent.
   a. Use a T-account to show the initial impact of this transaction on Bank of Montreal's balance sheet.
   b. Suppose that Bank of Montreal makes the maximum loan it can from the funds you deposited. Using a T-account, show the initial impact of granting the loan on Bank of Montreal's balance sheet. Also include on this T-account the transaction from part (a).
   c. Now suppose that whoever took out the loan in part (b) writes a cheque for this amount and that the person receiving the cheque deposits it in a branch of CIBC. Show the effect of these transactions on the balance sheets of Bank of Montreal and CIBC *after the cheque has been cleared*. (On the T-account for Bank of Montreal, include the transactions from parts (a) and (b).)
   d. What is the maximum increase in chequing account deposits that can result from your $2000 deposit? What is the maximum increase in the money supply? Explain.

3.4 Consider the following simplified balance sheet for a bank:

Assets		Liabilities	
Reserves	$10 000	Deposits	$70 000
Loans	$66 000	Shareholders' equity	$6 000

   a. If the desired reserve ratio is 0.10, or 10 percent, how much in excess reserves does the bank hold?
   b. What is the maximum amount by which the bank can expand its loans?
   c. If the bank makes the loans in part (b), show the immediate impact on the bank's balance sheet.

3.5 [Related to Don't Let This Happen to You on page 272] Briefly explain whether you agree with the following statement: "Assets are things of value that people own. Liabilities are debts. Therefore, a bank will always consider a chequing account deposit to be an asset and a car loan to be a liability."

3.6 [Related to the Making the Connection on page 268] An economist commented on the situation a bank faces when making personal loans to subprime borrowers: "You have to be alert to the trade-off between serving consumers and being viewed as taking advantage of them." If banks charge subprime borrowers a higher interest on loans than they charge prime borrowers, are the banks taking advantage of the subprime borrowers? Briefly explain.

Based on Ianthe Jeanne Dugan and Telis Demos, "New Lenders Spring Up to Cater to Subprime Sector," *Wall Street Journal*, March 5, 2014.

LO 10.4

4.1 The text explains that Canada has a "fractional reserve banking system." Why do most depositors seem to be unworried that banks loan out most of the deposits they receive?

4.2 Suppose that you are a bank manager, and because of an increase in the level of uncertainty in financial markets you want to hold more reserves. You raise your desired reserve ratio from 10 to 12 percent. What actions would you need to take? How would your actions (and perhaps similar actions by other bank managers) end up affecting the money supply?

4.3 Suppose that the Bank of Canada makes a $10 million discount loan to First National Bank (FNB) by increasing FNB's account at the Bank of Canada.

  a. Use a T-account to show the impact of this transaction on FNB's balance sheet. Remember that the funds a bank has on deposit at the Bank of Canada count as part of its reserves.

  b. Assume that before receiving the loan, FNB has no excess reserves. What is the maximum amount of this $10 million that FNB can lend out?

  c. What is the maximum total increase in the money supply that can result from the Bank of Canada loan? Assume that the desired reserve ratio is 10 percent.

4.4 When the Bank of Canada steps in as the lender of last resort to prevent a bank panic, does this constitute a "bail out of the banks"? Briefly explain.

4.5 An article in the *Wall Street Journal* reported in 2015 that the People's Bank of China, which is the central bank of China, "is freeing up cash by reducing the amount that banks must keep in reserve." What monetary policy tool was the People's Bank of China using? In what sense did this policy change "free up cash"? What was the People's Bank of China hoping the result of this policy action would be?

Based on Lingling Wei, "China Central Bank Checks Europe Playbook on Credit," *Wall Street Journal*, April 19, 2015.

LO 10.5

5.1 If the money supply is growing at a rate of 6 percent per year, real GDP is growing at a rate of 3 percent per year, and velocity is constant, what will the inflation rate be? If velocity is increasing 1 percent per year instead of remaining constant, what will the inflation rate be?

5.2 Suppose that during one period, the velocity of money is constant and during another period, it undergoes large fluctuations. During which period will the quantity theory of money be more useful in explaining changes in the inflation rate? Briefly explain.

5.3 In April 2009, the African nation of Zimbabwe suspended the use of its own currency, the Zimbabwean dollar. According to an article from the Voice of America, "Hyperinflation in 2007 and 2008 made Zimbabwe's currency virtually worthless despite the introduction of bigger and bigger notes, including a 10 trillion dollar bill." Zimbabwe's Economic Planning Minister, Elton Mangoma, was quoted as saying the Zimbabwean dollar "will be out for at least a year," and in January 2009, the government of Zimbabwe made the US dollar the country's official currency. Why would hyperinflation make a currency "virtually worthless"? How might using the US dollar as its currency help stabilize Zimbabwe's economy?

From Voice of America News, "Zimbabwe Suspends Use of Own Currency," voanews.com, April 12, 2009.

5.4 An article in the *Economist* notes that the government of Venezuela running a large budget deficit "caused the money supply almost to quadruple in two years and led to the world's highest inflation rate, of over 60% a year."

  a. Why would running a large budget deficit cause the money supply in Venezuela to increase so rapidly?

  b. If the money supply increased by 150 percent per year (or 300 percent over two years) while the inflation rate was 60 percent, what must have happened to velocity in Venezuela during this period?

Based on "Of Oil and Coconut Water," *Economist*, September 20, 2014.

5.5 [Related to Making the Connection on page 285] During the German hyperinflation of the 1920s, many households and firms in Germany were hurt economically. Do you think any groups in Germany benefited from the hyperinflation? Briefly explain.

Philippe Desmazes/AFP/
Getty Images

11

Monetary Policy

Chapter Outline and Learning Objectives

Why Would a Bank Pay a Negative Interest Rate?

In 2015, some banks in Europe were in an unusual—and unwel-come—situation: They were receiving negative nominal interest rates on loans. That is, the banks had to make interest payments to borrowers rather than receive interest payments from borrow-ers. One borrower in Spain boasted, "I'm going to frame my bank statement, which shows that Bankinter is paying me interest on my mortgage. That's financial history." Why would a bank pay someone to borrow money? The answer is that the interest rates on these loans were not fixed but were instead adjusted based on changes in short-term interest rates that depended on the actions of central banks in Europe. When some of these interest rates became negative, banks had to automatically make the interest rates on some of their mortgage loans negative as well.

Central banks, including the Bank of Canada, had driven interest rates to historically low levels as they tried to pull their economies out of the severe worldwide recession of 2007–2009. In conducting monetary policy, the Bank of Canada concentrates on the overnight interest rate, which is the interest rate that banks charge each other on short-term loans. In December 2008, the Bank of Canada reduced its target for the overnight interest rate to 1%, and kept it there for nearly seven years, before reducing further in 2015 to 0.5%.

In the fall of 2015, many businesspeople, policymakers, and economists were focused on predicting when Bank of Canada governor Stephen Poloz would reduce the target for the over-night interest rate again and by how much. Does this focus indi-cate that the Bank of Canada governor is more important to the Canadian economy than the prime minister of Canada? Most economists would answer "yes." The prime minister can take actions that affect the economy, but needs the approval of Parliament before enacting most polices. In contrast, the structure of the Bank of Canada gives the governor substantial control over monetary policy. As a result, the Bank of Canada governor can often have greater influence over the economy than the prime minister.

European banks paying negative interest rates on loans is a striking example of how central bank policy can affect businesses. Homebuilders like Stepper Custom Homes and car dealers like Ford that sell durable goods are also directly affected by changes in interest rates because their customers frequently borrow money to buy these goods. Other businesses will be affected indirectly because changes in interest rates cause changes in aggregate demand. Not surprisingly, many businesses watch the Bank of Canada carefully for signs of whether interest rates are likely to rise or fall.

In this chapter, we will study the Bank of Canada and how monetary policy affects GDP, employment, and inflation.

Based on Patricia Kowsmann and Jeannette Neumann, "Tumbling Interest Rates in Europe Leave Some Banks Owing Money on Loans to Borrowers," *Wall Street Journal*, April 13, 2015; and Min Zeng, "Government Bond Yields Turn Negative," *Wall Street Journal*, January 14, 2015.

Economics in Your Life

Should You Buy a House during a Recession?

Think ahead a few years to when you might be married and maybe even (gasp!) have children. You decide to leave behind years of renting apartments and buy a house, but then you read a *Globe and Mail* article that states that a majority of economists predict a recession is likely to begin soon. What should you do? Would it be a good time or a bad time to buy a house? As you read this chapter, try to answer these questions. You can check your answers against those we provide on page 318 at the end of this chapter.

I n Chapter 10, we saw that banks play an important role in providing credit to households and firms, and in creating the money supply. We also saw that the government established the Bank of Canada to stabilize the financial system and that the Bank of Canada is responsible for managing the money supply. In this chapter, we will discuss the Bank of Canada's main policy goals, and explore how the Bank of Canada decides which *monetary policy* actions to take to achieve its goals.

11.1 LEARNING OBJECTIVE

Define monetary policy and describe the Bank of Canada's monetary policy goals.

Monetary policy The actions the Bank of Canada takes to manage the money supply and interest rates to pursue macroeconomic policy goals.

What Is Monetary Policy?

The devastation of the Great Depression was fundamentally important to the creation of the Bank of Canada. Because the depth of the Great Depression was blamed on the operation of the country's financial system, the federal Conservative government established the Royal Commission on Banking and Currency in 1933 to study the country's banking and monetary system. Based on the commission's recommendation, Parliament passed the Bank of Canada Act in 1934, and the newly founded Bank of Canada started operations on March 11, 1935. The main responsibility of the Bank of Canada is to conduct monetary policy "in the best interests of the economic life of the nation."

Since World War II, the Bank of Canada has carried out an active *monetary policy*. **Monetary policy** refers to the actions the Bank of Canada takes to manage the money supply and interest rates to pursue its macroeconomic policy goals.

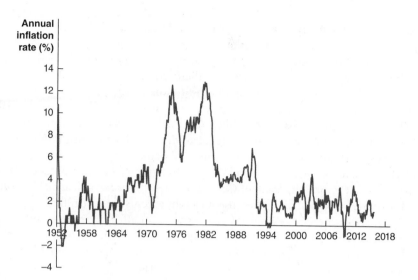

Figure 11.1

**The Inflation Rate,
January 1952–August 2015**

For most of the 1950s and 1960s, the inflation rate in Canada was 4 percent or less. During the 1970s, the inflation rate increased, peaking during 1979–1981. After 1992, the inflation rate was usually below 4 percent. The effects of the 2007–2009 recession caused several months of deflation—a falling price level—during the second half of 2009.

Note: The inflation rate is measured as the percentage change in the consumer price index (CPI) from the same month in the previous year.

Source: Statistics Canada CANSIM II series V41690914 and V41690926 (Accessed 1 October 2015). Reproduced and distributed on an "as is" basis with the permission of Statistics Canada.

The Goals of Monetary Policy

The Bank of Canada has four main *monetary policy goals* that are intended to promote a well-functioning economy:

1. Price stability
2. High employment
3. Stability of financial markets and institutions
4. Economic growth

We briefly consider each of these goals.

Price Stability. As we have seen in previous chapters, rising prices erode the value of money as a medium of exchange and a store of value. Especially after inflation rose dramatically and unexpectedly during the 1970s, policymakers in most industrial countries have had price stability as a policy goal. Figure 11.1 shows that, from the early 1950s until 1968, the inflation rate remained below 4 percent per year. Inflation was above 4 percent for most of the 1970s. In 1974–1975 and early 1979, the inflation rate increased to more than 12 percent, where it remained until late 1982, when it began to rapidly fall back to the 4 percent range. After 1992, the inflation rate was usually below 4 percent. The effects of the 2007–2009 recession caused several months of deflation—a falling price level—during the second half of 2009.

As we discussed in Chapter 10, the main goal of the Bank of Canada's current monetary policy is to keep the inflation rate within a target range of 1 percent to 3 percent, with the midpoint of the inflation target range, 2 percent, being the most desirable outcome. The Bank of Canada's approach to **inflation targeting** is **symmetric**, meaning that the Bank of Canada is equally concerned about inflation rising above the target as it is about inflation falling below the target. Such an approach to monetary policy guards against high inflation as well as against sustained deflation (a decline in the price level).

However, the Bank of Canada engages in **flexible inflation targeting**, in the sense that it does not rely on mechanical rules to achieve its inflation target, regardless of the shocks hitting the economy. The Bank of Canada (like most other inflation-targeting central banks) tries to meet its inflation target typically over a two-year period to minimize economic and financial volatility, which could be harmful to employment and economic growth in Canada.

High Employment. In addition to price stability, high employment (or a low rate of unemployment) is an important monetary policy goal. Unemployed workers and underused factories and office buildings reduce GDP below its potential level. Unemployment causes financial distress and decreases the self-esteem of workers who lack jobs. The goal of high employment extends beyond the Bank of Canada to other branches of the federal government.

Inflation targeting Conducting monetary policy so as to commit the central bank to achieving a publicly announced level of inflation.

Symmetric inflation targeting Conducting monetary policy based on equal concern about inflation rising above its target as about inflation falling below its target.

Flexible inflation targeting Conducting monetary policy that does not rely on mechanical rules to achieve its inflation target, but tries to meet the inflation target over some time horizon (typically a two-year horizon).

Stability of Financial Markets and Institutions. Firms need access to funds to design, develop, produce, and market their products. Savers look to financial investments to increase the value of their savings as they prepare to buy homes, pay for the education of their children, and provide for their retirement. The Bank of Canada promotes the stability of financial markets and institutions so that an efficient flow of funds from savers to borrowers will occur. As we saw in Chapter 10, the global financial crisis of 2007–2009 brought the issue of stability in financial markets to the forefront.

While the Bank of Canada doesn't regulate financial institutions, it does play a key role in providing liquidity to banks. Commercial banks can borrow from the Bank of Canada at the bank rate when they find themselves temporarily short of funds. By acting as a "lender of last resort" the Bank of Canada reduces the risk of a financial institution—that is otherwise healthy—failing because it cannot access short-term funds.

The events of the 2007–2009 financial crisis also affected investment banks and other financial firms in the *shadow banking system*. Investments banks, money market mutual funds, and other financial firms can be subject to *liquidity problems* because they often borrow for just a brief period—sometimes as briefly as overnight—and invest the funds in long-term securities. Just as commercial banks can experience crises if depositors begin to withdraw funds, investment banks and other financial firms can experience crises if investors stop providing them with short-term loans. In 2008, the Bank of Canada and other central banks around the world took several steps to ease the liquidity problems of these financial firms because they believed these problems were increasing the severity of the recession.

Economic Growth. We discussed in Chapters 6 and 7 the importance of economic growth to raising living standards. Policymakers aim to encourage *stable* economic growth because it allows households and firms to plan accurately and encourages the long-run investment that is needed to sustain growth. Policy can spur economic growth by providing incentives for saving to ensure a large pool of investment funds, as well as by providing direct incentives for business investment. The government, however, may be better able to increase saving and investment than the Bank of Canada. For example, the government can change the tax laws to increase the returns from saving and investing. In fact, some economists question whether the Bank of Canada can play a role in promoting economic growth beyond attempting to meet its goals of price stability and financial stability.

In the next section, we will look at how the Bank of Canada attempts to attain its monetary policy goal of price stability. We also look at how the turmoil in financial markets that began in 2007 led the Bank of Canada and other central banks around the world to put new emphasis on the goal of financial market stability.

11.2　LEARNING OBJECTIVE

Describe the Bank of Canada's monetary policy targets and explain how expansionary and contractionary monetary policies affect the interest rate.

The Money Market and the Bank of Canada's Choice of Monetary Policy Targets

The Bank of Canada aims to use its policy tools to achieve its monetary policy goals. Recall that the Bank of Canada's key monetary policy tools are open market buyback operations and lending to financial institutions. At times, the Bank of Canada encounters conflicts between its policy goals. For example, as we will discuss later in this chapter, the Bank of Canada can raise interest rates to reduce the inflation rate. But, higher interest rates typically reduce household and firm spending, which may result in slower growth and higher unemployment. So, a policy that is intended to achieve one monetary policy goal, such as reducing inflation, may make it more difficult to achieve another policy goal, such as high employment.

Monetary Policy Targets

The Bank of Canada tries to keep the inflation rate between 1 and 3 percent, but it can't affect the inflation rate directly. The Bank cannot tell firms how many people to employ or what prices to charge for their products. Instead, the Bank uses variables, called *monetary policy targets*, that it can affect directly and that, in turn, affect variables, such as real GDP and employment, that are closely related to the Bank's policy goal. The two main monetary policy targets are the money supply and the interest rate. As we will see, the Bank of Canada typically uses the interest rate as its policy target.

Bear in mind that while the Bank of Canada has typically used the interest rate as its target, this target was not central to the Bank of Canada's policy decisions during the global financial crisis of 2007–2009. As we will discuss later in this chapter, because financial markets suffered a degree of disruption not seen since the Great Depression of the 1930s, the Bank of Canada and other central banks around the world were forced to develop new policy tools. However, it is still important to have a good grasp of how the Bank of Canada carries out policy during normal times.

The Demand for Money

The Bank of Canada's two monetary policy targets are related. To understand this relationship, we first need to examine the money market, which brings together the demand and supply for money. Figure 11.2 shows the demand curve for money. The interest rate is on the vertical axis, and the quantity of money is on the horizontal axis. Here we are using the M1+ definition of money, which equals currency in circulation plus chequing account deposits. Notice that the demand curve for money is downward sloping.

To understand why the demand curve for money is downward sloping, consider that households and firms have a choice between holding money and holding other financial assets, such as Canada bonds. Money has one particularly desirable characteristic: You can use it to buy goods, services, or financial assets. Money also has one undesirable characteristic: It earns either no interest or a very low rate of interest. The currency in your wallet earns no interest, and the money in your chequing account earns either no interest or very little interest. Alternatives to money, such as Treasury bills, pay interest but have to be sold if you want to use the funds to buy something. When interest rates rise on financial assets such as Treasury bills, the amount of interest that households and firms lose by holding money increases. When interest rates fall, the amount of interest households and firms lose by holding money decreases. Remember that *opportunity cost* is what you have to forgo to engage in an activity. The interest rate is the opportunity cost of holding money.

We now have an explanation of why the demand curve for money slopes downward: When interest rates on Treasury bills and other financial assets are low, the opportunity cost of holding money is low, so the quantity of money demanded by households and firms will be high; when interest rates are high, the opportunity cost of holding money will be high, so the quantity of money demanded will be low. In Figure 11.2, a decrease in interest rates from 4 percent to 3 percent causes the quantity of money demanded by households and firms to rise from $90 billion to $95 billion.

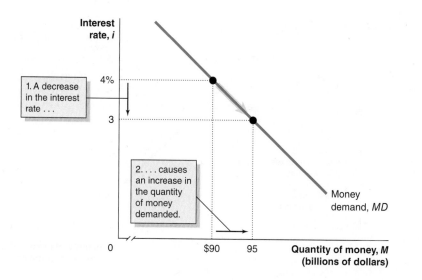

Figure 11.2

The Demand for Money

The money demand curve slopes downward because lower interest rates cause households and firms to switch from financial assets such as Treasury bills to money. All other things being equal, a fall in the interest rate from 4 percent to 3 percent will increase the quantity of money demanded from $90 billion to $95 billion. An increase in the interest rate will decrease the quantity of money demanded.

Shifts in the Money Demand Curve

We saw in Chapter 3 that the demand curve for a good is drawn holding constant all variables, other than the price, that affect the willingness of consumers to buy the good. Changes in variables other than the price cause the demand curve to shift. Similarly, the demand curve for money is drawn holding constant all variables, other than the interest rate, that affect the willingness of households and firms to hold money. Changes in variables other than the interest rate cause the demand curve to shift. The two most important variables that cause the money demand curve to shift are real GDP and the price level.

An increase in real GDP means that the amount of buying and selling of goods and services will increase. This additional buying and selling increases the demand for money as a medium of exchange, so the quantity of money households and firms want to hold increases at each interest rate, shifting the money demand curve to the right. A decrease in real GDP decreases the quantity of money demanded at each interest rate, shifting the money demand curve to the left. A higher price level increases the quantity of money required for a given amount of buying and selling. Eighty years ago, for example, when the price level was much lower and someone could purchase a new car for $500 and a salary of $30 per week put you in the middle class, the quantity of money demanded by households and firms was much lower than today, even adjusting for the effect of the lower real GDP and smaller population of those years. An increase in the price level increases the quantity of money demanded at each interest rate, shifting the money demand curve to the right. A decrease in the price level decreases the quantity of money demanded at each interest rate, shifting the money demand curve to the left. Figure 11.3 illustrates shifts in the money demand curve.

How the Bank of Canada Manages the Money Supply: A Quick Review

Having discussed money demand, we now turn to money supply. In Chapter 10, we saw how the Bank of Canada manages the money supply. If the Bank of Canada decides to increase the money supply, it purchases government of Canada securities. The sellers of these government securities deposit the funds they receive from the Bank of Canada in banks, which increases the banks' reserves. Typically, banks loan out most of these reserves, which creates new chequing account deposits and expands the money supply. If the Bank of Canada decides to decrease the money supply, it sells Canada securities, which decreases banks' reserves and contracts the money supply.

Figure 11.3

Shifts in the Money Demand Curve

Changes in real GDP or the price level cause the money demand curve to shift. An increase in real GDP or an increase in the price level will cause the money demand curve to shift from MD_1 to MD_2. A decrease in real GDP or a decrease in the price level will cause the money demand curve to shift from MD_1 to MD_3.

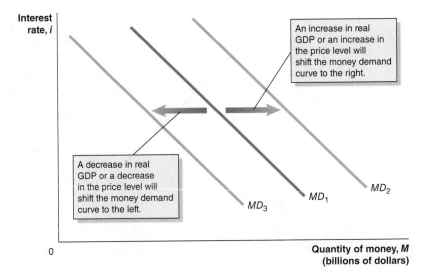

0

Quantity of money, M (billions of dollars)

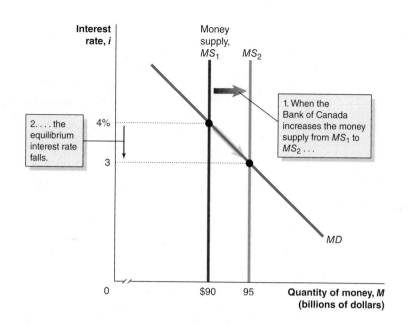

Figure 11.4

The Effect on the Interest Rate When the Bank of Canada Increases the Money Supply

When the Bank of Canada increases the money supply, households and firms will initially hold more money than they want, relative to other financial assets. Households and firms use the money they don't want to hold to buy short-term financial assets, such as Treasury bills, and make deposits in interest-paying bank accounts. This increase in demand allows banks and sellers of Treasury bills and similar securities to offer a lower interest rate. Eventually, the interest rate will fall enough that households and firms will be willing to hold the additional money the Bank of Canada has created. In the figure, an increase in the money supply from $90 billion to $95 billion causes the money supply curve to shift to the right, from MS_1 to MS_2, and causes the equilibrium interest rate to fall from 4 percent to 3 percent.

Equilibrium in the Money Market

In Figure 11.4, we include both the money demand and money supply curves. We can use this figure to see how the Bank of Canada affects both the money supply and the interest rate. For simplicity, we assume that the Bank of Canada is able to completely control the money supply. Therefore, the money supply curve is a vertical line, and changes in the interest rate have no effect on the quantity of money supplied. Just as with other markets, equilibrium in the *money market* occurs where the money demand curve crosses the money supply curve. If the Bank of Canada increases the money supply, the money supply curve will shift to the right, and the equilibrium interest rate will fall. In Figure 11.4, when the Bank of Canada increases the money supply from $90 billion to $95 billion, the money supply curve shifts from MS_1 to MS_2, and the equilibrium interest rate falls from 4 percent to 3 percent.

In the money market, the adjustment from one equilibrium to another equilibrium is a little different from the adjustment in the market for a good. In Figure 11.4, the money market is initially in equilibrium, with an interest rate of 4 percent and a money supply of $90 billion. When the Bank of Canada increases the money supply by $5 billion, households and firms have more money than they want to hold at an interest rate of 4 percent. What do households and firms do with the extra $5 billion? They are most likely to use the money to buy short-term financial assets, such as Canada bonds, or to deposit the money in interest-paying bank accounts, such as certificates of deposit. This increase in demand for interest-paying bank accounts and short-term financial assets allows banks to offer lower interest rates on certificates of deposit, and it allows sellers of Canada bonds and similar assets to also offer lower interest rates. As the interest rates on certificates of deposit, Canada bonds, and other short-term assets fall, the opportunity cost of holding money also falls. Households and firms move down the money demand curve. Eventually the interest rate will have fallen enough that households and firms are willing to hold the additional $5 billion worth of money the Bank of Canada has created, and the money market will be back in equilibrium. To summarize: *When the Bank of Canada increases the money supply, the short-term interest rate must fall until it reaches a level at which households and firms are willing to hold the additional money.*

Figure 11.5 shows what happens when the Bank of Canada decreases the money supply. The money market is initially in equilibrium, at an interest rate of 4 percent and a money supply of $90 billion. If the Bank of Canada decreases the money supply to $85 billion, households and firms will be holding less money than they would like, relative to other financial assets, at an interest rate of 4 percent. To increase their money holdings, they will sell Treasury bills and other short-term financial assets and withdraw funds from certificates of deposit and other interest-paying bank accounts. Banks will have to

Figure 11.5

The Effect on the Interest Rate When the Bank of Canada Decreases the Money Supply

When the Bank of Canada decreases the money supply, households and firms will initially hold less money than they want, relative to other financial assets. Households and firms will sell Treasury bills and other short-term financial assets and withdraw money from interest-paying bank accounts. These actions will increase interest rates. Eventually, interest rates will rise to the point at which households and firms will be willing to hold the smaller amount of money that results from the Bank of Canada's actions. In the figure, a reduction in the money supply from $90 billion to $85 billion causes the money supply curve to shift to the left, from MS_1 to MS_2, and causes the equilibrium interest rate to rise from 4 percent to 5 percent.

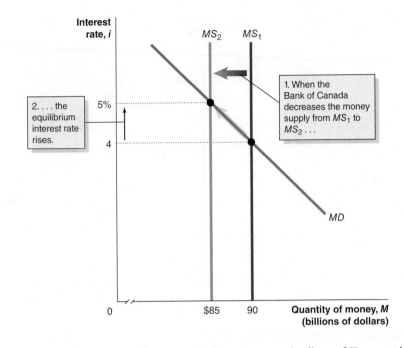

offer higher interest rates in order to retain depositors, and sellers of Treasury bills and similar securities will have to offer higher interest rates in order to find buyers. Rising short-term interest rates increase the opportunity cost of holding money, causing households and firms to move up the money demand curve. Equilibrium is finally restored at an interest rate of 5 percent.

A Tale of Two Interest Rates

In Chapter 6, we discussed the loanable funds model of the interest rate. In that model, the equilibrium interest rate is determined by the demand and supply for loanable funds. Why do we need two models of the interest rate? The answer is that the loanable funds model is concerned with the *long-term real rate of interest*, and the money market model is concerned with the *short-term nominal rate of interest*. The long-term real rate of interest is the interest rate that is most relevant when savers consider purchasing a long-term financial investment such as a corporate bond. It is also the rate of interest that is most relevant to firms that are borrowing to finance long-term investment projects such as new factories or office buildings, or to households that are taking out mortgage loans to buy new homes.

When conducting monetary policy, however, the focus is the short-term nominal interest rate because it is the interest rate most affected by increases and decreases in the money supply. Often—but not always—there is a close connection between movements in the short-term nominal interest rate and movements in the long-term real interest rate. So, when the Bank of Canada takes actions to increase the short-term nominal interest rate, usually the long-term real interest rate also increases. In other words, as we will discuss in the next section, when the interest rate on Canada bonds rises, the real interest rate on mortgage loans usually also rises, although sometimes only after a delay.

Choosing a Monetary Policy Target

As we have seen, the Bank of Canada uses monetary policy targets to affect economic variables, such as real GDP or the price level, that are closely related to the Bank of Canada's policy goals. The Bank of Canada can use either the money supply or the interest rate as its monetary policy target. As Figure 11.5 shows, the Bank of Canada is capable of affecting both. As we discussed in Chapter 10, the Bank of Canada has generally focused more on the interest rate than on the money supply.

There are many different interest rates in the economy. For purposes of monetary policy, the Bank of Canada has targeted the interest rate known as the *overnight interest rate*. In the next section, we discuss the overnight interest rate before examining how targeting the interest rate can help the Bank of Canada achieve its monetary policy goals.

The Importance of the Overnight Interest Rate

Recall from Chapter 10 that every bank likes to keep a fraction of its deposits as reserves, either as currency held in the bank or as deposits (settlement balances) with the Bank of Canada. The Bank of Canada pays banks a low interest rate on their reserve deposits, which (during normal times) is the bank rate less 50 basis points, $i_b - 0.50$, so banks normally have an incentive to invest reserves above the desired amounts. As the global financial crisis that began in 2007 deepened during 2008, bank reserves soared (especially in the United States) as banks attempted to meet an increase in deposit withdrawals and as they became reluctant to lend to any borrowers except those with the most flawless credit histories. These conditions were very unusual, however. In normal times, banks keep few excess reserves, and when they need additional reserves, they borrow in the *overnight funds market* from banks that have reserves available. The **overnight interest rate** is the interest rate banks charge one another on loans in the overnight funds market. The loans in that market are usually very short term, often just overnight.

The Bank of Canada does not set the overnight interest rate. Instead, it sets an **operating band** of 50 basis points wide for the overnight interest rate, and the rate is determined by the supply of reserves relative to the demand for them. Because the Bank of Canada can increase and decrease the supply of bank reserves through open market buyback operations, it can set a *target* for the overnight interest rate and usually comes very close to reaching it. The Bank of Canada operates under a system in which it announces the target for the overnight interest rate on eight "fixed" dates throughout the year. In April 2009, the Bank of Canada lowered the band for the overnight interest rate from 50 basis points to 25 basis points (from 0.50 percent to 0.25 percent) and instead of targeting the overnight interest rate at the midpoint of the band (as it does during normal times), it started targeting the overnight interest rate at the bottom of the operating band. On June 1, 2010, the Bank of Canada re-established the normal operating band of 50 basis points for the overnight interest rate, and the band currently is from 0.25 percent to 0.75 percent.

These very low overnight interest rates reflect the severity of the global financial crisis. Because only banks can borrow or lend in the overnight funds market, the overnight interest rate is not directly relevant for households and firms. However, changes in the overnight interest rate usually result in changes in interest rates on other short-term financial assets, such as Canada bonds, and changes in interest rates on long-term financial assets, such as corporate bonds and mortgages. A change in the overnight interest rate has a greater effect on short-term interest rates than on long-term interest rates, and its effect on long-term interest rates may occur only after a lag in time. Although a majority of economists support the Bank of Canada's choice of the interest rate as its monetary policy target, some economists believe the Bank of Canada should concentrate on the money supply instead. We will discuss the views of these economists later in this chapter.

Overnight interest rate The interest rate banks charge each other for overnight loans.

Operating band The Bank of Canada's 50-basis-point range for the overnight interest rate.

Monetary Policy and Economic Activity

Remember that the Bank of Canada uses the overnight interest rate as a monetary policy target because it can influence the overnight interest rate through **open market buyback operations** and because it believes that changes in the overnight interest rate will ultimately affect economic variables that are related to its monetary policy goals. It is important to consider again the distinction between the nominal interest rate and the real interest rate. Recall that we calculate the real interest rate by subtracting the inflation rate from the nominal interest rate. Ultimately, the ability of the Bank of Canada to use monetary policy to affect economic variables such as real GDP depends on its ability to affect real interest rates, such as the real interest rates on mortgages and corporate bonds. Because the overnight interest rate is a short-term nominal interest rate, the Bank of Canada sometimes has difficulty affecting long-term real interest rates. Nevertheless, for purposes of the following discussion, we will assume that the Bank of Canada is able to use open market buyback operations to affect long-term real interest rates.

11.3 LEARNING OBJECTIVE

Use aggregate demand and aggregate supply graphs to show the effects of monetary policy on real GDP and the price level.

Open market buyback operations Agreements in which the Bank of Canada, or another party, purchase securities with the understanding that the seller will repurchase them in a short period of time, usually less than a week.

How Interest Rates Affect Aggregate Demand

Changes in interest rates affect *aggregate demand*, which is the total level of spending in the economy. Recall that aggregate demand has four components: consumption, investment, government purchases, and net exports. Changes in interest rates will not affect government purchases, but they will affect the other three components of aggregate demand in the following ways:

- **Consumption**. Many households finance purchases of consumer durables, such as automobiles and furniture, by borrowing. Lower interest rates lead to increased spending on durables because they lower the total cost of these goods to consumers by lowering the interest payments on loans. Higher interest rates raise the cost of consumer durables, and households will buy fewer of them. Lower interest rates also reduce the return to saving, leading households to save less and spend more. Higher interest rates increase the return to saving, leading households to save more and spend less.

- **Investment**. Firms finance most of their spending on machinery, equipment, and factories out of their profits or by borrowing. Firms borrow either from the financial markets by issuing corporate bonds or from banks. Higher interest rates on corporate bonds or on bank loans make it more expensive for firms to borrow, so they will undertake fewer investment projects. Lower interest rates make it less expensive for firms to borrow, so they will undertake more investment projects. Lower interest rates can also increase investment through their effect on stock prices. As interest rates decline, stocks become a more attractive investment relative to bonds. The increase in demand for stocks raises their price. An increase in stock prices sends a signal to firms that the future profitability of investment projects has increased. By issuing additional shares of stocks, firms can acquire the funds they need to buy new factories and equipment, thereby increasing investment.

  Spending by households on new homes is also part of investment. When interest rates on mortgage loans rise, the cost of buying new homes rises, and fewer new homes will be purchased. When interest rates on mortgage loans fall, more new homes will be purchased.

- **Net exports**. Recall that net exports are equal to spending by foreign households and firms on goods and services produced in Canada minus spending by Canadian households and firms on goods and services produced in other countries. The value of net exports depends partly on the exchange rate between the Canadian dollar and foreign currencies. When the value of the dollar rises, households and firms in other countries will pay more for goods and services produced in Canada, but Canadian households and firms will pay less for goods and services produced in other countries. As a result, Canada will export less and import more, so net exports fall. When the value of the dollar falls, net exports will rise. If interest rates in Canada rise relative to interest rates in other countries, investing in Canadian financial assets will become more desirable, causing foreign investors to increase their demand for dollars, which will increase the value of the dollar. As the value of the dollar increases, net exports will fall. If interest rates in Canada decline relative to interest rates in other countries, the value of the dollar will fall, and net exports will rise.

The Effects of Monetary Policy on Real GDP and the Price Level

In Chapter 9, we developed the *aggregate demand and aggregate supply model* to explain fluctuations in real GDP and the price level. In the basic version of the model, we assume that there is no economic growth, so the long-run aggregate supply curve does not shift. In panel (a) of Figure 11.6, we assume that the economy is in short-run equilibrium at point *A*, where the aggregate demand (AD_1) curve intersects the short-run aggregate supply (*SRAS*) curve. Real GDP is below potential real GDP, as shown by the long-run aggregate supply (*LRAS*) curve, so the economy is in a recession, with some firms operating below normal capacity and some workers having been laid off. To reach

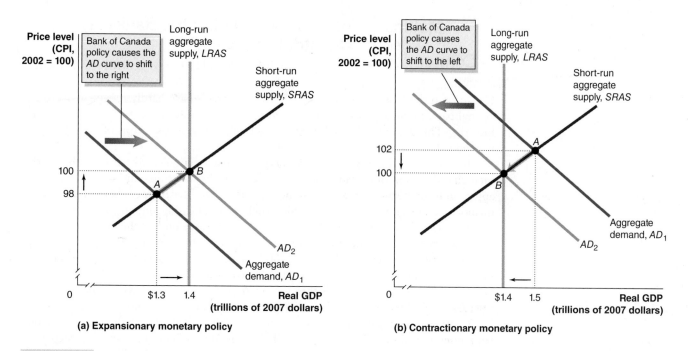

Figure 11.6 Monetary Policy

In panel (a), the economy begins in a recession at point *A*, with real GDP of $1.3 trillion and a price level of 98. An expansionary monetary policy causes aggregate demand to shift to the right, from *AD₁* to *AD₂*, increasing real GDP from $1.3 trillion to $1.4 trillion and the price level from 98 to 100 (point *B*). With real GDP back at its potential level, the Bank of Canada can meet its goal of high employment.

In panel (b), the economy begins at point *A*, with real GDP at $1.5 trillion and the price level at 102. Because real GDP is greater than potential GDP, the economy experiences rising wages and prices. A contractionary monetary policy causes aggregate demand to shift to the left, from *AD₁* to *AD₂*, decreasing real GDP from $1.5 trillion to $1.4 trillion and the price level from 102 to 100 (point *B*). With real GDP back at its potential level, the Bank of Canada can meet its goal of price stability.

its goal of high employment, the Bank of Canada needs to carry out an **expansionary monetary policy** by increasing the money supply and decreasing interest rates. Lower interest rates cause an increase in consumption, investment, and net exports, which shifts the aggregate demand curve to the right, from *AD₁* to *AD₂*. Real GDP increases from $1.3 trillion to potential GDP of $1.4 trillion, and the price level rises from 98 to 100 (point *B*). The policy successfully returns real GDP to its potential level. Rising production leads to increasing employment, allowing the Bank of Canada to achieve its goal of high employment.

In panel (b) of Figure 11.6, the economy is in short-run equilibrium at point *A*, with real GDP of $1.5 trillion, which is above potential real GDP of $1.4 trillion. With some firms producing beyond their normal capacity and the unemployment rate very low, wages and prices are increasing. To reach its goal of price stability, the Bank of Canada needs to carry out a **contractionary monetary policy** by decreasing the money supply and increasing interest rates. Higher interest rates cause a decrease in consumption, investment, and net exports, which shifts the aggregate demand curve from *AD₁* to *AD₂*. Real GDP decreases from $1.5 trillion to $1.4 trillion, and the price level falls from 102 to 100 (point *B*). Why would the Bank of Canada want to intentionally cause real GDP to decline? Because in the long run, real GDP can't continue to remain above potential GDP. Attempting to keep real GDP above potential GDP would result in rising inflation. As aggregate demand declines and real GDP returns to its potential level, upward pressure on wages and prices will be reduced, allowing the Bank of Canada to achieve its goal of price stability.

We can conclude that the Bank of Canada can use monetary policy to affect the price level and, in the short run, the level of real GDP, allowing it to attain its policy goals of high employment and price stability.

Expansionary monetary policy
The Bank of Canada's decreasing interest rates to increase real GDP.

Contractionary monetary policy
The Bank of Canada's increasing interest rates to reduce inflation.

**Making
the
Connection**

Too Low for Zero: Central Banks Try "Quantitative Easing"

In the aftermath of the global financial crisis and the Great Recession, policy rates such as the overnight interest rate in Canada and the federal funds rate in the United States have hardly moved at all, while central bank monetary policies have been the most volatile and extreme in their entire histories. This unpredictability has discredited policy rates as indicators of monetary policy and led central banks to look elsewhere.

In particular, the US Federal Reserve and many central banks around the world, including the Bank of Canada, have departed from the traditional interest-rate targeting approach to monetary policy and are now focusing on their balance sheet instead, using quantitative measures of monetary policy, such as credit easing and quantitative easing.

For example, in December 2008, the Federal Reserve pushed the target for the federal funds rate (the US equivalent of our overnight interest rate) to nearly zero and kept it there until now. Because the 2007–2009 recession was so severe, even this very low rate did little to stimulate the US economy. To lower the federal funds rate, the Federal Reserve buys Treasury bills through open market purchases, which increases bank reserves. Banks then lend out these reserves. As the figure below shows, however, in late 2008, many banks began piling up excess reserves rather than lending the funds out. Total bank reserves had been less than US$50 billion in August 2008, but with the deepening of the global financial crisis, they had soared to more than US$900 billion by May 2009.

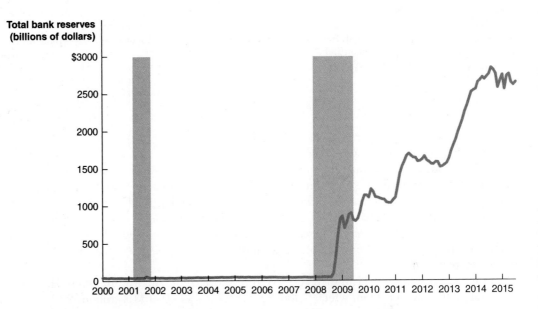

The increase in bank reserves was partly due to the Federal Reserve's decision in October 2008 to start paying interest of 0.25 percent on bank reserves held as deposits at the Federal Reserve. Primarily, though, the increase in reserves occurred because banks were reluctant to make loans at low interest rates to households and firms whose financial positions had been damaged by the recession. Some economists believed the Federal Reserve was facing a situation known as a *liquidity trap*, in which short-term interest rates are pushed to zero, leaving the central bank unable to lower them further. Some economists believe that liquidity traps occurred in the United States during the 1930s and in Japan during the 1990s.

Not being able to push the target for the federal funds rate below zero was a problem for the Federal Reserve. Glenn Rudebusch, an economist at the Federal Reserve Bank of San Francisco, calculated that given how high the unemployment rate was, the appropriate target for the federal funds rate was −5 percent. Because the federal funds rate can't be negative, the Federal Reserve turned to other policies. In particular, it decided to embark on a policy of *quantitative easing*, which involves buying securities beyond the short-term Treasury securities that are usually involved in open market operations. The

Federal Reserve began purchasing 10-year Treasury notes to keep their interest rates from rising. Interest rates on home mortgage loans typically move closely with interest rates on 10-year Treasury notes. It also purchased certain *mortgage-backed securities*. The Federal Reserve's objective was to keep interest rates on mortgages low and to keep funds flowing into the mortgage market in order to help stimulate demand for housing.

Later in this chapter, we will consider other new programs the Bank of Canada and many other central banks around the world put in place to deal with the global financial crisis of 2007–2009 and the slow recovery that followed, as the traditional focus on lowering policy rates to stimulate the economy proved ineffective.

Source: Based on Glenn Rudebusch, "The Fed's Monetary Policy Response to the Current Crisis," FRBSF Economic Letter, May 22, 2009.

Your Turn: Test your understanding by doing related problems 3.8 and 3.10 on page 322 at the end of this chapter.

MyEconLab

Can the Bank of Canada Eliminate Recessions?

Panel (a) of Figure 11.6 shows an expansionary monetary policy that performs perfectly by shifting the *AD* curve to bring the economy back to potential GDP. In fact, however, this ideal is very difficult for the Bank of Canada to achieve, as the length and severity of the 2007–2009 recession indicates. In practice, the best the Bank of Canada can do is keep recessions shorter and milder than they would otherwise be.

If the Bank of Canada is to be successful in offsetting the effects of the business cycle, it needs to quickly recognize the need for a change in monetary policy. If the Bank of Canada is late in recognizing that a recession has begun or that the inflation rate is increasing, it may not be able to implement a new policy soon enough to do much good. In fact, implementing a policy too late may actually destabilize the economy. To see how this can happen, consider Figure 11.7. The straight line represents the long-run growth trend in real GDP in Canada. On average, real GDP grows about 3 percent per year. The actual path of real GDP differs from the underlying trend because of the business cycle, which is shown by the red curved line. As we saw in Chapter 6, the actual business cycle is more irregular than the stylized cycle shown here.

Suppose that a recession begins in August 2017. Because it takes months for economic statistics to be gathered by Statistics Canada and the Bank of Canada, there is a *lag*, or delay, before the Bank of Canada recognizes that a recession has begun. Then it takes time for the Bank of Canada's economists to analyze the data. Finally, in June 2018, the Bank of Canada concludes that the economy is in recession and begins an expansionary monetary policy. As it turns out, June 2018 is actually the trough of the recession, meaning that the recession has already ended, and an expansion has begun. In these circumstances, the Bank of Canada's expansionary policy is not needed to end the recession. The ·

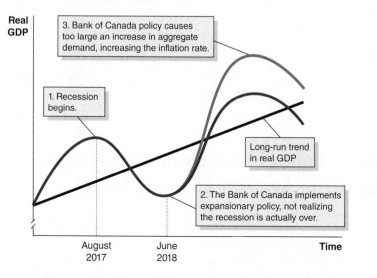

Figure 11.7

The Effect of a Poorly Timed Monetary Policy on the Economy

The upward-sloping straight line represents the long-run growth trend in real GDP. The curved red line represents the path real GDP takes because of the business cycle. If the Bank of Canada is too late in implementing a change in monetary policy, real GDP will follow the curved blue line. The Bank of Canada's expansionary monetary policy results in too great an increase in aggregate demand during the next expansion, which causes an increase in the inflation rate.

increase in aggregate demand caused by the Bank of Canada's lowering interest rates is likely to push the economy beyond potential real GDP and cause a significant acceleration in inflation. Real GDP ends up following the path indicated by the blue curved line. The Bank of Canada has inadvertently engaged in a *procyclical policy*, which increases the severity of the business cycle, as opposed to a *countercyclical policy*, which is meant to reduce the severity of the business cycle, and which is what the Bank of Canada intends to use.

Failing to react until well after a recession has begun (or ended) can be a serious problem for the Bank of Canada. In the case of the 2007–2009 recession, however, the Bank of Canada did promptly cut the overnight interest rate in response to the beginning of the global financial crisis, even though the recession did not actually begin until some months later.

A Summary of How Monetary Policy Works

Table 11.1 compares the steps involved in expansionary and contractionary monetary policies. We need to note an important qualification to this summary. At every point, we should add the phrase "relative to what would have happened without the policy." Table 11.1 isolates the impact of monetary policy, *holding constant all other factors affecting the variables involved.* In other words, we are invoking the *ceteris paribus* condition, discussed in Chapter 3. This point is important because, for example, a contractionary monetary policy does not cause the price level to fall; rather, a contractionary monetary policy causes the price level *to rise by less than it would have risen without the policy.* One final note on terminology: An expansionary monetary policy is sometimes referred to as a *loose* policy, or an *easy* policy. A contractionary monetary policy is sometimes referred to as a *tight* policy.

Don't Let This Happen to You

Remember that with Monetary Policy, It's the Interest Rates—Not the Money—That Counts

It is tempting to think of monetary policy working like this: If the Bank of Canada wants more spending in the economy, it increases the money supply, and people spend more because they now have more money. If the Bank of Canada wants less spending in the economy, it decreases the money supply, and people spend less because they now have less money. In fact, that is *not* how monetary policy works. Remember the important difference between money and income: The Bank of Canada increases the money supply by buying government securities, such as Canada bonds. The sellers of the Canada bonds have just exchanged one asset—Canada bonds—for another asset—a cheque from the Bank of Canada; the sellers have *not* increased their income. Even though the money supply is now larger, no one's income has increased, so no one's spending should be affected.

It is only when this increase in the money supply results in lower interest rates that spending is affected. When interest rates are lower, households are more likely to buy new homes and automobiles, and businesses are more likely to buy new factories and computers. Lower interest rates also lead to a lower value of the dollar, which lowers the prices of exports and raises the prices of imports, thereby increasing net exports. It isn't the increase in the money supply that has brought about this additional spending; *it's the lower interest rates.* To understand how monetary policy works, and to interpret news reports about the Bank of Canada's actions, remember that it is the change in interest rates, not the change in the money supply, that is most important.

MyEconLab
Your Turn: Test your understanding by doing related problem 3.11 on page 322 at the end of this chapter.

11.4 **LEARNING** OBJECTIVE

Use the dynamic aggregate demand and aggregate supply model to analyze monetary policy.

Monetary Policy in the Dynamic Aggregate Demand and Aggregate Supply Model

The overview of monetary policy we just finished contains a key idea: The Bank of Canada can use monetary policy to affect aggregate demand, thereby changing the price level and the level of real GDP. The discussion of monetary policy illustrated by

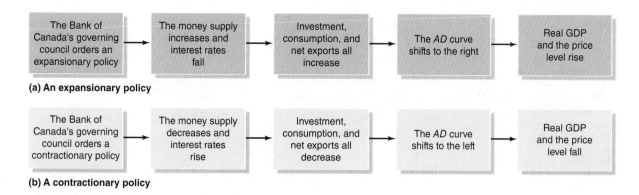

(a) An expansionary policy

(b) A contractionary policy

Table 11.1 Expansionary and Contractionary Monetary Policies

Figure 11.6 is simplified, however, because it ignores two important facts about the economy: (1) The economy experiences continuing inflation, with the price level rising every year, and (2) the economy experiences long-run growth, with the *LRAS* curve shifting to the right every year. In Chapter 9, we developed a *dynamic aggregate demand and aggregate supply model* that takes into account these two facts. In this section, we use the dynamic model to gain a more complete understanding of monetary policy. Let's briefly review the dynamic model. Recall that over time, the Canadian labour force and Canadian capital stock will increase. Technological change will also occur. The result will be an increase in potential real GDP, which we show by the long-run aggregate supply curve shifting to the right. These factors will also result in firms supplying more goods and services at any given price level in the short run, which we show by the short-run aggregate supply curve shifting to the right. During most years, the aggregate demand curve will also shift to the right, indicating that aggregate expenditure will be higher at every price level. Aggregate expenditure usually increases for several reasons: As population grows and incomes rise, consumption will increase over time. Also, as the economy grows, firms expand capacity, and new firms are established, increasing investment spending. Finally, an expanding population and an expanding economy require increased government services, such as more police officers and teachers, so government purchases will expand.

The Effects of Monetary Policy on Real GDP and the Price Level: A More Complete Account

During certain periods, *AD* does not increase enough during the year to keep the economy at potential GDP. This slow growth in aggregate demand may be due to households and firms becoming pessimistic about the future state of the economy, leading them to cut back their spending on consumer durables, houses, and factories. As we have seen, the collapse of the US housing bubble and the resulting global financial crisis had a negative effect on aggregate demand during the 2007–2009 recession. Other possibilities exist as well: The federal government might decide to balance the budget by cutting back its purchases, or recessions in other countries might cause a decline in Canadian exports. In the hypothetical situation shown in Figure 11.8, in the first year, the economy is in equilibrium, at potential real GDP of $1.4 trillion and a price level of 100 (point *A*). In the second year, *LRAS* increases to $1.6 trillion, but *AD* increases only to $AD_{2(\text{without policy})}$, which is not enough to keep the economy in macroeconomic equilibrium at potential GDP. If the Bank of Canada does not intervene, the short-run equilibrium will occur at $1.5 trillion (point *B*). The $100 billion gap between this level of real GDP and potential real GDP at $LRAS_2$ means that some firms are operating at less than their normal capacity. Incomes and profits will fall, firms will begin to lay off workers, and the unemployment rate will rise.

Economists at the Bank of Canada closely monitor the economy and continually update forecasts of future levels of real GDP and prices. When these economists

Figure 11.8

An Expansionary Monetary Policy

The economy begins in equilibrium at point A, with real GDP of $1.4 trillion and a price level of 100. Without monetary policy, aggregate demand will shift from AD_1 to $AD_{2(without\ policy)}$, which is not enough to keep the economy at full employment because long-run aggregate supply has shifted from $LRAS_1$ to $LRAS_2$. The economy will be in short-run equilibrium at point B, with real GDP of $1.5 trillion and a price level of 102. By lowering interest rates, the Bank of Canada increases investment, consumption, and net exports sufficiently to shift aggregate demand to $AD_{2(with\ policy)}$. The economy will be in equilibrium at point C, with real GDP of $1.6 trillion, which is its full employment level, and a price level of 103. The price level is higher than it would have been if the Bank of Canada had not acted to increase spending in the economy.

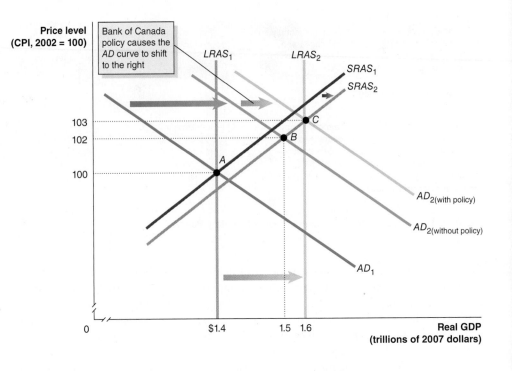

Governing council (of the Bank of Canada) A council with six members (including the governor) that is responsible for the management of the Bank of Canada.

anticipate that aggregate demand is not growing fast enough to allow the economy to remain at full employment, they present their findings to the Bank of Canada's **governing council**, which decides whether circumstances require a change in monetary policy. For example, suppose that the governing council meets and considers a forecast from the staff indicating that, during the following year, a gap of $100 billion will open between equilibrium real GDP and potential real GDP. In other words, the macroeconomic equilibrium illustrated by point B in Figure 11.8 will occur. The Bank of Canada may then decide to carry out an expansionary monetary policy to lower interest rates to stimulate aggregate demand. The figure shows the results of a successful attempt to do this: AD has shifted to the right, and equilibrium occurs at potential GDP (point C). The Bank of Canada will have successfully headed off the falling incomes and rising unemployment that otherwise would have occurred. Bear in mind that we are illustrating a perfectly executed monetary policy that keeps the economy at potential GDP, which is difficult to achieve in practice for reasons already discussed.

Notice in Figure 11.8 that the expansionary monetary policy caused the inflation rate to be higher than it would have been. Without the expansionary policy, the price level would have risen from 100 to 102, so the inflation rate for the year would have been 2 percent. By shifting the aggregate demand curve, the expansionary policy caused the price level to increase from 102 to 103, raising the inflation rate from 2 percent to 3 percent.

Using Monetary Policy to Fight Inflation

In addition to using an expansionary monetary policy to reduce the severity of recessions, the Bank of Canada can also use a contractionary monetary policy to keep aggregate demand from expanding so rapidly that the inflation rate begins to increase above the upper limit of the inflation rate target band of 3 percent. Figure 11.9 shows the situation during 2006 and 2007, when the Bank of Canada faced this possibility. During 2006, the economy was at equilibrium at potential GDP, but the Bank of Canada's economists and governing council were concerned that the continuing boom in the commodities sector might lead aggregate demand to increase so rapidly that the inflation rate would begin to accelerate.

Between January 2006 and July 2007, the target for the overnight interest rate rose from 3.25 percent to 4.5 percent as the Bank of Canada tried to slow the increase in

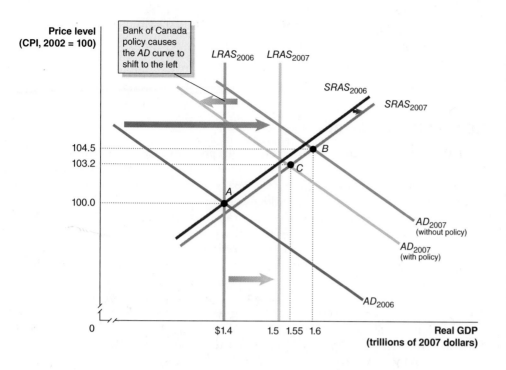

Figure 11.9

A Contractionary Monetary Policy in 2006

The economy began 2006 in equilibrium at point A, with real GDP equal to potential GDP of $1.4 trillion and a price level of 100.0. From 2006 to 2007, potential GDP increased from $1.4 trillion to $1.5 trillion, as long-run aggregate supply increased from $LRAS_{2006}$ to $LRAS_{2007}$. The Bank of Canada raised interest rates because it believed the commodities boom was causing aggregate demand to increase too rapidly. Without the increase in interest rates, aggregate demand would have shifted from AD_{2006} to $AD_{2007(without\ policy)}$, and the new short-run equilibrium would have occurred at point B. Real GDP would have been $1.6 trillion—$100 billion greater than potential GDP—and the price level would have been 104.5. The increase in interest rates resulted in aggregate demand increasing only to $AD_{2007(with\ policy)}$. Equilibrium occurred at point C, with real GDP of $1.55 trillion being only $50 billion greater than potential GDP and the price level rising only to 103.2.

prices. To see how the Bank of Canada can use this sort of monetary policy, let's work through Figure 11.9. Assume that the economy starts at point A with a real GDP of $1.4 trillion dollars and a price level of 100.0. We'll assume that the Canadian economy's potential GDP continued to grow during this period, which means that long-run aggregate supply and short-run aggregate supply both shift to the right. If the Bank of Canada takes no action, the aggregate demand curve will shift from AD_{2006} to $AD_{2007(without\ policy)}$ and the economy will be in equilibrium at point B. At point B, the economy is in a short-run equilibrium with real GDP of $1.6 trillion and a price level of 104.5.

A movement in the price level from 100.0 to 104.5 means an inflation rate of 4.5 percent, which exceeds the target range of 1 to 3 percent. The Bank of Canada used contractionary monetary policy to reduce inflation. In 2006, it began to increase its target for the overnight interest rate, which caused interest rates in the economy to rise. As a result investment, consumption, and net exports fell (or didn't increase as much as they would have), and the aggregate demand curve shifted to $AD_{2007(with\ policy)}$. As a result, the economy found equilibrium at point C, with real GDP of $1.55 trillion and a price level of 103.2. A change in price level from 100.0 to 103.2 meant that the inflation rate would be 3.2 percent, just a bit higher than the upper limit of the inflation target band.

Solved Problem **11.1**

The Effects of Monetary Policy

The hypothetical information in the following table shows what the values for real GDP and the price level will be in 2019 if the Bank of Canada does *not* use monetary policy:

Year	Potential GDP	Real GDP	Price Level
2018	$1.52 trillion	$1.52 trillion	114
2019	1.56 trillion	1.54 trillion	116

a. If the Bank of Canada wants to keep real GDP at its potential level in 2019, should it use an expansionary

policy or a contractionary policy? Should the trading desk buy Canada bonds or sell them?

b. Suppose the Bank of Canada's policy is successful in keeping real GDP at its potential level in 2019. State whether each of the following will be higher or lower than if the Bank of Canada had taken no action:

   i. Real GDP

   ii. Potential real GDP

   iii. The inflation rate

   iv. The unemployment rate

c. Draw an aggregate demand and aggregate supply graph to illustrate your answer. Be sure that your graph contains *LRAS* curves for 2018 and 2019; *SRAS* curves for 2018 and 2019; an *AD* curve for 2018 and 2019, with and without monetary policy action; and equilibrium real GDP and the price level in 2019, with and without policy.

Solving the Problem

Step 1: **Review the chapter material.** This problem is about the effects of monetary policy on real GDP and the price level, so you may want to review the section "The Effects of Monetary Policy on Real GDP and the Price Level: A More Complete Account," which begins on page 305.

Step 2: **Answer the questions in part (a) by explaining how the Bank of Canada can keep real GDP at its potential level.** The information in the table tells us that without monetary policy, the economy will be below potential real GDP in 2019. To keep real GDP at its potential level, the Bank of Canada must undertake an expansionary policy. To carry out an expansionary policy, the trading desk needs to buy Canada bonds. Buying Canada bonds will increase reserves in the banking system. Banks will increase their loans, which will increase the money supply and lower the interest rate.

Step 3: **Answer part (b) by explaining the effect of the Bank of Canada's policy.** If the Bank of Canada's policy is successful, real GDP in 2019 will increase from $1.54 trillion, as given in the table, to its potential level of $1.56 trillion. Potential real GDP is not affected by monetary policy, so its value will not change. Because the level of real GDP will be higher, the unemployment rate will be lower than it would have been without policy. The expansionary monetary policy shifts the *AD* curve to the right, so short-run equilibrium will move up the short-run aggregate supply (*SRAS*) curve, and the price level will be higher.

Step 4: **Answer part (c) by drawing the graph.** Your graph should look similar to Figure 11.8.

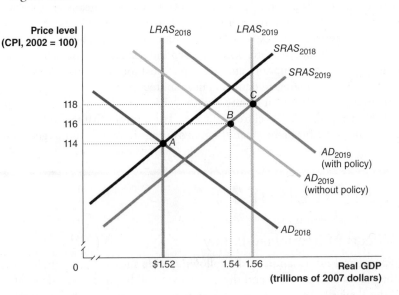

The economy starts in equilibrium in 2018 at point *A*, with the *AD* and *SRAS* curves intersecting along the *LRAS* curve. Real GDP is at its potential level of $1.52 trillion, and the price level is 114. Without monetary policy, the *AD* curve shifts to $AD_{2019(\text{without policy})}$, and the economy is in short-run equilibrium at point *B*. Because potential real GDP has increased from $1.52 trillion to $1.56 trillion, short-run equilibrium real GDP of $1.54 trillion is below the potential level. The price level has increased from 114 to 116. With policy, the AD curve shifts to $AD_{2019(\text{with policy})}$, and the economy is in equilibrium at point C. Real GDP is at its potential level of \$1.56 trillion. We don't have enough information to be sure of the new equilibrium price level. We do know that it will be higher than 116. The graph shows the price level rising to 118. Therefore, without the Bank of Canada's expansionary policy, the inflation rate in 2019 would have been about 1.8 percent. With policy, it will be about 3.5 percent.

Extra credit: Bear in mind that in reality, the Bank of Canada is unable to use monetary policy to keep real GDP exactly at its potential level, as this problem suggests.

Your Turn: For more practice, do related problems 4.2 and 4.3 on pages 322–323 at the end of this chapter.

MyEconLab

A Closer Look at the Bank of Canada's Setting of Monetary Policy Targets

11.5 LEARNING OBJECTIVE
Discuss the Bank of Canada's setting of monetary policy targets.

We have seen that in carrying out monetary policy, the Bank of Canada changes its target for the overnight interest rate depending on the state of the economy. During times when the economy is not experiencing a financial crisis, is using the overnight interest rate as a target the best way to conduct monetary policy? If the Bank of Canada targets the overnight interest rate, how should it decide what the target level should be? In this section, we consider some important issues concerning the Bank of Canada's targeting policy.

Should the Bank of Canada Target the Money Supply?

Some economists have argued that rather than use an interest rate as its monetary policy target, the Bank of Canada should use the money supply. Many of the economists who make this argument belong to a school of thought known as *monetarism*. The leader of the monetarist school was Nobel Laureate Milton Friedman, who was skeptical that central banks would be able to correctly time changes in monetary policy.

Friedman and his followers favoured replacing *monetary policy* with a *monetary growth rule*. Ordinarily, we expect monetary policy to respond to changing economic conditions: When the economy is in recession, the central bank reduces interest rates, and when inflation is increasing, the central bank raises interest rates. A **monetary growth rule**, in contrast, is a plan for increasing the money supply at a constant rate that does not change in response to economic conditions. Friedman and his followers proposed a monetary growth rule of increasing the money supply every year at a rate equal to the long-run growth rate of real GDP, which is about 3 percent. If the Bank of Canada adopted this monetary growth rule, it would stick to it through changing economic conditions.

Monetary growth rule A plan for increasing the quantity of money at a fixed rate that does not respond to changes in economic conditions.

But what happens under a monetary growth rule if the economy moves into recession? Shouldn't the Bank of Canada abandon the rule to drive down interest rates? Friedman argued that the central bank should stick to the rule even during recessions because, he believed, active monetary policy destabilizes the economy, increasing the number of recessions and their severity. By keeping the money supply growing at a constant rate, Friedman argued, the central bank would greatly increase economic stability.

Although during the 1970s some economists and politicians pressured the Bank of Canada to adopt a monetary growth rule, most of that pressure has disappeared in recent years. A key reason is that the fairly close relationship between movements in the money supply and movements in real GDP and the price level that existed before 1980 has become much weaker. Since 1980, the growth rate of narrow money supply measures (such as M1+) has been unstable. In some years, M1+ has grown more than 10 percent, while in other years, it has actually fallen. Yet despite these wide fluctuations in the

Figure 11.10

The Bank of Canada Can't Target Both the Money Supply and the Interest Rate

The Bank of Canada is forced to choose between using either an interest rate or the money supply as its monetary policy target. In this figure, the Bank of Canada can set a target of $90 billion for the money supply or a target of 5 percent for the interest rate, but the Bank of Canada can't reach both targets because it can achieve only combinations of the interest rate and the money supply that represent equilibrium in the money market.

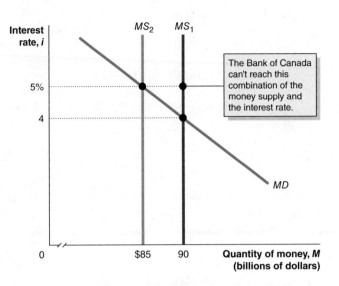

The Bank of Canada can't reach this combination of the money supply and the interest rate.

growth of this narrow money supply measure, growth in real GDP has been fairly stable, and inflation has remained low during most years.

Why Doesn't the Bank of Canada Target Both the Money Supply and the Interest Rate?

Most economists believe that an interest rate is the best monetary policy target, but other economists believe the Bank of Canada should target the money supply. Why doesn't the Bank of Canada satisfy both groups by targeting both the money supply and the interest rate? The simple answer to this question is that the Bank of Canada can't target both at the same time. To see why, look at Figure 11.10, which shows the money market.

Remember that the Bank of Canada controls the money supply, but it does not control money demand. Money demand is determined by decisions of households and firms as they weigh the trade-off between the convenience of money and its low interest rate compared with other financial assets. Suppose the Bank of Canada is targeting the interest rate and decides, given conditions in the economy, that the interest rate should be 5 percent. Or, suppose the Bank of Canada is targeting the money supply and decides that the money supply should be $90 billion. Figure 11.10 shows that the Bank of Canada can bring about an interest rate of 5 percent or a money supply of $90 billion, but it can't bring about both. The point representing an interest rate of 5 percent and a money supply of $90 billion is not on the money demand curve, so it can't represent an equilibrium in the money market. Only combinations of the interest rate and the money supply that represent equilibrium in the money market are possible.

The Bank of Canada has to choose between targeting an interest rate and targeting the money supply. For most of the period since World War II, the Bank of Canada has chosen an interest rate target.

The Taylor Rule

Taylor rule A rule developed by John Taylor that links the central bank's target for the overnight interest rate to economic variables.

How does the Bank of Canada choose a target for the overnight interest rate? John Taylor of Stanford University has analyzed the factors involved in central bank decision making and developed the **Taylor rule** to explain overnight interest rate targeting. The Taylor rule begins with an estimate of the value of the equilibrium real overnight interest rate, which is the overnight interest rate—adjusted for inflation—that would be consistent with real GDP being equal to potential real GDP in the long run. According to the Taylor rule, the Bank of Canada should set the target for the overnight interest rate so that it is equal to the sum of the inflation rate, the equilibrium real overnight interest rate, and two additional terms. The first of these additional terms is the *inflation gap*—the difference between current inflation and a target rate; the second is the *output gap*—the percentage difference between real GDP and potential real GDP. The inflation gap and output gap are each given "weights" that reflect their influence on the overnight interest rate target. With weights of 1/2 for both gaps, we have the following Taylor rule:

Overnight interest rate target = Current inflation rate + Equilibrium real

Overnight interest rate + ((1/2) × Inflation gap) + ((1/2) × Output gap).

The Taylor rule includes expressions for the inflation gap and the output gap because the Bank of Canada is concerned about both inflation and fluctuations in real GDP. Taylor demonstrated that if the equilibrium real overnight interest rate is 2 percent and the target rate of inflation is 2 percent, the preceding expression does a good job of explaining changes in the Bank of Canada's target for the overnight interest rate during most years. Consider an example in which the current inflation rate is 1 percent, and real GDP is 1 percent below potential real GDP. In that case, the inflation gap is 1 percent − 2 percent = −1 percent and the output gap is also -1 percent. Inserting these values in the Taylor rule, we can calculate the predicted value for the overnight interest rate target:

Overnight interest rate target = 1% + 2% + ((1/2) × −1%) + ((1/2) × −1%) = 2%.

It should also be noted that in the Taylor rule, the coefficient on the inflation gap is greater than zero. This means that when the inflation rate increases by 1 percentage point, the central bank increases the overnight interest rate by more than 1 percentage point (in the case of the above equation, by 1 + 1/2) so that the real interest rate also rises. This is known as the **Taylor principle** and is critical to the success of monetary policy as it ensures that monetary policy is stabilizing. For example, when the overnight interest rate increases by less than the increase in the inflation rate, then the real interest rate would decline, stimulating the level of economic activity and leading to more inflation.

Although the Taylor rule does not account for changes in the target inflation rate or the equilibrium interest rate, many economists view the rule as a convenient tool for analyzing the overnight funds target.

Taylor principle The principle that the central bank should raise the nominal interest rate by more than the increase in the inflation rate so that the real interest rate also increases.

Making the Connection | How Does the Bank of Canada Measure Inflation?

To attain its goal of price stability, the Bank of Canada has to consider carefully the best way to measure the inflation rate. The consumer price index (CPI) is the most widely used measure of inflation. But the CPI suffers from biases that cause it to overstate the true underlying rate of inflation. An alternative measure of changes in consumer prices can be constructed from the data gathered to calculate GDP. The GDP deflator is a broad measure of the price level that includes the price of every good or service that is in GDP. Changes in the GDP deflator are not a good measure of inflation experienced by the typical consumer, worker, or firm, however, because the deflator includes prices of goods, such as industrial equipment, that are not widely purchased.

The Bank of Canada uses the rate of change in the CPI to measure inflation because it is the most commonly used and understood price measure in Canada. The Bank of Canada's inflation targets are specified in terms of "headline CPI" (all items), but it also uses "core CPI," which excludes volatile components (such as food, energy, and the effect of indirect taxes) as a measure of the headline rate's trend. For example, prices of food and energy tend to fluctuate up and down for reasons that may not be related to the causes of general inflation and that can't easily be controlled by monetary policy. Oil prices, in particular, have moved dramatically up and down in recent years. Therefore, a price index that includes food and energy prices may not give a clear view of underlying trends in inflation.

The following graph shows movements in the CPI and the core CPI from January 1993 through August 2015. Although the two measures of inflation move roughly together, the core CPI has been more stable than the CPI. Note in particular the period in late 2009 when the CPI was indicating that the economy was experiencing deflation, but the core CPI was still showing moderate inflation rates of about 2 percent.

If you want to know what the Bank of Canada thinks the current inflation rate is, the best idea is to look at data on the core CPI.

The Bank of Canada excludes food and energy prices from its main measure of inflation.

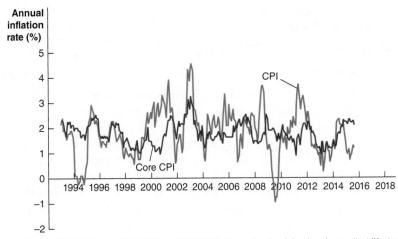

Source: Statistics Canada CANSIM II series V41690914 and V41690926. Reproduced and distributed on an "as is" basis with the permission of Statistics Canada.

MyEconLab **Your Turn:** Test your understanding by doing related problems 5.3 and 5.4 on page 323 at the end of this chapter.

11.6 LEARNING OBJECTIVE

Discuss the policies central banks used during the 2007–2009 global financial crisis.

Central Bank Policies during the 2007–2009 Global Financial Crisis

As we have seen, a country's central bank traditionally responds to a recession by lowering the target for the interest rate. The severity of the recession of 2007–2009, particularly the problems in global financial markets during those years, complicated the job of the Federal Reserve in the United States, the world's largest central bank. For example, by December 2008, the US Federal Reserve had effectively lowered the target for the overnight interest rate to zero, but the zero interest rate alone did not achieve the desired expansionary effect on the economy. In this section, we will discuss some of the additional policy measures the Federal Reserve took during the 2007–2009 recession. Some of these measures were used for the first time in its history.

The Inflation and Deflation of the Housing Market Bubble in the United States

To understand the 2007–2009 global financial crisis and the difficulties in financial markets that occurred during it, we need to start by considering the housing market in the United States. The US Federal Reserve lowered the target for its federal funds rate during the 2001 recession to stimulate demand for housing. The policy was successful, and most builders experienced several years of high demand. By 2005, however, many economists argued that a "bubble" had formed in the housing market. As we discussed in Chapter 6, the price of any asset reflects the returns the owner of the asset expects to receive. For example, the price of a share of stock reflects the profitability of the firm issuing the stock because the owner of a share of stock has a claim on the firm's profits and assets.

Many economists believe, however, that sometimes a *stock market bubble* can form when the prices of stocks rise above levels that can be justified by the profitability of the firms issuing the stock. Stock market bubbles end when enough investors decide stocks are overvalued and begin to sell. Why would an investor be willing to pay more for a share of stock than would be justified by its underlying value? There are two main explanations: The investor may be caught up in the enthusiasm of the moment and, by failing to gather sufficient information, may overestimate the true value of the stock; or the investor may expect to profit from buying stock at inflated prices if the investor can sell the stock at an even higher price before the bubble bursts.

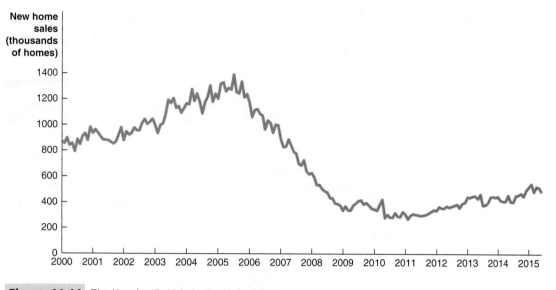

Figure 11.11 The Housing Bubble in the United States

Sales of new homes in the United States went on a roller-coaster ride, rising by 60 percent between January 2000 and July 2005, before falling by 80 percent between July 2005 and May 2010.

Note: The data are seasonally adjusted at an annual rate.

Source: Data from U.S. Bureau of the Census.

The price of a house should reflect the value of the housing services the house provides. We can use the rents charged for comparable houses in an area to measure the value of housing services. By 2005, in some US cities, the prices of houses had risen so much that monthly mortgage payments were far above the monthly rent on comparable houses. In addition, in some cities, there was an increase in the number of buyers who did not intend to live in the houses they purchased but were using them as investments. Like stock investors during a stock market bubble, these housing investors were expecting to make a profit by selling houses at higher prices than they had paid for them, and they were not concerned about whether the prices of the houses were above the value of the housing services provided.

During 2006 and 2007, it became clear that the air was rapidly escaping from the US housing bubble. Figure 11.11 shows new home sales for each month from January 2000 through August 2011. New home sales rose by 60 percent between January 2000 and July 2005 and then fell by 80 percent between July 2005 and May 2010; sales remained at low levels during the following year. Sales of existing homes followed a similar pattern. Prices of new and existing homes in most markets also began to decline beginning in 2006, and the inventory of unsold homes offered for sale soared. Some homebuyers began having trouble making their loan payments. When lenders foreclosed on some of these loans, the lenders sold the homes, causing housing prices to decline further. *Subprime loans* are loans granted to borrowers with flawed credit histories. Some mortgage lenders that had concentrated on making subprime loans suffered heavy losses and went out of business, and most banks and other lenders tightened the requirements for borrowers. This *credit crunch* made it more difficult for potential homebuyers to obtain mortgages, further depressing the market.

The decline in the housing market affected other markets as well. For example, with home prices falling, consumption spending on furniture, appliances, and home improvements declined as many households found it more difficult to borrow against the value of their homes.

Was the housing bubble the result of overly optimistic expectations by homebuyers and builders who believed that new residential construction and housing prices would continue to rise at rapid rates indefinitely? While overly optimistic expectations may have played some role in the housing bubble, many economists believe that changes in the market for mortgages may have played a bigger role.

The Changing Mortgage Market in the United States

Until the 1970s, the financial institutions that granted mortgages in the United States kept the loans until the borrowers paid them off. As we saw in Chapter 10, a financial asset such as a mortgage is a security only if it can be resold in a secondary market. Many politicians in the United States believed that home ownership could be increased by creating a secondary market in mortgages. If financial institutions could resell mortgages, then, in effect, individual investors would be able to provide funds for mortgages. The process would work like this: If a bank granted a mortgage and then resold the mortgage to an investor, the bank could use the funds received from the investor to grant another mortgage. In this way, financial institutions could grant more mortgage loans because they would no longer depend only on deposits for the funds needed to make the loans. One barrier to creating a secondary market in mortgages was that most investors were unwilling to buy mortgages because they were afraid of losing money if the borrower stopped making payments, or *defaulted*, on the loan.

To reassure investors, the US government used two *government-sponsored enterprises (GSEs)*: the Federal National Mortgage Association ("Fannie Mae") and the Federal Home Loan Mortgage Corporation ("Freddie Mac"), the equivalent of Canada's Canada Mortgage and Housing Corporation (CMHC). These two institutions stand between investors and banks that grant mortgages. Fannie Mae and Freddie Mac sell bonds to investors and use the funds to purchase mortgages from banks. By the 1990s, a large secondary market existed in mortgages, with funds flowing from investors through Fannie Mae and Freddie Mac to banks and, ultimately, to individuals and families borrowing money to buy houses.

The Role of Investment Banks in the United States

By the 2000s, further changes had taken place in the US mortgage market. First, investment banks became significant participants in the secondary market for mortgages. Investment banks, such as Goldman Sachs and Morgan Stanley, differ from commercial banks in that they do not take in deposits and rarely lend directly to households. Instead, investment banks concentrate on providing advice to firms issuing stocks and bonds or considering mergers with other firms. Investment banks began buying mortgages, bundling large numbers of them together as bonds known as *mortgage-backed securities*, and reselling them to investors. Mortgage-backed securities proved very popular with investors because they often paid higher interest rates than other securities with comparable default risk.

Second, by the height of the US housing bubble in 2005 and early 2006, lenders had greatly loosened the standards for obtaining a mortgage loan. Traditionally, only borrowers with good credit histories and who were willing to make a down payment equal to at least 20 percent of the value of the house they were buying would be able to receive a mortgage. By 2005, however, lenders were issuing many mortgages to subprime borrowers with flawed credit histories. In addition, "Alt-A" borrowers (those with mortgages that are riskier than prime mortgages but less risky than subprime mortgages) who stated—but did not document—their incomes and borrowers who made very small down payments found it easier to take out loans. Lenders also created new types of *adjustable-rate mortgages* that allowed borrowers to pay a very low interest rate for the first few years of the mortgage and then pay a higher rate in later years. The chance that the borrowers using these nontraditional mortgages would default was higher than for borrowers using traditional mortgages. Why would borrowers take out mortgages if they doubted that they could make the payments, and why would lenders grant these mortgages? The answer seems to be that both borrowers and lenders were anticipating that housing prices would continue to rise, which would reduce the chance that borrowers would default on the mortgages and would also make it easier for borrowers to convert to more traditional mortgages in the future.

Unfortunately, the decline in housing prices in the United States led to rising defaults among subprime and Alt-A borrowers, borrowers with adjustable-rate mortgages, and borrowers who had made only small down payments. When borrowers began defaulting on mortgages, the value of many mortgage-backed securities declined sharply. Investors feared that if they purchased these securities, they would not receive the promised payments because the payments on the securities depended on borrowers making their mortgage payments, which an increasing number were failing to do. Many commercial banks and investment banks owned these mortgage-backed securities, so the decline in the value of the securities caused these banks to suffer heavy losses. By mid-2007, the decline in the value of mortgage-backed securities and the large losses suffered by commercial banks and investment banks began to cause turmoil in the financial system. Many investors refused to buy mortgage-backed securities, and some investors would buy only bonds issued by the US Treasury.

Why Didn't Canada Have a Housing Bubble and Banking Crisis in 2008?

As already noted, during the subprime financial crisis, the value of mortgage-backed securities held by financial institutions in the United States plummeted. Moreover, the US government, as well as governments in some European countries, worked on full-scale banking bailouts and rescue packages in the trillions of dollars. Canada, however, did not have to bail out any banks, although Canadian banks also had their problems; their shares fell by almost 50 percent, and some of them experienced huge losses.

One reason the Canadian economy and banks have done much better than their US and European counterparts is that Canada's banking regulator, the Office of the Superintendent of Financial Institutions (OSFI), has been more conservative than banking regulators in other countries. As a result, Canadian banks have lower leverage and more conservative lending and acquisition practices. In fact, in the aftermath of the subprime recession, Canada's banking system has been viewed as the soundest in the world, with many countries considering Canadian-style reforms of their financial markets.

However, the low interest rates over the past seven years are creating distortions in the economy, such as a household debt-to-after-tax-income ratio of over 160 percent and an overheated housing market. These distortions have alarmed the Bank of Canada, the Department of Finance, and the Office of the Superintendent of Financial Institutions. So far, the Bank of Canada has resisted raising interest rates, because of the slow economic recovery and the uncertainty in the United States, Europe, and China. But there has been some coordination between monetary policy and financial stability policy. In particular, the Minister of Finance has tightened the country's mortgage insurance rules four times so far since the global financial crisis, in an attempt to cool the housing market and address financial imbalances in the economy.

Making the Connection | The Wonderful World of Leverage

Traditionally, most people taking out a mortgage make a down payment equal to 20 percent of the price of the house and borrow the remaining 80 percent. During a housing boom, however, many people purchase houses with down payments of 5 percent or less. In this sense, borrowers are highly *leveraged*, which means that their investment in their house is made mostly with borrowed money.

To see how leverage works in the housing market, consider the following example: Suppose that you buy a $200 000 house on January 1, 2017. On January 1, 2018, the price of the house—if you decide to sell it—has risen to $220 000. What return have you earned on your investment in the house? The answer depends on how much you invested when you bought the house. For example, if you paid $200 000 in cash for the house, your return on that $200 000 investment is the $20 000 increase in the price of the house divided by your $200 000 investment, or 10 percent. Suppose that rather than paying cash, you made a down payment of 20 percent, or $40 000, and borrowed the rest by taking out a mortgage loan of $160 000. Now the return on your investment

Making a very small down payment on a home mortgage leaves a buyer vulnerable to falling house prices.

in the house is the $20 000 increase in the price of the house divided by your $40 000 investment, or 50 percent. If the down payment is less than 20 percent, your return on investment will be higher. The second column in the table below shows how the return on your investment increases as your down payment decreases:

	Return on your investment from …	
Down Payment	A 10 Percent Increase in the Price of Your House	A 10 Percent Decrease in the Price of Your House
100%	10%	−10%
20	50	−50
10	100	−100
5	200	−200

An investment financed at least partly by borrowing is called a *leveraged investment*. As this example shows, the larger the fraction of an investment financed by borrowing, the greater the degree of leverage in the investment, and the greater the potential return. But as the third column in the table shows, the reverse is also true: The greater the leverage, the greater the potential loss. To see why, consider once again that you buy a house for $200 000, except that in this case, after one year the price of the house falls to $180 000. If you paid $200 000 in cash for the house—so your leverage was zero—the $20 000 decline in the price of the house represents a loss of 10 percent of your investment. But if you made a down payment of only $10 000 and borrowed the remaining $190 000, then the $20 000 decline in the price of the house represents a loss of 200 percent of your investment. In fact, the house is now worth $10 000 less than the amount of your mortgage loan. The *equity* in your house is the difference between the market price of the house and the amount you owe on a loan. If the amount you owe is greater than the price of the house, you have *negative equity*. A homeowner who has negative equity is also said to be "upside down" on his or her mortgage.

When the housing bubble burst in the United States and housing prices started to fall, many people found that they had negative equity. In that situation, some people defaulted on their loans, sometimes by simply moving out and abandoning their homes. Leverage had contributed to the housing boom and bust and the severity of the 2007–2009 recession.

MyEconLab **Your Turn:** Test your understanding by doing related problem 6.6 on page 324 at the end of this chapter.

The US Federal Reserve and the US Treasury Department Respond

Because the problems in financial markets resulting from the bursting of the housing bubble in the United States were so profound, the US Federal Reserve entered into an unusual partnership with the Treasury Department to develop suitable policies. Federal Reserve Chairman Ben Bernanke and Treasury Secretaries Henry Paulson (in the Bush administration) and Timothy Geithner (in the first Obama administration) responded to the crisis by intervening in financial markets in unprecedented ways.

Initial US Federal Reserve and Treasury Actions. The financial crisis significantly worsened following the bankruptcy of the investment bank Lehman Brothers on September 15, 2008. So it is useful to look at the actions taken by the US Federal Reserve and the Treasury before and after that date. First, although the Federal Reserve traditionally made loans only to commercial banks, in March 2008 it announced it would temporarily make discount loans to *primary dealers*—firms that participate in regular open market transactions with the Federal Reserve. This change was intended to provide short-term funds to these dealers, some of which are investment banks. Second, also in March, the Federal Reserve announced that it would loan up to US$200 billion of Treasury securities in exchange for mortgage-backed securities. This temporary program made it possible for primary dealers that owned mortgage-backed securities that were difficult or impossible to sell, to have access to Treasury securities that they could use as collateral for short-term loans. Third, once again in March, the Federal Reserve and the Treasury helped JPMorgan Chase acquire the investment bank Bear Stearns, which was on the edge of failing. The Federal Reserve agreed that if JPMorgan Chase would acquire Bear Stearns, the Federal Reserve would guarantee any losses JPMorgan Chase suffered on Bear Stearns's holdings of mortgage-backed securities, up to a limit of US$29 billion. The Federal Reserve and the Treasury were convinced that the failure of Bear Stearns had the potential of causing a financial panic, as many investors and financial firms would have stopped making short-term loans to other investment banks. Finally, in early September, the Treasury moved to have the federal government take control of Fannie Mae and Freddie Mac. Although Fannie Mae and Freddie Mac had been sponsored by the federal government, they were actually private businesses whose stock was bought and sold on the New York Stock Exchange. Under the Treasury's plan, Fannie Mae and Freddie Mac were each provided with up to US$100 billion in exchange for 80 percent ownership of the firms. The firms were placed under the supervision of the Federal Housing Finance Agency. The Treasury believed that the bankruptcy of Fannie Mae and Freddie Mac would have caused a collapse in confidence in mortgage-backed securities, further devastating this already weak housing market.

Responses to the Failure of Lehman Brothers.

Some economists and policymakers criticized the decision by the US Federal Reserve and the Treasury to help arrange the sale of Bear Stearns to JPMorgan Chase. Their main concern was with what is known as the *moral hazard problem*, which is the possibility that managers of financial firms such as Bear Stearns might make riskier investments if they believe that the federal government will save them from bankruptcy. The Federal Reserve and the Treasury acted to save Bear Stearns because they believed that the failure of a large financial firm could have wider economic repercussions. As we discussed in Chapter 10, when a financial firm sells off its holdings of bonds and other assets, it causes their prices to fall, which in turn can undermine the financial position of other firms that also own these assets. In September 2008, when the investment bank Lehman Brothers was near bankruptcy, the Federal Reserve and the Treasury had to weigh the moral hazard problem against the possibility that the failure of Lehman Brothers would lead to further declines in asset prices and endanger the financial positions of other firms.

The Federal Reserve and the Treasury decided to allow Lehman Brothers to go bankrupt, which it did on September 15, 2008. The adverse reaction in financial markets was stronger than the Federal Reserve and the Treasury had expected, which led them to reverse course two days later, when the Federal Reserve agreed to provide a US$85 billion loan to the American International Group (AIG)—the largest insurance company in the United States—in exchange for an 80 percent ownership stake, effectively giving the federal government control of the company. One important result of the failure of Lehman Brothers was the heavy losses suffered by Reserve Primary Fund, a money market mutual fund that had invested in loans to Lehman Brothers. The problems at Reserve Primary Fund led many investors to withdraw their funds from it and other money market funds. These withdrawals reduced the ability of the money market funds to purchase commercial paper from corporations. Because in recent years corporations had become dependent on selling commercial paper to finance their operations, the Treasury and the Federal Reserve moved to stabilize this market and ensure that the flow of funds from investors to corporations continued. The Treasury announced a plan to provide insurance for deposits in money market mutual funds, similar to the existing insurance on bank deposits. The Federal Reserve announced that for a limited time it would lend directly to corporations by purchasing three-month commercial paper issued by non-financial corporations.

Finally, in October 2008, Congress passed the *Troubled Asset Relief Program (TARP)*, under which the Treasury attempted to stabilize the commercial banking system by providing funds to banks in exchange for stock. Taking partial ownership positions in private commercial banks was an unprecedented action for the federal government.

Many of the Treasury and the Fed's new approaches were controversial because they involved partial government ownership of financial firms, implicit guarantees to large financial firms that they would not be allowed to go bankrupt, and unprecedented intervention in financial markets. Although the approaches were new, they were intended to achieve the traditional macroeconomic policy goals of high employment, price stability, and stability of financial markets. What remains to be seen is whether these new approaches represent a permanent increase in federal government involvement in US financial markets or whether the end of the recession will see policy return to more traditional approaches.

The US Federal Reserve Adopts Flexible Inflation Targeting

Inflation targeting has been adopted by the central banks of New Zealand (1989), Canada (1991), the United Kingdom (1992), Finland (1993), Sweden (1993), and Spain (1994), and by the European Central Bank. Inflation targeting has also been used in some newly industrializing countries, such as Chile, South Korea, Mexico, and South Africa, as well as in some transition economies in Eastern Europe, such as the Czech Republic, Hungary, and Poland. The results of inflation targeting have varied, but typically the move to inflation targeting has been accompanied by lower inflation (sometimes at the cost of temporarily higher unemployment).

Over the past decade, many economists in the United States had proposed using *inflation targeting* as a framework for conducting monetary policy in that country. As we have already discussed, with inflation targeting, the central bank commits to achieving a publicly announced inflation target of, for example, 2 percent. Inflation targeting does not impose an inflexible rule on the central bank. The central bank would still be free, for example, to take action in the case of a severe recession. Nevertheless, monetary policy goals and operations would focus on inflation and inflation forecasts.

Although Ben Bernanke's appointment as chair of the Federal Reserve in January 2006 signalled that the Federal Reserve would likely adopt a policy of inflation targeting, the necessity of dealing with the recession of 2007–2009 temporarily pushed the issue off the Federal Reserve's agenda. In 2011, however, the Federal Reserve adopted *flexible inflation targeting*, a strategy that has been practised for over 20 years by the Bank of Canada and a number of other central banks around the world.

Economics in Your Life

Should You Buy a House during a Recession?

At the beginning of this chapter, we asked whether buying a house during a recession is a good idea. Clearly, there are many considerations to keep in mind when buying a house, which is the largest purchase you are likely to make in your lifetime. Included among these considerations are the price of the house relative to other comparable houses in the neighbourhood, whether house prices in the neighbourhood have been rising or falling, and the location of the house relative to stores, work, and good schools. Also important is the interest rate you will have to pay on the mortgage loan you would need in order to buy the house. As we have seen in this chapter, during a recession, the Bank of Canada often takes actions to lower interest rates. So, mortgage rates are typically lower during a recession than at other times. You may want to take advantage of low interest rates to buy a house during a recession. But, recessions are also times of rising unemployment, and you would not want to make a commitment to borrow a lot of money for 15 or more years if you were in significant danger of losing your job. We can conclude, then, that if your job seems secure, buying a house during a recession may be a good idea.

Conclusion

Monetary policy is one way governments pursue goals for inflation, employment, and financial stability. The governor of the Bank of Canada may have a greater ability than the prime minister of Canada to affect the Canadian economy. The government and the prime minister, however, also use their power over spending and taxes to try to stabilize the economy. In Chapter 12, we discuss how *fiscal policy*—changes in government spending and taxes—affect the economy.

Chapter Summary and Problems

Key Terms

Contractionary monetary policy, p. 301

Expansionary monetary policy, p. 301

Flexible inflation targeting, p. 293

Governing council (of the Bank of Canada), p. 306

Inflation targeting, p. 293

Monetary growth rule, p. 309

Monetary policy, p. 292

Open market buyback operations, p. 299

Operating band, p. 299

Overnight interest rate, p. 299

Symmetric inflation targeting, p. 293

Taylor rule, p. 310

Summary

*LO 11.1 *Monetary policy* is the actions the Bank of Canada takes to manage the money supply and interest rates to pursue its macroeconomic policy goals. The Bank of Canada has four *monetary policy goals* that are intended to promote a well-functioning economy: price stability, high employment, stability of financial markets and institutions, and economic growth.

LO 11.2 The Bank of Canada's *monetary policy targets* are economic variables that it can affect directly and that in turn affect variables such as real GDP and the price level that are closely related to the Bank of Canada's policy goals. The two main monetary policy targets are the money supply and the interest rate. The Bank of Canada has most often chosen to use the interest rate as its monetary policy target. The Bank of Canada announces a target for the *overnight interest rate* on eight "fixed" dates throughout the year. The overnight interest rate is the interest rate banks charge each other for overnight loans. To lower the interest rate, the Bank of Canada increases the money supply. To raise the interest rate, the Bank of Canada decreases the money supply. In a graphical analysis of the money market, when the money supply curve shifts to the right, the result is a movement down the money demand curve and a new equilibrium at a lower interest rate. When the money supply curve shifts to the left, the result is a movement up the money demand curve and a new equilibrium at a higher interest rate.

LO 11.3 An *expansionary monetary policy* lowers interest rates to increase consumption, investment, and net exports. This increased spending causes the aggregate demand (*AD*) curve to shift out more than it otherwise would, raising the level of real GDP and the price level. An expansionary monetary policy can help the

Bank of Canada achieve its goal of high employment. A *contractionary monetary policy* raises interest rates to decrease consumption, investment, and net exports. This decreased spending causes the aggregate demand curve to shift out less than it otherwise would, reducing both the level of real GDP and the inflation rate below what they would be in the absence of monetary policy. A contractionary monetary policy can help the Bank of Canada achieve its goal of price stability.

LO 11.4 We can use the *dynamic aggregate demand and aggregate supply model* introduced in Chapter 9 to look more closely at expansionary and contractionary monetary policies. The dynamic aggregate demand and aggregate supply model takes into account that (1) the economy experiences continuing inflation, with the price level rising every year, and (2) the economy experiences long-run growth, with the *LRAS* curve shifting to the right every year. In the dynamic model, an expansionary monetary policy tries to ensure that the aggregate demand curve will shift far enough to the right to bring about macroeconomic equilibrium with real GDP equal to potential GDP. A contractionary monetary policy attempts to offset movements in aggregate demand that would cause macroeconomic equilibrium to occur at a level of real GDP that is greater than potential real GDP.

LO 11.5 Some economists have argued that the Bank of Canada should use the money supply, rather than the interest rate, as its monetary policy target. Milton Friedman and other monetarists argued that central banks should adopt a *monetary growth rule* of increasing the money supply every year at a fixed rate. Support for this proposal declined after 1980 because the relationship between movements in the money supply and movements in real GDP and the price level weakened. John Taylor analyzed the factors involved in central bank decision making and developed the *Taylor rule* for

*"Learning Objective" is abbreviated to "LO" in the end-of-chapter material.

overnight interest rate targeting. The Taylor rule links the central bank's target for the overnight interest rate to economic variables. The Bank of Canada adopted *inflation targeting*—conducting monetary policy so as to commit the central bank to achieving a publicly announced level of inflation—back in 1991, and its performance in the 1990s and 2000s generally received high marks from economists. Over the past decade, many economists and central bankers have expressed significant interest in using inflation targeting. A number of foreign central banks have adopted inflation targeting, including the US Federal Reserve.

LO 11.6 A bubble in the US housing market that began to deflate in 2006 led to the global recession of 2007–2009 and an accompanying global financial crisis. In response, central banks around the world, including the Bank of Canada, instituted a variety of policy actions to protect their economies. In a series of steps, the Bank of Canada cut the target for the overnight interest rate from 4.5 percent in July 2007 to 0.25 percent in April 2009. The US Federal Reserve also cut the target for the federal funds rate from 5.25 percent in September 2007 to effectively zero in December 2008. The decline in the US housing market caused wider problems in the global financial system, as defaults on home mortgages rose and the value of mortgage-backed securities declined. Central banks around the world implemented a series of new policies to provide liquidity and restore confidence. They expanded the types of firms eligible for loans from the central bank and began lending directly to corporations by purchasing commercial paper. In the United States, under the *Troubled Asset Relief Program*, the US Treasury provided financial support to banks and other financial firms in exchange for part ownership. The Treasury also moved to have the federal government take control of Fannie Mae and Freddie Mac, government-sponsored firms that play a central role in the US mortgage market. The failure of the investment bank Lehman Brothers in September 2008 led to a deepening of the global financial crisis and provided the motivation for some of the new monetary policies. Ultimately, the new policies stabilized the financial system, but their long-term effects remain the subject of debate.

MyEconLab Log in to MyEconLab to complete these exercises and get instant feedback.

Review Questions

LO 11.1

1.1 When the government established the Bank of Canada in 1934, what was its main responsibility?

1.2 What are the Bank of Canada's four monetary policy goals?

1.3 How can the government of Canada influence the conduct of monetary policy?

1.4 How can investment banks be subject to liquidity problems?

LO 11.2

2.1 What is a monetary policy target? Why does the Bank of Canada use policy targets?

2.2 What do economists mean by the *demand for money*? What is the advantage of holding money? What is the disadvantage?

2.3 Draw a demand and supply graph showing equilibrium in the money market. Suppose the Bank of Canada wants to lower the equilibrium interest rate. Show on the graph how the Bank of Canada would accomplish this objective.

2.4 What is the overnight interest rate? What role does it play in monetary policy?

LO 11.3

3.1 How does an increase in interest rates affect aggregate demand? Briefly discuss how each component of aggregate demand is affected.

3.2 If the Bank of Canada believes the economy is about to fall into recession, what actions should it take? If the Bank of Canada believes the inflation rate is about to increase, what actions should it take?

3.3 What is *quantitative easing* and what are the central banks' objectives in using it?

LO 11.4

4.1 What are the key differences between how we illustrate an expansionary monetary policy in the basic aggregate demand and aggregate supply model and in the dynamic aggregate demand and aggregate supply model?

4.2 What are the key differences between how we illustrate a contractionary monetary policy in the basic aggregate demand and aggregate supply model and in the dynamic aggregate demand and aggregate supply model?

LO 11.5

5.1 What is a *monetary rule*, as opposed to a *monetary policy*? What monetary rule would Milton Friedman have liked central banks to follow? Why has support for a monetary rule of the kind advocated by Friedman declined since 1980?

5.2 For more than 20 years, the Bank of Canada has used the overnight interest rate as its monetary policy target. Why doesn't the Bank of Canada target the money supply at the same time?

5.3 What is the Taylor rule? What is its purpose?

LO 11.6

6.1 What is a mortgage? What were the important developments in the mortgage market during the years after 1970?

6.2 Beginning in 2008, the US Federal Reserve, the Bank of Canada, and other central banks around the world responded to the financial crisis by intervening in financial markets in unprecedented ways. Briefly summarize the actions of the Federal Reserve.

Problems and Applications

LO 11.1

1.1 What is a bank panic? Why are policymakers more concerned about bank failures than failures of restaurants or clothing stores?

1.2 Why is price stability one of the Bank of Canada's main monetary policy goals? What problems can high inflation rates cause for the economy?

1.3 What is the difference between the Bank of Canada and commercial banks, such as CIBC, Royal Bank, TD Canada Trust, ScotiaBank, and Bank of Montreal?

1.4 Stock prices rose rapidly in 2005, as did housing prices in many parts of the country. By late 2008, both stock prices and housing prices were declining sharply. Some economists have argued that rapid increases and decreases in the prices of assets such as shares of stock or houses can damage the economy. Currently, stabilizing asset prices is not one of the Bank of Canada's policy goals. In what ways would a goal of stabilizing asset prices be different from the four goals of monetary policy listed on page 293? Do you believe that stabilizing asset prices should be added to the list of the Bank of Canada's policy goals? Briefly explain.

LO 11.2

2.1 In the following graph of the money market, what could cause the money supply curve to shift from MS_1 to MS_2? What could cause the money demand curve to shift from MD_1 to MD_2?

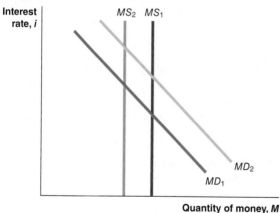

2.2 The following is the title of a July 15, 2015 *National Post* article: "Bank of Canada cuts benchmark interest rate to 0.5%, slashes economic outlook."

    a. What is the name of the "benchmark policy rate" mentioned in this article?

    b. Briefly explain who borrows money and who lends money at this "benchmark policy rate"?

    c. What is the "prime lending rate" and what is its relationship to the "benchmark policy rate" mentioned in the article?

Based on Gordon Isfeld, "Bank of Canada cuts benchmark interest rate to 0.5%, slashes economic outlook," National Post, July 15, 2015. (Accessed on October 2, 2015) http://www.nationalpost.com/Bank+Canada+cuts+benchmark+interest+rate+slashes+economic+outlook/11215945/story.html

2.3 If the Bank of Canada purchases $100 million worth of Canada bonds from the public, predict what will happen to the money supply. Explain your reasoning.

2.4 In response to problems in financial markets and a slowing economy, the Bank of Canada cut the target overnight interest rate to an all-time low. Jimmy Jean, senior economist at Desjardins Capital Markets, argued that the "rapidly emerging debate addresses the question of whether the Bank of Canada stands willing to step into the realm of unconventional policies, in case the evolution continues to stubbornly track the downside scenario and not the baseline."

    What is the relationship between the overnight interest rate falling and the money supply expanding? How does lowering the target overnight interest rate provide the banks with "extra money"?

Based on John Shmuel, "Will the Bank of Canada have to start looking at QE soon?" *Financial Post*, July 20, 2015. (Accessed on October 2, 2015) http://business.financialpost.com/investing/will-the-bank-of-canada-have-to-start-looking-at-qe-soon

LO 11.3

3.1 **[Related to the Chapter Opener on page 291]**. An October 2015 article in the *Financial Post* said:

> "Canadian household debt climbed to a record [high] relative to disposable income in the second quarter, underlining what the central bank has called a key vulnerability in the economy.
>
> Credit-market debt such as mortgages rose to 164.6 per cent of after-tax income from 163 per cent in the prior three months, Statistics Canada said Friday in Ottawa. Credit-market debt rose 1.8 per cent in the second quarter, outstripping growth in disposable income of 0.8 per cent."

What sort of "vulnerability" does a rising household debt create?

Reprinted with permission from Bloomberg News.

3.2 In explaining why monetary policy did not pull Japan out of a recession in the early 2000s, an official at the Bank of Japan was quoted as saying that despite "major increases in the money supply," the money "stay[ed] in banks." Explain what the official meant by saying that the money stayed in banks. Why would that be a problem? Where does the money go if an expansionary monetary policy is successful?

Based on James Brooke, "Critics Say Koizumi's Economic Medicine Is a Weak Tea," *New York Times*, February 27, 2002.

3.3 According to an article in *The Economist* magazine in 2013, the Japanese economy was experiencing falling prices "on everything from chocolate bars to salad."

    a. What is the term for a *falling price level*?

    b. The article also stated that Japanese Prime Minister Shinzo Abe was pressuring the Bank of Japan, the Japanese central bank, to take steps to hit an inflation target of 2 percent. Why would the Japanese government consider a falling price level to be undesirable? What steps could the Bank of Japan take to increase the price level?

Based on "Waging a New War," *The Economist*, March 9, 2013.

3.4 According to a recent article in *The Economist* magazine, "The central bank of New Zealand was the first to adopt an inflation target, in 1990. The Fed pursued an unofficial inflation target over a long period, only making its policy official in January of 2012, when it announced that it thought a policy which targets a 2% rate of inflation 'is most consistent over the longer run with the Federal Reserve's statutory mandate.'"

Why do the Fed and other inflation-targeting central banks around the world, including the Bank of Canada, target the inflation rate at 2%?

Republished with permission of The Economist Newspaper Ltd., from "Why the Fed targets 2% inflation?" *The Economist,* September 13, 2015; permission conveyed through Copyright Clearance Center, Inc.

3.5 William McChesney Martin, who was US Federal Reserve chairman from 1951 to 1970, was once quoted as saying, "The role of the Federal Reserve is to remove the punchbowl just as the party gets going." What did he mean?

William McChesney Martin

3.6 If monetary policy is so effective at helping the economy stabilize and protecting against recessions, why does recovery take so long? And why are the monetary policy effects not always readily apparent (effects can take years to determine)?

3.7 Former US president Ronald Reagan once stated that inflation "has one cause and one cause alone: government spending more than government takes in." Briefly explain whether you agree.

From Edward Nelson, "Budget Deficits and Interest Rates," *Monetary Trends,* Federal Reserve Bank of St. Louis, March 2004.

3.8 **[Related to Making the Connection on page 302]** John Maynard Keynes is said to have remarked that using an expansionary monetary policy to pull an economy out of a deep recession can be like "pushing on a string." Briefly explain what Keynes is likely to have meant.

3.9 A September 26, 2015 article in *The Economist* magazine said:

"This was supposed to be the year when the Federal Reserve would raise interest rates, which have sat between zero and 0.25% since late 2008. Shortly after the Fed allowed rates to lift off, pundits presumed that the Bank of England, which since March 2009 has held its base rate at 0.5%, a three-century low, would follow.

But on September 17th the Fed balked. Andrew Haldane, the Bank of England's chief economist, has meanwhile been airing the prospect of a further cut instead of a rise. Central banks that have raised rates in the past have had to retreat, including the European Central Bank and Sweden's Riksbank, which has since pushed rates into negative territory (see chart). Yet the longer rates remain so low, the louder the chorus of concern about financial instability, as investors in search of higher returns pile into ever riskier assets."

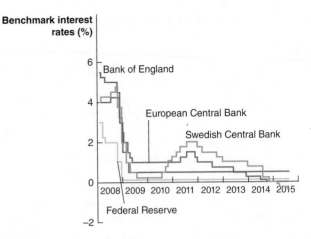

What are the negative interest rates mentioned in the article (and shown in the chart)?

Source: Republished with permission of The Economist Newspaper Ltd., from Repeat prescription: weighing the economic benefits of low interest rates against the financial risks." *The Economist,* September 26, 2015; permission conveyed through Copyright Clearance Center, Inc.

3.10 **[Related to Making the Connection on page 302]** If policymakers at the Bank of Canada are aware that GDP data are sometimes subject to large revisions, how might this affect their views about how best to conduct policy?

3.11 **[Related to Don't Let This Happen to You on page 304]** Briefly explain whether you agree with the following statement: "The Bank of Canada has an easy job. Say it wants to increase real GDP by $200 billion. All it has to do is increase the money supply by that amount."

LO 11.4

4.1 Explain whether you agree with this argument:

If the Bank of Canada actually ever carried out a contractionary monetary policy, the price level would fall. Because the price level has not fallen in Canada over an entire year since the 1930s, we can conclude that the Bank of Canada has not carried out a contractionary policy since the 1930s.

4.2 **[Related to Solved Problem 11.1 on page 307]** Use this graph to answer the following questions.

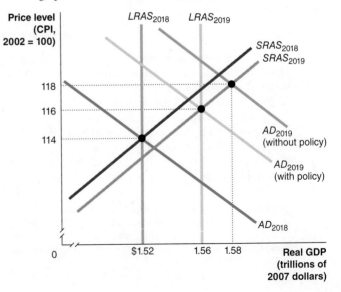

a. If the Bank of Canada does not take any policy action, what will be the level of real GDP and the price level in 2019?

b. If the Bank of Canada wants to keep real GDP at its potential level in 2019, should it use an expansionary policy or a contractionary policy? Should the Bank of Canada be buying Canada bonds or selling them?

c. If the Bank of Canada takes no policy action, what will be the inflation rate in 2019? If the Bank of Canada uses monetary policy to keep real GDP at its full-employment level, what will be the inflation rate in 2019?

4.3 [Related to Solved Problem 11.1 on page 307] The hypothetical information in the following table shows what the situation will be in 2019 if the Bank of Canada does *not* use monetary policy.

Year	Potential GDP	Real GDP	Price Level
2018	$1.52 trillion	$1.52 trillion	110.0
2019	1.56 trillion	1.58 trillion	115.5

a. If the Bank of Canada wants to keep real GDP at its potential level in 2019, should it use an expansionary policy or a contractionary policy? Should the trading desk be buying Treasury bills or selling them?

b. If the Bank of Canada's policy is successful in keeping real GDP at its potential level in 2019, state whether each of the following will be higher, lower, or the same as it would have been if the Bank of Canada had taken no action:
 i. Real GDP
 ii. Potential real GDP
 iii. The inflation rate
 iv. The unemployment rate

c. Draw an aggregate demand and aggregate supply graph to illustrate the effects of the Bank of Canada's policy. Be sure that your graph contains *LRAS* curves for 2018 and 2019; *SRAS* curves for 2018 and 2019; *AD* curves for 2018 and 2019, with and without monetary policy action; and equilibrium real GDP and the price level in 2019, with and without policy.

LO 11.5

5.1 Suppose that the equilibrium real overnight interest rate is 2 percent and the target rate of inflation is 2 percent. Use the following information and the Taylor rule to calculate the overnight interest rate target:

Current inflation rate = 4 percent
Potential real GDP = $1.4 trillion
Real GDP = $1.54 trillion

5.2 In 2013, John Taylor wrote: "I realize that there are differences of opinion about what is the best rule to guide policy and that some at the Fed (including Janet Yellen) now prefer a rule with a higher coefficient [on the output gap]."

a. If central bank policy were guided by a Taylor rule with a coefficient of 1, rather than 0.5, on the output gap, would the policy rate be higher or lower during a recession? Briefly explain.

b. Why might economist and policymakers disagree over the best rule to guide monetary policy?

Source: John Taylor, "Cross Checking 'Checking in on the Taylor Rule,'" www.economicsone.com, July16, 2013.

5.3 [Related to Making the Connection on page 311] If the core CPI is a better measure of the inflation rate than the CPI, why is the CPI more widely used? In particular, can you think of reasons the federal government uses the CPI when deciding how much to increase social security payments to retired workers to keep the purchasing power of the payments from declining?

5.4 [Related to Making the Connection on page 311] According to an article in the *Globe and Mail* in 2012, "Canada's statistics agency is refining the consumer price index, a key economic yardstick for matching pensions and salaries to the rising cost of living—and the result could mean sizable savings for governments and corporations that hike payments annually to keep pace with inflation."

Why do you think Statistics Canada would engage in this exercise? What kind of benefits do changes in the CPI affect?

Steven Chase and Tavia Grant, "Retooling of key inflation measure to influence pensions and wages," *Globe and Mail*, February 13, 2012.

LO 11.6

6.1 Some economists argue that one cause of the financial problems resulting from the housing crisis in the United States was the fact that lenders who grant mortgages no longer typically hold the mortgages until they are paid off. Instead, lenders usually resell their mortgages in secondary markets. How might a lender intending to resell a mortgage act differently than a lender intending to hold a mortgage?

6.2 William A. Barnett recently wrote the book *Getting It Wrong: How Faulty Monetary Statistics Undermine the Fed, the Financial System, and the Economy* (MIT Press, 2012). This book provides evidence that low-quality money supply measures produced and supplied by the Federal Reserve may have caused the subprime financial crisis in the United States and the global recession.

We discussed the money supply measures in Chapter 10. What are the problems with the money supply measures currently produced by most central banks around the world, including the Bank of Canada, that William Barnett is concerned with?

Based on James Pressley. "Fed's Poor Data, Not Greed, Drove Wall Street Off Cliff: Books," Bloomberg , February 16, 2012.

6.3 A recent article by leading economist Frederic S. Mishkin, "Monetary Policy Strategy: Lessons from the Crisis," concludes that:

the field of macro/monetary economics has become a hell of a lot more exciting. We are now faced with a whole new agenda for research that should keep people in the field very busy for a very long time. It has also made the work of central bankers more exciting as well. They now have to think about a much wider range of policy issues than they had to previously. This will surely be exhausting, but central banking will be a far more stimulating profession.

What are the policy issues that economists and central bankers are concerned with in the aftermath of the global financial crisis and the Great Recession?

Frederic S. Mishkin. "Monetary Policy Strategy: Lessons from the Crisis," Graduate School of Business, Columbia University and National Bureau of Economic Research, December 2010.

6.4 Recall that *securitization* is the process of turning a loan, such as a mortgage, into a bond that can be bought and sold in secondary markets. An article in *The Economist* notes:

> That securitization caused more subprime mortgages to be written is not in doubt. By offering access to a much deeper pool of capital, securitization helped to bring down the cost of mortgages and made home-ownership more affordable for borrowers with poor credit histories.

What is a "subprime mortgage"? What is a "deeper pool of capital"? Why would securitization give mortgage borrowers access to a deeper pool of capital? Would a subprime borrower be likely to pay a higher or a lower interest rate than a borrower with a better credit history? Under what circumstances might a lender prefer to loan money to a borrower with a poor credit history rather than to a borrower with a good credit history? Briefly explain.

"Ruptured Credit," *The Economist*, May 15, 2008.

6.5 In the fall of 2011, investors began to fear that some European governments, particularly Greece and Italy, might default on the bonds they had issued, making the prices of the bonds fall sharply. Many European banks owned these bonds, and some investors worried that these banks might also be in financial trouble. An article in *The Economist* magazine referred to the "prospect of another Lehman moment." The article noted that, "Governments are once again having to step in to support their banks." What did the article mean by another "Lehman moment"? Why might European governments have felt the need to support their banks in order to avoid another Lehman moment?

"Here We Go Again," *The Economist*, October 8, 2011.

6.6 **[Related to Making the Connection on page 315]** Suppose that you buy a house for $150 000. One year later, the market price of the house has risen to $165 000. What is the return on your investment in the house if you made a down payment of 20 percent and took out a mortgage loan for the other 80 percent? What if you made a down payment of 5 percent and borrowed the other 95 percent? Be sure to show your calculations in your answer.

MyEconLab   MyEconLab is an online tool designed to help you master the concepts covered in your course. It will create a personalized study plan to stimulate and measure your learning. Log in to take advantage of this powerful study aid, and to access quizzes and other valuable course-related material.

Chris Goodney/
Bloomberg/
Getty Images

CHAPTER

12

Fiscal Policy

Fiscal Policy as a 2015 Canadian Election Issue

During the election of 2015, fiscal policy became an election issue. GDP had shrunk in both the first and second quarters of the year, meaning a recession had occurred. Two of the three main national parties called for increases in federal government spending, in part to stimulate the economy. The Liberal Party, which won the election and formed the new government, promised to spend significantly and even run deficits in the process.

Many politicians and economists believe that changes in government spending and taxation can be used to manage the overall level of macroeconomic activity in a country. During 2007–2009, virtually all wealthy countries saw government spending increase in an effort to offset the drop in GDP associated with the global financial crisis.

Fiscal policy is not only used to stabilize the economy. It is also used to encourage investment and savings. For example, during the election campaign the Liberal Party promised that much of the new spending would be on infrastructure projects in an effort to provide the basics firms need to do business. Without high-quality infrastructure, firms will not undertake the risk of building new production facilities or upgrading existing equipment.

Economists and, more recently, politicians have also begun to worry about long-term deficit spending. When a government constantly spends more than it collects in taxes and other forms of revenue, more and more of its budget must be devoted to paying interest on past borrowing. The federal government has to attempt to balance its desire to stimulate the economy and foster economic growth with costs of borrowing to do so. Returning the budget to balance will be difficult if economic growth remains slow and incomes do not rise quickly.

Chapter Outline and Learning Objectives

Economics in Your Life

What Would You Do with $500 Less?

Suppose the federal government announces that it will ask every person in Canada over the age of 18 to pay an additional tax of $500 a year. You expect that this tax increase will be permanent; that is, you'll be required to pay this $500 tax every year in the future. How will you respond to this decrease in your disposable income? What effect will this tax increase likely have on equilibrium real GDP in the short run? As you read this chapter, see if you can answer these questions. You can check your answers against those we provide on page 351 at the end of this chapter.

I n Chapter 11 we discussed how the Bank of Canada uses monetary policy to pursue its main macroeconomic policy goals: (1) price stability, (2) high employment, (3) stability of financial markets and institutions, and (4) economic growth. In this chapter, we will explore how the government uses *fiscal policy*, which involves changes in taxes and government purchases, to achieve similar policy goals. As we have seen, in the short run, the price level and the level of real GDP and total employment in the economy depend on aggregate demand and short-run aggregate supply. The government can affect the levels of both aggregate demand and aggregate supply through fiscal policy. We will explore how Parliament and the prime minister decide which fiscal policy actions to take to achieve their goals. We will also discuss the disagreements among economists and policymakers over the effectiveness of fiscal policy.

12.1 LEARNING OBJECTIVE

Define fiscal policy.

What Is Fiscal Policy?

Since the Great Depression of the 1930s, federal, provincial, and territorial governments have been actively engaged in keeping their economies stable. The Bank of Canada closely monitors the economy and meets eight times a year to decide on any changes in monetary policy. Any time Parliament is in session, government can take action to change taxes and/or spending to influence the economy. Changes in taxes and spending that are intended to achieve macroeconomic policy goals are called **fiscal policy**.

Fiscal policy Changes in federal taxes and purchases that are intended to achieve macroeconomic policy objectives.

What Fiscal Policy Is and What It Isn't

In Canada, federal, provincial, territorial, and local governments all have the ability to levy taxes and spend money. Economists generally use the term *fiscal policy* to refer only to the actions of the federal government. Provincial, territorial, and local governments sometimes use their ability to tax and spend to aid their local economies, but only the federal government is focused on the economy of the whole country. The federal government also makes decisions about taxes and spending that are not related to the health of the economy. For example, a decision to tax junk food is a health policy, not a fiscal policy. Similarly, a decision to purchase new F-35 fighter jets to assert Arctic sovereignty is a national security policy, not a fiscal policy.

Automatic Stabilizers versus Discretionary Fiscal Policy

There is an important distinction between *automatic stabilizers* and *discretionary fiscal policy*. Some types of government spending and taxes, which automatically increase and decrease to counter the business cycle, are referred to as **automatic stabilizers**. The word *automatic* in this case refers to the fact that changes in these types of spending and taxes happen without actions by the government. For example, when the economy is expanding and employment is increasing, government spending on Employment Insurance payments to workers who have lost their jobs will automatically decrease. During a recession, as employment declines, this type of spending will automatically increase. Similarly, when the economy is expanding and incomes are rising, the amount the government

Automatic stabilizers Government spending and taxes that automatically increase or decrease along with the business cycle.

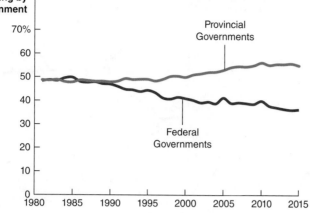

Figure 12.1

The Federal Government's Share of Total Government Spending, 1981–2015

The federal government's share of government spending has been falling for the past 35 years.

Source: Statistics Canada, Table 380-0080 – Revenue, expenditure and budgetary balance – General governments, quarterly (dollars), CANSIM (database). National Economic and Financial Accounts. Reproduced and distributed on an "as is" basis with the permission of Statistics Canada.

collects in taxes will increase as people pay additional taxes on their higher incomes. When the economy is in recession, the amount the government collects in taxes will fall.

With discretionary fiscal policy, the government takes actions to change spending or taxes. The increased spending and tax cut cuts for 2009–2010—along with the spending cuts of 2012—are examples of discretionary fiscal policy actions.

An Overview of Government Spending and Taxes

To provide a context for understanding fiscal policy, it's important to understand the big picture of government taxing and spending.

Over the past 35 years, the federal government's share of total government spending has been declining while the share of spending done at the provincial level has been rising, as Figure 12.1 shows. There are two reasons for the relative decline in federal spending: The federal government has been delegating the administration of certain responsibilities to provincial and territorial agencies (e.g., the regulation of interprovincial and international highway traffic, and the managements of forestry and natural resources), and the cost of health care.

Beginning in the late 1990s, overall government spending on health care rose rapidly. Figure 12.2 shows the percentage of total government spending on health care since 1981. According to the division of powers between the federal and provincial governments, health care is a provincial (and territorial) responsibility. However, the federal government supports provincial health care spending through the Canada Health Transfer, a payment program that provides money to provincial and territorial governments to pay for health care. Even though a significant portion of health care dollars come from the federal government, provincial and territorial governments are responsible for how the money is spent. In 2015, the Canada Health Transfer accounted for roughly 11 percent of federal government spending.

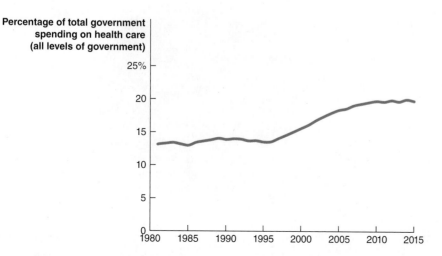

Figure 12.2

Total Government Spending on Health Care, 1981–2015

Like other levels of government, the federal government has been spending an increasing amount on health care over the past 20 years.

Source: Statistics Canada, Revenue, expenditure and budgetary balance – General governments, quarterly (dollars), CANSIM (database), Canadian Institute for Health Information National Expenditure Database. Reproduced and distributed on an "as is" basis with the permission of Statistics Canada.

Figure 12.3

Federal Government Expenditures as a Percentage of GDP

From the early 1960s until the mid 1990s, the government played an increasingly important role in the Canadian economy. The importance of government spending in the economy has fallen since the 1990s but still accounts for almost 40 percent of all economic activity in 2015.

Source: Statistics Canada, Table 380-0064 - Gross domestic product, expenditure-based, annual (dollars unless otherwise noted). Reproduced and distributed on an "as is" basis with the permission of Statistics Canada.

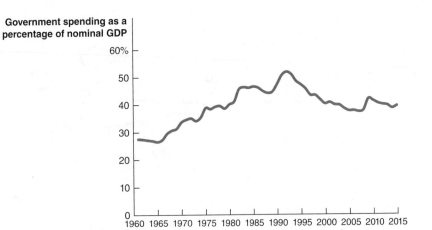

Economists often measure government spending relative to the size of the economy by calculating government spending as a percentage of GDP. Remember that there is a difference between government *purchases* and government *expenditures*. When the federal government purchases a new jet for the Canadian Armed Forces or hires an RCMP officer, it receives a good or service in return. Federal government expenditures include purchases plus all other forms of government spending, such as transfer payments to the provinces/territories and civil servants' paycheques. The change in the size of government spending relative to the Canadian economy is shown in Figure 12.3. The government was responsible for almost half the economic activity in Canada in 1992. From that time until 2008, the government played less of a role in the Canadian economy. In 2009, however, government spending increased in an effort to stimulate the shrinking economy, and the size of government spending relative to the Canadian economy rose significantly.

Where Does the Money Go?

The federal government spends money in a variety of areas. Figure 12.4 shows that in 2015, the largest area of federal spending was transfers to households, which accounted for $1 out of every $3 spent by the federal government. This spending includes Old Age Security payments and Employment Insurance payments. The second largest area of federal spending is purchases of Non-Defence Final Goods and Services—all government operations outside the Department of Defence. This would include spending by the Department of Fisheries and Oceans Canada and the Department of Justice. Spending on defence accounts for a relatively small portion of federal government spending, just 7 percent of the total. Transfers from the federal government to other levels of government

Figure 12.4

Federal Government Spending, 2015

Transfers to households, such as elderly support programs, Employment Insurance, and support for children, account for 33 percent of all federal government spending.

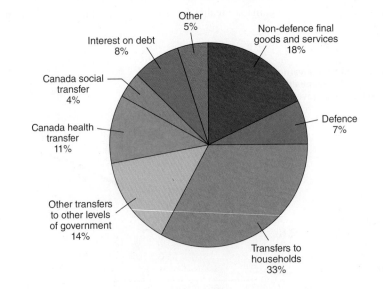

account for 29 percent of federal government spending. The two best known of these transfer programs are the Canada Health Transfer (11 percent) and the Canada Social Transfer (4 percent). These transfer programs are intended to help ensure all Canadians have access to high-quality health care and social services. Finally, interest on the debt owed by the federal government accounts for 8 percent of all federal government spending. Every time the federal government runs a deficit, it adds to the debt and adds to the interest that will have to be paid in the future.

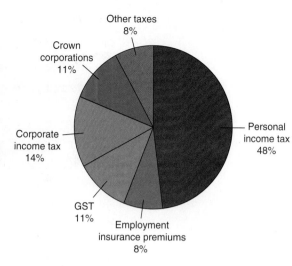

Figure 12.5

Federal Government Revenue

While all government revenue ultimately comes from people, almost half of the federal government's revenue comes from directly taxing personal income.

Source: Data from: Department of Finance, Government of Canada, http://www.fin.gc.ca/tax-impot/2011/html-eng.asp (accessed Feb. 7, 2012).

Where Does the Money Come From?

The short answer to this question is that the federal government's money comes from the people of Canada. The two main ways in which the federal government raises revenue are by taxing the population and charging for services. Figure 12.5 shows that in 2015 income taxes on individuals were the largest single source of government revenue, accounting for 48 percent of the total. Corporate income taxes, which are taxes on corporate profits before the companies owners are paid, were the second largest source at 14 percent. The Goods and Services Tax (GST) brought in 11 percent of federal government revenue. Crown corporations (businesses owned by the government) and the sale of goods and services also accounted for 11 percent of government revenue. Employment insurance premiums, which are paid as a portion of wages by everyone with a job, made up another 8 percent of government revenue. The remaining 8 percent of revenue came from consumption taxes (like taxes on alcohol and cigarettes), import duties, and energy taxes.

As the role of the federal government has shrunk, the role of provincial governments has increased. The Canadian system grants authority over health care and education to provincial, not federal, government. So while the federal government does transfer money to provincial government to help pay for health care and education, the provincial governments still have to take on a lot of this spending.

Where Does Provincial Revenue Come From?

Provincial governments have to generate revenue to pay for all the goods and services they provide. Figure 12.6 below shows the breakdown of provincial government revenue for the 2015–2016 budget year.

In the 2015–2016 fiscal year, Canadian provincial governments generated more revenue from personal income taxes, 27 percent, than from any other source. Transfers from the federal government, including the Canada Health Transfer, made up the second largest source at 21 percent. Sales taxes also made a significant contribution to provincial revenue in all provinces except Alberta, which does not levy a basic sales tax. Sales taxes contributed an average of 17 percent of provincial revenues across the country. Corporate incomes taxes contributed just 8 percent to revenue.

Where does Provincial Revenue Go?

Figure 12.7 shows provincial government spending by category, which is dominated by just two items–health care and education.

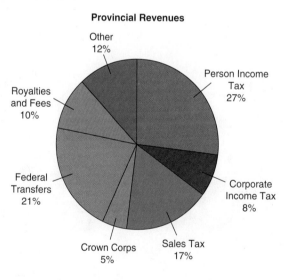

Figure 12.6

Aggregate Provincial Revenues by Source, 2015–2016

Provinces get almost half their revenue from just two sources, personal income taxes and transfers from the federal government. The importance of source of revenue varies widely by province, with some provinces relying heavily on natural resource royalties, others much more on personal income tax, and still others on the federal government.

Data from Estimates of the program expenditure and revenue of the consolidated Revenue fund 2015-16, The Department of Finance. http://www.budget.gov.nl.ca/budget2015/estimates/estimates_2015_16.pdf

Figure 12.7

Aggregate Provincial Spending by Theme, 2015–2016

Health care and education consume 61 percent of provincial budgets, while social services accounts for 9 percent. Debt service accounts for 7 percent of provincial budgets.

Data from Estimates of the program expenditure and revenue of the consolidated Revenue fund 2015-16, The Department of Finance. http://www.budget.gov.nl.ca/budget2015/estimates/estimates_2015_16.pdf

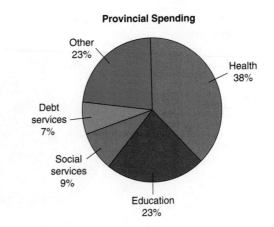

Provincial Spending

Other 23%
Health 38%
Debt services 7%
Social services 9%
Education 23%

Providing health care accounted for 38 percent of provincial budgets, while education (at all levels) accounted for 23 percent of spending. Social services, another important provincial responsibility, accounted for 9 percent of spending. The last notable category of spending was debt service at 7 percent. We can expect the share of provincial budgets consumed by servicing provincial debt to rise as provinces run deficits and interest rates rise.

Making the Connection

The Exploding Costs of Health Care

For many Canadians, public health care is central to Canadian identity. Under the current system, provincial, territorial, and federal governments collect taxes from a variety of sources (primarily people's incomes), and use the funds raised to pay for hospitals, doctors, nurses, and all other elements essential to providing health care services to the people of Canada.

While most Canadians agree that public health care is a good idea, doctors and nurses don't work for free, and drug companies don't either. Moreover, the costs of health care are increasing. The problem of paying for health care arises when we start to think about the distribution of health care spending by age. In 2009, health care spending in Canada was about $5500 per person. However, the health care system doesn't spend the same amount on everyone. In 2007, people younger than 64 cost an average of about $2000 per person. Those between 65 and 69 cost an average of $5589 per person. Those over 80 cost about $17 500 per person. Simply put, the older you are, the more it costs to provide you with health care, and the projected number of seniors as a percentage of Canada's population is growing (see panel (a), page 331), as is the projected spending on public health care (see panel (b), page 331).

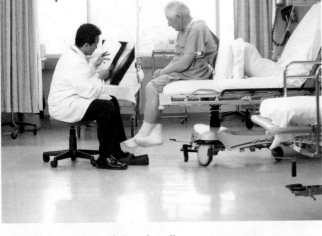

The aging population of Canada will lead to higher costs for health care.

If we combine data on the growing use of health care by older Canadians with data on the aging Canadian population, we get some explosive predictions on health care spending. Let's take Quebec as an example (the other provinces and territories aren't much different in terms of health care spending). In 1980, about 31 percent of Quebec government spending went to providing health care. By 2010, health care accounted for 45 percent of Quebec government spending and is projected to reach 67 percent by 2030. That means that by 2030, $2 out of every $3 spent by the government of Quebec will be spent on providing health care.

This projected level of health care spending can be maintained by provinces and territories in three ways. First, they could significantly cut back on spending in other areas, such as education and infrastructure. However, cutting back on investment in areas

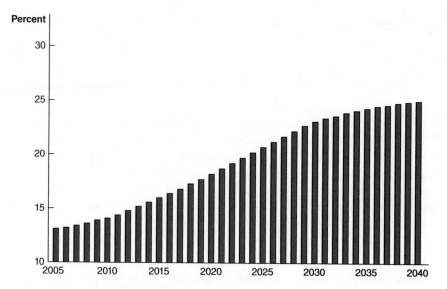

(a) Seniors as a percentage of Canada's population, 2005–2040

Source: Reproduced with permission of the Institute for Research on Public Policy www.IRPP.org.

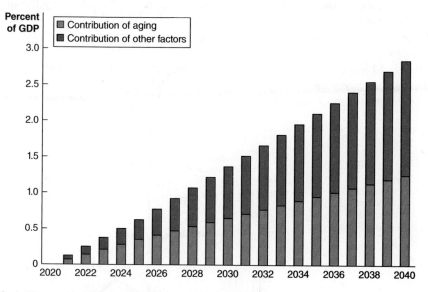

(b) Projected increase in public health care spending, 2020–2040

Source: Reproduced with permission of the Institute for Research on Public Policy www.IRPP.org.

such as education and infrastructure is likely to reduce the size of the economy in the future. Second, they could run a budget deficit. Provincial and territorial governments can run deficits by borrowing from investors. The problem with this approach is that future taxpayers will have to pay for today's health care costs, with interest. Finally, they could increase taxes. Doing so would also have a negative impact on the economy and inevitably make people unhappy.

The aging of Canada's population and the associated increase in health care costs will mean that different methods of delivering health care and/or paying for them will emerge. Most likely, provinces and territories will use a combination of the three options noted above and transfer more health care costs directly to patients.

Sources: Based on "The health care time bomb: Our aging population will make unthinkable reforms inevitable," by John Geddes on Monday, April 12, 2010; http://www2.macleans.ca/2010/04/12/the-health-care-time-bomb/; Two Policy Challenges Driven by Population Aging by Chris Ragan http://people.mcgill.ca/files/christopher.ragan/Oct2010PO.pdf.

Your Turn: Test your understanding by doing related problems 1.2 and 1.3 on page 353 at the end of this chapter.   MyEconLab

The Effects of Fiscal Policy on Real GDP and the Price Level

The federal government uses macroeconomic policies to offset the effects of the business cycle on the economy. We saw in Chapter 11 that the Bank of Canada carries out monetary policy through changes in the money supply and interest rates. Governments carry out fiscal policy through changes in government purchases and taxes. Because changes in government purchases and taxes leads to changes in aggregate demand, they can affect the level of real GDP, employment, and the price level. When the economy is in a recession, *increases* in government purchases or *decreases* in taxes will increase aggregate demand. As we saw in Chapter 9, the inflation rate may increase when real GDP is beyond potential GDP. Decreasing government purchases or raising taxes can slow the growth of aggregate demand and reduce the inflation rate.

Expansionary and Contractionary Fiscal Policy

Expansionary fiscal policy involves increasing government purchases or decreasing taxes. An increase in government purchases will increase aggregate demand directly because government expenditures are a component of aggregate demand. A cut in taxes has an indirect effect on aggregate demand. The income households have available to spend after they have paid their taxes is called *household disposable income*. Cutting the individual income tax will increase household disposable income and consumption spending. Cutting taxes on business income can increase aggregate demand by increasing business investment.

Figure 12.8 shows the results of an expansionary fiscal policy using the basic version of the aggregate demand and aggregate supply model. In this model, there is no economic growth, so the long-run aggregate supply (*LRAS*) curve does not shift. Notice

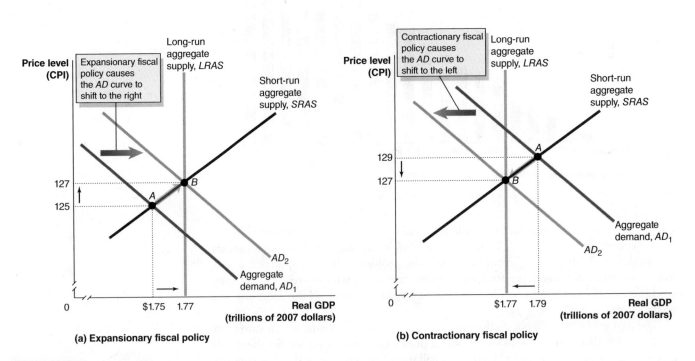

(a) Expansionary fiscal policy

(b) Contractionary fiscal policy

Figure 12.8 Fiscal Policy

In panel (a), the economy begins in recession at point *A*, with real GDP of $1.75 trillion and a price level of 125. An expansionary fiscal policy will cause aggregate demand to shift to the right, from AD_1 to AD_2, increasing real GDP from $1.75 trillion to $1.77 trillion and the price level from 125 to 127 (point *B*). In panel (b), the economy begins at point *A*, with real GDP at $1.79 trillion and the price level at 127. Because real GDP is greater than potential GDP, the economy will experience rising wages and prices. A contractionary fiscal policy will cause aggregate demand to shift to the left, from AD_1 to AD_2, decreasing real GDP from $1.79 trillion to $1.77 trillion and the price level from 129 to 127 (point *B*).

that this figure is similar to Figure 11.6, which shows the effects of monetary policy. The goal of both expansionary fiscal and expansionary monetary policy is to increase aggregate demand relative to what it would have been without a policy intervention.

In panel (a) of Figure 12.8, we assume that the economy is in short-run equilibrium at point A, where the aggregate demand curve (AD_1) intersects the short-run aggregate supply curve ($SRAS$). Real GDP is below potential GDP, so the economy is in recession, with some firms operating below capacity and some workers having been laid off. To bring real GDP back to potential GDP, the government can increase government purchases or decrease taxes, which will shift the aggregate demand curve to the right, from AD_1 to AD_2. Real GDP increases from \$1.75 trillion to potential GDP of \$1.77 trillion, and the price level rises from 125 to 127 (point B). The policy has successfully returned real GDP to its potential level. Rising production will lead to increasing employment, reducing the unemployment rate.

Contractionary fiscal policy involves decreasing government purchases or increasing taxes. Policymakers use contractionary fiscal policy to reduce increases in aggregate demand that seem likely to lead to inflation. In panel (b) of Figure 12.8, the economy is in short-run equilibrium at point A, with real GDP of \$1.79 trillion, which is above potential GDP of \$1.77 trillion. With some firms producing beyond their normal capacity and the unemployment rate very low, wages and prices will be increasing. To bring real GDP back to potential GDP, the government can decrease government purchases or increase taxes, which will shift the aggregate demand curve from AD_1 to AD_2. Real GDP falls from \$1.79 trillion to \$1.77 trillion, and the price level falls from 129 to 127 (point B).

We can conclude that government can attempt to stabilize the economy by using fiscal policy to affect the price level and the level of real GDP. It is, of course, extremely difficult to get the amount of fiscal expansion or contraction to exactly offset the business cycle and keep real GDP equal to potential GDP.

A Summary of How Fiscal Policy Affects Aggregate Demand

Table 12.1 summarizes how fiscal policy affects aggregate demand. Just as we did with monetary policy, we must add a very important qualification to this summary of fiscal policy: The table isolates the impact of fiscal policy *by holding everything else—including monetary policy—constant*. In other words, we are again invoking the *ceteris paribus* condition we discussed in Chapter 3. This point is important because, for example, a contractionary fiscal policy doesn't cause the price level to fall. A contractionary fiscal policy causes the price level *to rise by less than it would have without the policy.*

Fiscal Policy in the Dynamic Aggregate Demand and Aggregate Supply Model

12.3 LEARNING OBJECTIVE

Use the dynamic aggregate demand and aggregate supply model to analyze fiscal policy.

The overview of fiscal policy we just finished contains a key idea: Government can use fiscal policy to affect aggregate demand, thereby changing the price level and the level of real GDP. The discussion of expansionary and contractionary fiscal policy illustrated by Figure 12.8 is simplified, however, because it ignores two important facts about the economy: (1) The economy experiences continuing inflation, with the price level rising virtually every year, and (2) the economy experiences long-run growth, with the *LRAS* curve shifting to the right every year. In Chapter 10, we developed a *dynamic aggregate demand and aggregate supply model* that took these two facts into account.

Problem	Type of Policy	Action by Government	Result
Recession	Expansionary	Increase government spending or cut taxes	Real GDP and the price level rise.
Rising inflation	Contractionary	Decrease government spending or raise taxes	Real GDP and the price level fall.

Table 12.1

Countercyclical Fiscal Policy

Figure 12.9

An Expansionary Fiscal Policy in the Dynamic Model

The economy begins in equilibrium at point *A*, at potential GDP of $1.77 trillion and a price level of 127. Without an expansionary policy, aggregate demand will shift from AD_1 to $AD_{2(\text{without policy})}$, which is not enough to keep the economy at potential GDP because long-run aggregate supply has shifted from $LRAS_1$ to $LRAS_2$. The economy will be in short-run equilibrium at point *B*, with real GDP of $1.79 trillion and a price level of 129. Increasing government purchases or cutting taxes will shift aggregate demand to $AD_{2(\text{with policy})}$. The economy will be in equilibrium at point *C*, with real GDP of $1.80 trillion, which is its potential level, and a price level of 130. The price level is higher than it would have been without an expansionary fiscal policy.

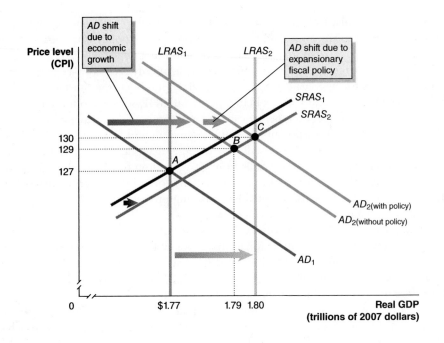

In this section, we use the dynamic model to gain a more complete understanding of fiscal policy.

To briefly review the dynamic model, recall that over time, potential GDP increases, which we show by the *LRAS* curve shifting to the right. The factors that cause the *LRAS* curve to shift also cause firms to supply more goods and services at any given price level in the short run, which we show by shifting the *SRAS* curve to the right. Finally, during most years, the *AD* curve also shifts to the right, indicating that aggregate expenditure is higher at every price level.

Figure 12.9 shows the results of an expansionary fiscal policy using the dynamic aggregate demand and aggregate supply model. Notice that this figure is very similar to Figure 11.10, which shows the effects of an expansionary monetary policy. The goal of both expansionary monetary policy and expansionary fiscal policy is to increase aggregate demand relative to what it would have been without the policy.

In the hypothetical situation shown in Figure 12.9, the economy begins in equilibrium at potential GDP of $1.77 trillion and a price level of 127 (point *A*). In the second year, *LRAS* increases to $1.80 trillion, but *AD* increases only to $AD_{2(\text{without policy})}$, which is not enough to keep the economy in macroeconomic equilibrium at potential GDP. Let's assume that the Bank of Canada doesn't react to this situation with expansionary monetary policy. In that case, without an expansionary fiscal policy of increased government spending or tax cuts, the short-run equilibrium will occur at $1.79 trillion (point *B*). The $10 billion gap between this level of real GDP and the potential level means that some firms are operating at less than their normal capacity. Incomes and profits will be falling, firms will begin to lay off workers, and the unemployment rate will rise.

Increasing government purchases or cutting taxes can shift aggregate demand to $AD_{2(\text{with policy})}$. The economy will be in equilibrium at point *C*, with real GDP of $1.80 trillion, which is potential GDP, and a price level of 130. The price level is higher than it would have been if expansionary fiscal policy had not been used.

Contractionary fiscal policy involves decreasing government purchases or increasing taxes. Policymakers use contractionary fiscal policy to reduce increases in aggregate demand that seem likely to lead to inflation. In Figure 12.10, the economy again begins at potential GDP of $1.77 trillion and a price level of 127 (point *A*). Once again *LRAS* increases to $1.80 trillion in the second year. In this scenario, the shift in aggregate demand to $AD_{2(\text{without policy})}$ results in a short-run macroeconomic equilibrium beyond potential GDP (point *B*). If we assume that the Bank of Canada does not respond to this situation with a contractionary monetary policy, the economy will experience rising inflation. Decreasing government purchases or increasing taxes can keep real GDP from

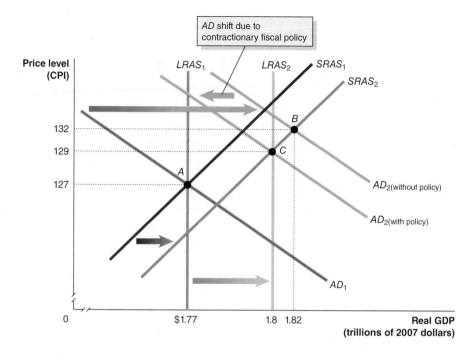

Figure 12.10

**A Contractionary Fiscal Policy
in the Dynamic Model**

The economy begins in equilibrium at point A, with real GDP of $1.77 trillion and a price level of 127. Without a contractionary policy, aggregate demand will shift from AD_1 to $AD_{2(\text{without policy})}$, which results in a short-run equilibrium beyond potential GDP at point B, with real GDP $1.82 trillion and a price level of 132. Decreasing government purchases or increasing taxes can shift aggregate demand to $AD_{2(\text{with policy})}$. The economy will be in equilibrium at point C, with real GDP of $1.8 trillion, which is its potential level, and a price level of 129. The inflation rate will be 1.6 percent, as opposed to the 3.9 percent it would have been without the contractionary fiscal policy.

moving beyond its potential level. The result, shown in Figure 12.10, is that in the new equilibrium at point C, the inflation rate is 1.6 percent rather than 3.9 percent.

Government Purchases and Tax Multipliers

Suppose that during a recession, the government decides to use discretionary fiscal policy to increase aggregate demand by spending $10 billion more on constructing roads and bridges in several cities. How much will equilibrium GDP increase as a result of this increase in government purchases? We might expect that the answer is greater than $10 billion because the initial increase in aggregate demand should lead to additional increases in income and therefore increases in consumer spending. To build the roads and bridges, the government hires private construction firms. These firms will hire more workers to carry out the new projects. Newly hired workers will increase their spending on cars, furniture, appliances, and other products. Sellers of these products will increase their production and hire more workers, and so on. At each step, real GDP and income will rise, thereby increasing consumption spending and aggregate demand.

Economists refer to the initial increase in government purchases as *autonomous* because it is a result of a decision by the government and does not directly depend on the level of real GDP. The increases in consumption spending that result from the initial autonomous increase in government purchases are *induced* because they are caused by the initial increase in autonomous spending. Economists refer to the series of induced increases in consumption spending that results from an initial increase in autonomous expenditures as the **multiplier effect**.

Figure 12.11 illustrates how an increase in government purchases affects the aggregate demand curve. The initial increase in government purchases causes the aggregate demand curve to shift to the right because total spending in the economy is now higher at every price level. The shift to the right from AD_1 to the dashed AD curve represents the impact of the initial increase of $10 billion in government purchases. Because this initial increase in government purchases raises incomes and leads to further increases in consumption spending, the aggregate demand curve will ultimately shift from AD_1 all the way to AD_2.

To better understand the multiplier effect, let's start with a simplified analysis in which we assume that the price level is constant. In other words, initially we will ignore

12.4 LEARNING OBJECTIVE

Explain how the government purchases and tax multipliers work.

Multiplier effect The series of induced increases in consumption spending that results from an initial increase in autonomous expenditures.

Figure 12.11

The Multiplier Effect and Aggregate Demand

An initial increase in government purchases of $10 billion causes the aggregate demand curve to shift to the right, from AD_1 to the dashed AD curve, and represents the effect of the initial increase of $10 billion in government purchases. Because this initial increase raises incomes and leads to further increases in consumption spending, the aggregate demand curve will ultimately shift further to the right, to AD_2.

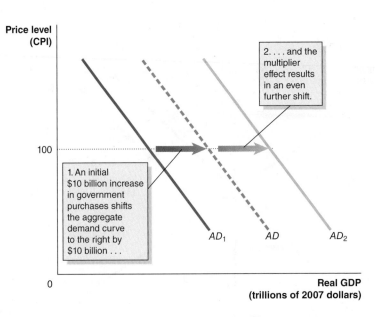

the effect of an upward-sloping *SRAS*. Figure 12.12 shows how spending and real GDP increase over a number of periods, beginning with the initial increase in government purchases in the first period. The initial spending in the first period raises real GDP and therefore total income in the economy by $10 billion. How much additional consumption will result from the $10 billion increase in incomes? We know that in addition to increasing their consumption spending on domestically produced goods, households will save some of the increase in income, use some to pay income taxes, and use some to purchase imported goods, which will have no direct effect on spending and production in the Canadian economy. In Figure 12.12, we assume that in the second period, households increase their consumption spending by one-half of the increase in income from the first period on domestically produced goods and services—or by $5 billion. This spending in the second period will, in turn, increase real GDP and income by an additional $5 billion. In the third period, consumption spending will increase by $2.5 billion, or one-half of the $5 billion increase in income from the second period.

Time Period	Additional Spending This Period	Cumulative Increase in Spending and Real GDP
1	$10 billion in government purchases	$10 billion
2	$5 billion in consumption spending	$15 billion
3	$2.5 billion in consumption spending	$17.5 billion
4	$1.25 billion in consumption spending	$18.75 billion
5	$0.625 billion in consumption spending	$19.375 billion
6	$0.3125 billion in consumption spending	$19.6875 billion
⋮	⋮	⋮
n	0	$20 billion

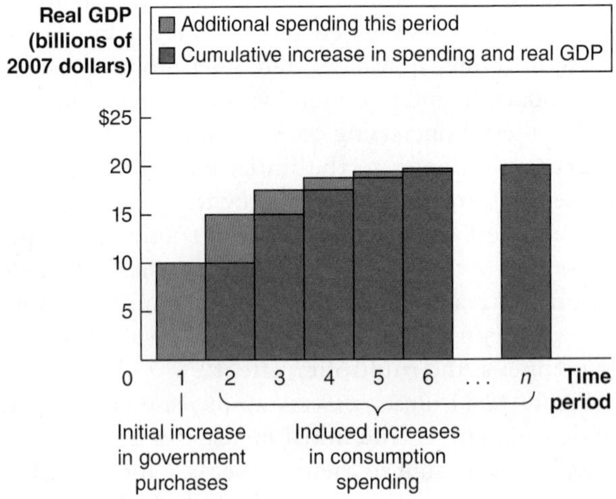

Figure 12.12 **The Multiplier Effect of an Increase in Government Purchases**

Following an initial increase in government purchases, spending and real GDP increase over a number of periods due to the multiplier effect. The new spending and increased real GDP in each period is shown in green, and the level of spending from the previous period is shown in orange. The sum of the orange and green areas represents the cumulative increase in spending and real GDP. In total, equilibrium real GDP will increase by $20 billion as a result of an initial increase of $10 billion in government purchases.

The multiplier effect will continue through a number of periods, with the additional consumption spending in each period being half of the income increase from the previous period. Eventually, the process will be complete, although we can't say precisely how many periods it will take, so we simply label the final period *n* rather than assign it a specific number. In the graph in Figure 12.12, the new spending and increased real GDP in each period is shown in green, and the level of spending from the previous period is shown in blue. The sum of the blue and green areas represents the cumulative increase in spending and real GDP.

How large will the total increase in equilibrium real GDP be as a result of the initial increase of $10 billion in government purchases? The ratio of the change in equilibrium real GDP to the initial change in government purchases is known as the *government purchases multiplier*:

$$\text{Government purchases multiplier} = \frac{\text{Change in equilibrium real GDP}}{\text{Change in government purchases}}$$

If, for example, the government purchases multiplier has a value of 2, an increase in government purchases of $10 billion should increase equilibrium real GDP by 2 × $10 billion = $20 billion. We show this in Figure 12.12 by having the cumulative increase in real GDP equal $20 billion.

Tax cuts also have a multiplier effect. Cutting taxes increases household disposable income. When household disposable income rises, so will consumption spending. These increases in consumption spending will set off further increases in real GDP and income, just as increases in government purchases do. Suppose we consider a change in taxes of a specific amount—say, a tax cut of $10 billion—with the tax *rate* remaining unchanged. The expression for this tax multiplier is

$$\text{Tax multiplier} = \frac{\text{Change in equilibrium real GDP}}{\text{Change in taxes}}$$

The tax multiplier is a negative number because changes in taxes and changes in real GDP move in opposite directions: An increase in taxes reduces disposable income, consumption, and real GDP, and a decrease in taxes raises disposable income, consumption, and real GDP. For example, if the tax multiplier is −1.6, a $10 billion *cut* in taxes will increase real GDP by −1.6 × −$10 billion = $16 billion. We would expect the tax multiplier to be smaller in absolute value (i.e., a smaller number) than the government purchases multiplier. To see why, think about the difference between a $10 billion increase in government purchases and a $10 billion decrease in taxes. The whole of the $10 billion increase in government purchases results in an increase in aggregate demand initially. But households will save rather than spend some portion of the $10 billion decrease in taxes, and they will spend some portion of the extra disposable income on imported goods. The fraction of the tax cut that households save or spend on imports will not increase aggregate demand. Therefore, the first period of the multiplier will lead to a smaller increase in aggregate demand than takes place after an increase in government purchases, and the total increase in equilibrium real GDP will be smaller.

The Effect of Changes in Tax Rates

A change in tax *rates* has a more complicated effect on equilibrium real GDP than does a tax cut of a fixed amount. To begin with, the value of the tax rate affects the size of the multiplier effect. The higher the tax rate, the smaller the multiplier effect. To see why, think about the size of the additional spending increases that take place in each period following an increase in government purchases. The higher the tax rate, the smaller the amount of an increase in income that households have available to spend, which reduces the size of the multiplier effect. So, a cut in tax rates affects equilibrium real GDP through two channels: (1) A cut in tax rates increases the disposable income of households, which leads them to increase their consumption spending, and (2) a cut in tax rates increases the size of the multiplier effect.

Taking into Account the Effects of Aggregate Supply

So far we've assumed that the price level didn't change when the *AD* curve shifted. However, because the *SRAS* curve is upward sloping, when the *AD* curve shifts to the right, the price level increases. As a result of the higher price level, the new equilibrium real GDP will not increase by the amount that the multiplier effect indicates. Figure 12.13 illustrates how an upward-sloping *SRAS* curve affects the size of the multiplier. To keep the graph relatively simple, we assume that the *SRAS* and *LRAS* curves do not shift. The economy starts at point *A*, with real GDP below its potential level. An increase in government purchases shifts the aggregate demand curve from *AD₁* to the dashed *AD* curve. Just as in Figure 12.11, the multiplier effect causes a further shift in aggregate demand to *AD₂*. If the price level remained constant, real GDP would increase from $1.69 trillion at point *A* to $1.79 trillion at point *B*. However, because the *SRAS* curve is upward sloping, the price level rises from 127 to 130, reducing the total quantity of goods and services demanded in the economy. The new equilibrium occurs at point *C*, with real GDP having risen to $1.77 trillion, or by $20 billion less than if the price level had remained unchanged. We can conclude that the actual change in real GDP resulting from an increase in government purchases or a tax cut will be less than indicated by the simple multiplier effect with a constant price level.

The Multipliers Work in Both Directions

Increases in government spending and cuts in taxes have a positive multiplier effect on equilibrium real GDP. Decreases in government purchases and increases in taxes also have a multiplier effect on equilibrium real GDP, but in this case, the effect is negative. For example, an increase in taxes will reduce household disposable income and consumption spending. As households buy fewer cars, furniture, refrigerators, and other products, the firms that sell these products will cut back on production and begin laying off workers. Falling incomes will lead to further reductions in consumption spending. A reduction in government spending on roads would set off a similar process of decreases in real GDP and income. The cutback would be felt first by construction contractors selling their services directly to the government, and then it would spread to other firms.

We look more closely at the government purchases multiplier and the tax multiplier in the appendix to this chapter.

Figure 12.13

The Multiplier Effect and Aggregate Supply

The economy is initially at point *A*. An increase in government purchases causes the aggregate demand curve to shift to the right, from *AD₁* to the dashed *AD* curve. The multiplier effect results in the aggregate demand curve shifting further to the right, to *AD₂* (point *B*). Because of the upward-sloping supply curve, the shift in aggregate demand results in a higher price level. In the new equilibrium at point *C*, both real GDP and the price level have increased. The increase in real GDP is less than indicated by the multiplier effect with a constant price level.

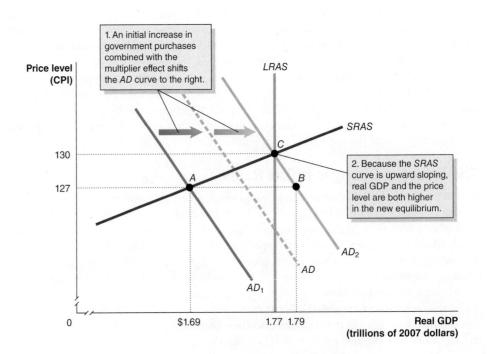

Don't Let This Happen to You

Don't Overestimate the Size of the Multiplier

The size of the multiplier depends on a wide variety of factors. As the income tax rate increases, the multiplier shrinks in value. As the share of new household disposable income that is saved falls, the multiplier increases in value. The more we import from other countries, the lower the value of the multiplier. Finally, as we've seen, the sensitivity of price levels to changes in demand has an impact on the multiplier—the steeper the *SRAS* curve, the lower the value of the final multiplier.

People arguing in support of specific government projects often ignore the influence of these factors when calculating the size of the multiplier for a given project in an effort to gain support for the project. In many cases, people arguing for new sports stadiums, harbours, or other large government-funded facilities claim that the multiplier associated with these projects is well over 2 or sometimes even 3. Because Canada is an open economy with moderate income taxes, these values are not reasonable for most regions in Canada. Statistics Canada estimates the multiplier size for different types of activities for different regions. These multipliers are generally below 1.5. The next time someone promotes a large project in your community using a multiplier as part of the project's justification, ask that person how that number was determined.

MyEconLab

Your Turn: Test your understanding by doing related problem 4.3 on page 354 at the end of this chapter.

Solved Problem **12.1**

Fiscal Policy Multipliers

Briefly explain whether you agree or disagree with the following statement: "Real GDP is currently $1.62 trillion and potential GDP is $1.64 trillion. If Parliament would increase government purchases by $20 billion ($0.02 trillion), the economy could be brought to equilibrium at potential GDP."

Solving the Problem

Step 1: Review the chapter material. This problem is about the multiplier process, so you may want to review the section "The Government Purchases and Tax Multipliers."

Step 2: Explain how the necessary increase in purchases or cut in taxes is less than $20 billion because of the multiplier effect. The statement is incorrect because it doesn't consider the multiplier effect. Because of the multiplier effect, an increase in government purchases or a decrease in taxes of less than $20 billion is necessary to increase equilibrium real GDP by $20 billion. For instance, assume that the government purchases multiplier is 2 and the tax multiplier is −1.6. We can then calculate the necessary increase in government purchases as follows:

$$\text{Government purchases multiplier} = \frac{\text{Change in equilibrium real GDP}}{\text{Change in government purchases}}$$

$$2 = \frac{\$20 \text{ billion}}{\text{Change in government purchases}}$$

$$\text{Change in government purchases} = \frac{\$20 \text{ billion}}{2} = \$10 \text{ billion.}$$

And the necessary change in taxes:

$$\text{Tax multiplier} = \frac{\text{Change in equilibrium real GDP}}{\text{Change in taxes}}$$

$$-1.6 = \frac{\$20 \text{ billion}}{\text{Change in taxes}}$$

$$\text{Change in taxes} = \frac{\$20 \text{ billion}}{-1.6} = -\$12.5 \text{ billion.}$$

MyEconLab **Your turn:** For more practice, do related problem 4.6 on page 355 at the end of this chapter.

Discuss the difficulties that can arise in implementing fiscal policy.

The Limits of Fiscal Policy as a Stimulus

Poorly timed fiscal policy, like poorly timed monetary policy, can do more harm than good. As we discussed in Chapter 11, it takes time for policymakers to collect statistics and identify changes in the economy. If the government decides to increase spending or cut taxes to fight a recession that is about to end, the effect may be to increase the inflation rate. Similarly, cutting spending or raising taxes to slow down an economy that has actually passed the peak of the business cycle can make the recession that follows longer and deeper.

Getting the timing right can be more difficult with fiscal policy than with monetary policy for two main reasons. First, control over monetary policy is concentrated in the hands of the Bank of Canada, which can change monetary policy at any of its meetings. By contrast, the prime minister and a majority of the members of Parliament have to agree on changes in fiscal policy. The delays caused by the legislative process can be very long.

Second, even after a change in fiscal policy has been approved, it takes time to implement the policy. Suppose the federal government decides to fund the building of new roads in several cities. It will probably take at least several months to prepare detailed plans for the construction. Local government will then ask for bids from private construction companies. Once winning bidders have been selected, they will usually need several months to begin the project. Only then will significant amounts of spending actually take place. This delay may push the spending beyond the end of the recession that the spending was intended to fight.

Does Government Spending Reduce Private Spending?

In addition to the problem of timing, using increases in government purchases to increase aggregate demand presents another potential problem. We have been assuming that when the federal government increases its purchases by $30 billion, the multiplier effect will cause the increase in aggregate demand to be greater than $30 billion. However, the size of the multiplier effect may be limited if the increase in government purchases causes one of the nongovernment, or private, components of aggregate expenditures—consumption, investment, or net exports—to fall. A decline in private expenditures as a result of an increase in government purchases is called **crowding out**.

Crowding out A decline in private expenditures as a result of an increase in government purchases.

Crowding Out in the Short Run

Consider the case of a temporary increase in government purchases. Suppose the federal government decides to fight a recession by spending $30 billion more this year on road construction. When the $30 billion has been spent, the program will end, and government spending will drop back to its previous level. As the spending takes place, income and real GDP will increase. These increases in income and real GDP will cause household and firms to increase their demand for currency and chequing account balances to

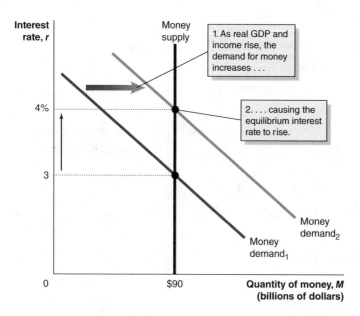

Figure 12.14

An Expansionary Fiscal Policy Increases Interest Rates

If the federal government increases spending, the demand for money will increase from Money demand$_1$ to Money demand$_2$ as real GDP and income rise. With the supply of money constant at $90 billion, the result is an increase in the equilibrium interest rate from 3 percent to 4 percent, which crowds out some consumption, investment, and net exports.

accommodate the increased buying and selling. Figure 12.14 shows the result, using the money market graph introduced in Chapter 11.

At higher levels of real GDP and income, households and firms demand more money at every interest rate. When the demand for money increases, the equilibrium interest rate will rise. Higher interest rates will result in a decline in each component of private expenditures. Consumption spending and investment spending will decline because households and firms will borrow less to purchase consumer durables and to make investments. Net exports will fall as the higher interest rates will attract foreign savers. German, Japanese, and American savers will want to exchange their currencies to Canadian dollars to purchase bonds and other Canadian financial assets. This increased demand for Canadian dollars will cause the exchange rate between the dollar and other currencies to rise. When the dollar increases in value, the prices of Canadian products in foreign countries rise, causing a reduction in Canadian exports. At the same time, the prices of foreign products in Canada fall causing an increase in Canadian imports. Falling exports and rising imports mean that net exports are falling.

The greater the sensitivity of consumption, investment, and net exports to changes in interest rates, the more crowding out will occur. In a deep recession, many firms may be so pessimistic about the future and have so much excess capacity that investment spending will fall to very low levels and will be unlikely to fall much further, even if interest rates rise. In this case, crowding out is unlikely to be much of a problem. If the economy is close to potential GDP, however, and firms are optimistic about the future, then an increase in interest rates may result in a significant decline in investment spending.

Figure 12.15 shows that crowding out may reduce the effectiveness of an expansionary fiscal policy. The economy begins in short-run equilibrium at point A, with real GDP of $1.73 trillion. Real GDP is below potential GDP, so the economy is in recession. Suppose that the government decides to increase government purchases to bring the economy back to potential GDP. In the absence of crowding out, the increase in government purchases will shift aggregate demand to $AD_{2(\text{no crowding out})}$ and bring the economy to equilibrium at real GDP of $1.77 trillion, which is the potential level of GDP (point B). But the higher interest rate resulting from the increased government purchases will reduce consumption, investment, and net exports, causing aggregate demand to shift back to $AD_{2(\text{crowding out})}$. The result is a new short-run equilibrium at point C, with real GDP of $1.76 trillion, which is $10 billion short of potential GDP.

Crowding Out in the Long Run

Most economists agree that in the short run, an increase in government spending results in partial, but not complete, crowding out. What is the long-run effect of a *permanent*

Figure 12.15

The Effect of Crowding Out in the Short Run

The economy begins in a recession, with real GDP of $1.73 trillion (point *A*). In the absence of crowding out, an increase in government purchases will shift aggregate demand to $AD_{2(\text{no crowding out})}$ and bring the economy to equilibrium at potential GDP of $1.77 trillion (point *B*). But the higher interest rate resulting from the increased government purchases will reduce consumption, investment, and net exports, causing aggregate demand to shift to $AD_{2(\text{crowding out})}$. The result is a new short-run equilibrium at point *C*, with real GDP of $1.76 trillion, which is $10 billion short of potential GDP.

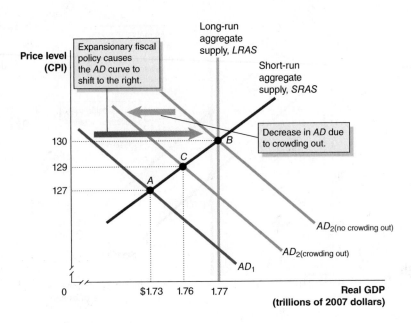

increase in government spending? In this case, many economists agree that the result is complete crowding out. In the long run, the decline in investment, consumption, and net exports exactly offsets the increase in government purchases, and aggregate demand remains unchanged. To understand crowding out in the long run, recall from Chapter 9 that *in the long run, the economy returns to potential GDP.* Suppose that the economy is currently at potential GDP and that government purchases account for 35 percent of GDP. In that case, private expenditures—the sum of consumption, investment, and net exports—will make up the other 65 percent of GDP. If government purchases are increased permanently to 37 percent of GDP, in the long run, private expenditures must fall to 63 percent of GDP. There has been complete crowding out: Private expenditures have fallen by the same amount that government purchases have increased. If government spending is taking up a larger share of GDP, then private spending must take a smaller share.

An expansionary fiscal policy doesn't have to cause complete crowding out in the short run. If the economy is below potential GDP, it is possible for both government purchases and private expenditures to increase. But in the long run, a permanent increase in government purchases must come at the expense of private expenditures. Keep in mind, however, that we don't know how long it will take to arrive at this long-run outcome. It may take several—possibly many—years to arrive at the new equilibrium.

Making the Connection | **Is Losing Your Job Good for Your Health?**

Recessions cause lost output and cyclical unemployment, which harms people. Any policy that leads to shorter recessions will also make people better at the same time. Someone experiencing cyclical unemployment will obviously have to live on less income. Will the unemployed have to deal with declining health too? As the energy industry in Alberta suffered large declines in 2015 and 2016, health experts warned that the lower incomes and unemployment could lead to an increase in obesity. When people lose their jobs and have to live on lower incomes, they make different choices at the grocery store. They opt for comfort and cheaper processed foods, which tend to be higher in sugar, fat, and salt. At the same time, they cut back on fresh fruits and vegetables—by as much as 20 percent in the 2008 global recession.

Suicide rates, particularly among men, also tend to rise during hard economic times. When people lose their livelihoods, they may become depressed. This and other forms of mental illness are contributing factors in most suicides.

Not all studies agree that recessions always lead to higher obesity. The work of Christopher Ruhm (professor of public policy and economics at the Frank Batten School of Leadership and Public Policy) shows that the unemployed during a recession may, on average, become healthier. Ruhm's analysis of American data found that during recessions, people smoke less, drink less alcohol, eat better, and even exercise more.

So while some people will be more stressed about money during a recession, it seems that others will have less stress about their bosses or the big presentation. If you're unemployed, you likely have more time to prepare meals instead of grabbing a burger on the drive home. Some may even find the time to go for walk instead of driving everywhere in a hurry.

There is another benefit of recession, too. Traffic congestion and pollution also tend to fall during recessions, making life less stressful for those still commuting to work and improving air quality. And having less job stress means you're less likely to have a job-related heart attack—Ruhm estimates that a 1 percent rise in the unemployment rate is associated with 3900 fewer American deaths from heart disease.

As with so many issues of economics, recessions have different effects on people. Some people are likely to get healthier and others likely become much less healthy. Overall, most economists agree that a fiscal or monetary policy that shortens a recession also improves the wellbeing (and health) of people.

Sources: Based on Christopher J. Ruhm, "A Healthy Economy Can Break Your Heart," *Demography*, Vol. 44, No. 4, November 2007, pp. 829–848; Christopher J. Ruhm, "Healthy Living in Hard Times," *Journal of Health Economics*, Vol. 24, No. 2, March 2005, pp. 341–363; and Christopher J. Ruhm, "Are Recessions Good for Your Health?" *Quarterly Journal of Economics*, Vol. 115, No. 2, May 2000, pp. 617–650; Sharon Kirkey, "Alberta's oil slump could trigger a spike in obesity as thousands cope with layoffs, specialists say." *National Post*, January 3, 2016.

Your Turn: Test your understanding by doing related problem 5.4 on page 355 at the end of this chapter.

Budget deficit The situation in which the government's current expenditures are greater than its current tax revenue.

MyEconLab

Deficits, Surpluses, and Federal Government Debt

The federal government's budget shows the relationship between its expenditures and its tax revenue. When the federal government's current expenditures are greater than its current tax revenue, a **budget deficit** results. If the federal government's current expenditures are less than its current tax revenue, a **budget surplus** results. As with many other macroeconomic variables, it is useful to consider the size of the surplus or deficit relative to the size of the economy.

Figure 12.16 shows that the federal government has tended to run a budget deficit since the 1960s. During the 1970s and 1980s it was common for governments around

12.6 LEARNING OBJECTIVE

Define federal budget deficit and federal government debt and explain how the federal budget can serve as an automatic stabilizer.

Budget surplus The situation in which the government's current expenditures are less than its current tax revenue.

Figure 12.16

The Federal Budget Deficit, 1967–2015

The federal government has run a budget deficit for most of the past 50 years. The federal budget balance tends to be more in deficit when the economy is in recession, and the deficit tends to be smaller when the economy is doing well. You should note that the federal government changed its accounting standards in fiscal year 1983–1984, which makes comparisons between years before 1983 to later years suspect.

Note: In this graph, the years represent the end of the fiscal year. For example, fiscal year 2009–2010 is identified as "2010."

Source: Data from Department of Finance, Fiscal Reference Tables, Table 2 http://www.fin.gc.ca/frt-trf/2015/frt-trf-15-eng.asp.

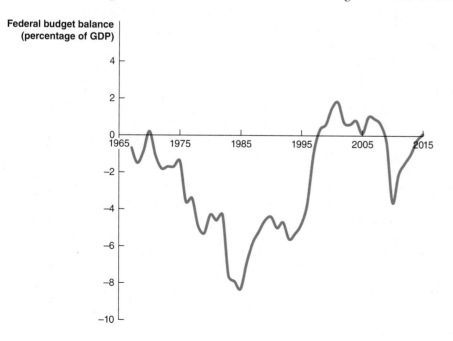

the world to run large budget deficits to finance a wide variety of government spending programs. The budget balance of the federal government began to improve in the late 1980s, but the deficit became larger in the early 1990s, as the Canadian economy entered a recession. In the late 1990s, the federal government began to run a surplus for the first time in decades.

You can clearly see the impact of the recent global recession and Canada's Economic Action Plan on the federal budget balance in Figure 12.16. The federal budget switches from surplus in 2008 to deficit in 2009, and the deficit grows to 3.6 percent of GDP in 2010. Remember that this increase in government spending was intended to stimulate the economy in the face of the global recession. The problem with a large deficit is that it can make funding new government initiatives difficult. The federal budget returned to balance briefly in 2015.

How the Federal Budget Can Serve as an Automatic Stabilizer

Discretionary fiscal policy actions can increase the federal budget deficit during recessions by increasing spending or cutting taxes to increase aggregate demand. Although the federal government delivered a fiscal stimulus package to counteract the effects of the global recession, in many milder recessions it takes no significant fiscal policy actions. In fact, most of the increase in the federal budget deficit during a small slowdown takes place without the federal government taking any deliberate action, but is instead due to the effects of the *automatic stabilizers* we mentioned earlier in this chapter.

Deficits occur automatically during recessions for two reasons. First, during a recession, wages and profits fall, causing government tax revenues to fall. Second, the government automatically increases its spending on transfer payments when the economy moves into recession. The government's contribution to the Employment Insurance program will increase as unemployment rises. Spending will also increase on programs to aid low-income people. These spending increases take place without the government taking any action. Existing laws already specify who is eligible for Employment Insurance and other programs. As the number of eligible persons increases during a recession, so does government spending on these programs.

Cyclically adjusted budget deficit or surplus The deficit or surplus in the federal government's budget if the economy were at potential GDP.

Because budget deficits automatically increase during recessions and decrease during expansions, economists often look at the *cyclically adjusted budget deficit or surplus* (sometimes referred to as the *structural budget balance*), which can provide a more accurate measure of the effects on the economy of the government's spending and tax policies than can the actual budget deficit or surplus. The **cyclically adjusted budget deficit or surplus** measures what the deficit or surplus would be if the economy were at potential GDP. An expansionary fiscal policy should result in a cyclically adjusted budget deficit, and a contractionary fiscal policy should result in a cyclically adjusted budget surplus.

Automatic budget surpluses and deficits can help stabilize the economy. When the economy moves into a recession, wages and profits fall, which reduces the taxes that households and firms pay to the government. In effect, households and firms have received an automatic tax cut, which keeps their spending higher than it otherwise would have been. In a recession, workers who have been laid off receive Employment Insurance payments, and households whose incomes have dropped below a certain level become eligible for government transfer programs. By receiving this extra income, households are able to spend more than they otherwise would have. This extra spending helps reduce the length and severity of the recession. Many economists argue that the absence of an employment insurance system and other government transfer programs contributed to the severity of the Great Depression of the 1930s and helps explain why the Canadian recession of 2008–2009 was not a lot worse. During the Great Depression, workers who lost their jobs saw their labour market incomes drop to zero and had to rely on their savings, what they could borrow, or what they received from private charities. As a result, many cut back their spending drastically, which made the downturn worse.

When GDP increases above its potential level, households and firms have to pay more taxes to the federal government, and the federal government makes fewer transfer payments. Higher taxes and lower transfer payments cause total spending to rise by less than it otherwise would have, which helps reduce the chance that the economy will experience high inflation.

Making the Connection

The Greek Debt Crisis and Austerity

Greece has spent much of the time since 2010 making financial news. In April of 2010, analysts and lenders started to become worried about high Greek government debt and whether or not the Greek government would continue to make interest payments. As a result, very few people were willing to lend to the Greek government, and those that were willing to lend would do so only at very high interest rates—rates as high as 15 percent at a time when most developed economies were borrowing at less than 5 percent. Faced with few lenders and high interest rates, the Greek government borrowed from the European Union and other international organizations instead. This loan came with many conditions— including reducing the government deficit and changing many regulations and laws. These reforms included changes to pension plans, reducing the pay received by government workers, selling government owned properties and businesses, and large changes to labour market laws. This situation is often referred to as a *bailout*.

The bailout of the Greek government led to many protests.

The measures to reduce the government deficit by cutting spending and raising taxes are often referred to as austerity. By 2015, the Greek government had been bailed out multiple times, and each time the spending plans and reforms the government accepted with the bailouts led to large-scale protests. Before the bailout agreed to in July 2015, the government of Greece refused to implement reforms or continue with austerity. The other governments of the European Union (led by Germany) refused to lend any more money to Greece unless they agreed to more austerity and reform. Prior to this agreement it was very possible that Greece would have to give up the Euro and return to printing its own currency. Things in Greece got so bad that banks shut down for three weeks and citizens were restricted to withdrawing only 50 euros a day (between $80 and $100 Canadian) from ATMs. Despite modest growth in 2014, the Greek economy shrank by an estimated 2 to 3 percent in 2015. In the end, Greece generally agreed to the terms demanded by the European Union and other creditors.

Greece has not been the only country to receive a bailout and be required to pursue austerity and reform. Ireland, Portugal, and Spain in particular have all received bailouts, suffered through austerity, and made substantive changes to their economies. These countries have had a very different experience than Greece. All three have returned to growth patterns that more closely match the broader European Union and, interestingly, Spain lead the European Union in economic growth in 2014–2015. It is unclear why the experience of Greece has been so radically different. Some economists argue that the spending cuts and tax increases required to deal with Greece's budget deficit are too big to be manageable, and reduce aggregate demand too much to be useful. Other economists argue that the reduced size of government and other reforms will create more opportunities for private business and private sector employment growth as has been the case in other countries receiving bailouts.

At the time of writing, the experts were still debating.

Your Turn: Test your understanding by doing related problem 6.4 on page 355 at the end of this chapter.   MyEconLab

Solved Problem **12.2**

The Effect of Economic Fluctuations on the Budget Deficit

The Canadian federal government's budget deficit was $35.3 billion in 1991 and $34.4 billion in 1992. A student comments, "The government must have acted between 1991 and 1992 to raise taxes or cut spending, or possibly both." Do you agree? Briefly explain.

Solving the Problem

Step 1: **Review the chapter material.** This problem is about the federal budget as an automatic stabilizer, so you may want to review the section "How the Federal Budget Can Serve as an Automatic Stabilizer" on page 344.

Step 2: **Explain how changes in the budget deficit can occur without government action.** If government takes action to raise taxes or cut spending, the federal budget deficit will decline. But the deficit will also decline automatically when GDP increases, even if the government takes no action. When GDP increases, rising household incomes and firm profits result in higher tax revenues. Increasing GDP also usually means falling unemployment, which reduces government spending on programs for the unemployed (Employment Insurance in Canada). So, you should disagree with the comment. A falling deficit does not mean that the government *must* have acted to raise taxes or cut spending.

Extra credit: Although you don't need this detail to answer the question, Canadian GDP rose from $696.9 billion in 1991 to $713.3 billion in 1992.

MyEconLab **Your Turn:** For more practice, do related problem 6.5 on page 355 at the end of this chapter.

Should the Federal Budget Always Be Balanced?

Although many economists believe that it is a good idea for the federal government to have a balanced budget when the economy is at potential GDP, few economists believe that the federal government should attempt to balance its budget every year. To see why economists take this view, consider what the government would have to do to keep the budget balanced during a recession, when the federal budget automatically moves into deficit. To bring the budget back into balance, the government would have to raise taxes or cut spending, but these actions would reduce aggregate demand, thereby making the recession worse. Similarly, when GDP increases above its potential level, the budget automatically moves into surplus. To eliminate this surplus, the government would have to cut taxes or increase government spending. But these actions would increase aggregate demand, thereby pushing GDP even further beyond potential GDP and increasing the risk of higher inflation. To balance the budget every year, the government might have to take actions that would destabilize the economy.

Some economists argue that the federal government should normally run a budget deficit, even when the economy is at potential GDP. When the federal budget is in deficit, the government sells bonds to investors to raise the funds necessary to pay the government's bills. Borrowing to pay the bills is a bad idea for a household, a firm, or a government when the bills are for current expenses, but it isn't necessarily a bad policy if the bills are for long-lived capital goods. For instance, most households pay for a home by taking a 15- to 25-year mortgage. Because houses last many years, it makes sense to pay for a house out of the income the household earns over a long period of time rather than out of the income received in the year the house is bought. Businesses often borrow the funds to buy machinery, equipment, and factories by selling long-term corporate bonds. Because these capital goods generate profits for the businesses over many years, it makes sense to pay for them over a period of years as well. By similar reasoning, when the federal government contributes to the building of a new highway, bridge, or subway, it may want to borrow funds by selling bonds. The alternative is to pay for these long-lived capital goods out of the tax revenues received in the year the goods were purchased. But that means that the taxpayers in that year have to bear the whole burden of paying for the projects, even though taxpayers for many years in the future will get to enjoy the benefits.

The Federal Government Debt

Every time the federal government runs a budget deficit, the government must borrow funds from investors by selling bonds. When the federal government runs a budget surplus, it pays off some existing bonds. Figure 12.16 shows that there are many more years of federal budget deficits than years of federal budget surpluses. As a result, the total number of bonds outstanding has grown over the years. The total value of bonds outstanding, which is equal to the sum of past budget deficits, is referred to as the **federal government debt**. Each year the federal budget is in deficit, the federal government debt grows. Each year the federal budget is in surplus, the debt shrinks.

    Figure 12.17 shows federal government debt since 1967. The debt has been increasing over virtually the entire period. The exception is the period from 2000 to 2008, during which the debt either fell or increased very little. You can see a major increase in the debt from 1980 to 1998. While federal government debt would have naturally increased during the recessions that took place in this period, it also increased when the economy was growing. In 2000, the debt actually began to fall. This trend continued until 2009, when the debt increased dramatically. This spike in the debt was a result of Canada's Economic Action Plan. When we consider the gross federal government debt, it's important to keep a couple of points in mind. First, we haven't controlled for changes in the value of the dollar: The total debt was fewer dollars in the 1960s, but those dollars were worth more. Second, the Canadian economy has been growing at the same time that the debt has been growing.

> **Federal government debt** The total value of bonds outstanding, which is equal to the sum of past budget deficits, net of surpluses.

Is Government Debt a Problem?

Debt can be a problem for a government for the same reasons that debt can be a problem for a household or a business. If a household has difficulty making the monthly mortgage payment, it will have to cut back on spending for other things. If the household is

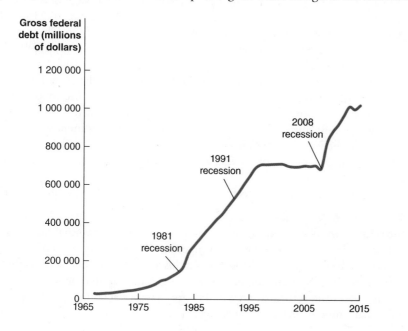

Figure 12.17

The Federal Government Debt, 1967–2015

The federal government debt increases whenever the federal government runs a budget deficit. The large deficits of the 1980s and 1990s increased the debt significantly. The debt actually began to fall in the 2000s, as the federal government brought budget deficits down and began to run budget surpluses. This trend continued until 2009, when the federal government engaged in expansionary fiscal policy to offset the global recession.

Source: Data from Department of Finance, Fiscal Reference Tables, Table 15 http://www.fin.gc.ca/frt-trf/2015/frt-trf-15-eng.asp.

unable to make payments, it will have to default on the loan and will probably lose its house. The federal government is in no danger of defaulting on its debt. Ultimately, the government can raise the funds it needs through taxes to make the interest payment on the debt. If the debt becomes very large relative to the economy, however, the government may have to raise taxes to higher levels or cut back on many other types of spending to make the interest payments on the debt. Interest payments are currently about 11 percent of total federal expenditures. At this level, tax increases or significant cutbacks in other areas aren't required.

In the long run, a debt that increases in size relative to GDP, as was happening after 2009, can pose a problem. As we discussed previously, crowding out of investment spending may occur if an increasing debt drives up interest rates. Lower investment spending means a lower capital stock in the future and a lower capacity of the economy to produce goods and services. This effect is somewhat offset if some of the government debt was incurred to finance improvements in *infrastructure*, such as bridges, roads, and ports; to finance education; or to finance research and development. Improvements in infrastructure, a better-educated labour force, and additional research and development can add to the productive capacity of the economy.

The Effects of Fiscal Policy in the Long Run

Some fiscal policy actions are intended to meet short-run goals of stabilizing the economy. Other fiscal policy actions are intended to have long-run effects by expanding the productive capacity of the economy and increasing the rate of economic growth. Because these policy actions primarily affect aggregate supply rather than aggregate demand, they are sometimes referred to as *supply-side economics*. Most fiscal policy actions that attempt to increase aggregate supply do so by changing taxes to increase the incentives to work, save, invest, or start a business.

The Long-Run Effects of Tax Policy

Tax wedge The difference between the pretax and posttax return to an economic activity.

The difference between the pretax and posttax return to an economic activity is known as the **tax wedge**. The tax wedge applies to the *marginal tax rate*, which is the fraction of each additional dollar of income that must be paid in taxes. For example, the Canadian income tax has several tax brackets, which are the income ranges within which a tax rate applies. In 2016, the federal personal income tax rate on the first $45 282 of income was 15%. The tax rate rose for higher income brackets until it reached 33% on income earned above $200 000. Suppose that you are paid a wage of $20 per hour. If your marginal income tax rate is 25 percent, then the after-tax wage is $15, and the tax wedge is $5. When discussing the model of demand and supply in Chapter 3, we saw that increasing the price of a good or service increases the quantity supplied. So, we would expect that reducing the tax wedge by cutting the marginal tax rate on income would result in a larger quantity of labour supplied because the after-tax wage would be higher. Similarly, we saw in Chapter 6 that a reduction in the income tax would increase the after-tax return to saving, causing an increase in the supply of loanable funds, a lower equilibrium interest rate, and an increase in investment spending. In general, economists believe that the smaller the tax wedge for any economic activity—such as working, saving, investing, or starting a business—the more of that economic activity will occur.

We can look briefly at the effects on aggregate supply cutting each of the following taxes:

- **Individual income tax.** As we've seen, reducing the marginal tax rates on individual income will reduce the tax wedge faced by workers, thereby increasing the quantity of labour supplied. Most households are taxed on their returns from savings at the individual income tax rates. Reducing marginal income tax rates, therefore, also increases the return to saving. Tax-free savings accounts allow households to earn small amounts of interest, tax-free.

- **Corporate income tax.** The federal government taxes the profits earned by corporations under the corporate income tax. In January 2012, the corporate income tax rate fell to 15 percent. Cutting the marginal corporate income tax rate may encourage investment spending by increasing the return corporations receive from new investments in equipment, factories, and office buildings. Because innovations are often embodied in new investment goods, cutting the corporate income tax can potentially increase the pace of technological change.

- **Taxes on dividends and capital gains.** Corporations distribute some of their profits to shareholders in the form of payments known as *dividends*. Shareholders may also benefit from higher corporate profits by receiving *capital gains*. A capital gain is the change in the price of an asset, such as a share of a stock. Rising profits usually results in rising stock prices and capital gains to shareholders. Individuals pay taxes on both dividends and capital gains (only half of dividend and capital gains are taxed, and they are taxed in the same way as other income). As a result, the same earnings are, in effect, taxed twice: once when corporations pay the corporate income tax on their profits and a second time when the profits are received by individual investors in the form of dividends or capital gains. Economists debate the cost and benefits of a separate tax on corporate profits. With the corporate income tax remaining in place, one way to reduce the "double taxation" problem is to reduce the taxes on dividends and capital gains. Lowering the tax rates on dividends and capital gains may increase the supply of loanable funds from households to firms, increasing saving and investment and lowering the equilibrium real interest rate.

Tax Simplification

In addition to the potential gains from cutting individual taxes, there are also gains from tax simplification. The complexity of the Canadian tax system has created an entire industry of tax preparation services such as H&R Block. Sean Speer estimates that it costs Canadians between $5.84 billion and $6.96 billion annually to comply with personal income tax regulations.[1] There are costs to complying with the corporate income tax and even the GST has costs associated with collecting, calculating net tax owed, and remitting the GST. The complexity of the tax code makes it unsurprising that over half of Canadians paid someone else to prepare their income taxes.

If the tax code were greatly simplified, the economic resources currently used by the tax preparation industry would be available to produce other goods and services. In addition to wasting resources, the complexity of the tax code may also distort the decisions made by households and firms. A simplified tax code would increase economic efficiency by reducing the number of decisions households and firms make solely to reduce their tax payments.

The Economic Effect of Tax Reform

We can analyze the economic effects of tax reduction and simplification by using the aggregate demand and aggregate supply model. Figure 12.18 shows that without tax changes, the aggregate supply curve will shift from $LRAS_1$ to $LRAS_2$. This shift represents the increases in the labour force and the capital stock and the technological change that would occur even without tax reduction and simplification. To focus on the impact of tax changes on aggregate supply, we will ignore any shifts in the short-run aggregate supply curve, and we will assume that the aggregate demand curve remains unchanged at AD_1. In this case, equilibrium moves from point A to point B, with real GDP increasing from Y_1 to Y_2 and the price level decreasing from P_1 to P_2.

If tax reduction and simplification are effective, the economy will experience increases in labour supply, saving, investment, and the formation of new firms. Economic

[1] Speer, Sean, Milagros Palacios, Marco Lugo, and François Vaillancourt (2014). The Cost to Canadians of Complying with Personal Income Taxes. Fraser Institute, http://www. fraserinstitute.org.

Figure 12.18

The Supply-Side Effects of a Tax Change

The economy's initial equilibrium is at point *A*. With no tax change, the long-run aggregate supply curve shifts to the right, from $LRAS_1$ to $LRAS_2$. Equilibrium moves to point *B*, with the price level falling from P_1 to P_2 and real GDP increasing from Y_1 to Y_2. With tax reductions and simplifications, the long-run aggregate supply curve shifts further to the right, to $LRAS_3$, and equilibrium moves to point *C*, with the price level falling to P_3 and real GDP increasing to Y_3.

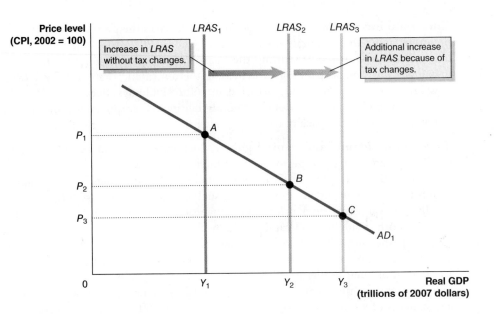

efficiency will also be improved. Together these factors will result in an increase in the quantity of real GDP supplied at every price level. We show the effects of the tax changes in Figure 12.18 by a shift in the long-run aggregate supply curve to $LRAS_3$. With aggregate demand remaining the same, the equilibrium in the economy moves from point *A* to point *C* (rather than to point *B*, which is the equilibrium without tax changes), with real GDP increasing from Y_1 to Y_3, and the price level decreasing from P_1 to P_3. An important point to notice is that compared with the equilibrium without tax changes (point *B*), the equilibrium with tax changes (point *C*) occurs at a lower price level and a higher level of real GDP. We can conclude that the tax changes have benefited the economy by increasing output and employment while at the same time reducing the price level.

Clearly, our analysis is unrealistic because we have ignored the changes in aggregate demand and short-run aggregate supply that will occur. How would a more realistic analysis differ from the simplified one in Figure 12.18? The change in real GDP would be the same because in the long run, real GDP is equal to its potential level, which is represented by the long-run aggregate supply curve. The results for price level would be different, however, because we would expect both aggregate demand and short-run aggregate supply to shift to the right. The likeliest case is that the price level would end up higher in the new equilibrium than in the original equilibrium. However, because the position of the long-run aggregate supply curve is further to the right as a result of the tax changes, the increase in the price level will be smaller; that is, the price level at point *C* is likely to be lower than at point *B*, even if it is higher than at point *A*, although—as we will discuss in the next section—not all economists would agree. We can conclude that a successful policy of tax reductions and simplifications will benefit the economy by increasing output and employment, while reducing inflation (increases in the price level) at the same time.

How Big Are Supply-Side Effects?

Most economists would agree that there are supply-side effects to reducing taxes: Decreasing marginal income tax rates will increase the quantity of labour supplied, cutting the corporate income tax rates will increase investment spending, and so on. The magnitude of the effects is the subject of ongoing debate. For example, some economists argue that the increase in the quantity of labour supplied following a tax cut will be limited because many people work a number of hours set by their employers and lack the opportunity to work additional hours. Similarly, some economists believe that tax changes have only a small effect on saving and investment. In this view, saving and investment are affected much more by changes in expectations of future profitability of new investment due to technological change or improving macroeconomic conditions than they are by tax changes.

Economists who are skeptical of the magnitude of supply-side effects believe that tax cuts have their greatest impact on aggregate demand rather than on aggregate supply. In their view, focusing on the impact of tax cuts on aggregate demand, while ignoring any impact on aggregate supply, yields accurate forecasts of future movements in real GDP and the price level, which indicates that the supply-side effects must be small. If tax changes have only small effects on aggregate supply, it is unlikely that they will reduce the size of price increases to the extent shown in the analysis in Figure 12.18.

Ultimately, the debate over the size of the supply-side effects of tax policy can be resolved only through careful study of the effects of differences in tax rates on labour supply and on saving and investment decisions. Recent US studies have arrived at conflicting conclusions. For example, a study by Edward Prescott concludes that differences between the United States and Europe with respect to the average number of hours worked per week and the average number of weeks worked per year are due to differences in taxes. The lower marginal tax rates in the United States compared with Europe increase the return to working American workers and result in a higher supply of labour. But another study by Alberto Alesina, Edward Glaeser, and Bruce Sacerdote argues that the more restrictive labour market regulations in Europe explain the shorter work weeks and longer vacations of European workers and that differences in taxes have only a small effect.

As in other areas of economics, differences among economists in their estimates of the supply-side effects of tax changes may narrow over time as additional studies are conducted.

Economics In Your Life

What Would You Do with $500 Less?

At the beginning of the chapter, we asked how you would respond to a new $500 tax and what effect this new tax would likely have on equilibrium real GDP in the short run. This chapter has shown that taxes decrease disposable income and that when there is a permanent decrease in disposable income, consumption spending decreases. So, you will likely respond to a permanent $500 decrease in your disposable income by decreasing your spending. How much your spending decreases depends in part on your overall financial situation. As mentioned in the chapter, people who are able to borrow usually try to smooth out their spending over time and don't decrease spending much in response to a one-time decrease in their income. But if you are struggling financially, your consumption may drop by the entire amount of the new tax. This chapter has also shown that tax cuts have a multiplier effect on the economy. That is, a decrease in consumption spending sets off further decreases in real GDP and income. Thus, this tax increase is likely to decrease equilibrium real GDP in the short run.

Conclusion

In this chapter, we have seen how the government uses changes in government purchases and taxes to achieve its economic policy goals. We have seen that economists debate the effectiveness of discretionary fiscal policy actions intended to stabilize the economy. Parliament and the Prime Minister share responsibility for economic policy with the Bank of Canada. In Chapter 13, we will discuss some of the challenges that the Bank of Canada encounters as it carries out monetary policy. In Chapters 14 and 15, we will look more closely at the international economy, including how monetary and fiscal policies are affected by the linkages between economies.

Chapter Summary and Problems

Key Terms

Automatic stabilizers, p. 326

Budget deficit, p. 343

Budget surplus, p. 343

Crowding out, p. 340

Cyclically adjusted budget deficit or surplus, p. 344

Federal government debt, p. 347

Fiscal policy, p. 326

Multiplier effect, p. 335

Tax wedge, p. 348

Summary

*LO 12.1 *Fiscal policy* involves changes in federal taxes and purchases that are intended to achieve macroeconomic policy objectives. *Automatic stabilizers* are government spending and taxes that automatically increase or decrease along with the business cycle. Since the 1960s, the federal government's share of total government expenditures has steadily declined from above 60 percent to almost 40 percent. Federal government *expenditures* as a percentage of GDP rose from the early 1960s to the early 1990s and fell between 1992 and 2009, before rising again. The federal government's share of total government spending has declined because (1) it has been delegating the administration of certain responsibilities to provincial and territorial agencies, and (2) the importance of health care in the budgets of other levels of government has grown. The largest sources of federal government revenue are income taxes. The federal government makes large-scale transfers to provincial and territorial governments, as they have larger burdens of expenditure without reciprocal revenue-generating power.

LO 12.2 To fight recessions, the federal government can increase government purchases or cut taxes. This expansionary policy causes the aggregate demand curve to shift out more than it otherwise would, raising the level of real GDP and the price level. To fight rising inflation, the federal government can decrease government purchases or raise taxes. This contractionary policy causes the aggregate demand curve to shift out less than it otherwise would, reducing the increase in real GDP and the price level.

LO 12.3 We can use the dynamic aggregate demand and aggregate supply model introduced in Chapter 11 to look more closely at expansionary and contractionary fiscal policies. The dynamic aggregate demand and aggregate supply model takes into account that (1) the economy experiences continuing inflation, with the price level rising every year, and (2) the economy experiences long-run growth, with the *LRAS* curve shifting to the right every year. In the dynamic model, an expansionary fiscal policy tries to ensure that the aggregate demand curve will shift far enough to the right to bring about macroeconomic equilibrium, with real GDP equal to potential GDP. A contractionary fiscal policy attempts to offset movements in aggregate demand that would cause macroeconomic equilibrium to occur at a level of real GDP that is greater than potential GDP.

LO 12.4 Because of the *multiplier effect*, an increase in government purchases or a cut in taxes will have a multiplied effect on equilibrium real GDP. The government purchases multiplier is equal to the change in equilibrium real GDP divided by the change in government purchases. The tax multiplier is equal to the change in equilibrium real GDP divided by the change in taxes. Increases in government purchases and cuts in taxes have a positive multiplier effect on equilibrium real GDP. Decreases in government purchases and increases in taxes have a negative multiplier effect on equilibrium real GDP.

LO 12.5 Poorly timed fiscal policy can do more harm than good. Getting the timing right with fiscal policy can be difficult because obtaining government approval for a new fiscal policy can be a very long process and because it can take months for an increase in authorized spending to take place. Because an increase in government purchases may lead to a higher interest rate, it may result in a decline in consumption, investment, and net exports. A decline in private expenditures as a result of an increase in government purchases is called *crowding out*. Crowding out may cause an expansionary fiscal policy to fail to meet its goal of keeping the economy at potential GDP.

LO 12.6 A *budget deficit* occurs when the federal government's expenditures are greater than its tax revenues. A *budget surplus* occurs when the federal government's expenditures are less than its tax revenues. A budget deficit automatically increases during recessions and tends to decrease during expansions. The automatic movements in the federal budget help stabilize the economy by cushioning the fall in spending during recessions and restraining the increase in spending during expansions. The *cyclically adjusted budget deficit or surplus* measures what the deficit or surplus would be if the economy were at potential GDP. The *federal government debt* is the total value of bonds outstanding, which is equal to the sum of past budget deficits. The national debt is a problem if interest payments on it require taxes to be raised substantially or other federal expenditures to be cut.

LO 12.7 Some fiscal policy actions are intended to have long-run effects by expanding the productive capacity of the economy and increasing the rate of economic growth. Because these policy actions primarily affect aggregate supply rather than aggregate demand, they are sometimes referred to as *supply-side economics*. The difference between the pretax and posttax return to an economic activity is known as the *tax wedge*. Economists believe that the smaller the tax wedge for any economic activity—such as working, saving, investing, or starting a business—the more of that economic activity will occur. Economists debate the size of the supply-side effects of tax changes.

MyEconLab   Log in to MyEconLab to complete these exercises and get instant feedback.

★"Learning Objective" is abbreviated to "LO" in the end-of-chapter material.

Review Questions

LO 12.1

1.1 **[Related to the Chapter Opener on page 325]** What is fiscal policy? Who is responsible for fiscal policy?

1.2 What is the difference between fiscal policy and monetary policy?

1.3 What is the difference between federal purchases and federal expenditures? Why have federal government expenditures as a percentage of GDP risen again since 2009?

LO 12.2

2.1 What is an expansionary fiscal policy? What is a contractionary fiscal policy?

2.2 If Parliament and the Prime Minster decide that an expansionary fiscal policy is necessary, what changes should they make in government spending or taxes? What changes should they make if they decide that a contractionary fiscal policy is necessary?

LO 12.3

3.1 What are the key differences between how we illustrate an expansionary fiscal policy in the basic aggregate demand and aggregate supply model and in the dynamic aggregate demand and aggregate supply model?

3.2 What are the key differences between how we illustrate a contractionary fiscal policy in the basic aggregate demand and aggregate supply model and in the dynamic aggregate demand and aggregate supply model?

LO 12.4

4.1 Why does a $1 increase in government purchases lead to more than a $1 increase in income and spending?

4.2 Define *government purchases multiplier* and *tax multiplier*.

LO 12.5

5.1 Which can be changed more quickly: monetary policy or fiscal policy? Briefly explain.

5.2 What is meant by crowding out? Explain the difference between crowding out in the short run and in the long run.

LO 12.6

6.1 In what ways does the federal budget serve as an automatic stabilizer for the economy?

6.2 What is the cyclically adjusted budget deficit or surplus? Suppose that the economy is currently at potential GDP, and the federal budget is balanced. If the economy moves into recession, what will happen to the federal budget?

6.3 Why do few economists argue that it would be a good idea to balance the federal budget every year?

6.4 What is the difference between the federal budget deficit and federal government debt?

LO 12.7

7.1 What is meant by *supply-side economics*?

7.2 What is the *tax wedge*?

Problems and Applications

LO 12.1

1.1 The BC government established the BC Scrap-It Program, which pays people between $750 and $2250 toward the purchase of a new car if they trade in older vehicles with poor fuel economy. The size of the payout is dependent on the size of the greenhouse gas benefit. Was this piece of legislation an example of fiscal policy? Does it depend on what goals the BC government had in mind when it enacted the legislation?

Based on Jeremy Cato, "Canada's cash-for-clunkers plan: Do nothing at all", *CTV News*, June 19, 2009, http://www.ctv.ca/CTVNews/Autos/20090618/AUTOS_cash_clunkers_090619/.

1.2 **[Related to Making the Connection on page 330]** According to Pierre Fortin, professor of economics at the University of Québec at Montréal:

> The passage of [the] large group of baby boomers into their golden years will push the percentage of senior citizens 65 and older from 13% of the total population in 2006 to 18% in 2020. . . . As a result, between now and 2020, there will be a 14% increase in annual provincial spending in health care and social services, this is above and beyond the already extremely rapid increase in spending over the past several years (on average 7% per year since 2000).

Who are the "baby boomers"? Why should their aging cause such a large increase in the growth rate of spending by the provincial governments on health care?

Pierre Fortin, "The Baby Boomers' Tab," *CBC News*, July 17, 2006, http://www.cbc.ca/news/background/canada2020/essay-fortin.html.

1.3 **[Related to Making the Connection on page 330]** According to Statistics Canada, "[b]y 2056, it is projected (based on a medium growth scenario) that there will be only 2 working-age people for every senior in Canada." Briefly explain the implications of this fact for federal government spending as a percentage of GDP in 2056.

StatsCan, Demographic change, January 14, 2010, http://www.statcan.gc.ca/pub/82-229-x/2009001/demo/int1-eng.htm.

LO 12.2

2.1 Briefly explain whether you agree with the following statements: "An expansionary fiscal policy involves an increase in government purchases or an increase in taxes. A contractionary fiscal policy involves a decrease in government purchases or a decrease in taxes."

2.2 Identify each of the following as (a) part of an expansionary fiscal policy, (b) part of a contractionary fiscal policy, or (c) not part of fiscal policy.

i. The corporate income tax rate is increased.

ii. The Bank of Canada lowers the target for the overnight interest rate.

iii. Individual income tax rate is decreased.

iv. The Quebec government invests in building a new highway in an attempt to expand employment in the province.

2.3 Use an aggregate demand and aggregate supply graph to illustrate the situation where the economy begins in equilibrium at potential GDP and then the demand for housing sharply declines. What actions can the federal government take to move the economy back to potential GDP? Show the results of these actions on your graph.

2.4 A political commentator argues: "Parliament is more likely to enact an expansionary fiscal policy than a contractionary fiscal policy because expansionary policies are popular and contractionary policies are unpopular." Briefly explain whether you agree.

LO 12.3

3.1 Use the graph to answer the questions that follow.

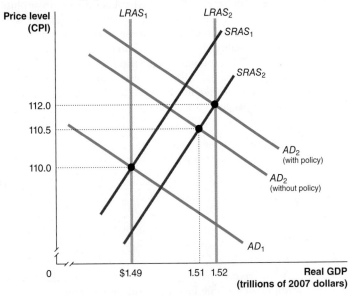

a. If the government takes no policy actions, what will be the values of real GDP and the price level in year 2?

b. What actions can the government take to bring real GDP to its potential level in year 2?

c. If the government takes no policy actions, what will be the inflation rate in year 2? If the government uses fiscal policy to keep real GDP at its potential level, what will be the inflation rate in year 2?

3.2 The hypothetical information in the following table shows what the situation will be in 2015 if the government does *not* use fiscal policy:

Year	Potential GDP	Real GDP	Price Level
2014	$1.50 trillion	$1.50 trillion	110.0
2015	$1.54 trillion	$1.50 trillion	111.5

a. If Parliament wants to keep real GDP at its potential level in 2015, should it use an expansionary policy or a contractionary policy? In your answer, be sure to explain whether the government should be increasing or decreasing government purchases and taxes.

b. If Parliament is successful in keeping real GDP at its potential level in 2015, state whether each of the

following will be higher, lower, or the same as it would have been if they had taken no action:

   i.   Real GDP
   ii. Potential GDP
   iii. The inflation rate
   iv. The unemployment rate

c. Draw an aggregate demand and aggregate supply graph to illustrate your answer. Be sure that your graph contains *LRAS* curves for 2014 and 2015; *SRAS* curves for 2014 and 2015; *AD* curves for 2014 and 2015, with and without fiscal policy action; and equilibrium real GDP and the price level in 2015, with and without fiscal policy.

LO 12.4

4.1 Why would the new bridge to the United States in Southern Ontario and similar construction projects elsewhere in the country be expected to help the economy in the short run? Proponents of government infrastructure projects often argue that government spending of this sort will have a "ripple effect" on employment. What do they mean by a *ripple effect*?

4.2 Suppose that real GDP is currently $1.31 trillion, potential GDP is $1.35 trillion, the government purchases multiplier is 2, and the tax multiplier is −1.6.

a. Holding other factors constant, by how much will government purchases need to be increased to bring the economy to equilibrium at potential GDP?

b. Holding other factors constant, by how much will taxes have to be cut to bring the economy to equilibrium at potential GDP?

c. Construct an example of a combination of increased government spending and tax cuts that will bring the economy to equilibrium at potential GDP.

4.3 **[Related to Don't Let This Happen to You on page 339]** Consider a local politician advocating for a local government-funded project. Suppose the politician justifies the cost by stating that for each dollar spent on the project, it will generate 2.5 dollars in economic activity.

a. Using the simple multiplier formula, derive the marginal propensity to consume (*MPC*). Is this reasonable?

b. Assume that, like most Canadian towns, the marginal tax rate is about 0.25 and the marginal propensity to import (*MPI*) can be conservatively estimated at 0.15. Find the *MPC*. Is this reasonable?

4.4 In many estimations of tax or expenditure multipliers, there are multiple values for different periods of time. These values generally increase as the time period gets longer. Briefly explain why a multiplier, such as the tax multiplier, might have a larger value after two years than after just one year.

4.5 In their efforts to stimulate the economy during the 2007–2009 global recession, countries around the world (including Canada, China, and the United States) spent trillions of dollars on new roads and other forms of infrastructure. Why would infrastructure spending be such a popular way for government to stimulate the economy?

4.6 [Related to Solved Problem 12.1 on page 339] Briefly explain whether you agree with the following statement:

> Real GDP is currently $1.65 trillion, and potential GDP is $1.64 trillion. If the federal government would decrease government purchases by $30 billion or increase taxes by $30 billion, the economy could be brought to equilibrium at potential GDP.

LO 12.5

5.1 In April 2008, the *Cape Breton Post* reported that it was widely believed that "Canada faces two lean years of slow growth, but will skirt a recession in the wake of the unfolding U.S.-centred financial crisis that is dragging down economies around the world." However, by December 2008, the *Toronto Star* reported that "Canada's economy evolved largely as expected during the summer and early autumn, it is now entering a recession as a result of the weakness in global economic activity." Does the idea that the definition of a recession comes from data released well after the fact tell us anything about the difficulty the federal government faces in implementing a fiscal policy that stabilizes rather than destabilizes the economy?

Based on Julie Beltrame, "IMF says Canada skirts recession, but growth to slow sharply to 1.3%", *Cape Breton Post*, April 10, 2008, http://www.capebretonpost.com/Economy/2008-04-10/article-772508/IMF-says-Canada-skirts-recession-but-growth-to-slow-sharply-to-13/1 and "Economy in recession, Bank of Canada says", *Toronto Star*, December 9, 2008, http://www.thestar.com/Business/article/550729.

5.2 In 2011, an article in *The Economist* argued that "heavy public debt risks more than just crowding out private investment. It can, in the extreme, bring on insolvency." What does the article mean by "heavy public debts"? How might heavy public debts lead to insolvency?

"Running Out of Road," *The Economist*, June 16, 2011.

5.3 Suppose that at the same time as Parliament pursues an expansionary fiscal policy, the Bank of Canada pursues an expansionary monetary policy. How might an expansionary monetary policy affect the extent of crowding out in the short run?

5.4 [Related to Making the Connection on page 342] Why might a recession be a reasonable time to reduce spending on health care?

LO 12.6

6.1 The federal government calculates its budget on a fiscal year that begins on October 1 and ends the following September 30. At the beginning of the 2003–2004 fiscal year, the Department of Finance forecast that the federal budget surplus for the fiscal year would be $4.0 billion. The actual budget surplus for the fiscal year was $9.1 billion. Federal expenditures were $1.7 billion less than the Department had forecast, and federal revenue was $1.5 billion more than the Department had forecast. The remainder of the surplus came from lower-than-forecast debt charges.

    a. Is it likely that the economy grew faster or more slowly during fiscal 2003–2004 than the Department of Finance had expected? Explain your reasoning.

    b. Suppose that the federal government were committed to balancing the budget each year. Does the surprise surplus during fiscal 2003–2004 provide any insight into difficulties that might arise in trying to balance the budget every year?

Data from http://www.fin.gc.ca/activty/pubs/oneil/oneil_3-eng.asp.

6.2 British Columbia passed a balanced budget law in 2001, and in February 2009 the provincial government announced that it would amend the law to allow deficit spending. *CBC News* reported that "[then BC Finance Minister Colin] Hansen and [then] Premier Gordon Campbell announced at a joint press conference that provincial revenues have fallen prey to the worldwide economic meltdown." Do you think that nothing is more important than a balanced budget, as was stated by British Columbia's initial law, or do you think it was reasonable to amend the law for fiscal flexibility?

"BC's Balanced Budget Law to Allow 2 Years of Deficits", *CBC News*, February 9, 2009, http://www.cbc.ca/canada/british-columbia/story/2009/02/09/bc-legislature-budget-deficit-vote.html#ixzz18k3CFTkV.

6.3 According to an article in the *Globe and Mail*, [then] Finance Minister Jim Flaherty stated at a meeting with provincial ministers in 2010: "Canada must avoid heading in the same direction as the European Union, where many countries are in the throes of a debt crisis." He also called on provincial ministers to eliminate their deficits by 2015. How might the economy suffer from large federal deficits? How can the provincial governments rein in their budget deficits?

Karen Howlett and Bill Curry, "Rein in Deficits or Risk EU-Style Crisis, Jim Flaherty Warns Provinces," *Globe and Mail*, December 20, 2010, http://www.theglobeandmail.com/news/politics/rein-in-deficits-or-risk-eu-style-crisis-jim-flaherty-warns-provinces/article1844649/.

6.4 [Related to Making the Connection on page 345] What impact do you think a major reduction in US government spending would have on the Canadian economy? Explain.

6.5 [Related to Solved Problem 12.2 on page 346] The federal government's budget surplus was $14.2 billion in 1999 and $19.9 billion in 2000. What does this information tell us about fiscal policy actions that the federal government took during those years?

Based on "Canada's Deficits and Surpluses, 1963–2012," *CBC News*, March 25, 2013, http://www.cbc.ca/news/interactives/canada-deficit/.

LO 12.7

7.1 It seems that both households and businesses would benefit if the federal income tax were simpler and tax forms were easier to fill out. Why then have the tax laws become increasingly complicated?

7.2 Suppose that an increase in marginal tax rates on individual income affects both aggregate demand and aggregate supply. Briefly describe the effect of the tax increase on equilibrium real GDP and the equilibrium price level. Will the changes in equilibrium real GDP and the price level be larger or smaller than they would be if the tax increase affected only aggregate demand? Briefly explain.

7.3 In a *CBC News* article on taxes—a major issue during the 2010 New Brunswick election—Craig Brett (professor of economics at Mount Allison University) stated: "There is a glimmer of hope for the supply-side myth in the case of corporate taxes. This is the only tax for which I have seen any plausible evidence that tax cuts might, I repeat might, be self-financing." Using a definition of "supply-side" tax cuts, explain how such cuts might lead to higher tax revenues and be self-financing. Why is Brett skeptical about the potential for supply-side tax cuts to be revenue generating for all types of taxes?

Craig Brett, "Talking Taxes: the Dirty Word in N.B.", *CBC News*, September 21, 2010, http://www.cbc.ca/canada/nbvotes2010/story/2010/09/20/nbvotes-analysis-craig-brett-taxes.html.

7.4 The majority of countries that have adopted a flat tax system of taxing individual incomes are Eastern European with historical links to the Soviet Union. Why do you think these countries might be more likely to adopt such a system than countries like Canada or the United States?

MyEconLab MyEconLab is an online tool designed to help you master the concepts covered in your course. It will create a personalized study plan to stimulate and measure your learning. Log in to take advantage of this powerful study aid, and to access quizzes and other valuable course-related material.

Appendix E

A Closer Look at the Multiplier Formula

LO

Apply the multiplier formula.

In this chapter, we saw that changes in government purchases and changes in taxes have a multiplied effect on equilibrium real GDP. In this appendix, we will build a simple economic model of the multiplier effect. When economists forecast the effect of a change in spending or taxes, they often rely on *econometric models*. As we saw in the appendix to Chapter 8, an econometric model is an economic model written in the form of equations, where each equation has been statistically estimated, using methods similar to those used in estimating demand curves, as briefly described in Chapter 3. In this appendix, we will start with a model similar to the one we used in the appendix to Chapter 8.

An Expression for Equilibrium Real GDP

We can write a set of equations that includes the key macroeconomic relationships we have studied in this and previous chapters. It is important to note that in this model, we will be assuming that the price level is constant. We know that this is unrealistic because an upward-sloping *SRAS* curve means that when the aggregate demand curve shifts, the price level will change. Nevertheless, our model will be approximately correct when changes in the price level are small. It also serves as an introduction to more complicated models that take into account changes in the price level. For simplicity, we also start out by assuming that taxes, T, do not depend on the level of real GDP, Y. We also assume that there are no government transfer payments to households. Finally, we assume that we have a closed economy, with no imports or exports. The numbers (with the exception of the *MPC*) represent billions of dollars:

1. $C = 100 + 0.8(Y - T)$	Consumption function
2. $I = 125$	Planned investment function
3. $G = 125$	Government purchases function
4. $T = 100$	Tax function
5. $Y = C + I + G$	Equilibrium condition

The first equation is the consumption function. The marginal propensity to consume, or *MPC*, is 0.8, and 100 is the level of autonomous consumption, which is the level of consumption that does not depend on income. We assume that consumption depends on disposable income, which is $Y - T$. The functions for planned investment spending, government spending, and taxes are very simple because we have assumed that these variables are not affected by GDP and, therefore, are constant. Economists who use this type of model to forecast GDP would, of course, use more realistic planned investment, government purchases, and tax functions.

Equation (5)—the equilibrium condition—states that equilibrium GDP equals the sum of consumption spending, planned investment spending, and government purchases. To calculate a value for equilibrium real GDP, we need to substitute equations (1) through (4) into equation (5). This substitution gives us the following:

$$Y = 100 + 0.8(Y - 100) + 125 + 125$$

$$= 100 + 0.8Y - 80 + 125 + 125.$$

We need to solve this equation for Y to find equilibrium GDP. The first step is to subtract $0.8Y$ from both sides of the equation:

$$Y - 0.8Y = 100 - 80 + 125 + 125.$$

Then, we solve for Y:

$$0.2Y = 270$$

or

$$Y = \frac{270}{0.2} = 1350.$$

To make this result more general, we can replace particular values with general values represented by letters:

$C = \overline{C} + MPC(Y - T)$	Consumption function
$I = \overline{I}$	Planned investment function
$G = \overline{G}$	Government purchases function
$T = \overline{T}$	Tax function
$Y = C + I + G$	Equilibrium condition

The letters with bars above them represent fixed, or *autonomous*, values that do not depend on the values of other variables. So, $\overline{C}$ represents autonomous consumption, which had a value of 100 in our original example. Now, solving for equilibrium, we get

$$Y = \overline{C} + MPC(Y - \overline{T}) + \overline{I} + \overline{G}$$

or

$$Y - MPC(Y) = \overline{C} - (MPC \times \overline{T}) + \overline{I} + \overline{G}$$

or

$$Y(1 - MPC) = \overline{C} - (MPC \times \overline{T}) + \overline{I} + \overline{G}$$

or

$$Y = \frac{\overline{C} - (MPC \times \overline{T}) + \overline{I} + \overline{G}}{1 - MPC}$$

A Formula for the Government Purchases Multiplier

To find a formula for the government purchases multiplier, we need to rewrite the last equation for changes in each variable rather than levels. Letting Δ stand for the change in a variable, we have:

$$\Delta Y = \frac{\Delta \overline{C} - (MPC \times \Delta \overline{T}) + \Delta \overline{I} + \Delta \overline{G}}{1 - MPC}$$

If we hold constant changes in autonomous consumption spending, planned investment spending, and taxes, we can find a formula for the government purchases multiplier, which is the ratio of the change in equilibrium real GDP to the change in government purchases:

$$\Delta Y = \frac{\Delta G}{1 - MPC}$$

or

$$\text{Government purchases multiplier} = \frac{\Delta Y}{\Delta G} = \frac{1}{1 - MPC}$$

For an MPC of 0.8, the government purchases multiplier will be

$$\frac{1}{1 - 0.8} = 5.$$

A government purchases multiplier of 5 means that an increase in government spending of $10 billion will increase equilibrium real GDP by $5 \times \$10$ billion = $50 billion.

A Formula for the Tax Multiplier

We can also find a formula for the tax multiplier. We start again with this equation:

$$\Delta Y = \frac{\Delta \overline{C} - (MPC \times \Delta \overline{T}) + \Delta \overline{I} + \Delta \overline{G}}{1 - MPC}$$

Now we hold constant the values of autonomous consumption spending, planned investment spending, and government purchases, but we allow the value of taxes to change:

$$\Delta Y = \frac{-MPC \times \Delta T}{1 - MPC}$$

Or:

$$\text{The tax multiplier} = \frac{\Delta Y}{\Delta T} = \frac{-MPC}{1 - MPC}$$

For an MPC of 0.8, the tax multiplier will be:

$$\frac{-0.8}{1 - 0.8} = -4.$$

The tax multiplier is a negative number because an increase in taxes causes a decrease in equilibrium real GDP, and a decrease in taxes causes an increase in equilibrium real GDP. A tax multiplier of −4 means that a decrease in taxes of $10 billion will increase equilibrium real GDP by $-4 \times -\$10$ billion = $40 billion. In this chapter, we discussed the economic reasons for the tax multiplier being smaller than the government spending multiplier.

The "Balanced Budget" Multiplier

What will be the effect of equal increases (or decreases) in government purchases and taxes on equilibrium real GDP? At first, it might appear that the tax increase would exactly offset the government purchases increase, leaving real GDP unchanged. But we have just seen that the government purchases multiplier is larger (in absolute value) than the tax multiplier. We can use our formulas for the government purchases multiplier and the tax multiplier to calculate the net effect of increasing government purchases by $10 billion at the same time that taxes are increased by $10 billion:

$$\text{Increase in real GDP from the increase in government purchases} = \$10 \text{ billion} \times \frac{1}{1 - MPC}$$

$$\text{Decrease in real GDP from the increase in taxes} = \$10 \text{ billion} \times \frac{-MPC}{1 - MPC}$$

So, the combined effect equals

$$\$10 \text{ billion} \times \left[\left(\frac{1}{1 - MPC} \right) + \left(\frac{-MPC}{1 - MPC} \right) \right]$$

or

$$\$10 \text{ billion} \times \left(\frac{1 - MPC}{1 - MPC} \right) = \$10 \text{ billion}.$$

The balanced budget multiplier is, therefore, equal to $(1 - MPC)/(1 - MPC)$, or 1. Equal dollar increases and decreases in government purchases and in taxes lead to the same dollar increase in real GDP in the short run.

The Effects of Changes in Tax Rates on the Multiplier

We now consider the effect of a change in the tax *rate*, as opposed to a change in a fixed amount of taxes. Changing the tax rate actually changes the value of the multiplier. To see this, suppose that the tax rate is 20 percent, or 0.2. In that case, an increase in household income of $10 billion will increase *disposable income* by only $8 billion [or $10 billion $\times (1 - 0.2)$]. In general, an increase in income can be multiplied by $(1 - t)$ to find the increase in disposable income, where t is the tax rate. So, we can rewrite the consumption function as:

$$C = \overline{C} + MPC(1 - t)Y.$$

We can use this expression for the consumption function to find an expression for the government purchases multiplier, using the same method we used previously:

$$\text{Government purchases multiplier} = \frac{\Delta Y}{\Delta G} = \frac{1}{1 - MPC(1 - t)}$$

We can see the effect of changing the tax rate on the size of the multiplier by trying some values. First, assume that $MPC = 0.8$ and $t = 0.2$. Then:

$$\text{Government purchases multiplier} = \frac{\Delta Y}{\Delta G} = \frac{1}{1 - 0.8(1 - 0.2)} = \frac{1}{1 - 0.64} = 2.77.$$

This value is smaller than the multiplier of 4 that we calculated by assuming that there was only a fixed amount of taxes (which is the same as assuming that the marginal tax *rate* was zero). This multiplier is smaller because spending in each period is now reduced by the amount of taxes households must pay on any additional income they earn. We can calculate the multiplier for an MPC of 0.8 and a lower tax rate of 0.1:

$$\text{Government purchases multiplier} = \frac{\Delta Y}{\Delta G} = \frac{1}{1 - 0.8(1 - 0.1)} = \frac{1}{1 - 0.72} = 3.57.$$

Cutting the tax rate from 20 percent to 10 percent increased the value of the multiplier from 2.77 to 3.57.

The Multiplier in an Open Economy

Up to now, we have assumed that the economy is closed, with no imports or exports. We can consider the case of an open economy by including net exports in our analysis. Recall that net exports equal exports minus imports. Exports are determined primarily by factors—such as the exchange value of the dollar and the levels of real GDP in other countries—that we do not include in our model. So, we will assume that exports are fixed, or autonomous:

$$\text{Exports} = \overline{Exports}$$

Imports will increase as real GDP increases because households will spend some portion of an increase in income on imports. We can define the *marginal propensity to import (MPI)* as the fraction of an increase in income that is spent on imports. So, our expression for imports is:

$$\text{Imports} = MPI \times Y.$$

We can substitute our expressions for exports and imports into the expression we derived earlier for equilibrium real GDP:

$$Y = \overline{C} + MPC(1 - t)Y + \overline{I} + \overline{G} + \left[\overline{Exports} - (MPI \times Y) \right],$$

where the expression $[\overline{Exports} - (MPI \times Y)]$ represents net exports. We can now find an expression for the government purchases multiplier by using the same method we used previously:

$$\text{Government purchases multiplier} = \frac{\Delta Y}{\Delta G} = \frac{1}{1 - [MPC(1 - t) - MPI]}$$

We can see the effect of changing the value of the marginal propensity to import on the size of the multiplier by trying some values of key variables. First, assume that $MPC = 0.8$, $t = 0.2$, and $MPI = 0.1$. Then:

$$\text{Government purchases multiplier} = \frac{\Delta Y}{\Delta G} = \frac{1}{1 - (0.8(1 - 0.2) - 0.1)} = \frac{1}{1 - 0.54} = 2.17.$$

This value is smaller than the multiplier of 2.5 that we calculated by assuming that there were no exports or imports (which is the same as assuming that the marginal propensity to import was zero). This multiplier is smaller because spending in each period is now reduced by the amount of imports households buy with any additional income they earn. We can calculate the multiplier with $MPC = 0.8$, $t = 0.2$, and a higher MPI of 0.2:

$$\text{Government purchases multiplier} = \frac{\Delta Y}{\Delta G} = \frac{1}{1 - (0.8(1 - 0.2) - 0.2)} = \frac{1}{1 - 0.44} = 1.79.$$

Increasing the marginal propensity to import from 0.1 to 0.2 decreases the value of the multiplier from 2.17 to 1.79. We can conclude that countries with a higher marginal propensity to import will have smaller multipliers than countries with a lower marginal propensity to import.

Bear in mind that the multiplier is a short-run effect which assumes that the economy is below the level of potential real GDP. In the long run, the economy is at potential real GDP, so an increase in government purchases causes a decline in the nongovernment components of real GDP but leaves the level of real GDP unchanged.

The analysis in this appendix is simplified compared to what would be carried out by an economist forecasting the effects of changes in government purchases or changes in taxes on equilibrium real GDP in the short run. In particular, our assumption that the price level is constant is unrealistic. However, looking more closely at the determinants of the multiplier has helped us see more clearly some important macroeconomic relationships.

LO A Closer Look at the Multiplier Formula

MyEconLab   Log in to MyEconLab to complete these exercises and get instant feedback.

Problems and Applications

12A.1 Assuming a fixed amount of taxes and a closed economy, calculate the value of the government purchases multiplier, the tax multiplier, and the balanced budget multiplier if the marginal propensity to consume equals 0.6.

12A.2 Calculate the value of the government purchases multiplier if the marginal propensity to consume equals 0.8, the tax rate equals 0.25, and the marginal propensity to import equals 0.2.

12A.3 Use a graph to show the change in the aggregate demand curve resulting from an increase in government purchases if the government purchases multiplier equals 2. Now, on the same graph, show the change in the aggregate demand curve resulting from an increase in government purchases if the government purchases multiplier equals 4.

12A.4 Using your understanding of multipliers, explain why an increase in the tax rate would decrease the size of the government purchases multiplier. Similarly, explain why a decrease in the marginal propensity to import would increase the size of the government purchases multiplier.

Ian Waldie/Bloomberg/
Getty Images

CHAPTER

13

Inflation, Unemployment, and Bank of Canada Policy

Chapter Outline and Learning Objectives

Can the Bank of Canada Balance the Risks in the Canadian Economy?

The Bank of Canada is continually balancing the risks in the Canadian economy. A contractionary monetary policy that would help rein in inflation risks pushing the economy into recession. An expansionary monetary policy that can reduce the effects of recession risks increasing inflation and spilling over into asset-price bubbles that can be damaging later on.

Consider the following example of the Bank of Canada's balancing act: In light of the fragile recovery and emerging global risks since the end of the global financial crisis, the Bank of Canada has kept interest rates historically low, and even surprised the markets twice in 2015 (in January and July) by its decision to further lower the policy rate from 1% to 0.5%, to counteract the negative effects of lower oil prices. It meant lower costs for consumers who borrow money to buy cars and houses. As a result, Canadians have loaded up on debt to historic levels; per capita debt levels at over 160% of disposal income are now higher than those of their American counterparts.

However, as a recent article in *The Economist* puts it, "in tempering one risk, Mr. Poloz has stoked another. Lower interest rates may encourage heavily indebted Canadian consumers to borrow even more, pushing up the ratio of household debt to disposable income, which is already at a record high. The Bank of Canada has also said that Canada's housing market is already overvalued by as much as 30%, so encouraging homeowners to borrow even more does not seem prudent. The central bank hopes that if it can cushion the fall in income and employment brought on by low oil prices, which it sees as a threat to financial stability, it will buy enough time for Canadian firms outside the energy industry to ride the coattails of America's recovery."

Monetary policy is not the only tool a central bank has at its disposal to mitigate risks. The Bank of Canada has highlighted the need for monetary policy to be coordinated with sound macro-prudential regulation to mitigate the externalities that arise from the spread of leverage cycles and the development of asset price bubbles. In fact, Canada has a tradition of sound macro-prudential regulation, recognized throughout the world for having allowed the country to emerge relatively unscathed from the financial crisis of 2008.

In regards to the housing market, which the Bank of Canada calls the most important risk to financial stability in Canada, in the aftermath of the global financial crisis, the Department of Finance tightened several regulations for real estate lending. The most significant regulatory changes are as follows: the maximum amortization period for a mortgage is now 25 years, down from 30; refinancing a home is allowed only up to 80% of its value, down from 85%; and homebuyers have to demonstrate their housing costs are no more than 39% of their gross household income. In addition, Canada's banking regulator, the Office of the Superintendent of Financial Institutions (OSFI), has placed a loan-to-value limit of 65% on borrowing against home equity.

Undoubtedly, the Bank of Canada had a tremendous amount of influence and input into this ex-ante intervention to target the housing bubble, or at least lean against it, to avoid future financial instability. If these regulatory changes fail to sufficiently mitigate risks in the Canadian economy, the Bank of Canada can still use the blunt hammer of monetary policy.

In this chapter, we will explore the Bank of Canada's attempts to balance its goals of inflation stability and high employment.

Source: "Lower oil prices prompt the Bank of Canada to loosen monetary policy," *The Economist,* January 22, 2015. http://www.economist.com/news/business-and-finance/21640394-lower-oil-prices-prompts-bank-canada-loosen-monetary-policy-risky-business (Accessed on December 2, 2015).

Economics in Your Life

Is It Wise to Delay a Job Search?

Your friend was recently laid off from her entry-level job as a computer analyst. You call to console her, but she does not seem very upset. "Employment Insurance offers workers up to 45 weeks of financial assistance. I have almost one year before i have to find a new job. With my education and job experience, I should be able to find a new job by then without much trouble." Your friend did well in school, but you are not sure that waiting almost one year to find a new job is a good idea. What advice would you give someone who has decided to wait nearly one year to look for a new job? As you read the chapter, try to answer this question. You can check your answer against the one we provide on page 382 at the end of this chapter.

An important consideration for the Bank of Canada as it carries out monetary policy is that in the short run, there can be a trade-off between unemployment and inflation: Lower unemployment rates can result in higher inflation rates. In the long run, however, this trade-off disappears, and the unemployment rate is independent of the inflation rate. In this chapter, we will explore the relationship between inflation and unemployment in both the short run and the long run, and we will discuss what this relationship means for monetary policy. We will also provide an overview of how monetary policy has evolved over the years and conclude with a discussion of the debate over Bank of Canada policy during the 2007–2009 recession.

Describe the Phillips curve and the nature of the short-run trade-off between unemployment and inflation.

The Discovery of the Short-Run Trade-off between Unemployment and Inflation

During most of the Bank of Canada's history, unemployment and inflation have been the two great macroeconomic problems it has contended with. When aggregate demand increases, unemployment usually falls, and inflation rises. When aggregate demand decreases, unemployment usually rises, and inflation falls. As a result, there is a *short-run trade-off* between unemployment and inflation: Higher unemployment is usually accompanied by lower inflation, and lower unemployment is usually accompanied by higher inflation. As we will see later in this chapter, this trade-off exists in the short run—a period that may be as long as several years—but disappears in the long run.

Although today the short-run trade-off between unemployment and inflation plays a role in the Bank of Canada's monetary policy decisions, this trade-off was not widely recognized until the late 1950s. In 1957, New Zealand economist A. W. Phillips plotted data on the unemployment rate and the inflation rate in Great Britain and drew a curve showing their average relationship. Since that time, a graph showing the short-run relationship between the unemployment rate and the inflation rate has been called a **Phillips curve**. (Phillips actually measured inflation by the percentage change in wages rather than by the percentage change in prices. Because wages and prices usually move together, this difference is not important to our discussion.) Figure 13.1 shows a graph similar to the one Phillips prepared. Each point on the Phillips curve represents a possible combination of the unemployment rate and the inflation rate that might be observed in a given year. Point *A* represents a year in which the inflation rate is 4 percent and the unemployment rate is 5 percent, and point *B* represents a year in which the inflation rate is 2 percent and the unemployment rate is 6 percent. Phillips documented that there is usually an *inverse relationship* between unemployment and inflation. During years when the unemployment rate is low, the inflation rate tends to be high, and during years when the unemployment rate is high, the inflation rate tends to be low.

Phillips curve A curve showing the short-run relationship between the unemployment rate and the inflation rate.

Explaining the Phillips Curve with Aggregate Demand and Aggregate Supply Curves

The inverse relationship between unemployment and inflation that Phillips discovered is consistent with the aggregate demand and aggregate supply analysis we developed in Chapter 9. Figure 13.2 shows why this inverse relationship exists.

Panel (a) shows the aggregate demand and aggregate supply model from Chapter 9, and panel (b) shows the Phillips curve. For simplicity, in panel (a), we are using the basic

Figure 13.1

The Phillips Curve

A. W. Phillips was the first economist to show that there is usually an inverse relationship between unemployment and inflation. Here we can see this relationship at work: In the year represented by point *A*, the inflation rate is 4 percent and the unemployment rate is 5 percent. In the year represented by point *B*, the inflation rate is 2 percent and the unemployment rate is 6 percent.

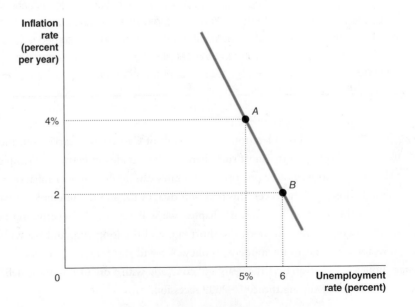

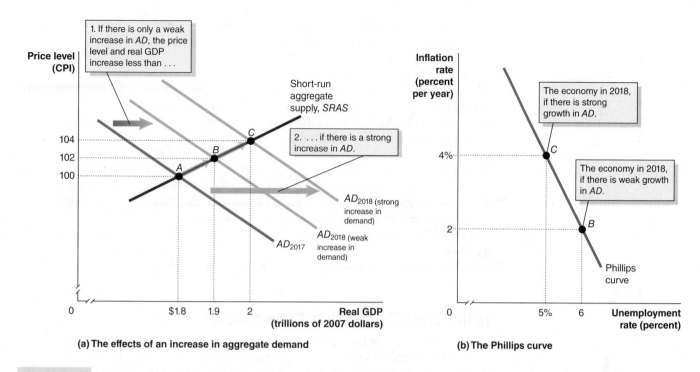

Figure 13.2 Using Aggregate Demand and Aggregate Supply to Explain the Phillips Curve

In panel (a), the economy in 2017 is at point *A*, with real GDP of $1.8 trillion and a price level of 100. If there is weak growth in aggregate demand, in 2018, the economy moves to point *B*, with real GDP of $1.9 trillion and a price level of 102. The inflation rate is 2 percent and the unemployment rate is 6 percent, which corresponds to point *B* on the Phillips curve in panel (b). If there is strong growth in aggregate demand, in 2018, the economy moves to point *C*, with real GDP of $2 trillion and a price level of 104. Strong aggregate demand growth results in a higher inflation rate of 4 percent but a lower unemployment rate of 5 percent. This combination of higher inflation and lower unemployment is shown as point *C* on the Phillips curve in panel (b).

aggregate demand and aggregate supply model, and we are assuming that the long-run aggregate supply curve and the short-run aggregate supply curve do not shift. To take a hypothetical example, assume that the economy in 2017 is at point *A*, with real GDP of $1.8 trillion and a price level of 100. If there is weak growth in aggregate demand, in 2018, the economy moves to point *B*, with real GDP of $1.9 trillion and a price level of 102. The inflation rate is 2 percent and the unemployment rate is 6 percent, which corresponds to point *B* on the Phillips curve in panel (b). If there is strong growth in aggregate demand, in 2018, the economy moves to point *C*, with real GDP of $1.2 trillion and a price level of 104. Strong aggregate demand growth results in a higher inflation rate of 4 percent but a lower unemployment rate of 5 percent. This combination of higher inflation and lower unemployment is shown as point *C* on the Phillips curve in panel (b).

To summarize, the aggregate demand and aggregate supply model indicates that slow growth in aggregate demand leads to both higher unemployment and lower inflation. This relationship explains why there is a short-run trade-off between unemployment and inflation, as shown by the downward-sloping Phillips curve. The *AD–AS* model and the Phillips curve are different ways of illustrating the same macroeconomic events. The Phillips curve has an advantage over the aggregate demand and aggregate supply model, however, when we want to analyze *changes* explicitly in the inflation and unemployment rates.

Is the Phillips Curve a Policy Menu?

During the 1960s, some economists argued that the Phillips curve represented a *structural relationship* in the economy. A **structural relationship** depends on the basic behaviour of consumers and firms and remains unchanged over long periods. Structural

Structural relationship A relationship that depends on the basic behaviour of consumers and firms and that remains unchanged over long periods.

relationships are useful in formulating economic policy because policymakers can anticipate that these relationships are constant—that is, the relationships will not change as a result of changes in policy.

If the Phillips curve were a structural relationship, it would present policymakers with a reliable menu of combinations of unemployment and inflation. Potentially, policymakers could use expansionary monetary and fiscal policies to choose a point on the curve that had lower unemployment and higher inflation. They could also use contractionary monetary and fiscal policies to choose a point that had lower inflation and higher unemployment. Because many economists and policymakers in the 1960s viewed the Phillips curve as a structural relationship, they believed it represented a *permanent trade-off between unemployment and inflation*. As long as policymakers were willing to accept a permanently higher inflation rate, they would be able to keep the unemployment rate permanently lower. Similarly, a permanently lower inflation rate could be attained at the cost of a permanently higher unemployment rate. As we discuss in the next section, however, economists came to realize that the Phillips curve did *not*, in fact, represent a permanent trade-off between unemployment and inflation.

Is the Short-Run Phillips Curve Stable?

During the 1960s, the basic Phillips curve relationship seemed to hold because a stable trade-off appeared to exist between unemployment and inflation. In the early 1960s, the inflation rate was low, and the unemployment rate was high. In the late 1960s, the unemployment rate had declined, and the inflation rate had increased. Then in 1968, in his presidential address to the American Economic Association, Milton Friedman of the University of Chicago argued that the Phillips curve did *not* represent a *permanent* trade-off between unemployment and inflation. At almost the same time, Edmund Phelps of Columbia University published an academic paper making a similar argument. Friedman and Phelps noted that economists had come to agree that the long-run aggregate supply curve was vertical (a point we discussed in Chapter 9). If this observation were true, the Phillips curve could not be downward sloping in the long run. A critical inconsistency exists between a vertical long-run aggregate supply curve and a downward-sloping long-run Phillips curve. Friedman and Phelps argued, in essence, that there is no trade-off between unemployment and inflation in the long run.

The Long-Run Phillips Curve

Natural rate of unemployment
The unemployment rate that exists when the economy is at potential GDP.

To understand the argument that there is no permanent trade-off between unemployment and inflation, first recall that the level of real GDP in the long run is also referred to as *potential GDP*. At potential GDP, firms will operate at their normal level of capacity, and everyone who wants a job will have one, except the structurally and frictionally unemployed. Friedman defined the **natural rate of unemployment** as the unemployment rate that exists when the economy is at potential GDP. The actual unemployment rate will fluctuate in the short run but will always come back to the natural rate in the long run. In the same way, the actual level of real GDP will fluctuate in the short run but will always come back to its potential level in the long run.

In the long run, a higher or lower price level has no effect on real GDP because real GDP is always at potential GDP in the long run. In the same way, in the long run, a higher or lower inflation rate will have no effect on the unemployment rate because the unemployment rate is always equal to the natural rate in the long run. Figure 13.3 illustrates Friedman's conclusion that the long-run aggregate supply curve is a vertical line at the potential real GDP, and *the long-run Phillips curve is a vertical line at the natural rate of unemployment*.

The Role of Expectations of Future Inflation

If the long-run Phillips curve is a vertical line, *no trade-off exists between unemployment and inflation in the long run*. This conclusion seemed to contradict the experience of the

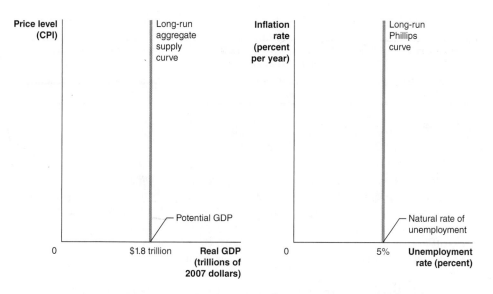

Figure 13.3

A Vertical Long-Run Aggregate Supply Curve Means a Vertical Long-Run Phillips Curve

Milton Friedman and Edmund Phelps argued that there is no trade-off between unemployment and inflation in the long run. If real GDP automatically returns to its potential level in the long run, the unemployment rate must return to the natural rate of unemployment in the long run. In this figure, we assume that potential GDP is $1.8 trillion and the natural rate of unemployment is 5 percent.

1950s and 1960s, which showed a stable trade-off between unemployment and inflation. Friedman argued that the statistics from those years actually showed only a short-run trade-off between inflation and unemployment.

Friedman argued that the short-run trade-off existed only because workers and firms sometimes expected the inflation rate to be either higher or lower than it turned out to be. Differences between the expected inflation rate and the actual inflation rate could lead the unemployment rate to rise above or dip below the natural rate. To see why, consider a simple case of Ford negotiating a wage contract with the Canadian Auto Workers (CAW) union. Remember that both Ford and the CAW are interested in the real wage, which is the nominal wage corrected for inflation. Suppose, for example, that Ford and the CAW agree on a wage of $31.50 per hour to be paid during 2018. Both Ford and the CAW expect that the price level will increase from 100 in 2017 to 105 in 2018, so the inflation rate will be 5 percent. We can calculate the real wage Ford expects to pay and the CAW expects to receive as follows:

$$\text{Real wage} = \frac{\text{Nominal wage}}{\text{Price level}} \times 100 = \frac{\$31.50}{105} \times 100 = \$30.$$

But suppose that the actual inflation rate turns out to be higher or lower than the expected inflation rate of 5 percent. Table 13.1 shows the effect on the actual real wage. If the price level rises only to 102 during 2018, the inflation rate will be 2 percent, and the actual real wage will be $30.88, which is higher than Ford and the CAW had expected. With a higher real wage, Ford will hire fewer workers than it had planned to at the expected real wage of $30. If the inflation rate is 8 percent, the actual real wage will be $29.17, and Ford will hire more workers than it had planned to hire. If Ford and the CAW expected a higher or lower inflation rate than actually occurred, other firms and workers probably made the same assumption.

If actual inflation is higher than expected inflation, actual real wages in the economy will be lower than expected real wages, and many firms will hire more workers than they had planned to hire. Therefore, the unemployment rate will fall. If actual inflation is lower than expected inflation, actual real wages will be higher than expected, many

Nominal Wage	Expected Real Wage	Actual Real Wage		
	Expected $P_{2018} = 105$	Actual $P_{2018} = 102$		Actual $P_{2018} = 108$
	Expected inflation = 5%	Actual inflation = 2%		Actual inflation = 8%
$31.50	$\frac{\$31.50}{105} \times 100 = \$30$	$\frac{\$31.50}{102} \times 100 = \$30.88$		$\frac{\$31.50}{108} \times 100 = \$29.17$

Table 13.1

The Effect of Unexpected Price Level Changes on the Real Wage

Table 13.2	If ...	then ...	and ...
The Basis for the Short-Run Phillips Curve	actual inflation is greater than expected inflation,	the actual real wage is less than the expected real wage,	the unemployment rate falls.
	actual inflation is less than expected inflation,	the actual real wage is greater than the expected real wage,	the unemployment rate rises.

firms will hire fewer workers than they had planned to hire, and the unemployment rate will rise. Table 13.2 summarizes this argument.

Friedman and Phelps concluded that *an increase in the inflation rate increases employment (and decreases unemployment) only if the increase in the inflation rate is unexpected.* Friedman argued that in 1968, the unemployment rate in the United States was 3.6 percent rather than 5 percent only because the inflation rate of 4 percent was above the 1 percent to 2 percent inflation that workers and firms had expected: "There is always a temporary trade-off between inflation and unemployment; there is no permanent trade-off. The temporary trade-off comes not from inflation per se, but from unanticipated inflation."

Making the Connection | Do Workers Understand Inflation?

A higher inflation rate can lead to lower unemployment if *both* workers and firms mistakenly expect the inflation rate to be lower than it turns out to be. But this same result might be due to firms forecasting inflation more accurately than workers do or due to firms understanding better the effects of inflation. Some large firms employ economists to help them gather and analyze information that is useful in forecasting inflation. Many firms also have human resources or employee compensation departments that gather data on wages competing firms pay and analyze trends in compensation. Workers generally rely on much less systematic information about wages and prices. Workers also often fail to realize this fact: *Expected inflation increases the value of total production and the value of total income by the same amount.* Therefore, although not all wages will rise as prices rise, inflation will increase the average wage in the economy at the same time that it increases average prices.

Nobel Laureate Robert Shiller of Yale University conducted a survey on inflation and discovered that, although most economists believe an increase in inflation will lead quickly to an increase in wages, a majority of the general public thinks otherwise. As part of the survey, Shiller asked how "the effect of general inflation on wages or salary relates to your own experience and your own job." The most popular response was: "The price increase will create extra profits for my employer, who can now sell output for more; there will be no effect on my pay. My employer will see no reason to raise my pay."

Shiller also asked the following question:

Imagine that next year the inflation rate unexpectedly doubles. How long would it probably take, in these times, before your income is increased enough so that you can afford the same things as you do today? In other words, how long will it be before a full inflation correction in your income has taken place?

Eighty-one percent of the public answered either that it would take several years for the purchasing power of their income to be restored or that it would never be restored. If workers fail to understand that rising inflation leads over time to comparable increases in wages, then when inflation increases, in the short run, firms can increase wages by less than inflation without needing to worry about workers quitting or their morale falling. Once again, we have a higher inflation rate, leading in the short run to lower real wages and lower unemployment. In other words, we have an explanation for a downward-sloping short-run Phillips curve.

Source: Robert J. Shiller, "Why Do People Dislike Inflation?" in *Reducing Inflation: Motivation and Strategy* by Christina D. Romer and David H. Romer, eds., (Chicago: University of Chicago Press, 1997).

Will wage increases keep up with inflation?

Paul Bradbury/OJO Images/Getty Images

MyEconLab **Your Turn:** Test your understanding by doing related problem 1.7 on page 385 at the end of this chapter.

The Short-Run and Long-Run Phillips Curves

13.2 LEARNING OBJECTIVE

Explain the relationship between the short-run and long-run Phillips curves.

If there is both a short-run Phillips curve and a long-run Phillips curve, how are the two curves related? We can begin answering this question with the help of Figure 13.4, which represents macroeconomic conditions in Canada during the 1960s. In the late 1960s, workers and firms were still expecting the inflation rate to be about 1.5 percent, as it had been in the early 1960s. Expansionary monetary and fiscal policies, however, had moved the short-run equilibrium up the short-run Phillips curve to an inflation rate of 4.5 percent and an unemployment rate of about 3.5 percent. This very low unemployment rate was possible only because the real wage rate was unexpectedly low.

Once workers and firms began to expect that the inflation rate would continue to be about 4.5 percent, they changed their behaviour. Firms knew that only nominal wage increases of more than 4.5 percent would increase real wages. Workers realized that unless they received a nominal wage increase of at least 4.5 percent, their real wage would be falling. Higher expected inflation rates had an effect throughout the economy. For example, as we saw in Chapter 10, when banks make loans, they are interested in the *real interest rate* on the loan. The real interest rate is the nominal interest rate minus the expected inflation rate. Banks will charge a nominal interest rate of 4.5 percent to receive a real interest rate of 3 percent on home mortgage loans when they expect the inflation rate to be 1.5 percent. If banks revise their expectations of the inflation rate to 4.5 percent, they will increase the nominal interest rate they charge on mortgage loans to 7.5 percent.

Shifts in the Short-Run Phillips Curve

A new, higher expected inflation rate can become *embedded* in the economy, meaning that workers, firms, consumers, and the government all take the inflation rate into account when making decisions. The short-run trade-off between unemployment and inflation now takes place from this higher, less favourable level, as shown in Figure 13.5.

As long as workers and firms expected the inflation rate to be 1.5 percent, the short-run trade-off between unemployment and inflation was the more favourable one shown by the lower Phillips curve. Along this Phillips curve, an inflation rate of 4.5 percent was enough to drive down the unemployment rate to about 3.5 percent. Once workers and firms adjusted their expectations to an inflation rate of 4.5 percent, the short-run trade-off deteriorated to the one shown by the higher Phillips curve. At this higher expected inflation rate, the real wage rose, causing some workers to lose their jobs, and the economy's equilibrium returned to the natural rate of unemployment of 5 percent—but now with an inflation rate of 4.5 percent rather than 1.5 percent. On

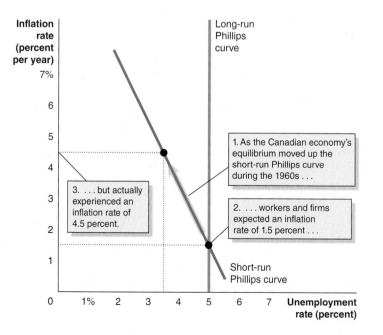

Figure 13.4

The Short-Run Phillips Curve of the 1960s and the Long-Run Phillips Curve

In the late 1960s, Canadian workers and firms were expecting the 1.5 percent inflation rates of the recent past to continue. However, expansionary monetary and fiscal policies moved short-run equilibrium up the short-run Phillips curve to an inflation rate of 4.5 percent and an unemployment rate of about 3.5 percent.

Expectations and the Short-Run Phillips Curve

By the end of the 1960s, workers and firms had revised their expectations of inflation from 1.5 percent to 4.5 percent. As a result, the short-run Phillips curve shifted up, which made the short-run trade-off between unemployment and inflation worse.

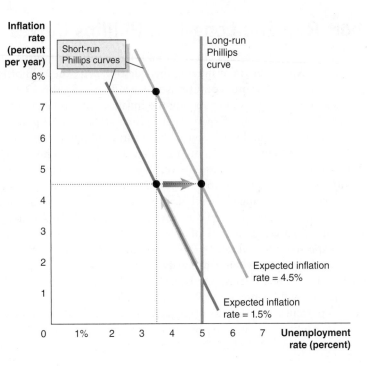

the higher short-run Phillips curve, an inflation rate of 7.5 percent would be necessary to reduce the unemployment rate to about 3.5 percent. An inflation rate of 7.5 percent would keep the unemployment rate at about 3.5 percent only until workers and firms revised their expectations of inflation up to 7.5 percent. In the long run, the economy's equilibrium would return to the 5 percent natural rate of unemployment.

As Figure 13.6 shows, there is a short-run Phillips curve for every level of expected inflation. Each short-run Phillips curve intersects the long-run Phillips curve at the expected inflation rate.

How Does a Vertical Long-Run Phillips Curve Affect Monetary Policy?

By the 1970s, most economists accepted the argument that the long-run Phillips curve is vertical. In other words, economists realized that the common view of the 1960s

A Short-Run Phillips Curve for Every Expected Inflation Rate

There is a different short-run Phillips curve for every expected inflation rate. Each short-run Phillips curve intersects the long-run Phillips curve at the expected inflation rate.

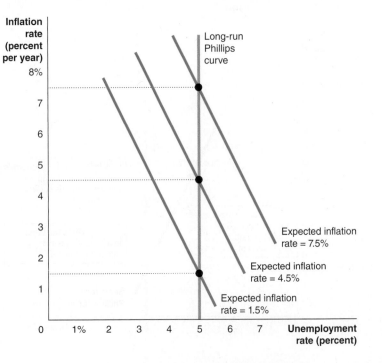

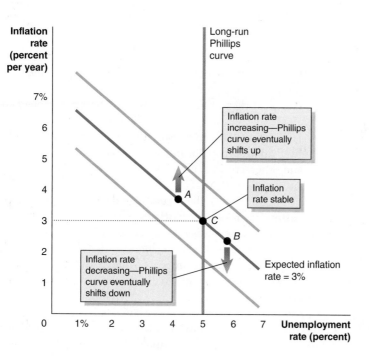

Figure 13.7

The Inflation Rate and the Natural Rate of Unemployment in the Long Run

The inflation rate is stable only if the unemployment rate equals the natural rate of unemployment (point *C*). If the unemployment rate is below the natural rate (point *A*), the inflation rate increases, and, eventually, the short-run Phillips curve shifts up. If the unemployment rate is above the natural rate (point *B*), the inflation rate decreases, and, eventually, the short-run Phillips curve shifts down.

had been wrong: It was *not* possible to buy a permanently lower unemployment rate at the cost of a permanently higher inflation rate. The moral is that *in the long run, there is no trade-off between unemployment and inflation*. In the long run, the unemployment rate always returns to the natural rate, no matter what the inflation rate is.

Figure 13.7 shows that the inflation rate is stable only when the unemployment rate is equal to the natural rate. If the Bank of Canada were to attempt to use expansionary monetary policy to push short-run equilibrium to a point such as *A*, where the unemployment rate is below the natural rate, the result would be a movement up the short-run Phillips curve with increasing inflation. If short-run equilibrium remained below the natural rate long enough, the short-run Phillips curve would shift up as workers and firms adjusted to the new, higher inflation rate. During the 1960s and 1970s, the short-run Phillips curve did shift up, presenting policymakers with a more unfavourable short-run trade-off between unemployment and inflation.

If the Bank of Canada used contractionary policy to push short-run equilibrium to a point such as *B*, where the unemployment rate is above the natural rate, the inflation rate would decrease. If short-run equilibrium remained above the natural rate long enough, the short-run Phillips curve would shift down as workers and firms adjusted to the new, lower inflation rate. Only at a point such as *C*, where the unemployment rate is equal to the natural rate, will the inflation rate be stable. Because the inflation rate has no tendency to increase or decrease when the unemployment rate equals the natural rate, the natural rate of unemployment is sometimes called the **nonaccelerating inflation rate of unemployment (NAIRU)**. We can conclude that *in the long run, the Bank of Canada can affect the inflation rate but not the unemployment rate*.

Nonaccelerating inflation rate of unemployment (NAIRU) The unemployment rate at which the inflation rate has no tendency to increase or decrease.

Making the Connection

Does the Natural Rate of Unemployment Ever Change?

Life would be easier for the Bank of Canada if it knew exactly what the natural rate of unemployment was and if that rate never changed. Unfortunately for the Bank of Canada, the natural rate does change over time. Remember that at the natural rate of unemployment, there is no cyclical unemployment, only frictional and structural unemployment.

Frictional or structural unemployment can change—thereby changing the natural rate—for several reasons:

An increase in the number of younger and less skilled workers in an economy can make the natural rate of unemployment increase.

- **Demographic changes.** Younger and less skilled workers have higher unemployment rates, on average, than older and more skilled workers. Because of the baby boom, Canada had an unusually large number of younger and less skilled workers during the 1970s and 1980s. As a result, the natural rate of unemployment rose from about 5 percent in the 1960s to about 6 percent in the 1970s and 8 percent in the 1980s and 1990s. As the number of younger and less skilled workers declined as a fraction of the labour force during the 2000s, the natural rate declined to about 6 percent.

- **Labour market institutions.** Labour market institutions such as the employment insurance system, labour unions, and legal barriers to firing workers can increase the economy's unemployment rate. Because many European countries have generous employment insurance systems, strong labour unions, and restrictive policies on firing workers, the natural rate of unemployment in most European countries has been well above the rate in Canada.

- **Past high rates of unemployment.** Evidence indicates that if high unemployment persists for a period of years, the natural rate of unemployment may increase. When workers have been unemployed for longer than a year or two, their skills deteriorate, they may lose confidence that they can find and hold a job, and they may become dependent on government payments to survive. It has been argued that in the mid-1930s, so many Canadian workers had been out of work for so long that the natural rate of unemployment may have risen to close to 15 percent. However, even though the unemployment rate in Canada was over 19 percent in 1933, the inflation rate did not change. Similarly, many economists have argued that the high unemployment rates experienced by European countries during the 1970s increased their natural rates of unemployment. As high rates of unemployment persisted more than two and a half years after the end of the 2007–2009 recession, some economists and policymakers were concerned that the natural rate of unemployment might eventually rise.

Sources: Based on Congressional Budget Office, "The Budget and Economic Outlook: Fiscal Years 2011 to 2021," January 2011; and "Damage Assessment," *Economist*, May 14, 2009.

MyEconLab   **Your Turn:** Test your understanding by doing related problem 2.2 on page 385 at the end of this chapter.

Solved Problem **13.1**

Changing Views of the Phillips Curve

Writing in a US Federal Reserve publication, Bennett McCallum, an economist at Carnegie Mellon University, argues that during the 1970s, the Federal Reserve was "acting under the influence of 1960s academic ideas that posited the existence of a long-run and exploitable Phillips-type tradeoff between inflation and unemployment rates." What does McCallum mean by a "long-run and exploitable Phillips-type tradeoff"? How would the Federal Reserve have attempted to exploit this long-run trade-off? What would be the consequences for the inflation rate?

Solving the Problem

Step 1: Review the chapter material. This problem is about the relationship between the short-run and long-run Phillips curves, so you may want to review the section "The Short-Run and Long-Run Phillips Curves," which begins on page 369.

Step 2: **Explain what a "long-run exploitable Phillips-type tradeoff" means.** A "long-run exploitable Phillips-type tradeoff" means a Phillips curve that in the long run is downward sloping rather than vertical. An "exploitable" trade-off is one that the Bank of Canada could take advantage of to *permanently* reduce unemployment, at the expense of higher inflation, or to permanently reduce inflation, at the expense of higher unemployment.

Step 3: **Explain how the inflation rate will accelerate if the Federal Reserve tries to exploit a long-run trade-off between unemployment and inflation.** As we have seen, during the 1960s, the Federal Reserve conducted expansionary monetary policies to move up what it thought was a stationary short-run Phillips curve. By the late 1960s, these policies resulted in very low unemployment rates. In the long run, there is no stable trade-off between unemployment and inflation. Attempting to permanently keep the unemployment rate at very low levels leads to a rising inflation rate, which is what happened in the late 1960s and early 1970s.

Source: Based on Bennett T. McCallum, "Recent Developments in Monetary Policy Analysis: The Roles of Theory and Evidence," Federal Reserve Bank of Richmond, *Economic Quarterly*, Winter 2002, p. 73.

Expectations of the Inflation Rate and Monetary Policy

13.3 LEARNING OBJECTIVE

Discuss how expectations of the inflation rate affect monetary policy.

How quickly does short-run equilibrium adjust from a point that is on the short-run Phillips curve but not on the long-run Phillips curve? It depends on how quickly workers and firms adjust their expectations of future inflation to changes in current inflation. The experience in Canada over the past 60 years indicates that how workers and firms adjust their expectations of inflation depends on how high the inflation rate is. There are three possibilities:

- **Low inflation.** When the inflation rate is low, as it was during most of the 1950s, the early 1960s, the 1990s, and the 2000s, workers and firms tend to ignore it. For example, if the inflation rate is low, a restaurant may not want to pay for printing new menus that would show slightly higher prices.

- **Moderate but stable inflation.** For the four-year period from 1968 to 1971, the inflation rate in Canada stayed in the narrow range between 4 percent and 5 percent. This rate was high enough that workers and firms could not ignore it without seeing their real wages and profits decline. It was also likely that the next year's inflation rate would be very close to the current year's inflation rate. In fact, workers and firms during the 1960s acted as if they expected changes in the inflation rate during one year to continue into the following year. People are said to have *adaptive expectations* of inflation if they assume that future rates of inflation will follow the pattern of rates of inflation in the recent past.

- **High and unstable inflation.** Inflation rates above 5 percent have been rare in Canadian history, but the inflation rate was above 5 percent every year from 1973 through 1982. Not only was the inflation rate high during those years, it was also unstable—rising from 6 percent in 1973 to about 13 percent in 1974, before falling below 6 percent in 1976 and rising again to above 11 percent in 1980. In the mid-1970s, Nobel Laureates Robert Lucas of the University of Chicago and Thomas Sargent of New York University argued that the gains from accurate forecasts of inflation had dramatically increased. Workers and firms that failed to correctly anticipate the fluctuations in inflation during these years could experience substantial declines in real wages and profits. Therefore, Lucas and Sargent argued, people should use all available information when forming their expectations of future

Rational expectations Expectations formed by using all available information about an economic variable.

inflation. Expectations formed by using all available information about an economic variable are called **rational expectations**.

The Implications of Rational Expectations for Monetary Policy

Lucas and Sargent pointed out an important consequence of rational expectations: An expansionary monetary policy would not work. In other words, there might not be a trade-off between unemployment and inflation, even in the short run. By the mid-1970s, most economists had accepted the idea that an expansionary monetary policy could cause the actual inflation rate to be higher than the expected inflation rate. This gap between actual and expected inflation would cause the actual real wage to fall below the expected real wage, pushing the unemployment rate below the natural rate. Short-run equilibrium would move up the short-run Phillips curve.

Lucas and Sargent argued that this explanation of the Phillips curve assumed that workers and firms either ignored inflation or used adaptive expectations in making their forecasts of inflation. If workers and firms have rational expectations, they will use all available information, *including knowledge of the effects of central bank policy*. If workers and firms know that an expansionary monetary policy will raise the inflation rate, they should use this information in their forecasts of inflation. If they do, an expansionary monetary policy will not cause the actual inflation rate to be above the expected inflation rate. Instead, the actual inflation rate will equal the expected inflation rate, the actual real wage will equal the expected real wage, and the unemployment rate will not fall below the natural rate.

Figure 13.8 illustrates this argument. Suppose that equilibrium is initially at point *A*, where the short-run Phillips curve intersects the long-run Phillips curve. The actual and expected inflation rates are both equal to 1.5 percent, and the unemployment rate equals the natural rate of 5 percent. Now suppose the Bank of Canada engages in an expansionary monetary policy. If workers ignore inflation or if they form their expectations adaptively (using only current and past information), the expansionary monetary policy will cause the actual inflation rate to be higher than the expected inflation rate, and short-run equilibrium will move from point *A* on the short-run Phillips curve to point *B*. The inflation rate will rise to 4.5 percent, and the unemployment rate will fall to 3.5 percent. The decline in unemployment will be only temporary because workers and firms will eventually adjust to the fact that the actual inflation rate is 4.5 percent, not the 1.5 percent they had expected. The short-run Phillips curve will shift up, and the unemployment rate will return to 5 percent at point *C*.

Figure 13.8

Rational Expectations and the Phillips Curve

If workers and firms ignore inflation, or if they have adaptive expectations (using only current and past information), an expansionary monetary policy will cause short-run equilibrium to move from point *A* on the short-run Phillips curve to point *B*; inflation will rise, and unemployment will fall. If workers and firms have rational expectations, an expansionary monetary policy will cause short-run equilibrium to move up the long-run Phillips curve from point *A* to point *C*. Inflation will still rise, but there will be no change in unemployment.

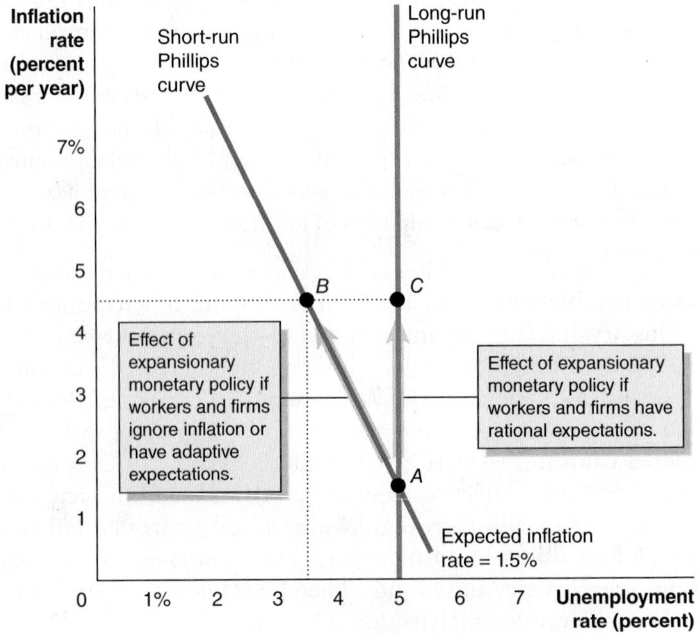

Lucas and Sargent argued that if workers and firms have rational expectations, they will realize that the central bank's expansionary policy will result in an inflation rate of 4.5 percent. Therefore, as soon as the central bank announces its new policy, workers and firms should adjust their expectations of inflation from 1.5 percent to 4.5 percent. There will be no temporary decrease in the real wage, leading to a temporary increase in employment and real GDP. Instead, the short-run equilibrium will move immediately from point *A* to point *C* on the long-run Phillips curve. The unemployment rate will never drop below 5 percent, and the *short-run* Phillips curve will be vertical.

Is the Short-Run Phillips Curve Really Vertical?

The claim by Lucas and Sargent that the short-run Phillips curve is vertical and that an expansionary monetary policy cannot reduce the unemployment rate below the natural rate surprised many economists. An obvious objection to the argument of Lucas and Sargent was that the record of the 1950s and 1960s seemed to show that there was a short-run trade-off between unemployment and inflation and that, therefore, the short-run Phillips curve was downward sloping and not vertical. Lucas and Sargent argued that the apparent short-run trade-off was actually the result of *unexpected* changes in monetary policy. During those years, central banks did not announce changes in policy, so workers, firms, and financial markets had to *guess* when the central bank had begun using a new policy. In that case, an expansionary monetary policy might cause the unemployment rate to fall because workers and firms would be taken by surprise, and their expectations of inflation would be too low. Lucas and Sargent argued that a policy that was announced ahead of time would not cause a change in unemployment.

Many economists have remained skeptical of the argument that the short-run Phillips curve is vertical. The two main objections raised are that (1) workers and firms actually may not have rational expectations, and (2) the rapid adjustment of wages and prices needed for the short-run Phillips curve to be vertical will not actually take place. Many economists doubt that people are able to use information on the central bank's monetary policy to make reliable forecasts of the inflation rate. If workers and firms do not know what effect an expansionary monetary policy will have on the inflation rate, the actual real wage may still end up being lower than the expected real wage. Also, firms may have contracts with their workers and suppliers that keep wages and prices from adjusting quickly. If wages and prices adjust slowly, then even if workers and firms have rational expectations, an expansionary monetary policy may still be able to reduce the unemployment rate in the short run.

Real Business Cycle Models

During the 1980s, some economists, including Nobel Laureates Finn Kydland of the University of California, Santa Barbara, and Edward Prescott of Arizona State University, argued that Robert Lucas was correct in assuming that workers and firms formed their expectations rationally and that wages and prices adjust quickly, but that Lucas was wrong in assuming that fluctuations in real GDP are caused by unexpected changes in monetary policy. Instead, Kydland and Prescott argued that fluctuations in "real" factors, particularly *technology shocks*, explain deviations of real GDP from its potential level. Technology shocks are changes to the economy that make it possible to produce either more output—a positive shock—or less output—a negative shock—with the same number of workers, machines, and other inputs. Real GDP will be above its previous potential level following a positive technology shock and below its previous potential level following a negative technology shock. Because these models focus on real factors—rather than on changes in the money supply—to explain fluctuations in real GDP, they are known as **real business cycle models**.

The approach of Lucas and Sargent and the real business cycle models are sometimes grouped together under the label *the new classical macroeconomics* because these approaches share the assumptions that people have rational expectations and that wages and prices

Real business cycle models
Models that focus on real rather than monetary explanations of fluctuations in real GDP.

adjust rapidly. Some of the assumptions of the new classical macroeconomics are similar to those held by economists before the Great Depression of the 1930s. John Maynard Keynes, in his 1936 book *The General Theory of Employment, Interest, and Money*, referred to these earlier economists as "classical economists." Like the classical economists, the new classical macroeconomists believe that the economy will normally be at its potential level.

Economists who find the assumptions of rational expectations and rapid adjustment of wages and prices appealing are likely to accept the real business cycle model approach. Other economists are skeptical of these models because the models explain recessions as being caused by negative technology shocks. Negative technology shocks are uncommon and, apart from the oil price increases of the 1970s, real business cycle theorists have had difficulty identifying shocks that would have been large enough to cause recessions. Some economists have begun to develop real business cycle models that allow for the possibility that changes in the money supply may affect the level of real GDP. If real business cycle models continue to develop along these lines, they may eventually converge with the approaches central banks use.

13.4 LEARNING OBJECTIVE

Use a Phillips curve graph to show how the Bank of Canada can permanently lower the inflation rate.

Bank of Canada Policy from the 1970s to the Present

Like the United States, Canada experienced high inflation rates in the late 1960s and early 1970s due in part to the Bank of Canada's attempts to keep the unemployment rate below the natural rate. By the mid-1970s, the Bank of Canada also had to deal with the inflationary impact of the Organization of the Petroleum Exporting Countries (OPEC) oil price increases. By the late 1970s, as the Bank of Canada attempted to deal with the problem of high and worsening inflation rates, it received conflicting policy advice. Many economists argued that the inflation rate could be reduced only at the cost of a temporary increase in the unemployment rate. Followers of the Lucas–Sargent rational expectations approach, however, argued that a painless reduction in the inflation rate was possible. Before analyzing the actual policies used by the Bank of Canada, we can look at why the oil price increases of the mid-1970s made the inflation rate worse.

The Effect of a Supply Shock on the Phillips Curve

The increases in oil prices in 1974 resulting from actions by OPEC caused the short-run aggregate supply curve to shift to the left. This shift is shown in panel (a) of Figure 13.9. (For simplicity, in this panel, we use the basic rather than dynamic *AD–AS* model.) The result was a higher price level and a lower level of real GDP. On a Phillips curve graph— panel (b) of Figure 13.9—we can shift the short-run Phillips curve up to show that the inflation rate and unemployment rate both increased.

As the Phillips curve shifted up, the economy moved from an unemployment rate of about 5.6 percent and an inflation rate of about 7.8 percent in 1973 to an unemployment rate of 6.9 percent and an inflation rate of about 10.7 percent in 1975. This combination of rising unemployment and rising inflation placed the Bank of Canada in a difficult position. If the Bank of Canada used an expansionary monetary policy to fight the high unemployment rate, the *AD* curve would shift to the right, and the economy's equilibrium would move up the short-run Phillips curve. Real GDP would increase, and the unemployment rate would fall—but at the cost of higher inflation. If the Bank of Canada used a contractionary monetary policy to fight the high inflation rate, the *AD* curve would shift to the left, and the economy's equilibrium would move down the short-run Phillips curve. As a result, real GDP would fall, and the inflation rate would be reduced—but at the cost of higher unemployment. In the end, the Bank of Canada chose to fight high unemployment with an expansionary monetary policy, even though that decision worsened the inflation rate.

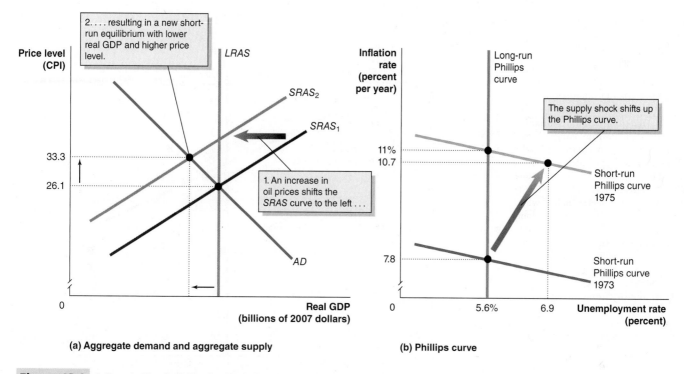

Figure 13.9 A Supply Shock Shifts the Short-Run Phillips Curve

When actions by OPEC increased the price of a barrel of oil from less than $3 to more than $10, panel (a) shows that the *SRAS* curve shifted to the left. Panel (b) shows that the supply shock shifted up the Phillips curve. In 1973, the Canadian economy had an inflation rate of about 7.8 percent and an unemployment rate of about 5.6 percent. By 1975, the inflation rate had risen to about 10.7 percent and the unemployment rate to about 6.9 percent.

The Canadian Disinflation, 1989–1993

By the late 1980s, the Bank of Canada had gone through two decades of continually increasing the rate of growth of the money supply. The Bank of Canada began fighting inflation in 1989 by adopting inflation targets, after a three-year public campaign to promote price stability as the long-term goal of monetary policy. During the Hanson Lecture at the University of Alberta in January 1988, newly appointed Bank of Canada Governor John Crow announced that the Bank of Canada would subsequently pursue an objective of price stability or zero inflation; "zero inflation" should be interpreted as a small positive rate of measured inflation.

In this attempt at lowering inflation, the Bank of Canada followed a different strategy, by announcing explicit targets for its ultimate goal—the inflation rate—rather than for an intermediate variable such as money growth. In particular, in February 1991, the Bank of Canada's governor and the minister of finance jointly announced a series of declining inflation targets, with a band of plus and minus one percentage point around them. The targets were 3 percent by the end of 1992, falling to 2 percent by the end of 1995, to remain within a range of 1 percent to 3 percent thereafter.

Figure 13.10 uses the Phillips curve model to analyze the movements in unemployment and inflation from 1989 to 1993. The Bank of Canada's contractionary monetary policy shifted the economy's short-run equilibrium down the short-run Phillips curve, lowering the inflation rate from 5 percent in 1989 to less than 2 percent in 1993—but at a cost of raising the unemployment rate from 7.5 percent to 11.4 percent. As workers and firms lowered their expectations of future inflation, the short-run Phillips curve shifted down, improving the short-run trade-off between unemployment and inflation. This adjustment in expectations allowed the Bank of Canada to switch to an expansionary monetary policy. By the late 1990s, the economy was back to the natural rate

Figure 13.10

The Bank of Canada Tames Inflation, 1989–1993

The Bank of Canada began fighting inflation in 1989 by adopting inflation targets. As workers and firms lowered their expectations of future inflation, the short-run Phillips curve shifted down, improving the short-run trade-off between unemployment and infla-tion. This adjustment in expectations allowed the Bank of Canada to switch to an expansionary monetary policy, which by the late 1990s brought the economy back to the natural rate of unemploy-ment, with an inflation rate of about 2 percent. The blue line shows the actual combinations of unemployment and inflation for each year from 1989 to 1993. Note that during these years, the natural rate of unemployment was esti-mated to be about 8 percent.

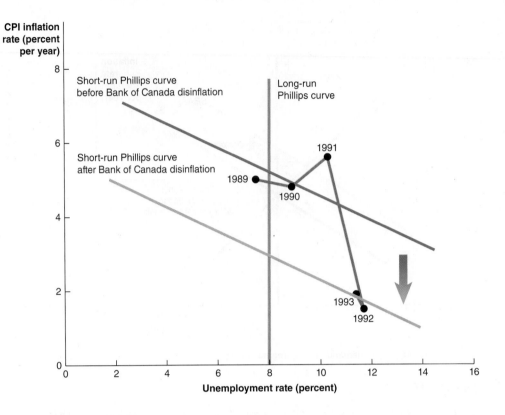

of unemployment, which during these years was about 8 percent. The orange line in Figure 13.10 shows the actual combinations of unemployment and inflation for each year from 1989 to 1993.

Disinflation A significant reduction in the inflation rate.

A significant reduction in the inflation rate is called **disinflation**. In fact, this epi-sode is often referred to as the "Canadian disinflation." The disinflation had come at a very high price, however. The unemployment rate increased from 7.5 percent in 1989 to above 11 percent in 1993, the first time this had happened since the end of the Great Depression of the 1930s and the severe 1981–1982 recession.

Don't Let This Happen to You

Don't Confuse Disinflation with Deflation

Disinflation refers to a decline in the *inflation rate. Defla-tion* refers to a decline in the *price level.* The Bank of Canada brought about a substantial disinflation in Can-ada during the years from 1989 to 1993. The inflation rate fell from over 5 percent in 1989 to below 2 percent in 1993. Yet even in 1994, there was no deflation: The price level was still rising—but at a slower rate.

The last period of significant deflation in Canada was in the early 1930s, during the Great Depression. The following table shows the consumer price index for each of those years.

Because the price level fell each year from 1929 to 1933, there was deflation.

Year	Consumer Price Index	Deflation Rate
1929	9.2	—
1930	9.1	–1.1%
1931	8.2	–9.9
1932	7.5	–8.5
1933	7.1	–5.3

MyEconLab

Your Turn: Test your understanding by doing related problem 4.2 on page 386 at the end of this chapter.

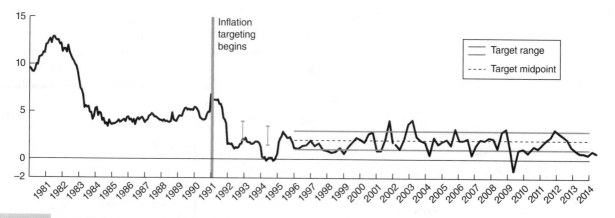

Figure 13.11 The Inflation Rate and Inflation Targets in Canada, 1980–2014

Canada has significantly reduced the rate of inflation and eventually achieved its inflation target.

Inflation Targeting, 1989–Present

The Bank of Canada was successful in achieving its inflation targets during the 1989–1993 disinflation. In fact, it renewed its 1 percent to 3 percent target range for inflation in December 1995, in early 1998, May 2001, November 2006, November 2011, and again in November 2016 to apply until the end of 2021. It is also to be noted that the 1995 and 1998 inflation-control agreements between the Bank of Canada and the government had a three-year horizon. However, the 2016 agreement, like the 2011, 2006, and 2001 agreements, has a five-year horizon, reflecting the wide acceptance of the targets after over 25 years of operation. The midpoint of the current inflation target range, 2 percent, is regarded as the most desirable inflation outcome.

What are the results of Canada's inflation-targeting monetary policy? Figure 13.11 plots the Canadian inflation rate for each year since 1980 and shows the Bank of Canada's target range since 1996. Clearly, inflation has fallen dramatically since the adoption of inflation targets, from above the 5 percent level in 1991 to a 1 percent rate in 1998, most of the time staying in the lower half of the target range. However, as already noted, this decline was not without cost: Unemployment soared to above the 10 percent level from 1991 until 1993, but has since fallen.

Solved Problem **13.2**

Using Monetary Policy to Lower the Inflation Rate

Consider the following hypothetical situation: The unemployment rate is currently at the natural rate of 5 percent, the actual inflation rate is 6 percent and, because it has remained at 6 percent for several years, workers and firms expect the inflation rate to remain at 6 percent in the future.

The Bank of Canada decides to reduce the inflation rate permanently to 2 percent. How can the Bank of Canada use monetary policy to achieve this objective? Be sure to use a Phillips curve graph in your answer.

Solving the Problem

Step 1: **Review the chapter material.** This problem is about using a Phillips curve graph to show how the Bank of Canada can fight inflation, so you may want to review the section "The Canadian Disinflation, 1989–1993," which begins on page 377.

Step 2: **Explain how the Bank of Canada can use monetary policy to reduce the inflation rate.** To reduce the inflation rate significantly, the Bank of Canada will have to raise the target for the overnight interest rate. Higher interest rates will reduce aggregate demand, raise unemployment, and move the economy's equilibrium down the short-run Phillips curve.

Step 3: **Illustrate your argument with a Phillips curve graph.** How much the unemployment rate would have to rise to drive down the inflation rate from 6 percent to 2 percent depends on the steepness of the short-run Phillips curve. In drawing the graph, we have assumed that the unemployment rate would have to rise from 5 percent to 7 percent.

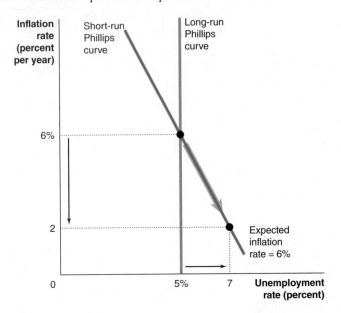

Step 4: **Show on your graph how the Bank of Canada can achieve a permanent reduction in the inflation rate from 6 percent to 2 percent.** For the decline in the inflation rate to be permanent, the expected inflation rate has to decline from 6 percent to 2 percent. We can show this decline on our graph:

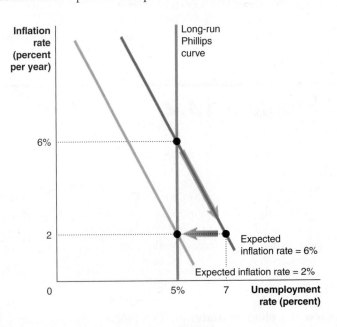

Once the short-run Phillips curve has shifted down, the Bank of Canada can use an expansionary monetary policy to push equilibrium back to the natural rate of unemployment. This policy is similar to the one carried out by the Bank of Canada in 1989 and the US Federal Reserve after Paul Volcker became chairman in 1979. The downside to these policies of disinflation is that they lead to significant increases in unemployment. In the United States, for example, the unemployment rate was above 10 percent from

September 1982 through June 1983, the first time that this had happened since the Great Depression.

Extra credit: A follower of the new classical macroeconomics approach would have a more optimistic view of the consequences of using monetary policy to lower the inflation rate from 6 percent to 2 percent. According to the new classical approach, the Bank of Canada's policy announcement should cause people to immediately revise downward their expectations of future inflation from 6 percent to 2 percent. Short-run equilibrium would move directly down the long-run Phillips curve from an inflation rate of 6 percent to an inflation rate of 2 percent, while keeping the unemployment rate constant at 5 percent. For the reasons discussed in this chapter, many economists are skeptical that disinflation can be brought about so painlessly.

Your Turn: For more practice, do related problem 4.4 on page 386 at the end of this chapter.   MyEconLab

---

The 2007–2009 Global Recession and the Crisis in Monetary Policy

Around the world, the 2007–2009 recession led many central banks (including the Bank of Canada) to move well beyond the short-term nominal interest rate as the focus of monetary policy. With the target overnight interest rate having been driven to the zero lower bound (the short-term nominal interest rate being zero or near zero) without much expansionary effect on the economy, some observers began to speak of a "crisis in monetary policy." We reviewed the Bank of Canada's new policy initiatives in Chapter 11. At this point, we can discuss some issues regarding the current approach to monetary policy.

The current approach to monetary policy is based on the new Keynesian model and is expressed in terms of the short-term nominal interest rate, such as the overnight interest rate in Canada and the federal funds rate in the United States. In recent years the New Keynesian model has also been extended to allow for interest rate channels (or corridors), and many central banks have changed the institutional structure within which monetary policy is conducted and now use a corridor system of monetary policy implementation such as the one we discussed for Canada in Chapter 11. For example, such systems are also used by the Reserve Bank of Australia, the Bank of England, the European Central Bank, the Bank of Japan, the Reserve Bank of New Zealand, Norges Bank (the central bank of Norway), and the Riksbank (the central bank of Sweden).

However, in the aftermath of the global financial crisis and the Great Recession, short-term nominal interest rates have hardly moved at all, while central bank policies have been the most volatile and extreme in their entire histories. This has discredited the short-term nominal interest rate as an indicator of monetary policy and led central banks to look elsewhere. For example, the US Federal Reserve, the European Central Bank, and many other central banks have departed from the traditional interest-rate targeting approach to monetary policy and are now focusing on their balance sheet instead, using quantitative measures of monetary policy, such as credit easing and quantitative easing. Because of these unconventional monetary policies, there is uncertainty about the future path of money growth and inflation. This uncertainty can be especially damaging to the economy, as it amplifies the negative response of the economy to unfavourable shocks and dampens the positive response to favourable shocks.

In fact, one problem with the current approach to monetary policy is that it ignores the role of money measures, known as *monetary aggregates*, that we discussed in Chapter 10. It is to be noted, however, that although current monetary policy is not expressed in terms of monetary aggregates, the central bank's adjustments of the short-term nominal interest rate translate into changes in the monetary aggregates. For example, when the Bank of Canada conducts open-market buyback operations to achieve the desired target for the overnight interest rate, it exchanges the monetary base (the monetary aggregate directly affected by the Bank of Canada's open-market operations) for government securities. The question then that arises is whether there is a useful role for monetary aggregates in today's approach to monetary policy, in the aftermath of the global financial crisis.

Another problem with the current approach to monetary policy is that it ignores the role of **leverage** (or collateral rates). Leverage, l, is defined as

Leverage A measure of how much debt an investor assumes in making an investment.

$$l = \frac{A}{A - L}$$

where A denotes total assets and L liabilities other than net worth (equivalently, capital). Thus, leverage is the ratio of assets to capital and is a measure of how much debt an investor assumes in making an investment; the reciprocal of leverage, $1/l$, is known as the *leverage ratio*.

To explore the leverage concept further, let's assume that you use $10 of your own funds to buy a house that is worth $100 by issuing a mortgage for the remaining $90 using the house as collateral. In that case, the down payment (also known as the *margin* or *haircut*) is 10 percent, the loan to value ratio is $90/$100 = 90 percent, and the collateral rate is $100/$90 = 111 percent. Leverage is the reciprocal of the margin, or the ratio of the asset value to the funds needed to purchase it, $100/$10 = 10. Clearly, when leverage is high, economic agents can buy many assets with very little money down, and asset prices increase. When leverage is low, they must have all (or nearly all) of the money in hand to purchase the same assets, and asset prices decline.

In the aftermath of the global financial crisis, leverage attracted a great deal of attention and it has been argued that leverage on Wall Street increased to 35 to 1 prior to the global financial crisis, though never before in the history of the United States had leverage exceeded 30 to 1. For example, in early 2007, Bear Stearns had a record-high leverage ratio of 35 to 1. Around the same time, (then) major Wall Street investment banks (Goldman Sachs, Morgan Stanley, Merrill Lynch, and Lehman Brothers) together averaged leverage ratios of 30 to 1, up from 20 to 1 in 2003. In fact, it is now widely recognized that leverage cycles (fluctuations in collateral rates) can have important effects on the level of economic activity.

With many central banks around the world implementing unconventional monetary policies in a zero lower-bound environment, having a level of excess reserves in the trillions of dollars, and having unusually high leverage ratios, no one is sure how things will unfold.

Economics in Your Life

Are There Benefits to Delaying a Job Search?

At the beginning of the chapter, we posed this question: What advice would you give someone who has decided to wait nearly one year to look for a new job? As we discussed in the chapter, evidence shows that many of those who are unemployed for longer than a year or two find it more difficult to find new employment than if they searched for a new job soon after they were laid off. The longer workers are unemployed, especially in a high-technology field, the more their skills deteriorate. By delaying her job search, your friend risks being unemployed for longer than one year. Eventually, she may have to be retrained or take additional courses in a different field in order to find a job. Tell your friend to start her job search right away!

Conclusion

The workings of the contemporary economy are complex. The attempts by the Bank of Canada to keep the Canadian economy near the natural rate of unemployment with a low rate of inflation have not always been successful. Economists continue to debate the best approaches for the Bank of Canada.

Chapter Summary and Problems

Key Terms

Disinflation, p. 378

Leverage, p. 382

Natural rate of unemployment, p. 366

Nonaccelerating inflation rate of unemployment (NAIRU), p. 371

Phillips curve, p. 364

Rational expectations, p. 374

Real business cycle models, p. 375

Structural relationship, p. 365

Summary

*LO 13.1 The *Phillips curve* illustrates the short-run trade-off between the unemployment rate and the inflation rate. The inverse relationship between unemployment and inflation shown by the Phillips curve is consistent with the aggregate demand and aggregate supply (*AD-AS*) model. The *AD-AS* model indicates that slow growth in aggregate demand leads to both higher unemployment and lower inflation, and rapid growth in aggregate demand leads to both lower unemployment and higher inflation. This relationship explains why there is a short-run trade-off between unemployment and inflation. Many economists initially believed that the Phillips curve was a *structural relationship* that depended on the basic behaviour of consumers and firms and that remained unchanged over time. If the Phillips curve were a stable relationship, it would present policymakers with a menu of combinations of unemployment and inflation from which they could choose. Nobel Laureate Milton Friedman argued that there is a *natural rate of unemployment*, which is the unemployment rate that exists when the economy is at potential GDP and to which the economy always returns. As a result, there is no trade-off between unemployment and inflation in the long run, and the long-run Phillips curve is a vertical line at the natural rate of unemployment.

LO 13.2 There is a short-run trade-off between unemployment and inflation only if the actual inflation rate differs from the inflation rate that workers and firms expected. There is a different short-run Phillips curve for every expected inflation rate. Each short-run Phillips curve intersects the long-run Phillips curve at the expected inflation rate. With a vertical long-run Phillips curve, it is not possible to buy a permanently lower unemployment rate at the cost of a permanently higher inflation rate. If the Bank of Canada attempts to keep the economy below the natural rate of unemployment, the inflation rate will increase. Eventually, the expected inflation rate will also increase, which causes the short-run Phillips curve to shift up and pushes the economy back to the natural rate. The reverse happens if the Bank of Canada attempts to keep the unemployment rate above the natural rate. In the long run, the Bank of Canada can affect the inflation rate but not unemployment. *The nonaccelerating inflation rate of unemployment (NAIRU)* is the unemployment rate at which the inflation rate has no tendency to increase or decrease.

LO 13.3 When the inflation rate is moderate and stable, workers and firms tend to have *adaptive expectations*. That is, they form their expectations under the assumption that future inflation rates will follow the pattern of inflation rates in the recent past. Robert Lucas and Thomas Sargent argued that during the high and unstable inflation rates of the mid- to late 1970s, workers and firms had *rational expectations*. *Rational expectations* are formed by using all the available information about an economic variable, including the effect of the policy being used by the central bank. Lucas and Sargent argued that if people have rational expectations, expansionary monetary policy will not work. If workers and firms know that an expansionary monetary policy is going to raise the inflation rate, the actual inflation rate will be the same as the expected inflation rate. Therefore, the unemployment rate won't fall. Many economists remain skeptical of Lucas and Sargent's argument in its strictest form. *Real business cycle models* focus on "real" factors—technology shocks—rather than changes in the money supply to explain fluctuations in real GDP.

LO 13.4 Inflation worsened through the 1970s. The Bank of Canada used contractionary monetary policy to reduce inflation. A significant reduction in the inflation rate is called *disinflation*. This contractionary monetary policy pushed short-run equilibrium down the short-run Phillips curve. As workers and firms lowered their expectations of future inflation, the short-run Phillips curve shifted down, improving the short-run trade-off between unemployment and inflation. This change in expectations allowed the Bank of Canada to switch to an expansionary monetary policy to bring the unemployment rate back to the natural rate.

In recent years, some economists have argued that monetary policy decisions in the United States may have contributed to the problems the financial system experienced during the 2007–2009 recession. It has been argued, for example, that central banks have lost their ability to lower long-term interest rates by lowering the overnight interest rate. Moreover, central banks have lost their usual ability to signal policy changes via changes in the overnight interest rate.

MyEconLab Log in to MyEconLab to complete these exercises and get instant feedback.

---

*"Learning Objective" is abbreviated to "LO" in the end-of-chapter material.

Review Questions

LO 13.1

1.1 What is the Phillips curve? Draw a graph of a short-run Phillips curve.

1.2 What actions should the Bank of Canada take if it wants to move from a point on the short-run Phillips curve representing high unemployment and low inflation to a point representing lower unemployment and higher inflation?

1.3 Why did economists during the early 1960s think of the Phillips curve as a "policy menu"? Were they correct to think of it in this way? Briefly explain.

1.4 Why did Milton Friedman argue that the Phillips curve did not represent a permanent trade-off between unemployment and inflation? In your answer, be sure to explain what Friedman meant by the "natural rate of unemployment."

LO 13.2

2.1 Suppose that the expected inflation rate increases from 4 percent to 6 percent. What will happen to the short-run Phillips curve?

2.2 What is the relationship between the short-run Phillips curve and the long-run Phillips curve?

2.3 Why is it inconsistent to believe that the long-run aggregate supply curve is vertical and the long-run Phillips curve is downward sloping?

LO 13.3

3.1 Why do workers, firms, banks, and investors in financial markets care about the future rate of inflation? How do they form their expectations of future inflation? Do current conditions in the economy have any bearing on how they form their expectations? Briefly explain.

3.2 What does it mean to say that workers and firms have rational expectations?

3.3 Why did Robert Lucas and Thomas Sargent argue that the Phillips curve might be vertical in the short run? What difference would it make for monetary policy if they were right?

LO 13.4

4.1 What was the "Canadian disinflation"? What happened to the unemployment rate during the period of the Canadian disinflation?

4.2 Why is the credibility of the Bank of Canada's policy announcements particularly important?

4.3 Why do most economists believe that it is important for a country's central bank to be independent of the rest of the country's central government?

Problems and Applications

LO 13.1

1.1 Use these two graphs to answer the following questions:

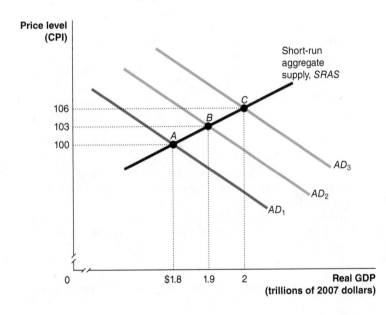

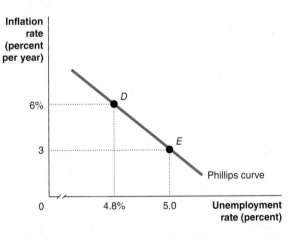

a. Briefly explain which point on the Phillips curve graph best represents the same economic situation as point *B* on the aggregate demand and aggregate supply graph.

b. Briefly explain which point on the Phillips curve graph best represents the same economic situation as point *C* on the aggregate demand and aggregate supply graph.

1.2 Given that the Phillips curve is derived from the aggregate demand and aggregate supply model, why do we use the Phillips curve analysis? What benefits does the Phillips curve analysis offer compared to the aggregate demand and aggregate supply model?

1.3 In a discussion of monetary policy in the United Kingdom, an article in *The Economist* quoted a publication of the British Institute for Economic Affairs as arguing that "to try to use monetary policy to reduce unemployment when inflation is already above target is playing with fire and could lead us down the road that we followed in the 1970s." What does the author mean by "the road that we followed in the 1970s"? How would trying to reduce unemployment at a time of rising inflation be travelling down that road?

"Mixed Reaction," *The Economist*, August 7, 2013.

1.4 General Juan Perón, the former dictator of Argentina, once said of the labour market in his country, "Prices have gone up the elevator, and wages have had to use the stairs." In this situation, what was happening to real wages in Argentina? Was unemployment likely to have been relatively high or relatively low?

Robert J. Shiller, "Why Do People Dislike Inflation?" in Christina D. Romer and David H. Romer, eds., *Reducing Inflation: Motivation and Strategy*, (Chicago: University of Chicago Press, 1997).

1.5 An article in the *Wall Street Journal* has the headline "Don't Look Now, but Market Inflation Expectations Are Falling." If inflation turns out to be lower than households and firms had previously expected, will the actual real wage end up being higher or lower than the expected real wage? Will employment in the short run end up being higher or lower? Briefly explain.

Based on Jon Hilsenrath, "Don't Look Now, but Market Inflation Expectations Are Falling," *Wall Street Journal*, August 10, 2015.

1.6 Why might leverage cycles have an effect on the level of economic activity? In other words, why are movements in collateral rates particularly important to economic activity in actual economies?

1.7 **[Related to Making the Connection on page 368]** Robert Shiller asked a sample of the general public and a sample of economists the following question: "Do you agree that preventing high inflation is an important national priority, as important as preventing drug abuse or preventing deterioration in the quality of our schools?" Fifty-two percent of the general public, but only 18 percent of economists, fully agreed. Why does the general public believe inflation is a bigger problem than economists do?

LO 13.2

2.1 Use the following information to draw a graph showing the short-run and long-run Phillips curves:

Natural rate of unemployment = 5 percent
Current rate of unemployment = 4 percent
Expected inflation rate = 4 percent
Current inflation rate = 6 percent

Be sure your graph shows the point where the short-run and long-run Phillips curves intersect.

2.2 In early 2015, an article in the *Economist* noted that it was possible that in the United States, "the NAIRU may already have been reached and inflation will start accelerating; the Fed should act soon."
a. What is the NAIRU?
b. If this evaluation of the economic situation is correct, what action should the Fed take?
c. If the Fed fails to act, what is likely to happen to the short-run Phillips curve over time? Briefly explain.

"Jobs Matter, Not the Dollar," *The Economist*, March 25, 2015.

2.3 Consider the long-run Phillips curve and the short-run Phillips curve in this graph. What would cause a movement from point *A* to point *B*? What would cause a movement from point *A* to point *C*?

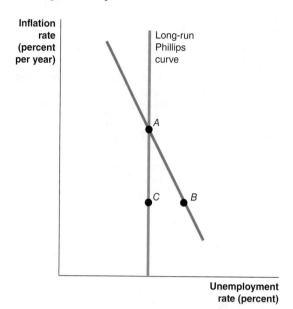

2.4 In 1968, Herbert Stein, who would later serve on President Nixon's Council of Economic Advisers, wrote: "Some who would opt for avoiding inflation would say that in the long run such a policy would cost little, if any, additional unemployment." Was Stein correct? Did most economists in 1968 agree with him? Briefly explain.

Herbert Stein, *The Fiscal Revolution in America*, Chicago: University of Chicago Press, 1969, p. 382.

LO 13.3

3.1 During a time when the inflation rate increases each year for a number of years, are adaptive expectations or rational expectations likely to give the more accurate forecasts? Briefly explain.

3.2 An article in *The Economist* states that: "Robert Lucas ... showed how incorporating expectations into macroeconomic models muddled the framework economists prior to the 'rational expectations revolution' thought they saw so clearly." What economic framework did economists change as a result of Lucas's arguments? Do all economists agree with Lucas's main conclusions about whether monetary policy is effective? Briefly explain.

"How to Know What Causes What," *The Economist*, October 10, 2011.

3.3 An article in *The Economist* observes that "a sudden unanticipated spurt of inflation could lead to rapid economic growth."
a. Briefly explain the reasoning behind this statement.
b. Does it matter whether a spurt of inflation is unanticipated? Might different economists provide different answers to this question? Briefly explain.

"How We Got Here," *The Economist*, January 21, 2013.

3.4 If both the short-run and long-run Phillips curves are vertical, what will be the effect on the inflation rate and the unemployment rate of an expansionary monetary policy? Use a Phillips curve graph to illustrate your answer.

LO 13.4

4.1 An article in the *New York Times* in 2015 quoted Minneapolis Fed President Narayana Kocherlakota as stating that "disinflation is worrisome." Most economists applaud the 1989–1993 Canadian disinflation. Why might disinflation have been a good thing in the early 1990s, but worrisome in 2015?

Based on Reuters, "Fed's Kocherlakota Sees Risk of U.S. Disinflation," *New York Times*, April 14, 2015.

4.2 **[Related to Don't Let This Happen to You on page 378]** Look again at the table on prices during the early 1930s on page 378. Was there disinflation during 1933? Briefly explain.

4.3 Suppose the current inflation rate and the expected inflation rate are both 4 percent. The current unemployment rate and the natural rate of unemployment are both 5 percent. Use a Phillips curve graph to show the effect on the economy of a severe supply shock. If the Bank of Canada keeps monetary policy unchanged, what will happen eventually to the unemployment rate? Show this on your Phillips curve graph.

4.4 **[Related to Solved Problem 13.2 on page 379]** Suppose the inflation rate has been 15 percent for the past four years.

The unemployment rate is currently at the natural rate of unemployment of 5 percent. The Bank of Canada decides that it wants to permanently reduce the inflation rate to 5 percent. How can the Bank of Canada use monetary policy to achieve this objective? Be sure to use a Phillips curve graph in your answer.

4.5 Robert Lucas said, "In practice, it is much more painful to put a modern economy through a deflation than the monetary theory we have would lead us to expect. I take this to mean that we have 'price stickiness.'"

  a. What does Lucas mean by "the monetary theory we have"?

  b. What events may have led Lucas to conclude that it is more painful to reduce the inflation rate than theory would predict?

  c. Why does he conclude that the U.S. economy apparently has "price stickiness"?

Paul A. Samuelson and William A. Barnett, eds., *Inside the Economist's Mind: Conversations with Eminent Economists*, Malden, MA: Blackwell Publishing, 2007.

MyEconLab   MyEconLab is an online tool designed to help you master the concepts covered in your course. It will create a personalized study plan to stimulate and measure your learning. Log in to take advantage of this powerful study aid, and to access quizzes and other valuable course-related material.

U.S. short sellers betting on Canadian housing crash: 'An accident waiting to happen'

Large Wall Street investors who made billions when the U.S. housing market collapsed in 2008 are now betting real estate values in Vancouver and other Canadian cities will crash, financial insiders say.

(a) The hedge fund investors, known as short sellers, are betting against what they believe is a housing bubble in Vancouver, Toronto, Calgary and other Canadian cities. They believe Canadians hold too much mortgage debt, and that Canadian banks, mortgage insurers and "subprime" private lenders will lose money on unpaid loans when property prices fall.

"The cross currents are beyond crazy in Vancouver — it's a mix of money laundering, speculation, low interest rates," said Marc Cohodes, once called Wall Street's highest-profile short-seller by *The New York Times*. "A house is something you live in, but in Vancouver you guys are trading them like the penny stocks on Howe Street."

He says Vancouver real estate has reached peak insanity, and any number of factors could trigger a collapse.

Local real estate professionals predicted the U.S. investors are likely to lose their shirts betting against Vancouver property, which they described as a special market thriving on international demand.

(b) But one Canadian housing analyst who advises U.S. clients, including Cohodes, said major investors are currently "building positions" against Canadian housing targets. They are forecasting a raise in historically low U.S. interest rates this fall will spill financial stress into Canada.

"All of the big global macro funds that were involved in betting against the U.S. in 2007 and 2008 and 2009, they've all studied Canadian housing for a few years," said the Canadian analyst, who asked not to be named because of client confidentiality. "I know a number of them are shorting Canadian housing. It looks like an accident waiting to happen."

This is although housing markets in Vancouver and Toronto have continued to rocket higher since international short-sellers started circling in 2013.

Short sellers use complex financial arrangements to make rapid profits when publicly traded stocks fall in value. In this case, they are betting against businesses connected to property and household debt. They are also betting against the Canadian dollar, because they believe it will decline significantly in a housing bust.

Most of these traders are employed by secretive New York investment funds that shy away from publicity, partly because they want to disguise how they lay their bets. A few though, like Cohodes, take the opposite approach.

He has come out of semi-retirement on his chicken farm in Northern California to make targeted bets against "subprime" Canadian lenders, who make loans to borrowers rejected by traditional banks.

(c) The Canadian housing analyst noted short-selling bets against big Canadian banks have doubled in New York markets in the past several months. And the risk of a sharp housing correction connected to Canadians' high household debt has risen since December, the Bank of Canada recently reported.

While short sellers point to Vancouver as the most extreme housing bubble in Canada, the analyst noted that some investors believe a massive flow of investment from Mainland China makes the market impervious to corrections.

Others speculate that if China's economy slows dramatically, the Vancouver housing will bust. "Toronto sees some offshore money from China, but definitely Vancouver is in its own world," the analyst said.

"Some of the guys that have timed this bet think that when China blows up Vancouver will blow up too, but I'm not sure that will happen."

Key Points in the Article

Many large international investors, including hedge funds (known as short sellers), think that the low interest rates in Canada in the nine years following the global financial crisis of 2007–2009 have encouraged excessive risk-taking and that a bubble has developed in the Canadian housing market, with house prices above levels that can be justified by the value of the housing services that houses provide.

During the global financial crisis, the Bank of Canada lowered its policy rate to 25 basis points (0.25 percentage points) to lessen the crisis by stimulating the level of economic activity. The policy was successful, although due to the severity of the 2007–2009 recession, this very low rate still did little to stimulate the economy, other than contribute to higher house prices. Today, almost nine years after the Great Recession, the policy rate is 0.50%.

The Bank of Canada recently reported that the risk of a sharp housing correction in Canada has risen because of Canadians' high debt-to-after-tax-income ratio which stands at over 160%, a ratio that is as high as the debt-to-income ratio of US households prior to the subprime financial crisis in the United States. If interest rates increase in the future, mortgage rates will also increase, leading to higher monthly mortgage payments and, therefore, less income to spend on other goods and services. Higher mortgage rates might also reduce house sales, and the decrease in demand may reduce housing prices.

Analyzing the News

(a) Large international investors are betting that a bubble is developing in the Canadian housing market (mostly in Vancouver, Toronto, and Calgary), as house prices seem to deviate significantly from fundamental market values. This bubble could be driven by overly optimistic expectations, which the former Federal Reserve chairman, Alan Greenspan, referred to as "irrational exuberance." However, the consensus is that this is a credit-driven bubble, similar to the housing price bubble in the United States that led to the global financial crisis and a number of banking crises around the world.

(b) The overnight interest rate is currently 0.5% and the 5-year (fixed-rate) mortgage rate is around 5%. The Bank of Canada has committed to keeping the overnight rate this low, and it seems that currently the only option for Canada is the use of financial stability policies, also known as macroprudential policies. In fact, banking regulators hope that tighter macroprudential policies will restrain excessive risk-taking and credit growth, and thereby promote financial stability for Canadians.

(c) Due to the slow economic recovery in Canada and the United States, as well as the economic uncertainty in Europe and China, the Bank of Canada cannot use monetary policy to raise interest rates to constrain the credit-driven housing bubble. Because the Bank is refraining from leaning on the bubble, investors are betting that the bubble will burst, which in turn will cause housing prices to decline. A burst bubble and decline in housing prices would have negative effects both on households and the balance sheets of banks, and thus would damage the economy.

Thinking Critically about Policy

1. As the increase in interest rates that are necessary to prick the housing bubble will affect not only the prices of housing, but all prices within the economy, the Bank is concerned that taking actions to prick the housing bubble could have harmful effects on the aggregate economy. Should the Bank of Canada pop the housing price bubble? Alternatively, in order to minimize the negative effect on the economy that will occur when the bubble bursts, should the Bank slow the bubble's growth?

2. There is a need for coordination between monetary policy and financial stability policy if the Bank of Canada is to achieve its objectives of price stability and financial market stability. How can such coordination between monetary policy and financial stability policy be achieved given that control of these policies rests with different government agencies?

Macroeconomics in an Open Economy

CHAPTER

14

Chapter Outline and Learning Objectives

IBM Sings the Dollar Blues

The company that became the International Business Machines Corporation (IBM) was founded in New York City in 1911. For decades, under the leadership of CEOs Tom Watson, Sr., and his son Tom Watson, Jr., IBM was best known for manufacturing large computer systems used by corporations. As business computing made the transition from mainframes to desktop computers, IBM established a new standard with its personal computers powered by Intel chips and using an operating system developed by Microsoft. In 2015, IBM was well into another transition, away from manufacturing hardware and toward selling cloud-based computing software services. As CEO Virginia Rometty put it, "We've reinvented this company one more time." Today, IBM has more than 375 000 employees, $90 billion in revenue, and $20 billion in profits.

Most people think of IBM as a giant of US business. However, as the company name indicates, IBM is an international company with offices throughout Europe, Latin America, Africa, and Asia. In 2014, more than two-thirds of IBM's revenue was earned outside the United States. As a result, the company's profits are affected by fluctuations in the value of the US dollar in exchange for other currencies. In some years, converting revenue from foreign currencies yields more dollars than in other years. For example, in 2014, IBM's global revenue was nearly $2 billion lower when measured in terms of US dollars than when measured in local currencies—Canadian dollars in Canada, pounds in Great Britain, euros in Germany, yen in Japan. Why the discrepancy? The value of the U.S. dollar had increased relative to most other currencies. So, converting Canadian dollars, pounds, euros, and yen into US dollars yielded fewer US dollars for IBM. As an article in the *Wall Street Journal* put it, "The company ... has run into a stiff headwind from the rising value of the dollar."

As we saw in Chapter 11, one reason for the increasing value of the US dollar in 2015 was actions taken by the Federal Reserve to increase interest rates. Higher interest rates made financial investments in the United States more attractive to foreign investors, which increased the demand for US dollars and the exchange rate between the US dollar and other currencies. But monetary policy is not the only reason that exchange rates fluctuate. In this chapter and the next, we will look more closely at how exchange rates are determined and at other important issues involving the international financial system.

Sources: Don Clark, "IBM Pumps $4 Billion into Cloud and Mobile Initiatives," *Wall Street Journal*, February 26, 2015; Steve Lohr, "IBM Revenue Falls 13% Despite Big Gains in New Fields," *Wall Street Journal*, July 20, 2015; and International Business Machines Corporation, *2014 IBM Annual Report*, February 24, 2015.

Economics in Your Life

The Norges Bank and Your Car Loan

Suppose that you are shopping for a new car, which you plan to finance with a loan from a local bank. While reading an article on Canadian bonds on your smartphone one morning, you see this headline: "Norges Bank, the central bank of Norway, announces it will sell its large holdings of Canada bonds. " Will Norges Bank's decision to sell its Canada bonds affect the interest rate you pay on your car loan? As you read this chapter, try to answer this question. You can check your answer against the one we provide on page 409 at the end of this chapter.

I n this chapter, we look closely at the linkages among countries at the macroeconomic level. Countries are linked by trade in goods and services and by flows of financial investment. We will see how policymakers in all countries take these linkages into account when conducting monetary policy and fiscal policy.

14.1 LEARNING OBJECTIVE

Explain how the balance of payments is calculated.

The Balance of Payments: Linking Canada to the International Economy

Today, consumers, firms, and investors routinely interact with consumers, firms, and investors in other economies. A consumer in France may use computer software produced in Canada, watch a television made in South Korea, and wear a sweater made in Italy. A firm in Canada may sell its products in dozens of countries around the world. An investor in London, England, may sell a Canada bond to an investor in Mexico City. Nearly all economies are **open economies** and have extensive interactions in trade or finance with other countries. Open economies interact by trading goods and services and by making investments in each other's economies. A **closed economy** has no interactions in trade or finance with other countries. No economy today is completely closed, although a few countries, such as North Korea, have very limited economic interactions with other countries.

A good way to understand the interactions between one economy and other economies is through the **balance of payments**, which is a record of a country's trade with other countries in goods, services, and assets. Just as Statistics Canada is responsible for collecting data on the gross domestic product (GDP), it is also responsible for collecting

Open economy An economy that has interactions in trade or finance with other countries.

Closed economy An economy that has no interactions in trade or finance with other countries.

Balance of payments The record of a country's trade with other countries in goods, services, and assets.

CURRENT ACCOUNT			**Table 14.1**
Exports of goods	523 631		The Canadian Balance of Payments, 2015 (millions of dollars)
Imports of goods	−547 277		
Balance of trade		−23 646	
Exports of services	99 201		
Imports of services	−122 954		
Balance of services		−23 753	
Income received on investments	90 582		
Income payments on investments	−103 934		
Net income on investments		−13 352	
Net transfers		−4 963	
Balance on current account		−65 714	
FINANCIAL ACCOUNT			
Increase of foreign holdings of assets in Canada	264 270		
Increase in Canadian holdings of assets in foreign countries	−209 055		
Balance on financial account		55 215	
BALANCE ON CAPITAL ACCOUNT		−106	
Statistical discrepancy		−10 605	
Balance of paymenrts		0	

Data from Statistics Canada CANSIM Tables 376-0101 and 376-0102 (Accessed 10 December 2015).

data on the balance of payments. Table 14.1 shows the balance of payments for Canada in the first quarter of 2015. Notice that the table contains three "accounts": the *current account*, the *financial account*, and the *capital account*.

The Current Account

The **current account** records *current*, or short-term, flows of funds into and out of a country. The current account for Canada includes exports and imports of goods and services (recall that the difference between exports and imports of goods and services is called *net exports*); income received by Canadian residents from investments in other countries; income paid on investments in Canada owned by residents of other countries (the difference between investment income received and investment income paid is called *net income on investments*); and the difference between transfers made to residents of other countries and transfers received by Canadian residents from other countries (called *net transfers*). If you made a donation to a charity caring for orphans in Afghanistan, it would be included in net transfers. Any payments received by Canadian residents are positive numbers in the current account, and any payments made by Canadian residents are negative numbers in the current account.

Current account The part of the balance of payments that records a country's net exports, net income on investments, and net transfers.

The Balance of Trade. Part of the current account is the **balance of trade**, which is the difference between the value of the goods a country exports and the value of the goods a country imports. The balance of trade is the largest item in the current account and is often a topic that politicians and the media discuss. If a country exports more goods than it imports, it has a *trade surplus*. If a country exports less than it imports, it has a *trade deficit*. In 2015, Canada had a trade deficit of $23 646 million (see Table 14.1). Figure 14.1 shows imports and exports of goods between Canada and its major trading partners and between the United States and its major trading partners. The data show that Canada ran a trade surplus in 2015 with the United States and the United Kingdom, but a trade deficit with its other major trading partners. The United States ran a trade deficit in 2015 with all its major trading partners and with every region of the world, except for the Middle East and Latin America (except Mexico). (Note

Balance of trade The difference between the value of the goods a country exports and the value of the goods a country imports.

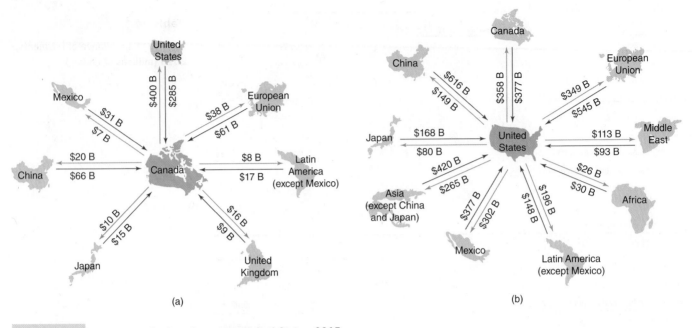

Figure 14.1 Trade Flows for Canada and the United States, 2015

Panel (a) shows that in 2015, Canada ran a trade surplus with the United States and United Kingdom and trade deficits with its other major trading partners. Panel (b) shows that the United States ran a trade deficit with all its major trading partners and with every region of the world, except for the Middle East and Latin America (except Mexico). In each panel, the green arrows represent exports from Canada or the United States, and the red arrows represent imports.

Source: Data from http://www.ic.gc.ca/eic/site/tdo-dcd.nsf/eng/Home (Accessed 13 March 2016).

that exports from Canada to the United States in panel (a) of Figure 14.1 should equal imports by the United States from Canada in panel (b). These two numbers are different because international trade statistics are not measured exactly.)

Net Exports Equals the Sum of the Balance of Trade and the Balance of Services. Recall that *net exports* is a component of aggregate expenditure. Net exports is not explicitly shown in Table 14.1, but we can calculate it by adding together the balance of trade and the balance of services. The *balance of services* is the difference between the value of the services a country exports and the value of the services a country imports. Notice that, technically, net exports is *not* equal to the current account balance because this account also includes net income on investments and net transfers. But as these other two items are relatively small, it is often a convenient simplification to think of net exports as being equal to the current account balance.

The Financial Account

Financial account The part of the balance of payments that records purchases of assets a country has made abroad and foreign purchases of assets in the country.

The **financial account** records purchases of assets a country has made abroad and foreign purchases of assets in the country. The financial account records long-term flows of funds into and out of a country. There is a *capital outflow* from Canada when an investor in Canada buys a bond issued by a foreign company or government or when a Canadian firm builds a factory in another country. There is a *capital inflow* into Canada when a foreign investor buys a bond issued by a Canadian firm or by the government or when a foreign firm builds a factory in Canada. Notice that we are using the word *capital* here to apply not just to physical assets, such as factories, but also to financial assets, such as shares of stock. When firms build or buy facilities in foreign countries, they are engaging in *foreign direct investment*. When investors buy stocks or bonds issued in another country, they are engaging in *foreign portfolio investment*.

Another way of thinking of the balance on the financial account is as a measure of *net capital flows*, or the difference between capital inflows and capital outflows. (Here we are omitting a few transactions included in the capital account, as discussed in the next section.) A concept closely related to net capital flows is **net foreign investment**, which is equal to capital outflows minus capital inflows. Net capital flows and net foreign investment are always equal but have opposite signs: When net capital flows are positive, net foreign investment is negative, and when net capital flows are negative, net foreign investment is positive. Net foreign investment is also equal to net foreign direct investment plus net foreign portfolio investment. Later in this chapter, we will use the relationship between the balance on the financial account and net foreign investment to understand an important aspect of the international economic system.

Net foreign investment The difference between capital outflows from a country and capital inflows, also equal to net foreign direct investment plus net foreign portfolio investment.

The Capital Account

A third, less important, part of the balance of payments is called the *capital account*. The **capital account** records relatively minor transactions, such as migrants' transfers—which consist of goods and financial assets people take with them when they leave or enter a country—and sales and purchases of nonproduced, nonfinancial assets. A nonproduced, nonfinancial asset is a copyright, patent, trademark, or right to natural resources.

Capital account The part of the balance of payments that records relatively minor transactions, such as migrants' transfers and sales and purchases of nonproduced, nonfinancial assets.

Why Is the Balance of Payments Always Zero?

The sum of the current account balance, the financial account balance, and the capital account balance equals the balance of payments. Table 14.1 shows that the balance of payments for Canada in 2015 was zero. It's not just by chance that this balance was zero; *the balance of payments is always zero*. Notice that the current account balance in 2015 was –$65 714 million. The balance on the financial account (which has the opposite sign to the balance on the current account) was $55 215 million. To make the balance on the current account equal the sum of the balance on the capital account and the balance on the financial account, the balance on capital account includes an entry called the *statistical discrepancy*.

Why does Statistics Canada include the statistical discrepancy entry to force the balance of payments to equal zero? If the sum of the current account balance and the financial account balance does not equal zero, some imports or exports of goods and services or some capital inflows or capital outflows were not measured accurately.

To better understand why the balance of payments must equal zero every year, consider the following: In 2015, Canada spent $65 714 million more on goods, services, and other items in the current account than it received. What happened to that $65 714 million? We know that every dollar of that $65 714 million was used by foreign individuals or firms to invest in Canada or was added to foreign holdings of dollars. We know this because logically there is nowhere else for the dollars to go: If the dollars weren't spent on Canadian goods and services—and we know they weren't because, if they had been, they would have shown up in the current account—they must have been spent on investments in Canada or not spent at all. Dollars that aren't spent are added to foreign holdings of dollars. Changes in foreign holdings of dollars are known as *official reserve transactions*. Foreign investment in Canada and additions to foreign holdings of dollars both show up as positive entries in the Canadian financial account. Therefore, a current account deficit must be exactly offset by a financial account surplus, leaving the balance of payments equal to zero. Similarly, a country that runs a current account surplus, such as China, must run a financial account deficit of exactly the same size. If a country's current account surplus is not exactly equal to its financial account deficit, or if a country's current account deficit is not exactly equal to its financial account surplus, some transactions must not have been accounted for. The statistical discrepancy is included in the balance of payments to compensate for these uncounted transactions.

Don't Let This Happen to You

Don't Confuse the Balance of Trade, the Current Account Balance, and the Balance of Payments

The terminology of international economics can be tricky. Remember that the *balance of trade* includes only trade in goods; it does not include services. This observation is important because Canada, for example, usually imports more *goods* than it exports, but it usually exports more *services* than it imports. As a result, the Canadian trade deficit is almost always larger than the current account deficit. The *current account balance* includes the balance of trade, the balance of services, net investment income, and net transfers. Net investment income and net transfers are much smaller than the balance of trade and the balance of services.

Even though the *balance of payments* is equal to the sum of the current account balance and the financial account balance—and must equal zero—you may sometimes see references to a balance of payments "surplus"

or "deficit." These references have two explanations. The first is that the person making the reference has confused the balance of payments with either the balance of trade or the current account balance. This mistake is very common. The second explanation is that the person is not including official reserve transactions in the financial account. If we separate changes in Canadian holdings of foreign currencies and changes in foreign holdings of Canadian dollars from other financial account entries, the current account balance and the financial account balance do not have to sum to zero, and there can be a balance of payments surplus or deficit. This discussion may sound complicated—and it is! But don't worry. How official reserve transactions are accounted for is not crucial to understanding the basic ideas behind the balance of payments.

MyEconLab

Your Turn: Test your understanding by doing related problem 1.2 on page 412 at the end of this chapter.

Solved Problem 14.1

Understanding the Arithmetic of the Balance of Payments

Test your understanding of the relationship between the current account and the financial account by evaluating the following assertion by a political commentator:

The industrial countries are committing economic suicide. Every year, they invest more and more in developing countries. Every year, more Canadian, US, Japanese, and European manufacturing firms move their factories to developing countries. With extensive new factories and low wages, developing countries now export far more to the industrial countries than they import.

Solving the Problem

Step 1: Review the chapter material. This problem is about the relationship between the current account and the financial account, so you may want to review the section "Why Is the Balance of Payments Always Zero?" which begins on page 393.

Step 2: Explain the errors in the commentator's argument. The argument sounds plausible. It would be easy to find statements similar to this one in recent books and articles by well-known political commentators. But the argument contains an important error: The commentator has failed to understand the relationship between the current account and the financial account. The commentator asserts that developing countries are receiving large capital inflows from industrial countries. In other words, developing countries are running financial account surpluses. The commentator also asserts that developing countries are exporting more than they are importing. In other words, they are running current account surpluses. As we have seen in this section, it is impossible to run a current account surplus *and* a financial account surplus simultaneously. A country that runs a current account surplus *must* run a financial account deficit and vice versa.

Extra credit: Most emerging economies that have received large inflows of foreign investment during the past two decades, such as South Korea, Thailand, and Malaysia, have run current account deficits: They import more goods and services than they export. Emerging economies, such as Singapore, that run current account surpluses also run financial account deficits: They invest more abroad than other countries invest in them.

The point here is not obvious; if the point were obvious, it wouldn't confuse so many intelligent politicians, journalists, and political commentators. Unless you understand the relationship between the current account and the financial account, you won't be able to understand a key aspect of the international economy.

Your Turn: For more practice, do related problems 1.3 and 1.4 on page 412 at the end of this chapter.

MyEconLab

The Foreign Exchange Market and Exchange Rates

14.2 **LEARNING** OBJECTIVE

Explain how exchange rates are determined and how changes in exchange rates affect the prices of imports and exports.

A firm that operates entirely within Canada will price its products in Canadian dollars and will use Canadian dollars to pay its suppliers' bills, wages and salaries to its workers, interest to its bondholders, and dividends to its shareholders. A multinational corporation such as BlackBerry, in contrast, may sell its products in many different countries and receive payments in many different currencies. Its suppliers and workers may also be spread around the world and may have to be paid in local currencies. In addition to exchanging currencies, corporations may also use the international financial system to borrow in a foreign currency. For example, during a period of rapid expansion in East Asian countries such as Thailand and South Korea during the late 1990s, many large firms received US dollar loans from foreign banks. When firms make extensive use of foreign currencies, they must deal with fluctuations in the exchange rate.

The **nominal exchange rate** is the value of one country's currency in terms of another country's currency. Economists also calculate the *real exchange rate*, which corrects the nominal exchange rate for changes in prices of goods and services. We discuss the real exchange rate later in this chapter. The nominal exchange rate determines how many units of a foreign currency you can purchase with \$1. For example, the exchange rate between the Canadian dollar and the Japanese yen can be expressed as ¥100 = \$1. (This exchange rate can also be expressed as how many Canadian dollars are required to buy 1 Japanese yen: \$0.01 = ¥1.) The market for foreign exchange is very active, with the equivalent of more than \$4 trillion worth of currency traded each day. The exchange rates that result from this trading are reported on a number of online sites devoted to economic news and in the business or financial sections of most newspapers.

Banks and other financial institutions around the world employ currency traders, who are linked together by computer. Rather than exchange large amounts of paper currency, they buy and sell deposits in banks. A bank buying or selling dollars will actually be buying or selling dollar bank deposits. Dollar bank deposits exist not just in banks in Canada but also in banks around the world. Suppose that the Crédit Agricole bank in France wants to sell Canadian dollars and buy Japanese yen. The bank may exchange Canadian dollar deposits that it owns for Japanese yen deposits owned by the Deutsche Bank in Germany. Businesses and individuals usually obtain foreign currency from banks in their own country.

Nominal exchange rate The value of one country's currency in terms of another country's currency.

Daisy Corlett/Alamy Stock Photo

You can find information on exchange rates on many online sites that report economic news and in the financial pages of most newspapers

<table>
<tr><td>**Making**
the
Connection</td><td>**Exchange Rate Listings**</td></tr>
</table>

You can find the exchange rates between the dollar and other major currencies on many online sites, such as wsj.com, Bloomberg.com, or finance.yahoo.com, as well as in the financial pages of most newspapers. The exchange rates in the following table are for December 10, 2015. The euro is the common currency used by 19 European countries, including France, Germany, and Italy, but not the United Kingdom.

Exchange Rate between the Canadian Dollar and the Indicated Currency		
Currency	Units of Foreign Currency per Canadian	Canadian Dollars per Unit of Foreign Currency
US dollar	1.3572	0.7368
Japanese yen	89.4657	0.0112
Mexican peso	12.5691	0.0796
British pound	0.4854	2.0602
Euro	0.6687	1.4954

Notice that the expression for the exchange rate stated as units of foreign currency per Canadian dollar is the *reciprocal* of the exchange rate stated as Canadian dollars per unit of foreign currency. So, the exchange rate between the Canadian dollar and the British pound can be stated as either 0.4854 British pounds per Canadian dollar or $1/0.4854 = 2.0602$ Canadian dollars per British pound.

Banks are the most active participants in the market for foreign exchange. Typically, banks buy currency for slightly less than the amount for which they sell it. This spread between the buying and selling prices allows banks to cover their costs from currency trading. Therefore, when most businesses and individuals buy foreign currency from a bank, they receive fewer units of foreign currency per dollar than would be indicated by the exchange rate shown on online business sites or printed in the newspaper.

Based on *The Globe and Mail: Report on Business*, December 10, 2015, http://www.theglobeandmail.com/report-on-business/rob-commentary/executive-insight/.

MyEconLab   **Your Turn:** Test your understanding by doing related problem 2.1 on page 412 at the end of this chapter.

The market exchange rate is determined by the interaction of demand and supply, just as other prices are. Let's consider the demand for Canadian dollars in exchange for Japanese yen. There are three sources of foreign currency demand for the Canadian dollar:

1. Foreign firms and households that want to buy goods and services produced in Canada.
2. Foreign firms and households that want to invest in Canada either through foreign direct investment—buying or building factories or other facilities in Canada—or through foreign portfolio investment—buying stocks and bonds issued in Canada.
3. Currency traders who believe that the value of the dollar in the future will be greater than its value today.

Equilibrium in the Market for Foreign Exchange

Figure 14.2 shows the demand and supply of Canadian dollars for Japanese yen. Notice that as we move up the vertical axis, the value of the dollar increases relative to the value of the yen. When the exchange rate is ¥150 = $1, the dollar is worth 1.5 times as much relative to the yen as when the exchange rate is ¥100 = $1. Consider, first, the demand curve for dollars in exchange for yen. The demand curve has the normal downward slope. When the value of the dollar is high, the quantity of dollars demanded will be low. A Japanese investor will be more likely to buy a $1000 bond issued by the Canadian

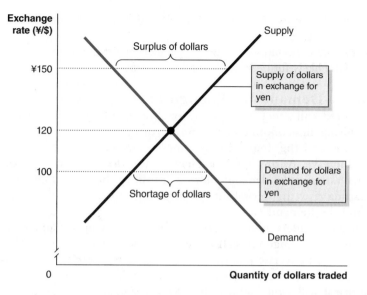

Figure 14.2

Equilibrium in the Foreign Exchange Market

When the exchange rate is ¥150 to the dollar, it is above its equilibrium level, and there will be a surplus of dollars. When the exchange rate is ¥100 to the dollar, it is below its equilibrium level, and there will be a shortage of dollars. At an exchange rate of ¥120 to the dollar, the foreign exchange market is in equilibrium.

government when the exchange rate is ¥100 = $1 and the investor pays only ¥100 000 to buy $1000 than when the exchange rate is ¥150 = $1 and the investor must pay ¥150 000. Similarly, a Japanese firm is more likely to buy $150 million worth of BlackBerrys when the exchange rate is ¥100 = $1 and the BlackBerrys can be purchased for ¥15 billion than when the exchange rate is ¥150 = $1 and the BlackBerrys cost ¥22.5 billion.

Now consider the supply curve of dollars in exchange for yen. The supply curve has the normal upward slope. When the value of the dollar is high, the quantity of dollars supplied in exchange for yen will be high. A Canadian investor will be more likely to buy a ¥200 000 bond issued by the Japanese government when the exchange rate is ¥200 = $1 and he needs to pay only $1000 to buy ¥200 000 than when the exchange rate is ¥100 = $1 and he must pay $2000. The owner of a Canadian electronics store is more likely to buy ¥20 million worth of television sets from Sony Corporation when the exchange rate is ¥200 = $1 and she must pay $100 000 to purchase the televisions than when the exchange rate is ¥100 = $1 and she must pay $200 000.

As in any other market, equilibrium occurs in the foreign exchange market where the quantity supplied equals the quantity demanded. In Figure 14.2, ¥120 = $1 is the equilibrium exchange rate. At exchange rates above ¥120 = $1, there will be a surplus of dollars and downward pressure on the exchange rate. The surplus and the downward pressure will not be eliminated until the exchange rate falls to ¥120 = $1. If the exchange rate is below ¥120 = $1, there will be a shortage of dollars and upward pressure on the exchange rate. The shortage and the upward pressure will not be eliminated until the exchange rate rises to ¥120 = $1. Surpluses and shortages in the foreign exchange market are eliminated very quickly because the volume of trading in major currencies such as the dollar and the yen is very large, and currency traders are linked together by computer.

Currency appreciation occurs when the market value of a country's currency increases relative to the value of another country's currency. **Currency depreciation** occurs when the market value of a country's currency decreases relative to the value of another country's currency.

Currency appreciation An increase in the market value of one currency relative to another currency.

Currency depreciation A decrease in the market value of one currency relative to another currency.

How Do Shifts in Demand and Supply Affect the Exchange Rate?

Shifts in the demand and supply curves cause the equilibrium exchange rate to change. Three main factors cause the demand and supply curves in the foreign exchange market to shift:

1. Changes in the demand for Canadian-produced goods and services and changes in the demand for foreign-produced goods and services;

2. Changes in the desire to invest in Canada and changes in the desire to invest in foreign countries; and

3. Changes in the expectations of currency traders about the likely future value of the dollar and the likely future value of foreign currencies.

Shifts in the Demand for Foreign Exchange. Consider how the three factors just listed will affect the demand for Canadian dollars in exchange for Japanese yen. During an economic expansion in Japan, the incomes of Japanese households will rise, and the demand by Japanese consumers and firms for Canadian goods will increase. At any given exchange rate, the demand for Canadian dollars will increase, and the demand curve will shift to the right. Similarly, if interest rates in Canada rise, the desirability of investing in Canadian financial assets will increase, and the demand curve for dollars will also shift to the right. **Speculators** are currency traders who buy and sell foreign exchange in an attempt to profit from changes in exchange rates. If a speculator becomes convinced that the value of the dollar is going to rise relative to the value of the yen, the speculator will sell yen and buy dollars. If the current exchange rate is ¥120 = $1, and the speculator is convinced that it will soon rise to ¥140 = $1, the speculator could sell ¥600 000 000 and receive $5 000 000 (= ¥600 000 000/¥120) in return. If the speculator is correct and the value of the dollar rises against the yen to ¥140 = $1, the speculator will be able to exchange $5 000 000 for ¥700 000 000 (= $5 000 000 × ¥140), for a profit of ¥100 000 000.

Speculators Currency traders who buy and sell foreign exchange in an attempt to profit from changes in exchange rates.

To summarize, the demand curve for dollars shifts to the right when incomes in Japan rise, when interest rates in Canada rise, or when speculators decide that the value of the dollar will rise relative to the value of the yen.

During a recession in Japan, Japanese incomes will fall, reducing the demand for Canadian-produced goods and services and shifting the demand curve for dollars to the left. Similarly, if interest rates in Canada fall, the desirability of investing in Canadian financial assets will decrease, and the demand curve for dollars will shift to the left. Finally, if speculators become convinced that the future value of the dollar will be lower than its current value, the demand for dollars will fall, and the demand curve will shift to the left.

Shifts in the Supply of Foreign Exchange. The factors that affect the supply curve for dollars are similar to those that affect the demand curve for dollars. An economic expansion in Canada increases the incomes of Canadians and increases their demand for goods and services, including goods and services made in Japan. As Canadian consumers and firms increase their spending on Japanese products, they must supply dollars in exchange for yen, which causes the supply curve for dollars to shift to the right. Similarly, an increase in interest rates in Japan will make financial investments in Japan more attractive to Canadian investors. These higher Japanese interest rates will cause the supply of dollars to shift to the right, as Canadian investors exchange dollars for yen. Finally, if speculators become convinced that the future value of the yen will be higher relative to the dollar than it is today, the supply curve of dollars will shift to the right as traders attempt to exchange dollars for yen.

A recession in Canada will decrease the demand for Japanese products and cause the supply curve for dollars to shift to the left. Similarly, a decrease in interest rates in Japan will make financial investments in Japan less attractive and cause the supply curve for dollars to shift to the left. If traders become convinced that the future value of the yen will be lower relative to the dollar, the supply curve will also shift to the left.

Adjustment to a New Equilibrium. The factors that affect the demand and supply for currencies are constantly changing. Whether the exchange rate increases or decreases depends on the direction and size of the shifts in the demand curve and supply curve. For example, as Figure 14.3 shows, if the demand curve for dollars in exchange for Japanese yen shifts to the right by more than the supply curve shifts, the equilibrium exchange rate will increase.

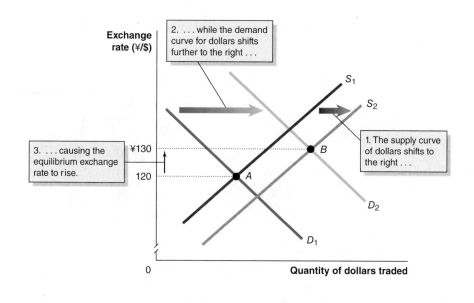

Exchange rate (¥/$)

2. . . . while the demand curve for dollars shifts further to the right . . .

3. . . . causing the equilibrium exchange rate to rise.

1. The supply curve of dollars shifts to the right . . .

¥130

120

S_1

S_2

B

A

D_2

D_1

0   **Quantity of dollars traded**

Figure 14.3

Shifts in the Demand and Supply Curve Resulting in a Higher Exchange Rate

Holding other factors constant, an increase in the supply of dollars will decrease the equilibrium exchange rate. Holding other factors constant, an increase in the demand for dollars will increase the equilibrium exchange rate. In the case shown in this figure, the demand curve and the supply curve have both shifted to the right. Because the demand curve has shifted to the right by more than the supply curve, the equilibrium exchange rate has increased from ¥120 to $1 at point A to ¥130 to $1 at point B.

Making the Connection | # Is a Strong Currency Good for a Country?

News stories often refer to a country as having a "strong" currency when the currency's value has been rising relative to other countries' currencies. Should a country want a strong currency? "Strong" certainly seems better than "weak," so most people would answer "yes" to that question. During late 2014 and 2015, as the price of oil declined in the global market and Canadian short-term nominal interest rates fell, the value of the Canadian dollar decreased, as shown in the graph below. The graph shows the Canadian-dollar *effective exchange rate index* (CERI), which is a weighted average of bilateral exchange rates for the Canadian dollar against the currencies of Canada's six major trading partners, the United States, the European Union, Japan, the United Kingdom, China, and Mexico. The index is based to 1992 = 100, and an increase in the index represents an appreciation of the Canadian dollar, while a decrease represents a depreciation of the Canadian dollar. The shaded areas indicate recessions.

The graph indicates that although the Canadian dollar lost value against other currencies for a brief period during the early 1980s and in the 1990s, and again in 2008 and 2015, overall it has not lost a lot of value since 1981. What explains the fluctuations in the value of the dollar? We have just seen that an increase in the demand by foreign investors for Canadian financial assets can increase the value of the dollar, and a decrease in the demand for Canadian financial assets can decrease the value of the dollar. The increase in the value of the dollar in the aftermath of the global financial crisis, as shown in the graph, was driven by strong demand from foreign investors for Canadian stocks and bonds. This increase in demand was not primarily due to higher Canadian interest rates but to problems in the international financial system that we will discuss in Chapter 15.

What explains the fall in the value of the Canadian dollar in the 1990s? Many investors and some central banks became convinced that the value of the dollar was too high in the late 1980s and that it was likely to decline in the future. As we will see later in this chapter, Canada ran large budget deficits and current account deficits in the 1990s. Many investors believed that the substantial increase in the supply of dollars in exchange for foreign currencies that resulted from these deficits would ultimately result in a significant decline in the value of the dollar. Once investors become convinced that the value of a country's currency will decline, they become reluctant to hold that country's financial assets. A decreased willingness by foreign investors to buy Canadian financial assets decreases the demand for dollars and lowers the exchange value of the dollar.

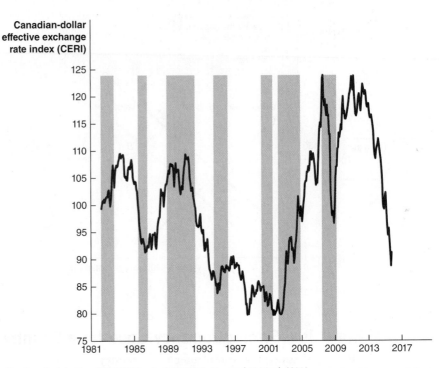

Source: Data from Statistics Canada CANSIM series V41498903. (Accessed 11 March 2016.)

What explains the increase in the value of the Canadian dollar from 2009 to early 2011? The increase has largely been the result of the good performance of the Canadian economy during the global financial crisis and the healthy and vibrant Canadian banking system that has become the envy of the world. Many investors saw Canadian securities as a safe haven and demanded dollars in order to invest in them. Also, worries that some European governments—particularly Greece— might default on their government bonds caused an increase in the value of the dollar since 2009. However, the recent decline in the price of oil has led to a significant decrease in the value of the Canadian dollar.

Although a strong Canadian dollar can be bad news for Canadian exporters, it can actually be *good* news for Canadian consumers. We can conclude that neither a "strong" currency nor a "weak" currency is all good or all bad for a country's businesses and households. Swings in exchange rates create both winners and losers.

MyEconLab **Your Turn:** Test your understanding by doing related problem 2.3 on page 412 at the end of this chapter.

Some Exchange Rates Are Not Determined by the Market

To this point, we have assumed that exchange rates are determined in the market. This assumption is a good one for many currencies, including the Canadian dollar, the US dollar, the euro, the Japanese yen, and the British pound. Some currencies, however, have *fixed exchange rates* that do not change over long periods. For example, for more than 10 years, the value of the Chinese yuan was fixed against the US dollar at a rate of 8.28 yuan to the US dollar. As we will discuss in more detail in Chapter 15, a country's central bank has to intervene in the foreign exchange market to buy and sell its currency to keep the exchange rate fixed.

How Movements in the Exchange Rate Affect Exports and Imports

When the market value of the dollar increases, the foreign currency price of Canadian exports rises, and the dollar price of foreign imports falls. For example, suppose that initially the market exchange rate between the Canadian dollar and the euro is $1 = €1. In that case, a BlackBerry that has a price of $200 in Canada will have a price of €200 in France. A bottle of French wine that has a price of €50 in France will have a price of $50 in Canada. Now suppose the market exchange rate between the Canadian dollar and the euro changes to $1.20 = €1. Because it now takes more dollars to buy a euro, the dollar has *depreciated* against the euro, and the euro has *appreciated* against the dollar. The depreciation of the dollar has decreased the euro price of the BlackBerry from €200 to $200/(1.20 dollars/euro) = €167. The dollar price of the French wine has risen from $50 to €50 × 1.20 dollars/euro = $60. As a result, we would expect more BlackBerrys to be sold in France and less French wine to be sold in Canada.

To generalize, we can conclude:

1. A depreciation in the domestic currency will increase exports and decrease imports, thereby increasing net exports. If real GDP is currently below potential GDP, then, holding all other factors constant, a depreciation in the domestic currency should increase net exports, aggregate demand, and real GDP.
2. An appreciation in the domestic currency should have the opposite effect: Exports should fall, and imports should rise, which will reduce net exports, aggregate demand, and real GDP.

Don't Let This Happen to You

Don't Confuse What Happens When a Currency Appreciates with What Happens When It Depreciates

One of the most confusing aspects of exchange rates is that they can be expressed in two ways. We can express the exchange rate between the dollar and the yen either as how many yen can be purchased with $1 or as how many dollars can be purchased with ¥1. That is, we can express the exchange rate as ¥100 = $1 or as $0.01 = ¥1. When a currency appreciates, it increases in value relative to another currency. When it depreciates, it decreases in value relative to another currency.

If the exchange rate changes from ¥100 = $1 to ¥120 = $1, the dollar has appreciated and the yen has depreciated because it now takes more yen to buy $1. If the exchange rate changes from $0.01 = ¥1 to $0.015 = ¥1,

however, the dollar has depreciated and the yen has appreciated because it now takes more dollars to buy ¥1. This situation can appear somewhat confusing because the exchange rate seems to have "increased" in both cases. To determine which currency has appreciated and which has depreciated, it is important to remember that an appreciation of the domestic currency means that it now takes *more* units of the foreign currency to buy one unit of the domestic currency. A depreciation of the domestic currency means it takes *fewer* units of the foreign currency to buy one unit of the domestic currency. This observation holds no matter which way we express the exchange rate.

MyEconLab

Your Turn: Test your understanding by doing related problem 2.5 on page 413 at the end of the chapter.

Solved Problem 14.2

Subaru Benefits from a Weak Yen

Today, most Japanese automobile companies have manufacturing plants in the United States. Honda, for example, exports from Japan only 21 percent of the cars it sells in the United States. Fuji Heavy Industries, whose main car brand is Subaru, is an exception in still producing most of its cars in Japan. An article in the *Wall Street Journal* observed that for Fuji Heavy Industries, "the plunging yen has turned

a problem—a shortage of production in the US—into an unexpected boon."

a. What does the article mean by a "plunging yen"?
b. Why would a plunging yen be a boon for Fuji Heavy Industries?
c. Briefly explain whether a plunging yen would help or hurt Honda.

Solving the Problem

Step 1: **Review the chapter material.** This problem is about changes in the value of a currency, so you may want to review the section "How Movements in the Exchange Rate Affect Exports and Imports" on page 400.

Step 2: **Answer part (a) by explaining what the article means by a "plunging yen."** In this case, a plunging yen means a yen that is worth less in exchange for the US dollar. With a plunging yen, a larger number of yen would be needed to exchange for one US dollar.

Step 3: **Answer part (b) by explaining how a plunging yen will affect Fuji Heavy Industries.** When Fuji Heavy Industries manufactures cars in Japan, it pays its production costs—including the salaries of its assembly-line workers and payments to its suppliers—with yen. With a falling value of the yen, the dollar price of cars Fuji sells in the United States decreases. As a result, Fuji will gain sales from other companies, particularly those that produce their cars in the United States. If Fuji produced its cars in the United States, it would not have gained this advantage.

Step 4: **Answer part (c) by explaining whether a plunging yen will help or hurt Honda.** Because most of the cars Honda sells in the United States are also produced here, most of the company's production costs and also most of the revenue it earns are in dollars. So, Honda will not be directly affected by fluctuations in the yen–dollar exchange rate. Honda will, though, likely lose some sales to Fuji as the dollar prices of Subarus declines.

Extra Credit: Of course, managers at Honda, Toyota, and Nissan are aware that when the value of the yen declines against the dollar, they would be better off producing in Japan the cars they planned to sell in the United States. But, unlike the managers of Fuji, the managers of these firms decided that moving production to the United States would allow them to plan better and to stabilize their profits because their sales would no longer depend on fluctuations in the exchange rate.

Based on Yoko Kubota, Why Subaru's Profit Is Surging, *Wall Street Journal*, November 15, 2014.

MyEconLab   **Your Turn:** For more practice, do related problem 2.6 on page 413 at the end of this chapter.

The Real Exchange Rate

Real exchange rate The price of domestic goods in terms of foreign goods.

We have seen that an important factor in determining the level of a country's exports to and imports from another country is the relative prices of each country's goods. The relative prices of two countries' goods are determined by two factors: the relative price levels in the two countries and the nominal exchange rate between the two countries' currencies. Economists combine these two factors in the **real exchange rate**, which is the price of domestic goods in terms of foreign goods. Recall that the price level is a measure of the average prices of goods and services in an economy. We can calculate the real exchange rate between two currencies as:

$$\text{Real exchange rate} = \text{Nominal rate} \times \left(\frac{\text{Domestic price level}}{\text{Foreign price level}} \right)$$

Notice that both changes in the nominal exchange rate and changes in the relative price levels cause movements in the real exchange rate. Suppose that the exchange rate between the Canadian dollar and the British pound is $1 = £1, the price level in Canada is 100, and the price level in the United Kingdom is also 100. Then the real exchange rate between the dollar and the pound is:

$$\text{Real exchange rate} = 1 \text{ pound/dollar} \times \left(\frac{100}{100} \right) = 1.00.$$

Now suppose that the nominal exchange rate increases to 1.1 pounds per dollar, while the price level in Canada rises to 105 and the price level in the United Kingdom remains 100. In this case, the real exchange rate will be:

$$\text{Real exchange rate} = 1.1 \text{ pound/dollar} \times \left(\frac{105}{100}\right) = 1.15.$$

The increase in the real exchange rate from 1.00 to 1.15 tells us that the prices of Canadian goods and services are now 15 percent higher than they were relative to British goods and services.

Real exchange rates are reported as index numbers, with one year chosen as the base year. As with the consumer price index, the main value of the real exchange rate is in tracking changes over time—in this case, changes in the relative prices of domestic goods in terms of foreign goods.

The International Sector and National Saving and Investment

14.3 **LEARNING** OBJECTIVE
Explain the saving and investment equation.

Having studied what determines the exchange rate, we are now ready to explore further the linkages between the Canadian economy and foreign economies. Until 1970, Canadian imports and exports were a small fraction of GDP. Imports and exports are now two to three times as large a fraction of Canadian GDP. Imports have also consistently been larger than exports, meaning that net exports have been negative.

Net Exports Equal Net Foreign Investment

If your spending is greater than your income, what can you do? You can sell some assets—maybe those 20 shares of stock in Rogers Communications that your grandparents gave you—or you can borrow money. A firm can be in the same situation: If a firm's costs are greater than its revenues, it has to make up the difference by selling assets or by borrowing. A country is in the same situation when it imports more than it exports: The country must finance the difference by selling assets—such as land, office buildings, or factories—or by borrowing.

In other words, for any country, a current account deficit must be exactly offset by a financial account surplus. When a country sells more assets to foreigners than it buys from foreigners, or when it borrows more from foreigners than it lends to foreigners—as it must if it is running a current account deficit—the country experiences a net capital inflow and a financial account surplus. Remember that net exports is roughly equal to the current account balance. Remember also that the financial account balance is roughly equal to net capital flows, which are in turn equal to net foreign investment but with the opposite sign. To review these two points, look again at Table 14.1, which shows that the current account balance is determined mainly by the balance of trade and the balance of services, and the financial account is equal to net capital flows. Also, remember the definition of *net foreign investment*.

When imports are greater than exports, net exports are negative, and there will be a net capital inflow as people in Canada sell assets and borrow to pay for the surplus of imports over exports. Therefore, net capital flows will be equal to net exports (but with the opposite sign), and net foreign investment will also be equal to net exports (with the same sign). Because net exports were negative for Canada during the 2009 to 2011 period, Canada was a net borrower from abroad, and Canadian net foreign investment was negative.

We can summarize this discussion with the following equations:

$$\text{Current account balance} + \text{Financial account balance} = 0$$

or

$$\text{Current account balance} = -\text{Financial account balance}$$

or

$$\text{Net exports} = \text{Net foreign investment}.$$

The last equation tells us, once again, that countries such as Canada, Japan, and China that usually export more than they import must lend abroad more than they borrow from abroad: If net exports are positive, net foreign investment will also be positive by the same amount. Countries such as the United States that import more than they export must borrow more from abroad than they lend abroad: If net exports are negative, net foreign investment will also be negative by the same amount.

Domestic Saving, Domestic Investment, and Net Foreign Investment

We can think of the total saving in any economy as equal to saving by the private sector plus saving by the government sector, which we called *public saving*. When the government runs a budget surplus by spending less than it receives in taxes, public saving is positive. When the government runs a budget deficit, public saving is negative. Negative saving is also known as *dissaving*. We can write the following expression for the level of saving in the economy:

$$\text{National saving} = \text{Private saving} + \text{Public saving}$$

or:

$$S = S_{\text{private}} + S_{\text{public}}.$$

Private saving is equal to what households have left of their income after spending on consumption goods and paying taxes (for simplicity, we assume that transfer payments are zero):

$$\text{Private saving} = \text{National income} - \text{Consumption} - \text{Taxes}$$

or:

$$S_{\text{private}} = Y - C - T.$$

Public saving is equal to the difference between government spending and taxes:

$$\text{Government saving} = \text{Taxes} - \text{Government spending}$$

or:

$$S_{\text{public}} = T - G.$$

Finally, remember the basic macroeconomic equation for GDP or national income:

$$Y = C + I + G + NX.$$

We can use this last equation, our definitions of private and public saving, and the fact that net exports equal net foreign investment to arrive at an important relationship, called the **saving and investment equation**:

Saving and investment equation
An equation that shows that national saving is equal to domestic investment plus net foreign investment.

$$\text{National saving} = \text{Domestic investment} + \text{Net foreign investment}$$

or:

$$S = I + NFI.$$

This equation is an *identity* because it must always be true, given the definitions we have used.

The saving and investment equation tells us that a country's saving will be invested either domestically or overseas. If you save $1000 and use the funds to buy a bond issued by BlackBerry, Blackberry may use the $1000 to renovate a factory in Canada (*I*) or to build a factory in China (*NFI*) as a joint venture with a Chinese firm.

Solved Problem **14.3**

Arriving at the Saving and Investment Equation

Use the definitions of private and public saving, the equation for GDP or national income, and the fact that net exports must equal net foreign investment to arrive at the saving and investment equation.

Solving the Problem

Step 1: **Review the chapter material.** This problem is about the saving and investment equation, so you may want to review the section "Domestic Saving, Domestic Investment, and Net Foreign Investment," which begins on page 404.

Step 2: **Derive an expression for national saving (S) in terms of national income (Y), consumption (C), and government purchases (G).** We can bring together the four equations we need to use:

1. $S_{private} = Y - C - T$
2. $S_{public} = T - G$
3. $Y = C + I + G + NX$
4. $NX = NFI$

Because national saving (S) appears in the saving and investment equation, we need to find an equation for it in terms of the other variables. Adding equation 1 plus equation 2 yields national saving:

$$S = S_{private} + S_{public} = (Y - C - T) + (T - G) = Y - C - G.$$

Step 3: **Use the result from Step 2 to derive an expression for national saving in terms of investment (I) and net exports (NX).** Because GDP (Y) does not appear in the saving and investment equation, we need to substitute the expression for it given in equation (3):

$$S = (C + I + G + NX) - C - G$$

and simplify:

$$S = I + NX.$$

Step 4: **Use the results of Steps 2 and 3 to derive the saving and investment equation.** Finally, substitute net foreign investment for net exports:

$$S = I + NFI.$$

Your Turn: For more practice, do related problem 3.4 on page 413 at the end of this chapter.   MyEconLab

---

A country such as Canada that has positive net foreign investment must be saving more than it is investing domestically. To understand why, rewrite the saving and investment equation by moving domestic investment to the left side:

$$S - I = NFI.$$

If net foreign investment is positive—as it is for Canada nearly every year—domestic investment (I) must be less than national saving (S).

In most years, the level of saving in Japan has also been well above domestic investment. The result has been high levels of Japanese net foreign investment. For example, Japanese automobile companies Toyota, Honda, and Nissan have all constructed factories in Canada and the United States. Sony purchased the Columbia Pictures film studio. Japan has made many similar investments in countries around the world, which has sometimes caused resentment in those countries. There were some protests in the United States in the 1980s, for example, when Japanese investors purchased the Pebble Beach golf course in California and the Rockefeller Center complex in New York City.

Japan needs a high level of net exports to help offset a low level of domestic investment. When exports of a product begin to decline and imports begin to increase, governments are often tempted to impose tariffs or quotas to reduce imports. In fact, many Japanese firms have been urging the Japanese government to impose trade restrictions on imports from China.

14.4 **LEARNING** OBJECTIVE

Explain the effect of a government budget deficit on investment in an open economy.

The Effect of a Government Budget Deficit on Investment

The link we have just developed among saving, investment, and net foreign investment can help us understand some of the effects of changes in a government's budget deficit. When the government runs a budget deficit, national saving will decline unless private saving increases by the amount of the budget deficit, which is unlikely. As the saving and investment equation $(S = I + NFI)$ shows, the result of a decline in national saving must be a decline in either domestic investment or net foreign investment. The algebra is clear, but why, economically, does an increase in the government budget deficit cause a fall in domestic investment or net foreign investment?

To understand the answer to this question, remember that if the federal government runs a budget deficit, the government must raise an amount equal to the deficit by selling bonds. To attract investors, the government may have to raise the interest rates on its bonds. As interest rates on government bonds rise, other interest rates, including those on corporate bonds and bank loans, will also rise. Higher interest rates will discourage some firms from borrowing funds to build new factories or to buy new equipment or computers. Higher interest rates on financial assets in Canada will attract foreign investors. Investors in the United States, Japan, or China will have to buy Canadian dollars to be able to purchase bonds in Canada. This greater demand for Canadian dollars will increase their value relative to foreign currencies. As the value of the dollar rises, exports from Canada will fall, and imports to Canada will rise. Net exports and, therefore, net foreign investment will fall.

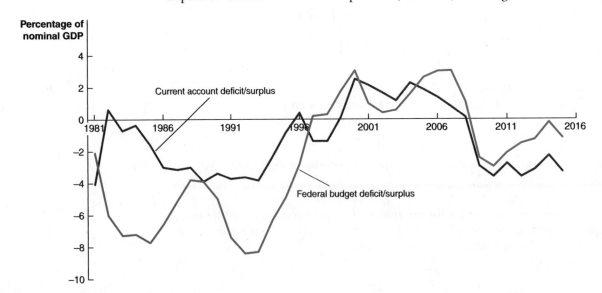

Figure 14.4 The Twin Canadian Deficits, 1981–2014

Before the mid-1990s, large federal budget deficits occurred at the same time as large current account deficits, but twin deficits did not occur in most other periods during these years, except for the 2008–2014 period, in the aftermath of the "Great Recession."

Sources: Data from Statistics Canada CANSIM series V61914609, V62425564, and V62295562. (Accessed 10 December 2015.)

When a government budget deficit leads to a decline in net exports, the result is sometimes referred to as the *twin deficits*, which refers to the possibility that a government budget deficit will also lead to a current account deficit. The twin deficits idea first became widely discussed in Canada during the early 1980s, when the federal government ran a large budget deficit that resulted in high interest rates, a high exchange value of the dollar, and a current account deficit.

Although there appears to be a tendency for twin deficits to occur in Canada (see Figure 14.4), the experience of other countries shows only mixed support for the twin deficits idea. For example, in the early 1980s, the United States had large federal budget deficits and large current account deficits. However, the twin deficits idea does not consistently match the experience of the United States after 1990. The large federal budget deficits of the early 1990s occurred at a time of relatively small current account deficits, and the budget surpluses of the late 1990s occurred at a time of then-record current account deficits. Both the current account deficit and the federal budget deficit increased in the early 2000s, but the federal budget deficit declined in the mid-2000s much more than the current account deficit. Beginning in 2008, the US federal budget deficit soared and then sharply declined, while the current account deficit declined.

Also, Germany ran large budget deficits and large current account deficits during the early 1990s, but Italy ran large budget deficits during the 1980s without running current account deficits. The saving and investment equation shows that an increase in the government budget deficit will not lead to an increase in the current account deficit, provided that either private saving increases or domestic investment declines.

| Making the Connection | Why Is the United States Called the "World's Largest Debtor"? |

The following graph shows the current account balance as a percentage of GDP for the United States for the period 1960–2014. The United States has had a current account deficit every year since 1982, with the exception of 1991. Between 1960 and 1975, the United States ran a current account deficit in only five years. Many economists believe that the current account deficits of the 1980s were closely related to the federal budget deficits of those years. High interest rates attracted foreign investors to US bonds, which raised the exchange rate between the US dollar and foreign currencies. The high exchange rate reduced US exports and increased imports, leading to current account deficits.

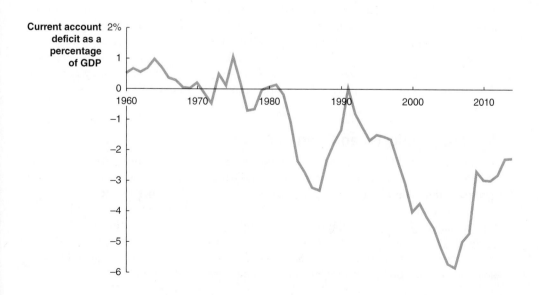

As the federal budget deficit in the United States narrowed in the mid-1990s and disappeared in the late 1990s, the foreign exchange value of the US dollar remained high—and large current account deficits continued—because foreign investors persisted in investing in the United States, despite low interest rates. In the late 1990s, a number of countries around the world, such as South Korea, Indonesia, Brazil, and Russia, suffered severe economic problems. In a process known as a *flight to quality*, many investors sold their investments in those countries and bought investments in the United States. In addition, the strong performance of the US stock market through the spring of 2000 attracted many investors. Finally, the sharp decline in private saving in the United States that began during the late 1990s also contributed to the US current account deficit. The fall in the value of the US dollar after 2008 helped reduce the size of the current account deficit. In late 2014 and 2015 though, the deficit was increasing along with the value of the dollar.

Are persistent current account deficits a problem for the United States? Current account deficits result in US net foreign investment being negative. Each year, foreign investors accumulate many more US assets—such as stocks, bonds, and factories—than US investors accumulate foreign assets. In 1986, for the first time since the nineteenth century, the value of foreign-owned assets in the United States became larger than the value of US-owned assets abroad. At the end of 2014, foreign investors owned about $7 trillion more of US assets than US investors owned of foreign assets, which is why the United States is sometimes called "the world's largest debtor." But the continued willingness of foreign investors to buy US stocks and bonds and of foreign companies to build factories in the United States can be seen as a vote of confidence in the strength of the US economy and the buying power of US consumers. When private saving rates declined in the United States to historically low levels in the mid-2000s, only the continued flow of funds from foreign investors made it possible for the United States to maintain the high levels of domestic investment required for economic growth. Beginning in 2009, private saving rates increased, but public saving turned sharply negative between 2009 and 2012 as the federal budget deficit soared. Even though public saving has been less negative in the past few years, domestic investment in the United States remains reliant on funds from foreign investors.

MyEconLab | **Your Turn:** Test your understanding by doing related problem 4.3 on page 413 at the end of this chapter.

Your Turn: Test your understanding by doing related problem 4.3 on page 413 at the end of this chapter.

14.5 LEARNING OBJECTIVE

Compare the effectiveness of monetary policy and fiscal policy in an open economy and in a closed economy.

Monetary Policy and Fiscal Policy in an Open Economy

When we discussed monetary policy and fiscal policy, we did not emphasize that Canada is an open economy (see Chapters 11 and 12). Now that we have explored some of the links among economies, we can look at the difference between how monetary policy and fiscal policy work in an open economy and how they work in a closed economy. Economists refer to the ways in which monetary policy and fiscal policy affect the domestic economy as *policy channels*. An open economy has more policy channels than a closed economy.

Monetary Policy in an Open Economy

When the Bank of Canada engages in an expansionary monetary policy, it typically buys government securities to lower interest rates and stimulate aggregate demand. In a closed economy, the main effect of lower interest rates is on domestic investment spending and purchases of consumer durables. In an open economy, lower interest rates will also affect the exchange rate between the dollar and foreign currencies. Lower interest rates will cause some investors in Canada and abroad to switch from investing in Canadian financial assets to investing in foreign financial assets. The result is a lower demand for the dollar relative to foreign currencies and a decline in the dollar's value. A lower exchange rate will decrease the price of Canadian products in foreign markets and increase the price of foreign products in Canada. As a result, net exports will increase. This additional policy channel will increase the ability of an expansionary monetary policy to affect aggregate demand.

When the Bank of Canada wants to reduce aggregate demand to reduce inflation, it engages in a contractionary monetary policy. The Bank of Canada sells government securities to increase interest rates and reduce aggregate demand. In a closed economy, the main effect is once again on domestic investment spending and purchases of consumer durables. In an open economy, higher interest rates will lead to a higher foreign exchange value of the dollar. The prices of Canadian products in foreign markets will increase, and the prices of foreign products in Canada will fall. As a result, net exports will fall. The contractionary policy will have a larger effect on aggregate demand, and therefore it will be more effective in slowing down the growth in economic activity. To summarize: *Monetary policy has a greater effect on aggregate demand in an open economy than in a closed economy.*

Fiscal Policy in an Open Economy

To engage in an expansionary fiscal policy, the federal government increases its purchases or cuts taxes. Increases in government purchases directly increase aggregate demand. Tax cuts increase aggregate demand by increasing household disposable income and business income, which results in increased consumption spending and investment spending. An expansionary fiscal policy may result in higher interest rates. In a closed economy, the main effect of higher interest rates is to reduce domestic investment spending and purchases of consumer durables. In an open economy, higher interest rates will also lead to an increase in the foreign exchange value of the dollar and a decrease in net exports. Therefore, in an open economy, an expansionary fiscal policy may be less effective because the *crowding out effect* may be larger. In a closed economy, only consumption and investment are crowded out by an expansionary fiscal policy. In an open economy, net exports may also be crowded out.

The government can fight inflation by using a contractionary fiscal policy to slow the growth of aggregate demand. A contractionary fiscal policy cuts government purchases or raises taxes to reduce household disposable income and consumption spending. It also reduces the federal budget deficit (or increases the budget surplus), which may lower interest rates. Lower interest rates will increase domestic investment and purchases of consumer durables, thereby offsetting some of the reduction in government spending and increases in taxes. In an open economy, lower interest rates will also reduce the foreign exchange value of the dollar and increase net exports. Therefore, in an open economy, a contractionary fiscal policy will have a smaller effect on aggregate demand and therefore will be less effective in slowing down an economy. In summary: *Fiscal policy has a smaller effect on aggregate demand in an open economy than in a closed economy.*

Economics in Your Life

The Norges Bank and Your Car Loan

At the beginning of this chapter, we posed this question: Will the Norges Bank's decision to sell its Canada bonds affect the interest rate you pay on your car loan? To sell its holdings of Canada bonds, Norway's central bank may have to offer them at a lower price. When the prices of bonds fall, the interest rates on them rise. As the interest rates on Canada bonds increase, the interest rates on corporate bonds and bank loans, including car loans, may also increase. So, the decision of the Norges Bank has the potential to increase the interest rate you pay on your car loan. In practice, the interest rate on your car loan is likely to be affected only if the Norges Bank sells a very large number of bonds and if investors consider it likely that other foreign central banks may soon do the same thing. The basic point is important, however: Economies are interdependent, and interest rates in Canada are not determined entirely by the actions of people in Canada.

Conclusion

At one time, Canadian policymakers—and economics textbooks—ignored the linkages between Canada and other economies. In the modern world, these linkages have become increasingly important, and economists and policymakers must take them into account when analyzing the economy. In Chapter 15, we will discuss further how the international financial system operates.

Chapter Summary and Problems

Key Terms

Balance of payments, p. 390

Balance of trade, p. 391

Capital account, p. 393

Closed economy, p. 390

Currency appreciation, p. 397

Currency depreciation, p. 397

Current account, p. 391

Financial account, p. 392

Net foreign investment, p. 393

Nominal exchange rate, p. 395

Open economy, p. 390

Real exchange rate, p. 402

Saving and investment equation, p. 404

Speculators, p. 398

Summary

*LO 14.1 Nearly all economies are *open economies* that trade with and invest in other economies. A *closed economy* has no transactions in trade or finance with other economies. The *balance of payments* is the record of a country's trade with other countries in goods, services, and assets. The *current account* records a country's net exports, net investment income, and net transfers. The *financial account* shows investments a country has made abroad and foreign investments received by the country. The *balance of trade* is the difference between the value of the goods a country exports and the value of the goods a country imports. *Net foreign investment* is the difference between capital outflows from a country and capital inflows. The *capital account* is a part of the balance of payments that records relatively minor transactions. Apart from measurement errors, the sum of the current account balance and the financial account balance must equal zero. Therefore, the balance of payments must also equal zero.

LO 14.2 The *nominal exchange rate* is the value of one country's currency in terms of another country's currency. The exchange rate is determined in the foreign exchange market by the demand and supply of a country's currency. Changes in the exchange rate are caused by shifts in demand or supply. The three main sets of factors that cause the supply and demand curves in the foreign exchange market to shift are (1) changes in the demand for Canadian-produced goods and services and changes in the demand for foreign-produced goods and services, (2) changes in the desire to invest in Canada and changes in the desire to invest in foreign countries, and (3) changes in the expectations of currency traders—particularly *speculators*—concerning the likely future value of the dollar and the likely future value of foreign currencies. *Currency appreciation* occurs when a currency's market value increases relative to another currency. *Currency depreciation* occurs when a currency's market value decreases relative to another currency. The *real exchange rate* is the price of domestic goods in terms of foreign goods. The real exchange rate is calculated by multiplying the nominal exchange rate by the ratio of the domestic price level to the foreign price level.

LO 14.3 A current account deficit must be exactly offset by a financial account surplus. The financial account is equal to net capital flows, which is equal to net foreign investment but with the opposite sign. Because the current account balance is roughly equal to net exports, we can conclude that net exports will equal net foreign investment. National saving is equal to private saving plus government saving. Private saving is equal to national income minus consumption and minus taxes. Government saving is the difference between taxes and government spending. As we saw in previous chapters, GDP (or national income) is equal to the sum of consumption, investment, government spending, and net exports. We can use this fact, our definitions of private and government saving, and the fact that net exports equal net foreign investment to arrive at an important relationship known as the *saving and investment equation:* $S = I + NFI$.

LO 14.4 When the government runs a budget deficit, national saving will decline unless private saving increases by the full amount of the budget deficit, which is unlikely. As the saving and investment equation ($S = I + NFI$) shows, the result of a decline in national saving must be a decline in either domestic investment or net foreign investment.

★"Learning Objective" is abbreviated to "LO" in the end-of-chapter material.

LO 14.5 When the Bank of Canada engages in an expansionary monetary policy, it buys government bonds to lower interest rates and increase aggregate demand. In a closed economy, the main effect of lower interest rates is on domestic investment spending and purchases of consumer durables. In an open economy, lower interest rates will also cause an increase in net exports. When the Bank of Canada wants to slow the rate of economic growth to reduce inflation, it engages in a contractionary monetary policy by selling government bonds to increase interest rates and reduce aggregate demand. In a closed economy, the main effect is once again on domestic investment and purchases of consumer durables. In an open economy, higher interest rates will also reduce net exports. We can conclude that monetary policy has a greater impact on aggregate demand in an open economy than in a closed economy. To engage in an expansionary fiscal policy, the government increases government spending or cuts taxes. An expansionary fiscal policy can lead to higher interest rates. In a closed economy, the main effect of higher interest rates is on domestic investment spending and spending on consumer durables. In an open economy, higher interest rates will also reduce net exports. A contractionary fiscal policy will reduce the budget deficit and may lower interest rates. In a closed economy, lower interest rates increase domestic investment and spending on consumer durables. In an open economy, lower interest rates also increase net exports. We can conclude that fiscal policy has a smaller impact on aggregate demand in an open economy than in a closed economy.

MyEconLab   Log in to MyEconLab to complete these exercises and get instant feedback.

Review Questions

LO 14.1

1.1 What is the relationship among the current account, the financial account, and the balance of payments?

1.2 What is the difference between net exports and the current account balance?

1.3 The late economist Herbert Stein described the accounts that comprise a country's balance of payments:

> A country is more likely to have a deficit in its current account the higher its price level, the higher its gross [domestic] product, the higher its interest rates, the lower its barriers to imports, and the more attractive its investment opportunities—all compared with conditions in other countries—and the higher its exchange rate. The effects of a change in one of these factors on the current account balance cannot be predicted without considering the effect on the other causal factors.

a. Briefly describe the transactions included in a country's current account.

b. Briefly explain why, compared to other countries, a country is more likely to have a deficit in its current account, holding other factors constant, for each of the following:
   i. A higher price level
   ii. An increase in interest rates
   iii. Lower barriers to imports
   iv. More attractive investment opportunities

LO 14.2

2.1 Suppose that the current exchange rate between the dollar and the euro is €0.7 = $1. If the exchange rate changes to €0.8 = $1 has the euro appreciated or depreciated against the dollar?

2.2 Why do foreign households and foreign firms demand Canadian dollars in exchange for foreign currency? Why do Canadian households and Canadian firms supply Canadian dollars in exchange for foreign currency?

2.3 What are the three main sets of factors that cause the supply and demand curves in the foreign exchange market to shift?

LO 14.3

3.1 Explain the relationship between net exports and net foreign investment.

3.2 What is the saving and investment equation? If national saving declines, what will happen to domestic investment and net foreign investment?

3.3 If a country saves more than it invests domestically, what must be true of its net foreign investment?

LO 14.4

4.1 What happens to national saving when the government runs a budget surplus? What is the twin deficits idea? Did it hold for Canada in the 1990s? Briefly explain.

4.2 Why were the early 2010s particularly difficult times for Canadian exporters?

4.3 Why is the United States sometimes called the "world's largest debtor"?

LO 14.5

5.1 What is meant by a "policy channel"?

5.2 Why does monetary policy have a greater effect on aggregate demand in an open economy than in a closed economy?

5.3 Why does fiscal policy have a smaller effect on aggregate demand in an open economy than in a closed economy?

Problems and Applications

LO 14.1

1.1 Use the information in the following table to prepare a balance of payments account, like the one shown in Table 14.1 on page 391. Assume that the balance on the capital account is zero.

Increase in foreign holdings of assets in Canada	$1181
Exports of goods	856
Imports of services	–256
Statistical discrepancy	?
Net transfers	–60
Exports of services	325
Income received on investments	392
Imports of goods	–1108
Increase in Canadian holdings of assets in foreign countries	–1040
Income payments on investments	–315

1.2 **[Related to the Don't Let This Happen to You on page 394]** In 2014, Germany had a balance of trade surplus of $217 billion and a current account surplus of $215 billion. Explain how Germany's current account surplus could be smaller than its trade surplus. In 2014, what would we expect Germany's balance on the financial account to have been? Briefly explain.

1.3 **[Related to Solved Problem 14.1 on page 394]** A news article notes, "China recorded a current-account surplus of $76.6 billion in the second quarter but that was offset by a deficit of the same amount on its capital and financial account." Is this outcome surprising? Briefly explain.

Reprinted with permission of China's Current-Account Surplus at $76.6 bln: SAFE," marketwatch.com, August 7, Copyright © 2015 Dow Jones & Company, Inc. All Rights Reserved Worldwide.

1.4 **[Related to Solved Problem 14.1 on page 394]** An article in the *Wall Street Journal* about China's balance of payments contained the following observations: "A country's balance of payments still has to add up to zero. If foreign investors wish to acquire assets denominated in yuan, the necessary implication is that China will have to run a trade deficit."
   a. Do you agree that the balance of payments must add up to zero?
   b. If China were to have a deficit in its balance of trade of –100 billion yuan, must it have a surplus in its financial account of +100 billion yuan? Briefly explain.

LO 14.2

2.1 **[Related to Making the Connection on page 396]** On January 1, 2002, there were 15 member countries in the European Union. Twelve of those countries eliminated their own individual currencies and began using a new common currency, the euro. For a three-year period from January 1, 1999, through December 31, 2001, these 12 countries priced goods and services in terms of both their own currencies and the euro. During that period, the value of their currencies was fixed against each other and against the euro. So during that time, the US dollar had an exchange rate against each of these currencies and against the euro. The information in the following table shows the fixed exchange rates of four European currencies against the euro and their exchange rates against the US dollar on March 2, 2001. Use the information in the table to calculate the exchange rate between the US dollar and the euro (in euros per US dollar) on March 2, 2001.

Currency	Units per Euro (Fixed)	Units per US Dollar (as of March 2, 2001)
German mark	1.9558	2.0938
French franc	6.5596	7.0223
Italian lira	1936.2700	2072.8700
Portuguese escudo	200.4820	214.6300

2.2 Use the graph to answer the following questions.

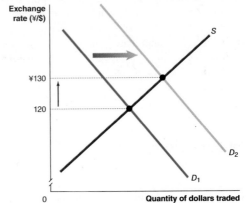

   a. Briefly explain whether the dollar appreciated or depreciated against the yen.
   b. Which of the following events could have caused the shift in demand shown in the graph?
      i. Interest rates in Canada decline.
      ii. Income rises in Japan.
      iii. Speculators begin to believe the value of the Canadian dollar will be higher in the future.

2.3. **[Related to the Making the Connection on page 399]** Paul De Grauwe, an economist at the London School of Economics, wrote in the *Economist* that the quantitative easing policies of the European Central Bank "will contribute to a further weakening of the euro vis-a-vis other currencies such as the dollar, the pound and the yuan, thereby increasing exports and boosting inflation."
   a. What does De Grauwe mean by "a weakening of the euro"?
   b. What is quantitative easing, and why should it lead to a weakening of the euro?
   c. If you ran a business in France that exported to Canada and Japan, would this development help you? If you were a consumer in France, would this development help you? Briefly explain.

Paul De Grauwe, "The Sad Consequences of the Fear of QE," *The Economist*, January 21, 2015.

2.4 According to an article in the *Wall Street Journal*, in 2014, "The Australian dollar tumbled after muted inflation data scotched investors' expectations that the central bank would raise interest rates."
   a. Why would the inflation rate being lower than expected make it less likely that the Australian central bank would raise interest rates?
   b. Why would the fact that it was less likely that the Australian central bank was going to raise interest rates cause the value of the Australian dollar to fall?

James Ramage, "Australian Dollar Tumbles after Data Scotches Rate-Increase Expectations," *Wall Street Journal*, April 23, 2014.

2.5 **[Related to Don't Let This Happen to You on page 401]** If we know the exchange rate between Country A's currency and Country B's currency and we know the exchange rate between Country B's currency and Country C's currency, then we can compute the exchange rate between Country A's currency and Country C's currency.

  a. Suppose the exchange rate between the Japanese yen and the Canadian dollar is currently ¥75 = $1 and the exchange rate between the British pound and the Canadian dollar is £0.62 = $1. What is the exchange rate between the yen and the pound?

  b. Suppose the exchange rate between the yen and dollar changes to ¥85 = $1 and the exchange rate between the pound and dollar changes to £0.55 = $1. Has the dollar appreciated or depreciated against the yen? Has the dollar appreciated or depreciated against the pound? Has the yen appreciated or depreciated against the pound?

2.6 **[Related to Solved Problem 14.2 on page 401]** An article in the *Wall Street Journal* notes, "For every one yen rise in the value of the dollar, Fuji Heavy's full-year operating profit increases by ¥9.7 billion, the company says." Would Honda's profits be likely to increase as much as a result of a rise in the value of the dollar versus the yen? Briefly explain.

Yoko Kubota, "Subaru Rides a Weaker Yen into the U.S.," *Wall Street Journal*, November 15, 2014.

LO 14.3

3.1 Writing in the *New York Times*, Simon Johnson, an economist at MIT, makes the argument that people outside the United States may at some point decide to "save less (in which case they may hold onto their existing United States government debt but not want to buy so much of new issues)." What does saving by people outside the United States have to do with sales of US government debt? Does the level of domestic investment occurring in foreign countries matter for your answer? Briefly explain.

Simon Johnson, "The Real Fiscal Risks in the United States," *New York Times*, December 6, 2012.

3.2 In 2014, domestic investment in Japan was 21.7 percent of GDP, and Japanese national saving was 22.4 percent of GDP. What percentage of GDP was Japanese net foreign investment?

3.3 In 2014, France's net foreign investment was negative. Which was larger in France in 2014: national saving or domestic investment? Briefly explain.

3.4 **[Related to Solved Problem 14.3 on page 405]** Look again at *Solved Problem 14.3*, in which we derived the saving and investment equation $S = I + NX$. In deriving this equation, we assumed that national income was equal to Y. But Y only includes income *earned* by households. In the modern Canadian economy, households receive substantial transfer payments—such as social security payments and Employment Insurance payments—from the government. Suppose that we define *national income* as being equal to $Y + TR$, where TR equals government transfer payments, and we also define government spending as being equal to $G + TR$. Show that after making these adjustments, we end up with the same saving and investment equation.

LO 14.4

4.1 An investment analyst recommended that investors "gravitate toward the stronger currencies and countries that are running current-account and fiscal surpluses," such as South Korea and Taiwan.

  a. Holding all other factors constant, would we expect a country that is running a government budget surplus to have a currency that is increasing in value or decreasing in value? Briefly explain.

  b. Holding all other factors constant, would we expect a country that has a currency that is increasing in value to have an increasing or decreasing current account surplus? Briefly explain.

  c. Is the combination of economic characteristics this analyst has identified likely to be commonly found among countries? Briefly explain.

Paul J. Lim, "Suddenly, BRIC Markets Are on a Shakier Foundation," *Wall Street Journal*, January 9, 2015.

4.2 According to an article in the *Economist*, "countries with persistent current-account deficits tend to have higher real interest rates than surplus countries." What do high interest rates have to do with current account deficits?

Source: "Carry on Trading," Economist, August 10, 2013. http://www.economist.com/news/finance-and-economics/21583294-why-nominal-interest-rate-differentials-are-important-currency-markets-carry

4.3 **[Related to Making the Connection on page 407]** Why might "the continued willingness of foreign investors to buy Canadian stocks and bonds and foreign companies to build factories in Canada" result in Canada running a current account deficit?

LO 14.5

5.1 An article in the *Economist* quotes the finance minister of Peru as saying, "We are one of the most open economies of Latin America." What did he mean by Peru being an "open economy"? Is fiscal policy in Peru likely to be more or less effective than it would be in a less open economy? Briefly explain.

Source: Hold on Tight," Economist, February 2, 2013. http://www.economist.com/news/americas/21571162-biggest-threats-latin-americas-economic-star-are-overconfidence-and-complacency-hold

5.2 Suppose that Bank of Canada policy leads to higher interest rates in Canada.

  a. How will this policy affect real GDP in the short run if Canada is a closed economy?

  b. How will this policy affect real GDP in the short run if Canada is an open economy?

  c. How will your answer to part (b) change if interest rates also rise in the countries that are the major trading partners of Canada?

5.3 Suppose the federal government increases spending without also increasing taxes. In the short run, how will this action affect real GDP and the price level in a closed economy? How will the effects of this action differ in an open economy?

MyEconLab   MyEconLab is an online tool designed to help you master the concepts covered in your course. It will create a personalized study plan to stimulate and measure your learning. Log in to take advantage of this powerful study aid, and to access quizzes and other valuable course-related material.

CHAPTER

15

The International Financial System

Chapter Outline and Learning Objectives

Bayer Uses a Weak Euro to Increase Sales

Most people in North America know the German firm Bayer mainly from its aspirin, which is sold in bottles with labels that display the firm's name in a distinctive cross. Although the chemical formula for aspirin had been known for decades, it was only in 1899 that Bayer began marketing aspirin as a pain reliever. Because no other effective over-the-counter pain relievers were available until the 1950s, Bayer aspirin was probably the most profitable medication ever sold.

Today, Bayer sells a variety of items, including prescription and over-the-counter pharmaceuticals and agricultural products. Bayer's acquisition of Merck & Company's over-the-counter unit in 2014 added brand names such as Coppertone, Dr. Scholl's, and Claritin to its product line. In addition to exports, Bayer has affiliates in North America, Latin and South America, Europe, and Asia that manufacture and sell its products. As a result, it receives revenue in many different currencies. As the exchange rate of each of the currencies changes relative to the euro, the value of Bayer's sales and profits change.

German manufacturers benefited from the introduction of the euro, the common currency of 19 members of the European Union. Because of the euro, Bayer and other German firms don't have to worry about fluctuations in exchange rates within most of Europe. Before the adoption of the euro, countries such as France, Italy, and Spain were able to bring about declines in the exchange values of their currencies, which made the output of their companies' products more competitive with those of Germany. These countries can no longer pursue this strategy in competing with Germany. When Bayer and other German companies export outside Europe, they still must deal with fluctuations in the value of the euro. When the value of the euro increases, as it did during 2012 and 2013, the prices of goods exported from Germany increase, and Bayer's sales can be hurt. But when the value of the euro falls, as it did during 2014 and 2015, it's good news for Bayer and other German exporters. For example, in the second quarter of 2015, Bayer's profits rose nearly 20 percent as a result of the lower value of the euro.

In this chapter, we will look more closely at the international financial system and at what determines fluctuations in exchange rates.

Based on Bryce Hoffman, "Bayer CEO Focuses On Company's Strengths," *Forbes*, April 4, 2015; Christopher Alessi, "Bayer Profit Rises on Healthy Currency Effects," *Wall Street Journal*, July 29, 2015; Peter Loftus, "Bayer Bulks Up Its Medicine Chest With Merck Brands," *Wall Street Journal*, May 7, 2014; and American Chemical Society, "Molecule of the Week: Aspirin," June 4, 2012.

Economics in Your Life

Exchange Rate Risk Can Affect Your Savings

Suppose that you decide to accept a job in Japan. You plan to work there for the next 10 years, build up some savings, and then return to Canada. As you prepare for your move, you read that economists expect the average productivity of Japanese firms to grow faster than the average productivity of Canadian firms over the next 10 years. If economists are correct, all else being equal, will the savings that you accumulate (in yen) be worth more or less in Canadian dollars than they would have been worth without the relative gains in Japanese productivity? As you read this chapter, try to answer this question. You can check your answer against the one we provide on page 430 at the end of this chapter.

A key fact about the international economy is that exchange rates among the major currencies fluctuate. These fluctuations have important consequences for firms, consumers, and governments. In Chapter 14, we discussed the basics of how exchange rates are determined. We also looked at the relationship between a country's imports and exports, and at capital flows into and out of a country. In this chapter, we will look further at the international financial system and at the role central banks play in the system.

Floating currency The outcome of a country allowing its currency's exchange rate to be determined by demand and supply.

Exchange Rate Systems

A country's exchange rate can be determined in several ways. Some countries simply allow the exchange rate to be determined by demand and supply, just as other prices are. A country that allows demand and supply to determine the value of its currency is said to have a **floating currency**. Some countries attempt to keep the exchange rate between their currency and another currency constant. For example, China kept the exchange rate constant between its currency, the yuan, and the US dollar, from 1994 until 2005, when it began allowing greater exchange rate flexibility. When countries can agree on how exchange rates should be determined, economists say that there is an **exchange rate system**. Currently, many countries, including Canada and the United States, allow their currencies to float most of the time, although they occasionally intervene to buy and sell their currency or other currencies to affect exchange rates. In other words, many countries attempt to *manage* the float of their currencies. As a result, the current exchange rate system is a **managed float exchange rate system**.

15.1 LEARNING OBJECTIVE

Understand how different exchange rate systems operate.

Exchange rate system An agreement among countries about how exchange rates should be determined.

Managed float exchange rate system The current exchange rate system, under which the value of most currencies is determined by demand and supply, with occasional government intervention.

Fixed exchange rate system A system under which countries agree to keep the exchange rates among their currencies fixed for long periods.

Historically, the two most important alternatives to the managed float exchange rate system were the *gold standard* and the *Bretton Woods system*. These were both **fixed exchange rate systems**, where exchange rates remained constant for long periods. Under the gold standard, a country's currency consisted of gold coins and paper currency that the government was committed to redeem for gold. When countries agree to keep the value of their currencies constant, there is a fixed exchange rate system. The gold standard was a fixed exchange rate system that lasted from the nineteenth century until the 1930s.

Under the gold standard, exchange rates were determined by the relative amounts of gold in each country's currency, and the size of a country's money supply was determined by the amount of gold available. To rapidly expand its money supply during a war or an economic depression, a country would need to abandon the gold standard. By the mid-1930s, in response to the Great Depression, Canada and most other countries had abandoned the gold standard. Although during the following decades there were occasional discussions about restoring the gold standard, there was no serious attempt to do so.

Bretton Woods system An exchange rate system that lasted from 1944 to 1973, under which countries pledged to buy and sell their currencies at a fixed rate against the dollar.

A conference held in Bretton Woods, New Hampshire, in 1944 set up an exchange rate system in which the United States pledged to buy or sell gold at a fixed price of $35 per ounce. The central banks of all other members of the new **Bretton Woods system** pledged to buy and sell their currencies at a fixed rate against the US dollar. By fixing their exchange rates against the US dollar, these countries were fixing the exchange rates among their currencies as well. Unlike under the gold standard, neither the United States nor any other country was willing to redeem its paper currency for gold domestically. The United States would redeem dollars for gold only if they were presented by a foreign central bank. Fixed exchange rate regimes can run into difficulties because exchange rates are not free to adjust quickly to changes in demand and supply for currencies. As we will see in the next section, central banks often encounter difficulty if they are required to keep an exchange rate fixed over a period of years. By the early 1970s, the difficulty of keeping exchange rates fixed led to the end of the Bretton Woods system.

Don't Let This Happen to You

Remember that Modern Currencies Are Fiat Money

Although Canada has not been on the gold standard since the beginning of World War I, many people still believe that somehow gold continues to "back" Canadian currency. Although the Canadian government still owns billions of dollars worth of gold bars, this gold no longer has any connection to the amount of paper money issued by the Bank of Canada.

As we saw in Chapter 10, Canadian currency—like the currencies of other countries—is *fiat money*, which means that it has no value except as money. The link between gold and money that existed for centuries has been broken in modern economies.

MyEconLab

Your Turn: Test your understanding by doing related problem 1.1 on page 431 at the end of this chapter.

15.2 LEARNING OBJECTIVE

Discuss the three key features of the current exchange rate system.

Euro The common currency of many European countries.

The Current Exchange Rate System

The current exchange rate system has three important aspects:

1. Canada allows the dollar to float against other major currencies.
2. Nineteen countries in Europe have adopted a single currency, the **euro**.
3. Some developing countries have attempted to keep their currencies' exchange rates fixed against the US dollar or another major currency.

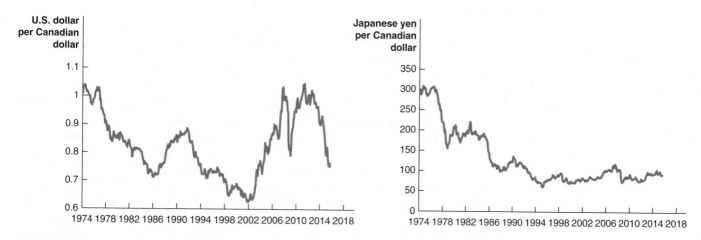

Figure 15.1 US Dollar–Canadian Dollar and Yen–Canadian Dollar Exchange Rates, 1974–2015

Panel (a) shows that from the end of the Bretton Woods system through November 2015, there have been a number of long swings in the US dollar per Canadian dollar exchange rate, but that overall the Canadian dollar did not lose value against the US dollar. Panel (b) shows that

during the same period, the Canadian dollar lost value against the Japanese yen.

Source: Data from Statistics Canada CANSIM II series V37426 and V37456 (Accessed December 7 2015).

We begin our discussion of the current exchange rate system by looking at the changing value of the Canadian dollar over time. In discussing the value of the dollar, we can look further at what determines exchange rates in the short run and in the long run.

The Floating Canadian Dollar

Since 1973, the value of the Canadian dollar has fluctuated widely against other major currencies. Panel (a) of Figure 15.1 shows the exchange rate between the Canadian dollar and the US dollar between January 1974 and November 2015, and panel (b) shows the exchange rate between the Canadian dollar and the Japanese yen for the same period. Remember that the dollar increases in value when it takes more units of foreign currency to buy $1, and it falls in value when it takes fewer units of foreign currency to buy $1. From January 1974 to November 2015, the Canadian dollar lost about 70 percent in value against the yen, and there have been a number of long swings in the US dollar per Canadian dollar exchange rate. Overall, however, the Canadian dollar did not lose much value against the US dollar over this period.

What Determines Exchange Rates in the Long Run?

Over the past 40 years, why has the value of the Canadian dollar fallen against the Japanese yen and fluctuated wildly against the US dollar? In the short run, the two most important causes of exchange rate movements are changes in interest rates—which cause investors to change their views of which countries' financial investments will yield the highest returns—and changes in investors' expectations about the future values of currencies. Over the long run, other factors are also important in explaining movements in exchange rates.

The Theory of Purchasing Power Parity. It seems reasonable that, in the long run, exchange rates should be at a level that makes it possible to buy the same amount of goods and services with the equivalent amount of any country's currency. In other words, the purchasing power of every country's currency should be the same. The idea that in the long run, exchange rates move to equalize the purchasing power of different currencies is called the theory of **purchasing power parity**.

Purchasing power parity The theory that in the long run, exchange rates move to equalize the purchasing powers of different currencies.

Consider a simple example: Suppose that a Hershey candy bar has a price of $1 in Canada and £1 in the United Kingdom and that the exchange rate is £1 = $1. In that case, at least with respect to candy bars, the dollar and the pound have equivalent purchasing power. If the price of a Hershey bar increases to £2 in the United Kingdom but stays at $1 in Canada, the exchange rate will have to change to £2 per $1 in order for the pound to maintain its relative purchasing power. As long as exchange rates adjust to reflect purchasing power, it will be possible to buy a Hershey bar for $1 in Canada or to exchange $1 for £2 and buy the candy bar in the United Kingdom.

If exchange rates are not at the values indicated by purchasing power parity, it appears that there are opportunities to make a profit. Suppose a Hershey candy bar sells for £2 in the United Kingdom and $1 in Canada and the exchange rate between the dollar and the pound is £1 = $1. In this case, it would be possible to exchange £1 million for $1 million and use the dollars to buy 1 million Hershey bars in Canada. The Hershey bars could then be shipped to the United Kingdom, where they could be sold for £2 million. The result of these transactions would be a profit of £1 million (minus any shipping costs). In fact, if the dollar–pound exchange rate does not reflect the purchasing power for many products—not just Hershey bars—this process could be repeated until extremely large profits were made. In practice, though, as people attempted to make these profits by exchanging pounds for dollars, they would bid up the value of the dollar until it reached the purchasing power exchange rate of £2 = $1. Once the exchange rate reflected the purchasing power of the two currencies, there would be no further opportunities for profit. This mechanism appears to guarantee that exchange rates will be at the levels determined by purchasing power parity.

Three real-world complications, though, keep purchasing power parity from being a complete explanation of exchange rates, even in the long run:

1. **Not all products can be traded internationally.** Where goods are traded internationally, profits can be made whenever exchange rates do not reflect their purchasing power parity values. However, more than half of all goods and services produced in Canada and most other countries are not traded internationally. When a good or service is not traded internationally, its price will not be the same in every country. Suppose that the exchange rate is £1 for $1, but the price for having a cavity filled by a dentist is twice as high in Canada as it is in the United Kingdom. In this case, there is no way to buy up the low-priced British service and resell it in Canada. Because many goods and services are not traded internationally, exchange rates will not reflect exactly the relative purchasing powers of currencies.

2. **Products and consumer preferences are different across countries.** We expect the same product to sell for the same price around the world, but if a product is similar but not identical to another product, their prices might be different. For example, a 3-gram Hershey candy bar may sell for a different price in Canada than a 3-gram Cadbury candy bar does in the United Kingdom. Prices of the same product may also differ across countries if consumer preferences differ. If consumers in the United Kingdom like candy bars more than consumers in Canada, a Hershey candy bar may sell for more in the United Kingdom than in Canada.

3. **Countries impose barriers to trade.** Most countries, including Canada and the United States, impose *tariffs* and *quotas* on imported goods. A **tariff** is a tax imposed by a government on imports. A **quota** is a government-imposed numerical limit on the quantity of a good that can be imported. For example, Canada has a quota on imports of milk. As a result, the price of milk in Canada is much higher than the price of milk in other countries. Because of the quota, there is no legal way to buy up the cheap foreign milk and resell it in Canada.

Tariff A tax imposed by a government on imports.

Quota A numerical limit that a government imposes on the quantity of a good that can be imported into the country.

Making the Connection

The Big Mac Theory of Exchange Rates

In a lighthearted attempt to test the accuracy of the theory of purchasing power parity, *The Economist* regularly compares the prices of Big Macs in different countries. If purchasing power parity holds, you should be able to take the dollars required to buy a Big Mac in the United States and exchange them for the amount of foreign currency needed to buy a Big Mac in any other country. The following table is for July 2015, when Big Macs were selling for an average price of $4.79 in the United States. The "implied exchange rate" shows what the exchange rate would be if purchasing power parity held for Big Macs. For example, a Big Mac sold for 49 pesos in Mexico and $4.79 in the United States, so for purchasing power parity to hold, the exchange rate should have been 49 pesos/$4.79, or 10.23 pesos = $1. The actual exchange rate in July 2015 was 15.74 pesos = $1. So, on Big Mac purchasing power parity grounds, the Mexican peso was *undervalued* against the US dollar by 35 percent: ([10.23 − 15.74]/15.74) × 100 = −35%). That is, if Big Mac purchasing power parity held, it would have taken 35 percent fewer Mexican pesos to buy a US dollar than it actually did.

Is the price of a Big Mac in Mexico City the same as the price of a Big Mac in New York?

Could you take advantage of this difference between the purchasing power parity exchange rate and the actual exchange rate to become fabulously wealthy by buying up low-priced Big Macs in New York and reselling them at a higher price in Mexico City? Unfortunately, the low-priced US Big Macs would be a soggy mess by the time you got them to Mexico City. The fact that Big Mac prices are not the same around the world illustrates one reason purchasing power parity does not hold exactly: Many goods are not traded internationally.

Country	Big Mac Price	Implied Exchange Rate	Actual Exchange Rate
Mexico	49 pesos	10.23 pesos per dollar	15.74 pesos per dollar
Japan	370 yen	77.24 yen per dollar	123.94 yen per dollar
United Kingdom	2.89 pounds	0.60 pound per dollar	0.64 pound per dollar
Switzerland	6.5 Swiss francs	1.36 Swiss francs per dollar	0.95 Swiss francs per dollar
Indonesia	30 500 rupiahs	6367 rupiahs per dollar	13 345 rupiahs per dollar
Canada	5.85 Canadian dollars	1.22 Canadian dollars per US dollar	1.29 Canadian dollars per US dollar
China	17 yuan	3.55 yuan per dollar	6.21 yuan per dollar

Based on The Big Mac Index," *The Economist*, July 16, 2015.

Your Turn: Test your understanding by doing related problem 2.4 on page 432 at the end of this chapter.

MyEconLab

Solved Problem **15.1**

Calculating Purchasing Power Parity Exchange Rates Using Big Macs

Fill in the missing values in the following table. Remember that the implied exchange rate shows what the exchange rate would be if purchasing power parity held for Big Macs. Assume that the Big Mac is selling for $4.79 in the United States. Explain whether the US dollar is overvalued or undervalued relative to each currency and predict what will happen in the future to each exchange rate if the actual exchange rate moves toward the purchasing power parity exchange rate. Finally, calculate the implied exchange rate between the Polish zloty and the Brazilian real (the plural of *real* is *reais*) and explain which currency is undervalued in terms of Big Mac purchasing power parity.

Country	Big Mac Price	Implied Exchange Rate	Actual Exchange Rate
Brazil	13.5 reais	_____	3.15 reais per dollar
Poland	9.6 zlotys	_____	3.77 zlotys per dollar
South Korea	4300 won	_____	1143.5 won per dollar
Sweden	43.7 kronor	_____	8.52 kronor per dollar

Solving the Problem

Step 1: Review the chapter material. This problem is about the theory of purchasing power parity, as illustrated by prices of Big Macs, so you may want to review the sections "The Theory of Purchasing Power Parity," which begins on page 417 and the *Making the Connection "The Big Mac Theory of Exchange Rates"* on page 419.

Step 2: Fill in the table. To calculate the purchasing power parity exchange rate, divide the foreign currency price of a Big Mac by the US price. For example, the implied exchange rate between the Brazilian real and the US dollar is 13.5 reais/$4.79, or 2.82 reais per dollar.

Country	Big Mac Price	Implied Exchange Rate	Actual Exchange Rate
Brazil	13.5 reais	2.82 reais per dollar	3.15 reais per dollar
Poland	9.6 zlotys	2.00 zlotys per dollar	3.77 zlotys per dollar
South Korea	4300 won	897.7 won per dollar	1,143.5 won per dollar
Sweden	43.7 kronor	9.12 kronor per dollar	8.52 kronor per dollar

Step 3: Explain whether the US dollar is overvalued or undervalued against the other currencies. The US dollar is overvalued if the actual exchange rate is greater than the implied exchange rate, and it is undervalued if the actual exchange rate is less than the implied exchange rate. In this case, the US dollar is overvalued against the real, the zloty, and the won, but it is undervalued against the krona. So, we would predict that in the future the value of the US dollar should rise against the krona but fall against the real, the zloty, and the won.

Step 4: Calculate the implied exchange rate between the zloty and the real. The implied exchange rate between the zloty and the real is 9.6 zlotys/13.5 reais, or 0.71 zlotys per real. We can calculate the actual exchange rate by taking the ratio of zlotys per US dollar to reais per US dollar: 3.77 zlotys/3.15 reais, or 1.20 zlotys per real. Therefore, the zloty is undervalued relative to the real because our Big Mac purchasing power parity calculation tells us that it should take fewer zlotys to buy a real than it actually does.

Based on The Big Mac Index," *The Economist*, July 16, 2015.

MyEconLab   **Your Turn:** For more practice, do related problem 2.5 on page 432 at the end of this chapter.

The Four Determinants of Exchange Rates in the Long Run. We can take into account the shortcomings of the theory of purchasing power parity to develop a more complete explanation of how exchange rates are determined in the long run. There are four main determinants of exchange rates in the long run:

1. **Relative price levels.** The purchasing power parity theory is correct in arguing that, in the long run, the most important determinant of exchange rates between two countries' currencies is their relative price levels. If prices of goods and services

rise faster in Canada than in the United States, the value of the Canadian dollar has to decline to maintain demand for Canadian products. Over the past 40 years, the price level in Canada has risen somewhat faster than the price level in the United States. This fact helps explain why the US dollar has increased in value against the Canadian dollar.

2. **Relative rates of productivity growth.** When the productivity of a firm increases, the firm is able to produce more goods and services using fewer workers, machines, or other inputs. The firm's costs of production fall, and usually so do the prices of its products. If the average productivity of Japanese firms increases faster than the average productivity of Canadian firms, Japanese products will have relatively lower prices than Canadian products, which increases the quantity demanded of Japanese products relative to Canadian products. As a result, the value of the yen should rise against the dollar. For most of the period from the early 1970s to the early 1990s, Japanese productivity increased faster than Canadian productivity, which contributed to the fall in the value of the Canadian dollar versus the yen.

3. **Preferences for domestic and foreign goods.** If consumers in the United States increase their preferences for Canadian products, the demand for Canadian dollars will increase relative to the demand for US dollars, and the Canadian dollar will increase in value relative to the US dollar. During the 1970s and 1980s, many Canadian consumers increased their preferences for Japanese products, particularly automobiles and consumer electronics. This greater preference for Japanese products helped to increase the value of the yen relative to the Canadian dollar.

4. **Tariffs and quotas.** The Canadian milk quota forces Canadian firms to buy expensive Canadian milk rather than less expensive foreign milk. The quota increases the demand for Canadian dollars relative to the currencies of foreign milk producers and, therefore, leads to a higher exchange rate. Changes in tariffs and quotas have not been a significant factor in explaining trends in the US dollar–Canadian dollar or yen–Canadian dollar exchange rates.

Because these four factors change over time, the value of one country's currency can increase or decrease by substantial amounts in the long run. These changes in exchange rates can create problems for firms. A decline in the value of a country's currency lowers the foreign currency prices of the country's exports and increases the prices of imports. An increase in the value of a country's currency has the reverse effect. Firms can be both helped and hurt by exchange rate fluctuations.

The Euro

A second key aspect of the current exchange rate system is that most countries in Western Europe have adopted a single currency. After World War II, many of these countries wanted to more closely integrate their economies. In 1957, Belgium, France, West Germany, Italy, Luxembourg, and the Netherlands signed the Treaty of Rome, which established the European Economic Community, often called the European Common Market. Tariffs and quotas on products being shipped within the European Common Market were greatly reduced. Over the years, Britain, Sweden, Denmark, Finland, Austria, Greece, Ireland, Spain, and Portugal joined the European Economic Community, which was renamed the European Union (EU) in 1991. By 2015, 28 countries were members of the EU.

EU members decided to move to a common currency beginning in 1999. Three of the 15 countries that were then members of the EU—the United Kingdom, Denmark, and Sweden—decided to retain their domestic currencies. The move to a common currency took place in several stages. On January 1, 1999, the exchange rates of the 12 participating countries were permanently fixed against each other and against the common currency, the *euro*. At first the euro was a pure *unit of account*. No euro currency was actually in circulation, although firms began quoting prices in both the domestic currency and euros. On January 1, 2002, euro coins and paper currency were introduced, and on June 1, 2002, the old domestic currencies were withdrawn from

Figure 15.2

Countries Adopting the Euro

The 19 member countries of the European Union (EU) that had adopted the euro as their common currency as of the end of 2015 are shaded with red hash marks. The members of the EU that had not adopted the euro are coloured tan. Countries in white are not members of the EU.

circulation. Figure 15.2 shows the 19 countries in the EU that had adopted the euro as of the end of 2015. These countries are sometimes called the *euro zone*.

A new European Central Bank (ECB) was also established. Although the central banks of the member countries continue to exist, the ECB has assumed responsibility for monetary policy and for issuing currency. The ECB is run by a governing council that consists of a six-member executive board—appointed by the participating governments—and the governors of the central banks of the 19 member countries that have adopted the euro. The ECB represents a unique experiment in allowing a multinational organization to control the domestic monetary policies of independent countries.

Making the Connection | **Greece and Germany: Diverse Economies, Common Currency**

Most of Europe experienced relative economic stability from the introduction of the euro in 2002 to the beginning of the global economic downturn in 2007. With low interest rates, low inflation rates, and expanding employment and production, the advantages of having a common currency seemed obvious. Firms no longer had to worry about exchange rate instability when selling within Europe, and the cost of doing business was reduced because, for example, it was no longer necessary for a French firm to exchange francs for marks to do business in Germany.

By 2008, however, some economists and policymakers questioned whether the euro was making the effects of the global recession worse. The countries using the euro cannot pursue independent monetary policies because the ECB determines those policies from its headquarters in Frankfurt, Germany. Countries that were particularly hard hit by the recession—for example, Spain, where the unemployment rate had more than doubled to 18 percent by 2009 and was 22 percent in mid-2015—were unable to pursue a more expansionary policy than the ECB was willing to implement for the euro zone as a whole. Similarly, countries could not attempt to revive their exports by allowing their currencies to depreciate because (1) many of their exports were to other euro zone countries, and (2) the value of the euro was determined by factors affecting the euro zone as a whole.

In 2010, a *sovereign debt* crisis developed when investors began to believe that a number of European governments, particularly those of Greece, Ireland, Spain, Portugal, and Italy, would have difficulty making interest payments on their bonds—or sovereign debt. The International Monetary Fund and the European Union put together aid packages to keep the countries from defaulting. In exchange for the aid, these countries were required to adopt *austerity programs*—cutting government spending and raising taxes— even though doing so sparked protests from unions, students, and other groups. The controversy was greatest over Greece, which had large debts and a high unemployment rate, and where political resistance to multiple rounds of austerity made it uncertain in 2015 whether the country would remain in the euro zone.

Did the euro contribute to the slow recovery from the 2007–2009 financial crisis? The figure below shows the average unemployment rate for the euro zone countries for the period 2007–2014 compared with the unemployment rates for the United States, the United Kingdom, and Iceland. The euro zone was still suffering from high unemployment rates more than seven years after the beginning of the financial crisis. The German economy, however, performed very well during and after the financial crisis, with its unemployment rate in 2014 being below what it had been in 2007. In fact, German firms, including Bayer, benefited from the euro because if the country had retained the deutsche mark as its currency, the deutsche mark would likely have increased in value during 2014 and 2015. The euro decreased in value during that period, thereby increasing German exports more than would have happened without the common currency. As the blue line shows, the performance of the euro zone looks significantly worse if Germany is left out.

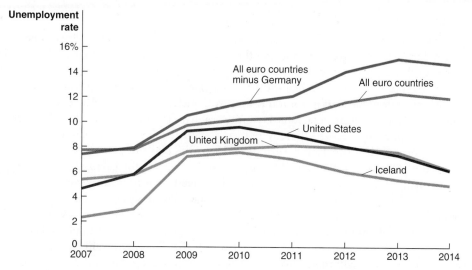

The United Kingdom, Iceland, and the United States all use their own currencies and all recovered more quickly from the financial crisis and recession than most of the countries using the euro. The United Kingdom is a member of the European Union but continues to use the pound as its currency. Iceland is not a member of the European Union and does not use the euro. The situation in Iceland is particularly interesting because no country was more severely affected by the global financial crisis. Although a small country, its banks aggressively made loans around the world in the years leading up to the crisis. By 2007, Icelandic banks had made loans equal to nine times the country's GDP. When many borrowers defaulted on those loans, the government of Iceland took over the banks and assumed their debt of about $100 billion—or more than $300 000 for each citizen of Iceland. Iceland's krona, the British pound, and the US dollar all depreciated against the euro in the period immediately following the financial crisis, which was good news for these countries because it helped them increase exports, but it was bad news for countries using the euro, many of which faced declining exports outside Europe.

The crisis over Greece highlighted another key problem facing the euro: the lack of coordinated government spending policies. The euro zone is a *monetary union*—the member countries all use the same currency and follow a joint monetary policy—but not a *fiscal union*—the member countries pursue independent fiscal policies. Although we don't usually think of countries in these terms, the provinces of Canada, the states of the United States, and the prefectures of Japan represent both monetary unions and fiscal unions. If during a recession Saskatchewan suffers a particularly sharp decline in production and employment, the federal government provides support to the economy of Saskatchewan through unemployment insurance and other transfer programs. Greece, by contrast, must fund such payments largely from its own revenues. The resulting large government budget deficits contributed to the sovereign debt crisis discussed earlier.

Some economists and policymakers wonder whether a monetary union of such diverse economies can survive in the absence of further fiscal integration. However, the political support for further fiscal integration of the euro zone countries has seemed lacking. In 2015, the ultimate fate of Europe's great economic experiment of having independent countries use a single currency was very much in doubt.

Note: Data for the figure are from the International Monetary Fund. The unemployment rate for the euro countries is for all members of the euro zone as of 2008, weighted by their shares in total employment in 2007.

Based on Nektaria Stamouli, "Greece Wants European Parliament Involved in Overseeing Bailout," *Wall Street Journal*, August 19, 2015; "A Third Bail-out Gets the Green Light," *Economist*, August 15, 2015; and Terence Roth, "Everything You Need to Know about European Political Union," *Economist*, July 27, 2015.

MyEconLab   **Your Turn:** Test your understanding by doing related problem 2.6 on page 432 and problem 2.12 on page 433 at the end of this chapter.

Pegging against Another Currency

A final key aspect of the current exchange rate system is that some countries have attempted to keep their exchange rates fixed against the US dollar or another major currency. Having a fixed exchange rate can provide important advantages for a country that has extensive trade with another country. When the exchange rate is fixed, business planning becomes much easier. For instance, if the South Korean won increases in value relative to the Canadian dollar, Korean car manufacturer Hyundai may have to raise the Canadian dollar price of cars it exports to Canada, thereby reducing sales. If the exchange rate between the Korean won and the Canadian dollar is fixed, Hyundai's planning is much easier.

In the 1980s and 1990s, an additional reason developed for having fixed exchange rates. During those decades, the flow of foreign investment funds to developing countries, particularly those in East Asia, increased substantially. It became possible for firms in countries such as South Korea, Thailand, Malaysia, and Indonesia to borrow US dollars directly from foreign investors or indirectly from foreign banks. For example, a Thai firm might borrow US dollars from a Japanese bank. If the Thai firm wants to build a new factory in Thailand with the borrowed US dollars, it has to exchange the US dollars for the equivalent amount of Thai currency, the baht. When the factory opens and production begins, the Thai firm will be earning the additional baht it needs to exchange for US dollars to make the interest payments on the loan. A problem arises if the value of the baht falls against the US dollar. Suppose that the exchange rate is 25 baht per US dollar when the firm takes out the loan. A Thai firm making an interest payment of US$100 000 per month on a US dollar loan could buy the necessary US dollars for 2.5 million baht. But if the value of the baht declines to 50 baht to the US dollar, it would take 5 million baht to buy the US dollars necessary to make the interest payment. These increased payments might be a crushing burden for the Thai firm. The government of Thailand would have a strong incentive to avoid this problem by keeping the exchange rate between the baht and the US dollar fixed.

Finally, in the 1980s and 1990s, some countries feared the inflationary consequences of a floating exchange rate. When the value of a currency falls, the prices of imports rise. If imports are a significant fraction of the goods consumers buy, a fall in the value of the

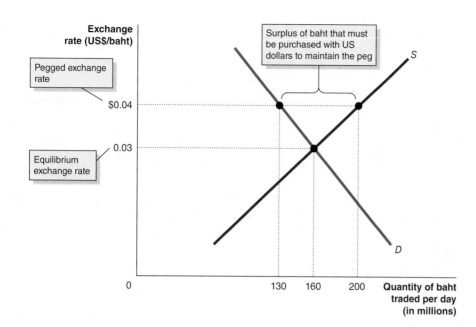

Exchange rate (US$/baht)

Pegged exchange rate

Equilibrium exchange rate

Surplus of baht that must be purchased with US dollars to maintain the peg

S

$0.04

0.03

D

0   130   160   200   **Quantity of baht traded per day (in millions)**

Figure 15.3

By 1997, the Thai Baht Was Overvalued against the US Dollar

The government of Thailand pegged the value of the baht against the US dollar to make it easier for Thai firms to export to the United States and to protect Thai firms that had taken out US dollar loans. The pegged exchange rate of US$0.04 per baht was well above the equilibrium exchange rate of US$0.03 per baht. In the example in this figure, the overvalued exchange rate created a surplus of 70 million baht, which the Thai central bank had to purchase with US dollars.

currency may significantly increase the inflation rate. During the 1990s, an important part of Brazil's and Argentina's anti-inflation policies was a fixed exchange rate against the US dollar. (As we will see, there are difficulties with following a fixed exchange rate policy, and, ultimately, both Brazil and Argentina abandoned fixed exchange rates.)

The East Asian Exchange Rate Crisis of the Late 1990s.
When a country keeps its currency's exchange rate fixed against another country's currency, it is **pegging** its currency. It is not necessary for both countries involved in a peg to agree to it. When a country has pegged the value of its currency against the US dollar, the responsibility for maintaining the peg is entirely with the pegging country.

Countries attempting to maintain a peg can run into problems, however. When the government fixes the price of a good or service, the result can be persistent surpluses or shortages. Figure 15.3 shows the exchange rate between the US dollar and the Thai baht. The figure is drawn from the Thai point of view, so we measure the exchange rate on the vertical axis as US dollars per baht. The figure represents the situation in the 1990s, when the government of Thailand pegged the exchange rate between the US dollar and the baht above the equilibrium exchange rate, as determined by demand and supply. A currency pegged at a value above the market equilibrium exchange rate is said to be *overvalued*. A currency pegged at a value below the market equilibrium exchange rate is said to be *undervalued*.

Pegging made it easier for Thai firms to export products to the United States and protected Thai firms that had taken out US dollar loans. The pegged exchange rate was 25.19 baht to the US dollar, or about US$0.04 to the baht. By 1997, this exchange rate was well above the market equilibrium exchange rate of 35 baht to the US dollar, or about US$0.03 to the baht. The result was a surplus of baht on the foreign exchange market. To keep the exchange rate at the pegged level, the Thai central bank, the Bank of Thailand, had to buy these baht with US dollars. In doing so, the Bank of Thailand gradually used up its holdings of US dollars, or its *US dollar reserves*. To continue supporting the pegged exchange rate, the Bank of Thailand borrowed additional US dollar reserves from the International Monetary Fund (IMF). The Bank of Thailand also raised interest rates to attract more foreign investors to investments in Thailand, thereby increasing the demand for the baht. The Bank of Thailand took these actions even though allowing the value of the baht to decline against the US dollar would have helped Thai firms exporting to the United States by reducing the US dollar prices of their goods. The Thai government was afraid of the negative consequences of abandoning the peg even though the peg had led to the baht being overvalued.

Although higher domestic interest rates helped attract foreign investors, they made it more difficult for Thai firms and households to borrow the funds they needed to finance

Pegging The decision by a country to keep the exchange rate fixed between its currency and another country's currency.

Figure 15.4

Destabilizing Speculation against the Thai Baht

In 1997, the pegged exchange rate of US$0.04 = 1 baht was above the equilibrium exchange rate of US$0.03 = 1 baht. As investors became convinced that Thailand would have to abandon its pegged exchange rate against the US dollar and allow the value of the baht to fall, they decreased their demand for baht, causing the demand curve to shift from D_1 to D_2. The new equilibrium exchange rate became US$0.02 = 1 baht. To defend the pegged exchange rate, the Bank of Thailand had to increase the quantity of baht it purchased in exchange for US dollars from 70 million per day to 140 million. The *destabilizing speculation* by investors caused Thailand to abandon its pegged exchange rate in July 1997.

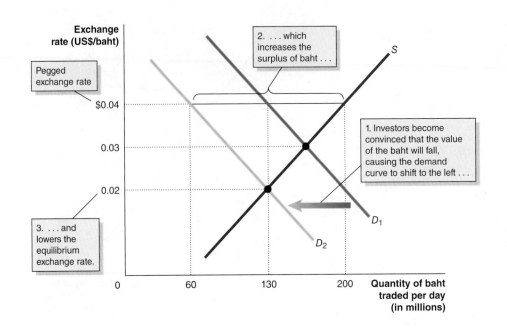

their spending. As a consequence, domestic investment and consumption declined, pushing the Thai economy into recession. International investors realized that there were limits to how high the Bank of Thailand would be willing to push interest rates and how many US dollar loans the IMF would be willing to extend to Thailand. These investors began to speculate against the baht by exchanging baht for US dollars at the official, pegged exchange rate. If, as they expected, Thailand was forced to abandon the peg, they would be able to buy back the baht at a much lower exchange rate, making a substantial profit. Because these actions by investors make it more difficult to maintain a fixed exchange rate, they are referred to as *destabilizing speculation*. Figure 15.4 shows the results of this destabilizing speculation. The decreased demand for baht shifted the demand curve for baht from D_1 to D_2, increasing the quantity of baht the Bank of Thailand needed to buy in exchange for US dollars.

Foreign investors also began to sell off their investments in Thailand and exchange their holdings of baht for US dollars. This *capital flight* forced the Bank of Thailand to run through its US dollar reserves. US dollar loans from the IMF temporarily allowed Thailand to defend the pegged exchange rate. Finally, on July 2, 1997, Thailand abandoned its pegged exchange rate against the US dollar and allowed the baht to float. Thai firms that had borrowed US dollars were now faced with interest payments that were much higher than they had planned. Many firms were forced into bankruptcy, and the Thai economy plunged into a deep recession.

Many currency traders became convinced that other East Asian countries, such as South Korea, Indonesia, and Malaysia, would have to follow Thailand and abandon their pegged exchange rates. The result was a wave of speculative selling of these countries' currencies. These waves of selling—sometimes referred to as *speculative attacks*—were difficult for countries to fight off. Even if a country's currency was not initially overvalued at the pegged exchange rate, the speculative attacks would cause a large reduction in the demand for the country's currency. The demand curve for the currency would shift to the left, which would force the country's central bank to quickly run through its US dollar reserves. Within a few months, South Korea, Indonesia, the Philippines, and Malaysia abandoned their pegged currencies. All these countries also plunged into recession.

The Decline in Pegging. Following the disastrous events experienced by the East Asian countries, the number of countries with pegged exchange rates declined sharply. Most countries that continue to use pegged exchange rates are small and trade primarily with a single, much larger, country. For instance, several Caribbean countries continue to peg against the US dollar, and several former French colonies in Africa that formerly pegged against the French franc now peg against the euro. Overall, the trend has been toward replacing pegged exchange rates with managed floating exchange rates.

Making the Connection

The Chinese Yuan: The World's Most Controversial Currency

In 1978, China began to move away from central planning and toward a market system. The result was a sharp acceleration in economic growth. Real GDP per capita grew at a rate of 6.5 percent per year between 1979 and 1995 and at the even more rapid rate of 8.8 percent per year between 1996 and 2014. An important part of Chinese economic policy was the decision in 1994 to peg the value of the Chinese currency, the yuan, to the US dollar at a fixed rate of 8.28 yuan to the dollar. Pegging against the US dollar ensured that Chinese exporters would face stable dollar prices for the goods they sold in the United States. By the early 2000s, many economists and policymakers argued that the yuan was undervalued against the US dollar—possibly significantly undervalued. Some policymakers claimed that the undervaluation of the yuan gave Chinese firms an unfair advantage in competing with US firms.

To support the undervalued exchange rate, the Chinese central bank had to buy large amounts of US dollars with yuan. By 2005, the Chinese government had accumulated more than $700 billion, a good portion of which it had used to buy US Treasury bonds. By this time, China was coming under pressure from its trading partners to allow the yuan to increase in value. Chinese exports of textile products were driving some textile producers out of business in Japan, the United States, and Europe. China had also begun to export more sophisticated products, including televisions, personal computers, and cellphones. Politicians in other countries were anxious to protect their domestic industries from Chinese competition, even if the result was higher prices for their consumers. In the United States and other countries, accusations that the Chinese government was intentionally undervaluing the yuan became a heated political issue. The Chinese government was reluctant to allow the market to determine the value of the yuan, however, because it believed high levels of exports were needed to maintain rapid economic growth.

In July 2005, the Chinese government announced that it would switch from pegging the yuan against the US dollar to linking the value of the yuan to the average value of a basket of currencies—the US dollar, the Japanese yen, the euro, the Korean won, and several other currencies. Although the Chinese central bank did not explain the details of how this linking of the yuan to other currencies would work, it declared that it had switched from a peg to a managed floating exchange rate. As the figure below shows, the value of the yuan gradually increased versus the US dollar for most of the period from 2005 to 2015. The exception is the period from July 2008 to May 2010, when the exchange rate stabilized at about 6.83 yuan to the US dollar, indicating that China had apparently returned to a "hard peg." This change in policy led to renewed criticism from policymakers in the United States. In mid-2010, President Barack Obama argued that "market-determined exchange rates are essential to global economic activity." In the face of this criticism, the Chinese central bank allowed the yuan to resume its slow increase in value versus the US dollar. (Note that the figure shows the number of yuan per US dollar, so an increase represents a *depreciation* of the yuan relative to the dollar and a decrease represents an *appreciation* of the yuan relative to the dollar.)

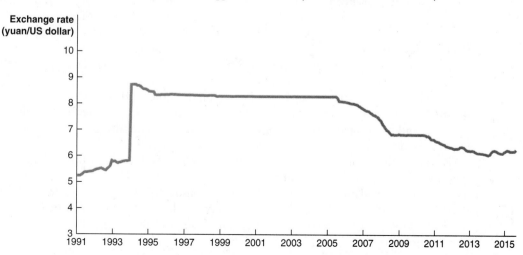

In 2015, the Chinese government was concerned that the growth rate of real GDP had slowed to about 7 percent, the lowest rate in more than six years. In August of that year, the yuan was once again in the news when the Chinese central bank made a surprise announcement that it would buy US dollars with yuan in order to reduce its value by about 3 percent, the largest one-day decline in the currency since 1994. The Chinese central bank again stated that it would allow the market to play a greater role in determining the value of the yuan. Many policymakers and economists were skeptical that the central bank truly intended to relax its control over the currency. And once again, politicians in the United States and elsewhere were critical of what they considered to be an attempt by the Chinese government to manipulate the value of yuan to gain an unfair advantage over its trading partners.

As long as the Chinese central bank continues to override the market to control the value of the yuan, controversy over Chinese exchange rate policies is likely to continue.

Based on "Yuan Thing after Another," *The Economist*, August 15, 2015; Lingling Wei, "China Moves to Devalue Yuan," *Wall Street Journal*, August 11, 2015; Greg Ip, "Why China's Yuan 'Reform' Merits Skepticism," *Wall Street Journal*, August 19, 2015; and Federal Reserve Bank of St. Louis.

MyEconLab | **Your Turn:** Test your understanding by doing related problem 2.10 on page 432 and problem 2.13 on page 433 at the end of this chapter.

15.3 **LEARNING** OBJECTIVE

Discuss the growth of international capital markets.

International Capital Markets

One important reason exchange rates fluctuate is that investors seek out the best investments they can find anywhere in the world. For instance, if Chinese investors increase their demand for Canada bonds, the demand for Canadian dollars will increase, and the value of the Canadian dollar will rise. But if interest rates in Canada decline, foreign investors may sell Canadian investments, and the value of the Canadian dollar will fall.

Shares of stock and long-term debt, including corporate and government bonds and bank loans, are bought and sold on *capital markets*. Before 1980, most Canadian corporations raised funds only in Canadian stock and bond markets or from Canadian banks. And Canadian investors rarely invested in foreign capital markets. In the 1980s and 1990s, European governments removed many restrictions on foreign investments in their financial markets. It became possible for Canadian and other foreign investors to freely invest in Europe and for European investors to freely invest in foreign markets. Improvements in communications and computer technology made it possible for Canadian investors to receive better and more timely information about foreign firms and for foreign investors to receive better information about Canadian firms. The growth in economies around the world also increased the savings available to be invested.

Today there are large capital markets in the United States, Europe, and Japan, and there are smaller markets in Latin America and East Asia. The three most important international financial centres today are New York, London, and Tokyo. Each day, the *Globe and Mail* and the *Financial Post* provide data not just on the S&P/TSX Composite Index of Canadian stocks but also on the Dow Jones Industrial Average and the Standard & Poor's 500 stock indexes of US stocks, the Nikkei 225 average of Japanese stocks, the FTSE 100 index of stocks on the London Stock Exchange, and the Hang Seng Index of stocks traded on the Hong Kong stock exchange.

Beginning in the 1990s, the flow of foreign funds into Canadian stocks and bonds— or *portfolio investments*—increased substantially. As Figure 15.5 shows, foreign purchases of stocks and bonds issued by corporations increased dramatically between 1995 and 2007. Foreign purchases of Canadian securities soared again after the global financial crisis, as fears that some European governments might default on their bonds led investors to a *flight to safety*, in which they sold other investments to buy Canadian securities. The fact that Canada ran current account deficits also fuelled some of the demand for Canadian government bonds. These current account deficits led to an accumulation of dollars by foreign central banks and foreign investors who used the dollars to purchase Canadian securities.

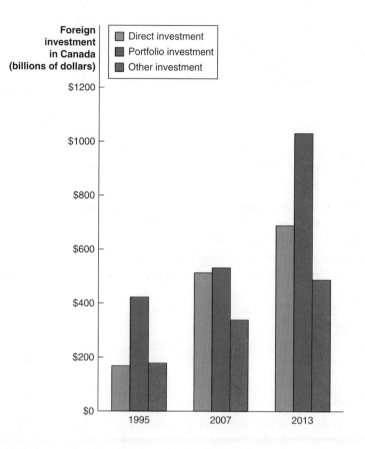

Figure 15.5

Growth of Foreign Portfolio Investment in Canada

Between 1995 and 2013, there was a large increase in foreign purchases of stocks and bonds issued by Canadian corporations and of bonds issued by the federal government.

Source: Data from Statistics Canada CANSIM II Table 3760141 (Accessed 8 December 2015).

Figure 15.6 shows the distribution during September 2015 of foreign portfolio investment in Canada by country. Investors in the United States accounted for 62 percent of all foreign purchases of Canadian bonds and money market instruments. The two other countries with the largest shares of foreign purchases were the United Kingdom, with 16 percent, and Japan, with 7 percent.

The globalization of financial markets has helped increase growth and efficiency in the world economy. Now it is possible for the savings of households around the world to be channelled to the best investments available. It is also possible for firms in nearly every country to tap the savings of foreign households to gain the funds needed for expansion. No longer are firms forced to rely only on the savings of domestic households to finance investment.

But the globalization of financial markets also has a downside, as the events of 2007–2009 showed. Because financial securities issued in one country are held by

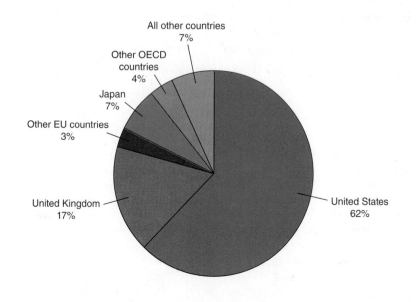

Figure 15.6

The Distribution of Foreign Purchases of Canadian Bonds and Money Market Instruments by Country, September 2015

Investors in the United States accounted for 62 percent of all foreign purchases of Canadian bonds and money market instruments, while investors in the United Kingdom accounted for 16 percent, and investors in Japan accounted for 7 percent.

Source: Data from Statistics Canada CANSIM II Table 3760145 (Accessed 8 December 2015).

investors and firms in many other countries, if those securities decline in value, the financial pain will be widely distributed. For example, the sharp decline in the value of mortgage-backed securities issued in the United States hurt not only US investors and financial firms but investors and financial firms in many other countries as well, including Canada.

Economics in Your Life

Exchange Rate Risk Can Affect Your Savings

At the beginning of this chapter, we posed this question: If economists are correct about the relative rates of average productivity growth between Japan and Canada in the next decade, then, all else being equal, will the savings that you accumulate (in yen) be worth more or less in Canadian dollars than the savings would have been worth without the relative gains in Japanese productivity? We saw in this chapter that when the average productivity of firms in one country increases faster than the average productivity of firms in another country, the value of the faster-growing country's currency should—all else being equal—rise against the slower-growing country's currency. But the savings that you accumulate in yen while you are in Japan are likely to be worth more in Canadian dollars than they would have been worth without the gains in Japanese productivity.

Conclusion

Fluctuations in exchange rates continue to cause difficulties for firms and governments. From the gold standard to the Bretton Woods system to currency pegging, governments have attempted to find a workable system of fixed exchange rates. Fixing exchange rates runs into the same problems as fixing any other price: As demand and supply shift, surpluses and shortages will occur unless the price adjusts. Nineteen countries in Europe are attempting to avoid this problem by using a single currency. Economists are looking closely at the results of that experiment.

Chapter Summary and Problems

Key Terms

Bretton Woods system, p. 416

Euro, p. 416

Exchange rate system, p. 415

Fixed exchange rate system, p. 416

Floating currency, p. 415

Managed float exchange rate system, p. 415

Pegging, p. 425

Purchasing power parity, p. 417

Quota, p. 418

Tariff, p. 418

Summary

★LO 15.1 When countries agree on how exchange rates should be determined, economists say that there is an *exchange rate system*. A *floating currency* is the outcome of a country allowing its currency's exchange rate to be determined by demand and supply. The current exchange rate system is a *managed float exchange rate system*, under which the value of most currencies is determined by

demand and supply, with occasional government intervention. A *fixed exchange rate system* is a system under which countries agree to keep the exchange rates among their currencies fixed. Under the gold standard, the exchange rate between two currencies was automatically determined by the quantity of gold in each currency. By the end of the Great Depression of the 1930s, every country had abandoned the gold standard. Under the Bretton Woods system, which was in place between 1944 and the early 1970s, the United States agreed to exchange US dollars for gold at a price of

★"Learning Objective" is abbreviated to "LO" in the end-of-chapter material.

$35 per ounce. The central banks of all other members of the system pledged to buy and sell their currencies at a fixed rate against the dollar.

LO 15.2 The current exchange rate system has three key aspects: (1) The Canadian dollar floats against other major currencies; (2) most countries in Europe have adopted a single currency; and (3) some countries have attempted to keep their currencies' exchange rates fixed against the US dollar or another major currency. Since 1973, the value of the Canadian dollar has fluctuated widely against other major currencies. The theory of *purchasing power parity* states that in the long run, exchange rates move to equalize the purchasing power of different currencies. This theory helps to explain some of the long-run movements in the value of the Canadian dollar relative to other currencies. Purchasing power parity does not provide a complete explanation of movements in exchange rates for several reasons, including the existence of tariffs and quotas. A *tariff* is a tax imposed by a government on imports. A *quota* is a government-imposed limit on the quantity of a good that can be imported. In 2016, 19 European Union member countries used a common currency, known as the *euro*. The experience of the countries using the euro will provide economists with information on the costs and benefits to countries of using the same currency.

When a country keeps its currency's exchange rate fixed against another country's currency, it is *pegging* its currency. Pegging can result in problems similar to the difficulties countries encountered with fixed exchange rates under the Bretton Woods system. If investors become convinced that a country pegging its exchange rate will eventually allow the exchange rate to decline to a lower level, the demand curve for the currency will shift to the left. This destabilizing speculation makes it difficult for a central bank to maintain a fixed exchange rate.

LO 15.3 A key reason exchange rates fluctuate is that investors seek out the best investments they can find anywhere in the world. Since 1980, the markets for stocks and bonds have become global. Foreign purchases of Canadian corporate bonds and stocks and Canadian government bonds have increased greatly in the period since 1995. As a result, firms around the world are no longer forced to rely only on the savings of domestic households for funds.

MyEconLab   Log in to MyEconLab to complete these exercises and get instant feedback.

Review Questions

LO 15.1

1.1 What is an exchange rate system? What is the difference between a fixed exchange rate system and a managed float exchange rate system?

1.2 How were exchange rates determined under the gold standard? How did the Bretton Woods system differ from the gold standard?

LO 15.2

2.1 What is the theory of purchasing power parity? Does the theory give a complete explanation for movements in exchange rates in the long run? Briefly explain.

2.2 Briefly describe the four determinants of exchange rates in the long run.

2.3 Which European countries currently use the euro as their currency? Why did these countries agree to replace their previous currencies with the euro?

2.4 What does it mean when one currency is "pegged" against another currency? Why do countries peg their currencies? What problems can result from pegging?

LO 15.3

3.1 What were the main factors behind the globalization of capital markets in the 1980s and 1990s?

3.2 Briefly describe the pattern of foreign investment in Canadian securities between 1995 and 2014.

Problems and Applications

LO 15.1

1.1 **[Related to Don't Let This Happen to You on page 416]** Briefly explain whether you agree with the following statement: "The Bank of Canada is limited in its ability to issue paper currency by the amount of gold the federal government has. To issue more paper currency, the government first has to buy more gold."

1.2 Canada and most other countries abandoned the gold standard during the 1930s. Why would the 1930s have been a particularly difficult time for countries to have remained on the gold standard? (*Hint:* Think about the macroeconomic events of the 1930s and about the possible problems with carrying out an expansionary monetary policy while remaining on the gold standard.)

1.3 After World War II, why might countries have preferred the Bretton Woods system over reestablishing the gold standard? In your answer, be sure to note the important ways in which the Bretton Woods system differed from the gold standard.

LO 15.2

2.1 An article in the *Toronto Star* discussed the Canadian teams that play in the National Hockey League, the National Basketball Association, Major League Baseball, and Major League Soccer. The article noted, "Under their collective agreements players get paid in US dollars. The majority of [team] revenue, however, is in Canadian currency." Are Canadian professional sports teams better off when the Canadian dollar increases in value relative to the US dollar or when it decreases in value? Briefly explain.

Josh Rubin, "MLSE, Blue Jays Deal with Dollar Dive," thestar.com, January 25, 2015.

2.2 Consider this statement:

> It usually takes about 98 yen to buy 1 Canadian dollar and more than 1.5 Canadian dollars to buy 1 British pound. These values show that Canada must be a much wealthier country than Japan and that the United Kingdom must be wealthier than Canada.

Do you agree with this reasoning? Briefly explain.

2.3 According to the theory of purchasing power parity, if the inflation rate in Australia is higher than the inflation rate in New Zealand, what should happen to the exchange rate between the Australian dollar and the New Zealand dollar? Briefly explain.

2.4 **[Related to Making the Connection on page 419]** Look again at the table on page 419 that shows the prices of Big Macs and the implied and actual exchange rates. Indicate which countries listed in the table have undervalued currencies and which have overvalued currencies versus the US dollar.

2.5 **[Related to Solved Problem 15.1 on page 419]** Fill in the missing values in the following table. Assume that the Big Mac is selling for $4.79 in the United States. Explain whether the US dollar is overvalued or undervalued relative to each of the other currencies and predict what will happen in the future to each exchange rate if the actual exchange rate moves toward the purchasing power parity exchange rate. Finally, calculate the implied exchange rate between the Russian ruble and the New Zealand dollar and explain which currency is overvalued in terms of Big Mac purchasing power parity.

Country	Big Mac Price	Implied Exchange Rate	Actual Exchange Rate
Chile	2100 pesos	_____	642.45 pesos per dollar
Israel	17.5 shekels	_____	3.78 shekels per dollar
Russia	107 rubles	_____	56.82 rubles per dollar
New Zealand	5.9 New Zealand dollars	_____	1.51 New Zealand dollars per U.S. dollar

Based on "The Big Mac Index," *The Economist*, July 16, 2015.

2.6 **[Related to the Making the Connection on page 422]** Britain decided not to join other European Union countries in using the euro as its currency. One British opponent of adopting the euro argued, "It comes down to economics. We just don't believe that it's possible to manage the entire economy of Europe with just one interest rate policy. How do you alleviate recession in Germany and curb inflation in Ireland?"

a. What interest rate policy would be used to alleviate recession in Germany?

b. What interest rate policy would be used to curb inflation in Ireland?

c. What does adopting the euro have to do with interest rate policy?

Alan Cowell, "Nuanced Conflict over Euro in Britain," *New York Times*, June 22, 2001.

2.7 When the euro was introduced in January 1999, the exchange rate was CDN$1.72 per euro. In December 2015, the exchange rate was CDN$1.45 per euro. Was this change in the dollar–euro exchange rate good news or bad news for Canadian firms exporting goods and services to Europe? Was it good news or bad news for European consumers buying goods and services imported from Canada? Briefly explain.

2.8 **[Related to the Chapter Opener on page 414]** The German firm Bayer reported that its pharmaceutical group experienced a 21 percent increase in profit for the second quarter of 2015. The firm stated that the increase was partly the result of "favourable currency effects."

a. Briefly explain what the firm means by "favourable currency effects."

b. How would favourable currency effects increase Bayer's profit?

c. Would these effects still have raised Bayer's profit if all of the firm's production and all of its sales were within Europe? Briefly explain.

Christopher Alessi, "Bayer Profit Rises on Healthy Currency Effects," *Wall Street Journal*, July 29, 2015.

2.9 Use the graph to answer the following questions.

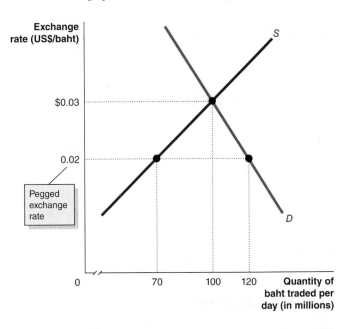

a. According to the graph, is there a surplus or a shortage of baht in exchange for US dollars? Briefly explain.

b. To maintain the pegged exchange rate, will the Thai central bank need to buy baht in exchange for US dollars or sell baht in exchange for US dollars? How many baht will the Thai central bank need to buy or sell?

2.10 **[Related to the Making the Connection on page 427]** In August 2015, after the Chinese central bank moved to decrease the value of the yuan in exchange for the dollar, a column in the *Wall Street Journal* offered this opinion: "China's trading partners are right to suspect that the real purpose of the so-called reform is a competitive devaluation that boosts exports and growth at the rest of the world's expense."

a. What does the writer mean by a "competitive devaluation"?

b. How would such a devaluation boost Chinese exports and growth?

c. Why would a boost in Chinese exports and growth come at the rest of the world's expense?

Greg Ip, "Why China's Yuan 'Reform' Merits Skepticism," *Wall Street Journal*, August 19, 2015.

2.11 *The Economist* observed the following: "In Argentina, many loans were taken out in [US] dollars: this had catastrophic consequences for borrowers once the peg collapsed." What does it mean that Argentina's "peg collapsed"? Why was the end of the peg catastrophic for borrowers in Argentina who had taken loans in US dollars?

"Spoilt for Choice," *The Economist*, June 3, 2002.

2.12 **[Related to the Making the Connection on page 422]** An article in *USA Today* argues, "Ironically, the euro's fall—and the benefit for German exports—is largely the result of euro zone policies that Germany has taken the lead in opposing … [including] easier money policies by the European Central Bank."

a. How does the "euro's fall" benefit German exports?

b. How is the euro's fall related to policies of the European Central Bank?

Mihret Yohannes, "Germany Benefits from Weak Euro Policies It Deplores," usatoday.com, March 4, 2015.

2.13 **[Related to the Making the Connection on page 427]** Graph the demand and supply of Chinese yuan for US dollars and label each axis. To maintain its pegged exchange rate, the Chinese central bank used yuan to buy large quantities of US dollars. Indicate whether the pegged exchange rate was above or below the market equilibrium exchange rate and show on the graph the quantity of yuan the Chinese central bank would have to supply each trading period.

2.14 Although it is a member of the European Community, Denmark is not part of the euro zone; it has its own currency, the krone. Because the krone is pegged to the euro, Denmark's central bank is obliged to maintain the value of the krone within 2.25 percent either above or below the value of the euro. To maintain the peg with the euro, in 2015 the Danish central bank was forced to offer negative interest rates on deposits of krone that it held. Was the Danish central bank's action in response to an increase or a decrease in the value of the euro? Briefly explain.

Based on Charles Duxbury and Josie Cox, "Denmark Cuts Rates Again to Protect Currency Peg," *Wall Street Journal*, February 5, 2015.

LO 15.3

3.1 Why are foreign investors more likely to invest in Canadian government bonds than in Canadian corporate stocks and bonds?

3.2 The text states that "the globalization of financial markets has helped increase growth and efficiency in the world economy." Briefly explain which aspects of globalization help to increase growth in the world economy.

3.3 The global financial crisis of 2007–2009 led some economists and policymakers to propose the reinstitution of capital controls—or limits on the flow of foreign exchange and financial investments across countries—which existed in many European countries prior to the 1960s. Why would a financial crisis lead to a reconsideration of using capital controls? What problems might result from reinstituting capital controls?

MyEconLab   MyEconLab is an online tool designed to help you master the concepts covered in your course. It will create a personalized study plan to stimulate and measure your learning. Log in to take advantage of this powerful study aid, and to access quizzes and other valuable course-related material.

Four ways the Fed's rate hike will affect our lives up north

The US Federal Reserve raised interest rates Wednesday for the first time in a decade, a move that sent the Canadian dollar lower, underscoring the widening gap between a strengthening US economy and our lackluster growth.

It was big news in the United States, but how much will the Fed's rate hike affect our lives up north? Here are four things to watch for.

Fixed-rate Mortgages

(a) Five-year fixed mortgage rates could rise. Banks are tied to long-term Canadian bonds, which are ultimately tied to US bond prices. When interest rates rise, bond prices fall. Banks sell bonds to loan money to mortgage holders. And as bond prices fall, the pot of money shrinks, lending tightens and mortgage rates rise. As a result, fixed mortgages rates have historically risen when the Fed makes an interest rate hike announcement.

The Loonie

(b) The already-battered loonie sank further after Wednesday's announcement to 72.54 cents (US). That's bad news for Canadians who want to spend their money in the US, but good news for the export sector, which is boosted when the loonie falls. Scott Guitard, a portfolio manager at Fiduciary Trust Canada, said climbing American interest rates will likely mean the opposite for the Canadian dollar.

Gas Prices

Conventional thinking is that a drop in oil prices results in lower prices for consumers at the pump. However, with the loonie plunging even further thanks to the Fed announcement—it was already dropping alongside oil prices—we aren't getting the expected break. The exchange-rate change more than offsetting the decline because imported gas is priced in US dollars. That is helping to keep gas price higher for Canadians.

Canadian Interest Rates

(c) Canadian interest rates have tended to move higher when the US pushes theirs higher. But most economists say the Canadian economy is performing so poorly that the chances are even that the central bank would raise or lower the overnight rate. Our low rate will keep the cost of borrowing low for longer on everything from variable-rate mortgages to lines of credit. Speaking earlier this week, Bank of Canada governor Stephen Poloz said that Canadian and American interest rate policies will continue to diverge as the gap widens between their relative economic performance. "We just want people to understand that usually we think of the Canadian economy following the U.S. economy fairly closely, and this will be one of those places where it really doesn't," he said.

Source: Reprinted with permission from Toronto Star Syndication Services.

Key Points in the Article

Canada is a diversified economy made up of significant contributions from the commodity (agriculture, energy, mining, and forestry) and manufacturing sectors. As a small open economy, Canada trades a large portion of its national output. In a typical year, Canada exports and imports around one third of its GDP. In recent years, however, falling commodity prices have caused Canada's currency, known as the loonie, to depreciate in value.

Also, Canadian consumers, in the face of historically low interest rates, have loaded up with debt to a point where their obligations (relative to income) now exceed those of their OECD counterparts. However, the largest risks to Canada's economic prosperity are external, due to its reliance on trade. Canada's future economic outlook is heavily dependent on global economic activity and events that occur outside its border and in particular in the United States.

Analyzing the News

(a) Because mortgages involve long-term funds, the mortgage market forms a subcategory of the capital markets. The interest rate that borrowers pay on their mortgages depends on the life (term) of the mortgage and current long-term market rates, with the latter being influenced by a number of national and global factors. Most of the time, mortgage rates tend to track along with the interest rates on the less risky Canada bonds, which in turn are ultimately tied to interest rates on US bonds. For these reasons, the article suggests that five-year fixed mortgage rates in Canada could rise if the Federal Reserve raises interest rates.

(b) The Canadian currency has depreciated in recent years because the relative demand for Canadian commodities and their prices have weakened. In fact, the Canadian currency is often referred to in the media as a petro currency given the observation that strong daily increases (or decreases) in the price of oil are often accompanied by an appreciation (or depreciation) of the Canadian dollar against the US dollar and other currencies. The article suggests that as a result of increases in interest rates in the United States, the Canadian dollar will depreciate further. This means that Canadians will likely reduce their purchases of foreign goods and increase their consumption of domestic goods. It also means, however, that Canadian businesses will become more competitive in global markets.

(c) When interest rates increase in the United States, the return on assets denominated in US dollars increases, holding the current exchange rate and everything else constant. In such cases, Canadians will want to hold fewer Canadian dollars assets and more US dollar assets. The decline in the demand for Canadian dollar assets and the increase in the demand for US dollar assets will lead to a depreciation of the Canadian dollar in the foreign exchange market. Of course, when Canadian interest rates move together with those in the United States, the exchange rate between the two currencies does not change, holding everything else constant. The article suggests that as the US economy is performing well and the Fed is moving away from the zero lower bound for the federal funds rate, and the Canadian economy is performing poorly and the Bank of Canada will likely stay close to the zero lower bound for the overnight interest rate, chances are that interest rate policies will diverge between the two countries.

Thinking Critically About Policy

1. Do you think consumer debt levels in Canada have been influenced by the values of the Canadian currency? What is the likely impact the depreciation of the Canadian dollar had on inflationary pressures in Canada? How would that influence Bank of Canada policy?

2. Have the costs of commodity prices and currency depreciation been felt equally across all of Canada? Are there any sectors and regions of the economy that have been hurt by these events—if so, where are they? Which provinces have the lowest unemployment rates in Canada? Why? What structural changes do we expect to see in the Canadian economy overtime if recent trends persist?

GLOSSARY

A

Absolute advantage The ability of an individual, a firm, or a country to produce more of a good or service than potential trading partners, using the same amount of resources.

Advances to banks Loans the Bank of Canada makes to banks.

Aggregate demand (AD) curve A curve that shows the relationship between the price level and the level of planned aggregate expenditure in the economy, holding constant all other factors that affect aggregate expenditure.

Aggregate demand (AD) curve A curve that shows the relationship between the price level and the quantity of real GDP demanded by households, firms, and the government.

Aggregate demand and aggregate supply model A model that explains short-run fluctuations in real GDP and the price level.

Aggregate expenditure (AE) Total spending in the economy: the sum of consumption, planned investment, government purchases, and net exports.

Aggregate expenditure model A macroeconomic model that focuses on the short-run relationship between total spending and real GDP, assuming that the price level is constant.

Allocative efficiency A state of the economy in which production is in accordance with consumer preferences; in particular, every good or service is produced up to the point where the last unit provides a marginal benefit to society equal to the marginal cost of producing it.

Asset Anything of value owned by a person or a firm.

Automatic stabilizers Government spending and taxes that automatically increase or decrease along with the business cycle.

Autonomous consumption The level of consumption that occurs no matter what disposable income is.

Autonomous expenditure An expenditure that does not depend on the level of GDP.

B

Balance of payments The record of a country's trade with other countries in goods, services, and assets.

Balance of trade The difference between the value of the goods a country exports and the value of the goods a country imports.

Bank of Canada The central bank of Canada.

Bank panic A situation in which many banks experience runs at the same time.

Bank rate The interest rate the Bank of Canada charges on loans (advances) to banks.

Bank run A situation in which many depositors simultaneously decide to withdraw money from a bank.

Board of directors (of the Bank of Canada) A board with 15 members (including the governor) that is responsible for the management of the Bank of Canada.

Bretton Woods system An exchange rate system that lasted from 1944 to 1973, under which countries pledged to buy and sell their currencies at a fixed rate against the dollar.

Budget deficit The situation in which the government's current expenditures are greater than its current tax revenue.

Budget surplus The situation in which the government's current expenditures are less than its current tax revenue.

Business cycle Alternating periods of economic expansion and economic recession.

C

Capital account The part of the balance of payments that records relatively minor transactions, such as migrants' transfers and sales and purchases of nonproduced, nonfinancial assets.

Capital Manufactured goods that are used to produce other goods and services.

Cash flow The difference between the cash revenues received by a firm and the cash spending by the firm.

Catch-up The prediction that the level of GDP per capita (or income per capita) in poor countries will grow faster than in rich countries.

Centrally planned economy An economy in which the government decides how economic resources will be allocated.

Ceteris paribus ("all else equal") condition The requirement that when analyzing the relationship between two variables—such as price and quantity demanded—other variables must be held constant.

Circular-flow diagram A model that illustrates how participants in markets are linked.

Closed economy An economy that has no interactions in trade or finance with other countries.

Collateralized transactions Transactions that involve property being pledged to the lender to guarantee payment in the event that the borrower is unable to make debt payments.

Commodity money A good used as money that also has value independent of its use as money.

Comparative advantage The ability of an individual, a firm, or a country to produce a good or service at a lower opportunity cost than potential trading partners.

Competitive market equilibrium A market equilibrium with many buyers and many sellers.

Complements Goods and services that are used together.

Consumer price index (CPI) An average of the prices of the goods and services purchased by a typical household.

Consumption (C) Spending by households on goods and services.

Consumption function The relationship between consumption spending and disposable income.

Consumption of capital The amount of capital that wears out (depreciates) during use.

Contractionary monetary policy The Bank of Canada's increasing interest rates to reduce inflation.

Crowding out A decline in private expenditures as a result of an increase in government purchases.

Crowding out A decline in private investment expenditures as a result of an increase in government purchases.

Currency appreciation An increase in the market value of one currency relative to another currency.

Currency depreciation A decrease in the market value of one currency relative to another currency.

Current account The part of the balance of payments that records a country's net exports, net income on investments, and net transfers.

Cyclical unemployment Unemployment caused by a business cycle recession.

Cyclically adjusted budget deficit or surplus The deficit or surplus in the federal government's budget if the economy were at potential GDP.

D

Demand curve A curve that shows the relationship between the price of a product and the quantity of the product demanded.

Demand schedule A table that shows the relationship between the price of a product and the quantity of the product demanded.

Demographics The characteristics of a population with respect to age, race, and gender.

Desired reserve ratio The minimum fraction of deposits banks desire to keep as reserves.

Desired reserves Reserves that a bank desires to hold, based on its chequing account deposits.

Discouraged workers People who are available for work but have not looked for a job during the previous four weeks because they believe no jobs are available for them.

Disinflation A significant reduction in the inflation rate.

E

Economic growth model A model that explains growth rates in real GDP per capita over the long run.

Economic growth The ability of an economy to produce increasing quantities of goods and services.

Economic model A simplified version of reality used to analyze real-world economic situations.

Economic variable Something measurable that can have different values, such as the price of coffee.

Economics The study of the choices people make to attain their goals, given their scarce resources.

Efficiency wage A higher-than-market wage that a firm pays to increase worker productivity.

Employment–population ratio A measure of the portion of the population engaged in paid work.

Entrepreneur Someone who operates a business, bringing together factors of production—labour, capital, and natural resources—to produce goods and services.

Equity The fair distribution of economic benefits.

Euro The common currency of many European countries.

Excess reserves Reserves that banks hold over and above the desired amounts.

Exchange rate system An agreement among countries about how exchange rates should be determined.

Expansion The period of a business cycle during which total production and total employment are increasing.

Expansionary monetary policy The Bank of Canada's decreasing interest rates to increase real GDP.

Expenditure approach Measuring GDP by adding up all the different types of expenditure in the economy.

Exports Goods and services produced in Canada that will be consumed by citizens of another country.

F

Factor market A market for the factors of production, such as labour, capital, natural resources, and entrepreneurial ability.

Factors of production The inputs used to make goods and services.

Federal government debt The total value of bonds outstanding, which is equal to the sum of past budget deficits, net of surpluses.

Fiat money Money, such as paper currency, that is authorized by a central bank or governmental body and that does not have to be exchanged by the central bank for gold or some other commodity money.

Final consumption expenditure Purchases of goods or services that will be used to satisfy individual or community needs and wants.

Final good or service A good or service purchased by a final user.

Financial account The part of the balance of payments that records purchases of assets a country has made abroad and foreign purchases of assets in the country.

Financial intermediaries Firms, such as banks, mutual funds, pension funds, and insurance companies, that borrow funds from savers and lend them to borrowers.

Financial markets Markets where financial securities, such as stocks and bonds, are bought and sold.

Financial system The system of financial markets and financial intermediaries through which firms acquire funds from households.

Fiscal policy Changes in federal taxes and purchases that are intended to achieve macroeconomic policy objectives.

Fixed exchange rate system A system under which countries agree to keep the exchange rates among their currencies fixed for long periods.

Flexible inflation targeting Conducting monetary policy that does not rely on mechanical rules to achieve its inflation target, but tries to meet the inflation target over some time horizon (typically a two-year horizon).

Floating currency The outcome of a country allowing its currency's exchange rate to be determined by demand and supply.

Foreign direct investment (FDI) The purchase or building by a corporation of a facility in a foreign country.

Foreign portfolio investment The purchase by an individual or a firm of stocks or bonds issued in another country.

Fractional reserve banking system A banking system in which banks keep less than 100 percent of deposits as reserves.

Free market A market with few government restrictions on how goods or services can be produced or sold, on who can buy or sell goods or services, or on how factors of production can be employed.

Frictional unemployment Short-term unemployment that arises from the process of matching workers with jobs.

G

GDP deflator A measure of the price level, calculated by dividing nominal GDP by real GDP and multiplying by 100.

Globalization The process of countries becoming more open to foreign trade and investment.

Governing council (of the Bank of Canada) A council with six members (including the governor) that is responsible for the management of the Bank of Canada.

Government spending (G) Spending on consumption goods and capital undertaken by government.

Gross domestic product (GDP) The market value of all final goods and services produced in a geographic area (country) during a period of time, typically one year.

Gross fixed capital formation Purchases of capital by firms, governments, and households.

Gross mixed income Paid to the owners of small business, this includes payments for labour and capital.

Gross operating surplus Payments made to the owners of capital.

H

Household production Goods and services people produce for themselves.

Human capital The accumulated knowledge and skills that workers acquire from education and training or from their life experiences.

I

Imports Goods and services produced by other countries that will be consumed by Canadians.

Income approach Measuring GDP by adding up all the income received by the owners of factors of production.

Income effect The change in the quantity demanded of a good that results from the effect of a change in the good's price on consumers' purchasing power.

Industrial Revolution The application of mechanical power to the production of goods, beginning in England around 1750.

Inferior good A good for which the demand increases as income falls and decreases as income rises.

Inflation rate The percentage increase in the price level from one year to the next.

Inflation targeting Conducting monetary policy so as to commit the central bank to achieving a publicly announced level of inflation.

Inflation A general increase in the prices of goods and services over time.

Intermediate good or service A good or service that is an input into another good or service, such as car seats.

Inventories Goods that have been produced but not yet sold.

Investment (I) The purchase of capital by firms.

K

Key policy rate The Bank of Canada's target for the overnight interest rate.

Keynesian revolution The name given to the widespread acceptance during the 1930s and 1940s of John Maynard Keynes's macroeconomic model.

L

Labour force participation rate The percentage of the working age population in the labour force.

Labour force The sum of employed and unemployed workers in the economy.

Labour productivity The quantity of goods and services that can be produced by one worker or by one hour of work.

Law of demand The rule that, holding everything else constant, when the price of a product falls, the quantity demanded of the product will increase, and when the price of a product rises, the quantity demanded of the product will decrease.

Law of supply The rule that, holding everything else constant, increases in price cause increases in the quantity supplied, and decreases in price cause decreases in the quantity supplied.

Leverage A measure of how much debt an investor assumes in making an investment.

Liability Anything owed by a person or a firm.

Long-run aggregate supply (LRAS) curve A curve that shows the relationship in the long run between the price level and the quantity of real GDP supplied.

Long-run economic growth The process by which rising productivity increases the average standard of living.

M

M1+ The narrowest definition of the money supply: It includes currency and other assets that have cheque-writing features—all chequable deposits at chartered banks, TMLs, and CUCPs.

M1++ This broader definition of the money supply includes everything that is in M1+ as well as all non-chequable deposits at chartered banks, TMLs, and CUCPs.

M2 A monetary aggregate that includes currency outside banks and personal deposits at chartered banks, non-personal demand and notice deposits at chartered banks, and fixed-term deposits.

M2+ A broader monetary aggregate that includes everything that is in M2 plus deposits at TMLs, deposits at CUCPs, life insurance company individual annuities, personal deposits at government-owned savings institutions, and money market mutual funds.

M2++ The broadest definition of the money supply: It includes everything that is in M2+ as well as Canada Savings Bonds and other retail instruments, and non-money market mutual funds.

M3 A category within the money supply that includes everything that is in M2 plus non-personal term deposits at chartered banks and foreign currency deposits of residents at chartered banks.

Macroeconomics The study of the economy as a whole, including topics such as inflation, unemployment, and economic growth.

Managed float exchange rate system The current exchange rate system, under which the value of most currencies is determined by demand and supply, with occasional government intervention.

Marginal analysis Analysis that involves comparing marginal benefits and marginal costs.

Marginal propensity to consume (MPC) The slope of the consumption function: The amount by which consumption spending changes when disposable income changes.

Marginal propensity to save (MPS) The amount by which saving changes when disposable income changes.

Market demand The demand by all the consumers of a given good or service.

Market economy An economy in which the decisions of households and firms interacting in markets allocate economic resources.

Market equilibrium A situation in which quantity demanded equals quantity supplied.

Market for loanable funds The interaction of borrowers and lenders that determines the market interest rate and the quantity of loanable funds exchanged.

Market A group of buyers and sellers of a good or service and the institutions or arrangements by which they come together to trade.

Market A group of buyers and sellers of a good or service and the institutions or arrangements by which they come together to trade.

Menu costs The costs to firms of changing prices.

Microeconomics The study of how households and firms make choices, how they interact in markets, and how the government attempts to influence their choices.

Mixed economy An economy in which most economic decisions result from the interaction of buyers and sellers in markets, but in which the government plays a significant role in the allocation of resources.

Monetarism The macroeconomic theories of Milton Friedman and his followers, particularly the idea that the quantity of money should be increased at a constant rate.

Monetary base The sum of the Bank of Canada's monetary liabilities (i.e., paper money in circulation and bank settlement balances) and the Canadian Mint's coins outstanding (i.e., coins in circulation).

Monetary growth rule A plan for increasing the quantity of money at a fixed rate that does not respond to changes in economic conditions.

Monetary policy The actions the Bank of Canada takes to manage the money supply and interest rates to pursue macroeconomic policy objectives.

Money Assets that people are generally willing to accept in exchange for goods and services or for payment of debts.

Multiplier effect The process by which an increase in autonomous expenditure leads to a larger increase in real GDP, or the series of induced increases in consumption spending that results from an initial increase in autonomous expenditures.

Multiplier The increase in equilibrium real GDP divided by the increase in autonomous expenditure.

N

Natural rate of unemployment The normal rate of unemployment, consisting of frictional unemployment plus structural unemployment.

Natural rate of unemployment The unemployment rate that exists when the economy is at potential GDP.

Net exports Exports minus imports.

Net foreign investment The difference between capital outflows from a country and capital inflows, also equal to net foreign direct investment plus net foreign portfolio investment.

Net operating surplus Payments to the owners of capital in excess of depreciation.

New classical macroeconomics The macroeconomic theories of Robert Lucas and others, particularly the idea that workers and firms have rational expectations.

New growth theory A model of long-run economic growth that emphasizes that technological change is influenced by economic incentives and so is determined by the working of the market system.

Nominal exchange rate The value of one country's currency in terms of another country's currency.

Nominal GDP The value of final goods and services evaluated at current-year prices.

Nominal interest rate The stated interest rate on a loan.

Nonaccelerating inflation rate of unemployment (NAIRU) The unemployment rate at which the inflation rate has no tendency to increase or decrease.

Normal good A good for which the demand increases as income rises and decreases as income falls.

Normative analysis Analysis concerned with what ought to be.

O

Open economy An economy that has interactions in trade or finance with other countries.

Open market buyback operations Agreements in which the Bank of Canada, or another party, purchases securities with the understanding that the seller will repurchase them in a short period of time, usually less than a week.

Open market operations The buying and selling of government securities by the Bank of Canada in order to control the money supply.

Operating band The Bank of Canada's 50-basis-point range for the overnight interest rate.

Opportunity cost The highest-valued alternative that must be given up to engage in an activity.

Overnight interest rate The interest rate banks charge each other for overnight loans.

P

Patent The exclusive right to produce a product for a period of 20 years from the date the patent is applied for.

Pegging The decision by a country to keep the exchange rate fixed between its currency and another country's currency.

Perfectly competitive market A market that meets the conditions of (1) many buyers and sellers, (2) all firms selling identical products, and (3) no barriers to new firms entering the market.

Per-worker production function The relationship between real GDP per hour worked and capital per hour worked, holding the level of technology constant.

Phillips curve A curve showing the short-run relationship between the unemployment rate and the inflation rate.

Positive analysis Analysis concerned with what is.

Potential GDP The level of real GDP attained when all firms are producing at capacity.

Price level A measure of the average prices of goods and services in the economy.

Producer price index (PPI) An average of the prices received by producers of goods and services at all stages of production.

Product market A market for goods—such as computers—or services—such as haircuts.

Production possibilities frontier (PPF) A curve showing the maximum attainable combinations of two products that may be produced with available resources and current technology.

Productive efficiency A situation in which a good or service is produced at the lowest possible cost.

Property rights The rights individuals or firms have to the exclusive use of their property, including the right to buy or sell it.

Purchase and Resale Agreements (PRAs) The Bank of Canada's purchase of government securities from primary dealers (i.e., banks or securities brokers/dealers), with an agreement to resell them later.

Purchasing power parity The theory that in the long run, exchange rates move to equalize the purchasing powers of different currencies.

Q

Quantity demanded The amount of a good or service that a consumer is willing and able to purchase at a given price.

Quantity supplied The amount of a good or service that a firm is willing and able to supply at a given price.

Quantity theory of money A theory about the connection between money and prices that assumes that the velocity of money is constant.

Quota A numerical limit that a government imposes on the quantity of a good that can be imported into the country.

R

Rational expectations Expectations formed by using all available information about an economic variable.

Real business cycle model A macroeconomic model that focuses on real, rather than monetary, causes of the business cycle.

Real business cycle models Models that focus on real rather than monetary explanations of fluctuations in real GDP.

Real exchange rate The price of domestic goods in terms of foreign goods.

Real GDP The value of final goods and services evaluated at base-year prices.

Real interest rate The nominal interest rate minus the inflation rate.

Recession The period of a business cycle during which total production and total employment are decreasing.

Reserves Deposits that a bank keeps as cash in its vault or on deposit with the Bank of Canada.

Rule of law The ability of a government to enforce the laws of the country, particularly with respect to protecting private property and enforcing contracts.

S

Sale and Repurchase Agreements (SRAs) The Bank of Canada's sale of government securities to primary dealers (i.e., banks or securities brokers/dealers), with an agreement to repurchase them later.

Saving and investment equation An equation that shows that national saving is equal to domestic investment plus net foreign investment.

Scarcity A situation in which unlimited wants exceed the limited resources available to fulfill those wants.

Seasonal unemployment Unemployment that is due to seasonal factors, such as weather or the fluctuation in demand for some products during different times of the year.

Securitization The process of transforming loans or other financial assets into securities.

Security A financial asset—such as a stock or a bond—that can be bought and sold in a financial market.

Settlement balances Deposits held by banks in their accounts at the Bank of Canada.

Shortage A situation in which the quantity demanded is greater than the quantity supplied.

Short-run aggregate supply (SRAS) curve A curve that shows the relationship in the short run between the price level and the quantity of real GDP supplied by firms.

Simple deposit multiplier The ratio of the amount of deposits created by banks to the amount of new reserves.

Speculators Currency traders who buy and sell foreign exchange in an attempt to profit from changes in exchange rates.

Stagflation A combination of inflation and recession, usually resulting from a supply shock.

Standing liquidity facilities The Bank of Canada's readiness to lend to or borrow from a bank.

Statistical discrepancy One-half of the difference between the estimates of GDP generated by the expenditure approach and the income approach.

Structural relationship A relationship that depends on the basic behaviour of consumers and firms and that remains unchanged over long periods.

Structural unemployment Unemployment that arises from a persistent mismatch between the skills and attributes of workers and the requirements of jobs.

Substitutes Goods and services that can be used for the same purpose.

Substitution effect The change in the quantity demanded of a good that results from a change in price making the good more or less expensive relative to other goods, holding constant the effect of the price change on consumer purchasing power.

Supply curve A curve that shows the relationship between the price of a product and the quantity of the product supplied.

Supply schedule A table that shows the relationship between the price of a product and the quantity of the product supplied.

Supply shock An unexpected event that causes the short-run aggregate supply curve to shift.

Surplus A situation in which the quantity supplied is greater than the quantity demanded.

Symmetric inflation targeting Conducting monetary policy based on equal concern about inflation rising above its target as about inflation falling below its target.

T

Tariff A tax imposed by a government on imports.

Tax wedge The difference between the pretax and posttax return to an economic activity.

Taxes less subsidies Payments to government by businesses net of transfers from government to businesses.

Taylor principle The principle that the central bank should raise the nominal interest rate by more than the increase in the inflation rate so that the real interest rate also increases.

Taylor rule A rule developed by John Taylor that links the central bank's target for the overnight interest rate to economic variables.

Technological change A change in the quantity of output a firm can produce using a given quantity of inputs.

Trade The act of buying and selling.

Trade-off The idea that because of scarcity, producing more of one good or service means producing less of another good or service.

Transfer payments Payments by the government to households for which the government does not receive a new good or service in return.

U

Underground economy Buying and selling of goods and services that is concealed from the government to avoid taxes or regulations or because the goods and services are illegal.

Unemployment rate The percentage of the labour force that is unemployed.

V

Value added The market value a firm adds to a product.

Velocity of money The average number of times per year each dollar in the money supply is used to purchase goods and services included in GDP.

Voluntary exchange A situation that occurs in markets when both the buyer and seller of a product are made better off by the transaction.

W

Working age population People 15 years of age and older who are legally entitled to work in Canada.

COMPANY INDEX

SUBJECT INDEX

Key terms and the page on which they are defined appear in **boldface.**